P9-BZV-269

BLOOD TO REMEMBER

AMERICAN POETS ON THE HOLOCAUST

Revised, second edition

Time Being Books®
10411 Clayton Road
St. Louis, Missouri 63131

Time Being Books® is an imprint of Time Being Press®, St. Louis, Missouri.

Time Being Press® is a 501(c)(3) not-for-profit corporation.

Time Being Books® volumes are printed on acid-free paper.

ISBN 9781568091129 (hardcover)
ISBN 9781568091136 (paperback)

Library of Congress Cataloging-in-Publication Data:

Fishman, Charles Adés
Blood to remember: American poets on the Holocaust / edited by Charles Adés Fishman — Revised, 2nd ed.
p. cm.
Includes bibliographical references and index.
ISBN: 9781568091129 (hardcover : alk. paper)
ISBN: 9781568091136 (pbk. : alk. paper)
1. Holocaust, Jewish (1939–1945)—Poetry. 2. American poetry—20th century. 3. Jews—Poetry. I. Fishman, Charles Adés.
PS595.H64B573 2007
811'.54080358—dc22

2007024078

Cover design by Jeff Hirsch
Cover illustration: Reva Sharon, "Valley of Lost Communities / Yad Vashem"
Dustjacket photo: FERLISE
Book design and typesetting by Sheri Vandermolen

Manufactured in the United States of America

First Edition, first printing (1991, Texas Tech University Press)
Second Edition, first printing (2007)

Choice blurb is an excerpt from my review of first edition of B+R

BLOOD TO REMEMBER

AMERICAN POETS ON THE HOLOCAUST

Revised, second edition

Edited by

CHARLES ADÉS FISHMAN

TIME BEING BOOKS
POETRY IN SIGHT AND SOUND

An imprint of Time Being Press
St. Louis, Missouri

IN MEMORY OF THE MILLIONS LOST
AND WITH GRATITUDE FOR THOSE
WHO SURVIVED

The more we know of the Holocaust, the more we change,
the more we find ourselves circumscribed by the event we sought
to transcend and from which we had hoped to pull free. . . .
— Terrence Des Pres

No gravestone stands on Babi Yar;
Only coarse earth heaped roughly on the gash.
Such dread comes over me; I feel so old,
Old as the Jews. Today I am a Jew . . .
And I too have become a soundless cry
Over the thousands that lie buried here.
I am each old man slaughtered, each child shot,
None of me will forget.
— Yevgeny Yevtushenko

It is blood to remember; it is fire
to stammer back.
— Hart Crane

CONTENTS

BLOOD TO REMEMBER

AMERICAN POETS ON THE HOLOCAUST

Revised, second edition

Preface to the Revised, Second Edition

This second edition of *Blood to Remember* is distinct from the 1991 original in several ways. Readers of that edition will notice that fewer than half of the poems in the two opening sections, "After the Holocaust — No Poetry" and "The Terrified Meadows," have been retained. In the early 1980s, when a full-length compilation of poems on the Holocaust was yet to be published, I saw those sections as necessary "framing" for the body of work by American poets I had found. The same readers will note that nearly one hundred fifty poems from the first edition appear in this revised collection and that a significantly larger number of poems — nearly all of them written or published after 1985 — have joined them. I have been lucky to discover so many moving and often stunning poems.

What is entirely new to *Blood to Remember* is its organization. With very few exceptions, poems now appear in alphabetical order under the names of the contributing poets, and this rule also governs the order in which poets are presented within the book. Early on, I decided to use this arrangement for the new edition because I wanted to allow the material I gathered to generate its own unanticipated links and points of resonance. I believe this structure will permit readers to find their favorite poets and poems more easily and that it simplifies the process of locating historical and biographical data, as well as the personal statements that many contributors to this volume have generously shared.

Poetry, at its best, resists abstraction and permits us to feel again, to be wounded again, and, though never entirely, to heal. I have seen this in the faces of audiences I have read for both in the United States and in Israel. I have heard it in the voice of a young German woman I met in Haifa, who read the poems in the first edition of this anthology as a guide to the darkest chapter in her country's past and as a light to guide her on the path of peace, reconciliation, and community service she had already begun to travel. And I have felt it when in the presence of survivors, who have encouraged me in my efforts to assemble the most powerful and evocative poems on the Holocaust. Always, they have spoken to me of their belief in this project. Their one-word mandate rings in my ears: *Continue.*

As with all serious attempts to comprehend the destruction of the Jews of Europe, in the end, Holocaust poetry is a bridge between that which can be known and expressed and that which cannot. The best use of our mother tongue is a form of spiritual resistance. It is memory given voice, and it is prayer.

My hope is that this new edition of *Blood to Remember: American Poets on the Holocaust* will startle and amaze, as often as it clarifies and deepens our sense of the Nazi genocide: what was lost and why it is essential that we deepen our understanding of all that was changed forever.

Charles Adés Fishman
Bellport, New York
May 2007

Marjorie Agosín

Bicycles

It began with the banning of your bicycles,
banning you from going out after eight at night,
restricting you to only buying goods in certain shops
for Jews,
to only walking down certain avenues
with a gold star between your open, blossoming
arms.
Your streets were filled with the thirsty and
fear-stricken.
Your feet quit crossing through windswept
pastures,
and yet
you loved life,
the butterflies,
dawns filled with all those wandering
in no particular direction,
the Star of David illuminating them.

Translated from the Spanish by Richard Schaaf

Cousins

My mother muttered
when she named them,
Julia, Silvia, Sonia,
Sonia, Julia, Silvia.
They were the names of rivers,
the names of fairies.
They were my cousins,
women we knew,
with whom we shared a history.
I loved them from a distance
and close by.

We know nothing about them.
Little was known about the obedient time
of war,
only certain clues,
a murmur,
a sigh.
They sent us encrypted addresses,

[stanza continues]

never deciphered,
false trails,
invisible names.

On holy days
there were empty seats
and my father, with his sacred cup,
invoked them,
Julia, Sonia, Silvia.

I also came to love them,
happy just
to see their handwriting
in threadbare postcards
from Vienna, then
Prague and
later, the cities of austere names.

My grandmother, Helena,
taciturn,
took out her photographs that
resembled amber-colored bones,
shining among absences.
Suddenly,
almost fifty years
later,
the cousin from Sweden calls,
and he can't help but remember.

He told us,
mute,
ethereal in the distance,
that he had seen them,
those cousins:
Julia, Sonia, Silvia.
He had found them
in the Holy Book of
the dead.
He had searched for
their last names,
and their crossings.

They had been transferred to those
trains of shadows
and shorn women,
singing in their blue clothes,
to Terezín,
later to be sent to
Auschwitz,

[stanza continues]

where there is no forgetting,
where there are no calendars,
where there is no memory,
where there is no voice,
where women keep silent,
are shorn,
are delirious
and carry on their heads the rituals
of dead birds.

The cousins from Sweden
found them.
They were dead and alive
or they arrived in an afternoon of amber,
wounded and dead.

He tells me hurriedly
that they killed them with blue gas
and that is all he knows about them.
He asks me to tell this to my mother
and also to Aunt Regina.

All of them
in Auschwitz,
and I don't know how to name them,
and I don't know how to remember them.

Anger blends with my screams.
I recognize them
Sonia, Julia, Silvia.
I cannot name them anymore,
I see them severed in those forests
of dead butterflies
and I think I do not deserve this life
without them.

I tell my mother
and my grandmother, who has remained
forgotten in the South,
that we should not
search for them,
not to imagine false
omens;
that they are here;
that upon their arrival
they made them burn;
their tiny bones were placed
without names in the minuscule ovens
of death.

I feel distressed when I tell you this story
and I can only say it in a poem
because I cannot tell it to anybody.
I don't want to hear things like
"Again, the Jews and their memories."
"That happened years ago."
"I don't know anything about that."
That is how they talked when the neighbor,
the grandfather,
his small grandchildren
disappeared.

Tonight
all of this turns in my head
like a gathering of wilted
poppies.
I don't know where Julia, Sonia, Silvia are.
I shall navigate those meadows.
My passion will kiss the grass
waiting to meet their lips.

Julia, Sonia, Silvia,
you shall not die among barbed wires.
You shall no longer be the hidden Jews
without hair or language.

I will return to the fields
to sprinkle them with prayers and holy water.
I shall give you a notebook, Julia,
a fan, Sonia,
a breath of light, Silvia.
My cousins, my blood cousins,
family that could no longer be loved.
I don't want lies for your names.
I don't want anybody to speak
on your behalf.
I ask for a second, a century of peace
and memory
for all
the dead Jews,
the Gypsies,
the women of Bosnia.
They are all named
Julia, Silvia, Sonia
and they are mine.

Translated from the Spanish by Laura Nakazawa

[Would it have been possible to take in the Jews,]

Would it have been possible to take in the Jews,
the squalid Gypsies?
Was it possible to whisper in their blackened ears
that even in Amsterdam torn asunder
someone loved them,
would rescue them from the chill of death?
Wasn't it possible to take in all the sick
who were waiting for misfortune's trains?
Was it possible to approach with an open heart
the destitute Jewish children?
Was it possible to be human?
Though, yes, it was possible
to accuse,
to denounce,
to banish,
to terrorize the sick, the crippled,
to destroy shops,
smashing windows, fire-bombing.
It was possible
to force them to undress,
with the prophecy of a Star tattooed
on their breasts.

Translated from the Spanish by Richard Schaaf

Sherman Alexie

from Inside Dachau

1. big lies, small lies

Having lied to our German hosts about our plans
for the day, Diane and I visited Dachau
instead of searching for rare albums in Munich.
Only a dozen visitors walked through the camp
because we were months away from tourist season.
The camp was austere. The museum was simple.

Once there, I had expected to feel simple
emotions: hate, anger, sorrow. That was my plan.
I would write poetry about how the season
of winter found a perfect home in cold Dachau.
I would be a Jewish man who died in the camp.
I would be the ideal metaphor. Munich

would be a short train ride away from hell. Munich
would take the blame. I thought it would all be simple
but there were no easy answers inside the camp.
The poems still took their forms, but my earlier plans
seemed so selfish. What could I say about Dachau
when I had never suffered through any season

inside its walls? Could I imagine a season
of ash and snow, of flames and shallow graves? Munich
is only a short train ride away from Dachau.
If you can speak some German, it is a simple
journey which requires coins and no other plans
for the day. We lied about visiting the camp

to our German hosts, who always spoke of the camp
as truthfully as they spoke about the seasons.
Dachau is still Dachau. Our hosts have no plans
to believe otherwise. As we drove through Munich
our hosts pointed out former Nazi homes simply
and quickly. "We are truly ashamed of Dachau,"

Mikael said, "but what about all the Dachaus
in the United States? What about the death camps
in your country?" Yes, Mikael, you ask simple
questions which are ignored, season after season.
Mikael, I'm sorry we lied about Munich
and Dachau. I'm sorry we lied about our plans.

Inside Dachau, you might believe winter will never end. You might lose faith in the change of seasons
because some of the men who built the camps still live in Argentina, in Washington, in Munich.
They live simple lives. They share bread with sons and daughters who have come to understand the master plan.

4. the american indian holocaust museum

What do we indigenous people want from our country?
We stand over mass graves. Our collective grief makes us numb.
We are waiting for the construction of our museum.

We too could stack the shoes of our dead and fill a city
to its thirteenth floor. What did you expect us to become?
What do we indigenous people want from our country?
We are waiting for the construction of our museum.

We are the great-grandchildren of Sand Creek and Wounded Knee.
We are the veterans of the Indian wars. We are the sons
and daughters of the walking dead. We have lost everyone.

[stanza continues]

What do we indigenous people want from our country?
We stand over mass graves. Our collective grief makes us numb.
We are waiting for the construction of our museum.

7. below freezing

Dachau was so cold I could see my breath
so I was thankful for my overcoat.
I have nothing new to say about death.

Each building sat at right angles to the rest.
Around each corner, I expected ghosts.
Dachau was so cold I could see my breath.

Everything was clean, history compressed
into shoes, photographs, private notes.
I have nothing new to say about death.

I wanted to weep. I wanted to rest
my weary head as the ash mixed with snow.
Dachau was so cold I could see my breath.

I am not a Jew. I was just a guest
in that theater which will never close.
I have nothing new to say about death.

I wonder which people will light fires next
and which people will soon be turned to smoke.
Dachau was so cold I could see my breath.
I have nothing new to say about death.

Karen Alkalay-Gut

Hitler Builds a City for the Jews

For Kurt Gerron, renowned director and actor, forced to direct a propaganda film on Theresienstadt, then exterminated in Auschwitz

If I make a perfect world,
my own life will have import

If I make a perfect world
out of the materials of hell

my life will once again become
valid

will have transcended the naiveté
of the medals I won for Fatherland
my films of Berlin love
my role as magician

If I make a perfect film
a chosen world
for the chosen people

from this concentration camp

I may be able to make it come true

If I show children eating bread
in the film
perhaps some day
they will have real food

and their smiles will emerge
from a joy beyond
the relief from hunger

They will be
the children I never conceived

Mr. Panitz

Even then I knew we were terribly cruel.
Even then it was clear our delight
at driving our teacher to acts of absurd violence
was wicked even as it wreaked our own petty revenge
on the terrible system that linked
great aging European scholars with
small unruly American children.

How shamed he must have felt, returning at night
to his wife and the morals and ethics he had been forced to forget
first in the Holocaust
and then in the fluorescent American schoolroom
half a world and a life away.

What good does it do now
for me to bow my head
for the tall slender man whose love
for God and books disappeared
to the rest of the world
when the *shtetl* that nurtured and admired him
vanished?

Night Travel

For my parents

On that night in Danzig the trains did not run.
You sat in the bus station till almost dawn,
knowing that if you could not get out
the invaders would find you, grind you among the first
under their heels.

Toward morning a bus was announced
and without knowing where it would go
you raced to the stop.
But the Nazis were there first, and you watched
as they finished their search —
checking each traveler for papers,
jewelry, a Jewish nose.

Among the passengers you recognized
a familiar face — a German woman sitting
with someone else you'd seen
in the neighborhood.
They winked a greeting,
waited for the soldiers to leave,
and jumped out,
pushing you up in their place.

Thus you escaped to Berlin, remaining alive
by keeping silent through the long train ride
from Berlin to Cologne in a car filled with
staring German soldiers

And arrived the next day in Holland,
black with fear and transportation.

Voices in My Skin

I.

"Where will I find another bed like this?
where will I find another view?
The Gestapo will get me
no matter what I do."

Years after the years of chase,
my father would mourn
the need to change
his hiding place.

II.

Ohio. The sign on the confused old lady says:
"*Rets zu mir Iddish*,"
and an expert is brought in
from the University of Michigan
to communicate with her, to
determine her identity.
The room is white, the nurses lean
over the bed to catch her fading voice.

"What is your name?" asks the professor.
"Hoffman, Anna," the voice responds like a bell rung.
"Where are you from?" "Bergen-Belsen."
"This is America, Mrs.
Hoffman. You are safe. This is a hospital,
1990. We do tests, not
experiments."

III.

"Here is a photo from after the Great War
all of us at New Year's with glasses raised high.
Only your father is not smiling.
Only he knows why."

IV.

"Why should that guttural language
disturb you now? Third
generation should be far enough away.
Well, keep it inside. There is too
much to be gained by listening."

V.

When I get old, I will speak
Yiddish like my mother. In the Home
I will revert to the tongue
in which I first suffered.

The staff will think me contrary,
senile, bothersome. But I will have
no choice.

Voyage Home

One afternoon in Zakopane, she took
the old diaries she had brought
from Israel and gave them to her cousin
to read to her.

She understood the Polish,
grasped at each word, and followed
Mother's writhing story
of wandering
through Czechoslovakia, Rumania,
all the way to Italy
and the *Altelana* —
the voyage to the land
of the Jews, and how Mother saw
Father there, waiting for her and their son.

But mother was empty-handed.
Between the diaries
and the cousins' visit
in the sleepy town of Zacopane
there were fifty years.

The child who vanished on the way
waited for that quiet afternoon
to appear, real
as the forests of Poland.

Michael Alpiner

David-Horodok

This town lives in me with the ache and cry of violin strings;
Gone now sixty years, it has the quivering stamina of memory.
A village once called *sweet* under white sky and dark omens,
Stained with the incessant ooze of mud and sabbath candles,
Blossomed with joy and color as the church bells
Knelled out their warnings like insolent children.

How does seven hundred years of history
Become extinguished like a wick between fingers so numb
They miss the flame's last stubborn crackle and hiss?
They should have listened to the bells, heeded their threats,
Left behind the bushels of raspberries, cherry trees,

[stanza continues]

A cleaver in the butcher block, allowed the geese to escape,
Chosen what to wear, what gets brought and what remains,
Circle stains on the walls where pictures once hung,
The thatched roofs shading the cow, the hollow echo of prayers
From the synagogue, the voices of the children,
The voices of the children, their hauntingly harmonious cries.

With every sunrise came the new day's crises,
Men at the dock, counting on fingers the haggled costs,
Yiddish swear words when mud swallowed a foot whole
Turning all shoes brown; barefoot children left their shoes home.
Good Samaritans would lay wood planks over the pools of mire
Turning pedestrians into circus performers, a medal of honor,
Washing daily in the Horin River, the true woman of valor.
It was the river that most defined Horodok, an artery
To the Europe that few would ever know: the steamers,
Barges, came daily, bringing goods and news from the West,
Lovers walked as slow as sunset on its banks,
Caressing the lip of creation, stealing a kiss under the wharf,
Bringing hope to a town that had more funerals than marriages.

In the town, little Hiah Leah sold fried goose skin and fat,
Lost herself among the livestock and religious students,
Grasses rich in pigment, all the jealous greens of the world.
Meir and Zev ran errands for the blacksmith,
Eager to learn a trade and earn a good wife,
Dream of pale skin and the miracle of woman.

Their mother taught them by example
That Horodok women are strong, shaped
Their destiny in bread dough with hands and fingers
Thick and gnarled as tree roots. They were sent to the ovens
Before they even had time to rise.

Pebbles from Auschwitz

They fit in the trench of my palm
As stoic survivors from a time in history,
Buried, exhumed, displaying their bony dust
With the shame of identification,
As if burned into an arm.
They came as a generous souvenir,
Wrapped with cloth and ribbon,
A gift for the creator.
Their memory burned tears in my hand.

My family missed the train to Auschwitz,
Could never have seen these stones
Or kicked them unaware, all too weak
To lift their knees and march properly.

Unlike these pebbles, they did not survive the war.
Pebbles simply wear away,
Through gentle breezes, soft caressing waves,
Almost humane, and take centuries.

Postcard from Poland

My father said the last postcard arrived in 1939.
Between newsreels, silence, the dark crackle of a radio,
Europe in shambles, silence, and soon the thud of reality,
An echo through the empty chamber of a gun.
Somewhere in Poland, the generation that preceded me,
All three thousand drew their last
Breath of moonlight on the Pripet Swamp.
They died as they were born,
Naked and screaming, swaddled
In each other's white shining skin.

Miles from David-Horodok,
Their bones wait to be found;
Fields now obscure the site,
Each wildflower a monument.
In Belarus, the ground still smolders,
All that was once Jewish is gone.
We inhabit the underground,
Noblemen in that dark kingdom
Whose only currency is memory,
For whom it is justice enough
That we survived.

Today I received a postcard from Poland.
It had been sixty years.
The mountain village of Sanok,
A medieval place where my friend thinks of me,
Longs to hear my voice.
Poland's southern frontier,
Two hundred miles south of David-Horodok;
Even if she had found the mass graves,
They all look alike now in a camouflage
Of thick grass, wildflowers and forgetfulness.

Her postcard, a cathedral in Kraków,
The mist upon the horizon,
A deep longing to have me there,
To see the spires and bell towers,
Hear songs in Polish,
Fill our mouths with kielbasa,
Kiss clean the powdered, sugary chin
Left from *chruscik*.

In 1939 it was no different.
Their village was the most beautiful place on Earth,
Before the rumble of wheels and boots,
Before the collaborative hatred of generations
Blackened every pebble, sent my people
Marching to the sound of their own martyrdom.

The last postcard —
There was so much that could not be said.

John Amen

Verboten

We are in Paris, my grandparents and I,
visiting his sister, the one who failed to
get out of Europe in 1938. I am seven
years old. My great-aunt's arms remind
me of spaghetti strands, and she speaks
in a high, labored voice, as if a little
pump inside her is not working right.
They are drinking wine and speaking
of French-U.S. relations when the long
sleeve on her arm falls down. Before
she can clutch it, I see the faded blue
tattoo on her flesh. "What are those
numbers?" I ask. A silence explodes
through the room like spores.
My aunt picks up a tray of empty
glasses and retreats into the kitchen.
"Some questions," my grandfather
says, rubbing his own unblemished arm,
"should not be asked." As life went on,
I learned that most of the questions
I wanted answers to fell into that category.
Still, I asked them; and I'm still asking.

Frieda Arkin

Pinochle Day

Max the music-hater rubs
the outdoors from his hands, gloves
pocketed. Unwinds the muffler
which since March has lain
dusted with crystals of naphthalene.
Luke's palsied hands chime the whiskey glasses.
Dave with age's lizard face
sets the cards and chips in place,
circling the bottle's golden heart.
Pulling chairs, the old men home
in on the table. They own
the new November dusk, and meld, and grunt,
toss chips, drink Scotch, crack jokes
seasoned like old oak until the dark
swells in between the cracks.
Luke gives the stereo a twist
and in the arc of Paganini-Liszt
smiles like an impresario. "How Richter plays
is enough to make your shoes fall off."
Dave waits, considers, nods.
Only Max. His cards slide flat.
This music is the silver tilt of time
that sweeps him back to Hildesheim,
his daughter's sounds. Sweet prodigy,
sweet child of fire. Her face
through his face: to this day
he has to turn his eye away from mirrors,
his ear from sounds like these.
Old man — who hears Beethoven's *Ode to Joy*
and sees gas chamber queues.
No waiting till the record stops.
Stands. Walks. Takes coat and muffler,
opens door and leaves. Old man —
smelling of mothballs and schnapps.

Brett Axel

Morning After a Fight, He Says

I'm sorry. I get angry
At only small things —
Being called a survivor . . .

I have no anger in me
For my sister's killer —
Raped her with the bayonet
On the end of his rifle —

Stuck it up her *nartik*
While two more held me
Making me watch.
When she hurt so much

She couldn't scream more —
Just panting like a bear,
Eyes big as grapefruits —
He pushed it deepest

And slid his finger like he
Was masturbating the trigger.
I was too scared
To hear an explosion —

Then he told me it was
Der orgasmus
Kurz und gut.
If I ever let myself

Have anger for him
I know I'll never feel
Anything other than that.
I won't hit you again

Just don't use that word.
Some of us lived
But the things they did
There was no surviving.

David B. Axelrod

The Suffering Cuts Both Ways

A swastika poem for Bill Heyen

The German-American boy,
what could he understand of war or pain —
his father, scraping swastikas off the front door.
The boy was only six. His immigrant father
worked in a defense plant on Long Island
riveting the fuselages of Douglas DC-3s.
What could a boy know of Bergen-Belsen,
Buchenwald? When the news came that Roosevelt
was dead, he cried because he couldn't go
to the picture show his mother promised.
But Hitler, hidden deep within the bunkers
beneath Berlin, stamped and screamed
the gods had sent a sign his Reich
would rise again from ashes and bombed-
out cities.
                    When the boy was twenty-three
he visited Germany and the family
who'd stayed behind. One older aunt
served tea and strudel which he savored,
but he had to ask her, what was she doing
during the war? How could it have happened?
It was then she dropped the smile —
the fond expression for this brother's son —
and, in a voice like testimony at a trial,
she explained:

> Your Uncle Max and I, we had
> a camera store. He was alive then.
> We had a family and our business.
> So I would walk to work, past the train
> tracks and the depot and I would hear
> moaning, and once I think I saw a hand
> sticking out of a boxcar. But it was
> the war. That wasn't anybody's business.
> What could I do? Only once . . . once
> I was walking home and the smoke —
> you know, the *smoke* — I smelled it,
> and I shouldn't say this. It was late,
> supper time, and I couldn't help myself
> from thinking: it smelled like pot roast cooking.

So very human her response, he finally understood.

Yakov Azriel

We, the *Tefillin* of Once-Was Europe

. . . and you shall bind them for a sign upon your hand,
and they shall be for frontlets between your eyes.
— Deuteronomy 11:18

We, the *tefillin* of once-was Europe, lament;
We, the black houses of *tefillin*,
Protest.
Our straps, black and long, no longer bind us to grateful, human muscle
But to a past
Suddenly snapped.
Forty years, fifty years, eternity
We have been waiting,
As if our Jews could return
From the black charcoal houses of scorching death.

We alone are left to mourn.
Black as cinders and soot,
We are small, but large enough to be
Our people's only tombstones.

Our Jews were snatched away from us in box-cars,
Transported through chimneys as death-cinder and death-soot
Smudging the unclouded blue sky.

We, the *tefillin* of once-was Europe,
Are as empty as box-cars without their cargo.

What was holy is now hollow.

Inside us
Only black echoes still whisper
Of what once was.

Crystal Bacon

Kristallnacht, 1991

Night of glass, Germany is broken.
Brothers of the new order pledge against foreigners.
Break the glass, burn the synagogues.
Whatever they think, they sniff

[stanza continues]

out of the German air. Berlin or Munich,
ashes of the not forgotten dead. This is their Fatherland.
This their ethnic purity. They eat the bread of bones.
Drink the wine of blood. This is the feast of fear.
The orgy of panic. The church of slash and burn.

Train wheels echo across the German landscape.
Treblinka, they hum. Dachau, comes the refrain.
Auschwitz, I am thinking, and liberation.
In Tutzing, my grandfather pledged himself
to the Voice of America, itself no small feat.
In Munich, Hitler held my mother up
on the running board of his parade car:
the stories I know about "the war."
Sixty years later, I am cut loose in America
with this past, a vast space where history
bares its teeth like the silent face of death.

Julius Balbin

Lament for the Gypsies

Their home was the endless
plains of Eurasia.
Their roof was the starlit sky
under which they slept in tribal embrace.
Like butterflies they would never settle
for the taste of one flower
but move on to the light
of ever new gardens.
They did not want to give up
their freedom to roam the continent
for the price of a homeland.
To rove without hindrance
from land to land
was as precious to them
as life itself.
They spoke a strange tongue
scholars count among the oldest
but they left no writings.
That they dared to be so different from others
remains their chief heritage.
Yet their love of music was as boundless
as their love of freedom.
The vibrant and melancholy tunes they fiddled and danced

[stanza continues]

as they wandered from country to country
found their way into notebooks
of many a famous composer.
Their nomadic ways aroused suspicion
and often they were persecuted.
Although innocent of any idolatry
many were forced to adopt alien creeds.
Their women possessed the art
of foretelling the future of others
yet had no foreboding of what
was in store for their own people.
Before they were consumed by crematoria
they bequeathed to us
a unique legacy:
that of a people
who practiced without preaching
what they believed —
that peoples should not be divided by frontiers.

Translated from the Esperanto by Charlz Rizzuto

Stanley H. Barkan

The Mothertree

For Blumke Katz

Prostrated
before the tree
in the middle
of the cemetery,
she prayed
for her mother,
buried somewhere
in that mass grave:
for her
and for so many other
mothers & fathers,
sisters & brothers,
grandparents
and grandchildren,
there in the middle of
Svintsyán, Lithuania,
lost shtetl
in the middle

[stanza continues]

of Eastern Europe
where Jews
bought & sold,
cooked & ate,
studied & prayed,
worked & dreamed.
Once.

Mama, where are you?
All those long years
alone,
far away in cold,
oh so cold, Siberia,
each night I spoke
with you
in my sleep.
You were just a dream.
Now — at last —
after the Germans
with their brownshirts left,
and the Russians
with their redshirts left,
I have returned,
I have awakened,
I am here —
but where are you?

Dear Tree,
            Dear Mother,
Yisgadal
            v'yiskadash . . .

Tony Barnstone

Parable of the Jew Without a Name

With our despised immigrant clothing, we shed also
our impossible Hebrew names.
— Mary Antin, *The Promised Land* (1912)

My great-uncle Vincent, son of the Milk Street tailor,
threw some fairy dust into the air and changed,
making it easy for me to go to the prom,
to grow up in Indiana and bite my tongue
when a hick would cuss at *the bastard who tried*
to Jew me down on the price for home-grown pot.

[stanza continues]

Like wool pants for blue jeans, Moshe, Shmuel and Lazar
traded in their names, and in exchange were changed
from cabbage-eaters into Americans, and why not?
"I never was a pumpkin!" cries the carriage.
"I never was a pauper!" shouts the prince.
In this fairy tale all the steins turn into stones, straw turns
to gold, stars warp into crosses, and the pauper trades up
and leaves the trades to the star-crossed Jews.

I'm a lousy Jew, ignorant of nearly everything
except that in another time the Klan would lynch me,
the Nazis flay me into yellow lampshades.
My white hide hides me, my baseball cap keeps greasy ash
out of my hair, and I'm glad for my nice name.
Who needs a life so grim? In the shtetl, the old Jews
would change their names so the Angel of Death
flying on black crape wings above the town,
fatal list in hand, would pass over them
— but not the ones who stayed behind
and kept their names, the Adelsteins, Eisensteins
or the one I'll never know, some cousin twice removed
born in Poland, some Maurice Bornstein. No way to gather
smoke out of the sky and give him flesh again.

I imagine him, with eyes like mine, intent
and studious, staring at the rusted cattle-car wall
in the rattling stink of packed bodies, trying not to breathe.
He'll get that wish soon enough.
Slender, bookish children aren't good workers
and it's too much trouble to take away their names
and write numbers in their skin.
They're gassed like fleas.
I'm a lousy Jew, but I'd like to disturb the grass,
unearth him from the crowded grave, and let his damp fingers
write this story, while his eyes like clouded marble roll.
I'd like to roll the story back to the dead boy
swaying in the train, to see him there imagining the sky
he hasn't seen for days, the white winter sky, like a page
he could write on again and again, practicing his name.

Willis Barnstone

Miklós Radnóti

Because time is a fiction in the mind,
I don't want to die, that is, in July
or Friday or last year. Farms and haystacks
are burning today. I Miklós Radnóti
write you a postcard with a poem. Darling,
I say to myself I won't lie down. The ox
drools blood. The shepherd girl is an orphan
when the troops stray over the wheatfields.
Wife, after they beat me to death, look through
my trenchcoat, in the mass grave, for the poems.

Maybe in two years, by 1946,
you will find our bodies. Today all over
Hungary and Poland I am dying. In taverns
I am already forgotten. How could the smell
of my hair linger? I hid in cellars too,
smoked in darkness, kissed kisses of the taste
of blackberries. When peace comes I won't be
at the Writers Club. Angels drink artillery.
Peasants dream among fleas, among worms. Wife,
the poems are time's wings. Spread them darkly.

The Rose of Blue Flesh

1

Facing a long Byzantine city wall,
the synagogue in Ioannina is white and bold
with Hebrew script over the portal.
Beyond the city,
the mountains lean like awkward ghosts,
ghost after ghost blurring into Albania
with its unmapped capital called Tirana.

2

The gatekeeper of the synagogue (a Greek word)
              is old, short,
a typical Epirote face.
I see his number tattooed on his left arm
which I lift to examine.
The ink is as fresh as the day of tattooing
in 1943.

"They shot my son in front of me.
A thousand of us were carried off.
Who are you?" he says, menacingly.
"I'm a Jew."

3

Paul came here. He proselytized in synagogues
in Corinth and nearby Thessaloniki,
speaking Aramaic and Greek to kinsmen of the first diaspora.
Only these Jews from Ioannina never spoke Ladino,
were never Sephardized when ships from Spain
poured into Greece after terrible 1492.
        Ladino
(there are four alive from one thousand).
A loudspeaker from a café is singing *agonia, agonia,*
        agonia.

"They put their pigs in the synagogue."
"How did you survive?"
"God wished it so."

4

The mountains are gray ghosts upon blue ghosts
over hunters' game and green tomato valleys.
The crooked fir and granite ghosts blue into
        Albania the Obscure,
whose unmapped capital is Tirana.
On the Greek side a trembling *tsamiko* flute
balloons wildly into the clouds.
White happiness tinkles down from the summit village wedding.

5

We say goodbye.
The little man picks up his cane and wobbles away
        behind the Byzantine wall.
The horror flower of tyranny,
the blue rose of the tattoo on the forearm
stays fresh and alive in 1986.

I wonder about forgetting at last.
Like the blue milk of morning and the black milk
        of night,
each number keeps its florid memory till death.

"Next year in Jerusalem!"
agonia, agonia, agonia!

Everyone is born with a blue rose number on the flesh.

Judith Barrington

Ineradicable

Sigmund Gundle 1915–96

He'll never forget their names: daughter
granddaughter, sister, late wife.
He'll always know where he parked the car
and what he went to the store for in the first place.

The President's name, today's date, his favorite
brand of coffee — all etched
like the names of the dead in a granite wall,
alphabetical. Memory's like that, isn't it? —

dark gray wall, file cabinet, a great room
with newspapers piled in rows by date and place
all of them recording news of a life
from gossip column to missile attack to the daily puzzle.

Or, of course, it's a computer: cerebral megabytes
swallow the story chapter by chapter
until the hard drive crashes . . .
What he thought could never be lost is lost:

names escape through paneless windows,
streets sprout unexpected turns
and faces float away from their old histories.
He turns his wheelchair to block the corridor;

nurses beg him to move but he waves them away
shouting in German. So much is erased
but this he'll remember and remember:
the camp; the guards; yellow star; dead mother.

History and Geography

For Ruth

1

Your finger skims the map
dense with villages, towns, cities
of Russia and Eastern Europe.
You lean towards the blond
head of your brother-in-law
as you search through Bessarabia
and your father hunches over
the littered dinner table
passing on pieces of your mother's history —
your mother, who was the family historian.
You all ask questions
to which, mostly, there are answers
or at least speculations.
Not like my relatives, I think,
who say "What's the use?"
and "The past is the past."

2

You have your father's zany laugh.
It comes down to you from before
the events which flung him
from camp to flight to new world,
his family decimated.
That laugh rings back through
Germany and Austria, pogroms and seders,
tracking the history that is your home
as no country can ever be.
Is this why my relatives discard
their history — rooted in land so long
they have no need of a people?
My parents, living abroad
much of their lives,
were sometimes called "expatriate" —
"away from the father land" —
but still and always
children of that father.
For you, changing countries without choice
is part of your history.
Surely there is no such thing
as an expatriate Jew
except, perhaps, a Jew outside history —
a Jew with no questions
wanting no answers.

3

The discarded map lies beside
pies and kugel, as the questions
and answers go on.
Leftovers become history.
This table becomes geography;
this room a small square, not marked
on the map, where countries each have
their own color: where countries
each have their own.
But what of this history,
this personal geography —
a patchwork of dining tables,
old documents, names culled from
telephone directories in strange cities?
Whose stories are missing
even from this family history,
where one unmarried aunt in Chicago
hides behind a post office box?
Has she chosen a life that does not fit
and written herself out
because she fears it will happen anyway?
Who will become the new expatriates
banished from the ranks of the banished?
Will your name be there, at some future table,
when they ask, "Who were they —
those who went before?"
And will mine?
We choose not to write ourselves out
but to record our presence here tonight —
my blond head leaning toward yours,
our curious intersection
on a map that is larger, even,
than the one your people trace
with such stubborn, loving care.

Marvin Bell

The Extermination of the Jews

A thousand years from now
they will be remembered as heroes.
A thousand years from now
they will still be promised their past.

Objects of beauty notwithstanding,
once more they will appear
for their ruin, seeking a purse,
hard bread or a heavy weapon

for those who must survive,
but no one shall survive.
We who have not forgotten,
our children shall outremember:

their victims' pious chanting —
last wishes, last Yiddish, last dreaming —
were defeats with which the Gestapo
continues ceasing and ceasing.

Oft-Seen Photo from the Liberation of Auschwitz

January 27, Holocaust Day

The masses of ill-fitting striped pajamas
could be clownish if in color. Hard now to recall
the long whiskers of rabbis, the men circling,
holding the ends of handkerchiefs while seeking
the passion of kabala. After the camps, what?
I see the melted rings, the scabs from kneeling,
the ephemeral notes one hears as the cantor
atones. I can't breathe for them,
they are rails, some are doll-sized, they emerge,
blinking, from shadow. The absence of a lawn,
the hollow cheeks, the sting of the wire fence
where hands grab for it, the lack of window glass —
these things lie this side of spectacle. The records
kept at headquarters rub salt into the wound.
The icy calculations — how many potatoes, what
volume of gas, a quart of water for how many.
The facts rest in the black that stained the negative
when the shutter clicked down over the light.

Lora J. Berg

Maschlacki

The boys in Bellingham like picking raspberries best.
They bob down among the bush rows, then pop up
To scare the girls. I tell what my father Alec tells,
How, out picking as a boy in the Tatras, he circled
The stout bushes with many uncles. Each uncle, a tooth-
Pick stuck between his teeth, would jauntily close in
On a berry, pick it, probe, flick the green worm out,
Pop the berry into his mouth. This story makes me laugh.
The boys here think it's just some crazy Polish joke,
But it's true, and none of those uncles are left.

When I go biking in the fall to harvest wild fruit,
I imagine myself a Great Uncle Jerzy, from Warsaw.
He is wise about things that grow. Maple leaves
Stick like starfish to his sleeves and fingertips;
In a basket we gather tart grapes for winter jam.
Bushels fall, tight as beads. At night, we boil
The glass, melt paraffin, squeeze the sour clusters
Through cloth until the whole kitchen turns purple!
As I soften the jam with caramel, I dream up cousins'
Names to print on the labels of the still steaming jars.

Or Jerzy and I, on our knees, quietly hunt mushrooms.
He uncovers a circle of maschlacki, a grey, dainty family
That must be harvested swiftly, before they melt back
Into the carpet of pine. In brine, their texture
Becomes like schleemak, the shy snails that emerge
After rain, inhabitants of water and dark, with no final
Texture of animal or plant. Then Jerzy talks of evolution:
How it is a way of saying all life descends from one Adam.
But what was he? Tell, Jerzy, how life in this new place
Corresponds to us, tell again what happened to my family.

Michael Blumenthal

Juliek's Violin

Was it not dangerous, to allow your vigilance to fail, even for a moment, when any minute death could pounce upon you? I was thinking of this when I heard the sound of a violin, in this dark shed, where the dead were heaped on the living.What madman could be playing the violin here, at the brink of his own grave? It must have been Juliek . . . The whole of his life was gliding on the strings — his lost hopes, his charred past, his extinguished future. He played as he would never play again.
— Elie Wiesel, *Night*

Ahnest Du den Schöpfer, Welt? (World, do you feel the Maker near?)
— Friedrich Schiller, "Ode to Joy"

In the dank halls of Buchenwald,
a man is playing his life.

It is only a fragment from Beethoven —
soft, melodic, ephemeral as the sleep
of butterflies, or the nightmares of
an infant, but tonight it is his life.

In one hand, he holds the instrument,
resonant with potential. In the other,
the fate of the instrument: hairs
of a young horse strung between wood,
as the skin of a lampshade is strung between wood.

Each note is a flicker of the lamp of his life,
and his father, an old conductor, listens
with the rapt attention of someone who knows
the finality of all moments, the power of music.

The bow glides over the strings, at first,
with the grace of a young girl brushing her hair.

Then, suddenly, Juliek leans forward
on his low stool. His knees quiver,
and the damp chamber fills with the voice
like the voice of a nightingale.

Outside, the last sliver of light weaves
through the fences. A blackbird preens
its feathers on the lawn, as if to the music,
and a young child watches from the yard,
naked and questioning.

But, like Schiller crying out
Ahnest Du den Schöpfer, Welt?
Juliek plays on.

And the children,
as if in answer,
burn.

George Bogin

Pitchipoi

So it was that through late July and August [1942], four thousand Jewish children, already orphans, some only a few months old and none above the age of twelve, were accumulated at Drancy [a concentration camp outside Paris]. George Wellers . . . witnessed the scene. 'They were dumped from buses in the middle of the courtyard, as though they were tiny beasts . . . the majority of the gendarmes did not hide sincere emotions at such a sight, nor their disgust at the work they were made to do.' Nonetheless, not one gendarme refused to carry out the assignment. Many children were too young to know their names and were entered as question marks on the train lists. They were in a constant state of panic; they were often screaming. Nobody could comfort them, nobody could tell them what their destination was, and they invented among themselves a name for the fearful place for which they were bound: 'Pitchipoi'. The word lingered in Drancy long after the children had been killed in Auschwitz.

— David Pryce-Jones, *Paris in the Third Reich: A History of the German Occupation, 1940–1944*

After such words
what further words?
The poem should stand as tall as the Eiffel Tower
and as wide as the city of light
and deep as the guilt of the French police.
The words must flame and smoke
like all the hells on earth,
the only hells we travel.
And fabulous should be the guilt
of a single gendarme
and fabulous the innocence
of the child plucked from its parents —
guilt perhaps like a dragon in the viscera,
innocence like a raindrop on a leaf.
And Pitchipoi? Pitchipoi?
Should the poet enter the imagination
of the child boarding the freight car?
But the least cannibal in New Guinea
has seen Pitchipoi.

[stanza continues]

And the poet, will he be this sad American
who is sinking under the weight
of the guilt that has been
and the terror to come?
Let these notes be incinerated
and the ashes scattered from the Arc de Triomphe
for the poem died in the epigraph.
Pitchipoi.

Emily Borenstein

Night Journey to Poland

I hear the heavy, rhythmical panting,
the fearful hissing of a coal locomotive
idling in the station.
I hear the geshrei of the engine's
whistle
as the train pulls out.
The way is strange and dislocated.
Mysterious fires are burning.
Even the moon hangs fire
casting evil shadows.
The thick, biting smoke is real.
The ashes are real.
A wounded songbird flies
into the forest
and doesn't return.

The Shoah

(Whirlwind-Holocaust)

Under an ominous sky trees uprooted themselves.
Dead branches whizzed by.

An old woman fell forward, blood dripping from
her forehead.

Great oaks bent down. They prayed like willows.
Their leaves streamed forward all in one direction.

Then everything fell on top of everything else.
The trees fell crown first.

The bark exploded. The trees screamed.
They split apart.

On the edge of town, trees fell on their knees
reciting the *Hineni*.

The wind blasted the trees.
It whipped, pounded, stripped them of leaves.

It trumpeted like a shofar:
Tekiah! Shevarim! Teruah! Tekiah!

Houses fell, mangled and twisted, under a sky
clenched like a blackened fist.

In a demolished synagogue a voice cried out
Ovinu Malkenu!

It was the voice of my mother praying for redemption,
chanting the *Yaaleh* and the *Shema Kolenu!*

It was life rising in outbursts into meaning
stumbling over the roots of trees.

It was my mother on her knees chanting the last
Shema Yisrael of the dying.

Triumph of the Dead

Purple smoke no longer belches from the smokestacks
of the crematoria.
The night sky is no longer red.
The smell of putrefaction no longer fills the air.
Prisoners who collapse no longer lie where they fall
or are thrown on carts and removed to a pyramid
of still-breathing corpses.
German prisoners are ordered to "Spread it.
Spread it!"
Instead of guns, they carry rakes.
They spread the ashes of Jewish prisoners
over the field.
High brick chimneys are beaten to the ground
with sledge hammers.
Signs above the showers are smashed with axes.
The electric current flowing through triple rows of
barbed wire no longer flows.
Signs that lied to newly arrived prisoners
declaring "Work will make you free"

[stanza continues]

are ripped down and burned on the spot.
For the Nazis, the world is fraught with incoherence
as scratchings and clawings become a tumult
of sound
rising from the ashes.

Verdi's Requiem Played and Sung by Jews in Terezín Concentration Camp / Summer, 1944

First there is the embryo of an orchestra
and a small choir.
Instruments are brought into the ghetto.
Some of them are smuggled in
under loads of hay.
A battered piano is already there.
A double bass is spirited in by an SS man.
Everything finally comes together —
sheet music, instruments and a rehearsal room.
The work grows in stature with the large roster of
professional Jewish musicians.
For many days the musicians rehearse the score
under Rafael Schächter, the orchestra's
conductor.

How was the Camp Commandant able to set up
a concert hall for the presentation
of Verdi's Requiem?
It came into being through a military order
of the SS.
The order stated: "Evacuate the Jewish Hospital."
Sick Jews are evacuated,
loaded into carts and carriages.
The bodies of the dead are carried to the
crematorium.
In front of the hospital there is confusion
and uproar
mingled with the cries of the dying.
The sick are dumped in attics
with no water, lights, beds or blankets.
The hospital is transformed into a theater
to provide entertainment
for the SS and the Nazi brass.

Eichmann is impressed that the Jews
want to put on a performance of Verdi's Requiem
and that it will take place in a theater
with a full stage and gleaming footlights.

[stanza continues]

He tries to keep a straight face.
He doubles up with laughter
at the thought of the Jews ringing their own death knell
in the Requiem with its ancient Catholic prayers
about sin, damnation and hell
but the Jewish prisoners know for whom the bell
really tolls.
They were alerted by reliable information from
outside sources.

Eichmann wonders how the Requiem
with its Christian beliefs and motifs
can be played and sung by Jewish prisoners
in Terezín.
"Don't the Jews know," he says, "that in the Requiem
they'll be singing for themselves in hell?"
Eichmann laughs again.
Schächter tells his musicians in a final
rehearsal before the performance
to remember those who were tortured
and murdered by the Nazis.
"Sing directly to the murderers, he tells them."

The performance begins.
The kettle drums thunder
"The day of wrath has come!"
Orchestra, chorus and soloists unite
as one.
"A final day will loose fire on the world
and leave it in ashes."
The Jews already know the terror that shakes
each heart when God, the Judge, sits
in judgment.
He will hold the Nazis accountable.
The *Tuba mirum* rings loud and clear.

Verses flame in the abyss of fate
for men who enslave, rob, murder and
humiliate.
Eichmann listens, transfixed.
The basso profundo thunders across
the room
"Confutatis maledictis,"
the verse Mozart whispered as he lay
dying.
The choir sings with passion
"Libera me"
reaching out to life.

Instead of conducting the music
quietly as a solo
the conductor raises his baton and brings
it down fortissimo
with full orchestra, choir and kettle drums.
The room is crowded with Jewish prisoners
who are seated in front of Eichmann
and the SS.

Schächter stands erect at the podium.
From the *Confutatis maledictis*
he moves to the *Recordare*.
A renowned Jewish opera singer,
a magnificent tenor, steps forward for his
grand aria.
"Groaning 'neath my sins,
I languish, Lord. Have mercy"
the singer prays.
He pleads and prays with desperate
groaning.
The music pierces every heart.

"Confutatis maledictis"
the singers thunder.
The kettle drums roll.
The baton draws lightning from
the score.
"Lacrymosa!"
Schächter can barely contain himself.
Under his breath he cries out:
Listen, you Nazi bastards,
you will not break us.
"Libera, Domine, de morte aeterna."

The choir is quiet. The soprano sings
"Tremens factus sum."
She repeats the words in a deep,
chilling recitative
as though an impartial judge were
pronouncing a death sentence
on the Nazis.
The cello joins in, taking up the melody.
The conductor lets his baton fall
and raises his hand clenched into a fist.
He shouts the last words of the
Dies irae.

Eichmann doesn't hear Schächter's
curses.
The conductor mutters to himself:
The day of wrath will come.
The German armies will be torn
to pieces.
Streams of blood will gush from
their wounds.
The whole world will witness the
downfall of Nazi Germany.
Justice will prevail.

The choir is singing fervently.
It stops singing.
The soprano's voice rings clear as
a great reverberating bell
"Libera me!"
Bells ring out in the orchestra.
Altos and tenors sing from all sides.

"Libera nos!
Libera nos!"
The huge choir thunders one last time.
The kettle drums boom —
three short strokes, one long.
Eichmann is visibly moved.
"Interesting. Very interesting"
he comments
as he applauds the musicians.

In early fall the train to Auschwitz stops
at the station in Terezín.
Schächter and his musicians are loaded
into the first cars of the first transport
to Auschwitz.

Laure-Anne Bosselaar

The Feather at Breendonk

I am praying again, God — pale God —
here, between white sky and snow, by the larch
I planted last spring, with one branch broken at the elbow.
I pick it up, wave winter away, I do things like that,
call the bluebirds back, throwing yarn and straw
in the meadow, and they do come, so terribly blue,
their strangled *teoo-teoo*

echoing my prayer *Dieu, Dieu* —
the same *Dieu* who stained the feather I found
in the barbed fields of the Breendonk Concentration Camp
near Antwerp in 1952. My father tried to slap it
out of my hand: *It's filthy*. But I held on to it —
I knew it was an angel's. *They only killed*
a few Jews here, he said, *seven, eight hundred, maybe.*

So I wave their angels away with my feather,
away from my father, away from the terribly blue skies
over the Breendonk Canal, where barges loaded bricks
for Antwerp, where my father loaded ships for Rotterdam,
Bremerhaven and Hamburg — as Antwerp grew,
and the port expanded, and his business
flourished, and all the while he kept repeating:

That's all we needed: a good war . . .

The Pallor of Survival

I'm lucky: autumn is flawless today,
sidewalks freckled rust and red, and the sun
gentle. I'll take the back streets
to the bookstore — it's a longer ride — but I avoid
the street where St. John the Evangelist Church
faces that seedy building with a sign flashing
Jews for Jesus
The last time I pedaled between them I felt
a draft there, something so chilling I gasped.

I don't know what happened to Lilianne,
placed in 1945 at the Mater Immaculata convent
in Brussels, after she was repatriated from Bergen-Belsen.
Judith who waited eleven years for some — any —
next of kin to claim her. No one ever came
to the black and brass door. And we

never saw her again after she turned eighteen
and left that very morning, still wearing the convent
uniform, but the blouse open three buttons down
and the socks low on her white ankles. She left
on a sleety day in October, years after —
from under a bed in the infirmary — I'd seen

what the nuns did to her when she confessed
she masturbated: bending her over, pulling down
her panties to ram the longest part of an ivory crucifix
into her, hissing: He is the Only One Who Can Come
Inside You — No One Else — You Hear?

She didn't let out a sound, not a sigh:
the pallor of survival carved into her face
when she pulled her panties up again.
I think she made it: she was of the stone
statues are made from. And yet, I still
search — Judith, I can't stop searching —
for signs we made it,
you, me and the others,
signs I find in the smallest things:
a flawless sky, a leaf autumn
turns, an open gate.

from Seven Fragments on Hearing a Hammer Pounding

Antwerp, 1947

My parents, hoarding
profits from what they call
the good war, are happy:

a million hammers, ten million
nails are needed to rebuild Europe,
and my father sells iron and steel.

One's misery is
another's happiness, he says
as we drive through

Pelican Street and what
had been the Jewish Quarter.
I am five.

(Fifty years later I remember winds blew dust
and ashes through the empty bellies of bombed houses.
Some walls still stood. For no one. Gutted doors
and windows were like screaming mouths caught in brick:
blocks of them. And blocks and blocks of them —)

Father spits out
his cigarette: Nothing's
changed here, only pigeons

and rats instead of Jews.
I don't know that word: *Joden*,
he says in Dutch, *Joden*.

I ask what kind
of animals *Joden* are. My parents
laugh, laugh.

(To think I spoke their tongue before finding mine —
O Gods of Grief, grant me this: some tongues will die,
some tongues must.)

Thief, 1950

Oxblood velvet drapes
frame Father's office windows.
Ten million hammers

pound nails in Belgium
France, Holland, Italy, England,
Russia, Poland,

and Germany — Germany,
too — building roofs, barns, houses,
churches, schools,

railroads, and bridges
after the war. Father loads iron
and steel onto Antwerp's ships —

he's a rich man now.
I wait for him to return
from meetings. I'm seven.

A dusk sun strokes
the drapes, his mahogany
desk gleams blood-red.

I open a drawer, see
Father's pen. I hear ships
from the harbor urge me —

Doo-it, dooo — so I
reach for it, gold and heavy,
take and uncap it,

draw a line in my palm —
the ink is green, a strong, hard
green. The door opens,

Father grabs his pen,
slaps my face, knees my chest,
but listen:

my need to write
started then, a hunger to write,
to own a pen.

Allen Brafman

Gardens of Smoke

There are Jews hidden in
the synagogue. Grasshoppers
hide in the grass. In which feather

does the song of the song sparrow
hide? Where is the salt hidden in
the ocean? Where is the smoke

hiding that hid my aunts and uncles,
tangled ghosts, screaming
Enough as they rose through Nazi

chimneys? How many leaves are in
hiding in the forest? How many trees?
To come home to his family for Shabbos —

every Shabbos — my grandfather's
grandfather fought wolves in the Hidden Forest.
Some say they were werewolves.

His beard was sparse, his long coat threadbare
but clean. Take me to the synagogues
built of ash. Deliver the smoke from my sleeves.

There is water hiding in the ocean. There are
gardens. Where are the people buried in the sky?
Where are the Jews buried?

Rivkah

Many times, I have seen this bird, or others like it, by itself,
 or in large numbers, standing on thin, yellow legs,
  in the shallows at the edge of one of the salt marshes
   I frequently visit.

The marsh I am visiting now is at the southern tip
of a narrow peninsula off the coast of New Jersey. The sun
setting in the background, an enormous orange disc,
makes the bird difficult to see.

Not only now, but every time I see the bird, I say its name,
as though in saying the name I am saying something significant
about the bird, but the fact is that when I pronounce its name,
it is not about the bird I am talking

but about myself — that I am the sort of person who calls a bird
by its proper name; that through its name, this bird and I
are bound essentially together. This bird and I,
we come from one another.

~ ~ ~ ~ ~

On the outskirts of town, along with the other women
and the elderly men and the children, my mother's
grandmother, a tiny person with spindly legs, a woman
I have never met, a woman I know only from photographs,

was shot to death by some neighbors and fell into a shallow ditch
half-filled with muddy water. She was killed for being Jewish,
and for a couple of fingers of whiskey. Her name was Rivkah.
Dovid, my mother's cousin Neshi's second husband,

told me the date. It was the same day but a few hours earlier
that he and the other men were taken from their homes
to a railway station and beaten. Then a long
train ride to slave labor and inexhaustible torture,

and a room filled with poison gas he escaped to survive.
Forty-seven years after Rivkah collapsed in the late
afternoon sun, dead from her neighbors'
bullets, Dovid told me. He told me everything.

~ ~ ~ ~ ~

Rivkah was the mother of his friend Leibel he had played with as a child;
my grandfather's baby brother, Leibel. My mother's uncle, Leibel,
she did not meet until he was an old man, leading a donkey
along a faraway road in a dusty place.

When the knock came on the door, Leibel went out the back window
into the forest. His wife had told him *Go. Leibish,*
they are coming for you.
He never saw his wife or children again.

Leibel — a name that means heart, a name that means dear heart.
My mother's grandmother's name is Rivkah —
in the language of this country, Rebecca. My great-grandmother.

The original meaning of the name is not entirely clear.
It is sufficient to know the name.
It is essential to know whose name it is.

~ ~ ~ ~ ~

The year Rivkah was murdered
was the year of my first birthday.

Dovid told me
forty-four years later.
He told me everything.

I was forty-five years old
when Dovid told me.

~ ~ ~ ~ ~

Eighteen years later while sitting shiva for my mother,
her cousin Sonya shakes her head — *To the day he died,*
Sonya whispers, *Leibish never forgave himself*

for going out that window. They had thought
the Nazis were coming for the men. But they came
for the women. And for the children.

~ ~ ~ ~ ~

Rebecca went to the well to draw water to fill her pitcher.
But when the water saw it was Rebecca, it rose on its own.
And Rebecca's pitcher was filled, without effort.
Rebecca did not bend. Nor did she labor.

~ ~ ~ ~ ~

The bird scratches its toes in the mud, lunges,
stabs its head into the water, pulls back in a moment — an eel
wriggling in its bill.

Rivkah and the bird take no notice of one another, go off
in different directions. Most of the time, I keep my eyes on Rivkah.
My younger sister's name is Rivkah.

Most of the time, I am alone in a marsh filled with ghosts.

Van K. Brock

The Hindenburg

This early showpiece of the Thousand Year Reich
used eight hundred fifty thousand skins of cattle
for hydrogen bags.

It is said that the night it burned
the thunder of panicking hooves
drowned the screams of passengers.

As far away as the buttes of Asia,
one old Siberian woman says that merely
the echo of their lowing still stirs
immense winds and whirlwinds.
                                        All the small
meadows of Europe remember their grazing;
cattle-cars and railway platforms shudder
still at their foreshadowings.
                                        Untold cobblers
recall the million seams glued and stitched
on screaming machines before their pockets
held enough hydrogen to kindle a conflagration.

The war on nature begun,
eventually, every country in Europe
and many in Africa and Asia were gutted:
in bombings, in battle, at sea, and in the fires,
filth, and hunger of virulent slave pens:
the outward rendering of ageless accumulations
sucked up from the cities and villages of earth,

and the ruins run in and out of us all,
stretching before and behind
for far more than a Thousand Years.

from This Way to the Gas

For Tadeusz Borowski (1922–51)

Tadeusz, the vice is still tight, and you
among those who show how it works — jaws, screw,
and lever — through what we do or don't do.
With you gone, we still write your life
and are written on, as it outlines us, still.
So many players, such footwork, kicked spheres,

[stanza continues]

the game in overtime, and Poland back and forth
for two hundred years, between new-risen czars mocking
Christ and Rome. And after our Armistice, Poland
fought on in rubble, then during the brief breath
of the republic of '22, you were born, a Pole
in the Ukraine, without a voice. Europe's lights
flickering after another long nightmare — reservoirs
of your spirit in libraries and museums elsewhere —
and bereft of tools, livestock, crops, Poland
stood up in debates and polls. Fields bloomed,
but the struggle against dead souls who still want
to live through us, goes on. I hear you, Tadeusz.

Your dad in the Polish army fought old gauntlets
making the game rules around you. You were four
when he was gulagged to dig canals from Leningrad
through tundra, to the White Sea, but already eight
when your mother, sent to Siberia, nearly died
among thousands who starved. You studied, tended
the cows until their calves calved, and you were ten.
Your dad came home, a stranger; mine died, and I
was born where white still taunted black; all that
in the year that became Hitler, Hitler a nation,
deepening poverty everywhere, darkening earth still.

Your mother returned; you were twelve, the years lost;
and all together in Warsaw, poverty sent you off
to school with the Brothers of Poverty, almost
as much an orphan as Poland. The blitz hit you
at seventeen, and east and west left you to SS squads
rounding up Poles for medals. In a close race,
a single squad shot one hundred and forty thousand
the first twenty-four hours.

All schools closed to Poles, in Warsaw's rooms
teachers rose tall to tell you the true heritage
of Europe, your struggle and trampling. On the way
to your finals, cars blocked streetcars, like tigers
tracking antelope, you said, as you spilled from wild
trolleys, ripe green pears, tearing up tilled fields,
spring scents. In jungle streets people were hunted.

It was 1940. At eighteen, in the underground university,
you read literature, translated *Twelfth Night* — "If music be the food
of love, play on, Give me excess of it, that surfeiting" —
learned love, "Methought she purged the air of pestilence."
And . . . "fell and cruel hounds / E'er since pursue me" —
and printed your own poems, among banned bulletins,
for us: *We will leave scrapiron behind us,*
in hollow mocking mouths of laughing generations.

In the rooms of a friend they tortured, the SS trapped
your fiancée, then you. From your cell by the ghetto
in Warsaw, you saw soldiers lob grenades into huge
tenements, burning houses edging anguish and hunger.

You, too, went to Auschwitz, she to Birkenau,
but gassing of Aryans had stopped. The long lines
to diurnal-nocturnal flames were reserved for Jews
and the living dead you called "muslims," the bigotry
of those dying in the teeth of bigotry. Dissident
Poles and others — from the nations of Europe — waited
their turn, with able, skilled Jews, working at death

to be free. They sent you to Birkenau with a crew
to collect the day's corpses of infants, and you saw
your betrothed, her head shaved, body a raw field
of drying sores, and holding her, you said,
"Don't worry. Our children won't be bald."

As the Allies neared, you were sent to Dachau,
then American camps, among ten million homeless.
Since she was safe in Sweden, you walked away
from all slants, to wander with books and notebook
by lakes, found Paris a lovely city, giddy whore,
and returned to Warsaw to publish your whole truth,
for the American 7th Army which freed us from hell.

Your truth was brutal, even to yourself, but others,
with you in the camps, called you a friend and hero.
At twenty-four — one of the best writer's in the east, risen
from death, deathless — your longing letters joined
you with your long betrothed. Enough! No more!
Nothing can ever be as before.

After your daughter's birth, you left
your wife in the hospital holding your bald innocence.
At home, not yet thirty, tattooed still, you opened the gas.
No one's laughing, Tadeusz. The dead are never right,
you once wrote, the living never wrong. Wrong.

Louis Daniel Brodsky

Learning the ABC's in Wartime Germany

A is for *Adam* and Eva Braun . . .
Is for *apple* a day, a minute, a zeptosecond,
Which keeps Dr. Mengele away
From dutiful Teutonic children,
Keeps teacher from reaching for her switch
To punish rosy-cheeked Brünhilde and Wolfgang,
Making them stay after school,
Writing six million names
Across the Third Reich blackboard
In disappearing crimson chalk . . .
Is for *Aryan*,
A master race of good little girls and boys like you . . .
Is for *Anschluss*, the annexation of Österreich,
Whose populace is fully sympathetic
To our racial policies
And eventual Endlösung . . .
Is for *Auschwitz*, a spa in the east,
Like Paradise or Valhalla,
Where Germany sends families of Juden
To collect their sweepstakes winnings and spend them.
B is for *beautiful Berlin boulevards,*
Berchtesgaden, blitzkrieg,
Bełżec, Bergen-Belsen, Buchenwald, Buna . . .
Is for the *bunker* of our *beloved* Führer . . .
And ***Z*** is for *zebras, zinnias, Zyklon B,*
And both backward pieces of our sacred swastika.

Phoenixes

For Menke Katz

My ears almost hear them crisping in the ovens,
Dissipating in acidic attrition
Above Auschwitz,
Entering the ancestral nimbus of Scripture,
Almost hear them crackling, sputtering,
Lifting into eviscerated whispers
Above the camps,
Almost hear their scattering ashes
Drifting through the blackest atmosphere
Toward the farthest galactic Canaan,

[stanza continues]

Where hearts beat
And the darkest planets in the sky
Glow like star sapphires backlighted by God.

My ears can almost hear those Jews,
Who, disguised as smoke, as ash,
And losing all hope,
Refused to die, to die
In me, in my poetry;
Almost, they come to life,
Keep coming alive
As I release them from history
To listen to me listening to them
Weeping for me,
Reminding me that I, too, am a Jew,
Issue of those stillborn
In the hissing wombs of Auschwitz.

Schindlerjuden

For Thomas Keneally

Yesterday, having arrived one hour early
For the 4 p.m. showing of *Schindler's List*,
Standing near the head of a rapidly extending line,
I scanned the faces of accumulating strangers
Patiently keeping their places,
Not bunching up, shoving, but not giving ground,
Jewish faces almost exclusively, like mine,
Waiting to be told to submit our tickets,
Proceed down the corridor, to the fourth door,
Assume spaces from which we'd watch
Our own potential futures pass in review,
As though they, it — destiny — were a Pathé newsreel
Reprising a normal *Judenrein*-day in Poland or Germany
From 1941 through April 1945 . . .

The ceaseless waiting grating on us,
Growing more enervating, until, en masse, we perked up,
Alert to phantoms, ghosts, poltergeists,
Dazed souls exiting through a narrow passage,
Those who'd just seen what we were about to witness —
Oh, those drawn, grim, gaunt, chalky faces,
So forlorn, morose, etched with inarticulate grief,
Their liberated spirits empty of tears, fear-ridden,
Groping to locate themselves in the hysterical mall
As though it were more than a matter of eyes
Accommodating to the bright lights

[stanza continues]

After all that black-and-white subjugation of the senses,
Trying to distinguish that haven from the eerie desolation
At whose depot gates they had just been jettisoned,
Corralled by what sinister manner of beast
Or sadistic executioner of crimes in the name of the Reich
None could begin to conceive . . . that crowd so somber
They might have made up a funeral procession
Or been the walking dead.

Now, a day later, I no longer rely on memory
So much as intuition to lead me to this conclusion:
Yesterday might as easily have been Auschwitz,
Not a theater, and I one of thousands
Led to the Zyklon B gassing showers,
Then dumped into Topf & Sons ovens,
Finally floating, sifting, spiraling inside the vast draft,
Up through that immense, roaring chimney stack
Spewing millions of tons of European Jew-ash into oblivion.

Speaking for Survivors

Yesterday at noon, a humid Sunday in St. Louis,
I performed my duties as the keynote speaker
For a gathering of Holocaust survivors,
A sacred congregation
Of more than a hundred aged waifs, devastated souls,
Whose glazed eyes still looked death in the face.

And I realized how inconsequential my life was
Compared with theirs, their disembodied lives,
Those people with the unpronounceable last names
Redolent of peasantry and ghetto-dweller stock
From Germany, Russia, Poland, Austria, Hungary,
How irrelevant the poems I was reading to them were,
Poems I'd invented with empathy and compassion,
Poems about those who died or outlasted the Shoah,
Poems of showers, furnaces, killing squads,

Poems depicting an entire panoply of disenfranchised spirits,
Ghosts wrested from parents,
Bereft of wife and children, possessions, dreams.
And as I read my poems to them,
I could see from the vantage of my podium,
From the vantage of my insularity,
From the vantage of half a century,
That those whom the angel of death had passed over
Were not listening to my verse,

Or, if they were, that my words were inaccessible,
Lost in the whirlwind of sixty years ago —
When they experienced the German scourge firsthand.
And so, I recited to them my pathetic poetic stories,
Hoping to let them know
I was paying tribute to their survivor lives,

That I care about their torments
And wish I could right the wrongs of the Endlösung,
Could soothe the lamentations of six million Jews
Sacrificed to the malevolent disease
Whose curse still plagues us all.
And I read my metaphors, my recreations,
My desperate approximations of the victimized psyche,
Hoping to strike a common chord in those survivors,
Who had gathered at a luncheon in their honor,

But nothing of substance changed fate one iota.
I, a poet born in 1941,
Too late to bear witness,
Looked out over my audience,
Looked into their eyes, and wept inside,
Helpless to rectify the sadness they've had to endure,
Wondering if I had any right to be there,
To write about their plight, to speak for them at all.

Yesterday, I tried to be of some use to those souls.
Tonight, a day after some praised me
For the humanity of my verse, the depth of my vision,
I reflect on what I read, my Holocaust poems,
Wondering what more I can do or say,
So battered were these survivors,
And knowing that not a word I had to say to them
Could possibly matter.

Yom Kippur for a Survivor

This dark, early Thursday a.m.,
There's fire in the sky,
An autumnal conflagration of disembodied spirits
Pulsating like northern lights
Reflecting across a lake's calm face,
A numinous cluster of depleted, incomplete souls
Orbiting their old home in a meteor shower,
Glowing particles that account for hued twilights,
Vermilion or hazy-pink dusks and dawns,
Depending on ice crystals and dust motes in the atmosphere,
Depending on parallaxes, angles of refraction,

[stanza continues]

Depending on willing suspensions of disbelief,
Depending on skepticism of science and religion,
Depending on the degree of forgiveness
Those who sacrificed their lives in the Shoah
Are willing to accord Elohim,

Since it's their celestial presences, their mandorlas,
Not His,
That cast a collective shadow at high noon,
Their raw, omniscient, unfinished mission
That promises first comings, eternal peace,
Not His,
Their ineffable vision of the ultimate infernal abyss
That he senses whenever, at Yom Kippur,
He asks God to repent,
To beg him for clemency from his final judgment of Him
For having abrogated His covenant,
Instead of beseeching Him
For dispensation from His Final Judgment of him.
This morning, his eyes cry tears of dry fire;
The Days of Awe, like Armageddon and Auschwitz,
Turn to Kaddish-flames, forgotten names, God-ashes.

Michael Dennis Browne

Mengele

Don't tell me about the bones of Mengele,
the bones are alive and well.
Don't think to thrill me with tales
of the drowned bones uncovered,
the bones are alive and well
inside the sleeves of a suit this day
and carving out the figures of a fat check
or severing a ribbon with the ceremonial scissors
or holding the head of a child;
I tell you, the bones are alive and well.

Don't expect me to get excited
concerning the skull of Mengele,
the skull is alive and well,
the skull is asquirm with schemes this day
and low words are leaving it at this moment
and other skulls are nodding at what they hear,
seated about the world table;
I tell you, the skull is alive and well.

Don't bother showing me pictures
of the remains of Mengele,
the remains are alive and well
and simmering in our rivers
or climbing into our houses out of the ground
where they will not be confined
or sliding inside the rain
out of the summer air; oh yes,
the remains are even there, I tell you,
are alive, are well, are everywhere.

Michael R. Burch

Pfennig Postcard, Wrong Address

We saw their pictures:
tortured out of our imaginations
like golems.

We could not believe
in their frail extremities
or their gaunt faces,

pallid as our disbelief.
They are not
with us now . . .

We have:
huddled them
into the backroomsofconscience,

consigned them
to the ovensofsilence,
buried them in the mass graves

of circumstancesbeyondourcontrol.
We have
so little left

of them
now
to remind us.

Olga Cabral

At the Jewish Museum

("Kaddish for the Little Children,"
an environment, consisting of a room 28 x 17 x 8 ft.,
by the sculptor, Harold Paris.)

Only what I bring to this room will exist here.
For the room is empty.
Empty as the inside
of a cold oven.
Narrow passageway in.
Narrow passageway out.
At the entrance, bronze scrolls.
Words:
the alphabet of mysterious
tablets.
May words guide me through this place.

Enter.
Did I expect to find
darkness?
Did I hope for blindness?
Worse than absence of light this
gloom and evil glint of some
metal object. Is it
a box?
a receptacle for —
what?
An artifact
of a door in the mind?
(Metal door that
clangs, clangs —.)
Walls bare.
Naked brick.
Nothing to see.
Nothing.

In this room there were never clocks or calendars
or daily lists of little things to be done.
No one ever had any birthdays.
No one ever put on a hat.
Neither star nor spider came here.
Nor mouse nor cricket.
There is no trace of the memory
of a swirl of dust
of a fly
crawling on the wall.

[stanza continues]

A room without history of furniture
of broken plates or cups
of diaries
lost buttons
of shreds of cloth
of colors.
A room filled with absence
a room filled with loss
a room with no address
in a city in a country
unknown to mapmakers.

Once and only once
God
a trembling old man leaning on a cane
passed by but did not dare
look in.

Perhaps the black metal object
is a box with names.
Perhaps nobody had a name.
It was all done with numbers.
It meant less that way.
Perhaps the box is filled with numbers.
Perhaps the walls and ceiling —
shadow walls and shadow ceiling
bulging with emptiness
are receding rapidly to the edge
of the visible universe where objects
tend to disappear —

where all the names have gone
the diminutives
the sweet
nicknames
beyond reach of our most cunning
telescopes
and nets to catch the whispers
of the stars.

Joan Campion

To Gisi Fleischmann
Rescuer of Her People

Courage in battle is an easy thing,
Compared to your gift —
You, who never would bow down
To your tormentors, and whose hand
Was always quick to save,
Though surely you endured
A million secret deaths
Before your own turn came
And you died with those you could not help.

When I imagine you, I do not dwell
Upon your end, so common to the times,
Yet so wretched in its loneliness.
Instead, I see your spirit
Burning as faithful as a candle
Whose flame is buffeted
But never quite put out.
For long and blood-drenched years
That candle gleamed:
For multitudes, the only light there was.

Those who will not bend
End by being broken;
And you were. Yet they could do no more
Than murder you. The radiance that was yours
Will glow forever in the hearts
Of those who search for righteousness.
And even if your very name should fade,
Wherever there is love, there you will live.

Cyrus Cassells

Auschwitz, All Hallows

Auschwitz-Birkenau, 1 November 2005

Look, we have made
a counterpoint

of white chrysanthemums,
a dauntless path

of death-will-not-part-us petals
and revering light;

even here,
even here

before the once-wolfish ovens,
the desecrating wall

where you were shot,
the shrike-stern cells

where you were bruised
and emptied of your timebound beauty —

you of the confiscated shoes
and swift-shorn hair,

you, who left,
as sobering testament, the scuffed

luggage of utter hope
and harrowing deception.

Come back, teach us.
From these fearsome barracks

and inglorious fields
flecked with human ash,

in the russet, billowing hours
of All Hallows,

let the pianissimo
of your truest whispering

(vivid as the crunched frost
of a forced march)

become a slowly blossoming,
ever-voluble hearth —

revealing to us,
the baffled, the irresolute,

the war-torn, the living,
more, more, more

of the fire and attar of what it means
to be human.

Juliek's Violin

For Elie Wiesel

Even here?
In this snow-bound barracks?

Suddenly, the illicit sounds
of Beethoven's concerto

erupt from Juliek's smuggled violin,
suffusing this doomsday shed

teeming with the trampled
and the barely alive,

realm of frostbite and squalor,
clawing panic and suffocation —

Insane, God of Abraham,
insanely beautiful:

a boy insisting
winter cannot reign forever,

a boy conveying his brief,
barbed-wired life

with a psalmist's or a cantor's
arrow-sure ecstasy:

One prison-striped friend
endures to record

the spellbinding strings,
the woebegone,

and the other,
the impossible Polish fiddler,

is motionless by morning,
his renegade instrument

mangled
under the haggard weight

of winterkilled, unraveling men.
Music at the brink of the grave,

eloquent in the pitch dark,
tell-true, indelible,

as never before,
as never after —

Abundance,
emending beauty,

linger in the listening,
the truth-carrying soul of Elie,

soul become slalom-swift,
camp-shrewd, un-crushable;

abundance, be here, always here,
in this not-yet-shattered violin.

Life Indestructible

For Etty Hillesum (1914–43)

1

It might have been a sibyl's voice,
Clear and winnowing:

We should be willing to act as a balm for all wounds.

All winter I've slept and labored
With those words.
Etty, you've haunted me —
I can't stop hearing your voice,
The last line of your diary,
Unshakable:

We should be willing to act as a balm for all wounds
We should be willing to act as a balm
We should be willing to act
We should be willing . . .

2

Your voice, Etty Hillesum,
A young Dutch Jew
Avid to weave a self
Whose ardent story
Refuses to end
In bleakness,
The final seep of ash,
Refuses to end
With your cloaked, anonymous death —

3

Like a wave long embedded in your body
Your urge to kneel,
Bear witness —

Dear *thinking heart of the barracks,*
When you started your diary
One loutish spring, in an occupied city,
You chose to listen to your soul:

Very well then, this new certainty
That what they are after
Is our total destruction.
I accept it. I know it now
And I will not burden others
With my fear.
I will not be bitter
If others fail to grasp
What is happening . . .
I work and continue to live
With the same conviction —

4

There was a man you came to love,
A priest of Jung,
Cherished by many women
For his warlock's gift:
        Unraveling the map of the hand —
        That second face, you called it.

Matchless union:
All at once you're negotiating a field
Of fierce clarity — lavender, lavender,
An ardor of lavender —

And you carried this strange sentience
Into a lovers' city
Of flower stalls, little bridges,
Become a city slowly siphoned of Jews . . .

Yet you stuck to your lucent journey,
As lovers might:
Reading the *Song of Solomon*
After rations,
Taking blackout paper from the window
To watch the stars —

You vowed to follow him
Even to flinty camps,
Sharing his fate —
Dear spoiled man,

Who died in his own bed
On the glowering day
The Nazis set for his capture —

5

You volunteered for Westerbork,
Way station to Poland:
No, not enough to love God from a garret,
When everywhere your people are reviled.
My people — yes, the words have a weight;
You feel them,
A well-worn treasured key
Cached between your breasts,
And so you go to your tribe,
Simply.

6

Behind barbed wire,
The one, unchanging task:
To value each
Who crosses your path —

Like the haggard, hunchbacked woman
In her green silk kimono,
Who came to you in Westerbork,
Moving with weird grace
From bed to bed,
Doing small services for the damned:

Surely God will understand my doubts
In a world like this . . .

7

Down on my knees, I begin to understand,
Dear girl who was learning to kneel —
With my forehead pressed
To the cool and charitable ground:
Yes, there are places the mind can't go,
Suffused as it is
With an inner debris,

[stanza continues]

Where only the soul can enter,
As the heart is crushed beneath the wheels
Of that juggernaut we call
        Past and Future:
The gutless Never Now,
The Never Here —

So you have to kneel
In the instant
When hush and humility are all;
You have to kneel
With a lilylike trust,

As you await the flutter of God . . .

8

Time and again, the trek to Poland,
The train's prey-cry,
Titanic, metallic —
Sometimes a rag or beloved hand
Waving from obstinate gaps
In box cars —

In brilliant, arduous light,
Now freight trains fill
With plundered heiresses, and bawling infants,
The old glazier, barely clothed,
Clutching a frayed, last-minute blanket —
The gruff boy who failed to escape,
And catapulted forty souls
Into the wide seine
Of corporal punishment,
The ex-soubrette adding hairdye
To her suitcase,
The fettered Gypsies, and the light-shy nuns,
The old women asking:

Will there be medical assistance in Poland?

9

At the threshold of banishment
There is so little to clasp,
Or carry.
Very well then,
You'll clear room in the rucksack
For Rilke, a Russian grammar,

[stanza continues]

A small, hardy Bible;
Opening the pages at random, you find:
The Lord is my high tower . . .

Is there room for Tolstoy on the train to Auschwitz?
You've made room.

* *

And now you toss from the train
An incandescent postcard:
We have left the camp singing

10

Today I went out into the sun,
With your injunction to *feel*,
Refuse every soporific,
To step into both
The bitter and the blossoming:

Beyond crocuses,
Always judges-and-juries,
The shadows of bully pulpits,
Of gallows trees —

And if I can hear long-voweled clues
Of blackbirds,
Red-wing clarions of spring,
Then I must hear
My neighbors groaning —

Etty, you journeyed to the core
Of havoc:

And if I should not survive,
How I die
Will show me who I really am:

Tell me what you found.
Tell me what it means
When a young man answers:
My AIDS — that's when the blessing began,
That's when I turned
To face my true self —

Today when I boarded a train,
I stood before a woman so deformed,
I felt the whole enormous weight —

Common fear, disgust, apathy, decorum —
The whole Valhalla of cruel culture
Against my cheek,
So that it took sheer strength
Not to turn away,
Sheer strength to let my eye veer
Into a place, a holiness
That was utterly hers —
Sheer strength for her to bare herself
To the workaday world —
Extraordinary woman,
Bloated mask,
Won-back heart
In her plain but confident business suit.

And it was your voice I imagined then:

If they speak of fate,
Terrific suffering,
Tell them:
We were never in anyone's "clutches";
Always, always,
We were in the arms of God.

Poem for the Artists of the Holocaust

The bone-white wind of this century
A prayer-shawl of human ash.
And still the hand lifts
The intrepid pencil,
The chip of charcoal,
Against the plunder, the ordure, the roaring.

And still the soul craves to make bridgeable
The space between the careworn
And the dead,
Craves never to quit the embattled earth
Unrecorded,
The unstainable soul:

This is the charnel house art,
The epistle,
Cached in the sleep-safe tin,
Inviolable, brought to air:

Dear Finder,

In Terezín,
By the meager bread-carts,
In Auschwitz,
Beside the rooms of shaved hair —
Tell someone I was here.

The Postcard of Sophie Scholl

There is the lightning-white moment
when you learn —

flint-like as the moment,
when your costive train to Kraków stopped

and you woke to find yourself,
in jostling twilight,

at the Auschwitz platform —
that the Italian postcard

you garnered in Milan years ago
as a genial talisman,

isn't of a pipe-dreaming
Italian boy,

no, no, but an androgynous
image of Sophie Scholl,

the young, intrepid Resistance heroine —
as if you registered,

in your Schubert-adoring daughter,
your school-bound son,

a fire undetected before:
Doric-strong nouns demanding

What would you undertake
to stop tyranny? —

stouthearted nouns:
integrity, probity, courage;

in benighted Munich,
the spit-in-the-eye swiftness,

the unflappable courage
of a crossed-out swastika,

a dissident leaflet,
the brash, the unbribable

integrity in the gust
of the word *freedom*

sprayed over the walls
and ramparts of a deranged

fatherland that rent flesh
as if it were foolscap —

Someday you will be
where I am now,

a steely, farseeing Sophie proclaimed
to the rapacious

Nazi tribunal that rushed her
to execution —.

Gazer, collector, in clarity's name,
look close, then closer:

it's not just a bud-sweet,
pensive beauty,

a *bel ragazzo's* charm;
all these years:

it's the spirit of unswerving truth
that you've cherished.

Judith Chalmer

The Archivist

I didn't expect it to be so
pretty. I didn't want it to be
so clean. It wasn't the Nazis
who fingered the needle,
stitched a neat cotton backing
to the coarse-grained star.
"It was my grandmother
who lined it," I told the archivist
when I dropped it on her table.

Slowly, as if lifting a thin yellow baby
from her bath, the archivist raised
the tired cloth to the light,
ran her finger over the little scars,
the tracks where my grandma pulled
a heavy thread around all six points
of the star. *Look!* She nodded
to where the window framed wild iris,
orchids banked in the yard, and the star
translucent against the light.

I'd missed the way people reach
inside, when even their faces are buried
in grime, to find something pretty,
something to shine — Beautiful! in the dirt,
in the stubble and smear, Bright! in the blade
of the knife. My eyes followed hers
in the late gray light to the curled free end
of the plain cotton thread my grandma hid
fifty years ago, tucked way inside, so in hands
like mine, it wouldn't come unraveled.

Personal to Kaplan

Kaplan, I saw your name
carved into the top bunk, the only scar
in the smooth white wood, the only
whiff of rotten flesh in the sweet incense
of fresh sawdust that lingers in the corners
of the reconstructed barracks at Dachau.

Half a century past and framed
signs remind us to be respectful
of the careful display, keep our breath
out of the bunks, and use quiet voices
while we tour the exhibit, as if we'd be
joking around like we were waiting
in line for the Tunnel of Love.

But I tell you, Kaplan, I left my blood,
which sprang like a poppy out of a trench,
when I gouged my finger with a point
of reconstructed barbed wire on the way
into this place, then smeared it on the wall
like the amputated stories my father
couldn't tell. Right where you leaned
yours, friend, I leaned my impious head,
stroked my finger down the rough side

[stanza continues]

of my father's drawn cheek in the picture
I held, sitting on the bottom bunk, looking up
at your name under the empty bowl
that hung from its hook.

And I can see you smiling after all,
clapping for me as I doubled over
the empty foundation of Barrack #9,
slamming my father's "No!"
against the concrete echo in the arid
roll-call square, spitting curses
over the caps of the cheerful
postcard concessionaires.

Kaplan, wherever you are, I'm carving
this message for you in the clean,
smooth side of God's unflinching sky:
We are here, you and I! Our coats on,
ready to go, our cheeks full and hot
against all that was planned. We're passing
notes across the tracks, through the fence,
bearing good hot food — big chunks of potato,
thick cream, fresh dill — steaming from the fire.

John Ciardi

The Gift

In 1945, when the keepers cried *kaput*,
Josef Stein, poet, came out of Dachau
like half a resurrection, his other
eighty pounds still in their invisible grave.

Slowly then the mouth opened and first
a broth, and then a medication, and then
a diet, and all in time and the knitting mercies,
the showing bones were buried back in flesh,

and the miracle was finished. Josef Stein,
man and poet, rose, walked, and could even
beget, and did, and died later of other causes
only partly traceable to his first death.

He noted — with some surprise at first —
that strangers could not tell he had died once.
He returned to his post in the library, drank his beer,
published three poems in a French magazine,

and was very kind to the son who at last was his.
In the spent of one night he wrote three propositions:
That Hell is the denial of the ordinary. That nothing lasts.
That clean white paper waiting under a pen
is the gift beyond history and hurt and heaven.

David Citino

Swastika

Forestry officials in the town of Zernikow
just found a huge swastika-shaped patch
of light-green larch trees . . .
— *Newsweek*

Aloft, we can read this world,
decipher our mean designs,
the glyphs and lines
we use to force earth
to wear our smallest ideas.

Some evils are seasonal.
Spring, the larches hope
against darker evergreens;
fall, they hold day's gold
like trembling hands.

Planted fifty-two years ago
by a troop of Hitler Youth,
stooping as one in cruel boots,
they grew, vicious whispers
outliving the war, the camps.

Can we pretend we've grown
beyond silent greeds,
shrill unisons of tribe,
a forest shouting out
a sign more obscene than money?

The crippled cross can't be
cut down, for in absence
it would glow louder,
a cold hole in the universe.
Only by clear-cutting

can these perennial acres
of unspeakable ache be erased.
Should we once and for all
fall to work with chainsaw, ax,
tree by lovely tree? No.

This scar must be preserved,
a monument to our talent
for twisting blessings
into curses, the very trees
saying *Hate, hate, hate*.

Vince Clemente

From the Ardeatine Caves

Nazi war criminal Herbert Kappler, 71, former police chief of Rome, died yesterday of stomach cancer. He had been serving a life term for the execution of 335 Italians, mostly Jews, in reprisal for the ambush killing of 32 German soldiers by Italian partisans in Rome. The execution was staged in the Ardeatine Caves, just outside of Rome. German engineers assisted in sealing the caves that entombed the victims. The execution was carried out on 24 March 1944, now observed in Italy as a national day of mourning.
— *New York Times*, February 1978

I. Above the Giardino alla Francese

From your window above the Giardino alla Francese
you muse through the cypress grove
to the pond, the footbridge
and think of Monet at Giverny —
the waterlilies like floating candles.

From your window above the Giardino alla Francese
you record in meticulous columns
your *todeskandidaten*,
these "candidates for death"
for the order that read:
"Ten Italians for every German dead
in today's ambush."

You've been up all night
listening to Wagner
remembering your boyhood in Stuttgart,
at 6 AM a vireo's song woke you
to the list incomplete —
and you had run out of Jews.

You have no stomach for this, Herr Kappler,
but a soldier like a monk
takes his solemn vows.
Out of some bizarre logic
you tell yourself that somehow
what you are doing is God's work —
this god red-eyed
all in pieces
seeding the fall harvest.

II. Inside the Ardeatine Caves

You learn, Herr Kappler
how one of your young officers
refused to shoot:
he looked too deeply
into the eyes of a boy,
the baker's helper from Rimini,
and saw for a second
his own brother
home from Dresden.
He could not fire.
The pistol froze
at the boy's temple.

At the bottom of the hill
you think you smell death.
It is only the mountain ash,
berries hemorrhaging.
The young officer is there
waiting for you at the cave's mouth,
double lightning bolt
on his helmet.

"Better I at your side
when you fire," you say,
then walk him
arm around waist
into the chamber.
Once inside, it is easy,
the cognac helps —
even the baker's helper falls.

The bodies are piled in rows
stacked like bread
and the caves are sealed tight.
"No resurrection here,"
you tell yourself,
"none tonight."

Helen Degen Cohen (Halina Degenfisz)

And the Snow Kept Falling

For my sister, who died at the age of two

Deep, deep in
the glass toy
there lies a river
warmer than diamonds
and we sit beside it
girls and boys
we sit in the snowy glass toy —

You lay down in the snow
leaving a human print when you rose,
and the snow kept falling
on the children, on their houses —
on Aunt Vera, who laughed like a movie star
coming in with her Warsaw shoes and chocolates,
on grandmother in her cooking house
folding her twenty children to sleep,
on Uncle feeling the oven-tile wall,
letting the warmth reach into his heart,
on Anna the nursemaid, who walked me to the park,
her legs like a goat's. It was summer, yet snow
fell on her freckles, on our braided hair,
on Nathaniel, soon to be sent to Siberia.
The streets were powdered white,
I was sucking an icicle
and the baker came out laughing
his arms high receiving the snow
as if it had just been made by God,
and it fell on the guts in the butcher shop,
on the tunnels where everyone ran to hide
when the planes came humming —
on the Thursday markets in the open square,
and the women who sat on the ground hawking
chickens and cheeses, on me
and my mother holding onto my hand,
and snow fell on the thunder and the flowers under it —
onto the schnapps in my father's hand,
and the card players humming
La Donna è Mobile, and on David and Rachel,
who were dancing the tango
in the middle of the living room,
Rachel, so modern no snow could reach her,
David, so smooth, that there was no snow —

[stanza continues]

The streets were already white,
whiter than the page I write on,
and it fell on grandfather rocking in prayer,
and the other, the atheist, in need of work,
as he stood at his window in Warsaw, where it fell
and would keep on falling,
on his youngest, who died in the famine,
on the figures below in their black coats,
on his wife's commodious breasts and hair
every year thinner and longer by an inch —
snow so radiant, it must be the snow
that fell on the shtetl,
and over the farms,
and the fiddlers, and the normal death of infants —

and this is when you came about, Mirenka,
when you suddenly appeared, behind the typewriter,
    white as a bride
    weightless and smiling
a woman, yet young as the day you died,
    first and only sister.

Goat sister, Chagall bride,
though we may be living in a different painting,
sit beside us, tell us what to know,
let us shake up, then enter, your bubble of snow —
as if we have never been lost in history.

Deep, deeper than the
    mothers of snow
there lies a river
    warmer than diamonds
and we sit outside it,
everyone I know —

we are sitting and staring into the snow.

Habry

Habry, peaceful Polish flowers,
Mine, yet I never belonged to that country.
Fraying, breezing in the quietest quiet,
Blue, all along the edge of the wheatfield,
Silken blue, among orange poppies,
And the sun is silent, silent as the night.

How can so much sunlight sink so quietly?
How can it be that no one is here?
I, after all, have never left that countryside

[stanza continues]

And not even the Poles are visible, and where
Are the girls who forever wove garlands
And ran through flowers as if they were air?

I return to Habry as if by candlelight,
Warmed, though I know they are nowhere near,
There is nothing like them in poor Illinois,
No Jews-and-gentiles, nothing to separate
Petal from petal — only hushed blue
Habry, hovering in the air.

I Remember Coming into Warsaw, a Child

out of a sheer, sunlit countryside
where sometimes a goat made the only sound in
all the universe, and a car engine would certainly
tear the wing of an angel. Entering burnt Warsaw
and the Sound of the World, how strange, how lonely
the separate notes of Everything, lost in a smell of
spent shots still smoking, a ghost of bombs, a silence
of so many voices, the ruined city singing not only
a post-war song but an Everything hymn of dogs wailing
a car, a horse, a droning plane, a slow, distant
demolition, hammers like rain, the hum, the hum
bells and levers and voices leveled and absorbed
into the infinite hum in which the ruins
sat empty and low like well-behaved children
the ruins, their holes, like eyes, secretly open
passing on either side, as we entered Warsaw, an air
of lost worlds in a smoky sweet light ghosting
and willing their sounding and resounding remains

David Curzon

The Gardens

By the rivers of Babylon, there we sat down, yea, we wept
when we remembered Zion. We hanged our harps upon the willows
in the midst thereof.
— Psalm 137:1-2

Melbourne's Botanical Gardens! where I came
to walk along the bordered paths with him,
and pose in short pants for the photos placed
into this album I'm now leafing through,

[stanza continues]

and eat my sandwiches beside the lake,
and cast bread on the waters for the swans.
And later, when we met on Sundays, we
went off to European movies, then
to his small room where we played chess. He cut
his dense black bread held close up to his chest.
One afternoon we passed the synagogue
and saw some litter scattered on its steps
including lobster shells. He said, 'This is
deliberate desecration. They must know
lobster isn't kosher.' — 'Daddy, it's not that,
it's an Australian picnic. Not cleaned up.'
I thought it was absurd he didn't know.
This must have been round nineteen fifty-five.
A mere ten years had passed. And in four years
he'd suicide, and I would read the documents
he kept inside their envelopes in a wood box —
certificates of immigration, change
of name, degrees, but mainly photographs
and letters from his parents and his friends.
And then I found a letter he had sent
to Poland. The final one. It said, *I wish*
I could protect you from the sadists and was stamped
"Unable to deliver." Somehow I
was not aware. He never talked of it.
And now I try to visualize what happened to
his parents and those smiling friends of his,
and try to understand how it would feel
orphaned, divorced, recalling, to walk in
the gardens of Babylon, and not weep.

Ruth Daigon

Dachau Revisited 1971

By the light of the ovens,
the neighbors are still dancing
and the ash cans have been enchanted into urns.
Shadows crowd the walls,
the scratch of men.

Below a frosted lens of sky,
ghosts tell stories.
Days expand to years,
years snap loose from digitals,
the landscape smolders.

Worm voices,
weed voices
whirl like feathered seeds
wreathed in the smoke of memory
in a pause that lasts forever.

Ashes still remind us
and gas sends sharper signals
of lullabies, of barbed wire,
of skins scribbled over with prayer,
of heaped bones calling.

And the silence from those bodies
curls in the mouth
like a mother tongue.

Susan Dambroff

There Were Those

There were those
who escaped to the forests
who crawled through sewers
who jumped from the backs of trains

There were those
who smuggled messages
who smuggled dynamite
inside breadloaves
inside matchboxes
inside corpses

There were those
who were shoemakers
who put nails
into the boots
of German soldiers

There were those
who wrote poetry
who put on plays
who taught the children

There were those
who fed each other

Enid Dame

Soup

After watching Josh Waletzsky's documentary, "Partisans of Vilna"

1

I am making chicken soup in the Vilna Ghetto.
You think it's easy? First
you've got to sneak in the chickens
feather by feather   bone by bone   and then the vegetables
root by root   leaf by leaf   next, the salt
past the Jewish police at the gate, and the Lithuanians,
the Nazis over their shoulders. You've got to be careful.
I keep the soup pot alive in the Vilna Ghetto
while all around buildings simmer
with meetings: young people, Zionists, leftists, rightists,
Communists, Bundists. My brother
tells me I'm on the wrong track.

He is sneaking guns into the Vilna Ghetto
part by part   scrap by scrap   and then the explosives.
This isn't easy, he says, but it's necessary.
Think of the working class, think of the revolution.
Think of the heroes at Warsaw, think of the pits at Ponar.
All we need here is a little solidarity.
All we need now is one good uprising.

2

She is sneaking Jews out of the Vilna Ghetto
into the forest   man by man   woman by woman
(there are no children left, no Jewish children).
The leader, a Jew with a Russian name, Yurgis,
doesn't like it at all.
But what can he do?
She is a hero, I guess. Here she is on TV,
on the documentary my daughter watches.

Me, I was somewhere nearby. I was making soup in the forest
for the Partisans, the peasants, the Jews, the Russians.
(I left my brother, he left me, back in the ghetto.)
Here, we trapped some rabbits, dug up a few wild scallions.
Yadwiga found us some mushrooms.
(They looked poisonous, but tasted like pine trees.)

3

I am warming up soup in Brooklyn,
in Brighton Beach, down by the worn-out ocean.
It's tomato-egg-drop soup from the Chinese take-out,
around the corner, next to the Russian deli
(where the man hums rock 'n' roll, counts change in Yiddish).
Beside me, my daughter watches the TV program.
I watch the tears break out on her face like a rash.
Why is she crying? What can she know of that time?
Me, all my tears are locked up behind my eyes,
rusted like all the words
in the mother language I don't even dream in now.
Me, I don't cry.

Me, I survive and survive.
How I survive! I've outlasted Vilna and Ponar,
the meetings   the sewer   the forest
the Judenrat   and my family
(except for this one, who came later).

My brother stares at us suddenly out of the screen,
out of that photograph I always hated.
He's twenty, he's serious, his ears are too big.
I can't look. I turn my back. I lower the flame
under the saucepan, the soup shouldn't burn.
You think it's easy, to concentrate on details?
Details, let me tell you, keep you alive.
Details, I thank God for them.

My daughter looks ugly and old, her face all muddy.
They've got someone else on there now, another story.
I could tell stories too, but I never talked much.
He talked all the time. He scattered his words like salt.
Words, he said, words are important, words can change things.
He sneaked his words in past the guards, he whispered, he shouted.
Think of the Jewish people, he said and he disappeared.
(And the Nazi troop train blew up, and they blamed the Russians.)

She's crying harder, my daughter; sobs choke in her throat like fishbones.
"Mama," she says, "Mama, why didn't you tell me?"
I say, "What's to tell? Have some soup."

Kate Daniels

For Miklós Radnóti: 1909–1944

1

When Radnóti wrote his last poem for his wife
he was weeks away from death,
and must have known it.
The landscape shook, green and terrible,
through the long retreat. The guards
pushed Radnóti and the other prisoners
harder, fed them less, whipped them more,
killed more frequently, with less thought,
the fear of their own death and defeat
making it easier to pull the trigger.

In the midst of it all, pissing blood,
hair and teeth falling out, Radnóti
kept writing his way out of the nightmare,
tiny poems on postcards and matchbooks.
On the road to Budapest, the guards tortured
a retarded Hungarian boy before they shot him in the mouth.
It was the same in the poems; the prisoners died there, too,
blood running from the ear of Radnóti's friend, the violinist,
the body abandoned in a drainage ditch.

At the end, in the common grave
scrambled up with the human bodies he loved so well,
his poems went down with him,
fierce scraps of life in his coat pockets
that refused defeat.
Two years later, the poet gone back
to the earth, the poems still lived,
exhumed and reborn,
when the widow plucked them
from the fresh, young skeleton.

2

In Harlem, housing projects shove their way up
out of the earth, all concrete and bricks,
iron bars at the windows, children locked inside
by themselves all day while their mothers work
and their fathers never come home.

I don't know how many people here
read poetry, or love it,
or know the name of Miklós Radnóti,
Hungarian poet dead forty years,
his one book out of print.
I know people love words and music,
listen to radios in the street,
jazz bands in the park,
memorize long passages of soul rap like poetry.
I know Radnóti would have loved my neighbors
who sit all night in Riverside Park
during the long weeks of the heatwave
singing and dancing in the breathless air.

From my window, I see a man on Broadway
propped against a concrete wall.
A brown joint dangles from his mouth.
Then traffic rushes by, obscuring him.
In the only photograph I've seen of Radnóti,
a homemade cigarette pokes between his lips,
his wide sexual mouth breathing
the putrid air of World War Two.

When I close the book,
the poems still sob around me.
When I turn off the light
the pages remain lit
like the blanched white slats
of a skeleton abandoned
in the war-torn night.
And across the street in Harlem:
the lights flickering off and
off, a chorus of frightened breathing,
a million human hearts
beating steadily in the darkness.

Sister Mary Philip de Camara

Yellow Starred

Approach the Holocaust
only with synecdoche:

not six million Jews —
just Anne Frank,

not hundreds of concentration camps —
but Buchenwald,

a single freight train,
one oven —

not millions of emaciated corpses,
but piled high human hair —

the unique color black
will stand for boots —

one madman — Hitler,
a lone symbol — twisted cross

one God,
one sound — silence.

Theodore Deppe

School of Music

For Zhanna Dawson

My first lesson: you won't even let me touch
the keyboard. You have me drum my fingers
against a table to work the stone from my wrists.

We all start with stone. For you
it was the laughter of Germans as the rabbi
danced. When the rope stopped, red bullwhips cracked,

and the rabbi danced again, briefly resurrected
in the sleet-backed wind of your childhood.
Or, say the stone is the wind

and the wind is the crying of children
loaded in open trucks. Even today you hate
wind. You are so still, sit such a long time

preparing to play. Your gold watch waits
silent as a heron over white keys.
You were one of thirteen thousand

marched out of Kharkov into the storm.
You wear the watch now to remind you of the one
your father gave a guard: barter for your life.

Almost imperceptibly it rises alone
over winter fields, and the music starts —
your fingers striking out

over unmarked graves, playing
for the demanding ears of your father
music that is first of all survival.

Norita Dittberner-Jax

Name Tag

As instructed, she brought only one
suitcase weighing no more than fifty kilograms
and wrote her name on it
in large block letters:
FANNY KLINGER

In the mountain of suitcases behind glass
other names are visible —
Bertha Eppinghausen
Franz Engler —
but the name *Fanny Klinger*
lodges like a splinter of bright glass
in my skin.

That name sings, even written
on a suitcase of brown cardboard.
Her parents must have practiced
saying it before she was born.
If the baby is a girl
we'll call her Fanny.
Fanny Klinger.
Das ist gutt.

She was someone's
childhood friend,
a shy schoolgirl, a young
woman of surprising passion
and long, dark hair.

When she packed the suitcase,
did she think, *Now at least*
the harassment
will stop? They would live
together in the labor camp,
her aunts and uncles,
her noisy cousins.

When the train stopped
and they piled out,
she walked with the others
down the *Lagerstrasse.*

She saw the SS men in their spotless
uniforms toss the suitcases
in the back of a truck and, ahead,
the leader, with a quick
glance, direct each prisoner
with a flick of his index finger:
left or right.

What good was her name then,
even a name as bright as a poppy,
against all the apparatus of death?

Sharon Dolin

Three Postage Stamps

All three are of Anne Frank.

The first one: *DEUTSCHE BUNDESPOST* across the top.
An odd drawing. Even wearing a dress, her torso seems bony.
Sitting at a writing table with a blank book
caught (or pausing) to look up. Her drawn face
in a thin smile revealing small spaces between her teeth,
the ridged bangs of her hair clipped so short
they seem an ill-fitted wig, her signature
scrawled in red across her book her watch-banded arm:
(*ANNE FRANK*-12.6.1929–31.3.1945) across the bottom.

Then *nederland* sideways, and then, simply, *ANNE FRANK*.
A close-up. Plump cheeks in a girlish grin, her wavy front-hair
pulled to one side with a barrette.
Here, Anne's young face — younger than the German one —
is the way her father, Otto, probably remembered her.
I'm certain it must have been her father
who took the photo of her almost giggling,
the trace of a dimple in her chin.
And how it must have lain in his memory:
a still in a father's mind of his youngest girl's face
beaming out at him with no sense of pain
before the hiding.

And I can imagine young girls everywhere
who grow up reading her diary and soon start their own,
who, loving their fathers and feeling, late at night,
their bodies developing in that painless, maddening way,
are less scared for it, imagining what could be:
days of total silence, nights when the family must stir
like cats, prowling in each other's hair.
Here, Anne is looking at nobody. There are no lights.
She is up in the attic with Peter
or she is alone with her words.

Wendy Drexler

On Hearing a String Quartet Written by Prisoners of Theresienstadt

I am cutting cucumbers
in the kitchen and crying.
I peel long green strokes
in the name of your grandfather,
murdered at Theresienstadt,
his life worth less than a sack
of wheat. I peel in the name
of your grandmother, lost
during the deportation.
The skins slap into the sink,
and I slice the flesh
in the name of the SS
officer who saved your mother
at the embassy in Rome —
Fraulein, don't go home now,
you wouldn't like the weather —
so your beautiful young mother
could meet your father.
My love, what a wide river
of blood has washed you here.
How sharp the blade. How cool the flesh.

Shoshana Dubman

Istanbul 1967

Above the Lemon Café
The rooftop was full of smoke
Full of travelers
Full of hopes and dreams
Adam said "Come to my room"
He was Jewish and much older
I felt a kinship
I went
I smoked
I dropped acid
We made love
I listened to his stories
Of loss
Of love
Of death
Of the Holocaust

Till my body was shaking
Till I knew I had to run
And run I did
On acid
On fear
On hope of finding
A truth that would set me free
Free of the Holocaust
Free of the nightmares
Free of the cries of my father
Free of the sadness of my mother

I knew the Holocaust
I knew the loss
I knew the pain
On my mother's face when she said
"No, he is not your father"
"No, you don't have any family"
"Yes, they were killed"
Killed like Adam's wife and kids
Killed like cattle that needed
To die

As I ran through the streets of Istanbul
I could feel myself crying for Adam's family   for my family
There were no fathers and mothers whose arms
I could jump into, who could help me understand
The loss,
The war,
The terror of not knowing
How to survive

Smoke filled the air from street vendors
Cooking kabob
Beggars waved their hands
Asking for money
And without thinking I answered
"Kash para yok"
"I have no money"
And I was not feeling the smoke
Of war
Or hearing the cries of my people
I was in Istanbul
Coming down off of acid.

Memories

What are the memories for
If they can't make you feel good?
What are the tears for
If they can't wash away the pain?
What is the pain for
If it only reminds you
Of the missing?

Please take these memories
And wash them with the tears
Of my father who I never knew
With the tears of my mother
Who gave me life
And the life that was taken

Dear god, give me memories
Of joy and forgiveness
And tears that fall from
The laughter of living
And pain that comes
From too much dancing

Jehanne Dubrow

Shulamith Rereads *The Shawl*

After Cynthia Ozick

After the broken world, we find
our honey in the warp of cloth.
We suck on wool until we're choked
and fed. Our unwound children wind
to butterflies against the wire.
No voice can pierce by speaking soft —
we've seen the velvet ones turned smoke
or rendered fat within the fire.
For us, only the tiger's growl
devours death, only a shard
of window glass can stitch our veins,
only the Name-of-absent-vowels
knows how to mend the silken yards
of silences, the twisted skeins.

Shulamith, in White

I won't wear ash this time but white
brocade sewn with forgetfulness,
to leave blackmilk for daylight.

What shadows does a bride invite
when she slips on her wedding dress?
Should I wear ash instead of white,

prepare for funerals, for night
and fog instead of wine and guests?
If I leave black behind for light,

I'll hide behind a veil or bite
my lip to ruby beads, a mess
of red and ash, my paperwhite

bouquet strangled inside the tight
ring of my hands that press and press
and press, like dusk against daylight.

> *O daughter of the camps, floodlights*
> *will follow you. Even your* Yes,
> I do *will cough with ash. In white,*
> *you'll breathe blackdust into daylight.*

Shulamith Writes *Fuck You*

Fuck you   you chimney stack
you living body made to choke
on prussian blue   blue face burned black
you rigor mortis turned to smoke
fuck you   you topos bent to make
a rhymed barbarity   go fuck
yourself   you charcoal comic book
you linearity   train track
which travels south while time runs back
to nil   fuck you   you stains of ink
across the page   you stack
of bleeding languages that stink
you gangrene words   fuck you black milk
fuck you   for all the worlds you broke

Shelley Ehrlich

Vilna 1938

On a photograph by Roman Vishniac

A woman leans in
the entry, wooden
door open to
the cobblestone street.
She dresses all
in black. Her face,
a distant star. Below,
her neighbor flings
open shutters to
a cellar shop. Carrots
glow near a burlap
sack of grain. No one
else on the street.

These two are no
strangers. My aunts
lived lives like these.
If I were to cross
the cobblestones, step
over the threshold,
where would the darkness
lead?

Kenneth Fearing

Ad

WANTED: Men
Millions of men are WANTED AT ONCE in a big new field;
NEW, TREMENDOUS, THRILLING, GREAT.
If you've been a figure in the chamber of horrors,
If you've ever escaped from a psychiatric ward,
If you thrill at the thought of throwing poison into wells,
have heavenly visions of people, by the thousands,
dying in flames —
YOU ARE THE VERY MAN WE WANT
We mean business and our business is YOU
WANTED: A race of brand-new men.
Apply: Middle Europe;
No skill needed;
No ambition required; no brains wanted and no character allowed;
TAKE A PERMANENT JOB IN THE COMING PROFESSION
Wages: DEATH.

— 1938

Frederick Feirstein

"Grandfather" in Winter

The overcoats are gone from Central Park
— In the sudden Spring.
A clump of leaves that lay in a white crypt
Of roots for months, loosens, looking for life.
Bare feet of hippies on the sunny walks,
Rock-heaps of pigeons bursting like corn, food
From brown bags, from white hands, from black hands,
Black and white kids kissing in the high rocks,
In the Rodin laps, in the hands of God
Above. Below, an old man, in a rough coat,
Wearing my grandfather's frown, lifts his face
Up to the sun and smiles smacking his lips.
His sky-blue Buchenwald tattoo has healed.
Below him, in the skating-rink, a small
Girl, Jewish, repeats the rings of the park:
The ring of her father skating around her,
The guard around him, the border of the rink

[stanza continues]

Around him, the rings of the pigeon-walks,
The rings of clouds, of jets, of the young
Sun around it. Me on the parapet,
The blood of the false Spring ringing my heart.
My wife beside me aims her camera at
The girl. The girl falls. The rope jerks. Nine
Iraqi Jews are falling through the air,
The Arab horde around them cheers. *Shema*.
The feet clump like leaves. The eyes turn up: white
Rocks. Israel in winter prepares again
For war. Around the gas-house are the guards,
Around the guards, pogroms: Deserts of dead,
Miles wide and miles thick. The rings around
Her border are of time. Grandfather knows.
His dead eyes scrutinize my eyes. He knows
Tomorrow snow will fall like lead, the news
Will be obituaries, Kaddish will
Be sung. It is the eve of war again:
Shema.

Irving Feldman

from **Family History**

Mit Dem Shpits Tsung Aroys

The pink clue of Mama's tongue,
the tip of it between her lips
when she concentrates, picking
at knots or threading a needle.
So she must have sat as a child,
a bit of sewing in her lap,
the tip of her tongue out showing
in imitation of her mother
or mother's mother — but I cannot
follow the clue any farther
and have nothing else to follow
into the lost domestic dark
of some small corner of the Pale.
Now she is patient but quick:
no false move, no motion wasted,
nothing that needs doing over,
nothing overdone or stinted,
everything measured so,
sized up by eye and no

[stanza continues]

anxiety, no pedantry.
Only now have I understood
I have no better measure for
the fitness of things than her gesture,
dreamy and alert and left-handed,
of pulling a thread to length
while the spool runs 'round in her hand.
She is proud of herself as a worker,
tireless, versatile, strong,
both craftsman and laborer.
When she aims her thread at the needle,
her wide gray eyes intensify
— in them no want, no waste, no withering —
and it pleases her to say,
Arbet macht dem leben ziess.
Oh if it does, if it did
— though smeared in iron on the gate to hell —
then of hers the overflowing sweetness,
like a sugar tit touched to battered lips,
has made something of the darkness sweet.

The Pripet Marshes

Often I think of my Jewish friends and seize them as they are and transport them in my mind to the shtetlach and ghettos,

And set them walking the streets, visiting, praying in shul, feasting and dancing. The men I set to arguing, because I love dialectic and song — my ears tingle when I hear their voices — and the girls and women I set to promenading or to cooking in the kitchens, for the sake of their tiny feet and clever hands.

And put kerchiefs and long dresses on them, and some of the men I dress in black and reward with beards. And all of them I set among the mists of the Pripet Marshes, which I have never seen, among wooden buildings that loom up suddenly one at a time, because I have only heard of them in stories, and that long ago.

It is the moment before the Germans will arrive.

Maury is there, uncomfortable, and pigeon-toed, his voice is rapid and slurred, and he is brilliant;
And Frank who is good-hearted and has the hair and yellow skin of a Tartar and is like a flame turned low;
And blond Lottie who is coarse and miserable, her full mouth is turning down with a self-contempt she can never hide, while the steamroller of her voice flattens every delicacy;
And Marian, her long body, her face pale under her bewildered black hair and

[stanza continues]

of the purest oval of those Greek signets she loves; her head tilts now
like the heads of the birds she draws;
And Adele who is sullen and an orphan and so like a beaten creature she
trusts no one, and who doesn't know what to do with herself, lurching
with her magnificent body like a despoiled tigress;
And Munji, moping melancholy clown, arms too short for his barrel chest, his
penny-whistle nose, and mocking nearsighted eyes that want to be
straightforward and good;
And Abbie who, when I listen closely, is speaking to me, beautiful with her
large nose and witty mouth, her coloring that always wants lavender,
her vitality that body and mind can't quite master;

And my mother whose gray eyes are touched with yellow, and who is as
merry as a young girl;
And my brown-eyed son who is glowing like a messenger impatient to be
gone and who may stand for me.
I cannot breathe when I think of him there.
And my red-haired sisters, and all my family, our embarrassed love
bantering our tenderness away.

Others, others, in crowds filling the town on a day I have made sunny for
them; the streets are warm and they are at their ease.

How clearly I see them all now, how miraculously we are linked! And
sometimes I make them speak Yiddish in timbres whose unfamiliarity
thrills me.

But in a moment the Germans will come.

What, will Maury die? Will Marian die?

Not a one of them who is not transfigured then!

The brilliant in mind have bodies that glimmer with a total dialectic;
The stupid suffer an inward illumination; their stupidity is a subtle tenderness
that glows in and around them;
The sullen are surrounded with great tortured shadows raging with pain,
against whom they struggle like titans;
In Frank's low flame I discover an enormous perspectiveless depth;
The gray of my mother's eyes dazzles me with our love;
No one is more beautiful than my red-haired sisters.
And always I imagine the least among them last, one I did not love, who was
almost a stranger to me.
I can barely see her blond hair under the kerchief; her cheeks are large and
faintly pitted, her raucous laugh is tinged with shame as it subsides;
her bravado forces her into still another lie;
But her vulgarity is touched with a humanity I cannot exhaust, her wretched
self-hatred is as radiant as the faith of Abraham, or indistinguishable
from that faith.
I can never believe my eyes when this happens, and I want to kiss her hand,
to exchange a blessing

In the moment when the Germans are beginning to enter the town.

But there isn't a second to lose, I snatch them all back,
For, when I want to, I can be a God.
No, the Germans won't have one of them!
This is my people, they are mine!

And I flee with them, crowd out with them: I hide myself in a pillowcase stuffed with clothing, in a woman's knotted handkerchief, in a shoebox.

And one by one I cover them in mist, I take them out.
The German motorcycles zoom through the town,
They break their fists on the hollow doors.
But I can't hold out any longer. My mind clouds over.
I sink down as though drugged or beaten.

Ruth Feldman

Survivor

For Giorgio Bassani

They would have mourned him, dead,
but could not quite forgive
his resurrection when the rest
had lain down quietly
under the marble plaque
on which their names were cut.

This numbered Lazarus whose blue tattoo
the gaping sleeve exposed indecently,
this gadfly with his flesh
hung on a scarecrow frame,
stung alive memories better left interred,
refused to love his enemies
or turn his cheek to one more blow.

The ones on whom his stubborn shadow fell
heartily wished him dead and safe in hell.

Charles Adés Fishman

Eastern Europe After the War

Wisps of memory   ragged dips in the grass

A few years earlier, millions died in sub-zero
temperature   Stripped to their underwear,

they were whipped   beaten with fists
and rifle butts   their infants ripped

from their arms   Their prayers to God
changed nothing   Shot in the neck,

they were kicked   into ditch after ditch
Those still living clutched at prayer shawls

or thrice-blessed amulets   but their words
their tears   called down no power

Their deaths did not alter the sky, which continues
to shelter their murderers   The earth

that churned for days afterward has yielded nothing
but fragments   The years swept by, blurring

the landscape   though, on occasion, something
in humanity   twitched   A list of the names

of the missing   slipped from official fingers
and drifted into history   In Eastern Europe,

not a stitch was mended   The gash
in the abandoned universe   could not be healed

A Jawbone from the Reich

If the voice speaks, then I know
the time has come to act.
— Hitler to Rauschning

All that remains is the bullet-pierced skull
and the jaw   that has never stopped
talking   even without the tongue
without larynx or throat   minus
even breath   The language
it spoke   was death.

The jaw is the jackpot   the pay-
off   the brass ring   the prize
and cannot be displayed   though
dental records were duly consulted
though it's been tagged   carbon-
dated   DNA'd.

So many years since the bullet
exited the brain   since gasoline
was poured on the body
and the corpse set alight   yet
the voice speaks   the voice
testifies   it jabbers away.

The Silence

After Claude Lanzmann's Shoah

I. Eli, Eli

In the beauty of Chelmno two thousand were burned
each day — two thousand Jews

On his third day unloading the dead
he saw his wife and children and asked
to die with them   to be buried
with them, laid out head-to-foot in ditches
like canned herring in a dark sauce
of blood

* * *

Ponari, Lithuania: thick fragrant evergreen forests
— here the Vilna Jews were murdered, here
there was a time when the trees were full of screams

* * *

In the first grave, twenty-four thousand bodies — they opened
the grave with their hands   The dead
were in layers, flatter as you dug,
flatter and less recognizable as you dug,
more than dead yet numb as death
as you dug

* * *

November 1942 Treblinka: red green yellow purple
flames   One who had been an opera singer
chanted "Eli, Eli," facing the flames

Pyres burned seven days, no, eight: a kind of miracle
a burning forest of decayed and broken limbs

The Narew River took the bone dust
from what was crushed when it would not burn

* * *

In Auschwitz, the Jews made up eighty percent of the prewar
population — but eighty percent of what? what animal
with back and legs, fur and femurs,
but without a head? without a head yet galloping
in place, its bloody mane flying away from it
in the wind

* * *

The cemetery of Sobibór is closed
Treblinka is closed
but in July 1942 the convoys rolled,
twenty cars at a time, an hour or so
to empty: the fish seller, the woodcutter,
the blacksmith, the shoemaker   Those
in the first twenty cars already dead

Sunshine flashed diamonds, and the vodka
was passed

On the morning of the second day, we saw we had left
Czechoslovakia . . .

* * *

The screaming burned into your mind
the crying burned   and the silence
that rose up between the cries: it, too,
left you sleepless

As you went on breathing, the transports
disappeared   the people disappeared
Outside the camp, the ground undulated
with decomposing bodies

Still the Jews waited — for deliverance or to be safely
murdered

* * *

Auschwitz I: bluish-purplish crystals scattered
between bodies

Camp B1, Birkenau, the women's camp: *Suddenly,*
water came up and swept the bodies down . . .

Each crematorium had fifteen ovens   a large undressing
room   Three thousand could be killed at once

* * *

Treblinka: Jewish bricklayers, Ukrainian
carpenters, German overseers built
the death camp

The commandant now sells beer!

* * *

Yes, it is true there were mountains
of corpses, a new and forbidding range
more romantic and mysterious than the Carpathians

And then it was winter at Auschwitz: the luminous
whiteness of snow   snow licking the barbed wire
snow in the frozen mouths of the murdered

* * *

The Nazis invented little, knew Luther's pronouncements
on the Jews of Europe, were intimates of the Church
Fathers, drew from this patriarchy the necessary
inspiration

* * *

Chelmno: Jews arrived half-frozen, caked
with filth, mesmerized by despair, orphaned
from the world but wedded to their fate: packed in
like firewood and ready to burn

In Kulmhof, green vans stood ready, their double-
leafed rear doors already opening

O who were the drivers who rushed
back and forth from the gates
of the ruined castle, delivering their
genome booty? Who were these fatal
angels who emptied the riches
of the Łódź Ghetto into the earth
of Rzuszow forest? *You couldn't hear*
a child squawk as the trucks flew by

* * *

In Grabow, the Jews have been gone
for sixty years: it was they who did the carvings
on these lovely houses

The synagogue is now a furniture warehouse:
today's sale, coffee tables cleverly disguised
as gravestones

The young tried to run but the Germans caught
them like hares   the streets steamed
with their blood

The rest understood: locked in the Polish church,
an elder muttered a prayer

They were tanners tailors sellers of eggs
When the trucks were ready, babies were tossed in
by their legs

II. No Jews

Polish men loved their "little Jewesses"
but for the SS even the prettiest were taboo,
though they could be toyed with — exquisite pain
or malevolence so complete neither the brain
nor the body could register it, but the spirit
would feel shamed

At Chelmno, the Jews were chained when the doors
were unbarred and the day broke on them — but only the workers
The rest, mainly women and children, were changed
immediately into lifeless things, then vaporized into smoke

* * *

At first light, huge green vans — unlocked but armored —
rolled right up to the church: Jews had been stored there,
held in the church and starved

You silent and forgetful ones, you gave only sidelong
glances, your eyes drawn by the moans

* * *

It is Mary's birthday in Chelmno and there are no Jews
no Jews save Mary and her child   Even now,
the scene is pastoral: a horse cart   the gray-green
of lichen-spattered trees   cross on the church spire
fifty vans to empty the church, each of them green, spacious,
punctual   fifty armored vans to relieve it of its burden . . .
and the Jews, too, are punctual though they bear the weight
of their God   How many have been remade
into cleverly crafted pots or wardrobes with false bottoms,
or louvered doors that open onto nothing   The white church
with its spire   its gold   its genocidal mysteries — how calmly
it floats on the sea of remembrance, as if the dead   the Jewish dead
might return to it

Green vans ran slowly over the dirt road so the Jews — eighty
to a van — would have ample time to die
Those not yet dead were thrown into the ovens alive —
They could feel the fire burn them

Such silence in the woods the deep still darkening Polish forest

* * *

In Łódź Ghetto, Jews took a step and fell: to be dead
was normal to survive was to desire and hunger
ate desire A survivor was a loaf of still-warm bread,
the only thing left in the world to be eaten

* * *

Treblinka: newly arrived Jews were taught a work song
to die to and twelve to fifteen thousand were murdered daily
Ice-rimmed cars shunted into the village station
barbed wire glittered on windows Ukrainians
and Latvians on the roofs of buildings clustered
on the ramp: twenty-five from the Blue Squad, ten Ukrainians,
five Germans The Red Squad carried the clothes
of the victims . . . a packed train was a puzzle
that took three hours to solve

* * *

The *Funnel*: thirteen feet wide maintained in terrible perfection
by the Camouflage Squad that wove pine branches
into the barbed wire At the top of a rise, the gas chamber
slumbered like a temple sunk beneath the soil

For Christmas the mercury dropped to 15° and colder

* * *

Prisoners forced to impersonate barbers cut hair
in the gas chambers the women completely naked,
naked with their children

To calm the women — to help them feel a future
was coming — the hair was clipped, not shaved:
two minutes a cut *no time to waste*: the Germans
needed hair for mattresses and U-boat sailors' socks

Sixteen barbers snipping in unison And if friends
from home came in — what then?

Stay a moment longer: one last caress of the steel

* * *

In the *Funnel*, panic overcame the women
who lost control of their bodies   Screamed at
by the guards, half blinded by pain and terror —
"a whiplash of beatings" — they forgot who they were

All they could see was bare flesh, slashes of blood,
driblets of shit and urine, and the flash of green life
in the twisted wire   life already dead

No mercy soothed this passage or stemmed the surge
of death, the churn and whipped-up slush   the raging
squalor of it   Jewish women   these Jewish women

but the sick and old were siphoned off   and the children
— they, too, were turned from the tidal crush and shifted
to the "Infirmary" with its white cloth flag and bright red cross
where they could be cured of Jewishness
and burned like rubbish

III. Be Still

Vrba at Auschwitz:
"We had to get out those bodies *running*!"
yet panic had to be avoided
so that blood on the ramp wouldn't delay
so that gas could seep unimpeded
so that murder could proceed as ordered

At Birkenau, in '44, even Zyklon B understood
the nuances of Hungarian
and kept up a dissolute muttering
until the dead were positioned securely
until corpses were properly elevated
until the bones could no longer talk

The crematoria looked like immigration centers
but were really full-service shopping plazas
featuring the world's best bakeries

LICE CAN KILL! promised the Disinfection Squad,
WASH YOURSELF!   The mouth of the gas chamber
had the mass of cathedral doors

CLEAN IS GOOD! promised the gas chamber:
Breathe deeply and be still . . .

* * *

The guards were poets: saw the dead
"packed together like basalt,"   like "blocks
of stone,"   saw how they "tumbled out"

Lights switched off in the chamber
The gas climbed the walls in darkness
Like blocks — like blocks of stone — they fell
like rocks falling from a racing truck
but a great void where the crystals had been tossed
as if the *burning bush* had spoken there:
the weakest of them crushed, smeared with excrement
and blood their stronger sisters and brothers
twisted and still above them

The dark gas of European history had done its work

* * *

Their murderers had believed in the valuelessness
of life and had lived as inhabitants of a planet
whose four unnamed winds were negation basking
in the typhus sun empathic with the community
of corpses

How they swam and splashed in the Lake of Ashes!

* * *

In the dark of the darkest night, the Jews waited
— on a remote uncharted star —
in the tomb of history they waited They waited
for the stone to be rolled back They waited
for black night to be divided to be torn
from the dead sky They waited for light
to shoot through their hearts needles of infinite
desire

They waited and in the night's terrible darkness
a woman's voice cried out:
she thought herself the last witness of darkness
the last Jew in the universe with eyes

and she cried out in the plain speech of their memories,
which sealed the borders of their lives
It was the silence that called to them it was the voice
of the pain that called to them

This was their native tongue

IV. Gone

My people, you are gone forever:
your faces smudged faded blurred
submerged in deepening drifts of winter,
your stunned silences, tendrils of fear and longing

[stanza continues]

that embraced all you loved   your tears and denials
and the brimming coldness that parched
the fiery stalks of your being

Such painful sweetnesses enter us
at thought of you: your hair that lives still
in the secret dreams of Europe   your songs
that have not learned to dull their yearning
the rich fragrances of your books and scrolls
your butcher shops and bakeries that were small
entire worlds   the tang and textures of Ladino Hebrew
Yiddish and all the ripped tongues of your dispersion,
all the haunted and unrecoverable names of your murdered
villages   the garments you wore on Sabbath evenings
and the chanted prayers you carried with you always,
folded like wings until the sun rose or set and they lifted free . . .

Ghost siblings, your vanished lives grow more silent
though we have become the paleontologists of words:
your absence is itself a rushing music that rises now and swells
a shadowing forest of branches that flourishes and flames
and each unsounded note unfurls like a burning leaf
so that speech and poetry will not name you   so that we mourn
as we sing.

Tamara Fishman

I Did Not Know, but I Remember

I can hear the clatter of the cattle cars.
It echoes forever in my mind.
My ears have never heard the sound,
and yet it is ingrained in my soul.
I did not know those who were tossed into the flaming inferno
and taken out,
black ashes.
I did not know those whose burning flesh smelled
for miles around,
still in the air.
I did not know those who were made to walk the death march,
slowly dying,
and were then gunned down not because of what they had done
but because of what they had been born.
I did not know those who were live guinea pigs for “doctors”
such as Josef Mengele

[stanza continues]

and later died or were permanently scarred
from the effects of the torture.
I did not know those who bravely fought
against a monstrous tyrant
and did not live to see it dwarfed.
I did not know those marked for death,
and yet they are a part of me.
I am bound to them with a special bond,
as still I think, "It could have been my grandparents,
parents, friends.
It could have been me, too."
A part of me died with those people whose faces I have never seen.
A part of me is dead and buried
in the grave of millions.

Ephim Fogel

Icon

Surely those eyes are of marble.
The exquisite hands
remember a score of mistresses in a dozen lands.
Who can believe that the lips —
merciless
thin —
have spoken except in the rasp of commands.

Impeccable uniform; face of ice;
staff work precise as angle of monocle;
statistics
at his fingertips.
He can tell you how many firing squads will execute a thousand Poles a day.
He can sacrifice a half a million troops without a tremor.
The murder of a million Jews is a problem in logistics
he has long ago considered, and solved.
Behind the marble eyes a hundred gallows glimmer.

Behold the man to conceive, and to gather and
consummate, new transfigurations in the mystery of killing.
And around the cerebrum ambitions revolve:
canonization in a Greater German Fatherland;
an Iron Cross for a more abundant chamber,
a quicker crematorium;
a bright medallion for weeding out a Region
ad maiorem Germaniae gloriam.

He would gleam in the amber of
a thousand-year chronicle.
His legends will be legion.
And millions of Aryan children
will contemplate his eyes, his dispassionate hands, his monocle.

Shipment to Maidanek

Arrived from scattered cities, several lands,
intact from sea land, mountain land, and plain.
Item: six surgeons, slightly mangled hands.
Item: three poets, hopelessly insane.

Item: a Russian mother and her child,
the former with five gold teeth and usable shoes,
the latter with seven dresses, peasant-styled.

Item: another hundred thousand Jews.

Item: a crippled Czech with a handmade crutch.
Item: a Spaniard with a subversive laugh;
seventeen dozen Danes, nine gross of Dutch.

Total: precisely a million and a half.

They are sorted and marked — the method is up to you.
The books must be balanced, the dispositions stated.
Take care that all accounts are neat and true.

Make sure that they are thoroughly cremated.

Yizkor

For all who died too soon.

For the early dead
The marine flyer from the Book of Kings
Sam Jacobson, Bernie Jacobs
For all the fallen airmen

For the martyrs
For the hostages lined up and shot, in the square,
        by the ditch
For the millions of Jews
For the circumcision and the uncircumcision torn
        by tanks
thrust under water
left on a gibbet for display

For the refugees
clogging the roads
strafed as they fled
For those who killed themselves
For those who were stronger
and died all the same of starvation and disease:
for all of these

For the valiant
For the dead at Guadalajara
For the soldiers who died in the Kasserine Pass
on Guadalcanal
the Normandy grass
For those who stopped short of the beaches, killed in
the lagoon

For all who died too soon:
fearful, inept
cursed by the sergeant
cursing the rain;
unwary: hit by the sniper at Samar
grenaded in the foxholes while they slept

For the nameless
For the thousands at Babi Yar
For the child who cried
Mother why are they throwing dirt on us
For the indistinguishable ashes in the camps:

May your souls be remembered,
both male and female,
whether killed, slain, or slaughtered
whether burnt, drowned, or strangled
for the sanctification of the name
for the constellation of a life
for the preservation of a hope

And may this prayer be spoken
in distant generations
And if its speech is no longer understood
may it be repeated in a living tongue
by men who say:
We are gathered in remembrance of our kindred
who died too soon.

— *May 1945*

Carolyn Forché

from The Angel of History

This is Izieu during the war, Izieu and the neighboring village of Bregnier-Cordon.
This is a farmhouse in Izieu.
Itself a quiet place of stone houses over the Rhône Valley, where between Aprils, forty-four children were
hidden successfully for a year in view of the mountains.
Until the fields were black and snow fell all night over the little plaque which does not mention
that they were Jewish children hidden April to April in Izieu near Bregnier-Cordon.

Comment me vint l'écriture? Comme un duvet d'oiseau sur ma vitre, en hiver.
In every window a blank photograph of their internment.

Within the house, the silence of God. Forty-four bedrolls, forty-four metal cups.
And *the silence of God is God.*

In Pithiviers and Beaune-la-Rolande, in Les Milles, Les Tourelles, Moussac and Aubagne,
the silence of God is God.

The children were taken to Poland.
The children were taken to Auschwitz in Poland
singing *Vous n'aurez pas L'Alsace et la Lorraine.*

In a farmhouse still standing in Izieu, *le silence de Dieu est Dieu.*

from The Notebook of Uprising

XIII

A two-hour queue for pears, a waxen hill of spent tapers where
Jan Palach immolated himself.
Meat lines, bridge lights in the Vltava.

In a child's leather prayer book from Terezín: V.K. 1940, hearts, a police doll wearing the star.

This is Hana Minka's field of flowers.
This Gabi Friová's imaginary house.

There are flowers growing on the roofs of the cell blocks, the low bricked grass-roofed
prisons,
the *au revoir* of the tunnels.

In starvation rooms along a wall of fading blue figures
a fresco of hair the blue of bread smoke.

On a wreath's black ribbon, the word for scaffold: *popraviště*.

Florence W. Freed

God's Death

during the Holocaust
along with the six million
God is slowly dying

golden glares of
Stars of David
blind Him

shattered glass
from Kristallnacht
cuts Him

devilish plans
in Hitler's ravings
deafen Him

Emanuel Ringelblum's pen
scratching his ghetto diary
crazes Him

shrieks of Jews
tortured in experiments
pierce Him

blood of victims
shot naked into pits
drowns Him

Zyklon B gas
shaken into "showers"
poisons Him

stench of smoke
rising from ovens
suffocates Him

even God almighty
can not go on
can not survive

closing Anne Frank's
innocent eyes
in Bergen-Belsen

God flings
Himself
to the four winds

hurls
Himself
beyond the Heavens

banishes
Himself
from the Universe

forever
I say
forever

Mike Frenkel

Quiet Desperation

my parents endured
the Nazi death blitz —
but barely.
my mother cushioned
the fatal tremors
of her mother,
her father,
her younger brother;
then on stick legs
exorcized the typhoid
from her own body.
my father
rested in a three-month coma,
eaten by bedsores and fever.
when he awoke,
he quietly longed for
that unconscious sanity.

their hands were mangled —
fingers un-
hinged and re-sewn.
to this day,
they are unable to
make a fist.
my mother,
who was a prodigy
and hammered out
sonatas —
allegro di bravura —
on a simple piano
long since looted
and burned,
now plays an occasional
listless bagatelle.

Sari Friedman

Skin

1

Mother, they say we never really leave you.
At the moment our bodies part
a new mutual dependence arises.

But from the look of you,
the limp color and dissonant rattling,
angers inflaming you for brief wild moments
from inside,
it seems impossible that I ever started
from one like you, or existed alongside.

2

I wasn't meant to see
that time you tried to kill yourself,
but I did, and that small thing
saved you.
I dragged you back
like picking through garbage.
What was left of you
didn't want to exist.

3

When you fled from the Germans,
and the gooseflesh fear,
their teeth sinking through your creamy layers,
you even escaped from yourself, and arrived
still burning inside like the ovens.

And you changed your name to Mary;
almost happy in a swirl of houses, clothes,
freckles, and a child . . .
the silly wet sponge, always crying.

4

You tried to be a good mother,
but like everything else in your life
it went wrong.
Breakfast after breakfast you piled
all the emptied eggshells back
into their original cartons,
and burnt all the eggs,
and became confused by our eyes.

If you were to read these words . . .
Would you understand? Would you see?
Would you collapse sobbing?
Freed?

5

You push back your hair,
palm up, a girlish gesture;
and I feel for the broken crunch of you,
the hurt of you;
my love, a salve or a stab,
washes over, relentless.
What is left of you?

6

I cannot know.
I am not you.
I am your American child,
and I want my mother.
I still look for your face,
that skin I know so well,
love, even if I love alone.

[stanza continues]

In one face, the shadows of another.
In swells and hollows,
hope.

Alice Friman

At the Holocaust Museum

December 1999

Like Dante, we too are led
down. The elevator that swooped us up
and spewed us out, leaves us —
clusters of strangers — to the inexorable power
of no way to go but with each other
and the relentless spiral of design.

We shuffle, slow as sludge
in a drain, winding to the bottom.
We gawk, not in disbelief but believing
this has little to do with us — our comfort
in the face of explanations that explain
nothing, the old jackboot footage
of rantings, book burnings, and the car
that waits for us, rattling with ghosts
on its siding, and the glass case
big as Germany, knee-deep in human hair.

We grow quiet. We have crawled
into our eyes. There is nothing
but what we see. And at base bottom,
what's to see but the dredged-up bottom
of ourselves that belongs only to ourselves
and the moving tide of each other.
We crowd in to look. The eye is hungry —
a dog dragging its belly through streets,
sniffing out its own vomit, not getting enough:
the experiments, the ovens, and all their

tattooed histories fidgeting in smoke
that rose like bubbles in a fish tank
to dissipate in air. Fingers pluck
at our sleeves. Gold teeth hiss
in their case. What do they want of us,
we who can give nothing, reduced to nothing

[stanza continues]

but dumb pupils staring at evidence —
the starved and naked dead, the bulldozers,
the British soldier throwing up in his hand?
We press to the TV monitors, mob in,

fit our bodies together like multiple births
in the womb, wanting the heat of each other,
the terrible softness beneath clothes.
Excuse me, *Pardon*, and the knot of us
slips a little, loosens to make room.
In the smallest of voices, *Sorry* we say
as if, battered back to three again,
all we have is what Mother said was good.
Pinkie in a dike. Bandaid on a gusher.
But what else do we know to do

at the end of another century that retrospect
will narrow to a slit, if this Holocaust —
this boulder big as Everest — isn't big enough
to change the tide that ran through it?

The Waiting Room

To speak of "crucial"
in a life of the merely interesting,
to have a yen for it, a calling you might say,
is to be perpetually involved
in the act of naming. And yet, when I went
to the one place where crucial happened
not once but over and over again,
I gagged on my own silence.

There is ash at Birkenau
under your every step. It hisses in the long
uncut grasses growing out of its mouths.
Nothing but this sibilance is left, this ocean
of wind-tortured tongues. The air
not big enough to hold it.

Never mind sixty years of museums
and memorials, vigils and eternal lights.
Never mind that everything to be said
has been said. My obligation was to translate.
The singed grass demanded it.

Birkenau means Place of Birches —
the grove in the meadow next to which
Crematorium IV was built and fired up to run

[stanza continues]

twenty-four hours a day, so busy gassing
and burning there'd be a back-up
waiting to go in.

Imagine the humiliations of the flesh
fumbling to cover up in that waiting room
of white trees, those totems of eyes. Imagine
your mother, her sparse patch. The unopened
pink purse that is your daughter. Then now,
with the wind up and the whipping grasses
wild at your knees, before the dogs come,
hurry write the choke of terror.

Patricia Garfinkel

The Tailor

Ulezalka, Ulezalka,
your head, laced with cancerous
tentacles like a spider's endless
web, remembers in nightmares
the Gestapo snapping commands
like castanets.

Your small head
fit so snugly in the guard's
palm, baseball in a mitt,
heaved against the camp wall;
the cancer shaken loose, resounding
against the bricks.

In Buchenwald
your bloodline was roasted
in ovens like the Christmas
goose, served in open graves,
the hot ashes melting
the snow to black water.

Only you,
last ink spot of the line,
were left, echoing the poison
of the walls. They carried you
from camp, a mass of papier-mâché,
shipped you to America.

They let you
keep your number and the threads
weaving in and out
of your brain. The numbers
counted disappearing
faces in the night.

The threads
grew until you became the thread,
they the body. After you put
the final stitches in my wedding
dress, the thread rose and floated
through the open window.

Kinereth Gensler

For Nelly Sachs

Every morning I took a shower
Every morning under the hot spray
tuned by my hand
I saw the valves
streaming gas
from the walls and ceilings
of rooms marked "BATH"
in Buchenwald   Bergen-Belsen

As if I'd been there
As if it were required of me
As if all Jews
were forced to start each day
stripped in a locked room
remembering in their skins
unable to stop it
just as one by one women
like me had stood
packed in a locked room
under the streaming gas

Give us this day
the grace
of showers

I can't remember when it stopped
in the crush of body-counts
in the years of drought & floods

[stanza continues]

& saturation bombing
I lost them all
they went up
in numbers

O the showers Nelly
the showers
where I stand alone graceless

This numbness
like the end of all desire
the terrible forgetting in my body

David Gershator

from The Akiva Poems

Postwar Mission

After the war
you were possessed:
you crisscrossed Poland
on a personal mission
gathering up Jewish children
foundlings orphans
prying them loose
from their adopters, foster parents
risk takers, simple folk
peasants or city people
saviors or bounty seekers;
you used persuasion
pleas and bribes
to save the children
from Poland
and send the remnant —
the saving remnant — to Palestine
(you a one time Bundist
who had no use for Palestine);
you knocked on so many doors
your only regret
the doors that didn't open
the children too young
to know their own name
the children baptized
in the waters of amnesia

[stanza continues]

the children born to oblivion
the children lost and found in Poland:
the children of Poland
lost to Poland
lost to the mercy of Poland

Last Night's Doubleheader

1990 and Lithuania's in the news again
morning noon and night —
it's Lithuania this and Lithuania that
more news from Lithuania
than I've heard in the last four decades
Hooray for Lithuanian independence!
But from 1939 to 1945
there was no news at all from Lithuania —
just waiting, waiting to hear something, anything
my father glued to the cathedral radio
his whole family out there in darkest Lithuania
hidden away behind the radio
coming on so boldly jauntily every evening
with its swinging March Slav and its mighty nightly news of war
and tanks and artillery and Stalin teaching the Germans
how to say uncle — *Oh Uncle Joe!* — and then it's over
and the radio carries no more tanks and planes and artillery
and I'll never get a chance to be a general now
and the radio is quiet and the radio doesn't tell
and the radio keeps its secrets to itself
and the radio plays games, telling nothing
hiding something —
fathers brothers mothers children
families and more families
lost in this strange cold dark place called Lithuania —
and one day the radio starts talking numbers
meaningless numbers
and my father waits and waits to find out
what's behind the numbers
and no numbers add up to anything
no news about what happened.
"My brother must've been a partisan, a fighter.
Maybe he escaped into the forests."
And then one day Father goes downtown
to look at official files big files
that arrived from somewhere with names
and numbers like a phone book and finds no name
no mention of anyone anywhere
and he comes home red-eyed

[stanza continues]

the only time I ever saw his tears
and there's no more talk
and no more singing psalms for the hell of it
and at night he bellows in his sleep like a bull —
"What is it? What is it? Wake up! Wake up!" —
and in the morning he recalls burning cities, flaming roofs
and running and chasing and buildings collapsing
and uniforms and identity papers
and this goes on for years after dark
but he never never admits to crying
and the night terrors the bellowing the burning cities
the panic the papers the police the uniforms
become part of the family — a familiar country
never in the news, never —
and over and over across the street from the Hook-and-Ladder
my night house my fire house my four-alarm house under fire
occupied by Lithuanians Poles Russians Germans
behind the refrigerator and up and down the fire escape
no escape until Brooklyn daybreak
and the ghosts break up in my father's skull
and all's quiet on the Eastern Front
and on the early morning radio news
it's baseball blesséd baseball

Jacob Glatstein (Yankev Glatshteyn)

Dead Men Don't Praise God

We received the Torah on Sinai
and in Lublin we gave it back.
Dead men don't praise God,
the Torah was given to the living.
And just as we all stood together
at the giving of the Torah,
so did we all die together at Lublin.

I'll translate the tousled head, the pure eyes,
the tremulous mouth of a Jewish child
into this frightful fairy tale.
I'll fill the sky with stars
and I'll tell him:
our people is a fiery sun
from beginning to beginning to beginning.
Learn this, my little one,
from beginning to beginning to beginning.

Our whole imagined people
stood at Mount Sinai
and received the Torah.
The dead, the living, the unborn,
every soul among us answered:
we will obey and hear.
You, the saddest boy of all generations,
you also stood on Mount Sinai.
Your nostrils caught the raisin-almond fragrance of each
word of the Torah.
It was Shavuoth, the green holiday.
You sang with them like a songbird:
I will hear and obey, obey and hear
from beginning to beginning to beginning.

Little one, your life is carved
in the constellations of our sky,
you were never absent,
you could never be missing.
When we were, you were.
And when we vanished,
you vanished with us.

And just as we all stood together
at the giving of the Torah,
so did we all die together in Lublin.
From all sides the souls came flocking,
the souls of those who had lived out their lives, of those
who had died young,
of those who were tortured, tested in every fire,
of those who were not yet born,
and of all the dead Jews from great-grandfather Abraham down,
they all came to Lublin for the great slaughter.
All those who stood at Mount Sinai
and received the Torah
took these holy deaths upon themselves.
"We want to perish with our whole people,
we want to be dead again,"
the ancient souls cried out.
Mama Sara, Mother Rachel,
Miriam and Deborah the prophetess
went down singing prayers and songs,
and even Moses, who so much didn't want to die
when his time came,
now died again.
And his brother, Aaron,
and King David
and the Rambam, the Vilna Gaon,
and Mahram and Marshal

[stanza continues]

the Seer and Abraham Geiger.
And with every holy soul
that perished in torture
hundreds of souls
of Jews long dead died with them.

And you, beloved boy, you too were there.
You, carved against the constellated sky,
you were there, and you died there.
Sweet as a dove you stretched out your neck
and sang together with the fathers and mothers.
From beginning to beginning to beginning.
Shut your eyes, Jewish child,
and remember how the Baal Shem rocked you
in his arms
when your whole imagined people
vanished in the gas chambers of Lublin.

And above the gas chambers
and the holy dead souls,
a forsaken abandoned Mountain Sinai veiled itself in smoke.
Little boy with the tousled head, pure eyes, tremulous mouth,
that was you, then, — the quiet, tiny, forlorn
given-back Torah.
You stood on top of Mount Sinai and cried,
you cried your cry to a dead world.
From beginning to beginning to beginning.

And this was your cry:
we received the Torah on Sinai
and in Lublin we gave it back.
Dead men don't praise God.
The Torah was given to the living.

I'll Find My Self-Belief

I'll find my self-belief in a dustpuff of wonder
flecking my view back
as far as dim sight
can imagine, can see.
In the bobbing
kindled dark
there rises up
a salvaged half-star
that managed not to be killed.
A chunk of exploded planet
that once had life,

[stanza continues]

green abundance, grazing luxury.
Witnesses: my tearfilled eyes,
the distant flora, grapestained with blood,
under a sky eternally sinking;
leaves rocking like bells
deafened, soundless,
on unlooked-at-trees
in an empty world.

I'll be stubborn,
plant myself
in my own intimate night
which I've entirely invented
and admired from all sides.
I'll find my place in space
as big as a fly,
and for all time
compel a cradle to stand there,
and a child
into whom I'll sing the voice
of a father drowsing
with a face in the voice,
with love in the voice,
with hazy eyes
that swim in the child's sleepy eyes
like warm moons.
And I'll build around this cradle a Jewish city
with a *shul*, with a God who never sleeps,
who watches over the poor shops,
over Jewish fear
over the cemetery
that's lively all night
with worried corpses.

And I'll buckle myself up with my last days
and, for spite, count them in you, my frozen past
who mocked me,
who invented my living, garrulous
Jewish world.
You silenced it
and in Maidanek woods
finished it off with a few shots.

Translated from the Yiddish by Ruth Whitman

Millions of Dead

If one plows and sows in burial ground,
it will yield dark grain,
but the wheat and rye will always taste of
millions of dead.
Over shame-drenched ground
new springtimes will one day bloom,
and sun and sky, lakes and forests,
will disport themselves radiantly.
Give a bird a tree
and it will sing foolishly to the sky.
But you — take a record book and write down
all the legendary tragedy.
Write quietly, with quiet words:
This is what man cold-bloodedly did to man;
this is what the year 5703 brought us,
when their murderous day
became our night of nights.

And remember — we have no words
for that tragedy.
How can you find words
to comfort us,
a people rooted in troubles
and cradled in sorrow.
Write it down dryly, sparely, sadly:
Here they died.
But sanctify each and every victim
and don't comfort yourself with the thought
that our people will survive. No! Forever will our living people
be dead with millions of dead.
And may we be accursed if we dissolve their sorrow
in the persistence of our luminous joy.
Do not desecrate and sadden the memory
of even the least human being.
Our glorious sky will be forever starred
with crowns of death.
Of course we will plow and sow,
plant and build;
of course we will count the days and years.
But may we be accursed if we let slip from our memory
even a single martyr.
Write it down: It's not that they died for us
but that we are condemned to live for them,
so that their death may flow in our veins,
so that we may horrify the world.

Translated from the Yiddish by Barnett Zumoff

Nightsong

Strangers' eyes don't see
how in my small room I open a door
and begin my nightly stroll among the graves.
(How much earth — if you can call it earth — does it take to bury smoke?)
There are valleys and hills
and hidden twisted paths,
enough to last a whole night's journey.
In the dark I see shining towards me
faces of epitaphs
wailing their song.
Graves of the whole
vanished Jewish world
blossom in my one-man tent.
And I pray:
Be a father, a mother to me,
a sister, a brother,
my own children, body-kin,
real as pain,
from my own blood and skin,
be my own dead,
let me grasp and take in
these destroyed millions.

At dawn I shut the door
to my people's house of death.
I sit at the table and doze off,
humming a tune.
The enemy had no dominion over them.
Fathers, mothers, children from their cradles
ringed around death and overcame him.
All the children, astonished,
ran to meet the fear of death
without tears, like little Jewish bedtime stories.
And soon they flickered into flames
like small namesakes of God.

Who else, like me, has
his own nighttime
dead garden?
Who is destined for this, as I am?
Who has so much dead earth waiting for him, as for me?
And when I die
who will inherit my small house of death
and that shining gift, an eternal deathday light
forever flickering?

Translated from the Yiddish by Ruth Whitman

Without Jews

Without Jews there is no Jewish God.
If we leave this world
The light will go out in your tent.
Since Abraham knew you in a cloud,
You have burned in every Jewish face,
You have glowed in every Jewish eye,
And we made you in our image.
In each city, each land,
The Jewish God
Was also a stranger.
A broken Jewish head
Is a fragment of divinity.
We, your radiant vessel,
A palpable sign of your miracle.

Now the lifeless skulls
Add up to millions.
The stars are going out around you.
The memory of you is dimming,
Your kingdom will soon be over.
Jewish seed and flower
Are embers.
The dew cries in the dead grass!

The Jewish dream and reality are ravished,
They die together.
Your witnesses are sleeping:
Infants, women,
Young men, old.
Even the Thirty-six,
Your saints, Pillars of your World,
Have fallen into a dead, an everlasting sleep.

Who will dream you?
Who will remember you?
Who deny you?
Who yearn for you?
Who, on a lonely bridge,
Will leave you — in order to return?

The night is endless when a race is dead.
Earth and heaven are wiped bare.
The light is fading in your shabby tent.
The Jewish hour is guttering.
Jewish God!
You are almost gone.

Translated from the Yiddish by Nathan Halper

Barbara Goldberg

Our Father

God Himself, in all His righteous wrath
could not have been more terrifying
than when you raised your fist and thundered,
"Donnerwetter noch einmal!"
Plates trembled, water spilled,
and we froze, waiting for
your lightning hand to strike.

True, we owe you our lives: paranoia's
useful in uncertain times. Hearing
distant troops, you forced Mother to flee
Czechoslovakia. How could you know
the shadows of those who died rose
at night to do their lone soft shoe?
And I, how could I know when I played
at your feet, you still heard boots.

Thomas A. Goldman

Rotterdam — 1946
The Pre-War Visa Files

In this grey vault
they lie preserved
in steel-walled tombs
against the years,
pressed tightly
one against another.
They are forgotten,
yet the names are here —
Tabakblad, Ferreira, Cohen, Frank —
name, address, occupation,
date and place of birth,
all details documented,
certified and sealed,
and here interred
in pale manila coffins.
Sad faces stare (in duplicate,
two inches square precisely)

[stanza continues]

from eyes the darkness
long since closed.
This room was but a station
on the bitter road.
We buried here one vital
organ, hope.
The numbed flesh that was left
went to the flames.

Rachel Goldstein

Prosciowiece, 1942

For Eliezer

My grandmother left him.
That was not the worst of it.
From that day on,
nothing was impossible,
even laughter. She left
him to be safe with neighbors.
Left him that day to be safe.
He will always be standing
behind a window, waving.
She left. He will always be
left with neighbors. Each day
will be that day. Where is he?
With neighbors. That was not
the worst of it. From that day on,
each day will be that day.
She left him.

There Is No Time

Crippled nights follow a starless path.
A wagon is filled with fields.
Trees, prayers leap like dust in the seam of this day.
Leaves escape the chase of wind.
I am in Schreniava, sitting at the edge of the river mill
with all of them, Yankush, Leah, Salek, and the rest.

I can see them dancing, dying too, before them and after, the children
repeating the burnt words of an ancient ceremony.

Willows may weep for centuries. Time is a velvet ribbon we tie,
try to remember.

There is nothing here. Everything they know is here.
No time to mourn, Grandmother Dosha says.

In train stations whistles blow then disappear in laddered smoke.
Luck is their obstinate companion. At least they call it that.

Those Who Remain

They named us for the dead,
tied red ribbons on our wrists
    to fool the evil eye.
Always carried extra bread,
bound us to their broken hearts.

They sang to us in bed:

Night trains emptied their loads.
    You were not there.
We disappeared into a wing of smoke
and the sun still rose like a red dress.
    You were not there.

Ber Green

The Martyrs Are Calling

The village ruined, its people dead;
the synagogue empty, its prayers unsaid.

Where are the grandparents, sisters and brothers, the children safe amid dreams?
Dead, brothers, dead they lie in meadows and streams.
Where are the shoemakers, tailors, tinsmiths, capmakers, teachers,
the bathhousekeepers, locksmiths, beggars, cantors, preachers?

Where is the inn, the bathhouse, the reading hall, the mill?
A hill of ashes, brothers, a skeleton-hill.
Over the holy graveyard I wander all alone;
my footstep quakes, my body becomes one heavy moan.

A door, a hinge, a picture-frame,
signs of a life that went up in flame.
A broken gate, a piece of wall —
the sands, the boards . . . grief fills them all.

I search through the wreckage of a home
and find a button, a shoe, a comb,
a rusty knife, a tattered boot,
and a Yiddish letter soiled by the brute.

Across the graveyard like a driven ghost I tread
where bayonets grew drunk and slaughter rioted;
I want to shriek, to roar, but on my tongue the word is dead.

And let us tell the might of — who can tell
of the heroes who hid in caves, of the martyrs who fell?
Some in fire — the unholy ones hurled babes into the flames
before their mothers' unbelieving screams.
Some in water — Don't you hear the rivers, how they thunder
with heroes drowned, with martyrs whom the tides dragged under?

And once again God's earth grows green
on the same spot where mother, child were slain.
Lush fields of cabbage and high grass arise
on the same spot where a whole city lies.
And quietly a little river flows
on the same spot where Jewish streets once rose.

And the sun shines, and leaves adorn the trees,
and the ashes are borne upon the wings of the breeze.
And everywhere wild plants take root —
and the God of Mercy is mute.

And suddenly there lifts a bitter moan
from every smoke-charred stone.
Within the holy ruins a rumbling comes alive:
"World, we shall yet arrive, we shall arrive!"

And suddenly the synagogue is filled with Jews, dead Jews at prayer:
swaying, wrapped in the white shawls they used to wear.
The holy congregation has risen at one word —
and your voice, too, my grandfather, is heard.

In the dark light of candles the ancient prayer-house gleams;
it trembles with the passion of a hundred holy screams.
And suddenly the whole earth's ripped asunder —
the skies turn black, as if with brewing thunder.

The sacred horn of the slain lamb rings out
a sob, a warning, and a wrathful shout:
over mountains of bodies and valleys of bones,
over ravaged market-places, and outraged cobblestones,

through slaughter-fields, and graveyard-neighborhoods,
through inferno-ghettos and partisan woods —
every hamlet, every little town
an altar on which grandfathers and schoolchums were cut down.

Through smoke and fire the shofar-call is hurled,
straining to reach its voice across the world.
Over grave-filled lands the notes are borne,
over corpse-filled meadows of fresh corn:

Repent, indifferent and stone-hearted ones!
Bow down at the ashes of six million daughters and sons!
Beneath ten layers of ash, bury your face:
then wash yourself, be cleansed of your disgrace!

Be cleansed at last, wash off the shame!
The martyrs' blood — can you not hear it scream?
Still unextinguished is Treblinka's flame . . .

World, wipe out forever the unholy one!
His memory begone, his name begone!
Remember: the spirit of revenge lives on.

And the notes console and cry:
Maidanek must not cause your dream to die.
Here where these ash-heaped ruins lie
there'll be a new birth to amaze the sky.

Long life to life! To death with death!
Into the dry bones is blown new breath.

Make strong, my tribe, your body and your soul!
Make yourself whole — a new life's to be charted,
oh partisans, oh Maccabean-hearted!

Translated from the Yiddish by Aaron Kramer

John Z. Guzlowski

How Early Fall Came This Year

Between the rows
of tomato plants
shrunken in their cages
and canna bulbs
buried in the snow
my daughter follows me

asks me at last
why I wear a coat
without buttons
shoes without laces

I tell her I'm a fool
in a dream of magic

drop to my knees
like a penitent seal

and while she laughs
I make up more

tell her the buttons
were stirred into soup
the laces when sold
bought the secret of bread

she doesn't need to know
my thoughts are always
with my mother and father
dying of the blood
that survived the camps
the memories of the baby
left in the field
with the beets

the real magic

only six she'd understand
their gray voices as I did
shaping a world out of
lightning and ashes

Hunger in the Labor Camps

1. What My Father Ate

He ate what he couldn't eat,
what his mother taught him not to:
brown grass, small chips of wood, the dirt
beneath his gray dark fingernails.

He ate the leaves off trees. He ate bark.
He ate the flies that tormented
the mules working in the fields.
He ate what would kill a man

in the normal course of his life:
leather buttons, cloth caps, anything
small enough to get into his mouth.
He ate roots. He ate newspaper.

In his slow clumsy hunger
he did what the birds did, picked
for oats or corn or any kind of seed
in the dry dung left by the cows.

And when there was nothing to eat
he'd search the ground for pebbles
and they would loosen his saliva
and he would swallow that.

And the other men did the same.

2. What a Starving Man Has

He has his skin. He has a thinness
to his eyes no bread will ever redeem.
He has no belly and his long muscles
stand out in relief as if they've been flayed.

He is a bony mule with the hard eyes
one encounters in nightmares or in hell,
and he dreams of cabbage and potatoes
the way a boy dreams of women's breasts.

There is always the empty sea in his belly, rising
falling and seeking land, and next to him
there's always another starving man who says,
"Help me, Brother. I am dying here."

3. Among Sleeping Strangers

The moon set early and it grew darker,
and the men settled to sleep in the cold
without blankets. Soon it would be spring
but it was still cold, and it was always cold

at night, and they did what men always did
at night when they were cold. They pressed their bodies
together and looked for warmth the way a man
who has nothing will look, expecting nothing

and thankful to God for the little he finds,
and the night was long as it always was
and some men crawled roughly across the others
to reach an outside wall to relieve themselves,

and some men started coughing and the coughing
entered the dreams of some of the other men
and they remembered the agony
of their mothers and grandfathers dying

of hunger or cholera, their lungs coughed up
in blood-streaked phlegm, and some men dreamt
down deeper and deeper against the cold
till they came somehow to that holy moment

in the past when they were warm and full
and loved, and the sun in those dreams rose early
and set late and the days were full of church bells
and the early spring flowers that stirred their lives

and in the morning the men shook away
from the cold bodies of their brothers
and remembered everything they had lost,
their wives and sisters, their lovers, their homes

their frozen fingers, their fathers, the soil
they'd been born on, the souls they'd been born with,
and then they crawled up out of the earth
and gathered together to work in the dawn.

4. The Germans

These men belonged to the Germans
the way a mule belonged to the Germans
and the Germans stood watching

their hunger and then their deaths,
watched them as if they were dead trees
in the wind, and waited for them to fall,

and some of the men did. They sank
to their knees like children begging
forgiveness for sins they couldn't recall,

or they failed to rise when the others did
and were left in the wet gray fields
where the Germans watched them

and the Germans stood watching
when the men who were still hungry
came back and lifted the dead men

and carried their thin bones to the barn,
and buried them there before eating the soup
that wouldn't have kept them alive.

The Germans knew a starving man
needed more than soup and more than bread
but still they stood and watched.

Night in the Labor Camp

Through the nearest window
he stares at the sky and thinks
of his dead father and mother,
his dead sister and brother,

his dead aunt and dead uncle,
his dead friend, Jashu, and the boy
whose name he didn't know
who died in his arms, and all

the others who wait for him
like the first light of the sun,
and the work he has to do
when the sun wakes him.

He hates no one, not God,
not the dead who come to him,
not the Germans who caught him,
not even himself for being alive.

He is a man held together
with stitches he's laced himself.

What the War Taught My Mother

My mother learned that sex is bad,
Men are worthless, it is always cold
And there is never enough to eat.

She learned that if you are stupid
With your hands you will not survive
The winter even if you survive the fall.

She learned that only the young survive
The camps. The old are left in piles
Like worthless paper, and babies
Are scarce like chickens and bread.

She learned that the world is a broken place
Where no birds sing, and even angels
Cannot bear the sorrows God gives them.

She learned that you don't pray
Your enemies will not torment you.
You only pray that they will not kill you.

Leo Haber

The Book of Lamentations

The event called the Holocaust was not made for poetry,
for the rhapsodizing and the charged emotion that
we associate with the form. It was beyond form

and beyond capturing with an apt phrase and even beyond
memorializing. I never met my father's brother face to face.
He, his wife, his two children were but brownish imprints

on a photo that came to us in the thirties from a
faraway place on the back of a picture postcard.
It must have been taken in a shop that made such fine

things for America, the golden land where we struggled
in the throes of the Depression. Photos do not show
height or even weight, only depth, and sometimes

the sequestered soul. My uncle must have been a little man
like my father. He was dressed in the black of believers,
black hat over furrowed brow and curled black sideburns,

black coat, black shoes. His eyes were piercing, perhaps
from all the time he spent looking deeply into holy books.
I confess that I had no interest in the figure of his wife,

but she was beautiful and young (in my mother's words)
though to me she looked like all the old ladies who
had been wearied by their own children, if not by me.

The two boys fascinated me because they seemed taller
than their father and had curled sideburns longer than his.
They would have made fine playmates with their ends of hair

flapping in the wind during touch-football season. But
they were not fated to spend their young days at play.
They ended up in furnaces struggling for breath

against the advanced science of gas, systematically,
routinely destroyed, by a master plan created by
a country of musicians and poets. This is what we

justly call "unspeakable," unworthy of words, of music,
of the art of poetry. Still, Jeremiah sang in poetic form
of ancient Jerusalem's destruction where other young cousins

of mine, playmates all, died too. He wept and proclaimed
the poetry of lamentation against the cruel triumphal song of
the destroyer. The old prophet's art prevailed as mine may —

pale consolation, dear God of poetry, of justice, of mercy,
of explanations, for the murder of little children.

Rachel at the Well

Is great art still possible in our century of death?
— Leonard Bernstein, *Norton Lectures at Harvard* (1973)

In the beginning, music was possible,
sex was possible, the coupling of the sons
of mighty gods with the daughters of men
whence came the giants in the earth.
Between ridges in the newly formed
mountains, grazing was possible,
and hunters aimed their jagged rocks
at flying fish vaulting toward blue heavens.
Fratricide was possible, stealing in across
the summits, and envy of the smallest ant
crawling noiselessly after a beloved queen.

Consider the explosive heavens in earliest
times, universal exemplars of destruction,
combustive blasts of dying stars in
the pot-boiling mystery of stellar birth,
and the gravitational pull of Abram's
star-gazing and Jacob's ladder to heaven
and Rachel's well, where work
was possible among the thirsty sheep,
prayer was possible, and love too —
fourteen years fleeing by like one day —
and the birthing of twelve sons
and a daughter, and an undying people
of the book in which poetry was possible,

artistry of art recited and renewed
and recast with and without
musical accompaniment many
times over up to and including
our century of death when
impossible Holocaust was possible.

Sanctification*

Let us mourn the murder of children together,
You and I, in the graceful form of the rhymed
Sonnet, dimensions of meaning, rigidly timed
Ritual of comfort at the brutal end of one's tether.
Young Alena Synkova tethered to L
410 spoke for all the children in free
Verse and fourteen short lines. Listen! See
the child in her innocent wisdom outwitting hell.

"Listen! / The boat whistle has sounded now / And we
Must sail / Out toward an unknown port / We'll sail a long
Long Way / And dreams will turn to truth . . . / Just look up

To heaven / And think about the violets." See
The child in the chamber of gas, listen to her song,
Mourn with the Kaddish; bless with the Kiddush cup.

**The quotations in this poem are from a fourteen-line poem, "To Olga," by L410, the number of one of the children's homes in the Terezín concentration camp, circa 1943–44.*

Israel I. Halpern

Being Seemingly Unscathed

To my communards at Little Sur and Misgav Am

We were singing
Blessed is the Holy Name   Barooch Ha-Shem
Celebrating the betrothal of our canyon companions
seated at long tables over bowls of hummus and cholent —
We were happy!

The drunken fiancé stood up, swaying, agreeing to say a few words;
admitting to being a little spaced out,
the soon-to-be-bridegroom spoke these words:
"As I have wandered, I have become aware of a responsibility
first held by our spiritual fore-parent, Avrooahm Avaynu;
Being a *Shomer* and a *Misgav*, I know exactly
what befell our people before we were born,
what recurred in each generation, and will occur with us,
in our generation."

We, who had been celebrating, stopped; we knew that toast quite well.
All around the room, we scanned each other's eyes,
we knew what had been,
we knew the phrase: *DO-ER V'DOER, AYLLEH TOLDOS;*
GENERATION TO GENERATION. THESE GENERATIONS.

This generation —
knowing Majdanek, Theresienstadt, Auschwitz, Buchenwald —
we know we are the seemingly unscathed generation.
We stopped singing, to look around,
wondering about ourselves,
celebrating
Ha-Shem.

Love in a Death Camp

For my Aunt Feigel

Swept along to the train in her pinafore,
Feigel braided her hair for the cattle car.

She found a space on the unwashed corner planks,
listened to the steam engine as everyone swayed.

Last last stop, Ravensbrück, arrived with a lurch.
An old woman from her village gave Feigel a wrinkled carrot.

There was smoke, ashes, and darkness.
Guards slammed truncheons into her back.

On her way to the showers, she saw a young man
staring at her, looking away, then looking again.

She smiled at him and lifted her still-delicate left hand
so her fingers seemed to wave at him.

He bowed and returned the gesture of three fingers,
he pantomimed his name and his admiration of her.

She pointed to an imaginary wristwatch, winked one eye,
then grimaced her mute-show of hunger and helplessness.

He indicated on his right hand an imaginary wedding ring,
fluttered his hands over his heart and pointed to her, then to himself.

They moved closer together whenever they could, until, in the soup
line, they spotted, among the doomed, a toothless tubercular rabbi.

For the swain's socks, they hired the *Maggid* to marry them,
as they trembled in line for the honeymoon chamber.

Annette Bialik Harchik

Earrings

A Bialik tradition back home   was
for a woman to wear   earrings
from birth to death.

Ears pierced in infancy   were
adorned in string;
small gold hoops for girlhood;
diamond studs with marriage.

When the trains pulled up
at Auschwitz
my mother was stripped, shorn,
and tattooed, leaving behind her   earrings
in a huge glittering pile of jewelry.

Under her wavy white hair,
her lobes hang heavy,
the empty holes
grown shut.

Requiem

Your names ring clearly,
carefully through my mind . . .
Sheyna, Pesach,
Chana, Yankel.
Your names my legacy:
my grandparents,
my aunts,
my uncles.
Your names echo
in my heart,
Helena, Gitl,
Miriam, Kreindl,
echo in my skin,
echo hollow vowels
and consonants,
naming the names.
Duvid, Nissum,
Zukkin, Shmuel.
Names
name
themselves,
not flesh.

I picture you
before me,
so strangely dressed
in the fashions of your time:
aged grandfolk in wrinkled clothes
stand stiff, stern, and unloving;
handsome uncles
smiling in sunlight;
tender aunts awkward
before the camera.
I ache to touch your faces,
and caress each feature;
to pull my fingers through
dark thicknesses of your hair.
I long to meet
the steady gaze of your eyes,
to meet — you.

Your names whisper clearly,
carefully through my mind,
tagging lost people
like missing baggage.
Sheyna, Pesach,
Chana, Yankel.
Helena, Gitl,
Duvid, Nissum,
Zukkin, Shmuel.
You who are not here
and yet
ever
with me.

Geoffrey Hartman

Day of Remembrance

This is the flat bread:
nothing rises.
This is the time:
nothing can rise.
Each year the clock
weeps, rattles again,
is wound up, goes on.

In the ovens
the loaves are
flattened corpses.
Only nightmares lurk:
words like a tired bell,
a maimed and graying sun.

Elijah's cup
stands untouched.
Through the door echoes fly
and unreadable ash.

The fiery table talk
of rabbis in the heights
wakes a hopeless morning's
blood-streaks of sound.

Hear me then:
what can I tell
— *vehigatta* — the one
who knows and does not wish
to know?

My gestures sit
and hold their tongue.

Hill unto hill
sea unto sea
no speech is heard.

We break words with each other
in the bitter dawn of night.

In Memory of Paul Celan

Someone will travel his book and turn its icy pages,
thinking of summer's green and invincible verse:
stricter the sky, black print — a storm that is mounting —
deadly the traveler's ear in the ghost-towns of Kadesh.

Under the worm of words corpses like proof-texts open,
blood from the rock will flow, though Belsen has drunk its cup;
a dream goes to the well where poppies and children slumber,
and unborn voices drown the Herod of waters.

Somewhere in Kadesh, color of shard and sound,
pen's mouth stopped up, my fingers broken teeth,
I who feed memories that rot like manna
strangle words near his darkened breast.

Anthony Hecht

"It Out-Herods Herod. Pray You, Avoid It."

Tonight my children hunch
Toward their Western, and are glad
As, with a Sunday punch,
The Good casts out the Bad.

And in their fairy tales
The warty giant and witch
Get sealed in doorless jails
And the match-girl strikes it rich.

I've made myself a drink.
The giant and witch are set
To bust out of the clink
When my children have gone to bed.

All frequencies are loud
With signals of despair;
In flash and morse they crowd
The rondure of the air.

For the wicked have grown strong,
Their numbers mock at death,
Their cow brings forth its young,
Their bull engendereth.

Their very fund of strength,
Satan, bestrides the globe;
He stalks its breadth and length
And finds out even Job.

Yet by quite other laws
My children made their case;
Half God, half Santa Claus,
But with my voice and face,

A hero comes to save
The poorman, beggarman, thief,
And make the world behave
And put an end to grief.

And that their sleep be sound
I say this childermas
Who could not, at one time,
Have saved them from the gas.

"More Light! More Light!"

For Heinrich Blücher and Hannah Arendt

Composed in the Tower before his execution
These moving verses, and being brought at that time
Painfully to the stake, submitted, declaring thus:
"I implore my God to witness that I have made no crime."

Nor was he forsaken of courage, but the death was horrible,
The sack of gunpowder failing to ignite.
His legs were blistered sticks on which the black sap
Bubbled and burst as he howled for the Kindly Light.

And that was but one, and by no means one of the worst;
Permitted at least his pitiful dignity;
And such as were by made prayers in the name of Christ,
That shall judge all men, for his soul's tranquillity.

We move now to outside a German wood.
Three men are there commanded to dig a hole
In which the two Jews are ordered to lie down
And be buried alive by the third, who is a Pole.

Not light from the shrine at Weimar beyond the hill
Nor light from heaven appeared. But he did refuse.
A Luger settled back deeply in its glove.
He was ordered to change places with the Jews.

Much casual death had drained away their souls.
The thick dirt mounted toward the quivering chin.
When only the head was exposed the order came
To dig him out again and to get back in.

No light, no light in the blue Polish eye.
When he finished a riding boot packed down the earth.
The Luger hovered lightly in its glove.
He was shot in the belly and in three hours bled to death.

No prayers or incense rose up in those hours
Which grew to be years, and every day came mute
Ghosts from the ovens, sifting through crisp air,
And settled upon his eyes in a black soot.

Leslie Woolf Hedley

Chant for All the People on Earth

Not to forget not to ever forget so long as you live
so long as you love so long as you breathe eat wash
walk think see feel read touch laugh not to forget
not to ever forget so long as you know the meaning
of freedom of what lonely nights are to torn lovers
so long as you retain the soul heart of a man so long
as you resemble man in any way in any shape not to
forget not to ever forget for many have already
forgotten many have always planned to forget fire
fear death murder injustice hunger gas graves for
they have already forgotten and want you to forget
but do not forget our beloved species not to forget
not to ever forget for as long as you live carry it
with you let us see it recognize it in each other's
face and eyes taste it with each bite of bread each
time we shake hands or use words for as long as we
live not to forget what happened to six million Jews
to living beings who looked just as we look men
people children girls women young old good bad evil
profound foolish vain happy unhappy sane insane
mean grand joyous all dead gone buried burned not
to forget not to ever forget for as long as you live
for the earth will never be the same again for each
shred of sand cries with their cries and our lungs
are full of their dying sounds for god was killed in
each of them for in order to live as men we must not
forget for if they are forgotten O if they are forgotten
forget me also destroy me also burn my books my
memory and may everything I have ever said or done
or written may it be destroyed to nothing may I
become less than nothing for then I do not want even
one memory of me left alive on cold killing earth for
life would have no honor for to be called a man
would be an insult —

Julie N. Heifetz

The Blue Parakeet

based on the tape of Ann Lenga, sent as a child
by her parents to hide in the Polish countryside

They knew what was coming to Radom, to all the Jews.
My parents paid to send me to a farm in the country
with a Gentile family. They treated me like
I was one of them. I learned to milk a cow
and churn my own butter. In the woods there were
mulberries and sweet clover. In the evening
I went to the edge of the property where Gypsies
played their violins and danced. I never saw
so much jewelry.

Because I talked to trees and said I heard
my father singing, they called me Dreamer.
I like to play games by myself, the games
I used to play with Papa. Especially the game
we called the Color Game. "I'm thinking of
something blue," I'd say. Papa had to guess
what I was thinking. "Your dress? Your eyes?
The book on the library table?" Until finally
I'd tell him "I'm thinking of the color blue.
Blue as the moonstone on your finger."
All the colors of home came back to me
playing the Color Game. The pale yellow grass
tall enough to hide in, Papa's cotton shirt,
embroidered like a silk bouquet
with every color of the rainbow.

Winter came. I heard Papa tell me, "Look
how the icicles are candles in the starlight.
Think of them as friends. Also,
slap yourself, move around, keep active.
You'll be warmer." With the first snowfall
I thought about my cousin Helga. We visited
winters in Cologne, flirted with boys
at the skating rink in our sophisticated dresses.
Helga was prettier than I was. I hoped
she was still pretty that winter.

Many nights the same dream came back to me.
I was in the forest, alone. On every tree
a sign with candy-striped colored letters.
LOST. A BLUE PARAKEET!!
I tried to see the treetops, a little spot

[stanza continues]

of blue in green leaves, but the limbs were
twisted fingers reaching out to grab me.
I ran faster and faster, until I woke up
whimpering, sad for the bird alone
in the world she hadn't been born to,
sad for the child who'd lost her.
Of all the nights I had the dream,
I never saw the bird.

One day some neighbors came. While I was
gathering eggs they saw me. "She has
a Jewish nose. You have Jews hiding here."
After that I hid in the hayloft,
but eventually the Germans found me.
I was sent to Auschwitz, the youngest
in my lager. Some would take bread
from the dead. I could never do this.
There was even cannibalism there. One old woman
tried to protect me. She put her arms around me.
"Cover your eyes. Nothing important is happening."
What I saw I did not see. What I felt
somedays I could not feel. I became like a robot,
empty, except for dreaming of hundreds of faces
streaked with color, melting in the rain.

To keep my spirits up, I started rumors.
"The war is over, someone with a radio told me
the liberators are coming." After a while,
whatever I said, nobody believed.
The Lagerführerin, our camp commander,
had the prettiest hair, hair like cotton candy.
You couldn't paint a doll that beautiful.
She loved to torture. The minute our hair
would grow a quarter of an inch, she'd cut it.
When she walked by, I imagined her bald and naked,
me holding the razor.

In 1945 after the war, I went back to Radom.
Our house was there, the Gentiles gave it back
for me to live in. Someone told me
while I was in the country they saw my father
on a transport. He was strong.
He was young enough to make it. I knew
where my strength had come from.
Three months I waited. One day I went
to an open window. Down below my mother was walking.
I must have screamed. She turned around.
I ran to the street where she was waiting.
Her hands were all over me. She was crying,
so much smaller than I remembered.

[stanza continues]

I thought she was a lie I wanted to believe in.
I held her very gently, the way a child would hold
a tiny bird in her hands.

Harry Lenga

based on the tape of his experiences

I. Kozienice, Poland 1939

We had a rabbi which was named the Kozienicer Rabbi.
The Hasidim believed in that rabbi. They used to come and . . .
on the holidays, especially the High Holidays,
they used to go and see the rabbi, the closest man to God.
Such a beautiful thing already
to sit by the table and study the Torah.
First thing, when the Germans came in to Kozienice,
they burned the synagogue. They assembled the most honored Jews,
my father included, and told them to bring twenty thousand zlotys
for ransom, and assembled them,
and lighted the synagogue, and told them to take out
all the books. Before they light the fire,
to take out all the books and throw them in.
Then they told them to take out the Torah scrolls
and they asked for the rabbi. He walked over —
and said, "I'm the rabbi."
"So," they said, "you take the scrolls and throw them in the fire."
The rabbi took the scrolls and went forward to the fire,
but when he came to the fire, he stopped.
The SS men commanded him "Throw it in . . . throw it in,"
and he didn't do nothing.
So finally they came and hit him over the head
and pushed him into the fire. The Torah scrolls fell
into the flames, and a few Jews close
grabbed the rabbi, and took him out of the fire.
Then they lighted up the synagogue — they throw gasoline —
and they light it, and the fire was burning,
and they told them to dance and sing happy songs.

II. Departure 1940

My mother she won't leave her mother.
Her sister can't go away and leave the mother with the sister.
My father can't go away and leave his wife with her mother.
That day after the synagogue was burned
my father took everything together and gave it to us,
tools, watches, rings, you know, whatever he had,

[stanza continues]

he gave it to my brothers and me.
Without his tools, a watchmaker is nothing.
"I don't need them — you're young, one day
you might have use for it."
My mother, she smiled. "It's not so bad, don't worry,
tomorrow we'll all probably go on the train
without having to pay for a ticket."
She took a photograph of my father in his caftan
and her in her new Shabbas dress,
and put it in my shoe, that they should always walk with me.
Then she kissed me goodbye.
It was the second night of Sukkoth.

III. Auschwitz

Fourteen hours, and suddenly,
the train stopped, and we thought —
we imagined we're already at wherever they're taking us.
Loud voices were talking from far away.
Everybody tried to listen, many people
what understood different languages,
but we couldn't make it out what kind of language it is.
We thought maybe they're taking us to some kind of crazy house.
Somebody what looked out of the one little window
in the dawn — in the morning light —
they told us they could see some Germans . . .
Gestapo coming up . . . Sturmführer, majors, big battalions of SS.
Suddenly the doors opened and they told us to step out . . . and . . .
we stepped out from those cars and they tried to —
with the rifles — whoever got close they hit.
They told us to line up and take everything out . . .
all our belongings — whoever had anything with them . . .

Then I saw from the other wagons, cars,
they started to carry out dead people.
We looked around and saw those high chimneys in the crematoriums —
the fire coming out of the chimney . . .
no matter how high the chimneys were, we saw the fire coming out . . .
spraying from the chimney.
And we thought, maybe we didn't know where we're going . . .
maybe it's our last moment already.
And they told us to undress and give up all the belongings.
Only thing was to keep our shoes.

They gave us soap, each one got a piece of soap,
for the showers. They checked us through,
they looked in our mouths, everyway,
with a flashlight and all the other places,
looked in where anything can be hidden . . .

[stanza continues]

for diamonds, for gold, for watches, whatever.
They looked in my shoes . . . a Jewish guy . . .
he saw the picture I had hidden,
and took it and threw it away, just like that.
And I asked . . . I said . . . "That's all I have left of my family . . .
Can I keep it?"
And he said, "Be glad they let you keep your shoes."

After the shower, they gave us a package of clothes,
and I dressed and walked outside, looking for my brothers.
The tall one, they gave him a pair of short pants
that reached him to his knees,
the one that was shorter, him they gave a pair of pants
covering his shoes, and I see them, I started laughing and laughing,
and they're looking at me in my big coat and round hat,
and they're laughing. For so long we never stopped laughing.
We see we're alive.

IV. Ebensee, Austria, May 1945

The ones what gave up — it's like a signal to their bodies.
We made a pact, my brothers, we shave, we look busy, healthy,
even not healthy, be strong and never give up thinking
We have to survive. We have to hold on.
We see a bowl of soup, a crust of bread,
every morning, maybe a butterfly,
we see a sign they cannot kill us.

When the Americans came,
all the people, Russians, Poles, French, Gypsies,
every nationality poured into the yard. They put up a flag,
each country, from nowhere, I don't know how they do this,
they saved a little flag. They waved their flags and each one
sang their national anthem, till one more nation,
the Jews, in such weak voices, skeletons of Jews from everywhere,
singing Hatikvah.

The Wheel

based on the tape of Jakob Szapszewicz,
who escaped from his town in Poland and lived
alone in the surrounding woods

I began to think
This is the way you should live.
For me it is normal, completely normal
to walk on these rocks in wooden shoes

[stanza continues]

not to have a shirt, to be so dirty
always dirty.
To live without food for a week
and don't feel sick, to sleep
outside in cold weather and not get a cold.
In the pine forest what smelled so sweet
in summertime, so peaceful,
maybe in the stone quarries,
in that hole filled with rain,
maybe here in the fog,
I can cover myself with leaves.
When the bullets fall, the dogs won't find me.

At night I feel in my surroundings
nobody could see me.
I walked around, with all those cold stars,
and see houses, a little light, I think
inside it's warm, and people are sitting,
maybe sleeping in a good bed, a clean bed.
And who am I? Even a murderer
when he escapes has someone,
parents, an uncle, a friend to exchange,
to talk to him before they kill him.

So many days I have not eaten.
I passed a meadow where cows were grazing.
An old stone well rose from the pastureland
like a voice, reminding me the way
we separated milk from cream before we had
machines at home, then set the vials into
cool streams, hot afternoons.

It was exactly like my mother's voice led me
to that well that day to feel inside
the darkness of the bricks
until my fingers found a string,
lifted bottle after bottle
of fresh cold milk and separated cream from the body of
the earth,
where peasants hid it just for me.
I drank maybe a gallon of that rich cream
beside the well, healthy in my belly,
empty so long. For two whole days
I was content thinking someone watches and
takes care of me.

So hungry for news,
I taught myself to read Gothic
from the Germans' newspapers.
I could sit in the dark on a stone,

[stanza continues]

my eyes lightening like a wolf's eyes
that light from the inside, and read
the fine print of the German paper.
Sometimes I was laughing to myself,
What am I doing here?
a Jewish boy from a good family,
who studied Torah fourteen years,
reading Gothic by the moon
longing for friends, for somebody else.
That's all I wanted, not to be the only one.

It came to my mind,
my family's mill, the happy occasions
when we were playing by the water wheel,
with children, as children of the mill.
I remembered every patch, every stone,
the key hidden under the stone,
the feel of the best flour.
New Year's Eve, in the dark,
I went back home.
There were Germans burning those bonfires
and skating on the ice of this lake
that belong to us, and singing.
I was lying on top of the hill
looking down, thinking, look those Germans,
dancing and skating, what I used to do sometimes.

Now I lie in this snow
in the dark, a thief who steals flour
from his own mill from a boy
what wouldn't even think to steal a pin.
How the world change. Sometimes we will be
in the top, like a wheel history turns around.
At the bottom, it's possible to go up.
As long as you live,
anything can happen.

Chaia Heller

A Jew's Love for Language

You convert, you expel,
you exterminate.
You said, "Jew, you'll burn in hell."
You said, "Jew, go live by yourself."

[stanza continues]

And just when you silenced her name,
she sang back into your world
beaming and book carrying
and wearing pearls.

Then one day you said,
"Jew, you are going to die —
all of you." And with gas in her mouth
she went under six million times.
And, finally, you inherited a meaner world,
silenced without our humor, without the sound
of our laughter, without our music.

And you almost won in the end.
You painted the walls of your world
with our saddest blood
till they glowed a glistening red
that dulled to their usual gray
when our blood washed off.

And it did wash off.
And you and your children will forget,
but I won't. Because I'm writing it all down
before the next generation of amnesiacs
comes rushing in, red-cheeked and smiling.

I'm writing letters to the would-be children
of all those artists, tailors, makers of poems
and ironic sayings. I'm thanking them
for my mother's Yiddishy expressions,
for my grandmother's chutzpah
and for my own love of the power of ideas.

We were the spice of the world's garden,
scattered over every land: spice you took
and ground into piles of cups and toothbrushes.
You finally sorted us out, converted us
into heaps of clothes and shoes, turned
the fillings of our teeth into fine, gold spoons.

The only monuments to our beautiful culture,
this rubble called Bergen-Belsen, Treblinka, Dachau,
Auschwitz, some horrible mecca
earnest pilgrims visit, offering their bouquets
of pity, disgust, and shame.

We will have learned nothing
if we do not remember the gifts of our humor,
our music, our ability to make orchards bloom.

I like to think of all those poets, storekeepers,
and yentas, gossiping and laughing.
Sometimes I can hear the echo
of their rowdy songs,
the banging of books,
the clatter of pearls.

The Yiddish I Know

1

The Yiddish I know is sugar-water
boiled down to a hard glaze
at the bottom of an iron pan.
The water burned away, twisted up
in six million puffs through a maze of cracks
in the ceiling. In my hand, chips of burnt sugar
glitter like diamonds.

My grandparents spoke fluently,
so that Yiddish poured like tea,
a gold stream eased down into tall glasses
they raised, laughing, a sugar cube blazing
between their teeth.

2

What couldn't be translated slipped through:
insults and irony, idioms that meant too many joys
or pain to coax into English.
These words my parents learned,
just a bit of colored glass
cut from the old country. Each facet,
a tiny window to a world of crooked streets
packed with houses bursting
with bowls of golden soup,
challah twisted into fat yellow braids
by a strong woman's hands
and oh, the sideways smiles, the endurance.

These words, a handful of stars plucked out
of a constellation, thrown across a kitchen table
like dice, thrown down to me.
What luck to know them.
I roll them in my hand, such a sweet light weight.
They tumble down in doubles.

Michael Heller

Bandelette de Torah

For Carl Rakosi

In honor of the Eternal One, it has been made, this band and cloak, by the young and dignified girl, Simhah, daughter of the cantor, Joseph Hay, son of the wise and noble Isaac.
— 1761, Musée de Judaïsm, Paris

The hunger is for the word between us,
between outside and in, between Europe
and America, between the Jew and his other,
the word and the non-word.

In the museum case, belief has been sealed
behind glass. The gold *yod,* fist-shaped
with extended finger, marks where the letter
is made free, *davar* twining *aleph* into thing.

The hunger was once for textured cloth, brocade
of thread, gold-webbed damask, tessellate fringe,
for sewn-in weight of lead or brass, the chanter
lifting all heaviness from the page, singing out

lost richness. He followed the gold *yod* of divining,
alchemic word intoning the throne's measure in
discarded lexicons of *cubits* and *myriads.* The cloth
lay over Europe's open scroll between Athens and Jerusalem,

between library and dream. What if Athens were to be
entered only via the syllogism or Jerusalem's sky
were written over in fiery labyrinth, in severe figures,
unerring texts? The hunger was for the lost world

that lay between Jerusalem and Athens. Later, terrors
came to be its portion, flames beyond remonstrance,
synagogue and worshiper in ash. Celan in the Seine
with its syllabary. The words were as burls in woven cloth.

They lay across the lettered scroll, ink on paper
enveloped in darkness, desperate to be inmixed
with matter. The words were between us, poised
to rise into constellated night as task unto the city,

to enter *this* place unshielded between the One
and nothingness, if only to exist as from an echo
between hope and horror, between sacred sound
and profane air. Between Athens and Jerusalem and America.

from Bialystok Stanzas

Burnt Synagogue

This light —
A river through which
Another life poured

Figure and ground
Of how the dark
Informs the light

Brings forth bodies, faces
Brings forth
The things of the earth
That we see to completion
— beloved, hated —

But that life was broken forever
Here, look, look, this is but
Its mirror

Only the mirror remains

And gone —
Whole peoples are gone
To horror beyond remonstrance —

Freitogdige
Donershtogdige
Shabbosdige
Consumed in those fires

Words can add nothing
That flame itself was without a light

Stephen Herz

Fried Noodles Topped with Raisins Cinnamon and Vanilla Cream

For Mina Pächter and the women of Terezín

Make a noodle dough from ½ kilogram flour,
2 eggs, 2-3 tablespoons white wine,
2-3 tablespoons thick sour cream . . .

We dig through the garbage heaps
rotting in the courtyard,
eat our watery pea powder soup,
our gray bread and potato peels.
But here in Terezín
we feed our minds with favorite recipes,
getting each ingredient just right, even arguing,
"cooking with the mouth."

Next, roll out the dough medium thick.
Cut short noodles and fry them in hot fat . . .

No eggs. No butter, cream, noodles.
But our recipes have them.
And we, the women of Terezín, have them as weapons
against a constant hunger. We write them
on scraps of paper, one of them across a picture
of Hitler.

Remove the noodles and put them into a
soufflé dish. Sprinkle them with sugar,
cinnamon and many raisins . . .

We fight back with Chocolate Strudel, with
Chicken Galantine garnished with aspic and caviar,
with Goose Neck stuffed with Farina, Goulash with
Noodles, Potato Herring, Nut Braid topped with
sugar icing, Liver Dumplings, Apple Dumplings,
Farina Dumplings, Cherry-Plum Dumplings, and
Mrs. Weil's Viennese Dumplings you can serve plain
or with roasts. Rye Schnapps, Macaroons, Linzer
Torte, Ice Cream à la Melba, Bean Cake, Czech Cake,
Butter Kindelin, and Cheap Real Jewish Bobe.

Now make a delicate vanilla cream, add a little
raw cream and pour over fried noodles.
Bake a little. Bring to table in dish.

In Your Lager Dream,

the black sun
turns orange and warm.
the stench of the cremo is gone.
the boils and pus and lice are gone.
the blue tattoo
fades from your wrist.

[stanza continues]

the green dye
fades from your eyes.
your long black hair is back,
you brush and comb it,
tie it with your favorite ribbon.
the SS man gives you back
your wool coat with the yellow star.
you give him back the paper bag
stuffed under your dress.
he doesn't take your number.
in your dream you're alone.
the Blockalteste is gone.
the Kapo is gone.
your Kommando is gone.
where are the Häftlinge?
you scream. and scream.
the loud speaker blares
Du Jude, kaputt!
the chimney belches red and black.
the guards sing *Deutschland über Alles*.
they sing the Horst Wessel song.
In your dream the snow is red.
Arbeit Macht Frei over the gate is red.
your red soup bowl floats. empty.
like iron words.

Jedwabne

based on the deposition of Szmul Wasersztajn,
the first at war's end to condemn his Polish neighbors,
rather than the Germans, for the massacre of nearly
the entire population of sixteen hundred Jews from
the Polish village of Jedwabne

With mine own eyes I see our local Polish
kill Chajcia Wasersztajn, fifty-three, Jakub Kac, seventy-three,
and Eliasz Krawiecki.
With bricks they stone to death Jakub Kac.
Krawiecki they knife,
then pluck his eyes and cut off his tongue.
He suffers terribly for twelve hours
before giving up his soul.
Wacek Borowski with his brother Mietk,
I see them with others walking from one Jewish dwelling to another,
they are playing accordion and flute
to drown the screams of our Jewish women and children.
The local Polish hooligans,

[stanza continues]

armed with axes, clubs studded with nails,
and other instruments of torture,
chase the Jews into the street where they are
clubbed and hacked to death.
Jews are ordered to dig a hole and bury all
previously murdered Jews,
then those are killed and in turn buried by others.
The beards of old Jews are burned,
newborn babies are killed at their mothers' breasts,
people are beaten and forced to sing and dance,
the Jews are ordered to line up in a column four in a row;
in front they put the ninety-year-old rabbi
and the shochet (Kosher butcher),
a red banner they give them —
and all are ordered to sing as they're bestially beaten
and chased into the barn.
Various instruments they are playing in order to drown out
the screams of the victims.
Some Jews try to defend themselves, but they're defenseless.
Bloodied and wounded, they're pushed into the barn,
the barn's doused with kerosene and lit.
Then the local Polish go around to search Jewish homes
to look for the remaining sick and children.
The sick they carry to the barn,
the little children they rope together by their legs,
carry them on their back,
put them on pitchforks and throw them into
the smoldering coals.

---

10 July 2002: on national TV from Jedwabne, Poland,
President Aleksander Kwasniewski asks forgiveness
for this "particularly cruel crime." A sign on several
doors in the village reads: "We do not apologize."

Marked

For Anita Schorr

at nine
you wore the yellow star,
the Star of David
that marked you *Jew*,
marked you for the cattlecar,
marked you for Terezín, for Bergen-Belsen,
marked you for Auschwitz
where you lost your name
for a number —
71569

will the tall chimney roar?
will it belch its stench red and black?
will you go to the showers
that aren't showers?
will you stand without falling
through the long *appels*?
will you avoid the dogs, the Kapo's blows?
will they take your number
at the next *selektion*?

a girl of fourteen
you say you're eighteen
like your mother tells you,
hiding your undeveloped body,
slipping out of Mengele's hands,
out of Auschwitz
into Hamburg slave labor,
a red stripe down your back,
the errant bomb burying you,
the German soldier
pulling you out, befriending you,
giving you half his sandwich
every day

until the day the cattlecar dumps you
into Bergen-Belsen,
into the living dead, the walking dead:
and the flesh of the dead
some are eating
before the British are coming,
and you tell yourself:
I'm going to make it!
willing yourself to survive,
to bear witness
for all of those who lost their names
who lost their lives
simply because
they were marked
like you:
Jew

Shot

shot in the synagogue
shot up against the wall in the headlights
        of the truck
shot in the farmyard by the dung heap

[stanza continues]

shot in the hospital, the maternity ward
shot in the city, the town, the shtetl
shot in the cemetery
shot in the warehouse after machine-gun muzzles
        were pushed through holes in the walls
shot in the roundups trying to escape
shot in bed
shot in their cribs
shot in the air, the baby thrown over its
        mother's head
shot because they stole a potato
shot because they were betrayed for a kilo of sugar
shot because they weren't wearing the yellow star
shot because they *were* wearing the yellow star

shot by the *Einsatzgruppen*
shot by the Reserve Battalion of the German
        Order Police
shot by the Gestapo
shot by the Waffen SS and the Higher SS
shot by the Hiwis — Ukrainian, Latvian, and
        Lithuanian volunteers
shot by the Hungarian Fascist Nyilas,
        the Arrow Cross
shot by the Romanian army, police, gendarmerie,
        border guards, civilians, and
        the Iron Guard
shot by the *Wehrmacht*
shot by old men in the German Home Guard
shot by young boys in the Hitler Youth
shot in "action" after "action," as if it was
        "more or less our daily bread"
shot in the search-and-destroy mission, the
        Jew Hunt
shot in the "harvest festival," the *Erntefest*
shot in order to make the northern Lublin district
        judenrein

shot in Zhytomyr, Poniatowa, Józefów, Trawniki
shot in Lomazy, Parczew, Bialystok, Kharkov
shot in Bialowieza, Luków, Riga, Poltava
shot in Miedzyrzec, Khorol, Kremenstshug
shot in Slutsk, Bobruisk, Mogilev, Vinnitsa
shot in Odessa, Lwóv, Kolmyja, Minsk, Rovno
shot in Majdanek and Brest-Litovsk
shot in Neu Sandau and Tarnopol and Rohatin
shot in Dnepropetrovsk
shot in Kovno, Pinsk, Berdichev, Tarnów
shot in Kamenets-Podolski

[stanza continues]

shot in Cracow, Szczebrzeszyn, Šiauliai
shot in Stolin, Kielce, Lutsk, Serokomla
shot in Drogobych, Luga, Delatyn
shot in the Warsaw Ghetto
shot in the ravine of Babi Yar
shot in Bilgoraj, Nadvornaya, Stanislawów
shot in David Grodek, Janów Podlesia
shot near Zamość

shot after nobody thought they would be shot because
    they were told "get ready, the entire Jewish
    population is going to spend the winter on a farm"
shot after being roped with their families, roped
    with barbed wire
shot after being told they would be spared if they
    came out of hiding and reported for a new
    identity card
shot after being tied together in threes — only the
    middle person shot, his weight pulling down
    the other two after being shoved in the river
shot marching to the shooting site because they
    lagged behind
shot after the Star of David was branded on their foreheads
shot lying face down, naked, waiting for hours
    in the hot August sun
shot after being paraded through the streets — the
    women, naked, arms in the air, marching through
    the snow and ice to the forest

shot walking across a plank laid over the grave
shot after being driven into the grave and made to
    lie down on top of those who
    had been shot before them
    layer on layer — the SS called this
    Sardinenpackung — sardine-packing
shot after their eyes were gouged out because they
    refused to undress
shot in the neck, their heads stuck in a pot
shot in the mouth after being forced to crawl through
    a mud hole, singing
shot in the back of the head, their brains splattering
    on the green uniforms
shot one after another, forcing the rabbi to watch,
    saving him for last
shot while the shooter ate an apple

shot because they were too weak to walk to the gas van
shot because they didn't take off their hats
    to the guards
shot when they sat down, after the guard told them:

[stanza continues]

"Take it easy. Rest a while."
shot marching to the *Umschlagplatz* because they walked
too fast, because they fell, because they strayed
out of line, because they turned their heads,
because they bent down, because they spoke too loud,
because they were children who cried
shot after being placed in a row for target practice,
bottles on their heads
shot after being raped — "going to peel potatoes,"
the Germans called it
shot after benches were placed at the shooting site
so local Lithuanians could get a good view
shot after uttering the first words of the Kaddish:
Yitgodal veyitkadach shmé . . .

shot in the courtyard of Block II at Auschwitz, at
the "Death Wall," after their breasts were singed,
their fingernails extracted
shot because the baby was alive at its mother's breast
after the doors of the gas chamber opened
shot because they couldn't walk a straight line
shot trying to scoop some soup from the bottom of the
empty pot
shot in the "hat trick" — the guard threw the prisoner's
hat in the air, ordered him to run after it, then
shot him trying to escape
shot after dismantling the camp
shot in the moments before liberation, the surrender
leaflets dropping into the camp, the commander
yelling: "We may have only two minutes to live,
but you have only one."

Walter Hess

Oma

1

She stayed in the village where they knew her worth —
sixteen and pregnant and no one reproached her

Once I saw the Gypsy at her door
skin like oil and beads of coral about her neck
who looked into her eyes and bowed her head
who saw her sorrows as the muted flint of fiery being
her joy, long flowing silence and calm knowing

We sat in front of bread and butter then
mothers and grandmothers rising like steam
from sweet creamy coffee
safety like raisins among the blue-lined china
and the nougat fathers dotted along the four o'clock napery

2

This is for my grandmother, an unimportant Jew
whose apron gathered morels in a green pine wood
who, in a walled city died of typhus
in Terezín, city of Therese, Empress of Typhus
eight days before the liberating Russian army came

Bulldozers may have shoveled her to stuff the pits
to stem the stench and sickness
from leaping beyond sane and certain borders —
laconic hands on throttles, shovels,
levers doing overtime, thin arms,

heads falling back in awkward postures
There must have been some scraping sound of gears
of metal on the hard-baked ground
of the resistance so much poundage makes
against an oily diesel energy

or, she just fell over, toppled in a heap
became a boulder,
a holy stone,
one of many dotting the parade ground
before which even the dark tanks halted

3

I think that someone picked her up —
a Russian soldier maybe —
persuaded beyond her rotting flesh
by memory and awe to place her gently with the others
to burn with others in the immense hollow of her grave
in other words in piety
doing what I do now

4

Grandmother, the cantillation of the rails
whistles in the three-starred night
enfilades where I am not,
and where I am the song evokes distance, borders, margins

[stanza continues]

winds of cloves, dark whistling winds
bearing cinnamon and plaited candles
Sabbath ends reflected in the half moon of your nails
and both your hands upon my shoulder
resting

William Heyen

The Candle

It would do me no good to travel to Auschwitz.
It would do the dead no good, nor anyone else any good.
It would do me no good to kneel there,
me nor anyone else alive or dead any good, any good at all.

I've heard that in one oven a votive candle
whispers its flame. When I close my eyes,
I can see and feel that candle, its pitch aura,
its tongues of pitch luminescence licking the oven's recesses.

A survivor, forty years later, crawled up into an oven and lay down.
What of his heart? Could it keep pumping its own pitch light
here where God's human darkness grew darkest?
Whoever you were, please grant me dispensation.

Rudolf Hess praised the efficiency of these ovens.
It would do me no good to travel to Auschwitz, to kneel or lie down.
It would do me or God or anyone else alive or dead,
or anyone else neither alive nor dead no good, no good at all.

The survivor did crawl back out of the oven.
He took his heart with him, didn't he not, it kept beating.
He left his heart in the oven, and it keeps beating, black-black,
black-black, the candle of the camps.

Eyes closed, staring up into this, eyebeams of pitch luminescence,
and the pulse of it, the heart, the candle — you and I,
haven't we not, have met him, the one who lay himself down there
where the Nazis had missed some, welcome, welcome home.

We have spoken the candle heart of the camps.
It does the dead no good, nor us any good, doesn't it not,
but it keeps, black-black, its watch of pitch light,
and will. Any good at all. Wouldn't we not? The candle.

The Legend of the Shoah

time came when
it was forgotten
for what it was
whatever it had been

no one remembered even
one ancestor who had spoken
of one survivor
to one descendent

libraries & museums
deaccessioned
photographs books
other memento mori
of that rumored past

the camps themselves
where the skeletal
bulldozed victims
had convened
for a century or two

or whose ash had been
spread into ponds
over fields into woods
into words
had changed their names
long before
& disappeared

a few of the devout
still lit candles
but to what

the whispering flames
interfused with prayer
couldn't find their homes
in the appalling beauty
of such memory

in whose story now
millions had willingly walked
into furnaces or ascended
into a paradise of vapor
singing — whole families
whole villages & cities

welcomed into the kingdom
made possible for them
by those in uniform
assisting them until

the legend grew of one
whose names were *Arbeit* & *Heil*
whose names were *Kristall* & *Reich*
the magnanimous one
who cleansed & forgave

who allowed them
despite their mephitic sins
this life they had forsaken
this life they had betrayed

Riddle

From Belsen a crate of gold teeth,
from Dachau a mountain of shoes,
from Auschwitz a skin lampshade.
Who killed the Jews?

Not I, cries the typist,
not I, cries the engineer,
not I, cries Adolf Eichmann,
not I, cries Albert Speer.

My friend Fritz Nova lost his father —
a petty official had to choose.
My friend Lou Abrahms lost his brother.
Who killed the Jews?

David Nova swallowed gas,
Hyman Abrahms was beaten and starved.
Some men signed their papers,
and some stood guard,

and some herded them in,
and some dropped the pellets,
and some spread the ashes,
and some hosed the walls,

and some planted the wheat,
and some poured the steel,
and some cleared the rails,
and some raised the cattle.

Some smelled the smoke,
some just heard the news.
Were they Germans? Were they Nazis?
Were they human? Who killed the Jews?

The stars will remember the gold,
the sun will remember the shoes,
the moon will remember the skin.
But who killed the Jews?

The Secret

For Chana Michaeli

The survivor spoke. I began to hear.
Not her cattlecar four eternal days from Budapest,
the dead buried under luggage in one corner —
I'd heard this before.
Not the shorning, the aberrant showers, the corpse stink of soup —
I'd heard this before.
Not the electrified barbed wire —
but as though her sentences
shorted themselves out,
phrases that buzzed & crackled
under her breastbone barracks. Not music,
the gaunt band playing the walking dead off to slave labor,
back from slave labor —
I'd heard this before, or tried to. But
red streaks of voice across
an ionized atmosphere,
gassed Hungarian clawhair & ribnails & tongues, a burst heart
breaking into static as she spoke,
into cancelling sparks,
her now never-ending speechlessness, never.

Simple Truths

When a man has grown a body,
a body to carry with him
through nature for as long as he can,
when this body is taken from him
by other men and women who happen to be,
this time, in uniform,
then it is clear he has experienced
an act of barbarism,

and when a man has a wife,
a wife to love for as long as he lives,
when this wife is marked with a yellow star
and driven into a chamber she will never leave alive,
then this is murder,
so much is clear,

and when a woman has hair,
when her hair is shorn and her scalp bleeds,
when a woman has children,
children to love for as long as she lives,
when the children are taken from her,
when a man and his wife and their children

are put to death in a chamber of gas,
or with pistols at close range, or are starved,
or beaten, or injected by the thousands,
or ripped apart, by the thousands, by the millions,

it is clear that where we are
is Europe, in our century, during the years
from nineteen-hundred and forty-five
after the death of Jesus, who spoke of a different order,
but whose father, who is our father,
if he is our father,
if we must speak of him as father,
watched, and witnessed, and knew,

and when we remember,
when we touch the skin of our own bodies,
when we open our eyes into dream
or within the morning shine of sunlight
and remember what was taken
from these men, from these women,
from these children gassed and starved
and beaten and thrown against walls
and made to walk the valley
of knives and icepicks and otherwise
exterminated in ways appearing to us almost
beyond even the maniacal human imagination,
then it is clear that this is the German Reich,
during approximately ten years of our lord's time,

and when we read a book of these things,
when we hear the names of the camps,
when we see films of the bulldozed dead
or the film of one boy struck on the head
with a club in the hands
of a German doctor who will wait
some days for the boy's skull to knit, and will enter

[stanza continues]

the time in his ledger, and then
take up the club to strike the boy again,
and wait some weeks for the boy's skull to knit,
and enter the time in his ledger again,
and strike the boy again,
and so on, until the boy, who,
at the end of the film of his life
can hardly stagger forward toward the doctor,
does die, and the doctor
enters exactly the time of the boy's death in his ledger,

when we read these things or see them,
then it is clear to us that this
happened, and within the lord's allowance, this
work of his minions, his poor
vicious dumb German victims twisted
into the swastika shapes of trees struck by lightning
on this his earth, if he is our father,
if we must speak of him in this way,
this presence above us, within us, this
mover, this first cause, this spirit, this
curse, this bloodstream and brain-current, this
unfathomable oceanic ignorance of ourselves, this
automatic electric Aryan swerve, this

fortune that you and I were not the victims, this
luck that you and I were not the murderers, this
sense that you and I are clean and understand, this
stupidity that gives him breath, gives him life
as we kill them all, as we killed them all.

Rick Hilles

Amchu

The velvet curtain was already falling, the twentieth
century losing its last gray hairs, when the man
brought back from death safely reentered
the war-ravaged city of his birth; the long shadows
flooded him, filling him with sparrows and broken glass.
He unwrapped himself to bandages of lilac cloud,
the ancient dirt road of river still there and shimmering.
The street-cleaners sprayed the sidewalk, and vendors
steadied their fresh flowers, and fruits, and meats;
one elderly woman's hands, like gloves the color
of crushed raspberries, held out a fat peach,

[stanza continues]

the best the season had to offer, or so it seemed —
it was all that he'd longed to touch again and taste
and see and would, he knew, soon mourn,
when he turned his back again on the great river,
the sun warm on his shoulders as he pushed through
the revolving glass doors to the library, imperceptibly
passing the distracted guards to one unlit corridor
where among the higher shelves he brushed off
the dusty volumes with an ecstasy that held him
wide awake in the nightmare; more than anything
now, he needed to fill in the years of his exile,
his appetite transforming his native tongue
to a new fluency — the readiness and dexterity
in him surpassed, nearly complete. He raced
through a language transcribed from fire
when on the next page framed in the window
by four sudden prison bar shadows, he saw
the photos — bleary, colorless, but images he knew
and recognized — the Warsaw Ghetto's first days:
a crowd of children's faces, some smiling and full;
electric cable car #61 wearing the Star of David
blurring beside a hand-drawn rickshaw; and after
the typhus, a headshot of the boy smuggler
who hid food in his knickers, lying in a black
pool of blood; a starving woman trying to hold
her grief and her newborn infant, already dead.

They were the photographs Tadzik had taken
half a century ago — in the first months
of his own captivity after he smuggled into
the ghetto his birthday present: a loaded
Leica camera with two rolls of film. Now
his left hand moved over the faces, the way
he tended them when they were still alive,
and he scanned the wreckage of a shelled-out
hospital for anything that might hold back
death, a spoon or handkerchief to improvise
a splint; overlooked laudanum for pain.
So that even as he stood holding the faces
of the ghetto dead, the buried lives returned,
resurfacing like water startled from the Carpathians.
The foreheads, still wet and feverish, pressed
back against his fingertips; and late Autumn
rattled the windowpanes. And he remembered
another runner: a man, like him, in the resistance.
But one with access to the outside world, a man
he somehow met and did not meet on a park bench.
Below a fruitless tree, along the ghetto wall
a suit, ashing a smoke, said "*Amchu*? — *Friend*?"

[stanza continues]

and Tadzik nodded, lowering his brim; the man
calmly sat and pocketed the shriveled bag of film.
And then, not looking up, the man rose slowly
(slowly!) and walked away. And that was that.
(Then fifty years.) The nightmare was exposed.
And the runner had made it, if only once,
back to the world of fruit and light.

Yom HaShoah in Florida

In remembrance of the Holocaust, observed in the Hebrew calendar on the anniversary of the Warsaw Ghetto Uprising

Here, the trees pay their respects, mourn openly,
        wear dreadlocks of hanging Spanish moss
sun bleached ash-blue and swaying; in seawind
        they become prayer shawls
salted with dust, grief threads of every kind
        of human hair, some washed ashore
in mollusk shells, some rescued from mass graves,
        appearing now as storm-torn curtains,
silver-blue and smoke-stained, as tattered
        boas flapper-thrown from some bygone

Mardi Gras, sweat-ruined scarves and handkerchiefs
        hanging like empty hives of dried lilac
& wisteria. Squinting and sweaty in the midday heat
        I can almost believe they shine for the
unlikely blessing on Tadzik, my Ohio pediatrician,
        who emerged from a Warsaw Ghetto
bomb-flooded cellar & walked out drenched
        into the clutches of laughing armed SS
and lived. The Gestapo, in laughing, forgot
        to shoot Tadzik and the nurses — Bela,

Sabinka — his fiancée, Fredzia, her brother, Henio.
        Maybe if I stare long enough I will see that
these trees wear the torn clothes of the vanquished
        like medals: Bela's torn blouse, her
skirt and underthings ruined at Umschlagplatz
        by Gestapo who pulled her by those prized
blond streaming curls into another room . . .
        and, later, on the train ride
to Treblinka, when Bela kissed Fredzia & said
        "Help me" and her hostaged

friends lifted her up together, up, like a child,
        up to the window without glass
— the train's pistons pumping furiously now —

[stanza continues]

her wish to fly finally fulfilled
when she pushed herself from the cattle car,
as Pinek had instructed her,
and how in leaping she became a paper moth,
before the rush of bullets pinned her
to the sky above the sun-scorched earth;
if I look hard enough, I will see

these heaps of Spanish moss are the spun
legacy of Henio Grin, the strewn yarn
of his lost story, for which there are still
not words enough. Not for Henio,
who was sixteen and would not live to see
another time. He was the first one
off the train at Maidanek, winning the prisoners'
race easily — by two whole lengths —
to the gated building beyond a field of dust,
turning around an instant to cheer on

his slower friends, certain his track-star speed
would save him, though it would not.
Only Tadzik, who stumbled, was saved
when the SS egging them on held out
a white-gloved hand to block Tadzik's last place
finish to the death showers, an act both
merciful and arbitrary. My doctor was shoved
aside, and the Gestapo said: "You
idiot" and "Don't be afraid, your death won't
amount to one flash of lightning

in the night sky." And what if the trees in Florida,
covered as they are with Hawaiian
leis and luau dancers' skirts & struck piñatas
whose treasures kids made off with
long ago, are also a kind of code still waiting
to be cracked, saved tickertape & streamers,
fanfare for homecoming parades that won't happen
till everyone comes home. Or they are
the nests of promises, each strand thrown
by a spouse whose marriage vows

extend beyond the grave; the mosses certainly are
woven of Bela's braids, and countless others,
which now smell forever of summer & brush
fires near Everglades. For each specter circling
the earth, and all who still believe blue Shoah smoke
shall block our way to Paradise, the trees
observe this breach, the break in covenant. Listen.
How gently they rattle their worry beads
for us on a day that begins in Hebrew at sunset
when the first three night stars are visible.

Edward Hirsch

Paul Celan: A Grave and Mysterious Sentence

Paris, 1948

It's daybreak and I wish I could believe
In a rain that will wash away the morning
That is just about to rise behind the smokestacks
On the other side of the river, other side
Of nightfall. I wish I could forget the slab
Of darkness that always fails, the memories
That flood through the window in a murky light.

But now it is too late. Already the day
Is a bowl of thick smoke filling up the sky
And swallowing the river, covering the buildings
With a sickly, yellow film of sperm and milk.
Soon the streets will be awash with little bright
Patches of oblivion on their way to school,
Dark briefcases of oblivion on their way to work.

Soon my small apartment will be white and solemn
Like a blank page held up to a blank wall,
A secret whispered into a vacant closet. But
This is a secret which no one else remembers
Because it is stark and German, like the silence,
Like the white fire of daybreak that is burning
Inside my throat. If only I could stamp it out!

But think of smoke and ashes. An ominous string
Of railway cars scrawled with a dull pencil
Across the horizon at dawn. A girl in pigtails
Saying, "Soon you are going to be erased."
Imagine thrusting your head into a well
And crying for help in the wrong language,
Or a deaf mute shouting into an empty field.

So don't talk to me about flowers, those blind
Faces of the dead thrust up out of the ground
In bright purples and blues, oranges and reds.
And don't talk to me about the gold leaves
Which the trees are shedding like an extra skin:
They are handkerchiefs pressed over the mouths
Of the dead to keep them quiet. It's true:

Once I believed in a house asleep, a childhood
Asleep. Once I believed in a mother dreaming
About a pair of giant iron wings growing

[stanza continues]

Painfully out of the shoulders of the roof
And lifting us into away-from-here-and-beyond.
Once I even believed in a father calling out
Names in the dark, restless and untransfigured.

But what did we know then about the smoke
That was already beginning to pulse from trains,
To char our foreheads, to transform their bodies
Into two ghosts billowing from a huge oven?
What did we know about a single gray strand
Of barbed wire knotted slowly and tightly
Around their necks? We didn't know anything then.

And now here is a grave and mysterious sentence
Finally written down, carried out long ago:
At last I have discovered that the darkness
Is a solitary night train carrying my parents
Across a field of dead stumps and wild flowers
Before disappearing on the far horizon,
Leaving nothing much in its earthly wake

But a stranger standing at the window
Suddenly trying to forget his childhood,
To forget a milky black trail of smoke
Slowly unravelling in the distance
Like the victory-flag of death, to forget
The slate clarity of another day
Forever breaking behind the smokestacks.

Jean Hollander

The Chosen

I try to tell them how it feels
to be chosen for death

how a child accepts
the policeman no longer friend,
that men, in and out of uniform
are looking for you —

how you've been prepared:
"Jud!" "Jude!" "Jüdin!"
with snowballs that didn't respect
even your parents. Streets were not safe,
gangs waiting at the last corner
each way home from school

how terror softens you
and laws anoint you
for your bitter fate

It is so hard to explain
how Jews accepted their heredity —
each child a Star of David
to the fire

how having been
in the jaws of that beast and spat out
does not make you kind,
how you bite back at the innocent
instead of the brute offender

how it has taken you a lifetime to shut
the pages of that bestiary,
to stop fearing
footsteps on the stairs

how you cannot find
a reason to have been spared.

Barbara Helfgott Hyett

And There Were Pits,

And there were pits,
I would say about fifty
yards long, and people
buried alive in there.
And they had German
civilians digging them
out — but they wouldn't
touch the bodies — with
shovels. Two at a time.
You could see that the
bodies were still warm.
The soldiers, the infantry
men were so angered by
what they had seen that
they made the civilians
throw the shovels away
and take them out by hand
and lay them gently down.

Too Weak to Stand, They Lay

Too weak to stand, they lay
on straw under heavy blankets,
skin stretched so taut
over joints they couldn't
bend their arms.
When we passed by they
cowered against the wall,
turned their faces
from the expected blow.

You Know, the Funny Thing Is

You know, the funny thing is
the memories I have —
I'm not sure that I could say
where I was, what I was doing.
The only thing I have
is the picture that I know
I took. I took the picture.
I had the camera. I had to
have been there. Otherwise
I wouldn't have known.

Thea Iberall

Keeping the Ground

At the New Jewish Cemetery, he cuts the grass,
tends trees, wears a baseball cap
backwards; the sun gets hot under the maples and poplars.
He smokes a Sparta, uses a wheelbarrow
or a motorized cart when there is lots of grass.
He drives along the path, past Leopold Pick 1866–1928,
Adolf Schulz 1867–1938. Does he think, how lucky
these people were, long lives, no torture?
He passes the 1950s, the 60s, the 70s.
He passes the 80s, he passes the 90s. People are still dying.
Anna Antonova 1908–2001.
Even a grave ready for Eva Povoridrova born 1943.
Does he worry whether the cemetery will fill up?

At the east end, the stones lean off,
tired, near the ground, covered in ivy.
An impenetrable word peeks through.
Olga Camperlikova 1878–1942 — Oświęcim
Erich Schild 1930–1944 — Oświęcim
And Ida Mermelsteinova's daughter, Juditha — Oświęcim

And there his task ends, a pile of grass by the wall, brick
and peeling. He pours the new cuttings over the old
though he knows compacted living material combusts.
When archeologists dig up these graves, what will they think
of the word — a disease perhaps — stamped
on the stones of the young and the old?
When they discover a handful of ashes,
will they say the grass exploded?

Judith Irwin

1985 — In a Small American Town

Sleeping beside you, I know a distance
without dimension. I reach out — you say
you do not dream. Your way is by no sound
I can follow.

I listen as you rise — your footfalls, throat clearing
and nose blowing, electric razor's whirr, change
jingling in your pocket where
I sometimes search
for answers in a wallet
stuffed with two forty-year-old photos —
faded, torn — of human skeletons tossed
in a common grave, piled too deep
for the eye to measure and, above,
someone in uniform holding between his fingers,
as you do now, a cigarette.

White as a bandage
rolled thin, it seems the smoke
is an inhalation, a kind of life
you draw into yourself
to cure the pain.

Dan Jaffe

In a Holocaust Memorial Garden

Temple Beth Sholom, Sarasota, Florida

After Genesis God's first role
was Gardener. He wove
tendrils and rivulets, orchid
and mangrove, hibiscus and bamboo,
a flowing of fountains and flora,
all flowering for the glory of the senses
and the iridescence of the soul.

What followed was the first Diaspora,
man's floundering through the foliage of the world,
a whole history of wanderings and missteps,
of flailing at the mysteries,
all the while the Garden growing distant,
the leaves shriveling, rising in drafts
across the desert, the Garden
lost somewhere, out of sight.

How did man come to this? To such forgetfulness,
to the double snakes of the SS,
to swastikas spiking the landscape?
When I think of the Garden gone,
of the world polluted, of the waste
of beautiful lives denied, of a child's face,
resplendent as a wet blossom, doomed,
I can hardly breathe.
I must restrain myself
or I will throw myself down among the stones
and water the weeds with my tears.

The ashes of Auschwitz, they say, drifted on the wind,
descended into streams and rivers,
into fields and forests. And so
the hydro-plankton flourished,
the land grew ripe from death.

In such lushness there is always pain,
as in this Holocaust Memorial Garden.
Here we are in Eden and in the loss of Eden,
and our grief fertilizes the present.
The spirits of Shoah
hover like hummingbirds among the plantings.

Katherine Janowitz

The Third Generation

For Jessie

And no blight on her
anywhere from the
beginning, almost
too bright as if
out of my packet
of mixed seeds
the most extravagant
was sown and
my father told me
not to wear red
and I listened
but I gave birth to
this red bird
impossible to miss,
I gave birth to this crimson flower
from my secret blood.

Sheila Golburgh Johnson

Shoes

U.S. Memorial Holocaust Museum

At the end
the shoes
powdered over with dust
or ashes
faded
splattered stained
worn cowhide canvas sandals
streaked velvet battered kidskin
pumps
oxfords wedgies boots sneakers
toe shoes Mary Janes
gaping throats torn tongues
spoke

Laurence Josephs

Passover at Auschwitz

Possibly they thought of it,
Remembering the old days; possibly
They could savor, still, the memory
Of spices, the clean bone, the glass
Of quiet wine left in the cool
Opacity of symbol, for the Guest.

Here were no calendars: perhaps
A knotted cord: more likely
That the stars alone beat time, aware and distant,
Or that clouds, like immaculate grandfathers,
Lay against the void of memory.
Here it was Passover all year long! What ghosts

Flamed in their blood, their terrible dreams!
The plague: life! The sea: tears! The serpent:
Hope! For in the dying
Center of history newer than theirs,
The world, like a wingéd horse, flew upside down.
They, then, firstborn, were prey of angels,

Where in an endless, idiot night
They waited for a sound of wings or feet.
Pass over! or Come down! they must have cried.
Or from their myth of sleep, reached out
To the angel death who once, in old bondage,
Did not forget, but held them more than dear.

Marilyn Kallet

After a While, at Theresienstadt

"After a while there were so many,
that the Nazis threw the ashes of the
nameless in the Ohře."

"So the river is filled with
the dead?" a woman asks.
The eyes of her troubled daughter

grow wide. We say Kaddish
at the bridge overlooking the Ohře.
Only the wild-eyed daughter

knows the prayer by heart.
How long does it take a river
to forget? The rich silt

of the Ohře has much to be grateful
for — last year
its banks flooded over.

We are grateful for our young
tour guide, his fine
dreadlocks and cocoa skin,

that he speaks five languages,
one of them ours,
that his parents and grandparents,

Czech Jews, survived
the Nazis, hidden by local farmers
for four years.

Grateful that our aunt Hedwig
survived Theresienstadt,
that her bones lie in the

shady ground at Rexingen,
near her mother.
That we can find the marker

and place a stone. Thankful
for names. For breathing daughters.
Blessed are You, O God.

— 2004

Mezuzah

In Memory, Hedwig Schwarz

In the doorpost of her house, a hollow
where the mezuzah used to hang.
I press my hand against the indentation,
my way of speaking to the past.

Touch the hollow where the mezuzah
used to hang. In Horb, Nazis renamed her street
Hitlerstrasse. My way of speaking to the past
is to listen, press the old men for answers.

1941, Jews were packed into Hitlerstrasse.
Now it's a winding picture postcard road,
Jew-free, pleasant as it seemed
before Nazis pressed my family into *Judenhausen*.

I press my hand against the indentation.
Over Horb, a hundred doorposts echo, hollow.

To My Poem of Hope

I don't blame you for hope,
for wanting the children
to have survived.
Because their names were not
inscribed in the "minority registration,"
you assumed they had slipped
through the net.
My dear, Horb was a hillbilly dot.
Everyone knew everyone.

Now we find this handwritten entry
by Hedwig Schwarz
in her daily book of prayer:
"On Friday, November 28, 1941
at 5:50 AM, our dear good daughter
Hilde Sara Lemberger and our dear
good grandson Siegfried Israel Lemberger
moved away from here.
We only wish that God may watch over them
and that they stay well."

Their grandmother kept "Sara" and "Israel"
in case of Nazi eyes.
Mother and son "moved away from here"
in early darkness.
The rooster couldn't crow.

The files reveal that Hilda
and Siegfried, called "Friederle,"
were deported "east for labor assignment,"
"that is to say, Riga,"
"declared dead on 4/1/1942."

Für tot erklärt.
Pronounced by anonymous agents
with past participles on their hands.

Dear poem, if we look again,
and we must,
we will find scraps,
scrawled words, secret histories,
the cry between the lines:
"Remember. They called me Freddie.
I was six years old.
Here's what really happened."

Survivor

The Night of Broken Glass,
thugs set fire to the Rexingen synagogue.
Scorched the Torah.
Officials blamed "outsiders."
Or kindergarteners playing with matches.
Jews on the fire brigade who doused the flames
were taken to Dachau.

Beginning of the end of three centuries
of Jewish life in Rexingen, Mühringen, Horb.
Sixty emigrated.
Ten "died on the spot."
Others were doomed to Theresienstadt,
Auschwitz, Riga.
After 1942, only one of the Schwarzes
from Horb survived deportation.

Hedwig had seen too much.
She died in Marienhospital,
Stuttgart, 1952,
fifty miles from her birthplace.
What held her to the land
of shards and ashes?

Was she lured by the
old cemetery, resting place
of her parents and grandparents?
Was the call of the dead more powerful
than Shavei Zion?
Perhaps the leaning firs
of the Black Forest reminded her
of her girlhood, her mother.

Nothing romantic about Terezín.
The ghetto taught her to decipher
tales of witches, children lured

[stanza continues]

to ovens. A few prisoners
had returned from Auschwitz,
told the truth about "the East."
No gingerbread houses.

But the Red Cross believed
in fairy tales.
For them, Theresienstadt
was a spa, overflowing with *Brundibár*,
soccer matches, cheerful kids.
After the official visits,
the children were transported to
Auschwitz-Birkenau.

The health care and retirement
package the Nazis had promised
turned out to be typhus, spotted fever,
starvation.

On Sunday, in hospital,
the Sisters of Saint Vincent de Paul
might have wheeled her out for a stroll.
Silence was good medicine,
they thought.

No words to ward off nightfall.
The dead were never far.

Rodger Kamenetz

My Holocaust

Don't remember talking about it much as a child.

Faces of men in striped pajamas
behind barbed wire, blinking at the light.
Their flesh soapy, unnatural. Their time
on earth slowed down to forever,
their waiting a new unit of time.

My eyes, their eyes. My flesh, their flesh.
My bones, their bones. My Holocaust
is a museum, a movie, a TV show.
A few old folks with tattoos who can say,
I was there, and soon enough
they will step out of the light.

My Holocaust is a book of fine print.
The names of dead relatives
I never knew recited in a small synagogue,
a chamber of memory where the chazzan
is fat and seedy in the shadows.

In a museum in Washington tourists
holding an ID card shuffle past cases
though no ID card will link me
to bits of crunched bone, crushed into flesh.

What can I take home as a souvenir?
Pity is too cheap and the history
of the Jews is not their deaths.

And I have no idea, dear chazzan,
how to join you in your reedy prayer, your chant
like a saxophone of spittle in your throat,
how to lift the obscure Aramaic of mourning
through seven heavens of praise
dragging the roll call of the dead
behind us like boxcars
through a Poland of smoke.

My Holocaust is a dozen wooden synagogues,
dollhouses on a table, for hundreds burned —
all of them, in Russia and the Ukraine.
The list of slaughtered towns
covers a wall that can't be read,
thick and obscure as dried blood.

My Holocaust is Europe without her Jews,
a pleasant Europe of shops,
prosperous boulevards,
fine art, and few Jews.

Judenstrassen where there are no *Juden*,
Jewless Jew towns, and in small shtetls,
the broken walls of a synagogue
pen pigs while an old man
who witnessed the slaughter
tends a cemetery of weeds.

Will my people reduced to a loud fraction
join their old friends the Hittites,
Jebusites, Moabites?
Lost tribes, lost language, ruined temples
gods and goddesses suspended
in a Lucite case.

When a people disappears, they leave
opaque, inexplicable names.
Ouachita.
Tallahassee. Mississippi.

Death is a solvent breaking the bonds
of word and object, fist and song,
marching orders and boots
that crushed small hands, the whips and dogs
whose teeth sank into particular flesh
and routed from an attic a trembling boy
whose name is lost. The cry of a child
and then the night was still
and the full moon continued its passage,
a great white boat carrying nothing.

The smoke left the chimneys rising
according to physical laws, and bodies in motion
remain in motion, and bodies at rest
disintegrate, their names break down
into letters and hollow breaths
of lost vowels. And bodies burned remain
ashes buried or scattered. So why should
memory be more permanent,
more sacred, than our flesh?

In my Holocaust Theme Park you will see
a river of blood, a mountain of gold crowns.
Here in the Fun House
it's a scary ride down into the tunnel
of broken teeth and children's shoes.

And what do I teach my children?
To be angry, not to be angry,
to hate the haters, to love them,
to love everyone, to hate everyone,
to remember, to be a little afraid,
to learn how to forget,
to be a Jew out of pure revenge,
to teach Hitler a lesson?
Who should I forgive and who
is now to be forgiven?
Naked bodies in piles that
cannot be untangled or unremembered . . .
The sparks in our souls are tired of leaping,
tired of bearing all these names
in Hebrew, Yiddish, Polish, and pure will.

When you leave the Fun House
you will get a blue tattoo,
souvenir of all lost memory,
to burn a day or two on your arm
and whatever you feel will be adequate,
for you bought your ticket for mercy
and had it stamped in sympathy,
though I wouldn't invest too many tears.
The Holocaust doesn't have a future.
Another fifty years and it's history.

Death is a great equalizer
and it is up to us to live against that fact
for the men in stripes have given me
their Holocaust to keep
and I don't know yet what to do with it.
The bodies with arms stamped with numbers
will be numbers again
unless an angel chazzan with a giant mouth of prayer
recites all their names, slowly one by one.
Or we will mourn with popcorn in a theater.

And someone is saying, "How many tickets were sold?"
And someone is asking, "Were there really six million?"
And someone is saying, "Are there really enough prayers?"

Marc Kaminsky

Medium

How do you do, delicate Roumanians!
You, with your large ovens,
where your girls sang, baking bread!

My grandmother sings your melodies,
but without your words:
they were in Hebrew, male and sacred,

which she never knew, and I,
sitting alone with her, on the other side
of two world wars, and two years

after the death of my grandfather,
am introduced to her grandfather:
Zalman of Kostuchohn, a lumber merchant,

and her father, Baruch, who sold wine
and farm tools, an old man
who couldn't keep up with the others,

forced to run towards the barbed wire —
fell,
and was shot.

Remembering her father's beautiful voice,
the silk *kapoteh* he wore, on Friday evenings,
and the Besarabian *tish mit mentshn*,

she sings as if her husky voice,
which can barely carry the *nign*,
is joyously nine years old and joining

in with her father's, and I, too,
will have sat at the Sabbath table
where my grandmother felt herself

happily loved, still happily loving,
in an old song,
though I will carry away

neither the words
nor the melody.
On the day that I met you,

Baruch of Kostuchohn,
how close you were
to never having existed.

Peretz Kaminsky

Bramble

I add my silence
to the spent years of my life.
I add my silence
to all the silences I have known.
I add my silence
to the ending of prayers I cannot say.
I add my silence
to the silence that speaks from unnamed graves.
I add my silence
to the unheard voices in gas chambers.
I add my silence
to the silence that weeps from crematoriums.

Memory makes a noise in my head
and words gather strength in my lungs
and sounds flood into my throat
and a wailing flows from my mouth
and my silence will not be silent
and I argue with God who is silent within me.

I light a bramble bush.
No voice speaks from its silence.
The fires of Auschwitz rise from the thorns.

Identifications

From shadows such as these I shape my songs:
"My hand wrote the message on Belshazzar's wall";
"The pen I use for poetry wrote psalms";
"My signet reads, 'Lord, from the depths I call'";
"My belt is braided from blind Samson's hair";
"I crawl up Jacob's ladder rung by rung";
"My sandals, made from scraps of parchment scrolls,
        use broken strings from David's harp for thongs."

I bless the Sabbath's end in candlelight
        and dip my pen into the kiddush cup.
The festive candles flicker as I write.
My written words are prayer, and wine, and bread.
They sound like looming thunder in my head,
        whispering the names of our sixmillion dead.

Rosa Felsenburg Kaplan

Kol Nidre

For an adolescent during the Holocaust

All the vows
And all the promises not kept
Because life was too short
Or too difficult,
Or we were too young,
Not wise enough, or too weak —
Let them be cancelled!

I remember being glad
To leave behind my friend and Europe.
When she told me how life was started,
She had sworn me to secrecy.
Now she would not have to know
That I had told our secret.

The choking void of unsaid farewells
Because we did not know
We were together for the last time —
Let it be closed!

Alice and Malka, twin cousins with whom I played,
And who I wished I looked like,
And whose parents, I thought,
Must love them more than mine loved me —
"One time," said their mother. "They mostly took
young girls . . ."

For the sins committed on them
Forgive us: *S'lach lanu, m'chal lanu, kaper lanu!*

The unsaid thanks
To those who gave to us,
Life, sometimes,
But to whom we could not give —
Let thanks be understood!

Twice I took another's name
To cross a border.
What happened to my namesakes?

And to Onkel Michel,
And Tante Esti
And Kati Neni —
Who took me in, housed me and fed me,
And whom I loathed and made fun of
Because they were not my parents,
Nor like them . . . ?

The tears unshed
Because we were too busy living
To mourn —
Let them now flow!

Trying to finish high school
And enter college,
Becoming American —
I shut my eyes to my parents' fears,
My heart to their losses as well as to my own . . .

To those of us who live,
To our families and friends,
And all of those whom we're supposed to love —
Father of mercy,
Give them life
And us, time enough
To make peace,
Perhaps even to love them.

Dori Katz

Line-Up

After Viewing Andrzei Munk's Film The Passenger

All this is history, the still disputed fate
of those who lived, then were deported, died
like you. Were you the third man
from the left, staring out of an old newsreel,
his long thin hands against the fence?
No, I said, but the face held me as though
it had a message I should understand.

Remember,
behind you stood the crematory buildings,
smoke rising from their stacks
like unrelenting ghosts forming and dispersing
the same question until I wanted to dig my hands
into the ground, hoping to unearth you still
breathing from a common grave, O frozen Auschwitz.

So many times since then I have gone back
into that film, trying to place you somewhere else,
perhaps with drivers of the Red Cross vans,
perhaps behind the calm and ancient trees
that stand evoked, fictitious, out of reach.
Each time, the same men carrying their clothes
line up before a smoking building. Absorbed,
an inmate string quartet plays Bach so lovingly
you would not notice all the guards,
the straining dogs baring their teeth,
were it not for that man staring out,
his hands grotesque against the fence,
his mouth an open grave waiting to be filled.

Father, the distance is so great between us;
light years from now, you'll still be standing
by that fence, I on the other side. Forgive me
if to release myself, I say it wasn't you
speaking to me with broken hands.

My Face Before

I think my father has the face
I had before I was born. Is it in Prague
that he carries it staring at the Vltava River?
I was in Prague once, staring at the same river
then looking for him in the ghetto's
narrow streets fifty years after he died.
Perhaps he sees my face among the aunts
and uncles sitting around the Seder table,
the half cousins and the stepmother passing
the bitter herbs, or in the grandparents,
a squat couple caught by the camera,
having no idea what life has in store
for them. Perhaps in Auschwitz he knows
that the high forehead, the narrow chin
the thin lips and deep-set eyes
will be his bequest to me,
so that someone who knew him then
seeing me, will say, surprised,
That's the face he had before he died.

The Return

The light I turn on to remember you these days
is small and distant in the dark.
I go back very deeply for you, and very carefully.
One false move and I fall off your shoulder
where I placed myself at three to be carried across
rain puddles; one inadvertent slip and you are gone
while I wait for you by the kitchen window,
angry because you promised to be right back,
and I never saw you again.
How you must have felt when they arrested you,
no time to say goodbye, send messages.
They took you to that public square in Malines,
made you line up with other Jews, then climb
into a box car: the doors are shut. Back home,

[stanza continues]

your wife, cursing your fate, burns your pictures,
your documents, packs my clothes in a basket,
then sends me to someone else's house. I squat
in a corner of a strange kitchen, crying for you.

Years pass. Your wife survives selling your things.
Converted, your daughter goes from house to home,
a different child now, quiet, tamed,
but at night she walks in her sleep
opening door after door to find you;
you are not there for you're living in Auschwitz now.
Your head is shaved, your hands swollen;
soon they will amputate a leg. You are 177679,
not Moise Chaim anymore, not anyone.

I waited for you.
I used to think of accidents, cured amnesia,
a hospital file that would turn up your name,
or that you had married again, forgotten us.
I pictured running into you on a deserted street;
you'd be walking against the wind,
dragging your bad leg behind you. As soon as
you'd recognize me the dark years would disappear like rain
drying up, or clouds pushed away by strong gusts. Other times,
I saw you as a one-legged man hopping around the house
outside, pressing his face against the window,
against my new life now all patched up.

And so I carried you for years, like salt upon the tongue,
a bitter taste always dissolving, always there;
I was afraid that you were lost, afraid you'd return,
old, crippled, gray, and we'd be singled out again.
Today it doesn't matter what I want; you have been dead
so long there's nothing left that could come back;
you are not flesh, not bone, not even dust of dust;
you are a light behind that kitchen window now,
behind that glass — a light that comes and disappears.

Eliot Katz

from **Liberation Recalled**

2

— Mom, tell me about your family.
— We were in our family ten people.
In 1944 Hitler came into
Hungary and we lived in a city
called Oradea Mare-Nagyvárad.
We were a family of ten, eight children
and my parents, six girls and two boys. I
was the oldest and the youngest was
about three years, two or three years. And when
Hitler came in, what he did, in a very
short time, he created a ghetto. All
the Jews had to go in one place to live.
What they did, the Germans, they took out all
the Jewish people from one district and
then they took out gentile people from
another district. The gentile people
had to get out of that district and they
put in the Jews there. And they put in one
room two families. Our neighbor was a
family of ten and we were ten, so
twenty people were put in one room. And
there was no furniture. The room was all
empty. It was a bit of a big room
but we almost slept on top of each other.
And the kids had to sleep there. My parents
had to sleep there. And we lived in that ghetto
in that house about three or four months.
— This was in Hungary?
— That was in Hungary, yes, in '44.
— Tell me if any questions I ask, you
don't feel like answering.
— Right, go ahead.

7

. . . .

To defy Himmler and bring history's secrets
    into animated light:
        does this build empowerment

[stanza continues]

alongside the overwhelming anguish
    from which one never
        fully recovers?
Should we remember Julius Streicher
    whose posters proclaimed
        without modern hesitation
"The Jews are our misfortune"?
    Wilhelm Marr, 1879 founder
        of pre-Nazi League of Anti-Semites?
Lanz von Liebenfels, 1901 author
    of *Theozoology* — founder
        of Aryan cult worship?
Does it help prevent future repeat to recollect cascadingly
    those who laid the asphalt path
        to annihilation's ovens?
Or does it simply provide the killers another
    fresh-poured concrete platform
        from which to throw their knives?

———

In his newspaper, *Attack*, 1928, Goebbels wrote: "We go into the Reichstag in order to acquire the weapons of democracy from its arsenal. We come as enemies! Like the wolf tearing into the flock of sheep, that is how we come."

———

Was it possible to realize at the time
    what a tragic forewarning
        this would become?

. . . .

10

— Could you tell who were the SS and who
were Hungarians?
— Sure, the SS men were in uniforms.
They had these, uh, swastikas, on their clothes,
and the Hungarians were not the soldiers
or police — just regular people.
— But the Hungarian police were not
resisting? They were helping?
— They were cooperating, cooperating.
They were helping the Germans to get us
faster out.
— So then your whole family was put on
one train car?
— Yes, we were all together in one wagon,
in one train. But not just one family:

[stanza continues]

They pushed us all in there. But one day they
said: Okay, now we're gonna take you all.
And it was before Passover. My poor
mother got together the Passover
dishes for taking into the ghetto
because Passover's coming. That was like
April. Then, they didn't let us have dishes.
They let us have whatever clothes we had —
to put everything on — so we took nightgowns,
dresses. They didn't let us have any packages,
just like one suitcase, and we took that suitcase
with us and we went. And that train stopped
in Auschwitz. Everything was lighted up.
But we didn't see any people around,
just wires. The whole thing was wired around
and we saw these chimneys — that was the
crematorium. And the light was on.
We didn't know what the hell was going on
and when we came off the trains then the SS
men were there. They put the men and the boys
on one side and the women and children,
the girls, on another side. And my mother
had three little girls, the babies, so I
went there to help her pick up the little
girl — helping with my sister. The SS men
took away my sister, dropped her to
my mother. And they took my two other
sisters and myself in one spot, because
we were older so we can go to work.
And the other kids went on the one side
and they went all right away in the
crematorium.

12

— And you saw them walking away?
— Yeah, just walking a little bit, like to
here from across the street.
— That was the last time you saw . . . ?
— That's the last I saw my parents, yes, my
mother and father.
— I remember once you told me that there
was an older woman when you were coming
into Auschwitz who saw the smoke in the
chimneys and said that's the crematorium
and no one believed her.
— Well, they took us in that night. They gave us
a bath, gave us showers, and my sister

[stanza continues]

Ann they took away separate to give
her a shower. And then Marcy and I
stayed for the next group to go under the
shower. Then I see my sister in
another group, all shaved up and naked.
So I said to Marcy, look they put us
with the crazy people. Because, in Europe,
the crazy people they shaved. They had no
hair. And then I went a little closer
and that was Ann, my sister. Then they put
us there. They shaved us. They took all the
clothes away, shoes, everything. And coats.
In April it was still cold. And they only
gave us a striped dress; that's all we had.
No underwear, no nothing. And then we
were sitting in that group all together.
A thousand girls shaved and it was cold and then
the SS men — were ladies in SS, too,
and men — then the ladies came and did something,
like with a sponge, and sponged us here and there
and all over where hair was, we shouldn't get lice.
But it was very painful, it was like . . .
I don't know . . . burned. It burned like. And then we
waited. Then they gave us wooden shoes, no
stockings, no nothing, and put us up in
a camp. No, not a camp, in a barn, where
the cows lived. They took out the cows and we
went into a barn. And then a thousand
people lived in one barn. And then they had
like this room each one, and six of us got
one blanket. So we had to sleep on top
of each other with one blanket. We were
freezing and crying, but we couldn't do
nothing.
— And this was your first night?
— First night.

14

— And by the first night, it was just you and
your two sisters?
— Yes, my mother and father were gone.
Then the next morning when we got up . . .
— This was still April?
— It was April, before Passover. Maybe
it was already Passover. But then
when we woke up, then each barrack — about
a thousand people was a barrack — each

[stanza continues]

had two ladies over us, Polish ladies.
Because they were there already so many
years. Two ladies had to take care of us
and then when we got up in the morning
we asked: "Where are my parents? Where can we
meet them?" And then the chimney was the flame
going out and they said, "They're in Himinlaga."
— What do you mean Himinlaga? — That means
they're in Heaven. And there they're burning.
That's what they, she, told us. They were very
angry at us.
— I think you first told me that people didn't
believe her when she said that.
— No, nobody believed it. We thought she
was so mean. Because she was mean to us.
She was very angry at us. How could
intelligent people figuring without
a fight to come here? Why didn't you struggle . . .
put up a fight and don't come here? We just,
we just went literally like lambs. Because
we were promised to go to work. And we
never went to work. As we went in the
wagon — my father was in World War I —
he recognized the mountains through the little
window the train has, that these mountains are
Polish mountains. We aren't going to work
this way, we're going to Poland.
— So you thought you were going to Germany?
— We thought we were going to Germany
to work, and meantime we went to Poland.
Auschwitz was Poland.
— Had you heard of Auschwitz before?
— Never. No, no, nobody heard of Auschwitz.
We couldn't *believe* it. Who would believe *that*?

30

— And where did you sleep on the way? You just
slept along the road?
— On the snow, along the road, wherever
we felt we laid down on the snow since we
couldn't walk. But all these kids who couldn't walk
anymore had to stay in the back. And Anna,
since she was still strong, had to dig the graves
to bury them. Because whoever couldn't
walk they just shot 'em, the SS men.
Because they couldn't walk no more, what
can you do with them? There was no wagon

[stanza continues]

to carry them, nothing. So he shot them
and buried them there. And quite a few,
my sister buried them. Her own girlfriend
they had to kill there and bury there.
— So then you went to Bergen-Belsen?
— Then we got to Bergen-Belsen. We slept
twelve in two rooms of beds. We slept there, with
very little food. And then they gave us
some kind of poison, not poison, some kind
of medicine that we should never get
our periods. So, nobody had
periods. They put us together with
Russian people, too, not Jewish. And they
went to work every day. They couldn't treat
them like us. They were fighting. They were shooting,
fighting. I don't know how they got guns, but
they were shooting, fighting.
— The Russians in the camp with you had guns?
— In the camp. Had hidden guns. Somehow, somewhere.
I don't know how they got them. Maybe they
slept with the SS men, who the hell knows?
And they were strong. We were so weak. They were
sleeping in the daytime and going to
work at night.
— Were they helping you at all?
— No, no. They felt sorry. They had to fight
for their own lives. But they had more food and
blankets. So in the daytime while they were
sleeping, I used to go and steal their food,
their bread, and blankets.
— And were you again on lines every day?
— Yes. Then, when I stole the blankets, I stole
some knives from them. They had knives, too, I don't
know how they had knives. Then the SS men
came and they said whoever — because the war
came so close — whoever has knives, they can
come in the kitchen and peel potatoes.
So I had a knife, I went to peel the
potatoes. But then they got very mad
and they came in to our camp again saying:
Who knows how to sew? So Anna volunteered
with other kids. And they took them to sew
their dresses, civilian dresses. The wives
or the SS ladies threw away the
SS clothes — the war came so close — and put
on civilian dresses. Then, when she finished
the dresses, he came and banged on the kitchen
and said: Who sewed my wife's dresses? And my
sister again volunteered. She thought she's

[stanza continues]

gonna get something for it. He started
beating her up. And beating her up so bad,
hitting with a screwdriver in the head.
And made holes in her head. And we couldn't cry,
because if we cry he sees a sister.
We didn't cry. He put her in a barrel
and hit her with an ice . . . with a screwdriver —
and bleeding. Then he went away. He hit
so many like that, and then they ran away
because the war was over. But we didn't know.
— So, the war was over at this time?
— Yes, but because we didn't know, he beat
all these kids up who'd sewed the dresses and
ran away. And then the war was over.
All of a sudden we had no SS
men with us. Then we saw other people
coming in. The English people came.

38

. . . .

— Did the pain of the memories come up
often through the years? And how did you
deal with it?
— Well, I couldn't talk about it for
about forty years. Till about five years
ago, I couldn't even talk about it.
You know that. Just a little bit I said.
When they asked me to go to speak in schools
here and there, I couldn't even talk about
it. The first time I spoke was about five
years ago in the local high school. Then
when I spoke about it, I said to the kids:
I probably was your age. I wasn't
any older than you and I went so
much through life and therefore please get your
education. Because that's very
important, and then you'll know that human
beings have to love each other, not hate.
— So, for forty years you tried not to think
about it too much?
— That's right. I thought about it. We had dreams,
many times we woke up.
— You woke up sometimes in the middle of
the night?
— Yeah, sure, lots of times, lots of times.
— Now, does it help you feel better to talk
about it?

[stanza continues]

— That's right. I feel better when I talk
about it. And I hope that people, the
way I talk, should never come to this
situation. We should never go through,
any nationality, any living
soul, should go through like that. Because this is
no good for anybody. We have to
have peace or else the whole world is . . .
— When you got out, did your friends and you talk
much about politics? Did you talk about
some of the signs to recognize so that
we would see when it's rising again: What
is fascism? Or why the Russians, who
were allies during the war, became enemies
of the United States with the Cold War soon
after the war was over?
— The Russian politics was never good,
because our father was captured during
World War I in Russia. All the Jewish
people were in a little shtetl, a
little town, like here, a little village.
He had a very good voice since he was
a cantor. He used to go up on the trees
singing for all the neighbors for this whole
village, all kinds of songs, Russian too, because
he was there four years in prison.
— Your father, your father was in prison?
— A prisoner of war, four years in Russia.
Then the people in Russia were very
good but the politicians were not.
They tried to kill Jews. Because of his
beautiful voice they let him live. When they
heard my father's voice singing, they let him live.
And he had to sing for the Russian people
with the dead people around him.

39

. . . .

Sophie Scholl, student cofounder of White Rose resistance,
    awaiting the Nazi firing squad, exclaimed with diamond defiance:
        "what we have written and said is in the minds of you all,
            but you lack the courage to say it aloud."
A common Holocaust survivor's refractive refrain:
    To understand you have to go through it —
        you cannot ever understand
            yet you must understand.

[stanza continues]

The multiple contradictions and cataclysmic voices
    are unresolvable. Memory's radical eyes never sleep.
        A century after slavery declared dead
            slaves still lie awake
with imperishable nightmares below deck.
    American Indians still see brothers & sisters falling
        along the trail of slaughtered tears.
            Oven smoke still stings the open eye.

. . . .

Alan Kaufman

My Mother Doesn't Know Who Allen Ginsberg Is

"Ginsberg?" she asks by phone, "Is that your friend from
    Israel?"
"He's a famous poet" I explain. "I've been invited with him
    and Kathy Acker to a Jewish festival in Berlin."
"Acker," says my mother, her voice cross, "This is a Jewish
    name?"

My Mother doesn't know
who Allen Ginsberg is.
She doesn't know who Anne
Waldman is, or Charles Bukowski.
My mother doesn't know that I make
a kind of living on stages
screaming my heart out
to strangers at five hundred dollars a pop,
and that there's some debate about whether
or not what I and others like me do should be considered
poetry. My mother was arrested by the Gestapo in 1942.
She was twelve then. She's sixty now. She lives in Florida,
where every so often a German tourist gets shot.
To my mother, that is poetry.

My mother doesn't like the idea of a Berlin
Jewish festival. She cannot understand what
Jews feel festive about over there.
"And what is this 'celebration' for?" she asks coldly.
And changes the subject before I can answer.
"So, what will you do there?" she asks, "Give lectures?"
"We'll read our works," I say, "talk in panel discussions."
"Talk?" she says. "In English, I hope!"

[stanza continues]

My mother doesn't like the sound of German.
"It's a funny thing," she says. "I see the tourists
on the beach, in their bathing suits . . . what could be more
harmless? But when I hear them speak, I
imagine them in uniforms, and become afraid."
My mother sees Germans in bathing suits
transformed into Germans in uniform,
and my mother fears that having once
narrowly missed killing her they might yet succeed
in killing me. As a child in war, she saw such things
as babies tossed through the air and shot.
"Like crying angels, they looked," she says.

My mother doesn't know who Allen Ginsberg is.
She watches German tourists sun themselves
on the shore. Sometimes they don uniforms
of German language, march to her condo,
call up through the intercom and order
her downstairs with one suitcase con-
taining six kilos of clothing, and food
for a journey of three days.

My mother doesn't know who
Allen Ginsberg is
and I wonder if she knows who
Alan Kaufman is.
She can't understand
why any Jew would ever
want to go to Germany.

My mother doesn't know who Allen
Ginsberg is. She looks older
than her years
but younger than the death she
still manages to escape
in retirement on the beaches
of Florida where there are not too many
round-ups for the camps, and one is safe,
generally speaking, if one stays indoors,
pretends not to be a Jew, even
to other Jews.

My mother doesn't know
who Allen Ginsberg is.
She has tended to regard most
'high' culture
as a kind of Disneyworld
for intelligent people —
to her, the three bolt locks

[stanza continues]

on her door are more important
than the collected works of Shakespeare.
She knows that she's supposed
to appreciate books and pretends
to, but my mother doesn't know who
Norman Mailer is, she doesn't know who
Maya Angelou is, she doesn't know who
wrote *On the Road* or *Leaves of Grass* or *The*
Awful Rowing Towards God.
She has seen six million of the best minds
of her generation gassed and burned.

She is making baked fish
in the oven tonight, regardless of what
my father says about the smell
and, tossing a nice salad,
she goes into the livingroom, sets down
the meal on the T.V. tray, and as she eats,
stares through the big plate glass
window filled with night, measuring the
distance between herself and the sprawling,
creeping lights out there, humming the Kaddish
in her throat, the prayer for the dead,
for so many, many illusions dressed as life.

Who Are We?

Into the past
I go like a stranger
to discover why at night
I lay alone as a child
waiting for the front door
to slam — my father gone
to night-shift work —
and my mother, Marie, to enter,
unable to sleep, and tell me
tales of childhood
war, pursued by those
who, as she spoke,
seemed to enter the room,
Gestapo men in leather coats
who ordered me to pack
and descend to a waiting truck,
for I am still going to Auschwitz
though a grown man in 1999
I am still boarding the freight,
crushed against numbed, frightened

[stanza continues]

Jews and Gypsies and Russian
soldiers and homosexuals
crossing frontiers to be gassed

I am her, in my heart,
though I am six-feet-two
and two hundred and ten pounds
and have played college football
and served as a soldier
and have scars from fights
with knives and jagged
bottles smashed on bars

I am still her, little girl,
hiding in chicken coops
and forests, asleep on dynamite
among partisans
I am still her, brushing teeth
with ashes
from the ruins of nations
gutted in war

I am still her brown eyes
and black hair of persecution
foraging scraps of thistle soup,
a star-shaped patch
sewn to my shirt

I am still my mother
every day in the streets
of New York or San Francisco:
the chimney skies glow and swirl
with soot like night above
a crematorium or the Bronx
incinerator chute where I
threw out trash in a brick
darkness shooting sparks

I am still her in the streets
of Berkeley, walking among
sparechangers, dyed-hair punkers,
gays in stud leather, Blacks,
Mexicans and Asians

I am still her rounded up
among poets and thieves
and politically incorrect
social deviants
on sun-drenched sidewalks
in the Mission and the Haight,

[stanza continues]

Greenwich Village, the Lower
East Side, or anywhere the weird
congregate in tolerance

And every day in this age
of intolerance,
in a mental ghetto
affirmed by the homeless,
I pass the dying
with the loud ring of my boots,
ashamed to think that perhaps
my heels are the last thing
they heard
Every day I am a
survivor of AIDS and poverty

Every day I sit in cafés
watching tattoos turn to numbers
and I grow angry
I want America back
I want America to be
the home I never had

And you, who are you
if you hear my voice?
Who are you, stranger,
if you read these words?

Who are we
who stand threatened
in these times of darkness?
Who are we, condemned to die,
who do not know ourselves
at all?

Melanie Kaye/Kantrowitz

from **Kaddish**

and when I told the woman — a survivor, a fighter in the Warsaw Ghetto Uprising — about the Holocaust conference in Maine, and how many of the people there had known nothing, *she said,* They still know nothing.

Yisgadal v'yiskadash sh'me rabbo,
b'olmo deevro chiruseh v'yamlick
malchuseh

if I said kaddish for each one

if I were to mourn properly
I would not be done

If I were to mourn
each artist seamstress schnorrer midwife baker
each fiddler talker tailor shopkeeper
each yente   each Communist   each Zionist
each doctor pedlar beggar Bundist rabbi
each prostitute   each file clerk   each lesbian
each fighter   the old woman in the photograph from
Hungary   holding the hand of the child whose
socks droop   each Jew

b'chayechon uvyo-mechon, uv'chayey
d'chol beys yisroel

I would not be done   yet
it was more than death   was more   the people's
heart   a language I have
to study   to practice speaking with
old people   songs   to collect   transcribing
from records or from the few
who know   a culture   which might have died
in this country   which eats cultures   a death
we call normal   a culture   *astonishing*
in its variety   a taste   a smell   a twist of song
that was   *Vilna*
Odessa
Cracow
Covner-Gberna
Warsaw
these were once Jewish sounds

Tsipi Keller

The Shower

Bergen-Belsen, April 1945

With such care she moves her hand
Over her skin, her bare breasts,
White and heavy in the cold sun.
Her nipples, a mother's nipples,
Like small towers defy the wire.

[stanza continues]

With such care she spreads lather
Between her breasts, moves her hand
As though her body isn't hers.

Habitual motions, yes,
Yet forgotten, now slowly retaking shape
With water splashing, drops sliding
Forever on her skin.

No matter that
She is in the open for all to see;
These men are soldiers who fought for her,
In a way, only for her. These men,
She knows, would understand
The simple fact of water,
The warmth in a hand.

Miriam Kessler

Yahrzeit

Your memory is leashed into my life,
lashed about me.
It strangles
like a morning-glory vine.
Six million muffled cries
smothered in the hiss of Zyklon B.

Today I will be joyful
for no good reason,
only because you were denied joy.
I live what you had a right to.
My presumption is your gift,
my debt inexhaustible,
though you were not.
My candle is not *Yahrzeit* enough.
I burn it anyway.

When day blinks down through grey shutters
and cardinals begin their red cantata;
when leaves curl away from rain,
you will not know it.
My voice,
my sobbing
will not shake you
from your Six Million sleeps.

Steve Klepetar

Burial

I wake this morning heavy as earth . . .
so many are buried inside me.
My grandmothers — their bones
and teeth and hair, acrid as Auschwitz
ash — are buried inside me.
I am a mass grave.
All night, I smell their burning flesh.
Nothing will grow in this place.
The hole is vast: a black chasm, a wound, a void.
There is nowhere to put the rage.
It spills over the sides of this canyon,
covers all the broken dead.
It is a shadow strapped to the back of my heel,
loaded on my back like a knapsack full of lead.
Sometimes my grandmothers try to rise
in the night, old lady phantoms,
frail and small.
I cannot look into their eyes.
They hold out bony hands
and I cringe.
Their silence is terrible.
It thunders in my ears, a river tumbling,
tearing down through mist
and rock, buried deep in a turbulent sea.
I want to sing for them,
I want to fill my lungs with air
and sing their names.

The Spells of Earth

I beat the green drum, tightly stretched skin of body's words.
I call on motion. Let it stream electric, soul of wind.
I cast the spells of earth.
Grandfather, I cast the spells of earth.
In the bones of your death, I cast the spells of earth.
I embrace your thin hands, against my cheek.
I embrace your sunken flesh, your rags, the ruin of your white hair.
Grandfather, dead at Auschwitz, I cast the spells of earth.
My face bleeds tears.
I climb into your torn pocket, crawl back deep into your broken life.
I breathe your smoke into my lungs. At Birkenau I cast the spells of earth.

[stanza continues]

At Auschwitz and Terezín I cast the spell. I beat the green drum,
the body's words, your daughter's strong life thread tenacious in the wind.
I cast the spells of earth.
Grandmothers, I cast the spells of earth.
I call you from the furnace, I call your blood from ash heaps and your bones from mass graves.
I cast the spell of earth.
I call up your faces from photographs, I call your bodies from story's breath,
I conjure your names: Herta and Theresa.
I call up your touch from past's black night.
Tears stream in the dust. I kneel and cast the spells of earth.

Irena Klepfisz

from **Bashert***

These words are dedicated to those who died

These words are dedicated to those who died
because they had no love and felt alone in the world
because they were afraid to be alone and tried to stick it out
because they could not ask
because they were shunned
because they were sick and their bodies could not resist the disease
because they played it safe
because they had no connections
because they had no faith
because they felt they did not belong and wanted to die

These words are dedicated to those who died
because they were loners and liked it
because they acquired friends and drew others to them
because they took risks
because they were stubborn and refused to give up
because they asked for too much

These words are dedicated to those who died
because a card was lost and a number was skipped
because a bed was denied
because a place was filled and no other place was left

These words are dedicated to those who died
because someone did not follow through
because someone was overworked and forgot
because someone left everything to God

[stanza continues]

because someone was late
because someone did not arrive at all
because someone told them to wait and they just couldn't any longer

These words are dedicated to those who died
because death is a punishment
because death is a reward
because death is the final rest
because death is eternal rage

These words are dedicated to those who died

Bashert

**Ba-shert (Yid.): inevitable, (pre)destined.*

These words are dedicated to those who survived

These words are dedicated to those who survived
because their second grade teacher gave them books
because they did not draw attention to themselves and got lost in the shuffle
because they knew someone who knew someone else who could help them and bumped into them on a corner on a Thursday afternoon
because they played it safe
because they were lucky

These words are dedicated to those who survived
because they knew how to cut corners
because they drew attention to themselves and always got picked
because they took risks
because they had no principles and were hard

These words are dedicated to those who survived
because they refused to give up and defied statistics
because they had faith and trusted in God
because they expected the worst and were always prepared
because they were angry
because they could ask
because they mooched off others and saved their strength
because they endured humiliation
because they turned the other cheek
because they looked the other way

These words are dedicated to those who survived
because life is a wilderness and they were savage
because life is an awakening and they were alert
because life is a flowering and they blossomed
because life is a struggle and they struggled
because life is a gift and they were free to accept it

These words are dedicated to those who survived

Bashert

1. Poland, 1944: My mother is walking down a road.

My mother is walking down a road. Somewhere in Poland. Walking towards an unnamed town for some kind of permit. She is carrying her Aryan identity papers. She has left me with an old peasant who is willing to say she is my grandmother.

She is walking down a road. Her terror in leaving me behind, in risking the separation, is swallowed now, like all other feelings. But as she walks, she pictures me waving from the dusty yard, imagines herself suddenly picked up, the identity papers challenged. And even if she were to survive that, would she ever find me later? She tastes the terror in her mouth again. She swallows.

I am over three years old, corn silk blond and blue eyed like any Polish child. There is terrible suffering among the peasants. Starvation. And like so many others, I am ill. Perhaps dying. I have bad lungs. Fever. An ugly ear infection that oozes pus. None of these symptoms are disappearing.

The night before, my mother feeds me watery soup and then sits and listens while I say my prayers to the Holy Mother, Mother of God. I ask her, just as the nuns taught me, to help us all: me, my mother, the old woman. And then catching myself, learning to use memory, I ask the Mother of God to help my father. The Polish words slip easily from my lips. My mother is satisfied. The peasant has perhaps heard and is reassured. My mother has found her to be kind, but knows that she is suspicious of strangers.

My mother is sick. Goiter. Malnutrition. Vitamin deficiencies. She has skin sores which she cannot cure. For months now she has been living in complete isolation, with no point of reference outside of herself. She has been her own sole advisor, companion, comforter. Almost everyone of her world is dead: three sisters, nephews, and nieces, her mother, her husband, her in-laws. All gone. Even the remnants of the resistance, those few left after the uprising, have dispersed into the Polish countryside. She is more alone than she could have ever imagined. Only she knows her real name and she is perhaps dying. She is thirty years old.

I am over three years old. I have no consciousness of our danger, our separateness from the others. I have no awareness that we are playing a part. I only know that I have a special name, that I have been named for the Goddess of Peace. And each night, I sleep secure in that knowledge. And when I wet my bed, my mother places me on her belly and lies on the stain. She fears the old woman and hopes her body's warmth will dry the sheet before dawn.

My mother is walking down a road. Another woman joins her. My mother sees through the deception, but she has promised herself that never, under any circumstances, will she take that risk. So she swallows her hunger for contact and trust and instead talks about the sick child left behind and lies about the husband in the labor camp.

Someone is walking towards them. A large, strange woman with wild red hair. They try not to look at her too closely, to seem overly curious. But as they pass her, my mother feels something move inside her. The movement grows and grows till it is an explosion of yearning that she cannot contain. She stops, orders her companion to continue without her. And then she turns.

The woman with the red hair has also stopped and turned. She is grotesque, bloated with hunger, almost savage in her rags. She and my mother move towards each other. Cautiously, deliberately, they probe past the hunger, the swollen flesh, the infected skin, the rags. Slowly, they begin to pierce five years of encrusted history. And slowly, there is perception and recognition.

In this wilderness of occupied Poland, in this vast emptiness where no one can be trusted, my mother has suddenly, bizarrely, met one of my father's teachers. A family friend. Another Jew.

They do not cry, but weep as they chronicle the dead and count the living. Then they rush to me. To the woman I am a familiar sight. She calculates that I will not live out the week, but comments only on my striking resemblance to my father. She says she has contacts. She leaves. One night a package of food is delivered anonymously. We eat. We begin to bridge the gap towards life. We survive.

4. Cherry Plain, 1981: I have become a keeper of accounts.

There are moments when I suddenly become breathless, as if I had just tricked someone, but was afraid the ruse would be exposed and I'd be hunted again. At those moments, the myths that propel our history, that turn fiction into fact, emerge in full force in me, as I stare into the eyes of strangers or someone suddenly grown alien. And when I see their eyes become pinpoints of judgments, become cold and indifferent, or simply distanced with curiosity, at those moments I hear again the words of the Polish woman:

Very accurate. Just like a Jew. You are perhaps a little Jewess?

At moments such as these I teeter, shed the present, and like rage, like pride, like acceptance, like the refusal to deny, I call upon the ancient myths and say:

Yes. It's true. All true. I am scrupulously accurate. I keep track of all distinctions. Between past and present. Pain and pleasure. Living and surviving. Resistance and capitulation. Will and circumstances. Between life and death. Yes. I am scrupulously accurate. I have become a keeper of accounts.

Like the patriarchs, the shabby scholars who only lived for what was written and studied it all their lives

Like the inhuman usurers and dusty pawnbrokers who were quarantined within precisely prescribed limits of every European town and who were as accurate as the magistrates that drew the boundaries of their lives and declared them diseased

Like those men of stone who insisted that the *goyim* fulfil the contracts they had signed and who responded to the tearful pleas of illness, weakness, sudden calamity and poverty, with the words: "What are these to me? You have made me a keeper of accounts. Give me my pound of flesh. It says on this piece of paper, you owe me a pound of flesh!"

Like those old, heartless, dried up merchants whose entire lives were spent in the grubby *shtetl* streets that are now but memory, whose only body softness was in their fingertips worn smooth by silver coins, whose vision that all that mattered was on pieces of paper was proven absolutely accurate, when their zloty, francs, and marks could not buy off the written words *Żyd, Juif, Jude*

Like these, my despised ancestors
I have become a keeper of accounts.

And like all the matriarchs, the wives and daughters, the sisters and aunts, the nieces, the keepers of button shops, milliners, seamstresses, peddlers of foul fish, of matches, of rotten apples, laundresses, midwives, floor washers and street cleaners, who rushed exhausted all week so that *shabes* could be observed with fresh *challah* on the table, who argued in the common tongue

and begged for the daughter run off to the revolution
and the daughter run off with a *shegetz*
who refused to sit *shiva* and to say *kaddish* for a living child
who always begged for life
who understood the accounts but saw them differently
who knew the power of human laws, knew they always counted
no matter what the revolution or the party or the state
who knew the power of the words *Żyd, Juif, Jude*

who cried whole lifetimes for their runaway children
for the husbands immobilized by the written word
for the brother grown callous from usury
for the uncle grown indifferent from crime, from bargaining,
from chiseling, from jewing them down

Like these, my despised ancestors
I have become a keeper of accounts.

I do not shun this legacy. I claim it as mine   whenever I see the photographs of nameless people. Standing staring off the edge of the picture. People dressed in coats lined with fur. Or ragged at elbows and collar. Hats cocked on one side glancing anxiously toward the lens. A peasant cap centered and ordinary. Hair styled in the latest fashion. Or standing ashamed a coarse wig awkwardly fitted. The shabby clothes. Buttons missing. The elegant stance. Diamond rings. Gold teeth. The hair being shaved. The face of humiliation. The hand holding the child's hand. A tree. A track. A vague building in a photograph. A facility. And then the fields of hair   the endless fields of hair   the earth growing fertile with their bodies   with their souls.

Old   rarely seen types. Gone   they say   forever. And yet I know they can be revived again   that I can trigger them again. That they awaken in me   for I have felt it happen   in the sight of strangers   or someone suddenly grown alien. Whenever I have seen the judgment   the coldness and indifference   the distanced curiosity.   At those moments   I teeter   shed my present self   and all time merges   and like rage like pride   like acceptance   like the refusal to deny   I answer

Yes. It is true.   I am a keeper of accounts.

Bashert

Solitary Acts

For my aunt,
Gina Klepfisz (1908?– 42)

"To garden is a solitary act."
— Michelle Cliff

1.

And to die
as you did   with the father
confessor   standing   waiting
patiently   for your death
for your final words
and you   watching the dissolution
around you   watching his eyes
his face   listening to his Latin words
said: "What have I to confess?
I am a Jew."

It was 1942   and you wanted someone
to know   though you'd be buried
in a Christian grave   with an Aryan name.

Such will to be known   can alter history.

2.

Today   I stand alone   planning my first garden
and think of you   buried on that other continent
rescued from the Christian plot
the only flesh of your family   to lie
in a marked grave   in the Jewish cemetery
in a Warsaw   almost empty of any Jews.
That ground   I know   is but a fragment
of the past   a place apart   the surroundings
long rebuilt   into a modern city
and I know   that even now
while I stand   and try to map this season's growth
that country   cleansed of our people's blood
intones the litany of old complaints.

Gina   they hate us still.

3.

You are to me   everything
that remains   outside my grasp
everything   in this world
that is destroyed   with no one
there to rescue the fragments
to hear the words.
So much of history   seems
a gaping absence   at best a shadow
longing   for some greater
definition   which will never come
for what is burned   becomes air
and ashes   nothing more.

So I cling   to the knowledge of your
distant grave   for it alone
reminds me   prods me   to shape that shadow.

4.

I have spent a life   disentangling from influences
trying to claim   what was original   mine:
from my mother's mastery   of daily survival
so subtly interwoven   with common gestures

[stanza continues]

few recognize it for what it is
from my father's more visibly heroic deed
of dying recorded in memoirs tributes
from the deaths of grandparents aunts uncles
anonymous in a heap indistinguishable
from all the others who died unmourned.

And now I remember you and face another:
Gina in those few months when you watched
over me before my consciousness learned
the danger into which I had just been born
and the label of who I was and while my mother
sick and weak teetered on the edge of life
in those few months as the meaning of the ghetto
walls grew more defined as you inched people
out of the *umschlagplatz* your chest contracting
gasping with fear yet certain that this needed to be done
I believe that in that short time something
passed between us Gina and you imparted to me
the vision the firm sense of self that gave
you strength to state your name.

5.

And who would say that I have mourned
enough that I have looked at the old
photographs enough yellowed and faded
and the green ink now a grey dullness
where Marek placed the flowers
on the rubble where my father's body
was buried and disappeared and Marek's head
looking down his profile etched against
an empty horizon for there was nothing left

who would say that I have mourned
enough?

And when I asked my mother if I
could have this album that holds it all
holds more than most have who are
without a witness to mark their spot in green
or whose graves have been overgrown by weeds
or forests or bulldozed for the sake
of modern cities or whose bodies were never
buried but were left for speechless animals
to devour there is no piece of earth
that does not have its nameless who lived
and died unnoticed beyond the grasp of history
who die today

And when I asked my mother if I
could have this album and she replied
this stays here in this apartment
until I die I glimpsed again the urgency
to be known.

6.

There have been many plots of ground
that formed me. This town's church
its cemetery the bare expectant earth
of my garden all remind me of that
other soil on which I grew.

The first was the green bush and grass
behind Marek's house in Łódź. It was
after the war and Elza orphaned and just recently
claimed from the Polish stranger stood proud
before me and brushed her long blond hair
her haughtiness her only power. I watched
ashamed and awkward my small hand trying
to hide my bald head shaved for reasons
I was never told. It was our first meeting.

More than two years later in the neutral
countryside that never saw the war in Neglinge
Moti and I crawled flat on our stomachs
to see the miniature wildflowers hidden
beneath the blooming lilac bush. They grew
for elves I said and bound him to me
with the secret not wanting anyone else
to know. He was alert then but only months
before had refused to eat was force fed
in a Stockholm hospital. When his appetite
returned he clung to me four years older
in a way no one could ever understand
and I responded as I never would again
unconsciously selflessly with complete
certainty. I knew that he must live
and inched him along.

And again a few years later in a park the Bronx
there was an unmowed field near a metal fence.
My mother would bring me here on warm summer Sundays
and spread a blanket that would billow
over the high resistant grass then finally settle
and flatten with the weight of our bodies.
We brought things to read books that warmed

[stanza continues]

with the sun   newspapers   that yellowed
as the day wore on.

These were the gardens of my childhood.

7.

Gina   I must tell you: today I
felt hopeful   as I knelt close
to the earth   and turned it
inch by inch   sifting the soil
clearing the way   for roots
of vegetables. I felt so hopeful
Gina   that with repeated years
and efforts   the monotony of daily
motion   of bending   and someday
the earth   would be uncluttered
the debris cleared.

There is   I know   no reason
for such hope   for nothing destroyed
is ever made up   or restored to us.
In the earth   are buried histories
irretrievable.   Yet what philosophy
can justify   any of our emotions?
Like the watercolors from Buchenwald —
if you can imagine! The stench
from the chimneys   just the sounds
of the place. And yet someone felt
a need to paint. And did.

So do not ask me to explain
why I draw meaning and strength
from these common gestures   why today
my hope is unwavering   solid   as if
I'd never lost it   or never would again
as if those dying   angry or stunned
at the stupidity of it   could be revived
as if their mortal wounds   could heal
as if their hunger   could be outlived
as if they were not dying   strangers
to others   strangers to themselves.

I need to hope. And do.

8.

I have been a dreamer   dreaming
of a perfect garden   of a family tree
whose branches   spread   through centuries
of an orderly cemetery   with no gravestones
missing. Tonight   as the sun sets   and I
turn towards evening   I have no such dreams.
Like the woman   who refused to trace
the ancient constellations   upon a clear
and crowded sky   because finding the stars
recording each in its place   the faint
and the brilliant   was enough
I too   Gina   have discarded all patterns
and blueprints. This night   I want only
to sleep   a dark   rich   dreamless sleep
to shelter   in me   what is left
to strengthen myself   for what is needed.

Cherry Plain, New York
August, 1982

Ruth Kluger

Halloween and a Ghost

I.

Unlike real people, ghosts are obvious,
Thinly disguised and come when most expected.
Must you stand at my door on Halloween,
With a sheet over your head like the other kids,
Asking for candy, brother?

Ripples of water where you were swimming,
Your questioning voice saying "Ampersand?"
These I recall and your sailor hat and
In a wintry schoolyard the shape of your breath.
But I never found out the shape of your death,
There being so many ways of killing.

Dead boys shouldn't walk the streets.
Real ghosts shouldn't wear real sheets.
The heart may break of tricks and can't give treats.

II.

You are the skipped sentence in the book I'm reading.
You are the kitchen knife that slips into the thumb.
Memory: the autonomous twitch of an aching muscle.
You are the word that is always mistyped
And, erased, defaces the page.

Tonight your two nephews play host here.
Candy and cookies are theirs to bestow
With shrieks of delight, for they do not know
That it's always you who is ringing the bell —
And the house turns into a pumpkin hell —
("There is no such thing as a ghost, dear").

Spilled ink I give.
Tears have run through a sieve.
Wine and milk are for lovers and children who live.

David Koenig

After the Holocaust, No Poetry

After the Holocaust,
No poetry —
That is what they say —
But I write poems about it.
What's that?
You do, too?
Come then,
Let us sit down together.
How do you spell your name
In this country,
With an *umlaut* or a vowel?
Shall we speak a bit
In the old tongue?
The one they tried to cut
Out of our parents' mouths?
Forgive me.
I'm not unstrung.
The poems keep me sane.
I guard them
Like torn and injured pages
From buried books of prayer.

Onkel Fritz Is Sitting

Onkel Fritz is sitting
Next to his cigarettes
On the table, here in Germany.
Onkel Fritz is sitting
On the terrace of his home
At dusk, smelling the
Tomato plants and roses,
Seventy-nine years old,
Staring out into the garden,
Thin shoulders propped up
On sharp bones, like barbed
Wire strung on posts.
Onkel Fritz, what are you seeing
As you wait for the dark
With your white handkerchief
Beside you on the table?
Do you see the white flag
Of surrender you couldn't
Wave when they came
And took you, the SS,
In Autumn, from your home?
Did you sit at a table, so
Long ago, next to your cigarettes,
And look up to see brown
Pants over black boots and
The red, hooked cross?
Did you smell food cooking
As they led you away
Without warm clothes,
Your stomach rumbling
With hunger you were yet
To feel, as they drove you
By the burning synagogue to jail?
Did you sit in jail, Onkel Fritz,
And wonder what you had done wrong,
Did you ask the jailer, an old Gentile
Friend, where you were being sent, and
Did he answer, "Buchenwald"?
Did you sit in Buchenwald
When you were not forced to stand
For hours in the dark, looking up
At a scaffold where the SS shouted down
At you all night about the man
They would hang before your eyes at dawn?
Did you sit at a table when
By some miracle your Dutch cousin
Brought you out, and the SS made

[stanza continues]

You swear in writing you had seen nothing?
Did you sit in the truck from Buchenwald
When the driver stopped for a moment
In memory of those left behind?
And then in the train where Jews
Were not allowed to sit, with
Shaved heads, while the conductor
Brought water for your dry lips
Because he too had a son in the camp?
Onkel Fritz, did you sit long
On the freighter to South America,
And years later, a sick old man,
On the ship back to Germany?
Did you sit with your fellow
Townsmen and neighbors and wonder
How you would ever feel at home again?
Did you sit in the dining room
Of city hall many times as the
Token remaining Jew? Did you
Sit when the Queen of England
On a visit to the occupation forces
In the town asked you, “How have you survived?”?
Onkel Fritz, are you sitting
In the dark tonight,
Under the sun gone under the earth,
Are you thinking that every time
One goes under another,
There is tyranny? Are you feeling
The chill of the night air?
Onkel Fritz, are you thinking
Of the miracle
Of standing up again?

Yala Korwin

The Little Boy with His Hands Up

Your open palms raised in the air
like two white doves
frame your meager face,
your face contorted with fear,
grown old with knowledge beyond your years.
Not yet ten. Eight? Seven?
Not yet compelled to mark
with a blue star on white badge
your Jewishness.

No need to brand the very young.
They will meekly follow their mothers.

You are standing apart
against the flock of women and their brood
with blank resigned stares.
All the torments of this harassed crowd
are written on your face.
In your dark eyes — a vision of horror.
You have seen Death already
on the ghetto streets, haven't you?
Do you recognize it in the emblems
of the SS-man facing you with his camera?

Like a lost lamb you are standing
apart and forlorn beholding your own fate.

Where is your mother, little boy?
Is she the woman glancing over her shoulder
at the gunmen by the bunker's entrance?
Is it she who lovingly, though in haste,
buttoned your coat, straightened your cap,
pulled up your socks?
Is it her dreams of you, her dreams
of a future Einstein, a Spinoza,
another Heine or Halévy
they will murder soon?
Or are you orphaned already?
But, even if you still have a mother,
she won't be allowed to comfort you
in her arms.
Her tired arms loaded with useless bundles
must remain up in submission.

Alone you will march
among other lonely wretches
toward your martyrdom.

Your image will remain with us
and grow and grow
to immense proportions,
to haunt the callous world,
to accuse it, with ever stronger voice,
in the name of a million youngsters
who lie, pitiful rag-dolls,
their eyes forever closed.

Noemi

In Memory of Noemi "Stefania" Meisels

You hid behind a borrowed name,
bleached your raven crown,
but there was no dye
to cover the pigment of doom
in your eyes.

Night after night I see you
alone in that place
guarded by a killer fence.
Night after night I am dying
all your deaths.

I didn't follow you, sister.
Can I ever be forgiven
the blueness of my irises,
the paleness of hair — hues of
Slavic fields?

I escaped to be your witness,
to testify: you were.
I live to carve your name
in all the silent stones
of the world.

Passover Night 1942

not a crumb of leavened
or unleavened bread
and no manna fell

no water sprang out
of the bunker's wall
the last potato was gone

we sat and we munched
chunks of potato-peels
more bitter than herbs

we didn't dare to sing
and open the door
for Elijah

we huddled and prayed
while pillars of clouds
massed above our heads

and pillars of fire
loomed like blazing traps

You, Who Did Not Survive

Volumes have been written
to explain how they
who murdered you
came to power
and the reason for their crusade
against you.

For you, the truth lay
in black rifle barrels
in crematorium fires.

None of you died because
of a great virtue
none because of a great sin.
You died because one dies
from exhaustion
because gas kills.

For you, the truth lay
in boxcars and ditches
and crematorium fires.

They accused you of greed,
then ordered you
to take off your clothes.
They extracted your gold teeth
after you died.

For you, the truth lay
in crematorium fires.

Aaron Kramer

Westminster Synagogue

Ears afire, I knock at Kent House door.
My hands could not protect them if I tried
except from the drone of Heathrow jets, the roar
of a bus marked “Kensington.” Too deep inside,
the tick of an Irish bomb at Harrod’s store,
the swords forever committing chivalricide
athwart Knightsbridge, the million-footed squall
from Victoria’s trains to Exhibition Hall.

The door shuts out those ghosts storming the Park
across the way; the dignity and calm
of my friend rabbi uncurtaining his Ark
halts the old swords, defuses the young bomb.
But smilingly he chooses to remark
that where the Torah blazes now, Madame
de St. Laurent enjoyed her fireplace,
herself enjoyed through long years by His Grace

the Duke of Kent. At once his royal groans
roll 'round the room, her murmured syllables
mock what the cantor loftily intones.
But now a door is opened; silence drills
my skull; it fills my rib-cage, chills my bones.
With dignity, with calm the rabbi tells
that in this room heal fifteen hundred holy
scrolls a scribe has been repairing slowly,

and as each wraith-loved Torah is repaired,
some living congregation takes it in.
— Not for such future were these writings spared,
the rabbi makes me understand: Berlin
had a museum in mind; these would be aired
as trophies of a tribe that once had been.
I ask: Might one be opened? — but at once
desist . . . No need! Madame de St. Laurent's

syllables, and the groans of her high lover,
are hammered into dust by the dear notes
that — scroll by scroll, rack under rack — recover
their Sabbath force. Seventy thousand throats
flame in my ears. The interview is over:
I'm at the bus stop; but around me floats
a choral fire from every synagogue
of Brno, Pilsen, Bratislava, Prague.

Zudioska

Smug in her Adriatic noon, Dubrovnik beams.
Within her walls, unconquered and intact,
was much to save — with guns or cunning.
It is all on file in the Rector's Palace.

The streets, in conscious harmony,
flow down from her twin hills
to merge in the Placa, where tourists go
marveling, that after a thousand years
in this world of wounded columns, ravished mausoleums,
no stone is vexed.

Here stands Zudioska, street of the Spanish Jews.
(Dubrovnik took in their banished scrolls;
not often made them wear the yellow badge,
pay special fees, stand trial for ritual murder.)

Ask no question of the stones. Go past.
You will find nothing peculiar on Zudioska.
Women dry their wash.
Children throw their ball.
A cartload rumbles down the narrow steps.
No room is vacant.
There are customers enough in the café.

Across from the café a door is open.
At the first landing the rabbi awaits you.
On the second landing is the synagogue —
six hundred eighteen years old.
The worshippers await you, though one cannot see them.

Ask no question of the stones.
The Jews had names, but what's the difference?
had women, children, trades — but what's the difference?
It is all on file, no doubt, in the Rector's Palace.
The rabbi could tell you:

> Two hundred Jews dwelled on this street.
> The Italians came, and put us on Rab.
> The Germans came, and took us to Auschwitz.
> Seventeen crawled home, and not one child.
>
> We sweep the floor of the synagogue each day.
> We hold our service without a minyan.
> Soon the synagogue will be perfectly silent,
> as silent as the perfect stones of the city,
> a museum with a guard collecting fees.
>
> God saved us from the quake of 1667.
> Nobody saved us in 1943.
> And you, if you were Dubrovnik, would you have cried
> *Shame!*
> as they checked off each name and shoved us into
> the boat?

Zudioska drowns in shadow.
The Placa runs in light.
Shield your eyes when you come back into the light
or the beaming stones will burn them as if you are crying.

Norbert Krapf

Tannenbaum, 1940

For Louis Daniel Brodsky

It stands in middle-class
dignity on a platform
glazed with cotton snow,
before lace curtains
gathered on the bay windows.

Burning wax candles give off
halos and add a romantic
glow to the glass globes
and a shimmer to the tinsel
dangling in elegance
from evergreen boughs.

Listen: you may even hear
a familiar Christmas melody
and the line *Wie treu sind*
deine Blätter! You may hear
the lullaby *Ihr Kinderlein*
kommet and *Stille Nacht,*
heilige Nacht! Yes, you
may hear the angelic voices
of a *Knabenchor* winging
through the air from
the radio in the corner.

Now look up. Do you see,
in all this glow, the image
of the Infant King,
the future Prince of Peace,
hanging near the crown
of this tall *Tannenbaum*?

Have a sip of *Glühwein*,
have a taste of *Stollen*,
but do not forget: This
is Deutschland. This is 1940.

Now look down. Look down
near the bottom boughs
of this evergreen wonder
and behold other ornaments
suspended in the haze.

See how these metal crosses
are hooked like angry claws?
Say *Hakenkreuz*. Say *Swastika*.
Now what songs do you hear?
What pastry do you taste?
What wine do you sip?
What boughs do you smell?
What light do you see?

The Name on the Wall

At the exhibit "The History and Culture of the Jews of Bavaria," Bavarian National Museum, Nuremberg, January 1989

Almost at the end, I pause in a replica
of a small, plain building that feels
like a train station located

near a concentration camp. When I move,
gravel crunches beneath my feet.
My Colombian-born children have fled

ahead after covering their eyes
before a blow-up of victims reduced
to skin stretched across bent

and twisted bones. Those who enter
this forlorn station do not stay
for long. Not many Germans stand

here with me. On the walls,
the names of all the Jews of Bavaria
who were deported to the camps.

The sound of any voice in this
hushed station sounds too loud.
Though we are Catholic, though

we left Bavaria one hundred fifty years ago,
though we should have known by now,
I can never not look. Can you ever

be sure exactly where you stood
or might have stood? When do you
ever know for certain who you

have been or what you might have
become? I can never not look.
Like many of my poems, the names

on the wall are grouped by place:
No Schmitts taken from Lohr am Main,
no Krapfs taken from the villages

of Hesslar, Kreuzthal or Tugendorf.
Near the end of the alphabet I find
myself drawn to my favorite Franconian

city, Würzburg, where I always return
for Frankenwein and the woodcarvings
of Riemenschneider and the statues

of the saints on the old stone bridge
across the Main. And there on the wall
is an entry I hear myself read in a language

I once knew, lost, and worked hard to re-
cover: *Krapf, Klara. 12.04.69. Wonfurt.*
18.01.43 Theresienstadt. But the name

on the wall has no face for me to view,
no voice to tell me her story. The simplest
questions multiply the fastest and can

be the hardest to answer. This familiar
yet strange name on the paper wall
of a replica of a train station in a museum

in the city where Albrecht Dürer walked
and worked has no voice to give
the details I need to hear, but raises

a chorus of questions I don't know
if I'll ever be able to answer:
Who was she? Why did she leave

her village for the city? Who were
her parents? Were they both Jewish?
Did she have brothers and sisters?

Was she married? Did she have children?
Was she my relative? One thing I know:
relationships run deeper than blood.

A Freight Yard in Würzburg

For Roland Flade

Old men and women climb
up a hill in Würzburg,
luggage in hand or strapped
across their shoulders.

[stanza continues]

Almost no one, except
uniformed Nazis marching
beside them on the sidewalk,
looks up. One member
of the Gestapo with unerring
aim trains a camera
like a high-powered rifle
at the top of the hill.

What could there be to
look forward to? Could
these old people really
believe at this point
in the war they were
being transferred to
a better home in spa
country to the east?

No wonder almost all heads
are turned at hard angles.
No wonder so many jaws
are set so hard.
No wonder so many people
are dressed in black.
No wonder so many shadows
have found faces to disfigure.
No wonder the cloth star
on the overcoat of the man
in the front row looks
so luminous and apocalyptic.

You are not among these
people, Klara Krapf, but five
months later, in your seventies,
you trudged up this hill.
You would not have seen
the spire of the Catholic
church pierce a gray sky
behind your bent back.

How could you make it
up this hill with all
your worldly possessions
shrunk into one bag?
With all the other luggage
you must have borne?

Your mother and father
were long dead. Your
brothers and sisters
were long gone to America.

[stanza continues]

There was no one left
to wonder where you
were going except friends
you'd made among the Jews
of Lower Franconia,
at the Altenheim
at Dürerstrasse 20, where
you'd lived a dozen
years, but most of them
came with you up this hill.

I stood at this empty
station, Klara, and looked.
Nothing but empty freight
cars and tracks curving
and stretching around a bend
toward invisible infinity.

As cars rushed by around
a curve in the road
I heard nothing but immense
and oppressive silence.
I was glad I could
not hear your voice.

I tried to fix my eyes
on wildflowers at my feet,
but they blurred. My usual
grasp of detail failed.
I saw almost nothing
but abstract colors. I could
not say in any language
the name of a single flower.

I stared at intersecting
tracks curving around
that ominous bend. I did
not want to follow you
where I knew you had gone.

Meditation in the Israelite Cemetery, Würzburg

Site of silence
away from the center.

Place of profound
and sacred quiet
where few
are left to come.

Hush of sorrow
and sadness welling up
from the earth.

Hush of leaf
and vine and sprig
of grass paying
their lush respect.

Silence in search
of restitution and reparation.

Silence of stories
wanting to be told.

Affection of weed
wanting to curl
against stone,

where almost
no one of
thousands
is left to lay
small stone
upon larger stone.

Silence of slow
and unending lament
and hope
evaporated like dew.

Silence of pink flowers
arranged to bloom
in the points of a star.

Silence of those
who were taken away
and had no one left
to have their names
cut in stone

but who returned
in spirit
nevertheless
from a place
to the east

with a beautiful
name which
nevertheless

has come to
signify
the cruelest
of fates.

Silence of annihilation
and desecration.

Silence of those
who had to endure
the thought
of the unthinkable.

Silence of you,
Klara, whose
family took
my last name

whose name
I bless and commemorate
with heavy words

I would lay
like stones
upon your tomb,
which would have
stood here
had there been

anyone left
to remember.

Carolyn Kreiter-Foronda

Leaving a Country Behind

I.

Rain over Munich, your plane's
clothed in a monk's black.
You look around the cabin
and wonder how the people
go on sleeping, rumors
over the radio of death
and hunger. Staring

[stanza continues]

into darkness, you see
your aunt cupping a fresh
bouquet, saying goodbye
to a stranger, someone
who knew about Dachau,
how long it takes to burn
the eyes shut. Again
there is lightning
and the murmur of her voice.
Father, how many times
must you leave a country
where the eyes praise nothing?

II.

I will always remember
the way your aunt said *Hitler*,
her lips drawn into a hiss
and then freed. Loving words,
I repeated *Hit* with a lilt
and then *ler*, too young
to understand the history
one man left behind
buried in this woman's heart.
I remember drawings hung
about the house, the time
she locked herself in the attic
to sketch a mad giant.
At the funeral, you placed
a rose in her lap.
The choirboy sang as if
the past were but a moment
he could bury with the dead.

III.

Drive twelve miles northwest,
the villager said, pointing
the way to the death camp.
I was six years old,
and today my mind returns
to Dachau, to the barbed
wire, ovens, and wooden bunks,
to iron bodies writhing
in a sculpture displayed
for the world's children.
Father, even now as the rains
fall, I hear sounds rising

[stanza continues]

from the dead and somewhere
beyond the rain, the voice
of a German offering her rose.

Maxine Kumin

The Amsterdam Poem

I.

All-Beethoven night at the Concertgebouw
is unashamedly schmaltz.
The audience melts into the Eroica
and we too, we the Americans
in our on-stage seats directly behind
five bass viols whose plucked strings set
the floorboards trembling, we sway
with mijnheer and mevrouw.

The conductor is Japanese.
When the firebombs fell on Tokyo
he was ten years old. Screaming.
Surely his hair, superfine, black,
grew forward then from his delicate crown.
His baton writes on air.
He conducts from the groin.
What his hips say, the violins seize:
Ars longa, my life is but a leaf.

In the morning we go to the gallery.
The exhibit is called *Bittere Jaren*,
1935 to 1941.
We who grew up in a safe place
expect the iron cross, the sealed boxcars
but the bitter years turn out to be
a rerun of the dustbowl by
Steichen, Walker Evans, Ben Shahn.

Remember the slogan, *The American Way*?
Here is the poster plastered on billboards,
the family of four in its brand-new car
smiling their toothpaste smiles
while a sharecropper across the hall
in a lovely grainy enlargement starves.
Here are the bloated babies

[stanza continues]

and the farms whipped into sand.
We two Americans, we two fools
taking in the town on our five-day week
hunch like turkey buzzards and
cannot lift our eyes and
cannot speak.

II.

Later, a pilgrimage
to Anne,
Anne Frank who was almost my age.
We go behind
the fake bookcase, climb
stairs that pitch
up to the little judas rooms
in which
they hid: Mother, sister,
the dentist, Peter,
and Papa who brought them to safety
from Frankfurt in '33
never dreaming of here,
never dreaming at all
of the makeshift kitchen, three
stools, a ladder
up to where Peter, "that boy,"
slept. I peer
at the w.c., its bowl
of blue-sprigged delft a beautiful
improbable toy.
In '33 I was eight years old,
soon to begin the Nazi nightmares
a hundred cold
wakings upstairs
in a warm bed in Germantown,
Pennsylvania.

We come down
into sunlight. There must have been
a few good years for Anne,
years of being a healthy animal
mooning along the estuaries,
skating on the canal
and eating cherries
in the Vondelpark
before, before
they went up in the dark.
I think of her

[stanza continues]

coming out, a prisoner,
a paradox
from behind the books
with the SS at her back . . .

III.

Along the canal that she could sometimes see
from Peter's window, a crowd has gathered.
The police arrive in a Volkswagen. A pigeon
has somehow blundered into the water. It floats
downstream, dumbly preparing to drown
but a girl guide fluent in five languages
dives in and bears it aloft like a pastry.
Everyone cheers.

In 1943, there wasn't a pigeon here
and the Dutch had begun to eat rats.
What can't I forgive? The rebirth of pigeons?
Of caring? Of live and let live? The carillons
in the Westerkirk on the corner ring out.
An old woman hawks eels from a pushcart.
For suffering there is no quantum. What heals
the city, its citizens, I know nothing about.

Tomorrow KLM can fly us out.

Aaron Kurtz

A Million Pairs of Shoes

A million pairs of shoes
lie thinking.
A million pairs of shoes, all that survived,
clambering,
creeping,
climbing to the sky.
A million Jews bore their wounds in these shoes.
A million children bore their future in these shoes.
A million pairs of shoes — forsaken, remembering
in the city of holocaust,
Lublin.

A million pairs of feet
hacked,
hewn,
charred.
But the shoes remained sound — intact
with poverty's corrosion upon them
or the patina of better days:
shoes with the sacred dust of the Warsaw Ghetto,
shoes of Viennese patent-leather elegance,
tough peasant boots that trudged hard roads,
children's shoes scuffed from childish games,
rubber boots of fishermen from the Volga, the Danube, the Vistula,
white-plastered boots of flour mill workers,
men's boots, women's shoes, children's slippers
twisted and worn,
shabby and torn.

No need to ask the coarse, clayed peasant boots
and the thick-soled shoes of toil
to what cities of the world they have been,
to what lands and why:
they speak
of ghettos and swamps,
basements and cemeteries,
blind attics and underground hideouts.
These boots are full of hopes and disappointments
from dangerous and bloody roads;
they pant, still hearing the hobnailed tread of fear,
and still pursuing hope
with faltering stride, heroic, sacred steps.

A million pairs of shoes
waiting.
These shoes will live.
These shoes will walk — over the world,
over the oceans and continents,
walk and walk
and never wear out!
They will be the shoes of history —
they will be the walking monument
of a people
on fire amid the flaming walls of hell.

Hell has fallen.
The people have survived.
The mountain of shoes
at the oven-graves of Lublin
is a mountain of rock split into a million fragments.
But the might of the rock lives on in every fragment:

[stanza continues]

a brotherhood of peoples that will arise and walk
that first day
of Genesis.

— *1945*

Translated from the Yiddish by the author and Olga Cabral

Christine Lahey

Dan's Shoe Repair: 1959

We know who her father is,
that bully, pushing, shoving,
shouting on the playground
at recess like a Valkyrie.
The nuns are extra nice
to her in compensation:
her father has no tongue.

He cannot command her
to keep quiet, to behave,
to pull up her socks,
do her multiplication tables,
dry the dishes before
she can watch *Popeye*.

I live one block from his shop,
am terrified of him,
dream of him: *he is trying*
to tell me something.
Yet always beg the errand,
enter his shop, stinky
with worn-out leather,
lathes whirring, shoelaces
jumbled up in
glass display cases,
the Norman Rockwell print
of the smiling shoemaker,
shoes, shoes, shoes
piled up everywhere,
in barrows, on shelves,
the shoes of the dead,
bundles of belongings,
hats, jackets, boots, gloves.

[stanza continues]

He learned his trade
from those cast-off shoes
heaped up at Bergen-Belsen;
the dead schooled the living.

Sweaty sleeves rolled up,
forearms covered
with blond hairs
I look at secretly,
his blue eyes see me,
much more than see,
they *talk* to me,
ask me my errand,
but I cannot repeat
my mother's instructions,
my mouth falls open,
cat's got my tongue.
He grabs my sister's pumps
and my summer sandals,
nods at me, nods at me,
marking white X's on the soles
with a piece of chalk,
the card with the day circled.
They'll be ready Thursday:
will I be there to pick them up?

He jerks his head past me
to the next customer,
who's decided to wait
while his heels are replaced.
He's taking no chances,
won't let that shoemaker
out of his sight.

I dawdle by the door,
wonder what it's like
to have Dan for a father,
thin as barbed wire,
fingers always dirty,
the big glass ashtrays
filling up as customers
look at photos in *LIFE*:
eyes behind barbed wire,
pictures stuck in his mind
that he cannot talk about.

Carole Glasser Langille

Babi Yar

For Anatoly Kuznetsov

They say the woman with black hair
shivered as she turned; the soldier
called out to her in German, told her to wait,
while others lined the front of the ditch, stripped off their clothes.
Body after body was shot then, limb upon limb.
By the time he reached the woman
(a matter of minutes)
her hair had turned completely white
and when she was finally shot
the bullets only wounded her
and she was buried like that, still breathing, an old lady
not quite twenty.

This happened thirty-nine years ago
and every woman who knows about her
has gone to sleep, one time or another,
hugging her shadow.

What substance do we have?

Alyssa A. Lappen

How It Happened

For Schmezell Zitser and his family

The crematorium's ashes, turned by tears to mud,
oozed into my veins. Masha told me of long-past
joyful Vilna days, how her boyfriend's twin
fooled her once in a dark movie house and stole
a kiss. The twins both died. Only her distant cousins
in Johannesburg remained. She never explained —
there was no need of it. Even a child of seven understood
that something unspeakable occurred.

Twenty years later, thinking myself lucky
to have been born later, and in America, I learned
the hollow solace of that lie: my forebears had died,
by dozens, in Ukraine — my great-great-grandfather,
Schmezell, tied by his beard to a horse's tail,

[stanza continues]

and dragged. In 1941, in Dobrinka — the little town,
they called it, though only the number who escaped
was small — murders were vast, open as the sky.

Days before, my few cousins rode on a strand of track
east to Omsk — the last train bound for life — and returned,
via Gorky, in '44, to precious Dobra of ash. Their Ukrainian
neighbors said how like pogroms it was. Except in 1941,
the year of Dad's Bar Mitzvah, Hitler's men
shot all, saving the horse only for the Zitser
patriarch, for whom Dad was named Saul.
I don't think he ever knew.

This, My Incarnation

For Masha Henley

At seventy-eight, you look ninety-three.
Your wrinkled face, folded in on hollow
Cheeks, tells in speechless phrases what
Besets you — of giant trees you felled

In sub-zero cold, beatings, the numbness
Of months and miles you walked in snow,
Following the long scar that was your son,
Buried nowhere but in your heart, his head

Crushed against Vilna Ghetto's sole tree. Your
Tree of life, anchored to vanished roots, sways
Branchless, leafless, fruitless — except for me,
Orphan soul, who found life on your birthday.

Denise Levertov

from During the Eichmann Trial

I. When We Look Up

When we look up
each from his own being
— Robert Duncan

He had not looked,
pitiful man whom none

pity, whom all
must pity if they look

into their own face (given
only by glass, steel, water

barely known) all
who look up

to see — how many
faces? How many

seen in a lifetime? (Not those
that flash by, but those

into which the gaze wanders
and is lost

and returns to tell
Here is a mystery,

a person, an
other, an I?

Count them.
Who are five million?)

'I was used from the nursery
to obedience

all my life . . .
Corpselike

obedience.' Yellow
calmed him later —

'a charming picture'
yellow of autumn leaves in

Wienerwald, a little
railroad station
nineteen-o-eight, Lemburg,

yellow sun
on the stepmother's teatable

Franz Joseph's beard
blessing his little ones.

It was the yellow
of the stars too,

stars that marked
those in whose faces

you had not
looked. 'They were cast out

as if they were
some animals, some beasts.'

'And what would disobedience
have brought me? And

whom would it have served?'
'I did not let my thoughts

dwell on this — I had
seen it and that was

enough.' (The words
'slur into a harsh babble')

'A spring of blood
gushed from the earth.'
Miracle

unsung. I see
a spring of blood gush from the earth —

Earth cannot swallow
so much at once

a fountain
rushes towards the sky

unrecognized
a sign —.

Pity this man who saw it
whose obedience continued —

he, you, I, which shall I say?
He stands

isolate in a bulletproof
witness-stand of glass,

a cage, where we may view
ourselves, an apparition

telling us something he
does not know: we are members

one of another.

III. Crystal Night

From blacked-out streets
    (wide avenues swept by curfew,
    alleyways, veins
    of dark within dark)

from houses whose walls
    had for a long time known
the tense stretch of skin over bone
as their brick or stone listened —

                    The scream!
The awaited scream rises,
the shattering
of glass and the cracking
of bone

a polar tumult as when
black ice booms, knives
of ice and glass
splitting and splintering the silence into
innumerable screaming needles of
yes, now it is upon us, the jackboots
are running in spurts of
sudden blood-light through the
broken temples

the veils
are rent in twain
terror has a white sound
every scream
of fear is a white needle freezing the eyes
the floodlights of their trucks throw
jets of white, their shouts
cleave the wholeness of darkness into
sectors of transparent white-clouded pantomime
where all that was awaited
is happening, it is Crystal Night
it is Crystal Night
these spikes which are not
pitched in the range of common hearing
whistle through time

smashing the windows of sleep and dream
smashing the windows of history
a whiteness scattering
in hailstones
each a mirror
for man's eyes

Philip Levine

On a Drawing by Flavio

Above my desk
the Rabbi of Auschwitz
bows his head and prays
for us all, and the earth
which long ago inhaled
his last flames turns
its face toward the light.
Outside the low trees
take the first gray shapes.
At the cost of such
death must I enter
this body again,
this body which is
itself closing on
death? Now the sun
rises above a stunning
valley, and the orchards
thrust their burning
branches into the day.
Do as you please, says
the sun without uttering
a word. But I can't.
I am this hand that
would raise itself
against the earth
and I am the earth too.
I look again and closer
at the rabbi and at last
see he has my face
that opened its eyes
so many years ago
to death. He has these
long tapering fingers
that long ago reached
for our father's hand
long gone to dirt, these
fingers that hold
hand to forearm,
forearm to hand because
that is all that God
gave us to hold.

The Survivor

In memory of my cousin,
David Ber Prishkulnick

Nîmes, August, 1966, and I
am going home. Home is here,
you say; your hand reaches
out and touches nothing.
Russia, New York, back,
that was your father; you
took up the road, moving
at dawn or after dusk
in the corrugated Citroën
loaded with shirts and ties.
Light broke in the fields
of poplars and up ahead
was one more village fair
and the peddling.

Once upon a day in 1940
a little man had to leave
his dinner and save his life
and go with his house
on his back, sleeping nowhere,
eating nothing, a shadow
running, a dark stop. That's
how Grandpa told the story.
Waking, I found you waiting,
your feet crossed and swinging,
like a child on the bench
outside the window, holding
a sack of warm rolls
for breakfast.

Gray suit, woolen vest,
collar, tie. Now you are
dispersed into the atoms
of gasoline and air
that explode an instant
and are always dispersed
to the earth that never
warmed you and the rain
drumming down on the hoods
of trucks stalled on the bridge
to Arles. You stop a moment
in my hand that cannot
stop and rise and stumble
onward toward the heart
where there is no rest.

Leatrice H. Lifshitz

A Few More Things About the Holocaust

Not only their money
was taken
a few more things
like beds and bathrooms
songs and stories
air

Not only their furniture
was taken
a few more things
like hallways and windows
bags and babies
hair

Not only their time was taken
a few more things
like hinges and handles
brothers and sisters
prayer

Not only their breath
was taken
a few more things
like shame and shadow
space and spirit
God

Alan Lupack

Auschwitz Reportaż

Today we went to Auschwitz. As we approached it, I could feel a heaviness, an oppressiveness in the air. We passed some railroad tracks. I could almost hear the screams and the moans and the dying gasps from trains whose people had been crammed like souls satanically stolen from heaven because of a sleeping God.

As I entered the lying gate and looked at the barbed wire — once electrified — and the zone of death, I could feel the bewilderment and the fear of those who had entered before, and then the anguish and terror when they were told by the sadistic SS officer that work would not make them free, that the only way out was through the poison gas and the ovens.

I saw in the buildings of Auschwitz the torn, filthy clothing of the men who weren't allowed to end their days with the dignity of men. I saw the hair cut from the heads of women so that it could be turned into cloth or be used to stuff mattresses. (What dreams those who slept on such mattresses must have had.) I saw the clothing of children and a broken doll — head torn off and mangled, arm cracked — which, if it could feel, would have suffered less than its owner. And I saw the pictures of hundreds of the millions who died there. There were names with each of those faces. And there were families and friends and loves and hates, there were moods and habits, there were lives with each of those names. Until they came to Auschwitz, where there were no names. I saw the wall where men were murdered, and the posts where men were hung like hunks of meat in the shambles of civilization, and the cells where men were starved and suffocated for crimes like stealing food from the pigs of the SS — but where one man gave his life for another. I saw the chambers where the prisoners thought they could escape for a few moments the filth and the stench but where, chaos having come again, water became gas and fire, and people became ashes.

I saw Barbara weep at Auschwitz. She wept for the faces of a family never seen, faces she could not find among the pictures on the wall and so would never see. She wept for the old who had worked and who had suffered the things that each man must, but who were not allowed to die with the dignity their endurance deserved. And she wept for the young who did not have a chance to suffer what men must because they were made to suffer what no man ever should, what it was once inconceivable that any man could at the hands of another. And she wept for a world where Auschwitz could exist.

Just across the road from Birkenau (Auschwitz II), whose wooden barracks and wooden bunk beds have none of the lying façade of Auschwitz I, whose gate, if it had a motto, would have said truthfully, "Abandon all hope . . ." —right across the road, I saw a farm with people working in the field.

As we drove away from Auschwitz, the farmers of the region were burning weeds. Billows of smoke filled the bus and burned our eyes. It was if we were escaping across the fiery river surrounding hell.

Yaacov Luria

There Is One Synagogue Extant in Kiev

They do not talk of loss at Babi Yar.
These aged men who blink into the sun
On benches in the courtyard of the *shul*
Have no more words or tears. *What's done is done.*

Their faces speak, each furrow slaughter-etched.
They sense the stranger's grief, yet know the cost
Of grief is small to him who merely sees,
Then journeys on his way. *What's lost stays lost.*

Their Ninth of Ab came early and stayed on.
There were forty temples once. Now one is all
That stands in Kiev, their Jerusalem,
A crumbling, wordless, tearless Western Wall.

So long ago their Queen of Sabbath fled,
All that's left is *kaddish* for the dead.

Arlene Maass

Opa the Watchmaker

Casper ten Boom's crime: "I will open my door
to any man in need who knocks."

Don't tell me the signs of the sky are against my back
and the rouge of the evening bears down on the mind's watchworks.
All of our lives now
are but rationed bones, like slivers of dice,
like blue bread rancid.
Life is in the palm of machinists.

He made me stalwart, but like Jacob the Patriarch
I move slower, leaning on the Maker who watches all,
leaning on the Maker for what I can't comprehend,
leaning on the Maker who personifies all wisdom
but I can't ask why this.

A babe arrives, smuggled into our home, unaware
that it is poor timing to be born Jewish in civilized Europe.
A soft spot crowns his head that a lifetime is meant to fill.
And I, an old man with hoarfrost beard tumbling,
caress the baby that must be wise and know not to cry!
I grasp the brass-bound Book
a watchmaker seeking precision
a watchmaker who looks to the One who created time
but is not bound to the brass moments — like the babe, like me.
Wisdom for understanding when there is no justice in the streets,
strength to love when there is no bread —
these are my requests clenched in the palms of the numbered days.
Love is numbing,

[stanza continues]

fields are barren even of turnips and squirrels,
bread is gold, worshipped in dug-out root cellars
and love goes hiding in the forests
like wild herbs against the wind
like a prophet's words rustling the reeds.
Charity is regarded as madness, or the play of fools.

I'm empty-handed now —
even the brass-bound Book is left behind
in our house guarded by the watchmen of the Third Reich.
They like our watches, but not us.
Thrown like sandbags in a cart, we leave Haarlem's market.
I carry nothing but what is buried in my heart —
how psalms are burnished in my eyes when I dare close them.
How resonant the words of King David
in the private conclaves of an old man's head!
How comforting the words of Jesus
to a Dutchman's burning heart.

They kept shoes, yanked gold from corpses,
burnt scrolls and flesh.
But they could not enter the hiding place
where the root of Jesse, the bruised reed, dwells.
No, they could not approach Moriah.

So many bones in this field of clay,
like a camp storeroom full of eyeglasses to the ceiling
from eyes that see the other side of time.

Channah Magori

from Holocaust Archives I

By My Father's Hand, in My Father's Name

My Father beside me —
On my shelf, in a frame
His pen hand tied to tubes
His heart hand tied to mine
In a hospital bed
Look, we're smiling
Me and Daddy —
And death, less than two weeks away

Tell me, Daddy
The stories flattened in time
Pressed into archives
By your hand
In your name:
What life could not bear to say
And what the living would not hear

———

"Die Aschen Heben Sich
Die Aschen Heben Sich"

Was this another planet
Was this heaven
What were they doing —
They were making a barrack, a beautiful barrack
They were putting in little beds, beautiful beds
They took in rolls
They took in milk

It was to be a children's barrack
It was to have a school
It was to teach them
To play catch

They took them in
And later
They took them out

Onto the Appellplatz
It was maybe two hundred
'Kleine Kinder'

And they were playing, you know, on the grass, playing
And they started throwing them around like garbage
They took them all
They took them all onto the *Appellplatz*
They played with them, catch

And after that — they shot them all
They was asking us
To open the graves and burn them

"Every one, he will get two breads when he will work during the night."

And I said,
I don't want the bread.

———

And by the open grave we said Yizkor for my father. And my brother lifted the holy earth of a burnt and blessed people and touched it to his death-dimmed eyes and put the lost and lifted ashes to their final rest.

In My Mother's Voice

Running to the grave
Pain *shtocht mir* in my side
Wanting to take a picture
With my eyes
For making me see
What I couldn't hear in words

My Tateh, I'm sorry, I'm sorry.
Not knowing who you are
They took your beard for
Nazi blankets
And for me no picture
For making me see
What I couldn't hear in words

Was it Rosh Chodesh Nisan
Was it Friday
What was it
It was windy
Yah, Ich gedenkt azoi
It was windy

On the hospital bed
Mit cuts on his face
Mit the sheets of the typhus
And his beard for Nazi blankets
The Fatherland warm in my Tateh's hair

And no one is knowing him at all
Not Dovid
Not Avrum
Not Levi-Yitzchak
And Mameh — not knowing him at all
But for the *tzeteleh* of paper tied on his big toe —
Zylberberg.

And after we came back from the gutten ort
We set stakes and wound strings
To mark his grave
Hoping we would return one day to erect a stone —

REB AHARON ZYLBERBERG: BELOVED HUSBAND, BELOVED FATHER

Mameh withered in the desolation of the abandoned.

Mameh started crying:
"Now is no one left
To call me be my name.
Now is no one left
To call me Channah'leh."

from **Holocaust Archives II**

The Voice Left in the Wall

The lost voice
Its markers on the wall

The lost song
Scratched thick through Zyklon Blue

Shadows
Singing on the wall

Its contour echoes
Slow and black and brackish in my ears
Black — the sound of bleeding.
And it sings

Come out, come out,
Wherever you are

And there are no windows in the gas chambers of Auschwitz — only spotlights that let you see the last scratching on death's walls. Spotlights that cast shadows on the walls. And I move closer to touch her dying marker. And my hand casts a shadow. And the shadow stares back and takes my hand as her own. And I move closer to the wall and the shadow stares back and takes me as her own. And I say —

Who are you?

And she says —

You —

Left in the wall
Your voice, left in the wall
Singing

Come out, come out
Wherever you are

And she takes me in and I take her out

Outside this wall
Outside this Auschwitz

And all at once the voice
And all at once the singing
And all at once the song

Ollie, Ollie, oxen
Free, free, free.

Ollie, Ollie, oxen
Free, free, free.

Sandra Cohen Margulius

Aunt Betty

Almost ninety-four, you remember
the Selections. You have survived the hunger,
stale bread, rancid water, biting leather
across your back, metal forceps that stole
the fetus from your body.

I see you ghost-walking near Brown Deer Plaza,
limping slightly in your tattered mink jacket.
You try to smile through the losing:
the baby torn from your uterus,
the daughter you couldn't adopt,
your mother's lost recipes,
too many deaths.

Aunt Betty, there will be no more cries
of *Juden Raus!* no Kristallnacht here,
no ovens. Yet you are still afraid to speak,
still afraid they will hunt you down,
burn your house, kill what's left
of your family, force you to wear a yellow star
over the endless tattoo of numbers, smoldering
black rows across your body.

David McKain

For the Children

In a painting by Brueghel
a hunter sights the hart
then strings his gut.

I would put him on a rooftop
as the king rides by — or, better,
near the Führerbunker:
Hitler loved the old masters,
hanging his favorites on the wall.

Did he see
the Brueghel of the hunters on the hill,
the children in the village?

He might have seen the red angle of their caps
and the cold blood deer hanging from a pole.

But in his final days
he'd stand at the window and gaze,
the winter woods a print
bled to the sash of their border.

His back to the Brueghel
the hunters could escape —
they could toast their venison under a hemlock,
scratch a plan in the snow with a stick.

Later they could slip back in
to do their work —
to parade the Führer
through the village,
slung on a pole like a deer,
upside down in the cold winter light
for all the children to see.

Robert Mezey

Terezín

In your watercolor, Nely Sílvinová
your heart on fire
on the grey cover of a sketchbook
is a dying sun or
a flower
youngest of the summer

the sun itself
the grizzled head of a flower
throbbing
in the cold dusk of your last day
on earth

There are no thorns to be seen
but the color says
thorns

and much else that is not
visible it says also
a burning wound at the horizon
it says Poland and winter
it says painful Terezín
SILVIN VI 25 VI 1944
and somehow
above the body on its bed of coals
it says spring
from the crest of the street it says
you can see fields
brown and green
and beyond them the dark blue line of woods
and beyond that
smoke
is that the smoke of Prague
and it says blood
every kind of blood
blood of Jews
German blood
blood of Bohemia and Moravia
running in the gutters
blood of children
it says free at last
the mouth of the womb it says
SILVIN VI 25 VI 1944
the penis of the commandant
the enraged color
the whip stock the gun butt
it says it says it says

Petrified god
god that gave up the ghost at Terezín
what does it say but itself
thirteen years of life
and your heart on fire

Nely Sílvinová

Richard Michelson

The Jews That We Are

. . . you have inherited its burden without its mystery.
— Elie Wiesel

I.

March 1979 and I am watching Nazis
march through Chicago. The bold type
of the *Sun-Times* describes a small band
of hoodlums, undereducated boy scouts, the better
to be ignored. My grandfather, back hunched
over his Bible, agrees. Jews like myself
should stay home, should lay down our stones
and pray like the Jews that we are.

II.

Grandfather, you are easy to love
with your long beard and the way you sway
like a palm branch in the storm. It is easy
to romanticize your spiritual search,
worldly naiveté and wise rabbinical words.
You belong in the books I read
by Singer, Peretz, Sholom Aleichem.
But their characters are ignorant
of the chapters to come. You know
where their prayers will lead.

III.

A circle. Six Nazis. Your wife in the middle.
One soldier says all *Jewesses* are whores
and the others agree. You say nothing.
Years later you'll decide to speak:
"Do we not serve Hitler's purpose, we
who would sooner renounce our beliefs
than assume our burdens?"

IV.

A generation after the Holocaust
and I know no Hebrew. No Yiddish. No Torah.
I fast only on the Day of Atonement
and even then I've been known to cheat.

[stanza continues]

A generation after the Holocaust
and I apologize for my grandfather's
bent back and wild gestures.
I used to tremble to the rhythm
of his prayers. I feared the mysterious
words that kept us from the devil.
Now, from my window I watch Nazis march.
Their feet strike the pavement
like the ticking of a clock. I am a Jew
a generation after the Holocaust.
Poorer, my grandfather says, without a past
than he, who has no future.

from Recital

Blessed is the Lord who trains my hands for battle, my fingers for warfare.
— Psalm 144

I. The Original Poem

My hands, French-braiding my daughter's hair before her recital,
are suddenly my grandmother's, kneading the ceremonial Friday night challah —
the same dark veins, the Tigris, the Euphrates, spreading life into each tributary.

Or, turned palms up, eight trains arriving at the same station, at the same time,
two others already emptied and heading back out, boxcars with pet names
like the racing boats of the wealthy: *Interior Affairs, Foreign Policy.*

Or elbows held close to the body, ten escape routes, and two shtetls
— my great-grandmother in one, my great-grandfather in the other.
I'm holding them both in my hands; I'm like God in the old camp song,
when my daughter starts to play, and I, forgetting myself, clap
and keep clapping, and I think maybe this world is like God's boat
and He calls it *Genocide*, and the next world is also His and ours to share.

III. Genocide

"Recital" is the name of the poem I was reading at my first recital,
when, in the back, I heard somebody's grandmother shuffling down the hallway,
her whole bridge game, Slavic barges, in tow, and suddenly
chairs were scraping all over the place. *Speak up,* she says, *what are you saying?*
I'm reading the numbers on her forearm, each numeral a poem written by God:
perfect, meaningless, and containing all meaning, just as you'd expect in a poem
by the Poet Laureate of all universes, of all religions, of all time.

V. Battles

All this, I'm remembering, was years ago, but years later I'm re-reading "Recital"
to my daughter, who turned out to be a pianist after all
and is practicing for her own recital, at the same North Shore Jewish Nursing Home,
her grandmother mired in the mud of the waiting list and the whole family conspiring
to maneuver her to the front of the line. She's the last soldier standing between me
and my death. She's the pre-Columbus boat heading over the edge of the horizon,
and I'm the nameless little boat following. Her husband died in the war of the streets
and her brother died in the war to end all wars and her father died in the war before that.
And the personal war my wife and I have waged between us for so long
that it's beginning to look like nostalgia, only seems never-ending. I want to die,
not like Saul, on the battlefield of my own sword, nor like Solomon, my house in disarray,
but like David, in his bed, reciting the psalms, at war only with his own soul.

VI. Lullabies

I'm standing in the back of the room listening to my daughter's recital,
her fingers furiously pumping up and down, and now, diminuendo toward the end,
controlling the strings and valves of my heart. Maybe I am the sheep,
sacrificing my inner life for the sake of her song. Or maybe her palms and fingers,
resting face down on the keys, are only her palms and fingers resting.

I'm alone in the back of the room, a sentry guarding the free cookies
which, according to policy, cannot be eaten except in the recreation hall
we call *The Afterlife*. Otherwise no one would sit still for the music,
half the audience deaf, and the rest already sailing home on the faint breath
of the small boats they've christened *Battles* and *Lullabies*. I want to die,
not like Goliath, a victim of modern warfare, nor like Uriah, turned love's collateral damage,
but like David himself, a shepherd leading his flock to feed among the flowers.

VII. The Revision

Would you still love me, my daughter asks, if I had played all the wrong notes?
She's wondering what it means to be her: Jewish, American, and upper-middle class
in a time of war, when all she really wants to think about is poetry and song.

Would you still love me, my wife asks, if I were old, ugly, too thin, toothless?
She's bombing her own body weekly, shrapnel embedded
in the roof and walls of the holy house where we prayed and made love.

Would you still love me, David asked his God, if I killed a man
for no better reason than to take his beautiful wife as my lover?

Would you still love me, I asked my father, if instead of fighting my own battles,
I deserted, conscientiously objected, sat on the sidelines, writing,
without even once harnessing the power to revise my life like words on a page?

Would you still love me, God asked my grandmother in the reception hall
before His grand recital, if I wiped out your entire family, let's say all at once,
leaving only one self-involved American tributary to tell the tale?

Life, my grandmother once explained to me, is not poetry, never was, and was
never meant to be. Now by way of answer I watch her wipe away the faint smudge
of chocolate still fresh on God's lips. *Your grandmother's one tough cookie,*
He whispers to me, while she rustles about, her chair scraping every which way.
What, she asks? *Speak up, or no one will hear a word you are saying.*
As for your certain and coming death, she adds,
I don't know if you're a religious man, but you might try praying.

Your steadfast love is eternal. Do not forsake the work of your hands. — Psalm 138

Bernard S. Mikofsky

Mame-Loshen, Yiddish

Long ago
We spoke a mother tongue;
Now its words, its warm words
Have grown cold
And trailed away
Into silence . . .

Those ancient sounds
From childhood's love —
They are dreams,
They are nightmares,
They laughed,
They cried,
They whispered then a while —
And they were gone.

They are wraiths,
They are ghosts,
Once warm and loving syllables:
Smoke . . .

1945

And that year
When the fires ceased
And the ovens were finally cool
A strange wind moved out
In slow, grief-laden eddies
And sooty swirls
Across Europe —
And even beyond.

And those with conscience
(And even those without)
Heard faint sounds from afar,
Echoes from an age-old abyss,
And sometimes these seemed to come
From inside one's ear —
So tiny and yet so persistent,
Echoes of the anonymous cries
Of numbered millions.

And far from the ovens
Far from the funeral fires,
This wind still carried
Wraiths of soot
Too fine to water the eye
Yet searing the heart.

That year the strange wind
Moved slowly across Europe —
And even beyond,
Now and then pausing
To eddy into the deepest corners
Of our minds
To remind us,
To stir us for an instant
From our dream of well-being.

Aaron Miller

Not Dachau

It is with curiosity, finally,
that man views his accomplishments:

as if this park
of spruce and new grass
were not of his own design;

as if these concrete markers
proclaiming acres of ashes,
mountains of bones,
concealed neither ashes nor bones,
but bits of moon
preserved in formaldehyde;

as if this statue
chiseled from death
were not of a man,
nor even man's work,
but some minor god's
ironic self-portrait;

as if these ovens
festooned with paper wreaths
never burned people;
old letters, perhaps,
bad books, rotten beams,
the refuse of a huge summer picnic —
but not people;

as if this were Atlantis,
not Dachau; a window,
not a mirror.

Marilyn Mohr

Tsena Tsena

There you are dancing with your child
the one you thought could never be born,
whirling her in tattooed arms,
your faces flushed with the joy
of her first year, rose-colored
sunrise after the long night,
twirling to the music of the Tsena,
holding her high, as if in thanks
to the God you thought had forsaken you.

This child, fondled and touched with awe,
each strand, each finger a miracle.
The three of you dancing in the dim lights
of a Brooklyn apartment, dancing away
the ashen smoke and hopeless years.
This child, this dance, this song
sweeping back the darkness,
Tsena!

Yiddish

They spoke in guttural tones,
muted notes echoing off tombstones.
Their words weaving through barbed wire
rose above gray smoke,

formed letters, words, poems
imprinted in blood on pages
of parchment and leather
read by the diminishing few.

A generation after destruction
almost vanquished it to silence,
the tongue of a people seeks speakers,
even whispers from their dying lips:

Rome died with Latin, Latin with Rome.
Remember the libraries of Łódź,
of Warsaw. Our language glows
in the cinders.

David Moolten

Photograph of Liberated Prisoner, Dachau, 1945

let none of it remain until the morning, anything
that remains until the morning you shall burn . . .
— Exodus 12:10

He has the look of Moses shambling down from God,
Barefoot in those ludicrous sackcloth pajamas,
Sparse and bitter as the Passover herbs that thrive
In a desert, his stare trekking beyond
The soldiers who shot this into a future

[stanza continues]

Where he leads us, no promise in stone,
Only his tattooed memory, only his fragile person
On which the broken laws are written. He stands
Out in a field, just a tedious field,
Overwhelmed by clover, saw grass, milk and honey,
Like a shepherd someone at the table
Years later will bless from a delicate glass
For his freedom, his return from the surly mountain
With its verboten pinnacle of smog, red wine
And horseradish for that inner holy ground
No picture could show, each sole black with Sinai,
His whole body an untouched burning bush.

Yellow Star

He saved it like a captured butterfly,
A medal decorating a box of yellowed black
And white snapshots, a souvenir of his first
Lost life, infernal and exquisite, a flared match
His hand could tolerate just a moment.
Up close it looked imperfect, homespun, fringed
With strands from the coat off which he'd torn it
The day the war ended, the long discarded coat
On which she slowly, carefully sewed
What she'd cut from cloth. Posted on walls
The edict said everyone must make their own,
Arbitrary and specific as any
In Leviticus, in the Torah that made him
Who he was, a noxious star, a hexagram,
Petaled like a sunflower, a saffron dahlia,
A bloom she might have pinned to his lapel
Were they going out to waltz. Maybe that's why
He kept it, as a mnemonic of her
Ordinary, singular soul, which imbued
Whatever her fingers touched, made it
Less horrific, less contemptible
Like the apple had Eve grown the tree herself
And the two of them stood before it scared
And hungry. Despite his teaching, her shift
In a shoe factory, they'd little to eat
With the rationing in Zagreb, no garden,
Not even a window box for their apartment,
Just bricks and dust, a candle in the glass
And the kiss it betokened, not much but savored
In a way that anywhere before became paradise
And this the flower he left with.

Sarah Traister Moskovitz

December

For Janet Hadda

For Yiddish it's December.
There's no more oven hearth.
The small fire sinks
and flames only in dreams.
The rebbe teaching little children there
died with them
on the other side of the Atlantic
in the great fires of hate.

And here, our Yiddish drowned
in roaring waves, in the crash and flood
of mass culture.

There is no cemetery for a language,
only for each speaker,
and every mouth becoming silent
takes with it a piece of world:
a client of the Yiddish Street
a teacher's effort, a mother's song,
a sister's comfort, a brother's help,
and hundreds of untold stories —
gifts ungiven,
carved from a thousand years of Yiddish history.

When Latin died
she was sanctified
in holy churches.
There are no holy walls
to honor my Yiddish . . .
only lonely professors
carrying the burden
of millions of silent graves
as single alien guests
in departments of German.

The Dress

I am sewing a dress for my high school graduation.
I've taken down my bedroom curtains —
floral seersucker on white background.
My parents come home.

[stanza continues]

They look shocked.
“What are you doing?”
“I want to go to my graduation.”
It doesn’t matter to them;
they don’t understand why it matters to me.
They look frustrated and disapproving.
Too late for me to hang the curtains back —
I’ve cut them dress-length.

It is spring 1944 and they are trapped in a fog
of worry for their families in Poland,
Warsaw and Biala Podlaska.
I live in a house inhabited by spirits of people who may be dead
and may not be dead:
my aunts, uncles and many cousins,
some my age.
Dead or alive, they come up
out of dark pits in the hall;
they are in the living room crying
where Yiddish newspapers with pictures
of concentration camp corpses are stacked.
They come up from under the kitchen table
where my parents sigh and talk softly:
“Nisht kayn vort shoin azoi lang.”
(Not a word, so long already.)
Their anxiety is a jagged black wall of broken glass
I cannot touch, let alone cross.

I go to the graduation myself in the dress I made.
I am not really good with the sewing machine
and have basted most of the dress by hand.
I pray the seams will hold.
After the ceremony, I watch the others meet
with parents, families. In cozy animated circles
they stand, talking, smiling, celebrating something.

White dogwoods and purple lilacs are in bloom.
The scent of fresh green around the auditorium is strong
Inside my blossoming young girl’s body —
a bare tree charred by fire in autumn.

I walk home slowly down Chestnut Street
to the quiet in our apartment.
Little brother having his afternoon nap.
Father sitting at his desk reading the newspaper.
Mother in the kitchen ironing.

It’s a long time before she asks
Nu, how was it?
I can find no words.

The Teaspoon

There is a shiny little metal teaspoon,
cold to the touch, in my kitchen drawer
reminding me of darkness in Germany;
reminding me of dark wood-paneled halls
in Nuremberg's main courthouse
where Nazi war criminals were tried
for crimes against humanity.

There, I listened to the guide recite:
names of judges, names of criminals,
types of crimes, numbers of victims, methods of murder.
But I stopped listening and heard only
the rumbling sounds of steel-wheeled trains
  too late, too late, too little, too late
        too late, too late, too little, too late
              too little, too little, too little, too late.

Silent, heavy with darkness
in the basement cafeteria afterward,
I stared into a teacup, sipping solace,
and saw the imprint facing me
on the handle front of a small teaspoon:
"Justiz NBG."

The spoon is little as justice was:
shrunken, crippled, blind to tens of thousands
of killers, like Mengele, and Eichmann . . .
helped by their supporters to flee from trial
and live
while those whose family trees they burnt to ash
are dead.
And their lonely red-eyed orphaned children
grow frail and gray around a stubborn core of sorrow.

Yesterday, I noticed engraved print
on the teaspoon handle's back.
At the window for better light
I held it close to read
what I had never seen before:

Stainless   Germany.

There is a little teaspoon in my kitchen
I hold captive in a drawer
and never use for eating.

At the United States Holocaust Memorial Museum

I came here well prepared
for work among the graves
the burial pits, the clouds of smoke and ash;
prepared my eyes for images of roads flooded with people
driven from their towns, their homes, their lives;
prepared my ears for sounds of broken glass
and fire raging in locked synagogues;
prepared my heart to break for sad-eyed, hungry children.

I brought with me a shawl from home
to pull around me like a prayer shawl,
a shield I have been knitting half a century
with good soft wool
to banish chill of death . . . warm wool wound around
steel wire and words.
I knit on fingers of my mother's love . . .

Here, at the library table
with the green-shade reading lamp
and a sign for SILENCE
I'm close to reference bookshelves
where murdered Yiddish poets live;
I feel the hovering presence of
my martyred aunts.
They warm me with my mother's soft brown eyes
and console me
with the same gentle hands.

Stanley Moss

Ghetto Theater, Vilnius, 1941

They offered *One Can't Know Anything.*
The players chose to wear something
about the person, a spoon, or since it was autumn
a large gold maple leaf that looked like a star of David
pinned to a shirt or blouse. Someone shouted,
"You are play-acting in a cemetery!"
But they went on: "To sit, to stand, to lie on the ground,
is it better to close or open your eyes, to listen or not,
to speak or not to speak? Those are the questions."

Fragments. A grave song: "I knew him well, Horatio.
Here hung the lips I have kissed I know not how often . . .
My Lord, I have some remembrances of yours."

Fifty-six years later in a sandlot where for three hundred years
the Great Synagogue stood, I watch children playing.
Perhaps God shows himself as hide and seek,
as wrestling, laughter, as children falling,
cutting their knees — the rush of tears.

A Visit to Kaunas

I put on my Mosaic horns, a pointed beard,
my goat-hoof feet — my nose, eyes, hair, and ears
are just right — and walk the streets of the old ghetto.
In May under the giant lilac and blooming chestnut trees
I am the only dirty word in the Lithuanian language.
I taxi to the death camp and to the forest
where only the birds are gay, freight trains still screech,
scream and stop. I have origins here, not roots,
origins among the ashes of shoemakers
and scholars, below the roots of these Christmas trees,
and below the pits filled with charred splinters of bone
covered with fathoms of concrete. But I am the devil;
I know in the city someone wears the good gold watch
given to him by a mother to save her infant
thrown in a sewer. Someone still tells time by that watch;
I think it is the town clock.

Perhaps Lithuanian that has three words for "soul"
needs more words for "murder" — murder as bread:
"Please pass the murder and butter" gets you to:
"The wine you are drinking is my blood,
the murder you are eating is my body."
Who planted the lilac and chestnut trees?
Whose woods are these? I think I know.
I do my little devil dance;
my goat hooves click on the stone streets.
Das Lied von der Erde
ist Murder, Murder, Murder.

Teresa Moszkowicz-Syrop

Lullaby

On a sleepless night
When the past and present
Mix together
As in a moving play,

[stanza continues]

Pictures from the Nazi horrors
Follow me,
Suffering
Beyond the limit
Of human endurance
Comes alive again.
I often
Don't believe that
All we experienced
Existed.
I still cannot speak
About it
In any clear way.
On such a night
I wish to be a child again,
To feel safe, without fear,
To reach out for my mother's
Soothing hands,
Resurrected from the ashes,
And listen to the lullaby
She used to sing for me:
Lulu lul, Lulu lul, Lulu lul . . .

The Tomatoes

Is it possible,
Do they still exist?
The real, red tomatoes
Which were shining in the sun
On some broken stands
In the corners
of the ruined streets
In Warsaw.
I still remember,
When we were marching by
After the uproar,
Taken from the hiding places
By the Gestapo,
To be sent away
To the unknown.
We were so hungry —
Many days without food.
The houses were ruined,
The streets smashed in disorder.
But,
Mostly what I noticed —
What I longed for —
Were the juicy, red tomatoes
Shining in the sun.

Elaine Mott

The Balcony

1

At the Anne Frank traveling exhibition
we're taken by surprise:
for five or six seconds on film, the velvet-eyed
dark-haired girl of twelve, whose story
we've all memorized, is alive
and looking at us,
all the way from 1941 Amsterdam, from before
the Secret Annex, before Bergen-Belsen
and the nightmare behind barbed wire, before
her own death. Her entire being is there,
fully alive in the flickering stars
of light falling across the film like snow,
though on that day, it was warm enough
for Anne to be wrapped in just a thin sweater,
chrysalis for her young woman's body about to reach
its awakening.

2

It must have been the unexpected sound
of celebration in wartime
that drew her to her balcony window
where she witnessed the dreamy swell of people
in fine clothes and top hats — a wedding party
being filmed on the sidewalk below.
Who knows why the cameraman turned from the crowd
to film the young girl leaning out of her second floor
balcony, looking down like a small dignitary
from the prow of a ship about to depart.

3

He saw her, as we see her, hesitate,
as if the spool of past, present, and future
were unrolling before her at once — the mysteries
of blood and salt, the warm life of the body
that would be taken from her. She looked
at the scene, the bride with flowers
and the smiling groom,
the blessing of clouds and light;
then — like a torchbearer for all the victims —
she waved goodbye to the world.

The Last Visa for Palestine

For my cousin, Gitl Frost,
who did not survive the Warsaw Ghetto

For a moment I saw my lover at the train station,
the yellow star blazing up
on the dark fabric of his jacket.
They were moving us along, children and old people,
pushing us into the train like cattle. The leaves
on the trees were opening out of winter.
Windflowers blown to the ground
were spreading a pale carpet under our feet.
My lover looked at me for the last time,
doors closing between us, and in the darkness
the answer in my eyes was lost.

Even over the smell of death
I can smell the green fields we are passing through,
near, yet further from me than the primal, locked bones
of my mother's pelvis, or the river of her
that I slid out of into the light.
In one green field the clouds were high and racing.
We ate apples and bread and wine,
and I let my lover's hand move under my dress,
white linen like a bride's.
The grass was our first bed
on which we dreamed our children, three small ghosts
swimming into the sun.
In a mirror I saw our breath mingle.
The mirrors have flown to the sky. The rivers
have carried away our breath.

On the Wings of the Wind

In Memory of Hannah Senesh

A man straps on her harness,
the parachute is folded back,
a bird, a butterfly, a white wing
tucked against her body.
She sways under the weight of the equipment
she carries. There are so many lives to save.
The airplane stops, and darkness draws her in.
She thinks of her father, her mother,
of going back to the beginning of herself,
of being small and curled and wet,

[stanza continues]

with solid lungs that won't breathe.
She hears her own thin cry,
sees the birth-stains on the sheets,
the placenta that fed her
stretched between the midwife's hands.
The cord is cut and slips off. She drops
out of the opened hatch. In the blue air
she falls free. There is no floor,
no ceiling, no wall to hold her anymore.
Her house has opened like petals and dissolved.
At the moment the cities below her
are being emptied of Jews, she falls
burning in the cool air. Her parachute unfurls.
Taking to the current,
she floats on the rushing silver light,
the airstream, home.

Mark Nepo

Hill Where the Lord Hides

In the summer of '41,
the same summer Ted Williams
hit 406, the city of Kovno
in Lithuania was being liquidated
by Germans whose fingers,
sore from firing, twitched.
The same summer
Joe DiMaggio hit safely
in fifty-six games, a notice
was posted in the ghetto
saying there was work
for educated Jews.

Hundreds assembled —
musicians, scholars, rabbis,
elders, architects, writers,
lawyers, engineers, doctors —
and on August 18, while Boston
played New York in a doubleheader,
the educated of Kovno crowded the gate
waiting for work, and as Ted
doubled off the right field wall,
a grey truck pulled up
and a squad of expressionless
Germans shot them all.

I don't know what to do with this.
I don't raise it to say
we shouldn't play ball.
But what can we do with
this kind of cruelty?

My grandmother's sister
and her husband and son
died in Treblinka. My grandmother
sent them steamship tickets in 1933,
and they sent them back.

Hitting, sending, giving back,
waiting for work — how do we
keep alive what is alive?

Does tenderness matter
when a throat is cut?

They say a great hitter's hands
pulse in the night and that
survivors hear shots forever.

But how do we find, tame, release
these things in ourselves? What
enabled Commandant Jäger
to kill so many and still
dab the corner of his mouth
with linen after dinner,
and what made Dr. Elkes
cough his heart into prayer
while starving in Dachau?

The whole world lives in each of us.
Where the Dachau? Where the sun?
How do we breathe in a sky
that has accepted it all?

I Wake from a Dream of Killing Hitler

I.

I have no numbers on my forearm.
I have only watched Grandma
with her thick tongue
sob in her Brooklyn apartment
while staring off.

I have watched her whisper
to her older brother, Louis,
butted off into a boxcar
no time for a wave or even a glance
just butt, butt, hop
the heavy door sliding
the padlocks fastened.

I only know of Grandma's
sister, Rifkah, who sent
back the steamship tickets
in 1933 because
Rumania was where she was born.
I only know of Grandma
ending the story there
sitting quietly
rocking inside
a sad flutter in her lip
mezuzah in her fallen hand.

I've thought too much.

II.

There can be no revenge
only relief
from a tension wound
across an era;
a tension strung
like an imperceptible copper leash
through the corner of every Jewish soul.

Who can say Kaddish for six million
without ever mentioning the dead?
Yahrzeit marks every calendar I know,
anniversaries of death outnumber the constellations,
the very planet marred
by a continent of scars
and only if the tissue
of every conscience
is seared;
only if for a century
we rub our lids with light;
only then might we not bleed in thought.

The sacred veils
behind which we walk this earth
are irretrievable.
Some gashes breach like canyons.

All my fathers' hands are broken
old prayers like knuckles broken
old prayers like bone resin.

Amos Neufeld

In the Heaven of Night

Chagall's villages float across the room,
curl into yesterday's clouds
and join the world destroyed
floating in the heaven of night.

The displaced figures and the silence of fiddles
join orphans and angels and sparks belched into the sky,
join a generation of capsized hearts, upturned towns
and inverted hopes, and mix with remnants
of memory, clouds and a sea breeze.
And all, all are rejoined
as dust and smoke
whirling silent in the heaven of night.

And we, the orphaned remnant, abandoned
to chambers of air, leaking memory,
lonely, beyond the frame of night still burning,
exiled to towns beyond our home,
beyond the capsized ghetto and shtetl uprooted,
we, who like a generation of smoke
have risen out of night's chamber furnace,
brother and sister to mounds
of heaving grass, tree and stone,
children of dust and stars, cannot believe
that we are part of this underworld,
this earth that would not have us,
that drove us out in chains of smoke,
and not part of the world destroyed,
that floats across the room
and curls in the heaven of night.

A Shade of Night

I am a shade,
a remnant,
here to recall
not explain.

[stanza continues]

The light is cast on others,
those responsible
for the darkness
and the pain
of the shadows
I try to recall.

I am a shade
cast
by the lost light
of my family,
a son
of ashes and memory
risen to fall
on the side of pain
and innocence;
not to forgive or forget
those
who created
the darkness and pain
in their image
over the mass graves
and under
the indifferent
silence:
only a shade,
the lost light
of that other world,
a blade of sadness,
fallen
on the side of the living.

When Israel Went Forth

(Psalm 114: *"When Israel went forth from Egypt")*

When Israel went forth
as smoke from Auschwitz,
when we were set free as ashes
from our bodies,
when we leapt up with the sparks,
the earth was sealed
and filled with gas.
Our pain was unnamable.
Death was our guardian.

When the red sea of our blood
flooded the earth
we did not have time to build an ark.

[stanza continues]

A rainbow did not vault the heavens
promising to shield us from harm.
That flood never receded.
The swelling sea never parted for us.

We took flight
on the wings of doves,
escaped through the chimneys
on ashes and sparks
and drifted on fugitive clouds of smoke
toward the heavens
where we settled on stars.

(More brilliant than the stars,
our light now fills the heavens.)

When Israel went forth
as smoke from Auschwitz,
when our life-breath was taken
in the fathomless silence of screams,
when we were drowned in a sea of gas,
darkness flooded the heavens and the earth.

When the earth trembled,
when our world vanished
as though it had never been,
when our nakedness
called out of the whirlwind,
Nothing liberated us.

Miriam Offenberg

Reforger

(REturn of FORces to GERmany — a U.S. military exercise)

I don't want to go
To streets that echo with forty-year-old cries
That went unheeded then
And go unheeded now,
Because who hears ghosts
But me?

I don't want to walk
On ground spongy with soaked up blood
Of my aunts and uncles and cousins.
There's no forgetting.

I can't eat the food
Heavy with pompous pride
Of a "new rebuilt Germany."
Nothing is new or rebuilt for me.
I still see the starved bodies
When I look at my full plate.

And how sleep at night
In a room too oven hot
Or too Black Forest cold.
I hear too many screams
And what others call a backfire
Sounds to me like gunshots.

Where can I hide
From memories of the tribe?
Why *should* I hide?
Let *them* hide
In shame.

Must I play hypocrite
And smile politely
As my hand is gripped
By a sixty-year-old solid citizen
Who once wore a black shirt
He's now conveniently forgot?

Must I greet him
On behalf of the United States government,
When I want to bury him
On behalf of the Holocaust?

I don't want to go
And dig up memories I can't escape —
Aunt Helen's arm with the blue numbers
And the stories she never told
About her sister
Whose shower was cyanide.

I don't want to go.
It's bad enough to be here
And say *yizkor*
And cry tears that don't bring back the dead.

I don't want to be there
Walking the streets with them
Feeling their murder
Sharing their agony
Unable to lay their ghosts
Or give them peace.

I don’t want to go
Feeling their helplessness
Feeling the guiltiness
Of my being alive.

Lois E. Olena

The Archivist

Note by note
        I type the history
of the victims of the
        Third Reich.
Misery
        plays out through my soft,
safe digits;
        haunting violin tones
fall away as the next song begins.
        Slowly,
sparingly,
        luscious chords
rock me, caress me, sway me
        side to side
like a cattle car fading into the distance.
        What is this caught in my throat?
Turnips?
        Raw potatoes?
Black bread?
        No matter . . .
move on; they’re waiting.
        Hurry! Finish!
Pay your bills.
        Feed your face.
Play your PC piano
        until weariness from the death march
lays you gently down in the snow
        for your afternoon nap
and you dream
        that the knock on your door
is the UPS man
        come to take you away.

Homeland

It was Christmas Eve
and there was no room in the inn,
the Oświęcim inn,
so the Arrow Cross
took the children,
barefooted
and in their nighties,
out to the Danube
and filled their little bellies
not with bread
but bullets,
flipping them
into the icy river.

It was the Red Danube
that night,
choking on the blood
of orphan Jews
who floated downstream
on their tour of Europe
until they washed up
on the shores of Eretz Yisroel
and came back to life,
their little blue-and-white
bodies
raised high,
flapping in the wind.

Jacqueline Osherow

Ponar

In the world to come, the forests won't have secrets.
Leaves will fall on soil made of leaves,
Stems, mud, sand, the usual substances
And everything that happens will be heard for miles:
Leaves rattling, trees falling, gunshots.
Only there will be no gunshots.
We are talking about the world to come.

And the people in Ponar will brush off the dirt
And return to the twenty-seven libraries
And sixty study halls of the Vilna synagogue

[stanza continues]

To run the gamut in their youth organizations
From right-wing Zionism to left-wing Zionism
And mimeograph avant-garde poetic tracts
On the beauty of the aspens at Ponar.

Mostly, they'll learn Mishnah and Gemara
At the oversubscribed lectures of Rabbi Akivah,
Who, though he was slaughtered like a beast
In the marketplace, according to the Midrash,
Was not hindered in the world to come
From astounding even Moses with his insights.

Not just the rabbis and the rich will study,
But butchers, tailors, shoemakers, musicians;
The air itself, weighted down with ash,
Will rifle through the aspens' skittish pages
For commentaries on the sacred texts
Derived from half-revealed illuminations
Lost before they could be copied down

Along with murals, stories, recipes,
Chemical formulae, dress patterns,
Melodramas, new prime numbers, poems
Crowded together in the rare, dark soil
That polishes the aspens' tarnished silver
To prepare a setting for the alef-bet

Or perhaps to make each leaf a tiny mirror
To shine, in miniature, an unclaimed face
Dreaming calmly of the world to come
Until it fills with gold and falls again —
This time gently — to its waiting place
And rests its secrets on the cluttered earth
Shaded by the forest at Ponar.

Villanelle from a Sentence in a Poet's Brief Biography

In '42 he was conscripted to work on trains.
An odd thing to mention in a poet's biography.
In *'42*? In Czechoslovakia? Trains?

I'm trying to figure out what this entry means,
If he sees himself as victimized or guilty.
In '42 he was conscripted to work on trains.

When Dutch workers wouldn't work *their* trains,
They found out that *work makes you free*.
In *'42*, in Czechoslovakia, trains

Weren't that busy. They didn't start the deportations
In earnest until 1943.
In '42 he was conscripted to work on trains.

But the next line says *after the war*, which means
That he was still at it in '43,
'44, '45. . . . In Czechoslovakia, trains

(What did he do? Run switches? Check the lines?)
Were as instrumental, let's face it, as Zyklon B.
In '42 he was conscripted to work on trains.
In '42. In Czechoslovakia. Trains.

Alicia Ostriker

The Eighth and Thirteenth

The eighth of Shostakovich,
Music about the worst
Horror history offers,
They played on public radio
Again last night. In solitude
I sipped my wine, I drank
That somber symphony
To the vile lees. The composer
Draws out the minor thirds, the brass
Tumbles overhead like virgin logs
Felled from their forest, washing downriver
And the rivermen at song. Like ravens
Who know when meat is in the offing,
Oboes form a ring. An avalanche
Of iron violins. At Leningrad
During the years of siege
Between bombardment, hunger,
And three subfreezing winters,
Three million dead were born
Out of Christ's bloody side. Like icy
Fetuses. For months
One could not bury them, the earth
And they alike were adamant.
The dead were stacked like sticks until May's mud
When, of course, there was pestilence.
But the music continues. It has no other choice.
Peer in as far as you like, it stays
Exactly as bleak as now. The composer

[stanza continues]

Opens his notebook. *Tyrants like to present themselves as patrons of the arts. That's a well known fact. But tyrants* understand nothing about art. Why? because tyranny is a *perversion and a tyrant is a pervert. He is attracted by the chance to crush people, to mock them, stepping over corpses . . . And so, having satisfied his perverted desires, the man becomes a leader, and now the perversions continue because power has to be defended against madmen like yourself. For even if there are no such enemies, you have to invent them, because otherwise you can't flex your muscles completely, you can't oppress the people completely, making the blood spurt. And without that, what pleasure is there in power?* The composer
Looks out the door of his dacha, it's April,
He watches farm children at play,
He forgets nothing. For the thirteenth —
I slip its cassette into my car
Radio . . . They made Kiev's Jews undress
After a march to the suburb,
Shot the hesitant quickly,
Battered some of the lame,
And screamed at everyone.
Valises were taken, would
Not be needed, packed
So abruptly, tied with such
Frayed rope. Soldiers next
Killed a few more. The living ones,
Penises of the men like string,
Breasts of the women bobbling
As at athletics, were told to run
Through a copse, to where
Wet with saliva
The ravine opened her mouth.
Marksmen shot the remainder
Then, there, by the tens of thousands,
Cleverly, so that bodies toppled
In without lugging. An officer
Strode upon the dead,
Shot what stirred.
How it would feel, such uneasy
footing, even wearing boots
that caressed one's calves, leather
and lambswool, the soles thick rubber —
Such the music's patient inquiry.
What then is the essence of reality?
of the good? The mind's fuse sputters,
The heart aborts, it smells like wet ashes,
The hands lift to cover their eyes,
Only the music continues. He scribbles

[stanza continues]

For the first movement,
A full chorus.
The immediate reverse of Beethoven.
An axe between the shoulder blades
Of Herr Wagner. *People knew about Babi Yar*
before Yevtushenko's poem, but they were silent. And when
they read the poem, the silence was broken. Art destroys
silence. I know that many will not agree with me, and will
point out other, more noble aims of art. They'll talk about beauty,
grace, and other high qualities. But you won't catch
me with that bait. I'm like Sobakevich in Dead Souls*: you can*
sugarcoat a toad and I still won't put it in my mouth.

Most of my symphonies are tombstones, said Shostakovich.

All poets are Jews, said Tsvetaeva.

The words *never again*
Clashing against the words
Again and again —
That music.

Poem Beginning with a Line by Fitzgerald/Hemingway

The very rich are different from us, they
Have more money, fewer scruples. The very

Attractive have more lovers, the very sensitive
Go mad more easily, and the very brave

Distress a coward like myself, so listen
Scott, listen Ernest, and you also can

Listen, Walt Whitman. I understand the large
Language of rhetoricians, but not the large

Hearts of the heroes. I am reading up.
I want someone to tell me what solvent saves

Their cardiac chambers from sediment, what is
The shovel that cuts the sluice

Straight from the obvious mottoes, such as *Love*
Your neighbor as yourself, or *I am human, therefore*

Nothing human is alien, to the physical arm
In the immaculate ambassadorial shirtsleeves

— We are in Budapest, '44 — that waves
Off the muddy Gestapo in the railroad yard

With an imperious, an impatient flourish,
And is handing Swedish passports to anonymous

Yellow-starred arms reaching from the very boxcars
That are packed and ready to glide with a shrill

Whistle and grate on steel, out of the town,
Like God's biceps and triceps gesturing

Across the void to Adam: Live. In Cracow
A drinking, wenching German businessman

Bribes and cajoles, laughs and negotiates
Over the workers, spends several times a fortune,

Saves a thousand Jews or so, including one
He wins at a card game and sets to work

In his kitchenware factory. A summer twilight
Soaks a plateau in southern France, the mountains

Mildly visible, and beyond them Switzerland,
As the policeman climbs from the khaki bus

To Le Chambon square, where the tall pastor
Refuses to give names of refugees;

Meanwhile young men slip through the plotted streets,
Fan out to the farms — it is '42 —

So that the houses empty and the cool woods fill
With Jews and their false papers, so that the morning

Search finds no soul to arrest. It happens
Over and over, but how? The handsome Swede

Was rich, was bored, one might have said. The pastor
Had his habit of hugging and kissing, and was good

At organizing peasants, intellectuals
And bible students. The profiteer intended

To amass wealth. He did, lived steep, and ended
Penniless, though the day the war ended,

The day they heard, over the whistling wireless,
The distant voice of Churchill barking victory

As the Russians advanced, his *Schindlerjuden*
Still in the plant, still safe, as he moved to flee,

Made him a small present. Jerets provided
His mouth's gold bridgework, Licht melted it down,

Engraved the circle of the ring with what
One reads in Talmud: *Who saves a single life,*

It is as if he saved the world; and Schindler
The German took it; he wears it in his grave;

I am reading up on this. I did not know
Life had undone so many deaths. *Now go*

And do likewise snaps every repercussion
Of my embarrassed heart, which is like a child

Alone in a classroom full of strangers, thinking
She would like to run away. Let me repeat,

Though I do not forget ovens or guns,
Their names: Raoul Wallenberg, Oskar Schindler,

André Trocmé. Europe was full of others
As empty space is full of burning suns;

Not equally massive or luminous,
Creating heat, nevertheless, and light,

Creating what we may plausibly write
Up as the sky, a that-without-which-nothing;

We cannot guess how many, only that they
Were subject to arrest each bloody day

And managed. Maybe it's like the muse, incalculable,
What you can pray in private for. Or a man

You distantly adore, who may someday love you
In the very cave of loneliness. We are afraid —

Yet as no pregnant woman knows beforehand
If she will go through labor strong, undrugged,

Unscreaming, and no shivering soldier knows
During pre-combat terror who will retreat,

Who stand and fight, so we cannot predict
Who among us will risk the fat that clings

Sweetly to our own bones —
None sweeter, Whitman promises —

Our life, to save doomed lives, and none of us
Can know before the very day arrives.

Christina Pacosz

Auschwitz: Oświęcim

Los Nasz Dla Was Przestroga
(Let Our Fate Be Your Warning)
— Majdanek Monument

We are leaving
flowers like messages:

what else to do
except fall down
with weeping
into a grieving
that will never
be done.

And how to live
in the world then?

So it is calendula
for memory here
with the children's
clothing they never
outgrew.

And here before
hundreds of neatly
lettered suitcases
with addresses from
every country in Europe
never claimed
by their owners
we leave
our innocence:
a single white daisy.

We should haul
larkspur by
the truckload
and fill every
exhibit room
from floor to ceiling
with levity
with light.

We must airdrop
hyacinth, purple
sorrow raining down
until this place
with the awful name
is smothered in
fragrance.

We should be weaving
miles of rosemary garlands
for remembrance
and planting olive trees
for peace.

The lilac leaves
are waving, try
to imagine
them blooming.

Poplar trees
are voices
in the wind:

Remember the ash
how it sifts down
to desks where bureaucrats
are stamping papers.

Linda Pastan

Landscape near Dachau

Adolf Hölzel, circa 1900

This is the innocence of blue —
pale blue sky, a blue river,
and of white —
snow unsullied yet
by human history.
See the farmhouses:
their humble roofs,
their chimneys.
The only shadows
are the shadows
of trees, wavering
on the pastel water.

Rachel (ra'chal), a Ewe

We named you
for the sake
of the syllables
and for the small boat
that followed the Pequod,
gathering lost children
of the sea.

We named you
for the dark-eyed girl
who waited at the well
while her lover
worked seven years
and again
seven.

We named you
for the small daughters
of the Holocaust
who followed their six-pointed stars
to death
and were all of them
known as
Rachel.

Response

A ban on the following subject matter:
the Holocaust, grandparents, Friday night
candle lighting . . . Jerusalem at dusk.
— From the poetry editor of *Response*

It is not dusk
in Jerusalem
it is simply morning

and the grandparents have disappeared
into the Holocaust
taking their sabbath candles with them.

Light your poems, hurry.
Already the sun is leaning
towards the west

though the grandparents and candles
have long since burned down
to stubs.

Mark Pawlak

Like Butterflies

After Charles Reznikoff; for Donna Brook

The Auschwitz “Angel of Death,” Josef Mengele,
would meet the trains delivering Jews to the camp
and select out from those destined for the gas
healthy pairs of twins. These he kept alive
in crowded cages for genetic experiments
to aid him in building a master race.

He gave them chemical injections
which made many nauseous and faint, and a few
became numb when the needles were put into their spines.
Some were given transfusions of blood
from one twin to another,
or he removed parts of their sexual organs;
yet others he sterilized by radiation.

He was especially interested in the colors of eyes.
If he noticed that twins' eyes were brown
but their mother's eyes were blue,
he might keep her alive in the cage with her children.
He would try to change their eye color
with injections of dye or with drops administered daily
that burned the eyes like acid,
and he would take blood samples from these subjects
several times each day.

One twin said she was stupefied
when ushered into Mengele's private laboratory.
There she saw an entire wall of eyes looking back at her,
human eyes of every color
mounted on the wall like butterflies.

Edmund Pennant

Thoughts Under the Giant Sequoia

(Yosemite National Park)

A shrub of tourists
gathers under “General Grant”
for the ranger's lecture. This patriarch
is at least two dozen centuries old,

[stanza continues]

a loner in a corner of the grove.
The general has heard the talk before.

It will not be about death's durance
inherent in the living, a subject
he could respect. It will not be
about strategies of attrition or political
whims of lightning lopping giants as if
they were dwarf skirmishers on the treeline.

The ranger — a romantic — commends us
to the lordly scene, citing
"silence of cathedrals"
which phrase we noted that morning
in the free brochure, pages made
from pulp of little brothers.

Thence to the usual chronicles building out
from natal core to delicate cambium:
William the Conqueror here, Charlemagne
and Columbus there, each to his ring concentric.
No mention, though, of the Massacre at York
of the Jews, while the tree was sleeping.

Francis Parkman and Emanuel Ringelblum:
there's a pair who took their scholarship al fresco.
One, pain-wracked on horseback, dared Indians
and forests, recapturing Pontiac's despair. The other,
historian of the Warsaw Ghetto, buried his diaries
in iron boxes before they took him in a bunker.

In what monstrosity of treetrunk, I wonder,
are all those martyrs marked, who died for
the Sanctification of the Name, unnamed?
Some day I'll come back alone and listen,
and look for a tree slightly older than Moses,
flaunting incredible veridians at the crown.

Tonight at Yosemite, though, I'll have to bushwhack
through dreams of the lovely greenbaums I have known
who rest securely under stone; and greenblatts
who huddled bleak by the grave they dug, waiting
for the guns; and greenwalds resting their tanks
in a grove of tamarisks near Sharm el-Sheik.

Yom Hazikaron

Day of Remembrance
for Israel's Fallen Soldiers

1

Because every monstrosity
is diminished by the next
which is the pathos of monuments

you lay a pebble
on top of the gravestone
before turning your back,

to tell the next visitor
you were there, to touch
the granite, to hear

the unspeakable, to leave
a forgotten nickname
inside a pebble.

2

The priests had to be fastidious
because the work of corrosion
goes on, all the washing of bodies
and donning of holy linens
was a war against corrosion.

And the blood and memory of blood
wash away best when done the same day.

Then the dirges and the elegies
are heard, and then they are drowned
by the sounds of children at play,
and the bleating of Azazel
by the silence of the desert.

3

Soldiers in the streets of Jerusalem
do not strut like Prussian officers;
you would have to look long
to find one whose body announces
he loves being a soldier.

They have the manner of quiet,
cool irregulars who would walk
away from camp at the drop of a hat,
like the farmer-fighters
of Washington's army;
and who could acquit themselves
well, under fire, for liberty.
They do not strut, neither do they slouch
like peddlars in the old ghettos
leaning against the pack. And yet,
if you look carefully, you will find
a posture inherent in the weight-bearing
bones, the knees and the hips,
bespeaking a pack, a burden
not easy to carry with grace.

It is the burden of the Law
and the burden of memories
become immemorial, that lie heavy
even on the very young,
those too young to remember.

In the pomp and necessary ceremonials
of Yom Hazikaron, they march, they turn,
they blow the trumpets, they stare
straight ahead, trying to see
the faces of parents who are mourners.

4

In one lifetime we have cringed
and we have crowed. Now, once again,
the surrounding, the moving in.
On the day of orations, between
the orations, is a silence
heavier than we have known before.

What was it the orators said? "Tried by fire."
"Stronger by loss." "Made brave by desperation."
The words disappear with the winds on Mount Herzl.

Not all the iron boxes buried in the ghetto
have been recovered. One of them has the history
that will never be known. The history eludes us.

5

In the struggle not to forget,
we are forgetting what it is
we are struggling to remember,

the thing which is like a stone
covered with wet slime
which must be held with a limber
grip or be lost forever.

The stone wants to sink
to the seabottom and burrow
deep in primordial silt

because it is not a stone
but an eye that remembers
everything that happened
which we want to forget.

Louis Phillips

Perhaps You Wish to Learn Another Language

Sometime in the late 20th century,
While you watch blue flowers tattoo a field,
An acquaintance will mention, offhand,
Trying to make it seem casual,
Auschwitz or Belsen & so many dead Jews.
Of course, the conversation must change.
The four-dimensioned world rattles.
"Yes, yes, it was all on television,
The cyanide that blossomed into bones." &
So you sigh & drink the final cup of coffee,
Lukewarm, sugared, black,
Like breathing that refuses to be stilled.
Perhaps you wish to learn another language?
A yellow star rises into our sky,
But there is no shining from it.

Words over the Entranceway to Hell

Halfway through my life, Dante returned to confess:
Constructing Hell he had made less,
Not more, of suffering. Hell could not hold the throng
Of dead brought to him via the 20th century. Among
The dead, too many Jews & innocents.
Words over Hell's entrance were clearly wrong,
So wrong in fact he took a stone

[stanza continues]

As large as the human heart, then — one by one —
Reduced each word to dust:
Abandon All Hope Ye Who Enter Here.
Upon new rock, with a chisel, he would try
The language of the times: ARBEIT MACHT FREI.
Then was done & waved good-bye.

Marge Piercy

Black Mountain

On Montagne Noire creeping everywhere under the beech trees
were immense black slugs the size and pattern
of blown truck tires exploded by the superhighway.
Diamonds patterned their glossy and glittering backs.

As we watched, leaves, whole flowers disappeared in three bites.
Such avidity rebuked our stomachs skittish with alien
water and strange food. In patches of sunlight filtered
down, the slugs shone like wet black glass.

Battlefields are like any other fields; a forest
where men and women fought tanks with Sten guns
houses as many owl and rabbit and deer as the next hill
where nothing's happened since the Romans passed by.

Yet I have come without hesitation through the maze
of lumbering roads to this spot where the small marker
tells us we have reached a destination. To die here
under hemlock's dark drooping boughs, better I think

than shoved into the showers of gas to croak like roaches
too packed in to flail in the intense slow pain
as the minutes like lava cooling petrified the jammed
bodies into living rock, basalt pillars whose fingers

gouged grooves in cement. Yes, better to drop in the high
clear air and let your blood soak into the rich leaf mold.
Better to get off one good shot. Better to remember trains
derailed, turntables wrecked with plastique, raids

on the munitions dump. Better to die with a gun
in your hand you chose to pick up and had time to shoot.
Dying you pass out of choice. The others come, put up
a monument decorated with crosses, no Mogen Davids.

I come avid and omnivorous as the shining slugs.
I have eaten your history and made it myth;
among the tall trees of your pain my characters walk.
A saw whines in the valley. I say kaddish for you.

Blessed only is the act. The act of defiance,
the act of justice that fills the mouth with blood.
Blessed only is the act of survival that saves the blood.
Blessed is the act of art that paints the blood

redder than real and quicker, that restores
the fallen tree to its height and birds. Memory
is the simplest form of prayer. Today you glow
like warm precious lumps of amber in my mind.

Growing Up Haunted

When I enter through the hatch of memory
those claustrophobic chambers,
my adolescence in the booming fifties
of General Eisenhower, General Foods
and General Motors, I see our dreams:
obsolescent mannequins in Dior frocks
armored, prefabricated bodies;
and I see our nightmares, powerful
as a wine red sky and wall of fire.

Fear was the underside of every leaf
we turned, the knowledge that our
cousins, our other selves, had been
starved and butchered to ghosts.
The question every smoggy morning
presented like a covered dish:
why are you living and all those
mirror selves, sisters, gone
into smoke like stolen cigarettes?

I remember my grandmother's cry
when she learned the death of all she
remembered, girls she bathed with,
young men with whom she shyly
flirted, wooden shul where
her father rocked and prayed,
red haired aunt plucking the
balalaika, world of sun and snow
turned to shadows on a yellow page.

Assume no future you may not have
to fight for, to die for, muttered
ghosts gathered on the foot
of my bed each night. What you
carry in your blood is us,
the books we did not write,
music we could not make, a world
gone from gristle to smoke, only
as real now as words can make it.

The Housing Project at Drancy

Trains without signs flee through Paris.
Wrong trains. The wrong station.
The world as microwave oven, burning from within.
We arrive. Drancy looks like Inkster,
Gary, the farther reaches of Newark.

In the station they won't give directions.
C'est pas notre affaire. We don't deal with that.
Outside five buses limp in five directions
into the hot plain drugged with exhaust.
Nobody ever heard of the camp. They turn away.

Out on the bridge, over marshaling yards:
Here Jews were stuffed into cars nailed shut.
Here children too young to know their names
were counted like so many shoes
as they begged the French police hemming them in,

Take me to the bathroom, please, please,
before I wet myself. Mother, I have been so good,
and it is so very dark. Dear concierge,
I am writing to you as everyone else
is dead now and they are taking me away.

Yes, to the land children named Pitchepois,
giant's skull land grimmer than Hansel came to.
On the bridge I saw an old bald workman
staring down and I told myself desperately,
He is a communist and will answer me.

I asked him where the camp was, now a housing
project. He asked, Why do you want to know?
I had that one ready. No talk of novels, research.
My aunt was there. Oh, in that case,
he pointed to distant towers. You want that bus.

Where we descended the bus, Never heard of it.
Eyes that won't look. Then a woman asked that
same question, Why do you want to know?
A housing project crammed with mothers.
The guard towers are torn down and lindens grow.

In flats now with heat and plumbing, not eighty
but one family lives. Pain still rises,
the groaning machinery deep underfoot.
Crimes ignored sink into the soil like PCBs
and enter the bones of children.

Heidemarie Pilc

Somewhere in Poland . . . Survivor's Lament

Lost in an alien forest
I pray at my people's tomb.
Lazy beams of sunlight
drift through autumn leaves,
vanish beneath darkening skies.

Murdered by thugs in uniform
half a century ago,
my parents and siblings reappear
in millions of heartaches,

their names chiselled
into a memorial stone —
towering monument
to a nation's shame.

I weep at my loved ones' grave,
want them as desperately
as the dark beneath the ground
wants light, want to dig
under the stone,

to stir their ashes alive,
to hear the earth — so still
these fifty-five years — turn
their cries to shouts of hallelujah.

I want you back, brothers
and sisters; mother and father,
I want to be your child again.

Long delivered from your tormentors,
one with the ancient walls and dust
of shtetl streets, you lie in whispers
of Kaddish and candle light.

William Pillin

Farewell to Europe

We, the captives of a thousand skies,
sang the airs of many peoples,
tango, waltz and leaping czardash;

but the waltz stumbles, the oboe
is poised on the point of a scream.

We whispered madrigals of woe
in sewers and cellars.
We learned sparrow wit, hangman humor,
at the bottom of scaffolds,
at the gates of stone chimneys.

Europe, the odor of your guilt
lingers in our nostrils.
You are a perspective of walls
diminishing in cold moonlight.

Vanish from our songs!

*

Will your pianos haunt us to the end?
The stars in your snows, O steppes?
the sunlight bleeding gold
on the rim of a snow-foaming mountain?

Façade of roses and wings,
shall we cloak our memories in blue
because your gardens sang to the sun?

The kaftaned companions of the Presence
are swept from the streets of your cities.
Our migrants kiss a new wind
scented with ancient cedars.

Farewell, the Vienna woods are no longer calling,
or the grimacing spires of Cologne,
or your gleaming cupolas, Kiev.

Your temples are Gothic stalactites,
frozen tears of eternity;
your gardens are lavender clouds;
your streetlamps shimmering buoys
of musical boulevards.

But you were never our motherland.
We were born
not on the Rhine or the Vistula
but in Abraham's tent
on a journey from Ur to Judea.

This you never ceased to remind us;
that we were alien,
remote from you, the light of a dead star
that faintly lingers upon this planet.

*

We are leaving. We take little with us;
some music, a few poems.

It is well that we stand under new arches
bequeathing to our children
our praises, our celebrations.

Our Einstein will toughen the mental sinews
　　of other continents.
Our Freud will plumb the dark soul of Asia.
Our Marx will rally the cadres of jungles
　　and savannahs.

*

We are leaving. No longer will you have to cross
　　yourself, people with pitchforks and cudgels,
　　as our huddled remnants trudge over your meadows.

O mother of white nights, after a millennium on
　　your steppes your hostages are pleading: let
　　us depart!

We are leaving our ancestral tombs, our shrines,
　　our wealth endlessly plundered by the card-
　　playing nobles.

We are leaving you forever, belching Siegfried,
　　Vladimir red-eyed from distilled potatoes!

*

Europe, you realm of carnivorous blonds!
Your grand canals are clogged by chemical silt.
The sculptures of your saints are eroded by
pigeon droppings.
Smokestacks spew their spittle on the
vineyards of Chateau de Rothschild.

Elegant bushmen celebrate your Requiem Mass
with tom-toms and banjos.

Even as you revel in your utopia of pig-fat,
blood-sausage and Pilsen
you look nervously over your shoulder
at the lean wolves of the east.

They will strip your flesh leaving
the bare bones of cathedrals.
What the wolves will not eat —
monuments, fountains, castles —
will be shipped stone by antique stone
to the Disneylands of America.

*

Basta! Genug! Assez! Dostatochno!

Farewell, blue-eyed maiden. You need no
longer exclaim on seeing the mark of our
ancient covenant: "You cheated me! You
never told me!"

Farewell, priests whose blood mysteries at Lent
goaded the tavern heroes to wield their
axes among us.

Zbignew, whom will your children curse?
Zoltan, astride a stallion, at whom will you
lash out galloping by?

You have no one to bludgeon but each other!

Miserere

I will not endow you with a false glow
ghetto
or say that only poets and seers
died in your ashes.
Many mourn the scholars and dreamers,
the beautiful innocent talented victims.

[stanza continues]

I will spare my tears for the
loudmouthed unhappy conniving
jews
the usurious lenders,

tuberculous hunchbacked
scum of the ghettos (the sweepings of Europe).
For them I will weep,
                    for the whores
pale in doorways, for the spiderous tradesmen
with their false measures
                    and for all the grey sparrows
hopping about the winters of Poland
                    the grief of whose eyes
went up in thin smoke like a final prayer.
For them I will weep, I want them returned,
the dwellers of dives, brothels and taverns.
I want them
back as they were, piteous, ignoble,
instead of this white ash
that like a winding sheet settles on shivering Europe.

A Poem for Anton Schmidt

*A German army sergeant, executed
in March 1942 for supplying the Jewish
underground with forged credentials
and military vehicles*

I have properly spoken
hymns for the dead, have planted
white roses in the high air.

And because my pen is a leech
to suck out blood's poison
I had a need to write

of death's clerks and doctors;
but my pen dissolved
in an inkwell of acid

and my paper, litmus of shame,
crumbled to ashes.
Anton Schmidt, I thank you

for breaking the spell that numbed
the singing mouth. I need not write
of the mad and the murderous.

That a vile camaraderie
caused streets and meadows to weep
no longer surprises us;

but a lone soldier's
shining treason
is a cause for holy attention.

I thank you that no poison
is burning my veins
but a wine of praise

for a living man
among clockwork robots
and malevolent puppets.

The Ascensions

You, Marc Chagall, should be able to tell us
what was cremated in Thor's ovens,
you who were always painting ascensions.

The ascension of priestly violinists,
the ascension of white-gowned brides,
the ascension of purple donkeys,
of lovers, of bouquets, of golden cockerels,
ascension into the clair-de-lune.

O this soaring
out of shanties and cellars!
the folk spirit ascending
through enchanted alphabets,
through magical numbers,
to a wandering in the bluest realm.

The ascension
(from sewers, dives, back-alleys)
of folk-songs to the new moon,
to the feast of lights,
to the silences of Friday evening . . .

. . . and suddenly
in the quietude of steppes
a thin column of smoke ascending
and after that
no more ascensions.

*

No more ascensions!

Only stone chimneys
heavily clinging
to the earth of Poland.
Not even a marker saying:
here the kikes
en masse ascended.

John C. Pine

The Survivor

After Seeing "Kitty Hart: Return to Auschwitz" on Public TV

She learned early that in order to survive
She would have to make herself
As small as possible and hide
Among the others, even if this meant
Concealing herself behind a corpse.
She learned also to appropriate
From the dead their bread
Ration and articles of clothing.
The sheer bureaucratic
Size and impersonality of the death camp
Worked to her advantage.
She survived also on animal instinct
And cunning. She knew that her elders
Thought too much about their situation.
Their fate could be read in the dazed
And vacant look on their faces.
After the inevitable selection they became
Spectral voices, disembodied hands
Between the iron bars of high windows.
Sometimes on warm spring days
When the foliage was beginning to turn green
And wildflowers were blooming in the woods,
She would sun herself within sight of the crematories
And observe the smoke rising from the chimneys,
And smell the stench of burning flesh
Which permeated the entire camp.
Almost thirty-five years later she returned
To Auschwitz-Birkenau with her son
From her home in Birmingham, England.
There was grass where before there had been only mud.

[stanza continues]

Some of the buildings had been torn down,
And the emptiness all round them
Was strange and unsettling. Nevertheless,
It soon came back to her. Unhesitatingly
She walked through the thick underbrush
To the pits which had been hastily dug
When the crematories could no longer
Dispose of people fast enough.
Many of those selected for extermination
Had been burned in these open pits —
Some of them while still alive.
Now poking in the ashes with a stick
She came upon a small fragment of bone
Bleached by the heat and cold of thirty-five years,
And gave it to her son as a memento
Of all that she had been witness to
And in memory of all those who nourished
The earth without even a whitish sliver
Of bone to be remembered by.

Karl A. Plank

Ash Wednesday

At Birkenau
the glass-eyed Cyclops
ordered pits to be dug
near Crematorium V.

Then bodies burned
behind a wall of wattle screens.

The Greek Jews could not see
the spring meadow nearby
as they entered the grey mist
with shovels

for the hot ash of kinsmen
rained down on their faces
and into their eyes,
blinding.

O priest!

You smudge my forehead
in Lenten gesture
of mortality,
unknowing.

The ash we bear
is not our own,
but those the flames
made dust.

It is again
the char of kinsmen
that burns and scars
the open face,

that sears now
our darkened cross.

Ginger Porter

I Am Babi Yar

My gold six-pointed star
is underground, bloodstained.
The sides of the pit are steep,
they reach to the
endless expanse of steely-blue sky.

The swastikas are gone —
they were washed away
by the tears of mourning.
The mad Führer is dead,
but his legacy lives;
my brethren all died with him.
I am alone here among ghosts.

Machine-gun fire echoes in my head.
My efforts to climb up are useless.
I feel the greasy dust of the dead around me.
I can taste the blood-soaked earth,
but I cannot feel it.

Here is where I will remain.
I can never die;
my soul cannot be at rest.
I am a memory, a message to posterity,
damned to haunt this pit
in the heart of Russia forever,
a sorrowful spirit,
a testimonial.
I am Babi Yar.

Evelyn Posamentier

Heinz Rosenberg on the Platform

Late at Night

went out again in history
looking for grandfather, asking for
grandmother, really just any clues
at all.
in a footnote i meet
heinz rosenberg of hamburg
who saw grandmother & grandfather
(he said so)
arrive in the minsk ghetto
in december of '41.
this is when i stop the film
say i've had enough, befriend the future:
their grandchildren shimmer at the end
of the century.
i take the footnote north
from vienna with that train to minsk.
heinz rosenberg is on the platform
witnessing.
of the trains that came, he says, that one
was the worst. all elderly, these jews, in shock.
any food brought with them was seized
at the station, eight days in transit.
their faces remember him & visit him
in hollow dreams down the years.
they rely on him, who else but
this heinz rosenberg of hamburg
to tell how he saw us?

Outreach

there is a portrait of heinz rosenberg that hangs
at the holocaust museum website, an identity photo
to match the man i met in a footnote, the boy
from hamburg deported to minsk in '41
just weeks before grandmother & grandfather.
the youngest of three, he could be my uncle.
arriving in minsk, he said, i saw guards
throwing loaves of bread into open cattle cars
full of soviet POWs. as the starving men fought
over the food, german guards shot at them.
i then realized we were never going to return.
you can visit heinz rosenberg by following
the holocaust museum's outreach link.

Arrival

heinz rosenberg was at the platform
when your train pulled in.
meine güte, tell me it isn't true.
finding this out i am learning my name
for the first time.
what is the low moan of one thousand
old jews? in forty below
zero? in a winter
that broke records. in the winter
of my grandparents. let them
have that.
heinz rosenberg on the platform.
this was the train that left vienna
on november 28, 1941.
eight days in transit.
i consider time travel.
want to touch grandmother's
skin, her fine cheek, a face
with a memory of mine &
all future possibility.
i will be with you forever.
promise me you will feel no pain.

Toska

Toska

went out again the other day looking for grandmother
on the internet & found toska feuchtbaum
instead, a seven-year-old girl, whose shy smile
was captured in the photo her father clutched
all those nights of not knowing, on the run.
the smile of surprise, perhaps a birthday party
later that day, not quite yet the end of vienna.
went out again the other day looking
for grandmother on the internet & saw
toska & her mother at the bahnhof
being shipped east to poland, held out till now.
same train as grandmother & grandfather:
the startled testimony of the photos of children
whispering *shoah.*
went out again, grandmother, looking
for you on the internet, & waited patiently
for the images to load on the browser.
this time it is the transit camp itself, typhus & all.
& still there is no word from you.

Toska, Again

this time, toska, i printed your picture off the internet
finding you, as i do, every time i go out looking
for grandmother. toska feuchtbaum, born april 8, 1935
in vienna, austria. that shy smile, fulfilling
the testimony of children's destinies.
when i dare, i insert your image beside one
in my head of grandmother, & both of you
nod to the future.

Toska at the Banhof

peek at sobibór on infoseek
(knock, knock, is grandmother there?)
& find the cybrary at remember.org
all calling, all silent.
the water ripples, the sky shudders in response.
toska at the bahnhof, toska on the page
of children's testimony (click on next ten, always
to the next citation) knock, knock, is
grandmother there? peek at sobibór
on infoseek, deportation statistics & the staccato
list of operation reinhard aktion dates.
toska at the collection point, grandmother
between the pages of a prayerbook
(daughter already escaped with photo)
peek at sobibór on infoseek
(toska & grandmother on the same load)
both last seen at the bahnhof: vienna, may 12, 1942.

Anna Rabinowitz

from **Darkling: A Poem**

Among remains —
　　　　　　the story builds — another and another —

　　　　　　　　　then another —

　　　　　　as if from a safekeeping —

　　　　　　　　　this mute parade of faces —
Tongues frozen in a dead of sepia —

profiles, three-quarters, head-
Ons of unpowderable nose, unshavable chin —

without
Name —
without
Context —

permanently impermanent,

imperfectly true —

this one
Endlessly fixed on possibility, a single ringlet
At her brow:
— *zum Abiken Andanken,*
Ostroleka, 1918
— *remember me forever* —

and this one —
no more than twenty,
perched on a ladder
in an orchard
pretending to pick apples:

— *I give you my photo, remember me* —

now in taffeta,
turning toward the
View:
woods-that-were or may-have-been —
— *life is a battle, so fight to win* —
— *my photo in remembrance* —
— *for the cousin I love*, 1922 —

and another, and another:

Our friend, we give you this photo —

— *remember us forever,* Warsaw, 1932 —
— *remember me* —
— *remember I wished you the best* —
from me, Isaac,
from me, Helena, Regina, Frank,
from me
and me,
Ostroleka, 1936 —
and me . . .

Is it re-entry they are after,
is it markers for their graves,
is it to remind us they burned
with the best possible light,

or is it to urge us to complete them —

"as they were . . . in great strong masses . . .

buttons are lost, but clothing remains;
Clothing is lost but figures remain;
figures are lost, but shadows remain;
shadows are lost but the picture remains,
and that,
night cannot
Efface . . ."

After their fact, after their thought, after their flesh —

Fotografia
Rafael, Lomza — Foto Bekker, Brok —
Cartolina Postale — Postkarte —
Briefkart — Tarjeta Postal —
Carte Postale — Pocztówka —

a little boy in a sailor suit clutches a ball — a young girl
smells a rose —

two women rest heads in their hands,
a third holds a drawstring purse —

a couple
lean against a plant stand,
a child
and a balustrade —

a man in high collar and striped tie —

a woman with blond hair cascading
to her waist —

beside a jagged shore: —

Once I had a love and I was loved —

my mother in a deckchair —

SS Hamburg —

wearing a fur-trimmed coat and a dark cloche
Edged with contrasting trim in a scallop motif —

but I've been left here
Abandoned and alone —

Masha peeking at me between hand-colored fronds
Of a potted palm —

a cottage in a distance of clouds nearing

Naomi in a lace dress — Moishe in a homburg —

Hersh in uniform —

Group photo:
friends — they must be friends —

twenty-four young men and women,
arms entwined —

three rows of eight —

most likely on an outing —
in the mountains —

just having finished
or just before

singing their songs —

from Dislocations

Friday, May 19, International Hotel, Cracow

I have come to visit the family graves
Where they may have been   the places

I nod as he tells me I cannot understand
How does one say *cry* in Yiddish
How does one say *howl*
How does one *know* when one hasn't witnessed
father kill son   son father   for a piece of bread

We tell you with our own eyes
we have seen such things in Auschwitz
that could not happen on this planet

Saturday, May 20, dinner with a tour group from Israel in the hotel restaurant

Survivors read poems discuss the Talmud
sing Polish Hebrew Yiddish

Welcome we are all Jews
Crawl into our eyes
They hoard what we remember

Poland you are the largest graveyard in the world

Under the chestnut trees
Under the oaks
Under the trolley tracks under the unkempt grass
Under the pavement where *Ulica Wotynska*
Turned to powder
Under the monument at *Umschlagplatz*

Where they rounded us up on the corners
where we talked beside the manhole cover
where as children we skittered like frantic mice
in and out of the ghetto to steal
potatoes radishes a few limp carrots

How many of us lifting the steel cap got a bullet
between the eyes in the back of the skull
through the heart scurrying legs wing-light feet
arms of shattered glass splatter of gravel on cobbled streets

One egg two eggs three eggs
pocket full of eggs
mouth full of broken teeth

Sunday, May 21, Auschwitz / Oświęcim

I am voyeur interloper
sculptor
of statistic
collator
of relic

Poland 1939
grandparents seated on a bench
About the rest
a window ajar
leans against the shutter
the sill tilts
a pot of violets oddly bent

[stanza continues]

their feet *out of focus*
breaking into rubble

Hairworks assemblage of matted strands
abhorrent province of haircloth
Wireworks spectacles gnarled
among charred lenses

Crate of gold teeth

Where are the heads
the Polish guide
asks then replies

In Heaven

Where is my grandmother's enamel wash basin
the pitcher for warm milk
where grandpa's *tallis* their names on the rosters
surname given name *Jude* birth date place of birth

We pass farmlands
women rake the grass
dust of green wire
rust on rocking fields
close by the rails

David Ray

Houses

They were beautiful houses, the ones confiscated
by Nazi fiat. Charles Lindbergh was tempted
to accept a Berlin mansion offered, not long after

Kristallnacht, but that would have been another
public relations disaster so Anne talked
him out of it. Lion Feuchtwanger the novelist

lost his home because he wrote a satire unkind
to Hitler. By good fortune he was in the U.S.
when the Gestapo arrived. Compounding

his offense, he wrote a letter to the new owner,
addressing him as *Dear Occupant*, asking if
the lucky fellow was enjoying the amenities,

the library — although he should not be caught
reading novels where they were written.
He asked if the silver carpets had been stained

and if jackboots of the Brownshirts had broken
any tiles. He warned against pipes freezing
in winter and cautioned the occupant not

to risk losing this home, now his by virtue
of laws that transferred title although the Jewish
ex-owner was obliged to go on paying the mortgage.

Even an Aryan, the novelist pointed out,
had better be careful in this new age of terror.
And lastly Feuchtwanger asked about his pets,

the turtles and lizards left behind, and the flower
beds and the rock garden, and he wanted to know
if the servants had screamed when they were shot.

You can tell me all, he said, for writing
is my profession, knowing the truth and telling it
even when it is bitter and hard as hell to bear.

A Photograph from 1935

For Kurt Klein

His parents sit at their kitchen table in Vienna
under a wall clock, its hands at five to twelve,
and when Kurt looks at the yellowed snapshot
he wishes he could go back and halt time itself,
since it galloped on to Auschwitz. He would leave
his father and mother there in their kitchen
with their hands on the table in their last days,
when they still thought of themselves as Germans.
He would leave his mother's hair up in a bun
and his father's mustache black, and he would know
the mustache had not been in honor of the dictator.

Kurt was a boy in knee pants when he saw the first bonfire,
books carried out and hurled into flames, gleeful faces aglow.
Later he saw the first Nazi motorcycle roar down the street,
and he still does not know how he survived to be
an old man in America. It took a number of miracles.
Had he not arrived at the factory just in time to disable
the bomb meant to blow up the young women inside?
Had he not been the first man to renew their faith

[stanza continues]

in humanity? And had he not found his bride there?
And yet it would not be kosher to claim miracles,
for it would not be fair to those who were given none.
He prefers just to say that even from boyhood
he always had a purpose in life.

A Song for Herr Hitler

Where did he kiss them, darling children,
as he held them on his knee, Adolf Hitler —

making his rounds, campaigning,
with a stop here and there while his aides

passed out ice cream and flowers,
flags to wave and bright arm-bands?

He did not say "Suffer the little children
to come unto me," but it was something

like that, as he patted and kissed them
like an uncle or affectionate father

or like Jesus. On the forehead, that's where
he kissed them, the children of Germany,

on their soft Aryan brows, and his fatherly palm
drew them close. And where, you might ask,

did he pat and caress them, the little children
who climbed on his knees or were placed there?

On their shoulders and rumps, on their knees
and their thighs — that's where he patted

and stroked them and caressed them,
on their hair most of all — the little children

of Germany, who were almost all perfect.
And what did he say to them, this master

of words, this leader so loved that he, Der Führer,
could do as he wished with the children,

pat them or poke them or send them on
some distant journey? What did he say

when he pinched their soft rosy cheeks
and their thighs? Not so much, really,

just short words of affection, like the ones
his dogs understood as he patted and petted them

as he did the children of Germany while he gazed
into their eyes, which gazed back, dazed,

often blue, sometimes brown or green
or hazel or sprinkled with stars. And where

you might well ask, did he send them,
the children, who were so plentiful and perfect?

Where did he, Der Führer, father of his Third
Reich, where in the world did he send them?

To Poland and Russia, that's where he sent them,
and to Denmark and France and to fly over England,

to fall in fuel fire, to spin onto the sea, that's where
he sent them. And to other lands too, for his hands

patted children but also reached far across oceans
and deserts and seas. And where did he scatter them,

the children, where did he, Adolf Hitler, scatter them?
On the snow, in the air, in the sea's darkest depths,

on the steppes and the mountains, in the fire,
in the mud and runoff from clay, in the rain

and hot sand, in the clouds and grey fogs,
on green trees and soft furs of four-legged creatures,

on feathers of birds and roofs of old tombs —
that's where he scattered them, and elsewhere as well.

And his fatherly hand may reach out through the years
seeking his children of ash and charred bone, lest

they be left alone with no father like him, rare indeed,
and unique, one of a kind. Or so we might hope.

Visitors from America

In a Ukrainian village a group
of Americans sought out what
had once been the home
of their loved ones who had
been rounded up by the Nazis,
all their possessions forfeited,
no legacy to pass on.

The current owner is genial, invites
the visitors in, seems glad to see
them. The wife serves drinks
and sweets. The children smile
at those their age. The hospitality
is flawless. And yet the nephew
of the uncle who was betrayed
by some neighbor risks being rude
by looking around, seeking
evidence. Had this been *their*
family furniture, their etchings
and paintings on the wall?
Should they ask for anything back?

The man of the family, this American,
wonders if his grandfather or the others
had glanced back, said farewell
to the house and all that was in it
as they left at gunpoint and soon
toppled into the open pit. He asks
his hosts how they had acquired
the house. The *pater familias*
does not seem to know, says he
was only a child at the time, shrugs,
looks puzzled. "After the war,"
he adds, and perhaps is glad his English
is so inadequate. He and his wife
exchange looks as if the other
might come up with magic words.

"From whom did you buy?"
the visitor persists. But it seems
he is dealing with owners who have
no idea how their house was acquired.
They look around at one another.
The children giggle in embarrassment.
The host lifts his shoulders, his eyebrows.
How should he know — it's been sixty
years. But his wife disappears, returns
with a bag of apples, hands them over
with a smile, apologetic, almost a grimace.

Were these the apples of guilt, forgiveness,
evasion, sorrow, reparation? Would apples
undo the past or serve as fair trade
for the house, the view of green hills,
the laden trees? Were these apples
the blood-red descendants of those
that grew in the yard that day in 1942
when the family came out, herded

[stanza continues]

at gunpoint, nudged along if they tried
to look back? The visitors on this path
taken by those rounded up climbed a knoll
and had no trouble finding the mass grave
though it was unmarked. It almost glowed
out of the earth. They stood gazing down,
eating apples. But they knew these
were not the golden apples of paradise.

Richard C. Raymond

And Nothing Moved

I know I saw those things.
Cunning in self-defense, the brain
Has kept its shutters tight,
But the eye knows.

I stood there and stared and stared:
At piles of sprawling shoes,
At sacks of hair, tagged for color,
At drawers of teeth with gold fillings;
At whitewash walls of a barren room
Black with stains of desperate palms
High as hands could reach;
At crouching rows of ovens,
At stakes for target practice live;
At bones in pits and trenches
And drums of lime;
At artificial flowers in a vase,
At curtains in a window.
And nothing moved.
Skeletons, breathing still, lacked strength
To crawl in rags from barracks,
No trees grew leaves for the wind to stir,
Stenches defeated the wind,
The barbed wire hummed.

I know I saw those things,
Stranded for years in my eye,
Marooned there, denied their full belief,
Although the cock has crowed, and more than thrice;
And now, against their pressure for entry,
This continual straining to strike for home,
Will the brain weaken,

[stanza continues]

Too long on guard grow slack,
And into screaming ducts and crannies
Sterile horror ooze for a thousand years?

Barbara Reisner

Sweet Savour

We look at pictures of the lost
relatives, the old black and white
photos from Russian Poland
with the elongated cursive
Yiddish on the back.
— *Your loving niece and nephew.*
— *Your remembering good friend.*
And from Nachem
— *This is a picture of me.*
My son Shavel. Don't
forget me. That I'm asking
for help. I should not perish
from hunger.

We are well fed.

A young cousin read from the Torah
this morning.
Her portion was from Leviticus,
the laws of sacrifice, the burnt-
offering.

The rabbi, a Jungian, regards
Leviticus as a wound —
acknowledge the past and let go, he says.
And so we are modern.
We do not make a sin offering.
We do not send up a sweet
savour unto the Lord.

We keep passing Nachem's
picture, as if
we could feed him
with our thumbprints.

Naomi Replansky

Korczak and the Orphans

(on a photograph)

He made his choice.
He went with them.
Their eyes so large,
Their ribs so plain.

They walked, a thin
and straggling line
past beefy,
booted,
grinning guards.

In the bookkeeping
of the butchers
how small an entry
this would make:
192 children,
10 adults.

The Six Million

They entered the fiery furnace
And never one came forth.
How can that be, my brothers?
No miracle, my sisters.
They entered the fiery furnace
And never one came forth.

They fell in the den of lions,
Of lions made like men.
No beast that wept, my brothers,
Nor turned to lamb, my sisters.
They fell in the den of lions
Of lions made like men.

The block of ice closed round them
And nothing kept them warm.
No god came down, my brothers,
To breathe on them, my sisters.
The block of ice closed round them
And nothing kept them warm.

No gods were there, nor demons.
They died at the hands of men,
The cold that came from men,
The lions made like men,
The furnace built by men.

How can that be, my brothers?
But it is true, my sisters.
No miracle to spare them,
No angel leaned upon them,
Their bodies made a mountain
That never touched the heavens.
Whose lightning struck the killers?
Whose rain drowned out the fires?
My brothers and my sisters,
No miracle to shield them
From cold human hands.

— *1946*

Lisa Ress

U.S. Army Holds Dance for Camp Survivors. Germany, 1945

We recognize each other, neighbors before the war,
schoolmates until the schools shut against us.
Our families hid past the coalbins,
the children's mouths taped, our heads swollen with sound.
You kept on with your piano lessons,
the silence of the Czerny exercises eroding
the black- and white-painted board.
G.I.s broke us from the camps.
Now we hold together, circling in time,
not the dead for whom we long, but like them.
Cracked open behind us, our cellars glow with our youth.

Elaine Reuben

After Generations After

Yom Hashoah 5755 / April 27, 1995

After Sinai,
Jewish men were of three kinds:
Kohen, Levi, Yisrael
each with roles and privileges and
their responsibilities.

After the *Churban*,
no Temple pilgrimage to make,
no offerings to accept there, and
only occasional blessings to bestow.

Distinctions of lineage
reduce to ritual echoes
in *galut*.

After the Shoah,
Jews are of four kinds:
Kohen, Levi, Yisrael and
Sheyres-Hapleyte, survivors

all with stony pilgrimages to make, burnt
sacrifices to remember,
burdensome blessings to bestow.

In exile from a world destroyed
distinctions disappear.

I wonder
what sort of
Jews there will be
after the generation
after.

Charles Reznikoff

from **Massacres**

2

Her father had a shop for selling leather
and was one of the notables in a Polish Jewish community
when the Germans entered.
They put their horses into the synagogue and turned it into a stable.
On a Saturday afternoon, peasants from neighboring villages
came to tell the Jews of the town
that the Germans were killing Jews: they should run away and hide.
But the rabbi and other elders of the town
thought running away useless;
besides, they thought the Germans might take a few of the young men to work for
them
but that no one would be killed.

The next day, before sunrise, a Jew from a neighboring village
ran into the town shouting:
"Jews, run for your lives!
The Germans are out to kill us,"
and the townspeople saw the Germans coming in.

The young woman's grandfather said, "Run and hide, children, but I will stay:
they will do no harm to me."
Those who could hid in a neighboring forest.
During the day they heard shooting —
single shots and cries;
but towards evening they thought the Germans would be leaving the town
and, sure enough, peasants from the neighborhood met them
and said: "You can go back now.
The Germans killed everybody left behind."

When the Jews came back,
they found that the Germans had rounded up about one hundred and fifty Jews,
including the rabbi and other notables.
They told the rabbi to take his prayer shawl along —
the other Jews had been gathered in the center of the town —
and he was told to put on his prayer shawl
and sing and dance. He would not
and was beaten up. And so were the other Jews.
Then they were driven to the cemetery.
Here a shallow grave had been dug for them.
They were told to lie down in fours
and were shot. But her father remained behind in the town — alive:

[stanza continues]

he had said he was cutting the leather in his shop for shoes
and was registered as a shoemaker.

Later, the Germans went into the town to take whatever they could find;
the place was swarming with Germans — four or five to every Jew.
Many were put upon a large truck;
those who could not climb on themselves
were thrown on; and those for whom there was no room on the truck
were ordered to run after it.
All the Jews were counted and the Germans searched for every missing person on their list.
The young woman was among those who ran,
her little daughter in her arms.
There were those, too, who had two or three children
and held them in their arms as they ran after the truck.
Those who fell were shot — right where they fell.

When the young woman reached the truck,
all who had been on it were down and undressed and lined up;
the rest of her family among them.
There was a small hill there and at the foot of the hill a dugout.
The Jews were ordered to stand on top of the hill
and four SS men shot them — killed each separately.
When she reached the top of the hill and looked down
she saw three or four rows of the dead already on the ground.
Some of the young people tried to run
but were caught at once
and shot right there.
Children were taking leave of their parents;
but her little daughter said to her,
"Mother, why are we waiting? Let us run!"

Her father did not want to take off all of his clothes
and stood in his underwear.
His children begged him to take it off
but he would not and was beaten.
Then the Germans tore off his underwear
and he was shot.
They shot her mother, too,
and her father's mother —
she was eighty years old
and held two children in her arms;
and they shot her father's sister;
she also had babies in her arms
and was shot on the spot.
Her younger sister went up to one of the Germans —
with another girl, one of her sister's friends —
and they asked to be spared,
standing there naked before him.

[stanza continues]

The German looked into their eves
and shot them both — her sister and the young friend;
they fell
embracing each other.

The German who had shot her younger sister
turned to her
and asked, "Whom shall I shoot first?"
She was holding her daughter in her arms and did not answer.
She felt him take the child from her;
the child cried out and was shot.
Then he aimed at her: took hold of her hair
and turned her head around.
She remained standing and heard a shot
but kept on standing. He turned her head around again
and shot her;
and she fell into the dugout
among the bodies.

Suddenly she felt that she was choking;
bodies had fallen all over her.
She tried to find air to breathe
and began climbing towards the top of the dugout,
and felt people pulling at her
and biting at her legs.
At last she came to the top.
Bodies were lying everywhere
but not all of them dead:
dying, but not dead;
and children were crying, "Mama! Papa!"
She tried to stand up but could not.

The Germans were gone.
She was naked,
covered with blood and dirty with the excrement of those in the dugout,
and found that she had been shot in the back of the head.
Blood was spurting from the dugout
in many places;
and she heard the cries and screams of those in it still alive.
She began to search among the dead for her little girl
and kept calling her name;
trying to join the dead,
and crying out to her dead mother and father,
"Why didn't they kill me, too?"

She was there all night.
Suddenly she saw Germans on horseback
and sat down in a field
and heard them order all the corpses heaped together;
and the bodies — many who had been shot but were still alive —
were heaped together with shovels.

Children were running about.
The Germans caught the children
and shot them, too;
but did not come near her. And left again
and with them the peasants from around the place —
who had to help —
and the machine-guns and trucks were taken away.

She remained in the field, stretched out.
Shepherds began driving their flocks into the field;
and threw stones at her,
thinking her dead or mad.
Afterwards, a passing farmer saw her,
fed her
and helped her join Jews in the forest nearby.

from **Mass Graves**

3

In the morning the Jews were lined up by an officer
and the officer told them:
"You are Jews, unworthy of life,
but are now supposed to work."
They were put upon trucks
and taken away to a forest
and set to digging.
After two or three spadefuls of earth,
the spade of one hit something hard,
and he saw that it was the head of a human being.
There was also a bad smell all around.
He stopped digging
and the officer in charge came towards him shouting:
"Why did you stop?
Didn't you know there are bodies buried here?"
He had opened a mass grave.

There were about ten thousand dead in that grave.
And after they had dug up the bodies
they were told to burn them.
Planks had been brought and beams — long and heavy.
The Germans also brought a grinding machine to grind the bones
and the ground bones would be sieved
for the gold fillings of teeth.
The dust of the bones would then be spread over the fields,
and the smell was dreadful.

They kept on working three months
opening mass graves;
and opened eight or nine.
In one those digging saw a boy of two or three,
lying on his mother's body.
He had little white shoes on
and a little white jacket,
and his face was pressed against his mother's.

One grave would remain open for new corpses
coming all the time;
a truck would bring bodies, still warm,
to be thrown into the grave —
naked as Adam and Eve;
Jewish men, many of them bearded, and Jewish women and children.
The graves they had opened would be refilled with earth
and they had to plant grass all over them;
as for the dead —
a thousand bodies would be put on a pyre;
and there were two pyres of bodies burning all the time.

from ***Inscriptions: 1944–1956***

Out of the strong, sweetness;
and out of the dead body of the lion of Judah,
the prophecies and the psalms;
out of the slaves in Egypt,
out of the wandering tribesmen of the deserts
and the peasants of Palestine,
out of the slaves of Babylon and Rome,
out of the ghettos of Spain and Portugal, Germany and Poland
the Torah and the prophecies,
the Talmud and the sacred studies, the hymns and songs of the Jews;
and out of the Jewish dead
of Belgium and Holland, of Rumania, Hungary, and Bulgaria,
of France and Italy and Yugoslavia,
of Lithuania and Latvia, White Russia and Ukrainia,
of Czechoslovakia and Austria,
Poland and Germany,
out of the greatly wronged
a people teaching and doing justice;
out of the plundered
a generous people;
out of the wounded a people of physicians;
and out of those who met only with hate,
a people of love, a compassionate people.

Liliane Richman

After Claude Lanzmann's *Shoah*

It was always peaceful
in those deep fir woods
where the sun playfully shot arrows
into slowly shifting shadows,
quiet day and night in the woods not far from my village,
still peaceful after they burned two thousand daily,
after the screams, the barking of dogs,
the hissing of hundreds of bullets
rising to vaulting branches above,
caught there, hanging, trapped in the trees' green canopy.

I thought, then, and now,
Don't they deserve axing, these trees,
not stretching their powerful limbs in protest,
not squelching the light twitter of birds?

When all was over
no one watched the mindless river
ferrying downstream kilos of powdered bones.

Michael D. Riley

Photograph of Bergen-Belsen, 1945

These rich shades, pasteled by the lens or morning mist,
Blur expectations out of place.
After all the grainy horrors, the inadmissible truths
In black and white that pierce like barbed wire —
Sleepwalking dwarfs and skeletons, lines of freight cars
Whose broken slats once bloomed with fingers,
Bulldozer drivers in surgical masks
Striving in self-defense to bury the past,
Greasy clouds above fields of snowy carrion —
This odd exposure captures something less, and more.

The single flatbed wagon filled with naked corpses
Sits right-center by itself, a memory in transit.
Grecoesque, the dead cling to one another
And refuse to horrify — in their rapt dignity,
Like paschal candles or bolts of ivory silk.

[stanza continues]

Fastidiously, their genitals and faces
Turn from the camera toward anonymity.
The war has ended here. On the lush grass of spring
A sprinkling of Americans in darker green
Smoke at their ease. But space grows between them
And no one speaks. They consider the lens
With noncommittal faces, these veterans of death.

A waist-high brick fence divides the foreground
From the barbed wire fence and corn field beyond.
All the rest is open, empty, serene.
Leaning upon the fence, a few more stragglers
Stare in while trying not to stare.
Not one looks at the dead. Studied indifference
Draws the quick and dead together, as if murder
has killed identity.

This held instant distances all the rest.
Of the thirty thousand dead the Allies found, only these few
Perhaps remain. Nor do these in their seraphic calm
Resemble those kept whole, as if by onionskin and thread,
Who crowded the earliest burials, the ten mass graves
Brimming with nameless thousands — entombed this time
By the death's-head guard themselves, yeasty men and women
Made to handle for once their zero sum of evil.

The Golgothas of clothing, gold fillings, and hair
Gone long ago, no more in view than the other thousands,
The living and barely living: the two hundred children
The camp contained sent away to feed their memories;
The local citizens lined up behind the city council
And the burghermeister, visitors at last
To the metropolis of death they denied so long,
Even when the lie fell in black snow upon their fields,
Then stank and soured in their mouths.
All gone except these few.

And the dead will not wait long. They bid the living haste.
These young Americans bore all this heavy news
In their arms and hearts, but their thoughts
Remain as distant as the thoughts of the dead.
They wear the blank disguise of combat soldiers
Everywhere, the ritual mask of the dead,
More out of place here with the burden of their lives
Than the dead could ever be. On this trimmed lawn
Set off like a tiny pleasure ground,
They ought to wear a woman on their arms,
Swing a wicker basket filled with pears,
Camembert, a fine chilled Rhine.

And in the end, what should anyone expect
When men murder for a cigarette
Or scrap of rotten bread, or just to kill an hour?
They who had held life so long against the trigger
Might well die to death, find no spirit left to feel
These pale presences vainly haunting lives
They had given over months or even years ago.
But no. They consider the considering lens,
Transposed by still another kind of knowledge.

In the springtime measure of light, the composed
Bodies glow from within, pull light
Into their thin shelves of flesh until the air
Vibrates with the luminous ivory depth
Of vigil candles ranged across an altar cloth.
The soldiers' faces, ruddy as the candle flames,
Complete the service here, redeeming and redeemed.
For an aching beauty animates this scene,
One conventional pieties cannot still.

By some trick of perspective, or of art,
Some extravagant promise of belief
Or blundering insight of the heart,
Even horror is not final. Reconciled by exhaustion
Into peace, time gives over even violence to beauty,
Lifts her up as the final sacrifice once the litter on the stage
Has been removed and the actors, living or dead,
Are left alone forever with their thoughts.

Nicholas Rinaldi

Auschwitz

Lucky the ones who were sick and in pain,
they would soon be out of their misery. The ones
who were deaf, there was nothing beautiful
for them to listen to. The ones who had no gold teeth,
they would not be robbed when they died.

The ones who still had warm breath
to blow on their fingers,
trying to keep warm. They could blow on their fingers,
try to keep warm. The ones who could dream,
imagining they were flowers
on the banks of the Nile. They could imagine
they were birds over Egypt, flying,
soaring, lost in the irreverent sky.

The ones who were hungry and dying,
and the ones past hunger, beyond the need to eat.
They were ruined trees, numb to the weather,
unmindful of the monotonous rain.

The ones who were old and senile,
humming to themselves, thinking the guards
were angels from heaven
come to avenge them. Lucky the ones
who were so lucky, the ones under whose feet
the ground opened up: they could fall and fall
and never be found.

Curtis Robbins

In der Nacht (In the Night)

For Rose Rosman, Pesach, 1988

You have come a distance to speak
Your heart of a life no man or woman would
Ever, should ever, relive. It's like day
And night. But, you see only Darkness —
Where no light can ever guide you —
Rosa, Rosa, in der Nacht,
The darkness is brighter than the flame.

A Nazi soldier was gathering your deaf friends,
Guiding them with his kindly, assuring hands,
To the trains of a certain destiny.
Rosa, Rosa, in der Nacht,
The darkness is brighter than the flame.

You were such an impeccable child —
Watching them come to take your family,
Acquiescent as silent drums.
Rosa, Rosa, in der Nacht,
The darkness is brighter than the flame.

The moon outshone by a distant fire
Glowing by night with kindlings of hearts —
Who knows where they went to witness the blackening sun.
Rosa, Rosa, in der Nacht,
The darkness is brighter than the flame.

Ner Tamid. Ner Tamid,
The eternal flame, has never dimmed.
The joys and smiles are never forgotten.
A new life reminisces the bitterness *in der Nacht*,
When the darkness was brighter than the flame.
Rosa, Rosa, in der Nacht,
The darkness is brighter than the flame.

William Pitt Root

Pastoral for the Twenty-first Century

Not far from Belsen the countryside
is forgetful and kind,
senile and green.

The air is clear as a natural's conscience.

Pastures are plotted out
like stamps in an old album so vast
only a pilot inclined to glance down
might appreciate its pattern.

Those on the ground require
sealed boots to inspect
fields in the flood plains.

Viewing them through binoculars
you might startle a moment
at the sight of farmers walking on water,
plodding like cattle.

The cattle graze unattended —
munching the tallest stalks,
sloshing about,
swishing their tails and swinging
their spiritual heads to and fro,
mooing as if they bore
the griefs of the world on their bones,
their eyes a constant reference
to those sufferings none can name.

The river that meanders there,
flushed back and forth
by floods from north and south,
gathers up flotsam and jetsam
— weeds here, sheaves of bark there —
hanging it up on barbed wire.

When eventually it cures
it is natural paper,
crude imperfect parchment,
sunbleached and rainbeaten,
where certain indigestible
fragments stubbornly
scrawl out the random glyphs
and tentative ciphers
cattle come upon in
their harmless ritual
testing of the fences.

They do this year after year,
flood after flood,
each ripening herd
bunched and huddled against
new rainfall, nibbling
a passage from
one text or another, lifting
the drooling magnificence
of heads stuffed
with scriptures assembled
by the flood.

And how inscrutably
they low
before the rainbow,
that tireless witness
their masters more knowingly
dismiss, one foot
in a pot of gold, the other

god knows where.

Marina Roscher

The Lanternman

Every evening without fail he
appeared and brought sleeptime
not by the clock
but according to the amount of darkness.
It was good at that hour to watch
by the window until
he arrived in his smock and red cap

[stanza continues]

climbed his ladder against the gas-lantern post and made
light by the touch
of a magic wand. He was a gnome and lived
in a fairytale, in a kind town
this friend of the sandman,
and he loved children. Sometimes
you might knock at your windowpane just
to see him doff that red cap.
He was better than a lullaby. His name was
Yaacov. Not a German name.

Once upon . . .
the nursery turned into schoolroom
the street grew wide
the comfort of lanterns
was chopped down. They gave him a broom
for his ladder and wand
but he kept the red cap. Now
doffing it often at all kinds of people
sweeping hard when tanks and boots
muddied the street. His name
was Yaacov. Gone one day
as if you'd only imagined him. It would
have been good in the hour of darkness
if the lanternman had come back
again. It would have been
good to think of ladders to heaven instead
of the gas-flame.

Jennifer Rose

At Dachau with a German Lover

I won't go with you to Munich's planetarium
though I have always loved a wandering moon.
I cannot bear to bless a German heaven.

Dachau. The sign appears, colloquial
amidst the traffic; the radio sputters
Stau — or is it *heil*?

Everything continues in this language!
Every chimney rises with a grudge.
The *Arbeit* gate swings slowly on its hinge.

This is the first time I feel at home
in your country, in this museum.
Elsewhere, the Nazis are innocuous — your neighbors.

You examine by yourself their careful orders.
Every road to death is neatly chartered.
You're horrified — not just by deaths of strangers,

but by the language, which killed them
before the gas or gunners;
your language, words you might have uttered.

Tell me what it says, this chart of stars:
Which color is my destiny of fire —
yellow, for the language of my prayers?

red, for the fury of my cares?
or pink, my crime of twin desires?
This is my planetarium, these pinned-on stars!

You won't go with me to Dachau's crematorium
though the ovens are cold, the fumes are gone,
and you're too young to have fired them.

The gas chamber, familiar as a dream
but smaller, is open at both ends.
I walk, without knees, without lungs, the brief

avenue. This is it. The vault, the safe
where they escaped, scratching
in the old direction of heaven.

At night our room is dark, the bed, a ditch.
The moon grows big in its hutch as we watch,
wide awake, tense. Your father was a soldier,

your mother, a Hitler youth who quit.
I'm a Jew. I'd be dead if we were older.
What shocked me most as we first slowed

to stop was not Dachau's walls or weight,
but its shamelessness at its own sight.
Had no one seen the guards guarding their flawed height,

the smoke drifting off, signaling in desperate code?
This is what I can't forget:
how public it was, how close to the road.

Harriet Susskind Rosenblum

After That Time

And it would never be over. After that,
time would stay fixed at three-seventeen
when the hands of the surgery clock pierced
her, and the huge man in a white lab coat
dropped his pants and climbed up on her.
She was eleven, nipples small as daisy hearts.

The bells sound, MENGELE, Mengele, mengele,
and the sour hunger and the sweat,
grunt and clinical odor, alcohol, formaldehyde
and semen made her afraid of the froth
of any sea. She was saved and would return,
over and over, to the table in the surgery.

In the soft washed light of the evening news,
the gravedigger stands in the pit, lifting
bones: a hip, two shanks and a rotting skull,
brown with soil. And is this the end of pity?

Almost as the light deepens, she wants
all the children to rise up and return,
to stand in a ring about the bones.
Then each one will touch that dark wrist
and each one will take his own hand,
close those missing eyes, and ask this of that sky:

Is this the final justice —
The moment the clock can move on?

Ritual at Auschwitz

1

History reveals itself
in the language of doors slammed
   against the night.
Skies blacken into a storm —
how can so many Jewish bodies
   be swept up?
God can invent a whirlwind?
   Then send God into exile.
Trains will carry this cargo

[stanza continues]

of husbands, neighbors,
their scared bellies pressed into
thin scapulas of children,
writing death on their eyelids.
Sleep or scream — even so,
night will follow.

Those final Warsaw Ghetto days:
mothers hid children,
tried to keep small hands
from shattered glass.
But, coming up to the landing,
to the last stair,
to the barred door —
boots of the *Einsatzgruppen*
kicked past the barricade.
As if hefting dolls,
men lifted babies
by their arms
and threw them, legs-first,
through windows,
bruising the eyes of the living.

2

The platform of Auschwitz station:
the living were dragged
from box cars while
a band of prisoners played Strauss.
Move faster! Form lines!
Taste the cattle prod.
Form lines — left, right —
Children will be all right.
Leave your clothes.
Walk to the showers.
Go swiftly, go
to the healing waters.
Afterwards,
be ready for sleep
in the tranquility of the countryside.

Under the shawl of steel
under the flames
of ovens, the smoke
the blood; under the mountains
of hair, shoes, caps, the names
of Anna and Sara, Moses and David.
Earth opened its troughs
to receive the seed of its children

[stanza continues]

in the bright sun
of the Polish countryside.
How green the crop is, how soft
the light bearing down upon calves,
tethered in chains to the road.
There is no water.
No one comes.

3

Poland, on the first day of spring,
declares a holiday from school.
Yellow buses carrying schoolchildren
line up in rows.
Children walk neatly in pairs
towards the museum at Auschwitz.
On the way in, or on the way out,
they buy ice cream, souvenirs.
A key chain? A book mark? A lock of hair?
All walk under a wrought iron arch:
ARBEIT MACHT FREI.
To the left, stone buildings
are cool and clean.
Their brown bricks do not exude
the stink of starvation.

On the clipped lawns outside,
beds of roses — perfect and red.
Only grass is uncannily green.
Will the stones bleed?
In dioramas, there are no sounds.
In photographs, there are
no cries, no coughs, no pleas —
and no weeping.
Whose long hair was woven
into the blue shawl?
Whose round glasses lie
in the midst of the heap?
Pulleys that once swept bodies
up and out are silent.
In the showers, no rust:
only a blue stain.

4

Here no lamps are muted by shades
of human flesh, or gloves
fashioned from a mother's soft white thigh.
Miles of silence:

[stanza continues]

some shreds of a tallith, human hair
piled high in crates like spoiled cotton.
Who were the prisoners? What was their crime?
The visiting schoolchildren are free
to return home,
to crisscross the countryside
back to Warsaw.

In Auschwitz at the firing line,
the wall stays shattered;
on the sturdy lookouts, windows
still watch.
And at night,
barbed wire cries.

Menachem Z. Rosensaft

Birkenau Barracks

cold wind blows
through crumbling barrack walls
rotted wood soaked with
vomit
blood
rain
dew
cracking under the sun
dust covering ashes in unswept corners

they crumble, the barracks
as ice wind blows
past flames no longer burning
now without screams
without shadows
not even echoed whispers

so let them crumble, the barracks
let them collapse
disintegrate into their corpses' earth
leaving only frozen wind
to mourn

The Second Generation

true, we are the children
of a nocturnal twilight
the heirs of Auschwitz and Ponar
but ours is also the rainbow:
in us the storm meets sunlight
to create new colors
as we add defiant sparks
to an eternal fire

Sosnowiec Visited

light cuts the rain grey
semi-darkness
through curtains
sixty years old

from across the street
that should have been
but never will be
mine
I see shadows move
behind windows where
another family once lived
same rooms
same walls
same bricks
perhaps even the same furniture

here the good church-going citizens
watched and waited
until the non-believers
the non-Poles
were finally taken away,
then they stole
my mother's home
her bed
her clothes
my brother's toys

dead Jew reborn
to refuse to knock on their door
any door
I came to curse
only to find
them cursed already

my final victory: I can leave

even the air tastes bitter

Yad Vashem Museum Opening, March 15, 2005

cool wind blowing colder
becoming ice
sun fading into darkness
under Judean clouds
grey against black
we sit shivering in our
coats
hats
woolen socks
knowing that
coffee
brandy
a warm bed
are only an hour or two away

cool winds blew colder
became ice
sun fading into darkness
grey clouds against black
there
sixty years before
shivering naked in barracks
on wooden planks
praying for death as respite
from hunger
from pain
from tomorrow's hunger
tomorrow's pain

images I never saw
but remembered from words
whispers
of the almost murdered
now etched forever
inside a hill
where my daughter
will walk through shadows
know reflections
hear echoes
of her grandparents' memories
fading

[stanza continues]

dark grey against black
as cool winds blow colder
becoming ice
under the Jerusalem sun

Elizabeth Rosner

Almost Beautiful

Our hotel is on Schäferkampsallee, a street in Hamburg
where my father used to live. From the cab window
he points and says he doesn't remember the street being
this wide, says he is surprised the trolley cars are gone.
I imagine spidery arms reaching into a tangled web
of charged wires, tracks embedded in cobblestone streets,
electricity crackling overhead. We listen to the silence.
My father is a German who will speak no German, and I,
forbidden to learn it in school, studied Spanish instead.
There were no German products in the house, not for
twenty-five years after the war, not until he bought
that steel-blue Krups shaver to hold against
his cheek in the harsh bathroom light after another
almost forgotten nightmare. "You've got to admit,"
he said, "Germans are good at what they do."

The subway, he tells me, still smells the same:
overripe fruit and wet leaves and salty air damp
from the sea. At Gänsemarkt we rise blinking
into the sunlight and my father points to a bakery
across the street. "They make a special pastry
I've never found anywhere else in the world . . ."
He looks for the nearest place to cross, an eager
child promised a favorite sweet. "It's called
a binnenstück," he explains between mouthfuls.
I take a small bite of cream, butter and honey.
"Too rich," I murmur, and he agrees, wrapping
the rest into a napkin, then into the shoulder bag
he carries everywhere, stuffed with newspapers,
magazines, books, maps. Ballast for this journey.

We take a ferry ride on the Alster and his expressions
change like the sky. "I came back here once thinking
I would spend a weekend just visiting the city. But
I felt so lonely and strange I didn't even stay overnight."
Ghosts everywhere and the sound of broken glass
under his feet. We pass under several bridges where

[stanza continues]

children stand waving and giggling; the ferry passengers
all smile up at them. My father looks bitter, as though
thinking Yes, they can grow up here as if nothing
happened. "Over there," he says, pointing, "we used
to play along that bank. I fell in once. Not long
after that we weren't allowed to go swimming anymore."
We glide past mansions whose rose gardens slope gracefully
toward the water's edge. "It's almost beautiful," he says.

Anything

The Swedes who knew you after
the war tell me you were lucky because
you got out in time. I can't think what
they mean at first until I realize they
think you didn't survive what you
survived, they think you didn't ever
get sent to a camp, and I can't think why
they think that until I realize
maybe you didn't talk about it then,
when it was so recent you still
woke sometimes in the night thinking
it was time to be counted again.
Maybe you thought it was so obvious
it didn't need to be said out loud,
when the fact that all of your bones
showed through your clothing
seemed to speak for itself. Didn't it?
I tell them they must not mean
what they mean, tell them
you were there, in Buchenwald, for
the last year of the war, and they say
No, he wasn't, we would have
known that, and I say, Yes, of course
he was, I should know, I'm his daughter.
And we sit silently around their dining
room table, trying to understand how
such a thing could be forgotten, or mis-
taken, or kept a secret. I keep thinking
about that picture of you with Mom
just after you'd met in Stockholm
where you're both standing on some
seashore with the wind blowing so hard
that the legs of your pants are pressed
against your ankles which look like
a young girl's ankles they're so terribly
thin and fragile. And I don't understand anything
about anything.

Chocolate

My father hoards it,
needs a stash of dark
nougat hidden in shoeboxes
on high closet shelves, under
piles of winter hats, behind
unmatched socks, trapped
between old bills and
unanswered letters.
Instead of lint or loose
change, his pockets store
gold and silver foil:
the shed skin of secret feasting
against the memory of hunger.

Homework

What do I say to them, the ones who say they
didn't know about the ovens and the gas chambers,
the ones who say *I didn't know they were actually*
killing people, I mean I just didn't know. What do
I say? It happens all the time: casual announcements
at various gatherings, pieces of conversation floating
lightly into the air as if I am someone they can confess
to and be reassured *It's all right, it's all right.* Is it?
I never had the luxury of not knowing. I knew even
before I knew, had this feeling in my bones that
something was terribly wrong and there was
nothing anyone could do about it, especially me.
Nothing. I mean fifth grade, studying about World
War Two on a worksheet, filling in the blanks, and there
is one sentence about Hitler invading Poland, one
sentence. I'm thinking about my mother, about how
that one sentence is supposed to summarize being
herded into the ghetto and the cousins killed and
the hiding in the basement of the peasants' house and
the aunts killed and the dogs barking and the terror
of every moment — one sentence on a worksheet is all.
I'm ten years old but I know this blank can't be
so easily filled in, and I'm noticing another sentence
about America entering the war, and I'm thinking
What took so long? And where is the part about all
the dead people? Where is the part about yellow stars
and Zyklon B and the soap made from burning bodies?
Where is the story that people keep telling me they
didn't hear until they were older, until just recently
in fact, when they saw *Schindler's List* on TV?

My Father's Souvenirs

One.

A mustard-yellow tattered star, and
JUDE mimicking the Hebrew alphabet.
A rectangular patch for
a faded blue prison number.
A pale yellow file card with a
small, passport-size "mug shot"
of a fifteen-year-old boy with a newly shaved head
and protruding ears, a mouth held tightly closed
and wide, wide dark eyes.

Two.

When I was eight years old,
my father came to my Hebrew school class.
He asked how many people
lived in our city; a few of us mumbled
uncertain guesses, no one knew.
He took a piece of chalk and wrote 80,000
on the board, said this was how many.
I thought about shopping malls and schools
and neighborhoods, about the vastness of my world.
Then he wrote another number on the board: 6,000,000.
I don't know what else he talked about that
Sunday morning, what stories he told; I just remember
all those zeroes lined up against each other.

Three.

In my eleventh grade history class,
a room full of bored adolescents,
we are about to see a film and the teacher refuses,
for once, to tell us anything about it.
The projector hums and flutters, the room is dark
and full of whispers, giggles, chairs scraping the floor.
When I realize the film is *Night and Fog*,
my body stiffens. I have seen it before;
I know about the mass graves, piles of eyeglasses and
suitcases and shoes, the living skeletons
huddled behind barbed wire.
The film gets caught in the mechanism and begins
to flap and sputter; someone gets up
to fix it but I'm already out of my chair and
heading for the hall where I can lean against
the cold metal lockers and close my eyes.
It's the only way to stop myself
from wondering which emaciated face is his.

Jerome Rothenberg

Dibbukim (Dibbiks)

spirits of the dead   lights
flickering (he said) their ruakh
will never leave the earth
instead they crowd the forests the fields
around the privies the hapless spirits
wait millions of souls
turned into ghosts at once
the air is full of them
they are standing each one beside a tree
under its shadows or the moon's
but they cast no shadows of their own
this moment & the next they are pretending
to be rocks   but who is fooled
who is fooled here   by the dead   the jews
the gypsies   the leadeyed polish patriot
living beings reduced to symbols
of what it had been to be alive
"o do not touch them" the mother cries
fitful, as almost in a dream
she draws the child's hand to her heart
in terror   but the innocent dead
grow furious they break down doors
drop slime onto your tables
they tear their tongues out by the roots
& smear your lamps your children's lips
with blood a hole drilled in the wall
will not deter them
from stolen homes stone architectures
they hate they are the convoys of the dead
the ghostly drivers still searching
the roads to malkin   ghost carts overturned
ghost autos in blue ditches
if only our eyes were wild enough
to see them our hearts to know their terror
the terror of the man who walks alone
their victim whose house whose skin
they crawl in   incubus & succubus
a dibbik leaping from a cow to lodge inside
his throat   clusters of jews
who swarm here mothers without hair
blackbearded fathers
they lap up fire   water   slime
entangle the hairs of brides

[stanza continues]

or mourn their clothing hovering
over a field of rags   half-rotted shoes
& tablecloths   old thermos bottles   rings
lost tribes in empty synagogues
at night their voices
carrying across the fields
to rot your kasha your barley
stricken beneath their acid rains
no holocaust because no sacrifice
no sacrifice to give the lie
of meaning   & no meaning   after auschwitz
there is only poetry   no hope
no other language left to heal
no language   & no faces
because no faces left   no names
no sudden recognitions on the street
only the dead still swarming   only khurbn
a dead man in a rabbi's clothes
who squats   outside the mortuary house
who guards their privies who is called
master of shit   an old alarm clock
hung around his neck   who holds
a wreath of leaves under his nose
from eden   "to drive out
the stinking odor of this world"

Dos Oysleydikn (The Emptying)

at honey street in ostrova
where did the honey people go?
empty   empty
miodowa empty
empty bakery & empty road to warsaw
yellow wooden houses & houses plastered up with stucco
the shadow of an empty name still on their doors
shadai & shadow shattering the mother tongue
the mother's tongue but empty
the way the streets are empty where we walk
pushing past crowds of children
old women airing themselves outside the city hall
old farmers riding empty carts down empty roads
who don't dispel but make an emptiness
a taste of empty honey
empty rolls you push your fingers through
empty sorrel soup dribbling from their empty mouths
defining some other poland
lost to us the way the moon

[stanza continues]

is lost to us
the empty clock tower measuring her light four ways
sorrel in gardens mother of god at roadsides
in the reflection of the empty trains
only the cattle bellow in
like jews the dew-eyed wanderers
still present still the flies
cover their eyeballs
the trains drive eastward, falling
down a hole (a holocaust) of empty houses
of empty ladders leaning against haystacks no one climbs
empty ostrova & empty ostrolenka
old houses empty in the woods near vyzhkov
dachas the peasants would rent to you
& sleep in stables
the bialo forest spreading to every side
retreating the closer we come to it to claim it
empty oaks & empty fir trees
a man in an empty ditch who reads a book
the way the jews once read
in the cold polish light the fathers sat there too
the mothers posed at the woods' edge
the road led brightly to treblinka
& other towns beaches at brok
along the bug
marshes with cattails
cows tied to trees
past which their ghosts walk
their ghosts refuse to walk
tomorrow in empty fields of poland
still cold against their feet
an empty pump black water drips from
will form a hill of ice
the porters will dissolve with burning sticks
they will find a babe's face at the bottom
invisible & frozen imprinted in the rock

IN THE DARK WORD, KHURBN

all their lights went out

their words were silences,
memories
drifting along the horse roads
onto malkiner street

a disaster in the mother's tongue
her words emptied
by speaking

returning to a single word
the child word
spoken, redeyed on
the frozen pond

was how they spoke it,
how I would take it from your voice
& cradle it

that ancient & dark word

those who spoke it in the old days
now held their tongues

The Other Secret in the Trail of Money

& all true all true the poet's vision
proven in the scraps. Bank notes & zlotys strewn
over the field. Papers buried. Testaments
to death & to the acquisitive nature of the guards
its passage from hand to hand, to make a picnic
in the Jewish State. Imagine.

That he is again in the field leading to the showers & that the field is strewn with money. Those who are dead have left it, & the living bend to pick it up. The rhythms of Gold's orchestra drift past him, as in the woods sometimes the squeals of children & women or the deeper bellows of the men. He bends to lift a coin or to remove a bag of chocolates & raisins from a dead girl's coat. Butter. Cheese. White rolls. Roast chicken. Cognac. Cream. Sardines. "More sugar & tea than in the whole Warsaw Ghetto." The Jewish workers & their guards feast in the woods. A child is with them — turns her mouth to you — that by gematria becomes a hole.

from Peroration for a Lost Town

[May 1988]: *"On this road thou camest . . ."*

what will I tell you sweet town?
that the sickness is still in you
that the dead continue to die
there is no end to the dying?
for this the departed would have had an answer:
a wedding in a graveyard
for you sweet town
they would have spoken they who are no longer among us
& would have shown forth in their splendor
would have danced pellmell

[stanza continues]

over your stones sweet town
the living & the dead together   feathers
would have blown like feathers
from their fingers   no   like gold   like roses
like every corny proposition
fathers or uncles ever gave us   they gave us
to call your image back to life
sweet town their voices twittering
like bats over your little houses
is this the sound then that the breath makes
in its final gasp that the dead make
having lived a whole life under water
now coming up for air, to find themselves
in poland in the empty field
bathers who had their bodies torn apart
& ran from you   their long guts
hanging, searching the forgotten woods
for houses & the consolation
that death brings   children in a circle
dancing   without tongues   the meadow that had once stood open
shut in remembrance now sweet town
the screams of the cousins carried by the wind
lost in the gentile cities
in the old men's dreams of you
each night sweet town who rise up from their beds
like children   bellowing   their words
stuck in their beards like honey
who drift up brok street past the russian church
the doctor's house beside it heavy
& whitebricked in the dream   who glide above
napoleon square o little orchards little park
where lovers once walked with lovers   children
still capture fishes in thy little pond
its surfaces still green with algae
o sounds of church bells — bimbom — through the frozen air
that call forth death o death o pale photographer
o photos of the sweet town rubbed with blood
o of its streets the photographs its vanished folk
o wanderers who wandered o bodies of the distant dead who stayed
o faces o dimming images lost smiles o girls embracing girls
in deathless photographs   o life receding
into images of life   you beautiful & pure   sweet town
I summon & I summon thee to answer

Larry Rubin

The Nazi in the Dock, at Sixty

Incensed, he clutches at his innocence,
Created out of years of careful lies.
The court is less important than his age:
Living with the skulls and cordoned flesh
Is possible; dying with them, something
Else. A poet of the past, he tames
The truth, shapes it to his need, makes
Lambs of dinosaurs. A Jewess on
The jury knows; she burns behind her eyes,
Like him. What more awaits?
The year grows thin; they lead him downward
To a camp where old men should not go —
To bits of hair and wire, acrid smells
Of something in his skin he can't recall.

Mark Rudman

Easy Living in Terezín

I am almost finished with my essay on chaos and the threshold . . .
— Martin Heidegger

I wake with my ears held:
It's that dream about the Terezín Ghetto, where the little
Children are being encouraged to express themselves.
Words like *shekl* and *shetl* crisscross and scatter.

Practiced artists supervise.
Guards pretend not to watch.
Red Cross workers beam.
It isn't low rent, it's no rent,

An art colony where you're admitted
Without application: "Ideally situated
Between city and country, nature and culture."
Gaily pack your gear.

I dream I am sent on a photographic mission to Terezín.
Diplomatic immunity, WAC brunette and jeep
At my disposal.
Idyllic two hour ride from Prague.

She chooses to wait outside the gates.
When I catch sight of something that makes me retch,
I cover my ears until the next shot.
This helps not at all.

There is no one with whom I can share my disturbance
That what I am allowed to see doesn't reflect the reality.
The children seem to be absorbed.
With the adults, it is not so clear.

They take a little more time with the children
Than would appear, at first
Glance, and without history, necessary.
"So this is what I prayed for: more time to concentrate on my art!"

The children's laughter twitches the guards like an explosion.
It is this that had to be rooted out.

Not long before the end, Heidegger could still
Boast of Terezín in letters to Arendt and Sartre:

"And yet, art is more valued here than in . . ."
It was like an art school with everyone floated on full scholarship.
Transportation included.
Meals provided in a timely way.

There was an order to the day that induced concentration.
The children were giddy, art-crazed, until it was time to leave camp.
The supply of chalk and paper and pastel seemed inexhaustible.
And words like *shekel* and *shtetl* I never learned to spell.

Biff Russ

The Way to Be Haunted

For M.F.

I. Yom Ha-Shoah

They are like small children,
bringing you strange treasures,
asking hard questions, the dead.
Today they enter you like air
forcing your lungs wide open, startling them
into the shape of wings
inside your flesh. Fly.
This is the way to be haunted

[stanza continues]

by those you love. They move your eyes
towards a sky as fragile as blue glass
in which they must teach you to move
carefully, like an angel. *Kristallnacht*.
The world is easily broken.

You think of your American childhood
as if you were not safe yourself.
You cradled your sister's head
while your mother told of the gone ones,
the family's dead children, the treasures.
She spoke of separations. Parent
from child. Like the skull of an infant
your horror slowly sealed itself
filling in her silences with details
she did not tell — the red of a young girl's hair,
the scent of tea and candle wax, the sound
of a particular window breaking. Inside you,
your ghosts are as beautiful as glass.
Like family crystal
they are handed down by your mother intact.
Grown up now, a father yourself,
you fear their preciousness.
Carefully. Turn completely
towards their pain. Promise each beloved ghost,
as you would promise a real child,
that nothing will ever take them from you.

II. The Gates of Hell

Rodin chose scenes from Dante, mixing them
with modern scenes, to illustrate the realm
of the damned. This great unfinished work
takes the form of sealed doors in a portal.
After Rodin's death, the incomplete structure
was cast in bronze, exactly as it stood.

The guard's bootsteps
move from room to room frightening
the dead children. They do not know
why you brought them here, or why
you do not take them away
now, before they think of keys.
You are yourself frightened
by certain echoes
as you look at the shining figure
on the bottom of the left-hand door,
a door which neither opens nor closes.
Your hand reaches down to touch the cold skin

[stanza continues]

of the figure of Ugolino
which feels as if it has been long dead, and yet
he is alive. You can see the pain on his face
as his face stops forever
here, at its worst point. He is locked
in a tower where he must starve
together with his four children.
The guard's bootsteps echo, and voices.
And now, the dusk light closes
though there is no longer any tower
or key or living bones.
Only Ugolino's bronze story
which cannot move
forward. His beautiful face surprises you,
so great that he is found
in the lowest circle of Hell. You think of the faces
of those who killed Jews. Your family's ghosts
flock wildly around you, no bigger than
your own sons and daughter. They grasp you
away from him. They recognize evil. Ugolino's body
arches like a shield over his own small children
who are forbidden by the sculptor's dead hand
ever to finish dying. One of them
reaches out to him, but Ugolino
can do nothing to save it, nothing
to help the child escape. This is the punishment
of art: he enters the Gates of Hell forever.

And like a shriek
against your will
something in your heart
                                        goes out to him,
some almost impossible fragment of mercy
through which like a door
you lead your astonished dead.

Luada Sandler

A Scene From *Shoah*

For Claude Lanzmann

It is spring, and a boatman is rowing down the river
singing a song of his childhood, of the land
and his people, his sweet voice filling the air
with a haunting melody.

He moves serenely along the peaceful river
and a light wind that once had carried the ashes
of his family now wafts his song ahead of him
like a greeting to his village.

But, beneath his boat, the river is poisoned
with the refuse of war and the camp,
with the ashes of millions of victims.

There are wildflowers in the meadow that lies
between the camp and the village, a setting
of natural beauty bordered by the quiet river,
a landscape of innocence in pastoral Poland.

But the soil is tainted as deep down as silence.
The land is hallowed with its millions dead,
yet it is forever stained with their murder.

The boatman is gliding down the river, sweetly singing
in the midst of horror. He is a survivor of those times,
but his memory — his memory perished in the camp,
except for the song he is singing.

Reg Saner

Aspen Oktoberfest

Through an amber dazzle of aspen
the sun delves and paddles. The eye opens,
walks with that sun in its circles,
and closes.

Along the streambed I listen: crag chunks, pebbles, boulders
breasting torrent, whacking back at it, memorizing
the full past of a creek trailing from them like robes
as their fracture lines blunt and decide
on the strange, voluptuous forms of believers in water.

Trunk shadows zebra the dirt. Within planes of blue umber, then light,
then umber, the blurred twirl of a leaf
winks twenty, thirty yards, descending. A scintilla. An eye,
like the others. Autumn opens as radiance, closes
as stone. Under a pressure nobody can imagine
there's a central cubic inch of this planet, a black incandescence
towards which everything falls,
yet I've never been, can never be, happier

[stanza continues]

and no reason — or none weightier than mountain air
leaking gold. Which no sooner seems an "Oktoberfest"
than out of the word's transparent German
a girl's smile comes to me, surviving only as name, Lily Tofler,
luckless and radiant — just as, thinking of stone,
I step into sunlight
traversing exactly these branches to reach me.

Ultramarine rings off the summits, their scree slopes.

The eye opens to brilliance like that, animal and happy
it walks in the sun's perfect circles
helping photons pour from their center out of some vast, casual joy
while our share infinitesimal strikes this earth
and keeps going. That I touched them for others
in me, the words on those gates, or passed through them,
wife and sons with me unharmed, reading *Arbeit Macht Frei*
written in iron on eyes closed as stone
back of the black hinges at Dachau
teaches nothing but luck. Moment to moment
light's witnesses dismantle, annihilate, while every particle
illumined survives, eternal
as matter.

Along faults in this creek making gravity its entire career
fire breaks from pebbles that quench and rekindle
darkness in granite, this sparkling
inside the stream.

with high tides and leaf spills flecking shrub clumps
like pollen, I see warehouses of shoe leather
emptied, bales of shorn hair, gold teeth shoveled up
like shelled corn. But this isn't that light —
in which the shadow of a bullet nine millimeters small
entered the shadow of a girl.

It's just that within the outline of each, the sun
burns to a focus on me
for a moment, never happier.

And the ashen lids of Jewish women squint shut,
wombs injected with mixtures, fine sand in quicklime, hardening
to history. It happened. My kinsmen, the Germans.

Further upslope toward the quarry
I tour the afternoon's plumed and luminous festival,
each aspen a sunburst, a shock, a fire curd I pass through
while October's least breath
offers windfalls of spattered translucence.

In a camp only my kinsmen the Germans could've imagined
I never saw Lily Tofler. It's just that her smile
there became a by-word. Talismanic and mine
now, as it was then for others. A style, a daily impossible courage
making even the officer's name a matter of record.
Whose name was Boger. Who raped her
then killed her.

Lapping right up to timberline, the highest trees
seem a gray haze of twig, standing wind-stripped, naked,
accomplished.

In light so dust-free, so moteless these spruce cones
one hundred and fifty yards off cluster their bough tip, glittering
an absolute clarity
what would I know about suffering?
It's just that out of that firebrick and soot-centered camp,
through this blind rightness of trees
yellow-breasted as meadowlarks, the name of a girl
comes to me.

Within an amber dazzle of aspen, the sun's circle
half eclipses, trembles — then flares. The eye opens
and closes. And creekwater flashes, leaping down off the peaks,
making up new lives as it runs.

May Sarton

from The Invocation to Kali

3

The Concentration Camps

Have we managed to fade them out like God?
Simply eclipse the unpurged images?
Eclipse the children with a mountain of shoes?
Let the bones fester like animal bones,
False teeth, bits of hair, spilled liquid eyes,
Disgusting, not to be looked at, like a blight?

Ages ago we closed our hearts to blight.
Who believes now? Who cries, "merciful God"?
We gassed God in the ovens, great piteous eyes,
Burned God in a trash-heap of images,
Refused to make a compact with dead bones,
And threw away the children with their shoes —

Millions of sandals, sneakers, small worn shoes —
Thrust them aside as a disgusting blight.
Not ours, this death, to take into our bones,
Not ours a dying mutilated God.
We freed our minds from gruesome images,
Pretended we had closed their open eyes

That never could be closed, dark puzzled eyes,
The ghosts of children who went without shoes
Naked toward the ovens' bestial images,
Strangling for breath, clawing the blight,
Piled up like pigs beyond the help of God . . .
With food in our stomachs, flesh on our bones,

We turned away from the stench of bones,
Slept with the living, drank in sexy eyes,
Hurried for shelter from a murdered God.
New factories turned out millions of shoes.
We hardly noticed the faint smell of blight,
Stuffed with new cars, ice cream, rich images.

But no grass grew on the raw images.
Corruption mushroomed from decaying bones.
Joy disappeared. The creature of the blight
Rose in the cities, dark smothered eyes.
Our children danced with rage in their shoes,
Grew up to question who had murdered God,

While we evaded their too attentive eyes,
Walked the pavane of death in our new shoes,
Sweated with anguish and remembered God.

Rebecca Seiferle

"A lonely man in his greatness"

Pius XII, who for some unknown reason
always hated flies, rotted in his coffin.
He who had been crowned with such ceremony,
glittering in a bejeweled, ascetic pose, had
the tip of his nose fall off while he reposed
in state. He who had such a delicate stomach
that trains of food stuffs traveled with him
and yet who, as Europe starved, faced
every heaping plate as if *opening a warrant*;

[stanza continues]

who was so parsed, he said nothing of the Jews;
who *smelled of the absence of all scents*,
who lifted his arms in a gesture of immolation
and said nothing for the Jews, who had himself
filmed carrying a lamb on his shoulders, who
required that *no human presence should mar*
his daily stroll in the gardens, whose odor
of sanctity was antiseptic doused on his hands
and linens, from whom the workers hid
in the bushes rather than disturb the *pure white wraith*,
who would not sanctify those who smoked
or uttered a single curse, who would say nothing
to the Jews, rotted in his coffin. The doctor
who tended to his strange undiagnosed ailments
embalmed his body with a technique
that failed like the Concordat with Hitler,
though, in a sense, it was successful,
elevating the absolute power of the Pope,
as his coffin was elevated through the streets
of Rome. As the trinity of coffins, one nested
inside the other, passed from the caecum
of St. Peter's, past the appendix of the archives,
to the colic streets, through the gates of Ileum,
the bowels of the city itself, strange noises
of belches, flatulence, erupted from the corpse
of the Angelic Shepherd — like the earth
in many places in Europe, even in 1958
still rising and falling to the noises of death.

David Shapiro

For Victims

They have used the bodies
Of children as improvised bridges
Which, later, they cross
First the sun and the moon,
            then the earth comes in
But they have lost the atmosphere
Which belongs to them

Light passers-by

Gregg Shapiro

Tattoo

My father won't talk about the numbers
3-7-8-2-5 between the wrist and elbow
blue as blood on his left forearm
Instead, he spreads himself over me
spilling his protection, like acid, until it burns
I wear him like a cloak, sweat under the weight

There were stories in the lines on his face
the nervous blue flash in his eyes
his bone-crushing hugs
I am drowning in his silence
trying to stay afloat on curiosity
Questions choke me and I swallow hard

We don't breathe the same air
speak the same language
live in the same universe
We are continents, worlds apart
I am sorry my life has remained unscathed
His scars still bleed, his bruises don't fade

If I could trade places with him
I would pad the rest of his days
wrap him in gauze and velvet
absorb the shocks and treat his wounds
I would scrub the numbers from his flesh
extinguish the fire and give him back his life

Harvey Shapiro

Ditty

Where did the Jewish god go?
Up the chimney flues.
Who saw him go?
Six million souls.
How did he go?
All so still
As dew from the grass.

Natural History

The dinosaurs, to survive,
became birds. The Jews
of Europe became
smoke. What can you
do as smoke?

Reva Sharon

In the Absence of Yellow

The last, the very last
so richly, brightly, dazzlingly yellow,
Perhaps if the sun's tears would sing
against a white stone . . .
Only I never saw another butterfly.
— Pavel Friedmann, 4 June 1942

It is summer and it is quiet
where I am standing in the yard
several feet from the wall
scarred by executions
It is quiet now . . .
more than forty years
have passed since you arrived
that Spring — late in April
Pavel, how long did you live
here? In only seven weeks
you grasped the universe
within these ramparts
and etched a page of sorrow
with your poem

Pavel, I have just come
from your city . . .
the glorious buildings of Prague
are unscathed by the War
In the narrow winding
streets of the Jewish Quarter
where you were born
centuries-old synagogues
are museums —
one thousand only
of your people live there now

[stanza continues]

On a wall in Pinkas Synagogue
your name is inscribed
with nearly eighty thousand others

In remembrance
Pavel, the light
is tarnished with ashes
and every stone is stained
Here in Terezín
wings the color of rust
are fluttering . . .

Holocaust Remembrance Day

— Jerusalem

Everything
even the wind
through the trees
through the dry clouds scudding
over the face of the waters
even the birds' songs
stopped

Stopped like the drivers
who stepped from their cars
like the workers
who stopped at their desks
like the farmers
who stood erect in their fields
We stopped

in our tracks
like their whisks in the batter
like their pens on their pages
in mid-stream
like the laughter of the children
like the embraces of the lovers
were stopped

Like their dreams
like their hopes
like their memories
like their footsteps
like their voices
. . . we stopped

And the sirens wailed *remember*
And again they wailed *remember*

Shoshana

for Shoshana Schreiber, who bears number A-25415 on her arm

Leaning on her cane   and into
the wind of two continents
that lifts the leaves of Jerusalem
and sweeps by her in
the streets of New York,
wisps of blond hair
straying from under
an elegant hat,
she listens
as the wind carries
the refrain
    Shoshi Shoshi
    you will survive

At end of day she removes
hairpins   and as she brushes
remembers a scarf
long lost   white and crimson
rescued from a heap
of abandoned clothes
and stuffed   (verboten)
in the toe of her shoe
as she passed (otherwise
innocent   naked and shorn)
the armed guards of Auschwitz
    Shoshi Shoshi
    you will survive

On her high hard bunk
she tied the scarf
securely around her head
crimson and white   in a sea of sick gray
caught the eye of the kapo
who selected her for
work in the kitchen
where she ate what she could scrape
and wondered why   with a scarcity of bread
the stacks always smoked at the bakery ovens
    Shoshi Shoshi
    you will survive

She remembers   the hands of her mother
and the eyes of her father
and recalls the clatter
of wheels on tracks

[stanza continues]

and the voice of her brother
in the cavedark of the boxcar
"Shoshi Shoshi
you will survive"
The faces their faces she remembers
the last time she glimpsed them
when she gazes into
her grandchildren's faces
(eight in New York thirteen in Jerusalem)

And she leans
into the wind of two continents
which rises
bypasses Europe
lifts the leaves
under a stone-heavy sky
and shifts

Unanswerable Questions

Along the path where your light feet passed
your footsteps have been lost forever . . .
— Haim Guri

It was here Jhirka
in that black yesterday
after your fists were torn

from your mother's shirt
and you were ripped
from her breast

when your eyes were dark
and your mouth was full
of questions

you shared the hard wood bunk
of a starving man
who had no answers

for a boy of five
with no memory
of life under a wide sky

beyond this
barbed electric fortress
But he captured you

in a sketch
that survives
framed and protected under glass

Oh Jhirka
do your ashes
nourish wild vermilion poppies

or eddy endlessly in the River Ohře?
Your image stays
and haunts

the silence
of an unlit place
where we walk now

and cry out “why”
. . . but Jhirka
who will ask your questions?

Enid Shomer

Women Bathing at Bergen-Belsen

— April 24, 1945

Twelve hours after the Allies arrive
there is hot water, soap. Two women bathe
in a makeshift, open-air shower while nearby
fifteen thousand are flung naked into mass graves
by captured SS guards. Clearly legs and arms
are the natural handles of a corpse. The bathers,
taken late in the war, still have flesh
on their bones, still have breasts. Though nudity was
a death sentence here, they have undressed,
oblivious to the soldiers and the cameras.
The corpses push through the limed earth like upended
headstones. The bathers scrub their feet, bending
in beautiful curves, mapping the contours
of the body, that kingdom to which they’ve returned.

Joan I. Siegel

Haggadah

After reading Primo Levi

If not death
    still there would be winter

If not winter
that burns a man's lips blue
and freezes excrement and blood
winter that roars through cloth
slashes the weft of flesh
the warp of sleep
    still there would be hunger

If not hunger
growling like a wild beast
in the empty belly
in the bones
in the eyes
in the ears
    still there would be fear

If not fear
in the eyes of the mothers
in the eyes of the fathers
in the eyes of the daughters
in the eyes of the sons
all eyes
crawling in the mud
slouching toward nothing
    still there would be hope

If not hope
when spring rains came
and washed the air
and washed the earth
and washed the fire
and washed the blood
and punished all with memory
so that one might recall
he was once a man
    still there would be shame

If not shame
for what one has thought
or not thought
shame for what one has done
or not done
shame for what one has become
or not become
among the living
and the dead
    still there would be death

And if not death
    still there would be memory

Maurya Simon

Letter to Vienna from Paris, 1942

Grandmother,
your face is dangerous,
is a chameleon blushing
the color of red onions.

You missed the last exodus:
it's obvious your teeth
won't last.

Look at the world's compass.
The needle's nose trembles.
Here, children cut yellow stars
from old scarves, their topaz
eyes turn brass and tarnish.

Grandfather,
they left your white dish
dark with foreboding.
You're too cold to carry fire:
all your weapons sold
for fake diplomas.

The iron wings stretch out
across France, Poland, Russia.
The thin hand of each man
is clasped to fodder.

Louis Simpson

The Bird

"Ich wünscht', ich wäre ein Vöglein,"
Sang Heinrich, "I would fly
Across the sea . . ." so sadly
It made his mother cry.

At night he played his zither,
By day worked in the mine.
His friend was Hans; together
The boys walked by the Rhine.

"Each day we're growing older,"
Hans said, "This is no life.
I wish I were a soldier!"
And snapped his pocket-knife.

War came, and Hans was taken,
But Heinrich did not fight.
"Ich wünscht', ich wäre ein Vöglein,"
Sang Heinrich every night.

"Dear Heinrich," said the letter,
"I hope this finds you fine.
The war could not be better,
It's women, song and wine."

A letter came for Heinrich,
The same that he'd sent East
To Hans, his own handwriting
Returned, and marked *Deceased*.

*

"You'll never be a beauty,"
The doctor said, "You scamp!
We'll give you special duty —
A concentration camp."

And now the truck was nearing
The place. They passed a house;
A radio was blaring
The *Wiener Blut* of Strauss.

The banks were bright with flowers,
The birds sang in the wood;
There was a fence with towers
On which armed sentries stood.

They stopped. The men dismounted;
Heinrich got down — at last!
"That chimney," said the sergeant,
"That's where the Jews are gassed."

*

Each day he sorted clothing,
Skirt, trousers, boot and shoe,
Till he was filled with loathing
For every size of Jew.

"Come in! What is it, Private?"
"Please Sir, that vacancy . . .
I wonder, could I have it?"
"Your papers! Let me see . . ."

"You're steady and you're sober . . .
But have you learned to kill?"
Said Heinrich, "No *Herr Ober-*
Leutnant, but I will!"

"The Reich can use your spirit.
Report to Unit Four.
Here is an arm-band — wear it!
Dismissed! Don't slam the door."

*

"*Ich wünscht', ich wäre ein Vöglein*,"
Sang Heinrich, "I would fly . . ."
They knew that when they heard him
The next day they would die.

They stood in silence praying
At midnight when they heard
The zither softly playing,
The singing of the Bird.

He stared into the fire,
He sipped a glass of wine.
"Ich wünscht'," his voice rose higher,
"Ich wäre ein Vöglein . . ."

A dog howled in its kennel,
He thought of Hans and cried.
The stars looked down from heaven.
That day the children died.

*

"The Russian tanks are coming!"
The wind bore from the East
A cannonade, a drumming
Of small arms that increased.

Heinrich went to headquarters.
He found the Colonel dead
With pictures of his daughters,
A pistol by his head.

He thought, his courage sinking,
"There's always the SS . . ."
He found the Major drinking
In a woman's party dress.

The prisoners were shaking
Their barracks. Heinrich heard
A sound of timber breaking,
A shout, "Where is the Bird?"

*

The Russian was completing
A seven-page report.
He wrote: "We still are beating
The woods . . ." then he stopped short.

A little bird was flitting
Outside from tree to tree.
He turned where he was sitting
And watched it thoughtfully.

He pulled himself together,
And wrote: "We've left no stone
Unturned — but not a feather!
It seems the Bird has flown.

"Description? Half a dozen
Group snapshots, badly blurred;
And which is Emma's cousin
God knows, and which the Bird!

"He could be in the Western
Or in the Eastern Zone.
I'd welcome a suggestion
If anything is known."

*

"Ich wünscht', ich wäre ein Vöglein,"
Sings Heinrich, "I would fly
Across the sea," so sadly
It makes his children cry.

A Story About Chicken Soup

In my grandmother's house there was always chicken soup
And talk of the old country — mud and boards,
Poverty,
The snow falling down the necks of lovers.

Now and then, out of her savings
She sent them a dowry. Imagine
The rice-powdered faces!
And the smell of the bride, like chicken soup.

But the Germans killed them.
I know it's in bad taste to say it,
But it's true. The Germans killed them all.

*

In the ruins of Berchtesgaden
A child with yellow hair
Ran out of a doorway.

A German girl-child —
Cuckoo, all skin and bones —
Not even enough to make chicken soup.
She sat by the stream and smiled.

Then as we splashed in the sun
She laughed at us.
We had killed her mechanical brothers,
So we forgave her.

*

The sun is shining.
The shadows of the lovers have disappeared.
They are all eyes; they have some demand on me —
They want me to be more serious than I want to be.

They want me to stick in their mudhole
Where no one is elegant.
They want me to wear old clothes,
They want me to be poor, to sleep in a room with many others —

Not to walk in the painted sunshine
To a summer house,
But to live in the tragic world forever.

Myra Sklarew

from Lithuania

2

There is no way
to make the journey to this place. We circle
it, we read it like a map of a district, we name
its alleyways and its houses. We draw in closer
like the camera's eye but we describe
shadows, we describe air fence
lattice petrol cudgel wooden club
water hose gully blood we describe
a man, hardly more than a boy.

He leans on a wooden club, resting —
his murdered lie at his feet his dying
at his feet, his club thick as an arm
high as his chest, he is wearing
a fine suit of clothing his hair
is combed. A group of Jewish men guarded
by armed civilians wait their turn. Within forty-five
minutes the young man has beaten

them to death. And when he is done,
he puts his club to one side
and climbs on the corpses and plays
the Lithuanian national anthem
on his accordion to the clapping
and singing of the nearby civilians —
women hold up their small children to see.
At Keidan in order to cover the cries

of the Jews forced to strip at the mouth
of a mass grave, the Lithuanians started up their tractor
motors. Those not killed by machine guns were buried
alive. All this was watched by the principal
of the high school, the mayor, and a young
priest. Afterwards, the Lithuanians told that when
the pit was covered with a bit of earth, the surface
heaved up and down as if a live pulse

emanated from that mass grave. In order to stop
the heaving of the blood earth, the Lithuanians
used rollers to press the earth down . . .

6

Be wary of old forts — they have a history
of killing; their walls are used to the screams
of prisoners, the silence of death. Their walls
are impervious to the last messages
scrawled in blood. There is no poetry in any
of this. These forts have witnessed
the deaths of over a hundred thousand Jews. Be wary
of names. Those who took the long

road from ordinary life to the ghetto and
from the ghetto to the Ninth Fort called that way
Via Dolorosa — Christ's walk
to Golgotha. The road that led uphill from
Kovno to the Ninth Fort. The Germans called it
the Way to Heaven — *Der Weg*
zur Himmel-Fahrt. And in secret they named it
Place of Extermination No. 2, *Vernichtungstelle*, nr. 2.

Not existing place, *vernichtungstelle*. No,
that's not quite it. A transitive word, more active —
place to make nothing, to nullify, cancel, annul.
You must say these names yourself. Taste
the strange mixtures of annihilation, the Jew
using Christian iconography, going in columns
of a hundred along the sorrowful way.
In the Ninth Fort the power went off. We

stood in the cold dark, in the cold, in the
dark. We could smell the air they had breathed.
I wanted, above all, to escape. But I kept
my feet on the ground. We lighted candles
and we walked through the steel blackness.
The woman with me had worked there twelve years.
Her face had no expression as she talked about what
happened there, the voice drilling into my head.

In the barracks, dug deep into the ground, heavy
steel doors. Deep trenches surrounding the
fortifications. High concrete walls, rows of barbed
wire. Trucks whose motors were run to drown
out the sound of crying, of shooting. Guards
who beat and chased them into the paths of the guns
of the Lithuanian partisans. *October 4: Kovno, 9th fort —*
315 Jewish men, 712 Jewish women,

818 Jewish children (punitive action because
a German policeman was shot at in the ghetto). October 29:
Kovno, 9th fort — 2,007 Jewish men, 2,920 Jewish women,

[stanza continues]

4,273 Jewish children (removal from the ghetto of surplus Jews).
Digging and burning. What was
buried had to be unburied. The Master of Fire,
the expert on burning supervised the firemen,
three hundred bodies exhumed and burned

each day until the flour of dead souls disappeared
in the earth or fled upward into the air.

8

What I remember is not how they were
rounded up like animals, caught
like fish in a net, beaten and shouted at, dragged
over the fallen bodies of their kind, not how
they stood against a wall or at the edge
of a ravine or a pit or a trench they themselves
were forced to dig, knowing
it was for their own graves, not how they were

bludgeoned or blasted out of this life,
nor what they thought or felt as they breathed
in the air of their last moments, but
what happened afterward. The single human
acts that came afterwards. We know about the killings,
we have seen the pictures, read the descriptions, heard
the testimonies. We know nothing about the killings.
How could we? But what happened afterward.

How the women who were not burned
alive in the school house or the church or their villages
sent the smallest children home and walked up
to the edge of the ravine to see
for themselves. How they stepped carefully
among the bodies until they found their own: brothers, sons,
fathers. How they tenderly held their hands,
their heads, still warm. How they did not know

what to do. How they removed the wedding rings
from the fingers before they grew stiff and wore,
from that day on, two rings on their wedding finger.
How that night they came with candles
and kept a vigil so their dear ones would not
be alone all night. How in the morning they came with water
and cloths and washed their dead and prepared them
for burial. How they carried each of them on a palette

to the graveyard, thirteen hundred of them. How the other villagers
came to help them. And they set them in the center
of the cemetery and with the stones of the stony fields

[stanza continues]

they built a wall around them, to keep them from wild
animals, to give them the burial every dead one deserves.
But for mine, the tender acts afterward were not
possible, not the hands on their faces, nor the white
cloths to wash them, nor a few drops of water,

nor their faces turned upward to the opening
sky, but thrown down, eyes wide against the blood earth,
in whatever state they happened to fall, whatever moment
of surprise or pain. Nor were there any to find them, to carry
them, to console my dead. Afterward, to cover their actions,
those barely alive were forced to dig up the bodies out of the
pits, the ravines, to prepare a place for burning, a stack of logs,
a row of bodies, logs, bodies, orderly but for the power of the

odor of death, but for the decay of death, the fires taking them,
taking the living, not even washing
the dead, not even burying our dead, not even, not

Joan Jobe Smith

Hollow Cost

My mother told me about the hollow cost
one Saturday morning as I lay
in her bed beside her where I read
comic books while she moaned
for just forty more winks, it her
day off from the Payless Café,
and when she finally yawned,
stretched and woke, after I'd
turned the Little Lulu pages
as loudly as I could, sometimes
she told me stories about when
she was a little girl in Texas
riding horses, milking cows,
cooking on a wood-burning stove.
But that one morning she cleared her throat
the way she always did before she scolded me
and she told me she had something to tell me
that I should hear first from my mother
hunger
gas showers
shaven-headed women
human-skin lampshades

[stanza continues]

the war so much more
than white oleo
F.D.R. speeches on the radio
letters from my father in Algeria. Oh,
how you wish you had never heard
some of the things your mother told you
that six million were more
than all the stars in the sky
on a clear winter night

Kirtland Snyder

"City Children at a Summer Camp. Slonim, 1936"

The naked girls
lift their arms
above their heads.

Are they under
arrest?

No, they are showering
at the Jewish camp,
hands held up

deflecting drops of water.

Light makes of their arms
fine porcelain.

They could be Dresden
dolls
were they not
living children.

Heads bowed,
they stand on wooden
planks
on porcelain feet,
one girl up on tip-toe.

Water sparkles
in their hair,
shines on their fine
skin.

Porcelain dolls,
easily broken.

No fruit to come,
ever,
from their plump vulvas.

"Selma . . . A Pot of Soup . . . A Bottle of Milk. Łódź, 1938"

Look
how Selma holds
the bottle
out to us.

Shall we sip
the milk,
so white!
so cold!

Look
how she holds
the soup
beneath her shawl,

keeping its warmth
for the walk home.

Can you smell it? Barley!

Selma's smile
is all we need
to know her happiness,
the happiness
of all her family
who today will eat and drink.

But what of the swelling
sleeplessness
about her eyes,

The mark above her brow
that seems
a bullethole —

what of that?

J. R. Solonche

Another Book on the Holocaust

Is it the duty
Of every survivor

To write a book?
The stories are

The same. Read one,
You've read them all.

Why should we be
Different from

The earth itself
That has already

Forgotten, in a shorter
Time than the life

Of a witness, how
Its new grass was grown,

Where its wounds
Had been, and what

Had filled them in?
I can't believe

They think we don't believe.
Surely we believed

From the very beginning,
At the sight of the first

Pictures: those shreds
Of people, fingers

Of bodies staring through
The wire as if it

Weren't there, those bodies
Of fingers curled around

The air in lost fists.
We sickened at the sight.

The bodies, the parts
Of the bodies, the whole

Bodies, the naked bodies,
The bodies recognizable

And the bodies unrecognizable,
The piles of bodies, bodies

Heaped on bodies heaped on
Bodies, bodies in mounds

As though swept there by
A broom made for sweeping bodies.

They sickened us. The facts
Of bodies. Statistics of

Bodies. Arithmetic of bodies.
They sickened us until

They numbed us. The dead proof.
How can they, the living proof,

Believe we don't believe?

Jason Sommer

from Mengele Shitting

III. Speaking of the Lost

I cannot look at Lilly as I ask
my father about his younger brother Shmuel,
whom she knew only a little,
the brother also of her husband Harry
sitting on my left. Of these
survivors of slave-labor and war,
her history may be the worst,
and she never speaks of it, not of Auschwitz
or the brothers of her own she lost there,
so it's her eyes I avoid as I break the etiquette
forbidding anyone to ask for speech
when speech is memory and memory is pain.

Alone among them, I try to think of myself
as an adult with a right to speak, a man
who has paid a price and waited long enough,
and I have children of my own, off somewhere
in the house with their mother and my mother,

[stanza continues]

but I feel like a child demanding a story,
teased with the half-promise of my father's
stories, wanting the one he cannot tell —
the one which has been told to him
by witnesses in that vague way they have
of passing on essentials only, the barest news.

I want whatever else can be recovered
to hold Shmuel at the center of a final scene,
but Harry and my father have begun
now with the boyhood of someone
who is already the hero of a tale —
handsome as he was tall, as strong as he was both,
at home in the forests around Kustanovice,
gifted with understanding the language of animals,
and I continue romance to the end,
imagining him a wild creature,
gnawing his very life away to be free
of the trap, undoing the web of barbed wire
over the window of — not a cattle car,
I knew already — a Karlsruhe freight, one hundred
tons, a number chalked up outside
on the weathered boards, forcing himself
out awkwardly, dropping — how far down? — to the water.

If they suffer memory for me,
maybe I can give them something in return,
the date they need to commemorate
the true anniversary of Shmuel's death
with *yahrzeit* candles — my bookishness of use
to them with SS diaries, maps of train routes.
As they grow older, more and more
they want the ritual.
I want the discipline of facts,
about that train to Auschwitz, to anchor Shmuel
in the drift of others' memory where he swims
across an unnamed river to his death
in a flood of gunfire on the farther shore.

I have a plan to follow rivers
if only on the maps, until they intersect
the lines of track, and I will have the place
he died among those crossings.
How many trestle bridges can there be,
crossing as the rivers bend?
I run to get an ordinary atlas,
which shows the possibilities in blue
meandering lines and red lettering:
The Tisza, too soon out of Munkács, or the Latorica,

[stanza continues]

Laborec, Ondava, Topl'a, Torysa,
as if I could name a river to go back along
against the current of forgetting.
Nervous, I talk and talk, babbling over
the map of Eastern Europe between us on the table:
how, rate by time equaling distance, the date
must lead to the place, but either will give the other,
how at first I thought that it was winter,
filling in with images from movies,
the shot man tumbling down the incline
of the tracks, or rolling into snow.

May Lilly says abruptly *May*
between the twentieth and the twenty-second,
two days, two nights to Auschwitz
from the station at the brickworks.
She was on the transport. She was there.
Nobody looks stunned that she has harbored this
for more than forty years. No voice but mine
determined to recover Shmuel,
to rescue the hero from her silence.
How could she have kept it all these years?
Lilly, there was shooting. The train was halted
on a trestle bridge — think, the twentieth,
the twenty-first, day or night? —
Brakes shrieking. *Polizei* shouting in German.
The splashing below in the water.
Surely she would recall which day that was?
No, says Lilly mildly, *there was shooting*
many times, many times the train would stop
without a reason. In our car, everyone,
old people and children, pressed together.
The women held rags out of the window to catch
rainwater we could drink. The train had many cars.
No one thing happened I could tell from where I was.

IV. *from* **Lilly, Reparations**

There may be hints that God exists in some diminished form, humorous.

At the railhead Lilly saw him first, the binary motion of the stick,
among the stumbling shoals *raus*ed from the boxcars,
doling general death and fishing for his special interests —
twins, any anomaly: the hunchback father and clubfooted son —
unrhythmic metronome sending people to the left or right
onto different lines — death, life, death, death, death death, death —
or with a jerk of the thumb, a flick of the finger in white kid gloves,
arms in a half embrace of himself, left arm across his waist propping
the right, which moved only from the wrist as he parted the living stream,

[stanza continues]

fingertip flick of the finger, jerk of the thumb, or conducting with that baton,
humming opera, *tall* Lilly thought and *handsome*, in his monocle
 and gloves —
not merely handsome, courtly in the way my aunt described him.

Because survivors say some of the worst of the dailiness
the SS enforced involved the bowels,
because in terror of the latrines at night or too weak or diarrheal anyway,
people relieved themselves in the precious containers they used for soup,
or, kept at attention for hours at roll call, soiled themselves where
 they stood —
or at the work details, no break provided, and begging requests refused —

bear with me, Lilly, there is a reason for the coprology, and this is it:
Years later after his brief internment, every day a new name when
 the Americans
called the roll, after his release undetected and all the years of names,
Ullman, Holman, Gregor, Gregori, Hochbicler, Gerhard, Alvez, and the rest,
he acquired the habit, a kind of grooming out of fear, of biting on his
 moustache-ends,
severing bits of hair and swallowing, but since he was not animal enough
 to cough it up,
the hair lodged in his lower bowel and grew and grew as he kept chewing
until it valved the passage closed with a hairball, *tricho-bezoar*,
an asylum condition usually of the stomach — but in this case happily
 otherwise.
So Mengele shitting would have to lean forward with his precise fingers
 in his rectum
to guide stools past, sometimes, of course, not stools but a pouring
 over his hands,
hot as his own insides, bathing him as he should be bathed.

Lilly, rejoice in what he felt arriving at the dispensary in Jundiai, Brazil,
the filth of the surroundings bad enough (the town itself, the outer office) —
a surgeon, too, to shudder at, small-town absurd in cowboy boots,
but worst of all when he reached the sanctum of the operating room,
 around the walls
he saw disposable rubber gloves adhering to tiles, drying for re-use. But
 he had little choice.
Here he would be cut open to get at what he thought was cancer.

So, Lilly, a kind of symmetry that will pass for justice in its absence,
irony's schadenfreude, ours by interpretation of what occurs,
as good as construing Providence out of the luck of chance survival —
yours, say, Harry's, or my father's — or constructing a God
who happens to care for some and takes care of others with a little quittance.
In Dante effluvia doesn't seem that much, serious enough for the *Inferno* —
Canto 18, Ring 8, Trench 2 — frauds swim it.
Who would wish for hell just to have Mengele in it?

[stanza continues]

What Mengele did was not done to him, nothing was done to him by anyone,
but he was unhappy, abandoned, fearful, startled at the least sound:
a car backfiring, being addressed by someone unexpectedly —
a small hell in the body, such as the innocent also experience,
and that hand, which motioned thousands toward death,
those fingers reaching up his ass for years,
this thing I tell you that few people know.

Meyer Tsits and the Children

In the gone world of Roman Vishniac's book
of photographs of Jewish Eastern Europe,
which we sit down to look over,
my father recognizes for certain only
the village idiot of a Munkács neighborhood,
Meyer "Tsits," whom they used to tease:
"Your mother has breasts,"
the children would say as they passed,
and frothing with rage he would give chase
some years before breasts and Meyer were ash.

In the picture, though, Meyer is
contentedly on his way to a meal at the home
of the prosperous burgher who walks beside him
wielding a cane and wearing a *shtreimel*.
(My father thinks the fur hat means it must be *Shabbos*.)
Meyer's benefactor protects the sable tails
from the drizzle with a draped handkerchief
and performing his mitzvah, taking
an unfortunate home to dinner,
he looks more foolish than the fool.

Even in the still one can tell how Meyer moves
on rain-glossed Boco Corsi,
hands tucked into opposite sleeves
making a muff, shuffling the spanceled
steps of a Chinese woman
when Vishniac sights him,
transfers his photographer's gaze down through
the viewfinder of the hidden reflex camera
held at his solar plexus
and out through the lens that peers through
the gap in his overcoat.
In the direction of the background,
straight back until the stacks of firewood,
up stairs behind wrought iron,
through the tiled entry,

[stanza continues]

rooms burst with Rabinovitz's court
where Hassidim argue passionately
over matters of indifference
to those outside their picture
of the world to come, the Messiah,
and the immortality of the soul.

Out of the book open on a table
in the dining room of this house,
I extend the scale of the photograph
into the world —
and my father's cellar rooms
in 1937 would be somewhere
in the schoolyard of this suburban
New York neighborhood.
But my father would not yet have been there.
Even at the late hour of the photograph,
age fifteen, he welded in Fisher's bike shop
on Kertvarosh, which crosses a few blocks
from where Meyer walks,
and my grandmother Yitta Feiga
still launders clothes in someone's basement.

Vishniac clicks his shutter.
Meyer is caught especially unaware,
after and before — no children near to show him
stripped to his oedipal machinery,
though here in this moment, as in his rage
or his final agony, he was incapable of other modes than candor.

Meyer himself would have survived no selection.
He would have been among the first,
as in 1940 they practiced Holocaust
on his sort just to get the knack.
The picture has been hidden, captured,
liberated, restored while other negatives perished
in the journey from their moments.

My father, who has come through much to get here,
prepares to turn the page.
His own escape and liberation
may not be on his mind now.
There are so many losses and Meyer is little to him,
so few survivals and a picture something but not enough.
The dearest faces to him from then
are faces not in this book,
faces of which there are no extant images
outside of memory.

Meyer Tsits and the children
may not signify to him that before the astounding
cruelties are the ordinary ones,
which have been restored to us at least —
the cruelties of sons and fathers,
cruelties which may be partially redeemed
by forgiveness, and therefore for which
forgiveness is seldom sought,
cruelties not on a street which leads to streets
which lead to the camps
where Meyer still and always in his first
childhood, in his first love and jealousy,
was first for the gas.

I delay with questions the turning of the page.
What does the sign behind them — Mydlow — mean? How old was Meyer?
And it comes to me suddenly that I want
my father to ask forgiveness of Meyer Tsits
for peasant amusements,
for laughing the blank laugh
at those one thinks one never will become,
and that I must ask, too, for having made
some part of his life and death
into coin, capital for speculation.
And to ask forgiveness of Meyer Tsits is to
imagine him restored to faculties
he may never have had,
and to believe for a photographic instant
in the immortality of the soul.

The Property of the World

The beam that found her, masking her weeping face
suddenly white in the dark room like a searchlight,
should have meant surprise, did surprise
him, the child shuffling from sleep, the fading
bad dream drowned in new alarm at the flash
of the TV on his mother's face —
simply
some shot more sky than earth: up through wire
to the watchtowers, the gate's *Arbeit Macht Frei*
arching above in wrought iron, and then
downward the widened light was instead
the limp ivory of limbs, bodies entrenched
and shining out of the ground, a second flare
glimpsed just as he turned.
Not yet for him

[stanza continues]

what will come: a teacher's careful introduction,
the documentary — years ahead — the way
he'll be astonished at this nakedness
which is the property of the world, his eyes
drawn to midpoint, the shock at the undiminished
pubis in the fork of the withered legs.
For when
he looked away from her face to see
what she saw, that night it was the shoes,
and only for the moments she allowed
not noticing him there. He saw with her
the shapely heap, the pyramid of shoes
which rose in a mounting absence: antique
high-buttons, work boots, pumps, a small sandal,
all paired invisibly somewhere inside.

Centered in the steady regard of the lens,
the shoes trembled a little. On the abraded
surface of the film, dust leaped back
and forth and a strand of hair appeared, held,
quivering, and whisked away.
The light moved most,
though, as the screen changed on her face,
the icy glint of tears gone in shadow,
and in that shadow the deeper shadows passing
were the film's gray blur and blackout turned to shoulders,
backs, heads: a procession of townspeople
to interrupt the dim light of the shoes
in pyramid, of the hair and clothes in bales,
the glitter of granary heaps of eyeglasses,
watches, jewelry. Beneath the cold gaze
of the G.I.s a few of the women in tears, but most
faces of the town composed to show
nothing, as if the blankness were for inscription —
since somewhere it must be written — that those
who need to see these things will not,
and those
who do not need will see them constantly.
Sometimes his mother cried at gatherings
of children: ordinary events at the Jewish school,
the boys and girls in two lines entering
the room, and he would find her weeping eyes —
the child could feel the sympathy that lay
between his mother and some others who
were gone, that stood between his mother
and him, her living child who might have been
among those other children, if everyone
they knew were someone else,
if that could be.

[stanza continues]

This is his mother's other life and secret,
in which she made a vow, her faithfulness
betrayal to him, as if there were another
child he might have been, a better child
than he has ever been: never sullen,
preferring nothing to a piano lesson,
who wore without demur in summer, long shorts
and knee socks, the sailor coat during winter,
allowed his hair to be cut straight across
his forehead like an English schoolboy's.

Partly on account of that other child
she made her vow about remembering —
and because she wasn't there, but bystanding
here in America in ignorance,
what was it then she had to swear to do
or to forego? — sometimes to put off joy —
to weep without reserve — never to see
without remembering her distant witness
to the story recorded in that shaking light.

She caught sight of him, eager and fearful
at his own looking in, leaped up, hands fluttering:
switching off the set, sweeping her eyes,
taking his hand to lead him back to bed.
Startled at the movement and the sound
the chair made scraping on the floor,
                                                            he thought
he heard his father stir in the next room.
His father's sleep is delicate, forbidden
to disturb. He had been somewhere terrible
and narrowly come through, someplace to do
with what was on the films.
                                                  He might emerge,
disheveled, struggling for focus, looking like anger,
as he once had, naked from the waist,
dark around his genitals like the bodies
in the open graves he nearly was among.
So many dead, how was his father not?
He wondered even as a child,
                                                      and later,
less than halfway to what he has become,
a man considering memory now, the boy
he was at fifteen could think his father slept
as badly as a Nazi guard should sleep —
and worse — could even say to a friend, that he
had heard of them: men who, as the armies
arrived from east and west, threw away
their uniforms, took on the striped pajamas

[stanza continues]

of the camps, made Jews of themselves,
stayed in expiation Jews for years,
but could not fully burn away their sins
or what they'd been — which must sometimes have showed.
What could he do, having told a friend
his evil theory? What penance would be sufficient
for such a wrong except to live as a Jew
trying to imagine his father's guiltless life?

From that night he remembers often the shoes
at first, as if the rest were the parts of a dream
forgotten, gradually recovered in
the certainty that there was one night,
no matter if it resembled others, he knows
the one: the light opening and closing on
his mother's face, the people passing, and her
alarm, the screen blackening to a star,
a dot, then nothing, her wiping the stipple of tears
to a glaze high across her cheeks and temples,
giving him the water he asked for, taking
him to his bed, where he heard from their room
the scrape of whispers breaking into voice
and down again to whispers, over and over
before he slept, but nothing of what they said.

What They Saw

In the midst of, out of the depths of, through
        the strands of wire, beneath and
                between the towers and chimneys,
while they stood roll call under
        the round stars in the earliest daylight,
                or marched out to gather or break stones,

the gaze could go to the low sun gaining,
        a few trees sun-backed, leaves aswarm,
                burning and unconsumed,
or the slender flashes of birch.
        Stronger than the fear, for moments
                at a time, a particle of will summoned

out of them, a secret willing there's no help for,
        they tell me, they who were there
                in that place, or places like it,
eyes lifted toward the hills from where
        came nothing, or following a bird
                or bird song, drawn up

to a sky without smoke —
        not the yellow autumn smoke
                of burning off the potato fields
after the harvest, not the white smoke
        of the blowing snowfall —
                spring the season most often.

A flock of a hundred and more turn
        on a single edge at once,
                slicing back and forth through the spaces beneath
the clouds, dangerous to be lost
        in it, however briefly, but someone is.
                An afternoon, straight ahead of them —

among other stick figures in tatters,
        parting those shufflers and staggerers,
                come striders in uniform:
the head of the head of the women's camp,
        a hint of the blond pennant of her hair
                in a stray lock from under her cap.

Mengele, too, movie-star handsome,
        and beyond the sexual flutter as he
                passes through the women's barracks,
whatever his actual errand, whatever he had
        done or would do, gone for
                a trance instant in his beauty.

Even downcast eyes might find
        something in a frame of vision: the yellow
                star of one dandelion beside
the pure centrifugal burst
        of another's globe of seed,
                like a little puff of smoke.

Gizela Spunberg

Memories of December

Like a very fine, white dust snow was falling
that memorable December night, when we were saying "Good-bye."
We walked the desecrated, violated streets
of our conquered city and knew
that we were parting forever maybe.
I held you under your arm, pressed to your shaking body.

[stanza continues]

In the soft lights of the city lamps I saw your eyelids trembling;
tears were running down your cheeks.
You stopped, turned facing me and said,
"So you are leaving me, that I cannot believe!"
"I must go, my destiny is calling me, Mother!"
And destiny it was — it led me towards life and
yours brought you to your untimely death.
It did not seem that way then —
yours was the safe road, mine the dangerous one.

We returned home, sat holding hands.
You stroked my head, I kissed you on the cheek.
The softness, the feel of it is still on my lips.
Your face is before my eyes, the straight chiseled nose,
the generous chin. I have your mouth and
hairline, exactly to the thinnest angle.

Did I fail you? Did I betray you by my absence?
Would I have been of any help?
There is so much to regret, so much to be sorry for.
You have never been in my home —
I have never cooked a meal for you —
And what is most regrettable, you never saw him,
your grandson, and he never knew you.
There is so much of you in him in looks and traits.
That happiness you deserved — it was torn away from you.

When, again in December, four years after we parted,
they, the cold-blooded killers, took you
for your last walk, you left a message, a legacy:
"Tell my daughters, I was not afraid."

Hans Jörg Stahlschmidt

November Rain

For Patricia

Today I am grateful for the rain — heavy like
milky sheets thrown down from heaven — the rain
that didn't come when the Wannsee Conference met
and the boxcars left for Bergen-Belsen.

These are the tears my parents never cried,
nor their neighbors, nor their uncles and co-workers,
nor the students when their classmates did not return,

[stanza continues]

when their neighbors were picked up in midnight fog,
when books disappeared from libraries
and stores closed forever while storm-troopers
marched proudly down clean streets.

These are the tears I cried with you,
German and Jewish tears together washing the dust
from Hebrew letters on the gravestones in Prague,
stones stacked on top of each other as if even in death
there was no room to be, tears falling onto the deaf tunnel walls
in Theresienstadt and on the Appellplatz in Dachau.

These are the tears that mourn absence, the life
that could have been, the richness of friendships never made,
the Jewish quarters which vanished, the German-
Jewish thoughts never thought, the sound of Yiddish
that could have warmed the long Prussian winters.

This is a grief which does not have a grave
nor a monument nor a museum,
a grief without a name, a photograph or a song;
it is the grief of murdered possibilities, of a strangled unborn,
of books not written, of a painting burnt to ashes,
of orchards that never bloomed. It is the loss
of a brother and a sister I never had.

Visit to the Fatherland

For Patricia

We all had a lot to drink: there were half-empty bottles, breadcrumbs,
laughter, wild conversations. My father, neglected,
became cranky like a child while the darkness was falling
warm and soft upon the poplars and our family
gathered around the large dinner table.

My father rising above the permanent thick haze
of his mind turned to you and I translated
that he was *glad you were with me — you an American woman*
whose country was once an enemy and I said *und eine Jüdin.*
Ja, he said after a long pause, *eine Jüdin.*

You were looking at him with your large green eyes
as if thousands of your tribe were looking through you
as I translated: *I am sorry for what the Germans did to your people;*
it was inhuman, and I want you to know that I never did anything
to any Jew. He took your hand from the green and white
checkered tablecloth and you both cried and my sisters cried.

An old warrior had finally reached out before his mind
faded into a lasting night. I sat still, looking across
the darkening lake and the gray silhouette of the Alps
trying to catch the last vanishing light, unsure
if I could fully believe what he had said, knowing
that there was no one left to erase my doubts.

When we walked out, I held you tightly, as if to press your
body into mine, leaving marks no one could ever erase.

Jan Steckel

The Maiden Aunts

My grandmother was alive again,
the one who said to me on her deathbed,
"You must write!" and
"Don't waste your life cooking, honey;
it's all over in ten minutes."
She told me again
about her rich Latvian aunts
who visited her in the squalor
of the Lower East Side.
Dressed in black, the maiden aunts
bent and kissed her eight-year-old head
saying, "Never forget, Selma,
you are one of the *höcher Menschen*."
What they meant was,
You come from a line of ten chief rabbis
of the city of Riga.
Your grandfather wrote a treatise on Maimonides
that is in the Library of Congress.
Your family, the Widow Romm and Sons,
is the largest publisher of Yiddish books
in Eastern Europe. They own the lumber mills
that make the paper that makes the books.
Though you live in poverty here,
you are part of a civilization.
They kissed my grandmother's head
and sailed back to Europe.
For two decades, they wrote monthly to their faraway niece.
My grandmother sailed on a steamer to California
and joined the Anti-Fascist League,
but she couldn't make her gentile neighbors understand
what was happening in Europe.
She remembered the day the letters stopped.

After the war, she learned
that all the Romms in Europe,
every last one,
had perished in the concentration camp
outside of Riga.
She and her sister
were the only ones left.
She dreamed of the last rabbi of Riga
turning from the door of the gas chamber,
as he shepherded his congregation in.
Beyond him, her two old-maid aunts
clutched each other's hands
and stared at her past the rabbi's shoulder,
whispering "Never forget, Selma."

Martin Steingesser

The Three

For Miroslav Kosek, 12, Hanus Löwy, 13, and one Bachner,
three children who died in German concentration camps

Koleba, you signed your dreams,
raids over the wall
                    for green meadow smell
and the warm hum of bees.
You craved these, not like sweets
but the way fawns forage snow for shoots
and so under one name
                         wrote other lives, brilliant as air
burning like a star
                    over Terezín, over Prague.
And your voices — such thin arms!
                                   straws across the Holocaust,
             reeds weaving into light —
under this sign, your star
          pulses
                    Ko.le.ba
                                   pulses
bright yellow, a burr
                      — your star in the throat of Death

Gerald Stern

Adler

The Jewish King Lear is getting ready
for some kind of horror — he is whispering
in the ears of Regan and Goneril: I know
the past, I know the future, my little hovel

will be in Pennsylvania, I will be
an old man eating from a newspaper,
I will stop to read the news, my fish
will soak the petty world up, it will stretch

from Sears on the left to Gimbels on the right,
my table will be a crate and I will cover
the little spaces with tape, it is enough
for my thin elbows. They will look at him

with hatred reminiscent of the Plains
of Auschwitz — Buchenwald — and drive him mad
an inch at a time. Nothing either in England
or Germany could equal his ferocity,

could equal his rage, even if the Yiddish
could make you laugh. There is a famous picture
of a German soldier plucking a beard; I think
of gentle Gloucester every time I see

that picture. There is a point where even Yiddish
becomes a tragic tongue and even Adler
can make you weep. They sit in their chairs for hours
to hear him curse his God; he looks at the dust

and asks, What have I done, what have I done,
for Him to turn on me; that audience murmurs,
Daughters, daughters, it cries for the sadness that came
to all of them in America. King Lear,

may the Lord keep him, hums in agony,
he is a monster of suffering, so many holes
that he is more like a whistle than like a king,
and yet when sometimes he comes across the stage

crowned with burdocks and nettles and cuckoo flowers
we forget it is Adler, we are so terrified,
we are so touched by pity. It is said
that Isadora Duncan came to worship him,

that John Barrymore came to study his acting,
that when he died they carried his coffin around
from theatre to theatre, that people mourned in the streets,
that he lay in a windsor tie and a black silk coat.

One time he carried Cordelia around in his arms
he almost forgot his words, he was so moved
by his own grief, there were tears and groans
for him when they remembered his misfortune.

I thank God they were able to weep
and wring their hands for Lear, and sweet Cordelia,
that it happened almost fifty years
before our hell, that there was still time then

to walk out of the theatre in the sunlight
and discuss tragedy on the bright sidewalk
and live awhile by mercy and innocence
with a king like Adler keeping the tremors alive

in their voices and the tears brimming in their eyes.
Thank God they died so early, that they were buried
one at a time, each with his own service,
that they were not lined up beside the trucks

or the cattle cars. I think when they saw him put
a feather over her lips they were relieved
to see her dead. I think they knew her life
was the last claim against him — the last delusion,

one or two would say. Now he was free,
now he was fully changed, he was *created*,
which is something they could have to talk about
going back to their stairways and their crowded tables

with real streaks of remorse on their faces —
more than forty years, almost fifty,
before the dead were dragged from their places
and dumped on the ground or put in orderly piles —

I think they used a broom on the charred faces
to see if there was breath — and a match or two
was dropped on the naked bodies. For the sake of art
there always was a German or Ukrainian

walking around like a dignified Albany,
or one made sad repentant noises like Kent
and one was philosophical like Edgar,
giving lectures to the burning corpses,

those with gold in their mouths, and those with skin
the color of yellow roses, and those with an arm
or a hand that dropped affectionately on another,
and those whose heads were buried, and those whose black tongues —

as if there were mountains, as if there were cold water
flowing through the ravines, as if there were wine cups
sitting on top of the barrels, as if there were flowers —
still sang in bitterness, still wept and warbled in sorrow.

Soap

Here is a green Jew
with thin black lips.
I stole him from the men's room
of the Amelia Earhart and wrapped him in toilet paper.
Up the street in *Parfumes*
are Austrian Jews and Hungarian,
without memories really,
holding their noses in the midst of that
paradise of theirs.
There is a woman outside
who hesitates because it is almost Christmas.
"I think I'll go in and buy a Jew," she says.
"I mean some soap, some nice new lilac or lily
to soothe me over the hard parts,
some Zest, some Fleur de Loo, some Wild Gardenia."

And here is a blue Jew.
It is his color, you know,
and he feels better buried in it, imprisoned
in all that sky, the land of death and plenty.
If he is an old one he dances,
or he sits stiffly,
listening to the meek words and admiring the vile actions
of first the Goths and then the Ostrogoths.
Inside is a lovely young girl,
a Dane, who gave good comfort
and sad support to soap of all kinds and sorts
during the war and during the occupation.
She touches my hand with unguents and salves.
She puts one under my nose all wrapped in tissue,
and squeezes his cheeks.

I buy a black Rumanian for my shelf.
I use him for hair and beard,
and even for teeth when things get bitter and sad.
He had one dream, this piece of soap,

[stanza continues]

if I'm getting it right,
he wanted to live in Wien
and sit behind a hedge on Sunday afternoon
listening to music and eating a tender schnitzel.
That was delirium. Other than that he'd dream
of America sometimes, but he was a kind of cynic,
and kind of lazy — conservative — even in his dream,
and for this he would pay, he paid for his lack of dream.
The Germans killed him because he didn't dream
enough, because he had no vision.

I buy a brush for my back, a simple plastic
handle with gentle bristles. I buy some dust
to sweeten my body. I buy a yellow cream
for my hairy face. From time to time I meet
a piece of soap on Broadway, a sliver really,
without much on him, sometimes I meet two friends
stuck together the way those slivers get
and bow a little, I bow to hide my horror,
my grief, sometimes the soap is so thin
the light goes through it, these are the thin old men
and thin old women the light goes through, these are
the Jews who were born in 1865
or 1870, for them I cringe, for them
I whimper a little, they are the ones who remember
the eighteenth century, they are the ones who listened
to heavenly voices, they were lied to and cheated.

My counterpart was born in 1925
in a city in Poland — I don't like to see him born
in a little village fifty miles from Kiev
and have to fight so wildly just for access
to books. I don't want to see him struggle
half his life to see a painting or just to
sit in one of the plush chairs listening to music.
He was dragged away in 1940
and turned to some use in 1941,
although he may have fought a little, piled
some bricks up or poured some dirty gasoline
over a German truck. His color was rose
and he floated for me for days and days; I love
the way he smelled the air, I love how he looked,
how his eyes lighted up, how his cheeks were almost pink
when he was happy. I loved how he dreamed, how he almost
disappeared when he was in thought. For him
I write this poem, for my little brother, if I
should call him that — maybe he is the ghost
that lives in the place I have forgotten, that dear one
that died instead of me — oh ghost, forgive me! —

[stanza continues]

Maybe he stayed so I could leave, the *older* one
who stayed so I could leave — oh live forever!
forever! — Maybe he is a Being from the other
world, his left arm agate, his left eye crystal,
and he has come back again for the twentieth time,
this time to Poland, to Warsaw or Bialystok,
to see what hell is like. I think it's that,
he has come back to live in our hell, if he could
even prick his agate arm or even weep
with those crystal eyes — oh weep with your crystal eyes,
dear helpless Being, dear helpless Being. I'm writing this
in Iowa and Pennsylvania and New York City,
in time for Christmas, 1982,
the odor of Irish Spring, the stench of Ivory.

Bradley R. Strahan

Yom Kippur

In this great synagogue
on this great Sabbath
of the year,
the altar is spread
with flowers.

Not white alone
that mourns endless martyrs
but blues and yellows,
orange and purple,
litany of a people
various as these blossoms,
picked over by some
merciless angel.

Here I count my sins
in silence like cut flowers.
Walking slowly,
I measure my distance
from the stench
of Auschwitz
by the sweet purity
of this day.

Early fallen leaves
litter the path,
abandoned follies

[stanza continues]

of summer.
Still clinging
to this great tree
I feel the surge
that year by year
pushes heavenward
in scorn of ax and saw.

Rabbi Michael Strassfeld

Who Knows One?

A Passover reflection,
April 2006

Who knows one? One is the Janjaweed militia cleansing Darfur

Who knows one? Two is the stealing and killing of livestock

Who knows one? Three is the poisoning of wells and the destruction of crops

Who knows one? Four is the use of rape to destroy and humiliate families

Who knows one? Five is the creation of two-and-a-half million people: displaced,
hungry, susceptible to disease

Who knows one? Six is the over four hundred thousand people who have
already died.

These and more are the plagues of Darfur.

Who knows one?
I know one.
Send a postcard to President Bush. Urge him to take leadership on this issue.
lo dayenu — but it is not enough.

Who knows one?
I know one.
Encourage institutions to hang *Save Darfur* banners outside their buildings.
lo dayenu — but it is not enough.

Who knows one?
I know one.
Attend the rally in Washington, DC on April 30th.
lo dayenu — but it is not enough.

Who knows one?
I know one — Rwanda

Who knows one?
I know one — Bosnia

Who knows one?
I know one — Cambodia

There are too many ones.
And I am the child who does not know how to count:
One. Two. Four hundred thousand. Six million.
For six million are the lips of our dead mouthing "never again" in eternal silence.

Who knows one? I know one.
For I am that one.
One person created in the image of God.
It is for me alone to speak out. I and no other.
Not a messenger, not a congressperson, not a president.

I alone am here to tell the tale.

Who knows one? I am that one.

And who knows — I may be the one who will make the difference.

Lynn Strongin

I met Bergie in my early thirties in Berkeley. It was the first time I had seen the blue numbers on a person's arm. These poems are dedicated to her memory.

Erasing the Blue Numbers

When it snows, Bergie walks into the yard & holds out her arm which held the violin bow.
She lets snow thorns touch her skin
the purple-blue numbers.

When it rains,
She opens her palms   long bird-like hands, which pressed the flute-stops
in blue-silver rain:
        The fingers burn
  the numerals: too, they have a sound: eerie, otherworldly
        they ring
        not the small goat's bell
to the falling rain
but echoing a larger & larger bell   which finally engulfs the world:

[stanza continues]

It is then that
the archangel, Language, spreading wings, burnt-sienna, umber, bruise-
violet   has power to   shade & swallow the death-knell:
        The incessant sound
of snow falling in pines
is still
unable to bury the lies they told for salvation: First Communion for
Jewish girls with assumed names: convent schools near Brussels
Father Bruno sheltering children in Belgium
girls in the Garden of Convents, Franciscan Sisters, Bruges
the Dutch policeman looking out of the entrance latch of the hiding place
discovered by the Germans a day earlier
The *Volksdeutsch*, Ethnic Germans, hated, are buried but the Angel's shadow
cannot completely swallow them:
denounced by the chaplain while righteous rescuers went on
to transit camps   transport trains   the smallest of Jewish children at highest risk:
the yellow star shining in their eyes: its light
the air piercingly sharp, a whip
All rescuers' names would be inscribed in the book of life
but none could eradicate the sound
almost inaudible
of cherry petals falling
touching the blue numbers in spring.

Her Velocity Had Been Taken

Her velocipede parked   in the sepia hallway
the gas-lamp flickering on with its little people
melancholy background of an accordion in Prague playing
smokier than a hazy Sunday in Brussels

The children catch hands, Lisi & Elizabeth, twirl till they grow dizzy
and fall down.
But why have they left Belgium?
Lisi has *jamais vue*: epileptic fits, *petit mal*.
Bergie is the picture of health.

A musical girl. She likes to be in a dusky room damasked,
composing on flute & violin.   Lisi hums.
Until   Burnless sky above Terezín
ignites the notes like parchment. She writes a mazurka for the prisoners,
tries to compose   but tears block her breath & bowing:

The wounded, still standing, hold hands
in Terezín; she wakes screaming with nightmares
of Lisi with her at ages five and nine in Brussels, the park, star sapphire sky sparkling.

Her hundred-year-old doll, Halie, is mauled, shoved in the bin stares
upward into rag & bone pickings
blue glass eyes, cracked bisque skull.
A rat scuttles across the bread.

Steadying her hand with ferocious patience,
Bergie, the blue numbers under her skin
after the dawn nightmare
has a waking vision, an apparition: reaches for the first apple-

blossom of spring
to hand Lisi through the glass of separation, Lisi who has just had another
jamais vue smiling through tears:
Bergie has a bent spine from crouching:
her speed taken, broken like a wing torn off to be thrown into the fire,
which is how the arms & legs of the men & women were, the dead
whose limbs snapped brittle wood

in the conflagration which used all the flames in the world
the sobbing
which used all the tears Lisi cups her hands over her mouth in the silent
scream.

Theresienstadt

There are stones like souls.
— Rabbi Nachman

Were those stones once souls of the small fortress?
Star-shaped thick-walled
with cypress like rows of black torches:
“The Paradise of the camps”

Even the Red Cross was duped into thinking this was a Spa.
This once military prison sucking souls from the shtetls.

The winds form a gallows:
gray vaulted cloisters it dares mimic church
from which to watch the humans
melt away.

*

Parting hours like grasses or the part in a child’s hair.
People like Bergie know shops are back there in the village: cereal & tea.
Here air is granular grains of ice, which rub flesh till it bleeds.
These dough-pale hours.

There was Martha   there Sabine, Marie:
they walk   exhaling fragile breath, which leaves a small cloud
upon the air
soon sharpening whiter & whiter
as though their Bas Mitzvah dresses
have been exchanged for burial robes.

Look once
down the gray stone well & you will never look again:
but look away from the reflections
which ice will seal over
like the happiness of our people
driven into permanent exile
to reflect like copper branches
in iridescent ice, hallucinatory,   frozen.

What a Waste of World

Yesterday Mother still drew
Sleep toward them like a white moon,
There was the doll with cheeks de-rouged by kisses
— Nelly Sachs, "O the Night of the Weeping Children!" from *O the Chimneys*

Translated by Michael Hamburger

I. Bleeding thru the Roses on Your Quilted Vest

O Lord of burning, how permit this conflagration?

At intervals through day, glancing at sun through barbed wire birds,
Bergie, you brusht the hair from your eyes, thin as smoke or nerves.

Fifty springs ago, you were a girl opening a new cake of lustrous rosin.
At Yom Kippur air was flammable kerosene.
Then you were taken
Rounded up.

*

This, walking from the beginning,
your shoes ripped off your feet:
the outer world harsh, the inner not forgiving.

Whiteout love's name   snow had fallen during night.
It was in brick crevices
of this star-shaped fortress
which was your hell:
a trio was rehearsing chamber music.
Despite the music, despite the theatre, despite the dancing

[stanza continues]

it was all macabre theatre, aglitter
Like that snow world at the Town Gate of Nuremberg
into which Casper Hauser came.
You too had been stabbed to the heart
bleeding
through the roses on your quilted vest.

II. Closing Both Eyes You Imagined

Bleeding thru the roses on your quilted vest,
closing both eyes you imagined first snow back home mirror-like
flake-after-flake
six-sided
spinning
dizzily
melting:

language, speech forming, before you lost them
&
the triage workers came.

Old Father, his pipes & leathers, old Mother, her yarns of colors
their names will be written in the book of life
You had no sweethearts, only Lisi, little sister: you were too young
to have lain with a boy.

III. Fire Bit the Legs off the Horse

To have lain with a boy came later, was haven.
But early in childhood.
fire bit the legs off the horse.
Schwesterlein kissed the cheeks from the doll
long ago.
Now,
bronze sunrise finds the rooster crowing from his own dunghill.
The unanswered questions
far outnumber the answered ones:
being taken in a gas-van
in a locked cage No one lit the sun those days:
only, on lowest branches, filaments of wiry angels
while Sabine, your bunk-mate, committed suicide throwing her head back
upon barbed wire
one Arctic morning.

Ishmael knocking at the gate, shivering.
You knew
hod carriers would come
the first Monday of Forever:

[stanza continues]

without God
Where were you?
At this terrible ignition
you were at the junction
of Hope & Despair
& cried out
Where are you
O Lord of all burning things?

Yerra Sugarman

Because

There were days the color of numbers, of runny ink
marks on the arms, the color of iris and storm,
of cattle brand. When I was small,

I thought some people come numbered.
There was the silent ticking of stars, their clear
constant trails, memories floating up from nowhere:

Gedenkst du? Remember? He was a socialist
before the war. Gey shoyn. Go on . . . There were stories
from the Torah, a Sabbath candelabra (the one thing saved).

Why? Because our minds are like planted fields.
Candy dishes of crystal, rose and blue, bone china,
a bad painting of the Champs Élysées (purchased with care)

the people in it just a few quick brushstrokes. Kosher
bakery cookies, tea served in glass cups, its darkness lightened
by wheels of lemon. There were the swirling rhythms

of the Bible. *When you pray you should move*
your lips. Why? Because God must hear
each word. You should shuckle back and forth,

sway. Why? Because the spirit of man
is a candle. There was the rush to Yizkor services
when children were hushed and filed out of the sanctuary.

Why? Because the dead are asked to intercede.
Early cherry blossoms pawed the suburban fences.
Crocuses speared through late snow where we found ghost

boot-holes, paths that made you know
someone had lived before and now you were taking
their place. The voices of my parents and their friends

hard as iron, soft as pulp. The languages
they spoke pellets of hail against a window.
I met him in the camp, in lager.

Prosze Pani, please Madam, take more cake.
Bardzo ladny. Very good.
He looked like a Pole, that's how he survived.

Beautiful dress! To jest piekna, Pani Regina. Sheyn.
She ran from one hiding place to another. That's why she's so nervous.
Dziekuje bardzo. A sheynem dank. Thank you very much.

What I still don't understand — the simultaneity:
beauty fringing horror, the everyday
lined like a coat with the fabric of the extraordinary. A glitter

of lakes, the plush of trees alongside the route of freight trains
from Drancy to Auschwitz. On Deportation Convoy 23,
there was a girl with my name, my name exactly,

just another language. *Convoy*, I look up
the meaning: *To accompany on the way*
for protection. A protecting force. There were skies

opalescent as the insides of oyster shells, clouds
like schools of newly hatched fish.
Some of the children were listed only by number. Why?

Because the infants were too young
to say their names. Why? Because there was light
reaching through the ribs of the library chairs.

Because there was light.

Yuri Suhl

. . . And the Earth Rebelled

News item: A great number of Jewish prayer-shawls, many of them blood-stained, were given burial in the Jewish cemetery in Yavar, Lower Silesia. . . . Together with the prayer-shawls, there were also buried several small cakes of soap which the Nazi murderers had made out of Jewish bodies.

The earth rebelled.
The good and patient earth,
Which knows so well
Death's varied look, its every shape and mold,

[stanza continues]

Had never taken to itself
A corpse of soap,
Enshrouded in a prayer-shawl's bloody fold.

The Grave was stunned,
And beat the earth with frantic cry:
"And where is body? Where is bone?"
But earth had no reply.
The Grave insisted: "I have always been
The confidant of Death, his trusted kin,
I know the turn of all his harrowed lines:
Death with gaping holes instead of eyes,
Death with shape of life, or cruelly torn,
And tender, cherished infants dead, new-born,
And those who died by gas, the 'peaceful' dead,
'Efficient' Death, with bullet-hole in head,
And Death imprinted with the hangman's rope.
But never have I seen a corpse of soap,
Nor heard that Jewish prayer-shawls can die!" . . .
But earth had no reply.

The earth was stark
In soundless shock
From drop of dew to mountain mass;
And all the leaves on all the trees were numb,
And all the winds arrested in their paths.

The birds in all their secret nests
Were stricken dumb,
As though the Grave, by disbelief,
Had turned the pulse of earth to stone,
And now moaned lonely in his grief:
"Whence this *tallis*? Why this soap?
And where is body? Where is bone?"

But suddenly a blast of thunder split
The clotted silence of the earth to bits,
And over all of Europe's fields and seas,
From ocean beds to misty mountain peaks,
Was heard the throbbing of the Grave's demand:
"For every bit of soap there was a soul,
For every *tallis* there was once a man!
Now earth and Grave must call the awful roll,
And never will the reckoning be done,
Till all the dead are counted,
One by one!"

And thus the Grave spake to the wondering Wind:
"Get ye into that land of frightful sin,
Where German Nazi — forever cursed name —

[stanza continues]

Destroyed a people in a flame of pain.
Awaken all the martyrs, tortured, bled,
Bestir the crumbling ashes in the pits,
And ask the ashes, ask the restless dead,
And ferret out the traces, find a way
To recognize the *tallis* and the corpse
Of human soap that came to me today!"
And thus it was that in a herald's guise,
The Wind pressed forward into Polish skies.

The grasses wept, and all the stalks of grain,
And every threshold, suffering memory's pain,
And all the splintered ruins, charred and burned,
And all the ancient hallowed streets, upturned,
And anywhere the searching Wind appeared,
Arose the sound of sobbing and of tears.

The Wind, perplexed, turned here and there.
So many graves on Polish earth!
Lublin or Łódź or Warsaw first?
Or maybe Maidanek? Or where?
"Where!" the echo came from far and near,
And from the disembodied multitude
A million-voiced reply resounded; "Here!
Our corpse, an image of six million Jews!
The tortured dead of Warsaw, Vilna, Łódź,
The bitter weeping and the tears unshed,
Each smouldering ash, each drop of blood,
Are all one corpse, one body of our dead!"

But still the doubting Wind did not believe,
And tarried, unconvinced, to hear the truth.
Again the echoes cried, "Go back!
And take along these signs as proof."
And then the heavens shook
And from the emptiness
Came forth the witnesses:
A speck of glowing ash.
A letter from a sacred Book.
A last *Shema*.
And shifting in his course, the Wind returned
To tell the waiting Grave what he had learned.

But as the Wind moved past a Polish wood,
A voice arose: "Your work is not yet done!
Add to the prayer, the ashes, and the Book,
the thunder of a Jewish Fighter's gun!"

Translated from the Yiddish by Max Rosenfeld

Zahava Z. Sweet

Dark Whispers

In memory of my mother
— Łódź Ghetto, 1941

Grandmother
sorts potato peels in the sink
for our supper.
"My children gone," she sighs.
"The oldest and the youngest gone."
I hide in the black folds of her dress —
will my mother come back?

The light of day faded
in Grandmother's house,
the room dark as her dress.
I sleep in the empty bed,
my mother's hair
in the blankets.
Her fragrance of konwalia. If I wait
the door might open.
She will appear in her seal coat,
her voice,
pearls of the sea.
Perhaps she'll come
through a window in the sky,
fly in on wings,
a raven or an angel.
Maybe I could take
a strand of her hair
to wear
on my finger.

The Line

We stood
in a long
line
moving slowly.

A crooked
line
bulging
from inside
and outside.

Skin
on our faces
white tissue
bodies
bones
without
marrow

feet
dragging
in
oversized
shoes
hardly
stirring
the dust.

In a line
moving
slowly
we stood still.

In Ravensbrück

After "Two Winds" by Julian Tuwim

Perhaps there were leaves rustling in a field.
I couldn't see
through the windows covered with soot.
Maybe a wind blew in the meadow,
though I didn't hear it.

Inside the barrack,
(an anxious rectangle)
three sips of water in a tin can,
five crumbs of blind bread.
A sack full of straw: a bed.
The flimsy gray jacket
full of lice: a blanket.

One wind in the meadow blew.
There must have been a sky somewhere,
children going to school,
drinking milk in the morning.
In this anxious rectangle
two sips of water in a can,
three crumbs of bread.

Words tumbled in my head,
at night when nothing stirred —
words, heavy at first,
from a forgotten well.
One wind in the meadow blew.
A second wind in the garden flew.
Leaves chased and embraced
the second wind.

Marie Syrkin

Niemand*

You with the cross and you without the cross,
Come quietly.
We go to Maidanek; all roads lead there
And every sea.
The summons is for all; the pilgrims wait.
It is not far.
You will find stations: shelter in Zbonzyn,
A bed in Babi Yar.

Niemand will greet you; *Niemand* knows the way
From ditch to doom.
(Hear the Annunciation: cursed art thou,
And cursed thy womb.)
A little child shall lead you — it is he,
No one, my son.
No one, Nobody, Nothing — now he calls
On everyone.
The house of death is big; its walls will hold
A multitude;
And of this sacrament you must partake,
Body and blood.

You with the cross and you without the cross,
On each the sin.
Seek absolution in no other place.
Come, enter in.

**In 1938, a Jewish woman driven out of the Sudeten area gave birth to her son in a ditch. She named him* Niemand, *Nobody.*

The Reckoning

In the hour of reckoning
You will have to count them one by one.
Not a single figure dare be lost,
Not one old man
Or frightened child that ran.
You will have to count them everyone
Till the sum be done.

The total has been quickly made too long:
The lethal chambers filled, the ovens stoked,
And the six million tripping from the tongue.

But you will have to count them one by one,
Without a census or machines that add
A golden girl unto a golden lad.
Upon the fingers of your outstretched hand
The reckoning will stand.

Marilynn Talal

Another Holocaust Poem

What drives me? One more poem won't change anything.
I spit out grief, trying to send it away like worshipers
at a Shinto shrine tying paper strips with bad fortunes
onto bare branches that flutter with bad luck.

For years, one photo lit up memory: four men in sunlight,
three laughing in uniforms creased like wire, the fourth drowning
in a coat as he danced, one ripped shoe showing toes
like a tongue.

Then I remembered, realized I had conflated at least two:
the four men on that sunny street and another of soldiers
machinegunning the feet of men in hats and long coats,
white beards wild, feet spinning in air.

The picture stands, an open gate where I hear something.
Last night, I closed the curtains, shutting out the darkness,
and heard the hooks groan. I think it is that sound. The picture
will not let me go.

For Our Dead

1

The air where their ashes have gone
is a mirror against our faces.
Each breath carries mute pleading, hear it, hear
this pathetic rebuke to inadequacy
and constant failure.

These ashes stop our mouths.
The dead lay claim to us
who must not let go the millions of destroyed worlds
that, unredeemed, call and call.
There is no answer.

How can we say Kaddish? Praise God?
The bitterness breaks our teeth.

Torn from this life, the ties
to this world not tenderly laid aside,
these ghosts hover over the surface of the earth
tethered to the fragrance of a pot of soup
steaming on the stove,
the horse's harness on a nail to be mended,
the severed rope of a toy pull-wagon
wheels spinning on finger-sized axles.

They died many deaths at each
hopeless point: roundup, the clanging doors,
whips and loud, rude calls: "Heraus! Heraus!"
Slowly their suffering reshapes our being
and we are helpless children
in a world without guidance.

2

O, our loved ones, the places shorn of you
cry out. They are not vacant but burn
as witnesses of torment.
The very stones tremble with damnation.

Our lives will always be in disarray
around this great wound. Particles
in the mass, we make small
arrangements at the edges.
Evil has become too large.

The Kaddish is supposed to comfort, to begin
to mend the tear. What blood song
can redeem this blood lesson?

Ripped out of lives in mid-step,
that hole in the air hangs, shaping itself
into a mouth twisted with weeping.

My Mother as Superhero

Faster than a fleeing cattle car, she flies to smash tracks.
Her bare hands destroy swaths of barbed wire. At the gas chambers,
she tears out canisters of Zyklon B, not leaving one whiff
to poison the air. With her superhuman breath, she blows out
fires in the crematoria. A careless throw tosses Hitler
into space where he tumbles, slowly disintegrating.

Pleased with her feats, her Krypton strength,
she trucks loads of nourishing food to feed the starving.
She transports frightened refugees home, builds comfortable houses,
answers cries of the tortured, locates the lost, reunites families,
uses her strength, speed, fantastic vision and hearing to help
the helpless and soothe the broken, flying everywhere, never stopping.

Throughout the night, she holds the weeping in her embrace,
yet all this saving leaves her empty unless the rescued love her,
unless they praise her with superheroic gratitude that covers up
self-loathing and stops the demon anvil banging in her head.
How I wish I could have helped her to enjoy miracles of unheroic
achievement: a lifetime with loving friends, the hosting of happy parties.

Her dearest wishes never brought contentment. She could never rest
with her own goodness.

Sean M. Teaford

A Pure Breath

What matters is that all this did happen.
— Janusz Korczak

The boy pushed away sleep and,
blinking his eyes in the candlelight,
listened to Korczak's voice.

Echoing above the soldier's
ash-muffled steps,
the only sound in the camp

[stanza continues]

was the doctor's paper cracking
like a stiff flag in a sharp breeze
as he chiseled the lead
onto what once was white.

Despite his arthritic fingers
he had written hundreds of
pages in the ghetto,
but these were the first
curled letters of his Kaddish.
This was his last leaf of script,
the last journal entry
which would never leave his hand.

This was his voice that would rain
down with his body and rest
in the lungs of Treblinka

Warsaw Epidemic

I used to write at stops, in a meadow under a pine tree, sitting on a stump. Everything seemed important and if I did not note it down I would forget. An irretrievable loss to humanity.
— Janusz Korczak

The sun peeled gray
from the clouds,
burned their pewter lining.

Mid-day February
and sick students were having
troubled afternoon naps.
Their dry heaves echoed
in the doctor's ears — he had
nothing to cure a cough,
no antidote for a fever.

The flu flooded the ghetto
like a forgotten fog.

The children lay tightly
curled in their cots, restlessly
immobile. With every turning
groan, their clothes ruffled
like wet paper.

Some orphans cried but
nobody made a sound.
Many prayers are silent.

Below the venting glass
panes, standing on the sleet-
encrusted sidewalk, soldiers
laughed while slurping soup —
Korczak's stomach twisted
as he heard uneaten broth
splash and sizzle in the snow.

The fragrant steam slid
through cracked windows;
he listened as his children
sniffed and moaned. He had
no bowls to scrape with spoons
they did not possess.

Philip Terman

The Jewish Quarter in Budapest

I. The Orthodox Synagogue

In this former Jewish neighborhood,
where Kazinczy Street curves
hardly wider than an alley,

in a Sunday quiet, hidden in its own
shadows, sun climbing its back,
across the street a gate opened

to a courtyard, a mother and child
sweeping up a cobbled walkway.
Under Reconstruction, a sign says,

near a partially covered open door where
a heavy-set man hauling an electric cord
waves me inside through mounds of plaster,

pieces of stone and lumber. Upstairs,
in the woman's section, tarped pews.
Soft morning light is muted through stained glass.

The chandeliers are sheeted and drooping
lopsided from the ceiling over the sanctuary,
shaped like wrapped bells. In front,

two workers crouch on a scaffold, delicately
painting Jewish stars with blue paint on thin brushes.
Something is putting back this house

of worship piece by piece, star by star.
They don't look like angels. They chatter back
and forth, sometimes climb down to take

a piss or bring up more paint to continue
their task on this eastern wall above where
the cantor would mourn and the holy scrolls.

If they drop a brush, they don't raise
its silken hairs to their lips the way a yarmulke
must be kissed each time it falls.

The sanding, the plastering, the staining,
the Sabbath Bride. In the loose wires
and sawdust, the Lord is One.

II. At the Kosher Restaurant

Where you can sit elbow to elbow
with ancient rabbis in beards
and sidelocks, the guidebook says

but instead there are cats in the courtyard
behind the synagogue. They scatter
at my approach, experts in survival.

Upstairs the empty dining area
and, beyond, the narrow kitchen
where a tiny man, ancient, rabbinical,

black suit and black yarmulke
that covers his whole head, sits alone
at a small table against the window,

sipping soup from a white bowl.
His face is cracked parchment,
back hunched over as if

he's been carrying the Torah
above his head during all the years
of darkness. He's so small,

perhaps he survived in a refrigerator,
a cabinet, the ark of the holy scrolls;
maybe he folded himself up into a word,

a single letter — it's possible
he became the hardly distinguishable
silence between the call and the response.

I pause at the doorway and stare
the way, at the museum, I studied
photographs of the round-ups

and the trains, recognized shofars
and circumcision knives behind
protective glass. He won't pose

as I snap the camera but stays
his place, sipping his soup, as if
I was the one who didn't exist.

What We Pass On

I was a Bilfield, she begins,
starting with the name her father
gave her, *before I was a Terman.*

She is sitting at the kitchen table,
facing the clock with the Hebrew letters,
its poorly tuned motor a perpetual moan

in the background when the house
is full, louder when she's alone
among furniture and portraits.

The names of Jews, she says, *were for*
their occupation, what they did.
A "felt" meant a large field. My grandparents

worked in a large field, green,
wildflowers, in summer. Austria-
Hungary. The shtetl I'm not sure of.

I have it written down somewhere.
What happened to that name: Bilfield,
Field? My mother keeps it tucked

between other names. Whenever
I do anything right — get up early,
set the table before she comes home —

I'm a Bilfield, a field with yellow
and blue and white, a meadow
in a country no longer there,

divided and portioned out like
its people scattered under the grass
or in other lands, their names diminished,

their language attenuating to hushes,
breaths stuttered into the ears
of children — phrases from a Yiddish

they strain to hear, like the story she tells now
about her grandparents Shmu-el
and Malka. Their portraits hang on the wall:

Shmu-el: gray streaks in a beard
that bunches past his white collar,
the black coat of the peasant

and the black square hat
because wherever he was
he was in the House of God.

His eyes stare into the future
as if it were an obligation.
And the other, Malka, for whom

my mother was named:
Malka, Mildred —
the first letter of the most recent dead

passes on, the rest of the name
we fill in for ourselves — so what
is left of us is an initial, one capital

letter, a sound signifying human
to remind us that we are spelled out
of those who came before —

Malka, sad faced, babushka
wrapped around thin hair, looped
across tired breasts, the forehead

wrinkled and around the eyes
marks of claws, pupils staring
in slightly different directions,

the right tilted upward signaling
worship, the left off to the side
signaling caution and there's something —

these figures, inside their original frames,
sketched in pencil and charcoal,
dusted with one-hundred-year-old light,

something, not in the noses or chins,
the mouths fixed as if the barest smile,
a grin would be an effort — but something

in my mother's voice: *Shmu-el*
was an elder — I have it written down
somewhere — and the Germans

lined him up and they shot him
and Malka came across with a son
they discovered to be tubercular

so the officials at Ellis Island
wouldn't let him in. Imagine —
she left these portraits with a relative

and made the long journey back
so the son shouldn't make the trip alone,
coughing up blood, both disappearing

on the other side of the waters
in the country of hardship, but where —
we can only guess. My mother's eyes

turn and lock into mine: *Yes —*
her head nods to the rhythm
of the clock moaning: *we can guess.*

With the Survivors

At the service in the Rehmuh Synagogue,
the last one left in Kraków, Poland
not a museum, across from kosher-
style cafés and trained klezmers,

the dozen ancient men don't rise
at the appropriate passage in the liturgy;
they don't read responsively with the rabbi
or follow along in the prayer book.

They kibbitz, as if their gossip
and news were more significant
than whatever God is telling them.
In the back pew I attempt to follow

the Hebrew above the Polish-Yiddish
muttering of these men in stained
sweaters, untucked shirts, ties
barely knotted as if they had no one

to dress them. Suddenly, the *Shema:*
The Lord is our God, the Lord is one,
the prayer you must remember after
you have forgotten everything else.

The Ark opens, as if from a wind.
All at once each worshipper grips
his seat's edge, forearms quivering,
struggling to lift their body's weight

of resistance to confront the Holy Book.
No one hoists it out of the sanctum
and heaves it above his shoulders,
no one bears it around the sanctuary

for the congregation to touch it
with their tallises or caress its scroll
with their kissed prayer books.
Who was it closed the curtains?

We retire to a back table set
with cake and vodka, shot glasses
filled to the brim, recite in cracked
voices the blessing for the fruit

of the vine, throw back the clear fire.
Over our thin slice, we chant words
for the earth, the morning liquor
lightening my head, the dusty air swirling

the table a few inches above the ground,
the room tilting, spinning, these faces
floating on the air's surface — flat, as if
what they witnessed had frozen their expressions.

One beside me — hair tousled, skin rough
like coarse paper, speaks, half Yiddish,
half English, shrugs his right arm: *East.*
To Ruskie. Vork. The vodka goes around.

Someone murmurs: *Shabbat shalom.*

The Wounds

Our wounds are according to instructions.

The recipe calls for one scar each, a searing
of our sex, a cut where it would most hurt,
our lives starting with a scream, a loss,
pieces of skin we pay with in advance.

If it's our blood we bequeath,
will we live lives of holiness?

Will we be rewarded for our severings?

Will we be called out of the congregation
to open the curtains of Your Book?

Will we carry it on our shoulders
around the synagogue in the Days of Awe?

What will You do with these wicks, these tips
of grass, these flecks of light?

Will You write on our accumulated flesh
the words You did not say concerning Auschwitz?

Elaine Terranova

1939

A woman takes a small girl's hand.
The leaves pull away and fall,
separate, stiff with color.
Out of the smoky, distant forest
the train brings its load of passengers,
the passengers, their burdens.
A horse nuzzles the fence of every field,
at peace within its boundaries.
There is the woman's beautiful fair hair,
a certainty that's braided into it.

At the crossing, the stationmaster's wife
aligns the bars
of any misdirected night.
A girl is walking by her mother's side.
She knows from fairy tales
the shape that evil takes —
stretched in shadow, giants, witches,
wolves — the weight of poisoned fruit,
the irrevocable claim of fire.

The hill twists and flattens.
The little girl tugs at the funny hooks
of weeds like fingers pointing down,
down. She hears the snap of branches

[stanza continues]

underfoot, the whistling stalks
that pull the air into
their tubular, dry bodies. Sometimes
in the wind the trees reach up
on tip-toe to the sky like tall, lost girls.

These are the easy days. Heaven
comes to meet the earth
in such a bountiful accord. The sun
so near it pulls the water taut
until the river shines. The two walk on.
They walk into the clouds, an ample white,
into a sky that has already forgotten them.

Susan Terris

Train to Oświęcim

She heard the grass mumble
Imagined fields of fainting burdocks
And the cathedral coiled like a snail
They'd left in haste
No soft ferns on the hillside
Only sounds of breaking glass
Where they were
No windows
Only the stutter of rails
They'd packed in a hurry
Only asked which station
And if the luggage would be safe
Trust was important
And singularity of vision
But not anger
No indulgence
Nothing voluptuous
No sweetness of Queen Anne cherries
Or other taste of summer
The sulk of sun from behind cloud
No peaches fresh from the tree
No windows to frame the size of doom
Only dark depths to plumb
No tickets
No passports
No poem

Hilary Tham

Daughter of Survivors

For Elaine, Helen, Myra

She is screaming again.
You stand at your bedroom door,
shivering; you will her to stop, will it
to go away. Your father's voice rises
and falls with the burden of her name.

She is awake. You hear her voice cling
to his. You hear the creak of bedsprings
as they rise.

Soon, the kettle whistles in the kitchen.
When you peer in, they are huddled together
over the table. Her pale hands clenched
around the teacup, she whispers her dream.

He has heard it six million times,
but he listens, his arm clamped around her.
He, too, has bad dreams.

You are afraid of this trembling woman
who replaces your mother each night —
you want the daylight woman
who bakes honeycake and brushes your hair,
smiling, as if you are her good dream.

Your father does not change at night,
but he, too, fears the knock on the door.
He makes you learn street maps
by heart, sends you out alone
on the New York subway

so that if you should come home from school
and find them missing, you would know
how and where to run.

Susan Tichy

Gaby at the U.N. Observation Post

. . . you find yourself always standing
Between the much-praised landscape
And the one who praises it and explains it
— Yehuda Amichai

1.

On the border
you're posed and poised as a model
who has no idea where she is.

You cross your legs. One elbow
rests on the telescope mount
where a newspaper is tucked
and folded: the news
is startling and old, news of a year
in which love joined hands with her sister
and both went down to death.

On the Day of Atonement
thirsty hands drank from the eyes,
and those who had nothing to grieve for
received a gift.

The gift you wanted? To win the world
by leaving it alone.

2.

You're not alone.

To one side, shadows of things that happened.
To the other, dreams that didn't come true.
The land is dry because of them. They live
on the surface of things, like Gypsies
drinking all the moisture from the air.

Here, give them a loaf of bread
and wine from an earthen jar. Say,
"This is no longer the border.
This is no longer the war." Tell them
in each of your four languages,

"I want to go home alone."
What if a man is waiting for you?
What if your body
could be his whole country —
two countries, for night and for day?

On the Day of Atonement
you painted your face with make-up
and walked to the top of the city wall.
Everyone saw you mourn
for having your hands and feet.

3.

Two hands, two feet —
you are never alone.

Out of your father's country
you marched
at the head of a million dead.

But when you tried to lead them
to the future,
they ran back, disappearing
through a small crack in the earth.

Don't rub your toe in the dust
like that. Show respect.
Turn your face away from the wind
when it blows
their loose hair in your eyes.

Alfred Van Loen

Auschwitz #1

With gradual rhythm snowflakes
Fell on barracks and roads,
Covering trees, surrounding
With merciful cold.
Within the white blanket,
Death and peace:
Wintertime and soon expected
Christmas.
Christmas without candles

[stanza continues]

Without music
Without food and without warm clothes.

At this time a young woman
Dragged herself into the field
Through the cold snow
To be alone,
To give birth to her first child
Without help, without love.
The crying infant came into life.

Along came three drunken Nazis
And watched with amusement
This miracle happening before their eyes,
And they took the baby
And threw it in the oven —
A sacrifice to their Führer.

This happened while the young mother
Froze to death:
Around Christmastime,
After nearly two thousand years
Of Christianity.

Auschwitz #6

Tortured, sick, and hungry,
yet as long as there was the sun
and the moon at nights feelings
were alive
and even in this place of horror
and death
people hoped, prayed, and loved.

A man found a woman he had known
years ago when there was food,
when there was peace and life,
and love blossomed for each other.

Men and women were separated
and looking was punished
with burned out eyes
and talking meant a slashed tongue.
But love knows no fear
and they were surprised
in each other's arms.

Endless tortures . . .

The woman was raped, the man forced
to watch,
and she was sentenced as a prostitute
to burn at the stake he
had to build
and to which he had to put the fire.

Refusing, he was tied
to the same stake
and the flames leaped with the laughter
of the Nazis.

Derek Walcott

from ***Midsummer '81***

XXXVIII

The camps held their distance of brown chestnuts and grey smoke
that coiled into thorns. The industry of guilt continues.
Wild pigeons gurgle, the squirrels pile up acorns like little shoes,
and moss, voiceless as smoke, hushes the bodies
of abandoned kindling; in the clear pools, fat
trout, rising to flies, bubble in umlauts.
Over forty years ago in the islands, I felt
that the gift of poetry had made me one of the Chosen,
but that all mankind was one kindling to the fire of the Muse,
now, I see her again, on that pine-bench where she sits,
the nut-brown ideal, in silence, with her coppery braids,
the blood-drops of poppies embroidering her white bodice,
essence of smoke and autumn, the spirit of Keats,
whose gaze raked the level fields where the smoky cries
of ravens were almost human. I knew then she was
goddess of the golden stubble, of the cornflower iris,
the winnower of chaff for whom the flashing blades
fell in whole harvests. Had I known what I know now,
the palm-fronds of my island would have been harrows, and
the sand of the beaches as warm and white as ashes,
and at fifteen I would have put down my pen,
since this century's pastorals were already written
at Auschwitz, Buchenwald, at Dachau, at Sachsenhausen.

George Wallace

An Apple for Wolfgang Granjonca

I was two hours out of Oroville, driving over the hills and
sleek yellow crests of Jameson Canyon on the back road
to Napa and thinking about Wolfgang Granjonca, eleven years old,
who'd escaped the Nazis, crossed the Pyrenees — thinking about
how a man may face fear and failure after he has faced death
because in 1942 Wolfgang Granjonca faced the Holocaust
and he survived: a survivor who found his way to America
where he grew up and went west to San Francisco and changed
his name and made his fortune. In the Bay area
the psychedelic rock and roll era was mushrooming and about
to spread all over the world and when it did there was Wolfgang
with his new name — Billy Graham — sitting atop the stone cold
psychedelic mushroom cloud with his survivor's grit, with his
sweet and utter fearlessness, and Wolfgang was the king,
Wolfgang was the king-maker: Joplin Airplane Zeppelin Cream
and even Jerry Garcia and the Dead — he backed them all,
yes, Wolfgang Granjonca promoted them and presented
them: love peace music power were his and he gave it all
away: with Live Aid concerts and Human Rights concerts
and with concerts supporting the poor and the oppressed
and farmworkers and earthquake victims and the starving
people of Africa and the indigenous people of the world
and people with AIDS — he brought the power of music
to the mission of human compassion — and all that goodness
came back to Wolfgang Granjonca, major concert promoter
of the world, who handed out free apples at every concert
and became enormous, earth shattering, mindblowing:
he was the Wolfgang the Nazis couldn't stop, and nothing
could stop him except death itself, which takes everybody's hand
eventually, and one black October day in 1991 death did take
Wolfgang's hand as he was returning from a concert
and bearing in on San Francisco along the northeast flight
corridor: in an instantaneous flash of light, his helicopter
crashed into an electrical tower in the marshflats of Vallejo
and thousands were left lightless — and then Wolfgang was
dead, and the rock world lost a pulsar for eternity,
and five hundred thousand came to San Francisco's Golden Gate Park
to hear Ken Kesey read a poem for Wolfgang — Cummings's
"and what i want to know is how do you like your blueeyed boy
Mister Death" — and Jerry Garcia was there, he played "Crashing
the Dark Star" — yes, the Grateful Dead played and
they played and they couldn't stop playing and they
couldn't bring the man back to life, because death stops
everybody, but it can't stop love — which is why to this day
people leave apples at the grave of Wolfgang Granjonca.

Michael Waters

Dachau Moon

1

There is a place like Germany in the body
that wants to remain a secret,
where all the tremendous weight of a life
is a kiss buried in the eyes,
pale moons that drift like Heaven
across this bastard landscape

& I am flying to this place
on an overcast morning
when nothing is ready to rise,
so it's easy to imagine a moon
blue & romantic as a dead woman.

This country is full of surprises.
My parents have told me to keep an eye
for the family star,
the remains of dark bone charcoal
thumbed like a mole
on the left side of the forehead.

2

Three days in Munich
& my head begins to split,
the beer tastes like a railroad
& I have been too fucking polite
like a child come home from death.

I am astonished by the number of gold teeth
taken from the mouths of the dead
& placed in the heads of fine German women.
There is a beauty in gold
when found in a dark forgotten place

& a fear
when the moon resembles a gold tooth
lodged in the skull like a light.

The smile of the engineer is a killer,
precise as a military operation,
all the way to Dachau.

3

The stillness is so complete
not even the dead are here anymore.

All the fathers are gone,
having kissed their daughters like fever,
to a room where the moon is seen as a face
blue & almost romantic in mist.

So unlike the photograph in the museum:
someone, maybe an uncle,
strapped in a chair
with his forehead neatly sliced
& opened like a jewelry box,
the brain & its still water
exposed to the hands . . .

His mouth shapes a small *o*
that could be a moon
disappearing for the last time.

4

The sad Jews
who may be our fathers
haul themselves across New York City
as if weighted with stones,

& in my pocket is a stone
selected that day in Dachau
that contains all the darkness of a family,

& I remember the moon is a skullcap
not placed properly on the head
like this, Lord, like this.

Florence Weinberger

Marrowbones

The fat women in the Coney Island steam bath
pinched my cheek and laughed at nothing,
sweat gleaming off their skin and coarse, curly hair,
not a bone to be seen anywhere,

not in my aunt's long breasts, none in the flesh
of my mother's belly. I grew up in the shelter
of kitchen gossip, amplitude nourished by yeasty smells,
pillows of soft rising dough, a feminine language

that taught me where the body begins, its armature
concealed, its health augmented like good soup.
By sixth grade, I knew I was fat. I married a man
with a flat stomach and an unrequited hunger.

The soup the Nazis fed him in their concentration camp
was thin as silk, what floated there thinner still.
From the aunts and mothers I learned wisdom is liquid,
rescue, a recipe they give to their daughters.

When the soup is done, I remove the bones,
scoop out the glutinous marrow, every last shred.
I spread it on fresh rye bread.
I watch him eat, and my heart gets fat.

Speak to the Children

You meet them wherever you go.
On a cruise ship of a thousand people,
the one other survivor
sits down at your table.
You start comparing notes, camps,
liberation dates. Nearby,
a survivor's granddaughter eavesdrops,
then joins your conversation — soon
everyone around you is in tears.

Survivors' children find you.
You look like their uncle; they want to hear
your story. You seldom tell. Meanwhile,
the survivors dwindle. They're down to a handful.
Tell, I urge you, tell it
on paper, on tape, but you'd rather
speak to the children, speak to the children
without faltering, if you can bear to;
you'd rather look into their eyes,
where they carry, carelessly revealed,
everything they own.

Survivor

He knows the depths of smokestacks,
from their bleak rims down
their spattered walls, from their ash cones
to the bone-bottom ground.
Once he could see under skin,
inside the body, where deprivation
thins the blood of all desire
except hunger.
For years he wanted to forget
everything. He knows it is possible
to live only at the surface,
it is possible to work,
to marry and have daughters.
But his daughters
look like people he once knew,
and he dreams them.
He dreams them opening doors,
sending letters. When he wakes,
he knows he has been dreaming.
This year, he will show his daughters
where he was born. He will show them
the chimney, the iron gate,
the deep oven where his mother baked bread.

Theodore Weiss

The Late Train

What is it like?

A horn suddenly jammed
in a car junked years
ago.
            An alarm
gone off in a town
that a volcano leveled.

A siren snarling
out in me that must
belong to a time, a far-
off place
            I've
never known, shrieking

[stanza continues]

like a jet-black van
lurching
                to the wrecks
it's most successful in,
my countless relatives
minus
                faces, names,
crying out of flowers,
birds, this windy smoke
clotting up our sky.

Throttled before
they got the word out,
it must break through
some way.
                How satisfy
except to let it go,
listen
                till it runs
its course, father,
mother,
                else a curse
choking itself, choking
him it's locked up in.

Ruth Whitman

The Death Ship

The Struma.
It lay in the harbor at Istanbul
without food or coal.

Don't let it land,
said the Ambassador.

Jews are enemy aliens,
said the British.
Tow them out to the Black Sea,
send them to Crete, Mauritius,
to Rumania, Germany, Jamaica,
but don't let them come to Palestine.

That was December 1941.

Safe in my kibbutz at Sdot Yam
(meadows of the sea),
I looked
at the peacock-blue Mediterranean
and cried, let them come,
we have room.

No, said Lord Moyne,
if one ship comes
they'll all want to come.

Let the children come.

Children?
What will we do with children?

The hold was airless.
Sickness, filth,
layers of excrement, vomit.
The ship could not sail.
the ship could not stay.
No land would take them.

In February the ship exploded
outside the harbor at Istanbul.
Eight hundred lives flew up,
their rags, arms, legs, hopes,
falling like rain.

One was saved.
He was allowed to enter
Palestine.

Maria Olt

On a hillside in Jerusalem
under the hammer sun, she lifts

a little carob tree, the tree of John
the Baptist, and sets it

into its hole. Solid as a house,
she is called Righteous, a Christian

who hid Jews in Hungary. Her hair clings
around her broad face as she bends

with the hoe, carefully heaping the soil
around the roots. She builds a rim of dirt

on the downhill side and pours water from
the heavy bucket. She waits until the earth

sucks the water up, then pours again
with a slow wrist. The workmen

sent to help her, stand aside, helpless.
She straightens up. Her eyes are wet.

Tears come to her easily.
The small Jewish woman she saved
stands beside her, dryeyed, beyond tears.
Thirtyfive years ago, as they watched

the death train pass, faces and hands
silent between the slats, the girl

had cried, I want to go with them!
No, said Maria, you must understand,

if you go, I will go with you.

C.K. Williams

Spit

. . . then the son of the "superior race" began to spit into the Rabbi's mouth so that the Rabbi could continue to spit on the Torah . . .
— The Black Book

After this much time, it's still impossible. The SS man with his stiff hair and his uniform;
the Rabbi, probably in a torn overcoat, probably with a stained beard the other would be clutching;
the Torah, God's word, on the altar, the letters blurring under the blended phlegm;
the Rabbi's parched mouth, the SS man perfectly absorbed, obsessed with perfect humiliation.
So many years and what is there to say still about the soldiers waiting impatiently in the snow,
about the one stamping his feet, thinking, "Kill him! Get it over with!"
while back there the lips of the Rabbi and the other would have brushed
and if time had stopped you would have thought they were lovers,
so lightly kissing, the sharp, luger hand under the dear chin,
the eyes furled slightly and then when it started again the eyelashes of both of them

[stanza continues]

shyly fluttering as wonderfully as the pulse of a baby.
Maybe we don't have to speak of it at all, it's still the same.
War, that happens and stops happening but is always somehow right there, twisting and hardening us;
then what we make of God — words, spit, degradation, murder, shame; every conceivable torment.
All these ways to live that have something to do with how we live
and that we're almost ashamed to use as metaphors for what goes on in us
but that we do anyway, so that love is battle and we watch ourselves in love
become maddened with pride and incompletion, and God is what it is when we're alone
wrestling with solitude and everything speaking in our souls turns against us like His fury
and just facing another person, there is so much terror and hatred that yes,
spitting in someone's mouth, trying to make him defile his own meaning,
would signify the struggle to survive each other and what we'll enact to accomplish it.

There's another legend.
It's about Moses, that when they first brought him as a child before Pharaoh,
the king tested him by putting a diamond and a live coal in front of him
and Moses picked up the red ember and popped it into his mouth
so for the rest of his life he was tongue-tied and Aaron had to speak for him.
What must his scarred tongue have felt like in his mouth?
It must have been like always carrying something there that weighed too much,
something leathery and dead whose greatest gravity was to loll out like an ox's,
and when it moved, it must have been like a thick embryo slowly coming alive,
butting itself against the inner sides of his teeth and cheeks.
And when God burned in the bush, how could he not cleave to him?
How could he not know that all of us were on fire and that every word we said would burn forever,
in pain, unquenchably, and that God knew it, too, and would say nothing Himself ever again beyond this,
ever, but would only live in the flesh that we use like firewood,
in all the caves of the body, the gut cave, the speech cave:
He would slobber and howl like something just barely a man that beats itself again and again onto the dark,
moist walls away from the light, away from whatever would be light for this last eternity.
"Now therefore go," He said, "and I will be with thy mouth."

Barbara Wind

Hating Shakespeare

Because he always scowled
At the mention of Shakespeare
I thought my father ignorant
Of western literature.

As a youth, he read the translations
Yet he called the bard a "thief"
Who stole others' stories. Moreover,
The Englishman was "a big anti-Semite."

I argued the beauty of words and ideas
How Shakespeare made Shylock human.
Daddy fiercely disagreed. He had lost all
His family in the war against the Jews

And believed the playwright deserved some
Of the blame. Now I, named for his
Pious mother who read Goethe and Schiller
On Sabbath afternoons, was being seduced

By the same false world.
It took years until I understood.
His father had worn the Austrian uniform —
The decorated jacket was still

In the wardrobe the day the Nazis
Sent a bill for his cremation.
Postmarked *Auschwitz*, it included
A little envelope filled with ash.

Math Test

The teacher cannot understand why I failed.
I remain silent, satisfied
Because I know my math too well.

I could tell her numbers set me dreaming.
I do not see white marks on blackboard
But blue ink tattooed on flesh.

I could rattle off numbers I've memorized.
I could confess I'm counting my mother's
Sisters and brothers, her nephews, nieces, uncles, aunts . . .

Wondering how many cousins
I might have if they and others had been spared.
I could admit I'm adding

Those on my father's side.
I could say I'm multiplying, subtracting, dividing,
Learning how to square my roots.

Betty Wisoff

Sanity

Jack, I never knew you
Until yesterday:
It was your face I saw on TV —
Holocaust survivor.

Your grocery store my weekly trysting place.
Your cheer the reason I return —
But now I know you.
You tell me of your sick dog, the fortune spent
To cure.
Why do you tell me *this*?

*

They traveled for ten days in a sealed boxcar.
On the tenth day, Auschwitz: not a dread word yet
— Here was daylight.

The cattle doors slid open.
Most were unable to move quickly from cramped
Positions, but moved toward fresh open air,
Unknowing, glad for anything.

A woman cradling her babe took cautious footholds,
Stumbled, prodded by an elegantly dressed SS man.
Before a thousand eyes, before she could scream,
Before realization, the terror, the shock,
Bayonet poised, he pierced her baby's breast,
Lifted it from her arms, tossed the child
As one tosses hay in a field.

I seek a word for the man's act.
I seek a word for the mother.
I seek a word for the then thirteen-year-old Jack,
Now grown, who says "I see that act daily
All of my days. I must do mundane things
For the sanity of my days."

Kenneth Wolman

The Drapers: A History Lesson

Silent, they measure the windows,
pass tape and yardstick back and forth,
silent, the father and son,
heavily, heavy, to shut out the light,
filling the room with their silence.

Only their numbers speak:
jagged, purple, like wounds that themselves are knives
seeming even now to stab the wearers' arms.
When I hand the father the tape he has dropped,
I stare at the numbers, then into his face:
and his eyes jump as from a soft shock,
swirling away from the question he fears.

But I am only nine, the ignorant son
who cannot conceive, so cannot ask.
And seeing so, he takes the tape, nods,
then turns to his son who watches:
and in their faces, the smiles of knowledge
harden like putty lips on a sacrificial mask:
not from mockery of an ignorant boy,
but from hiding still that special place
where nothing grew, not even questions.

Carolyne Wright

After Forty Years

Don't tell me about the bones of Mengele,
the bones are alive and well.
— Michael Dennis Browne

They've found the body
of the Angel of Death,
a bundle of brown bones
and scraps of skin
tossed like market produce
in the gravedigger's tray.

He can be himself now
for his loved ones — those

[stanza continues]

who took no chances
with the forged passports, bribes,
code words filing past the censors,
never breaking the family silence.

Himself now, for those
whose mouths gaped on silence,
survivors staring through barbed wire
in the abandoned camps,
stumbling chance their messenger,
those for whom the bones
will always be alive and well.

Finally, the tribunal of Embú,
plain light of the TV anchor's day.
Cameras cross-haired on the throats
of witnesses who shrugged
and said nothing, while for years
ash drift, fosses of lime,
the dead kept listening.

He was never sorry.
Death had grown old by the end,
familiar with his dreams:
water burning blue
off the coast of Brazil
like gas jets turned on full.

Strange how the bones are blameless,
the body dissolved as anyone's —
those who walked into the flames
with the prayer for the dead in their mouths,
the angel in his name
passing over the gates of the camps.

KZ

ARBEIT MACHT FREI
— Motto over the entrance of Auschwitz,
Dachau, Terezín, and several other Nazi
concentration camps

We walk in under the empty tower, snow
falling on barbed-wire nets where the bodies
of suicides hung for days. We follow signs
to the treeless square, where the scythe blade, hunger,
had its orders, and some lasted hours in the cold
when all-night roll calls were as long as winter.

We've come here deliberately in winter,
field stubble black against the glare of snow.
Our faces go colorless in wind, cold
the final sentence of their bodies
whose only identity by then was hunger.
The old gate with its hated grille-work sign

walled off, we take snapshots to sign
and send home, to show we've done right by winter.
We've eaten nothing, to stand inside their hunger.
We count, recount crimes committed in snow —
those who sheltered their dying fellows' bodies
from the work details, the transport trains, the cold.

Before the afternoon is gone, the cold
goes deep, troops into surrendered land. Signs
direct us to one final site, where bodies
slid into brick-kiln furnaces all winter
or piled on iron stretchers in the snow
like a plague year's random harvest. What hunger

can we claim? Those who had no rest from hunger
stepped into the ovens, knowing already the cold
at the heart of the flame. They made no peace with snow.
For them no quiet midnight sign
from on high — what pilgrims seek at the bottom of winter —
only the ebbing measure of their lives. Their bodies

are shadows now, ashing the footprints of everybody
who walks here, ciphers carrying the place of hunger
for us, who journey so easily in winter.
Who is made free by the merciless work of cold?
What we repeat when we can't read the signs —
the story of our own tracks breaking off in snow.

Snow has covered the final account of their bodies
but we must learn the signs: they hungered,
they were cold, and in Dachau it was always winter.

Rajzel Zychlinsky

I Remember

I remember —
It was a day
like today —
I was alone in a park.

[stanza continues]

The benches were empty and abandoned,
as if they knew
that never again
would anyone sit on them.
Slowly the leaves were falling,
counting the autumns on the earth.
Silence was all around,
as before a storm.
In what country was that?
In what city?
It was a temple
without a God
and without worshipers.
And how did I, from there
escape?

The Undarkened Window

In the daytime, I see him in the street
in a dark suit,
shaved,
combed,
wearing a tie —
at night the light shines in his window
across from my window.
A survivor
of Hitler's gas chambers,
he sails at night around
his undarkened window —
a wandering ship
on oceans of darkness,
and no port
allows it to enter,
so it may anchor
and darken.

Only in the mornings
does it go out,
the sickly yellow light
in his window.

Translated from the Yiddish by Barnett Zumoff

God Hid His Face

All the roads led to death,
all the roads.

All the winds breathed betrayal,
all the winds.

At all the doorways angry dogs barked,
at all the doorways.

All the waters laughed at us,
all the waters.

All the nights fattened on our dread,
all the nights.

And the heavens were bare and empty,
all the heavens.

God hid his face.

Translated from the Yiddish by Aaron Kramer

Glossary

I have limited this section to historically significant references that recur in the poems and that are not common knowledge or easily gleaned from a good college dictionary. Less frequently occurring words are defined and explicated in the *Notes to Poems* section that follows this one.

Appellplatz [also spelled "Appelplatz"] (Ger.). The place for roll call, used in English in its Holocaust context. *"Appell!"* was one of the most dreaded words of a day. Upon the call, the inmates had to arrange themselves into neat columns, and this process could take several hours. After that, the command "Attention! Caps off!" followed. From that moment on, any slight disorder in the rows could lead to heavy beating or death.

Arbeit Macht Frei (Ger.). Work Makes [You] Free. The slogan *"Arbeit Macht Frei"* was placed over the entrances to a number of Nazi concentration camps, including, most notoriously, Auschwitz. Although it was common practice in Germany to post inscriptions of this sort at entrances to institutional properties and large estates, the slogan's use in this instance was ordered by SS General Theodor Eicke, inspector of concentration camps and first commandant of Dachau Concentration Camp. The slogan can still be seen at several sites, including the entrance to Auschwitz I — although, according to *Auschwitz: a New History*, by BBC historian Laurence Rees, it was placed there by commandant Rudolf Höss (Hess / Ger.: Höß), who believed that doing menial work during his own imprisonment under the Weimar Republic had helped him through the experience. At Auschwitz, the "B" in "Arbeit" is placed upside-down. The slogan can also be seen at the Dachau concentration camp, Gross-Rosen, Sachsenhausen, and the Theresienstadt Ghetto-Camp. At Buchenwald, however, "Jedem das Seine" ("To each his own") was used instead.

Auschwitz-Birkenau. Konzentrationslager Auschwitz was the largest of the Nazi concentration camps. Located in southern Poland, it took its name from the nearby town of Oświęcim (*Auschwitz* in German), situated about fifty kilometers west of Kraków and two hundred eighty-six kilometers from Warsaw. Following the Nazi occupation of Poland in September 1939, Oświęcim was incorporated into Germany and renamed Auschwitz. The camp complex consisted of three main camps: Auschwitz I, the administrative center; Auschwitz II (Birkenau), an extermination camp or *Vernichtungslager*; and Auschwitz III (Monowitz), a work camp. There were also around forty satellite camps, some of them tens of kilometers from the main camps, with prisoner populations ranging from several dozen to several thousand. An unknown, but very large, number of people were killed at Auschwitz. The camp commandant, Rudolf Höss (Hess), testified at the Nuremberg Trials that three million had died there. The Auschwitz-Birkenau State Museum revised this figure in 1990, and new calculations now place the figure at 1.1–1.6 million, about ninety percent of them Jews from almost every country in Europe. Like all Nazi concentration camps, the Auschwitz camps were operated by Heinrich Himmler's SS. Höss provided a detailed description of the camp's workings during his interrogations after the war and also in his autobiography. He was hanged in 1947 in front of the entrance to the crematorium of Auschwitz I.

Babi Yar. A ravine in Kiev, the capital of Ukraine, remembered today as the site where more than one hundred thousand Soviet citizens were executed by the Nazis during the Second World War. On 29–30 September 1941, 33,771 Jewish civilians were murdered. This two-day massacre was one of the largest single mass killings of the Holocaust, second only to the Romanian extermination of more than forty thousand Jews in Bogdanovka in 1941. In the months that followed, many more thousands of Jews were seized, taken to Babi Yar, and shot.

Bergen-Belsen. A Nazi concentration camp in Lower Saxony, southwest of the town of Bergen near Celle. Although there were no gas chambers in Bergen-Belsen because the mass executions took place in the camps further east, between 1943 and 1945, an estimated fifty thousand Jews, Czechs, Poles, anti-Nazi Christians, homosexuals, and Roma and Sinti (Gypsies) died in the camp. Among them were Czech painter and writer, Josef Čapek, as well as Amsterdam residents Anne Frank (who died of typhus) and her sister, Margot, who died there in March 1945. The average life expectancy of an inmate was nine months.

Buchenwald. A Nazi concentration camp established on the Ettersberg (the Etter Mountain) located near Weimar, Germany, in July 1937, and opened by American troops on the morning of 11 April 1945. The word "Buchenwald" (Ger.: "beech forest") was chosen because of the close ties of the location to Goethe, who had been idealized as "the embodiment of the German Spirit." Between July 1937 and April 1945, approximately two hundred fifty thousand people were incarcerated in Buchenwald by the Nazi regime. The number of deaths is estimated at fifty-six thousand. Although the prisoners were primarily used as slave labor in local armament factories, many inmates died during human experimentations, or fell victim to arbitrary acts of brutality perpetrated by the SS guards. The camp was also the site of large-scale testing of vaccines for epidemic typhus in 1942 and 1943.

Buna. The largest sub-camp of Auschwitz. Between 1942 and 1945, the Nazis sent thousands of prisoners from various countries to Buna, the majority of them Jewish (there were approximately ten thousand prisoners in this camp in 1944). A significant proportion of them died because of arduous slave labor, starvation, savage mistreatment, and executions. Those who were unable to go on working fell victim to selection and were taken to their deaths in the Birkenau concentration camp gas chambers.

Bundist. A member of the Jewish Labor Zionist movement, especially in Warsaw, prior to World War II.

Chelmno / Kulmhof. Nazi death camp, established December 1941. The first commandant was Herbert Lange. The camp consisted of two parts: an administration section, barracks and storage for plundered goods and a burial and cremation site. It operated three gas vans that used carbon monoxide to kill. The camp began operations on 7 December 1942, and conclusively ended operations on 17 January 1945. The estimated number of people murdered at this camp is one hundred fifty thousand to three hundred thousand, most of them Jews.

Dachau. A Nazi German concentration camp located on the grounds of an abandoned munitions factory near the medieval town of Dachau, about ten miles northwest of Munich in southern Germany. Opened on 22 March 1933, the Dachau camp was the first regular concentration camp established by the National Socialist (Nazi) government. Dachau served as a prototype and model for the other Nazi concentration camps that followed. In total, over two hundred thousand prisoners from more than thirty countries were housed in Dachau. Soviet prisoners of war were summarily executed by the thousands; civilians were assigned by the Gestapo to the camp for *Sonderbehandlung* ("Special Treatment," a Nazi euphemism that signified "killing"); and a great many died in evacuation marches and death marches. These deaths were never registered. The International Tracing Service in Arolson reports 31,591 dead among the prisoners who were registered, but the total number of dead will never be known. On the day of liberation, some twenty-five hundred of the thirty-two thousand remaining inmates were Jewish. [Source: declassified U.S. Army report].

Eichmann. Karl Adolf Eichmann (1906–62) headed Gestapo Department IV B4 for Jewish Affairs and was the man responsible for keeping the trains rolling from all over Europe to the death camps during the Holocaust. Following the surrender of Nazi Germany in May 1945, Eichmann was arrested and confined to an American internment camp but managed to escape because his name was not yet well known. In 1950, with the help of the SS underground, he fled to Argentina and lived under the assumed name of Ricardo Klement for ten years, until Israeli Mossad agents abducted him on 11 May 1960. Eichmann went on trial in Jerusalem for crimes against the Jewish people, crimes against humanity and war crimes. During the four-month trial, over one hundred witnesses testified against him. Eichmann took the stand and used the defense that he was just obeying orders. He was found guilty on all counts, sentenced to death, and hanged at Ramleh Prison, on 31 May 1962. Sachar states: "It was the trial of Adolf Eichmann in 1961, conducted in [Jerusalem] Israel, that most effectively recreated for the short-memoried world all the bestiality of the Nazi period" (140).

Jude[n] (Ger.). Jew[s].

Kaddish (Aram. and Heb.). Holy, sanctified. A traditional prayer in the Jewish service that praises God and expresses a yearning for the establishment of God's kingdom on earth. The term "Kaddish" is often used to refer specifically to "The Mourners' Kaddish," recited as part of the mourning rituals in Judaism in all prayer services, as well as at funerals and memorials. When mention is made of "saying Kaddish," this unambiguously denotes the rituals of mourning. The opening words of this prayer are inspired by Ezekiel 38:23, a vision of God's becoming great in the eyes of all the nations.

Kapo. A term used for certain prisoners who worked inside the Nazi concentration camps during World War II in various lower administrative positions. The German word may also mean "foreman" and "non-commissioned officer" and is derived from French for "Corporal" (Caporal) or the Italian word *capo*. Kapos received more privileges than normal prisoners, towards whom they were frequently brutal.

[Janusz] Korczak. The memorial at Treblinka is comprised of seventeen thousand stones of different sizes and shapes, some with names of towns whose entire civilian populations were murdered. According to Michael Berenbaum, "Only one rock is etched with the name of an individual. He is Dr. Janusz Korczak, the famed director of the orphanage in the Warsaw Ghetto, who was offered personal refuge but refused to abandon the children he could not save. He boarded the train and went to Treblinka with them" (Midstream, March/April 2007, 15-16).

Kristallnacht. Also widely known as "Crystal Night" and the "Night of Broken Glass," "Kristallnacht" was a State-organized pogrom that took place throughout Germany and in parts of Austria on the nights of 9–10 November 1938. The pogrom was ostensibly triggered by the following sequence of events: On 28 October 1938, seventeen thousand Polish Jews living in Germany (some for more than a decade), were arrested and taken to the river marking the Polish-German border and forced to cross it. The Polish border guards sent them back over the river into Germany and this stalemate continued for days in the pouring rain, the Jews marching without food or shelter between the borders until the Polish government admitted them to a concentration camp. Herschel Grynszpan, a German-Polish Jew living in Paris, received a letter from his family describing the horrible conditions they had been experiencing during this deportation. Seeking to alleviate their situation, he appealed repeatedly over the next few days to Ernst vom Rath, Third Secretary of the German Embassy in Paris, who could not help him. On Monday, 7 November

1938, Grynszpan shot vom Rath in the stomach. He attempted and missed three additional shots. Two days later, vom Rath died.

Vom Rath's assassination served as a pretext for launching a rampage against Jewish inhabitants throughout Germany. Jewish homes and stores were ransacked throughout Germany and also in Vienna, with a mixture of German citizens and Stormtroopers destroying Jewish-owned buildings with sledgehammers and leaving the streets covered in smashed windows. This pogrom damaged, and in many cases destroyed, more than fifteen hundred synagogues (constituting nearly all Germany had), many Jewish cemeteries, more than seven thousand Jewish shops, and twenty-nine department stores. Some Jews were beaten to death while others were forced to watch. More than thirty thousand Jewish males were arrested and taken to concentration camps, primarily Dachau, Buchenwald, and Sachsenhausen. The treatment of prisoners in the camps was brutal, but most were released during the following three months, on condition that they leave Germany. In addition to the estimated ninety-one Jews killed in the rioting, there are believed to have been hundreds of suicides. Counting deaths at the concentration camps, between two thousand and twenty-five hundred deaths were directly or indirectly attributable to the Kristallnacht pogrom. A few non-Jewish Germans mistaken for Jews were also killed.

Synagogues, some centuries old, were also victims of considerable violence and vandalism. Fires were lit, and prayer books, scrolls, and works of art were thrown upon them, and the precious buildings were either burned or smashed until unrecognizable. Even graveyards were not spared, and tombstones were uprooted and graves violated. After this, the Jewish community was fined one billion marks to clean up the mess the Nazis had made. Events in Austria were no less horrible. Most of Vienna's ninety-four synagogues and prayer-houses were partially or totally destroyed, and Jews were subjected to all manner of humiliations, including being forced to scrub the pavements while being tormented by their fellow Austrians, some of whom had been their friends and neighbors.

Historian, Lucy Dawidowicz stresses the power of Kristallnacht as a metaphor or template for future actions: "The Germans reenacted the Kristallnacht in every town and city they invaded and occupied. All over Poland, synagogues went up in flames. (Those spared the fire were desecrated, turned into stables, garages, and public latrines.) Everywhere the Germans organized pogroms, rounding-up the non-Jewish population to witness and learn how to mock, abuse, injure, and murder Jews" (200).

Lager (Ger.). Camp.

Lublin. A major city in eastern Poland and Poland's ninth largest city. After the 1939 German invasion of Poland the city found itself in the General Government. During the German occupation the city's population was a target of various repressions by the occupiers, with a particularly grim fate reserved for the Jewish inhabitants. The city served as a German headquarters for Operation Reinhard, the main German effort to exterminate the Jews in occupied Poland. Lublin's Jewish population was forced into the Lublin ghetto established around the area of Podzamcze. The majority of the ghetto's inhabitants, about twenty-six thousand people, were deported to the Bełżec death camp between 17 March and 11 April 1942. The remainder were moved to facilities around Majdanek, a large concentration camp established at the outskirts of the city. Most of them were killed by the war's end.

Łódź. Poland's second largest city. During the Invasion of Poland, the Polish forces of the Łódź Army of General Juliusz Rómmel defended Łódź against initial German attacks. However, the Wehrmacht captured the city on 8 September. Despite plans for the city to become a Polish enclave, attached to the General Government, the Nazi hierarchy respected the wishes of the local governor of Reichsgau Wartheland, Arthur Greiser, and of many of the ethnic Germans living in the city, and annexed it to the Reich in November 1939. Soon the Nazi authorities set up the Łódź Ghetto in the city and populated it with more than two hundred thousand Jews from the Łódź area. Only about nine hundred people survived the liquidation of the ghetto in August 1944. Several concentration camps and death camps arose in the city's vicinity for the non-Jewish inhabitants of the regions, among them the famous Radogoszcz prison and several minor camps for the Roma people and for Polish children. By the end of World War II Łódź had lost approximately four hundred twenty thousand of its pre-war inhabitants: three hundred thousand Jews and one hundred twenty thousand Poles.

Maidanek / Majdanek. German and Polish spellings of the Nazi extermination camp located in German-occupied Poland, about two miles from Lublin. It was regarded as in the same class as Bełżec and Sobibór. Like Bełżec, Maidanek was originally a labor camp but was transformed into a death camp. Unlike Bełżec, it had some industrial activity and non-Jewish prisoners were admitted. At first, death was induced by carbon monoxide asphyxiation, but later, following successful tests at Bełżec, hydrocyanic, or prussic, acid fumes were used. It is estimated that as many as 1.5 million inmates were gassed at Maidanek.

Mengele. Dr. Josef Mengele (1911–79). A German SS officer and a physician in the Nazi concentration camp Auschwitz-Birkenau. He gained notoriety chiefly for being one of the SS physicians who supervised the selection of arriving transports of prisoners and determined who was to be killed and who was to become a forced laborer, and for performing human experiments of dubious scientific value on camp inmates, amongst whom Mengele was known as the "Angel of Death." After the war, he first hid in Germany under an assumed name, then escaped and lived in South America, first in Argentina (until 1959) and finally in Brazil, where he accidentally drowned. Mengele's death was confirmed after DNA testing was used on his remains.

Onkel (Ger.). Uncle.

Oświęcim. The Polish name for Auschwitz.

Ponar[y]. The Ponary massacre (or Paneriai massacre) was the mass-murder of about a hundred thousand people perpetrated by German SD and SS and their subordinate Lithuanian Sonderkommando collaborators (Special SD and German Security Police Squad units) during the Second World War in German-occupied Lithuania. The executions took place between July 1941 and August 1944 near the railway station of Paneriai (Pol.: Ponary), now a suburb of Vilnius. The vast majority of the victims, who were usually brought to the edges of huge pits and shot to death with machine gun fire, were Jews and Poles, many from the metropolis of Vilnius.

Sabbath Queen / Sabbath Bride. In Jewish observance, doors are opened during Friday night prayer services to welcome the Sabbath Queen. Shabbat is compared to a bride given to us by God, and worshippers long for her arrival.

Selections / Selektions (Ger.). Daily mass executions at the Nazi concentration camps, but also initial selections of prisoners for slave labor or immediate death.

Shabbat (Heb.) / **Shabbos** (Yid.). The Jewish Sabbath.

Shema (Heb.). Hear. "Shema Yisrael" are the first two words of a section of the Torah that is used as a centerpiece of all morning and evening Jewish prayer services. It is considered the most important prayer in Judaism, and its twice-daily recitation is a *mitzvah*, a religious commandment. Its main focus is loving the one God with all one's heart, soul and might, and the rewards that come from doing this.

Shoah (Heb.). Literally, a "catastrophic upheaval." The Holocaust. The Khurbn.

Shtetl (Yid.). A small town with a large Jewish population in pre-Holocaust Eastern Europe.

Tante (Yid.). Aunt.

Terezín / Theresienstadt. A Nazi concentration camp during World War II. The camp was established by the Gestapo in the fortress and garrison city of Terezín (Ger.: Theresienstadt), located in what is now the Czech Republic. The function of Terezín was to provide a front for the extermination of Jews. Of the approximately one hundred forty-four thousand Jews sent there, about eighty-eight thousand were deported to Auschwitz and other extermination camps and a mere seventeen thousand inmates survived. Terezín was distinct in the universe of camps maintained by the Nazis. Many educated Jews were imprisoned there, and the camp was known for its rich cultural life. On 23 June 1944, the Nazis permitted a visit by the International Red Cross, in order to dispel rumors about the death camps. To minimize the appearance of overcrowding at Terezín — before the war, the population of the town of Terezín had hovered around five thousand people, whereas at the height of the war, the Ghetto/Concentration Camp Terezín held over fifty-five thousand Jews — the Nazis deported many Jews imprisoned there to Auschwitz. They also erected fake shops and cafés to give the visiting officials the impression that the Jews lived in relative comfort. The Danes whom the Red Cross visited lived in freshly painted rooms, and the guests enjoyed the performance of *Brundibár*, or *Bumble Bee*, a children's operetta, which had been written by inmate Hans Krása. In fact, there were so many musicians in Terezín, there could have been two full orchestras performing simultaneously daily. In addition, there were a number of chamber orchestras playing at various times.

The Red Cross hoax was so successful for the Nazis that they went on to make a propaganda film at the camp. Directed by Jewish prisoner, Kurt Gerron (a director, cabaret performer, and actor who had appeared with Marlene Dietrich in *The Blue Angel*), it was intended to show how well the Jews lived under the "benevolent" protection of the Third Reich. After the film was completed, most of the cast, and even the filmmaker himself, were deported to Auschwitz, where Gerron and his wife were executed in the gas chambers. See *Hitler Builds a City for the Jews*, by Karen Alkalay-Gut, and Emily Borenstein's poem, "Verdi's Requiem Played and Sung by Jews in Terezín Concentration Camp / Summer, 1944."

Treblinka. A Nazi extermination camp in German-occupied Poland during World War II. Extermination camps like the one at Treblinka were used in the Holocaust for the systematic genocide of people categorized as "sub-humans" by the Nazis. It operated from July 1942 until October 1943. Over seven hundred eighty thousand people were killed there, an amount second only to Auschwitz II (Birkenau) as the site with the most victims killed in the Holocaust. Treblinka was one of four camps of Operation Reinhard, the other three being Bełżec, Sobibór and Majdanek. Chelmno extermination camp was originally built as a pilot project for the development of the other three camps. Operation Reinhard was overseen by

Heinrich Himmler, commander of the SS, and headed by Odilo Globocnik in Poland. Unlike other concentration camps, Operation Reinhard camps reported directly to Himmler's office (the Reichs Sicherheits Hauptamt) in Berlin. Himmler maintained overall control of the program close to him but delegated the work to Globocnik. Operation Reinhard used the euthanasia program (Action T4) as a model for site selection, construction and the training of personnel. Before Operation Reinhard, over half a million Jews had been killed by the *Einsatzgruppen*, mobile SS units whose main purpose was to murder Jews and Communist officers in territories conquered by the German army. It became evident, however, that they could not handle millions of Jews that the Nazis had concentrated in the ghettos of Poland. So Treblinka, like the other Operation Reinhard camps, was especially designed for the rapid elimination of Jews who were imprisoned in ghettos. Treblinka was ready on 24 July 1942, when the shipping of Jews began. According to SS Brigadeführer Jürgen Stroop's report, a total of approximately three hundred ten thousand Jews were transported in freight trains from the Warsaw Ghetto to Treblinka from 22 July to 3 October 1943. See *The Stroop Report: The Jewish Quarter of Warsaw Is No More!* Trans. and annotated by Sybil Milton (1979).

Umschlagplatz (Ger.). Collection point or reloading point. The place in the Warsaw Ghetto where Jews were gathered for deportation to the Treblinka extermination camp. Beginning on 22 July 1942, as many as seven thousand Jews were shipped daily in freight cars under the most barbaric conditions. An estimated eight hundred thousand Jews were taken to the Treblinka gas chambers, and some sources describe it as the largest slaughter of any single community in World War II. The deportations ended on 12 September 1942. In 1988, a stone monument resembling an open freight car was built to mark the Umschlagplatz.

Yahrzeit (Yid.). From the German (jahr + zeit). Year's time. The anniversary of someone's death, usually a parent or other close relative whom one is obligated to mourn. On this day, a memorial candle is lighted in the home, where it burns from sunset to sunset.

Yellow Badge / Yellow Star. The yellow badge, also referred to as a Jewish badge, was a mandatory mark or a piece of cloth of specific geometric shape, worn on the outer garment in order to distinguish a Jew in public. It is associated with antisemitism in Christian countries and with humiliation of Jews in Muslim ones. In some countries, at different times, a badge was accompanied or replaced by identifying garb or a special hat. Although during the Holocaust the requirement for Jews to display the yellow star on their clothing was inconsistently enforced, the yellow star, inscribed with the word "Jude," has become a symbol of Nazi persecution.

Yizkor (Heb.). May (God) remember. A memorial service that is recited as part of the prayer service four times during the year. This is based on the Jewish belief in the eternal life of the soul — that although a soul can no longer do good deeds after death, it can gain merit through the charity and good deeds of the living. Yizkor is said following the Torah and Haftarah readings on Yom Kippur, on the last day of Passover, on the second day of Shavuot (a holiday that celebrates the harvest season), and on the eighth day of Sukkot (Shemini Atzeret). It is said on Yom Kippur because it is believed that the dead as well as the living need atonement on this day. Yizkor is said by every observant Jew who loses a parent or other loved one, although some authorities hold that one need not say it in the first year following a death.

Yom Kippur. The Day of Atonement when Jews gather in their places of worship to confess their sins before God and to ask forgiveness for sins against God and their fellow man.

Zyklon B (also spelled Cyclon B). The trade name of a cyanide-based insecticide and pesticide notorious for its use by Nazi Germany to kill over one million people in the gas chambers of Auschwitz and other death camps during the Holocaust. It consisted of hydrocyanic acid (prussic acid), a stabilizer, and a warning odorant that were impregnated onto various substrates, typically small absorbent pellets, fiber discs, or diatomaceous earth. It was stored in airtight containers; when exposed to air, the substrates evolved gaseous hydrogen cyanide (HCN). Zyklon B was manufactured by a firm called Degesch, which was largely owned by I.G. Farben, and it had been brought to Auschwitz in the summer of 1941 as a vermin-killer and disinfectant.

Notes to Poems

I have limited these annotations to factual details that are not common knowledge or easily gleaned from a good college dictionary or the daily news. I have placed more personal reflections by the authors in the section immediately following this one, "Poets' Statements." A number of references that recur in the text have been placed in the glossary, which precedes this section.

Sherman Alexie
from* "Inside Dachau"**: ***Sand Creek. The "Sand Creek Massacre" (also known as the "Chivington Massacre" or the "Battle of Sand Creek") occurred on the morning of 29 November 1864, when Colorado Territory militia, under the command of Colonel John Chivington (1821–94), surrounded a village of Cheyenne and Arapaho encamped on the eastern plains. Colonel Chivington and his eight hundred troops attacked the village and massacred the majority of its mostly unarmed inhabitants, even though their chief, Black Kettle (?–1868) was flying an American flag and a white truce flag over his lodge, as Federal army officers had demanded. Before the attack, Chivington had ordered his men to "Kill and scalp all, big and little," and about two hundred Cheyenne — most of them women, children, and elderly men — were slaughtered. Later, in the Apollo Theater and the saloons of Denver, Chivington and his men displayed scalps and other body parts from the dead they had mutilated. ***Wounded Knee***. The "Wounded Knee Massacre" was the last major armed conflict between the Dakota Sioux and U.S. military forces. On 29 December 1890, five hundred troops of the 7th Cavalry, supported by four Hotchkiss guns (lightweight artillery capable of rapid fire), surrounded an encampment of Lakota (Miniconjou and Hunkpapa Sioux), with orders to escort them to the railroad for transport to Omaha, Nebraska. The cavalry commander had been ordered to disarm the Lakota before proceeding, and shooting broke out near the end of the disarmament. Although accounts differ regarding who fired first and why, the encounter was subsequently described as a "massacre" by General Nelson A. Miles in a letter to the Commissioner of Indian Affairs. By the time the incident was over, twenty-five troopers and approximately three hundred Lakota Sioux lay dead, including men, women, and children.

Karen Alkalay-Gut
"Voyage Home": ***Zakopane***. A well-known skiing and hiking center in the Tatra mountains.

Michael Alpiner
"Postcard from Poland": ***Chruscik***. A crunchy Polish pastry.

John Amen
"Verboten": ***Verboten*** (Ger.). Forbidden.

Frieda Arkin
"Pinochle Day": ***Hildesheim***. A city in Lower Saxony, Germany. The city, which had retained its medieval character until the beginning of World War II, was heavily damaged by air raids in 1945. ***Ode to Joy***. ***"An Die Freude."*** The choral finale of Beethoven's Ninth Symphony.

Brett Axel
"Morning After a Fight, He Says": ***Nartik*** (Yid.). Apparently, a slang or invented word for vagina. ***Kurz und gut*** (Ger.). Literally, *brief and good*, but in this context, an idiomatic expression meaning *end of discussion*.

Yakov Azriel
"We, the *Tefillin* of Once-Was Europe": ***Tefillin*** (Heb.). Phylacteries. Two small black leather boxes containing Biblical verses; black leather straps are attached to them. One box is worn on the arm, the other on the forehead. For observant Jews, they are an essential part of morning prayers.

Julius Balbin
"Lament for the Gypsies": Like the Jews, Gypsies were singled out by the Nazis for racial persecution and annihilation. To a degree, they shared the fate of the Jews in their ghettos, in the extermination camps, before firing squads and as medical guinea pigs. The Nuremberg Laws of 1935 aimed at the Jews were soon amended to include the Gypsies and, in 1937, they were classified as "asocials": second-class citizens, subject to concentration camp imprisonment. After 1939, Gypsies from Germany and from the German-occupied territories were shipped, by the thousands, to Jewish ghettos in Poland. It is not known how many were killed by the Einsatzgruppen charged with speedy extermination by shooting. Like Jews, Gypsies were usually made to strip naked, then shot while facing pre-dug graves. There are few authoritative sources about the fate of Gypsies in the Holocaust of the type widely available in regard to Jewish victims of the Nazi terror. However, it is known that perhaps two hundred fifty thousand Gypsies were killed, mainly at Auschwitz, though some estimates place the number as high as five hundred thousand. Whatever the exact number, it's clear that, proportionately, they suffered losses greater than any group of victims, except the Jews.

Stanley H. Barkan
"The Mothertree": ***Yiskadal v'yiskadash*** (Heb.): Magnified and sanctified (the first two words of the mourner's prayer).

Tony Barnstone
"Parable of the Jew Without a Name": ***Mary Antin*** (1881–1949). An American author and immigration rights activist. Born to a Jewish family in Polotsk, she emigrated to the Boston area with her mother and siblings in 1894. She later moved to New York City where she attended Teachers College of Columbia University and Barnard College. Antin is best known for her 1912 autobiography *The Promised Land*, which describes her assimilation into American culture.

Willis Barnstone
"Miklós Radnóti": ***Radnóti*** (b. Miklós Glatter, 1909). Hungary's major poet of the twentieth century. A Jewish slave laborer during the war, he was beaten to death by his German captors in 1944 while on a forced march and left in a ditch. Two years later, he was identified by a letter and poems he'd written to his wife that were found in his overcoat pocket. These "postcard" poems are considered to be among the most beautiful and poignant in the Hungarian language.

"The Rose of Blue Flesh": ***Terrible 1492***. In March 1492, the Jews of Spain were given the choice between renouncing their faith — and submitting to baptism as Christians — and exile from their home country. As many as one hundred sixty-five thousand Sephardim (Spanish Jews) chose exile and emigrated from Spain to Portugal, Italy, Greece, Turkey, and North Africa. ***Tsamiko flute***. A traditional Greek instrument. ***Agonia*** (Grk.). Agony.

Emily Borenstein

"Night Journey to Poland": ***Geshrei*** (Yid.). A scream, a shout.

"The Shoah": ***The Hineni*** (Heb.). A prayer, "Here I am [as I stand before God]." ***Tekiah! Shebarim! Teruah! Tekiah!***. The notes of the shofar — the ram's horn —sounded in the synagogue during Rosh Hashanah (the New Year) and at the end of services on Yom Kippur (Day of Atonement). ***Ovinu Malkenu!*** (Heb.). Our Father, our King. A prayer recited on the New Year and Day of Atonement, in which worshippers acknowledge their sins and pray for God's forgiveness. ***Yaaleh*** (Heb.). Let us go up. A High Holiday prayer — that our words might ascend to God. ***Shema Kolenu*** (Heb.). Hear our voice. A plea for God to listen to our prayers.

"Verdi's Requiem Played and Sung by Jews in Terezín Concentration Camp / Summer, 1944": ***Requiem*** (L.). Rest. The first word in the Mass for the dead or the musical setting for a mass of this kind. ***Tuba miram*** (L.). A large brass wind instrument. ***Confutatis maledictis*** (L.). Cursed are the wicked ones. ***Libera me*** (L.). Release me. The absolution belongs not to the Mass itself but to the burial service. Many important Masses were composed between 1816–1874 including Verdi's Requiem in 1874. ***Recordare***. The Offertory Antiphon for the Feast of the Compassion of Mary on the Friday before Holy Week: ***Recordare Virgo mater, dum steteris in conspectu Dei, ut loquaris pro nobis bona, et ut avertas indignationem suam a nobis***. "Remember, Virgin Mary, when you stand in the presence of God, to speak well of us so as to turn his wrath from us." ***Lacrymosa!*** (L.). Painfully sad (causing tears). ***Libera, Domine, de morte aeterna*** (L.). Save me, Lord, from eternal death. ***Tremens factus sum*** (L.). I'm frightened. I tremble. ***Dies irae*** (L.). Day of wrath. ***Libera nos!*** (L.). Liberate us!

Van K. Brock

"The Hindenburg": LZ-129 was completed in 1936 and offered the first commercial air service across the North Atlantic. It was eight hundred three feet long, had a cruising speed of seventy-eight mph, and could transport more than a thousand passengers per flight. On 6 May 1937, while landing at Lakehurst, New Jersey, on the first crossing of the 1937 season, the Hindenburg burst into flames and was completely destroyed. ***Thousand Year Reich***. Hitler had predicted that the Third Reich would last for a thousand years.

from This Way to the Gas*:** ***Tadeusz Borowski (1922–51). A Polish Christian writer and journalist, and a Holocaust survivor. The English translation of his book, *This Way to the Gas, Ladies and Gentlemen*, was published in 1922 by Penguin Books and has been in print ever since.

Louis Daniel Brodsky

"Learning the ABC's in Wartime Germany": ***Anschluss*** (Ger.). Annexation. ***Österreich*** (Ger.). Austria. ***Endlösung*** (Ger.). Final Solution [the code words used by Hermann Göring in a letter to Reinhard Heydrich to refer to a plan to extirpate the Jews of Europe that was later codified at the Wansee Conference, an eighty-seven-minute meeting attended by fifteen leading Nazi bureaucrats, including Adolf Eichmann, that was held on 20 January 1942, at a villa in a Berlin suburb].

"*Schindlerjuden*": ***Schindlerjuden*** (Ger.). Schindler's Jews. Oskar Schindler (1908–74) was a German businessman who saved more than twelve hundred Jews from almost certain death. Schindler made a fortune on military contracts during World War II (1939–45) and spent nearly all of it to save the Jewish slave workers in his factory, who produced pots and pans for the German army. **Schindler's List**. A 1993 film directed by Steven Spielberg that was based on the book of the same title by Thomas Keneally. ***Judenrein*** (Ger.). Literally, "free of Jews." Establishments, villages, cities, and regions were declared *Judenrein* after they were ethnically cleansed of Jews. ***Pathé***. Pathé Frères is the name of various businesses established and originally run by the Pathé Brothers of France. Founded as Société Pathé Frères in Paris, France, in 1896 by brothers, Charles, Émile, Théophile and Jacques Pathé, Pathé became the largest film equipment and production company in the world, as well as a major producer of phonograph records, during the first part of the twentieth century. ***Topf and Sons***. A German firm that produced crematorium furnaces.

"Speaking for Survivors": ***Endlösung*** (Ger.). See above.

Michael R. Burch
"Pfennig Postcard, Wrong Address": ***Pfennig*** (Ger.). A penny.

Olga Cabral
"At the Jewish Museum": At an exhibition of art on the theme of the Holocaust, one of the exhibition pieces was a large, brick-lined, darkened room that was totally empty. This environment was the sculptor's monument for the children who had perished in the death camps that blighted Germany, Poland, and parts of Eastern Europe during the Holocaust.

Joan Campion
"To Gisi Fleischmann: Rescuer of Her People": ***Gisi Fleischmann***. Leader of the Slovakian Jewish resistance group known as the Arbeitsgruppe (Working Group) and one of the heroic figures of the Holocaust. She is especially known for her efforts to save children and to negotiate with the Nazis for Jewish Lives. Fleischmann was murdered at Auschwitz 18 October 1944.

Cyrus Cassells
"Life Indestructible": ***Etty Hillesum***. Ester "Etty" Hillesum (1914–43) was born to a Dutch Jewish father and a Jewish Russian mother and lived in Holland during her short but courageous life. In March 1941, nearly a year after the beginning of the German occupation, she began a diary, and in July 1942 she volunteered to work at Westerbork concentration camp to help the Jews interned there. In October 1942, she stopped writing in her diary, and some months later, her travel permits were withdrawn and she and her family, and also those she had tried to help, were summarily interned in the camp. On 7 September 1943, Hillesum, her family, and about nine hundred other prisoners were transported to Auschwitz, where she died later later that year. Her letters to friends and family deal mainly with her views on the treatment of Jews, her experiences in Westerbork, and her life as a young Jewish woman in the occupied country. ***Juggernaut***. An incarnation of the Hindu god Vishnu, whose idol so excited his worshipers when it was hauled along on a large car during religious rites that they threw themselves under the wheels and were crushed. ***Soubrette*** (Fr.). Lady's maid.

"The Postcard of Sophie Scholl": ***Sophie Scholl*** (1921–43). A German college student, who became an international symbol of resistance when she was swiftly executed, along with her brother, Hans, and their friend, Christopher Probst, for distributing anti-Nazi leaflets at Munich University and for their part in the White Rose resistance movement. Her brief, dedicated life has been the subject of four dramatic films and several documentaries. Recently-released transcripts of her trial and interrogation reveal a young woman of enormous vision, strength, and integrity. Her last words, on facing the guillotine, were *"Die Sonne Scheint noch"* ("The sun still shines"). ***Bel ragazzo*** (Ital.). Pretty boy. [The art referred to in the poem is a lithograph by Bruno Bruni (Italian artist, born 1935).]

Judith Chalmer
"Personal to Kaplan": ***Tata*** (Pol.). Dad.

John Ciardi
"The Gift": ***Josef Stein***. According to American poet, Miller Williams, Ciardi based his poem on the experience of an actual poet-survivor. ***Kaput*** (Ger.). Dead (the correct German spelling is "Kaputt").

Vince Clemente
"From the Ardeatine Caves": ***Giardino alla Francese*** (It.). French-style garden. ***Monet at Giverny***. Claude Monet (b. 1840) settled at Giverny in 1883 and died there in 1926. The garden at Giverny inspired some of his best works.

Helen Degen Cohen (Halina Degenfisz)
"And the Snow Kept Falling": ***La Donna è Mobile*** (It.). Woman is fickle. An aria in Giuseppe Verdi's opera, *Rigoletto*.

"Habry": ***Habry*** (Pol.). Cornflowers.

Jehanne Dubrow
"Shulamith Rereads *The Shawl*," "Shulamith, in White," "Shulamith Writes *Fuck You*": ***Shulamith***. Shulamith is the "black and comely" princess in the Song of Songs in the Old Testament, whose name holds echoes of the Hebrew words "shalom" (peace) and "Yerushalayim" (Jerusalem). According to John Felstiner, Shulamith is often understood to represent the Jewish people itself: See *Paul Celan: Poet, Survivor, Jew* (New Haven: Yale University Press, 1995), p. 38. **The Shawl**. A short story first published in the *New Yorker* in 1981; "Rosa," its longer companion piece, appeared in that magazine three years later. Together, they tell a story of a woman who survived the Holocaust but who has no life in the present because her existence was stolen away from her in a past that does not end.

Shelley Ehrlich
"Vilna 1938": In 1938, Roman Vishniac traveled secretly to photograph the Jews of Poland. Edward Steichen wrote of this trip: "It gives a last-minute look at the human beings he photographed just before the fury of Nazi brutality exterminated them." According to the poet's husband, Dr. Frederick M. Ehrlich, the photograph that inspired this poem is entitled "Vilna, Poland" and appears on page 62 of *Roman Vishniac*, ICP Library of Photographers (New York: Viking, 1974). ***Vilna***. Now called Vilnius, this city had been a leading center of Jewish

culture in Eastern Europe since the sixteenth century. Napoleon had called it "the Jerusalem of Lithuania." The shifting geopolitical borders of Eastern Europe during the twentieth century account for the fact that Vilna has been identified as Polish, Lithuanian, and Russian within the course of a single lifetime. See "Ponary" under *Glossary*.

Frederick Feirstein
"'Grandfather' in Winter": ***Nine Iraqi Jews***. Nine Jews were hung publicly in Iraq in 1978, the year this poem was written.

Irving Feldman
from* "Family History":** ***Mit dem shpits tsung aroys (Yid.). With the tip of the tongue out. ***The Pale***. The Pale of Settlement, an area in the western portions of Tsarist Russia, in which Jews were permitted to settle. ***Arbet macht dem leben ziess***. (Yid.) Work makes life sweet.

"The Pripet Marshes": The area near Lake Narocz in Poland, east-northeast of Vilnius (Vilna), and the site of a great, but disastrous, offensive by the Russian Second Army in the spring of 1916. Concerning World War II, Hilberg states: "We know that only a few thousand Jews escaped from the ghettos of Poland and Russia; that only a few hundred Jews hid out in the large cities of Berlin, Vienna, and Warsaw; that only a handful of Jews escaped from camps. Von dem Bach mentions that in Russia there was an unguarded escape route to the Pripet Marshes, but few Jews availed themselves of the opportunity. In the main, the Jews looked upon flight with a sense of futility. The great majority of those who did not escape early did not escape at all" (1036).

Ruth Feldman
"Survivor": ***Giorgio Bassani*** (1916–2000). An Italian novelist, poet, essayist, editor, and international intellectual. In 1956, the collection *Cinque storie ferraresi* (*Five Stories of Ferrara*; reissued as *Dentro le mura [Inside the Wall]*, 1973), five novellas that describe the growth of fascism and anti-Semitism, brought Bassani his first commercial success and the Strega Prize (offered annually for the best Italian literary work). The Ferrara setting recurs in Bassani's best known book, the semiautobiographical *Il giardino dei Finzi-Contini* (*The Garden of the Finzi-Continis*, 1962) and in the 1971 Vittorio de Sica film of the same name. The narrator of this work contrasts his own middle-class Jewish family with the aristocratic and decadent Finzi-Continis, also Jewish, whose sheltered lives end in annihilation by the Nazis.

Charles Adés Fishman
"A Jawbone from the Reich": ***Rauschning***. Hermann Rauschning (1887–1982) was a German conservative and reactionary who joined the Nazi Party and became the president of the Danzig Senate. After resigning, he fled Germany and became an opponent of Nazism. He wrote several books warning the world about the nihilistic nature of Hitler's movement. Rauschning is most famous for his work *Hitler Speaks* where he describes the many meetings and conversations he had with Adolf Hitler. A number of historians now regard this book with suspicion (Wikipedia). See *Sources Cited*.

"The Silence": ***"Eli, Eli."*** A traditional Hebrew song, which has been attributed to Hannah Senesh, a hero of the Holocaust who was tortured and executed by the Nazis in 1944, after she parachuted into Hungary, in a desperate attempt to save Jews. Her words can be translated as follows: "Oh Lord, my God, I pray that these things never end: / The sand and the sea, / The rush of the waters, / The lightning from heaven, / The prayer of man." ***Vrba***. Rudolf Vrba was a Slovakian Jew who, with his friend Alfréd Wetzler, a Hungarian Jewish leader, escaped from Auschwitz on 7 April 1944. Their eyewitness testimony, known by various names, including the "Vrba-Wetzler Report" and "The Auschwitz Protocols," is a thirty-two-page document about the Auschwitz-Birkenau extermination camp that was written by hand and dictated in Slovak between 25 and 27 April 1944 and then typed up in the form of a report by Dr. Oscar Krasniansky of the Slovak *Judenrat* (Jewish Council), who simultaneously translated it into German. The report represents one of the first attempts to estimate the numbers of people being killed in the death camp. Dr. Vrba died at the age of eighty-two in 2006. ***Sobibór***. Sobibór was a Nazi extermination camp that was part of Operation Reinhard (see note under "Posamentier," below). It is also the name of the village outside which the camp was built. Jews, including Jewish Soviet POWs, and possibly Gypsies, were transported to Sobibór by rail and suffocated in gas chambers that were fed with the exhaust from a gas engine. At least two hundred fifty thousand people were killed in Sobibór.

Ephim Fogel

"Icon": ***Ad maiorem Germaniae gloriam*** (L.). To the greater glory of Germany — a take-off on the the unofficial Jesuit motto: *Ad Maiorem Dei Gloriam* ("for the greater glory of God").

"Yizkor": ***Guadalajara***. The Battle of Guadalajara (8–23 March 1937) saw the Spanish Popular Army defeat Italian and Nationalist forces attempting to encircle Madrid during the Spanish Civil War. ***Guadalcanal***. The Guadalcanal campaign, also known as the Battle of Guadalcanal, was fought between 7 August 1942 and 9 February 1943 in the Pacific Theater of World War II. This campaign, fought on the ground, at sea, and in the air, pitted Allied forces against Imperial Japanese forces, and was a decisive, strategically significant campaign of World War II. ***Kasserine Pass***. The Battle for Kasserine Pass took place in World War II during the Tunisia Campaign. It was actually a series of battles fought around Kasserine Pass, a two-mile-wide gap in the chain of the Atlas Mountains in west central Tunisia, and significant as the first large-scale meeting of American and German forces in World War II. ***Normandy***. The Battle of Normandy was fought in 1944 between Nazi Germany and the invading Allied forces, as part of the larger conflict of World War II. Over sixty years later, the Normandy invasion (code-named "Operation Overlord"), which involved almost three million troops crossing the English Channel from England to Normandy in then German-occupied France, still remains the largest sea-borne invasion in history. It is most commonly known by the name D-Day. ***Samar***. The Battle of Samar was the final stage of the Battle of Leyte Gulf, the largest naval battle in history. The battle took place in the Philippine Sea near the Samar area of Leyte Island in the Philippines on 25 October 1944 and involved warships from the United States Navy and the Imperial Japanese Navy. With the assistance of air units from other task forces, the U.S. Navy ships succeeded in causing enough damage to drive back a force they were not equipped to fight.

Carolyn Forché

from* "The Angel of History":** ***Izieu. Izieu and Bregnier-Cordon were villages in the Free Zone. The children were arrested on 6 April 1944 by the Lyon Gestapo and were sent to Drancy for deportation to the extermination camps. ***Comment me vint . . . hiver*** (Fr.). A line from the poet Rene Char: "How does writing come to me? / Like a feather to the window pane in winter." ***Le silence de Dieu est Dieu*** (Fr.). "The silence of God is God." A line from Elie Wiesel's poem "Ani Maamin."

Pithiviers, Beaune-la-Rolande, Les Tourelles. Internment camps in Vichy France. Most of the Jews rounded up — including thousands of children under sixteen — were deported to Auschwitz by order of Adolf Eichmann (see *Glossary*). ***Les Milles***. The Camp des Milles was opened in September 1939, in a former tile factory near the village of Les Milles. It was first used to intern Germans and ex-Austrians living in the Marseilles Area, and by June 1940, some thirty-five hundred artists and intellectuals were detained there. Between 1941 and 1942, Le Camp des Milles was used as a transit camp for Jews, mainly men (women were kept at the Centre Bompard in Marseilles, while they waited for visas and authorizations that would allow them to emigrate). About two thousand of the inmates were shipped to the camp at Drancy on the way to Auschwitz. For a detailed discussion of the French camps and the deportation process, see Hilberg, 609–660 ("The Semicircular Arc"). ***Vous n'aurez . . . Lorraine*** (Fr.). You shall not have Alsace-Lorraine. During the German occupation, the provinces of Alsace-Lorraine were ruled as quasi-incorporated areas, which facilitated the deportation of the Jewish population of the region. According to Hilberg, "twenty-two thousand Jews were involved in these movements from Alsace alone. The victims were piled on trucks, driven across [borders to unoccupied France], and dumped out at night on a deserted country road" (614).

from* "The Notebook of Uprising":** **"XIII":** ***Jan Palach (b. 1948). A Czech student who committed suicide by self-immolation as a political protest on 16 January 1969. The Soviet-led invasion of Czechoslovakia in August 1968 was designed to crush the liberalizing reforms of Alexander Dubček's government during the "Prague Spring." Palach died after setting himself on fire in Wenceslas Square.

Florence W. Freed

"God's Death": ***Emanuel Ringelblum*** (1900–94). A Polish-Jewish historian, politician and social worker, known for his *Notes from the Warsaw Ghetto*, *Notes on the Refugees in Zbąszyn*, and the "Ringelblum Archives" of the Warsaw Ghetto, which was buried in three milk cans and ten metal boxes, just prior to the destruction of the Warsaw Ghetto in spring 1943. The *Archives* consists of approximately twenty-five thousand pages — government documents, literature, scientific papers, works of art, private correspondence, and materials concerning Jewish resistance and testimonies on the fate of Jewish communities during the Holocaust — that were retrieved from the ruins of the ghetto, following the war. This collection is absolutely unique, both in terms of its origin and its historic value. One of the milk cans has still not been recovered.

Mike Frenkel

"Quiet Desperation": ***Allegro di bravura***. Used to mark a technically difficult piece or passage to be executed swiftly and boldly (in contrast to "bagatelle," a short piece of light music).

Kinereth Gensler

"For Nelly Sachs": ***Nelly Sachs*** (1891–1970). Sachs was a German Jewish poet who found asylum in Sweden during World II. In 1966, when she was seventy-five, she shared the Nobel Prize for Literature with Israeli novelist S. Y. Agnon. Sachs received the award for her life's work as a poet, playwright, and translator — work that culminated in the moving lyrics of *O the Chimneys*, a deeply metaphoric book of elegies for the victims of the Holocaust.

David Gershator
from* "The Akiva Poems": *Akiva Gershater. The spelling is correct.

Jacob Glatstein (Yankev Glatshteyn)
"Dead Men Don't Praise God": *Rambam*. Maimonides (1135 or 1138–1204). A rabbi, physician, and philosopher in Spain, Morocco, and Egypt during the Middle Ages. He was one of the principal medieval Jewish philosophers who also influenced the non-Jewish world. Although his copious works on Jewish law and ethics were often met with opposition during his lifetime, he was posthumously acknowledged to be one of the foremost rabbinical arbiters and philosophers in Jewish history. Today, his works and his views are considered a cornerstone of Orthodox Jewish thought and study. Maimonides' full Hebrew name was *Moshe ben Maimon*, but he is most commonly known by his Greek name, Moses Maimonides ("Moses, son of Maimon"). Most Jewish works refer to him by the Hebrew acronym of his title and name — Rabbi Moshe ben Maimon — and call him the "Rambam." ***Vilna Gaon***. A prominent rabbi, Talmud scholar, and Kabbalist (1720–97). His real name was Elijah (Eliyahu) ben Shlomo Zalman, but he is commonly referred to in Hebrew as *ha'Gaon ha'Chasid mi'Vilna*, "the saintly genius from Vilna." ***Mahram*** (Heb.). Our master. As with "Gaon," used when referring to a great rabbinical teacher. ***Marshal the Seer***. A famous rabbi in eigthteenth-century Poland, but possibly a further reference to an ancient Jewish sage who was reputed to have the ability to see into the future. ***Abraham Geiger*** (1810–74). A German rabbi who laid the foundation for Reform Judaism by seeking to remove all nationalistic elements from Judaism; he stressed that Judaism is an evolving religion. ***Baal Shem*** (Heb). Master of the Name. A title that is almost always used in reference to Israel ben Eliezer, the Rabbi who founded Hasidic Judaism and was called the Baal Shem Tov (Master of the Good Name).

"Millions of Dead": The year 5703 is the date, according to the Jewish calendar. According to the Gregorian calendar, it is 1943.

"Without Jews": *The Thirty-Six*. In Jewish mystical tradition, the "Lamed Vav Tzaddikim": the thirty-six righteous individuals in each generation, whose very existence in the world protects it from destruction.

Barbara Goldberg
"Our Father": *Donnerwetter noch einmal* (Ger.). Thunderstorm again! (expression of anger).

Leo Haber
"Sanctification": The author of the lines quoted in this poem was probably Alena Synkova, a teenage girl from Prague who was deported to Terezín in 1942 and managed to return home after Liberation. Of fifteen thousand children under fifteen who passed through Terezín, only one hundred to one hundred thirty-two survived. The poem was translated from the Czech by Jeanne Nemcova. ***Kiddush***. The Hebrew prayer of blessing recited over the wine cup at the beginning of every festive meal on a holy day. The root of the word is the same as for *Kaddish* (see *Glossary*) and also refers to "sanctification."

Israel I. Halpern
"Being Seemingly Unscathed": ***Ha-Shem*** (Heb.). Literally, "The Name": substituted for "God" by Orthodox Jews, who are not supposed to speak or write the word. ***Maggid*** (Heb.). An itinerant preacher, skilled as a narrator of stories. ***Misgav*** (Heb.). Guardian. ***Shomer*** (Heb.). Custodian.

Geoffrey Hartman
"Day of Remembrance": Author's note — "The Passover seder, a festive family evening, which each year marks the liberation of the Hebrews from Egypt and slavery, is based on the Biblical commandment 'vehiggata': 'you shall tell' [that story to everyone in the household]. The official Day of Remembrance for the Holocaust falls close to Passover, and the poem applies the 'you shall tell' to the deliverance of the Jews from death under the Nazi regime. Images from the Passover ritual mingle, therefore, with anniversary symptoms reflecting what became public knowledge at the opening of the camps. Yet liberation, despite the faith, hope, and joy that make the Passover ceremony more poignant than ever, is often overshadowed by the nearness of the memory of the Holocaust, a memory that revives with every renewed act of genocide."

"In Memory of Paul Celan": ***Kadesh***. Qadesh. An ancient city of the Levant, located on the Orontes River, in what is now western Syria.

Anthony Hecht
"'It Out-Herods Herod. Pray You, Avoid It.'": ***Out-Herods Herod***. Out-does in wickedness, violence, or rant, the tyrant, Herod, who is remembered for ordering the "Massacre of the Innocents," following the birth of Jesus. See Matthew 2. See also *Hamlet*, iii. 2 (Shakespeare). ***Heinrich Blücher*** (1899–1970) ***and Hannah Arendt*** (1906–75). Arendt was a German political theorist and philosopher, perhaps best known for her book, *Eichmann in Jerusalem*, in which she coined the phrase, "the banality of evil." She was married to the German poet and Marxist philosopher Heinrich Blücher.

"'More Light! More Light!'": Author's note — "The title is composed of what are reputedly the last words of Johann Wolfgang von Goethe (1749–1832), German poet, scientist, critic, man of letters, and probably chief representative of what was once called the 'German Enlightenment.' The first three stanzas concern details conflated from several executions, including those of Latimer and Ridley (Anglican bishops executed for heresy in 1555), whose death at the stake are described by John Foxe in *Acts and Monuments* (S. R. Cattley and George Townsend, eds.), a Protestant martyrology. Neither of these men wrote poems just before their deaths, though others did." ***Kindly Light***. A phrase from a hymn by Cardinal Newman, "Lead, Kindly Light." According to Hecht, the events described in the remaining stanzas of the poem are transcribed as exactly as possible from a book called *The Theory and Practice of Hell*, by Eugen Kogon (trans. by Heinz Norden [New York: Farrar, Straus & Co., 1950]). Buchenwald concentration camp was built only a few miles from Goethe's home at Weimar, and prisoners sent to that camp were unloaded from trains at the Weimar station and marched the rest of the way to the camp.

Julie N. Heifetz
"The Blue Parakeet": ***Lagerführerin*** (Ger.). Female camp commandant.

"Harry Lenga": ***Sturmführer*** (Ger.). Storm Leader. A paramilitary rank of the Nazi Party which began as a title used by the Sturmabteilung in 1925 and became an actual SA rank in 1928. By 1930, Sturmführer had become the first officer paramilitary rank of several Nazi Party organizations. ***Ebensee***. A dark point in Ebensee's history was the placement of a Nazi concentration camp — part of the Mauthausen network — in Ebensee. Roughly twenty thousand inmates were worked to their deaths to construct giant tunnels in the surrounding mountains. These tunnels were designed for moving Penemünde's rocket research into bomb-proof surroundings. Together with the Mauthausen subcamp of Gusen, Ebensee is considered to be one of the most diabolic concentration camps ever built. ***Hatikvah***. *Hatikvah* or *Hatikva* (Heb: "The Hope") is the national anthem of Israel.

Michael Heller
from **"Bialystok Stanzas":** The Yiddish names in the penultimate stanza were those given by the citizens of Bialystok to the victims of three mass executions: "the Friday dead," "the Thursday dead," "the Saturday dead." ***Davar*** (Heb.). Author's note — "Davar is a key Hebrew word used for both 'word' and 'thing'; hence the line 'davar twining aleph into thing.' A lot of commentary exists on this word, the concepts often focusing on the physical literariness of the Hebrew language. 'Aleph' is also often seen as the first word, containing all the other words." ***Yod***. The tenth letter of the Hebrew alphabet. It rhymes with 'mode' and has the sound of 'y' as in 'yes.' In the Jewish mystical tradition, yod represents a divine point of energy, but since Yod is used to form all the other letters — and since God uses the letters as the building blocks of creation — yod indicates God's omnipresence."

Stephen Herz
"In Your Lager Dream,": ***Blockalteste*** (Ger.). Block elder. A position of authority that evolved at Ravensbrück and other early camps that were built to house women prisoners. Although the SS was responsible for the overall management of these camps, the administration of day-to-day activities was relegated to prisoners who had been appointed to positions of leadership. An authorized prisoner usually acted as a mediator between the SS and her fellow prisoners. She imposed discipline, supervised labor, and made numerous decisions that influenced the fate of the women under her command. ***Kommando***. Any group of prisoners in the camps that was assigned to a specific task, which could range from constructing prisoner barracks and sorting clothes to removing the newly-killed from gas chambers. ***Häftlinge***. Prisoners. ***Du Jude, kaputt!*** (Ger.). Literally, You Jew, dead! The sense is: You are as good as dead. ***Deutschland über Alles***. "Das Lied der Deutschen" ("The Song of the Germans" or "The Song of Germany") has been used wholly or partially as the national anthem of Germany since 1922. Outside Germany, the hymn is sometimes informally known by the opening words and refrain of the first stanza, "Deutschland, Deutschland über alles," but this was never the title of the original work nor is the first stanza part of the current German national anthem. ***Horst Wessel song***. Horst Wessel was twenty-two when he dropped out of law school and defied his mother by joining the Nazis and becoming an SA storm trooper. On 23 February 1930, someone broke into his apartment and mortally wounded him. Joseph Goebbels, the Nazis' propaganda chief, claimed Wessel had been murdered by a Communist and made him a martyr in the party's struggle with their Communist opponents. Wessel was given an elaborate funeral, which was interrupted by stone-throwing Communists. The murder and reaction helped turn public opinion in favor of the Nazis and against the Communists. A poem Wessel had written was put to music and became the marching song of the SA and later the official song of the Nazi Party and the unofficial national anthem of Germany.

"Shot": ***Zhytomyr . . . Zamość***. Many of the place names come from Daniel Jonah Goldhagen's *Hitler's Willing Executioners* (New York: Knopf, 1996); others occur in Christopher Browning's *Ordinary Men: Reserve Police Battalion 101 and the Final Solution in Poland* (New York: HarperCollins, 1992), and Martin Gilbert's *Atlas of the Holocaust* (New York: Viking Penguin, 1982). Most are names of villages, towns, and cities located in Poland, Lithuania, Ukraine, Belarus, and Russia where roving killing units, the *Einsatzgruppen*, massacred entire communities. ***Einsatzgruppen*** (Ger.). Paramilitary groups operated by the SS before and during World War II. Their principal task was the annihilation of Jews, Gypsies, and political prisoners. According to their own records, the Einsatzgruppen operatives were responsible for killing over one million people, almost exclusively civilians, starting with the Polish intelligentsia and quickly progressing by 1941 to target primarily the Jews of Eastern Europe. Raul Hilberg estimates that between 1941 and 1945 the Einsatzgruppen murdered over 1.4 million Jews in open air shootings. ***German Order Police***. In January 1934, the National Socialist government began to reorganize all police authorities in Germany by placing them under direct national (Reich) control. Heinrich Himmler was appointed by Adolf Hitler to be the commander in chief of all police organizations in Germany. This was the origin of the the association and close working relationship between the German Order Police and the deadly "Protections Squads" (Schutzstaffeln-SS). ***Waffen SS***. The combat arm of the Schutzstaffel. Headed by Reichsführer-SS Heinrich Himmler, the Waffen-SS saw action throughout the Second World War. After beginning as a protection unit for the NSDAP leadership, the Waffen-SS eventually grew into a force of thirty-eight combat divisions comprising nearly a million men. ***Fascist Nyilas***. The Arrow Cross: a pro-German, antisemitic, fascist party led by Ferenc Szálasi, which ruled Hungary from 15 October 1944 to January 1945. During its short rule, eighty thousand Jews, including many women, children and old people were deported from Hungary to their deaths. After the war, Szálasi and other Arrow Cross leaders were tried as war criminals by Hungarian courts. ***Iron Guard***. An ultranationalist, antisemitic, fascist movement and political party in Romania in the period from 1927 to the early part of World War II. ***German Home Guard***. The *Volkssturm* (literally, the *People's Storm*) was a German national militia during the last months of Germany's Third Reich. It was founded on Adolf Hitler's orders on 18 October 1944 and effectively conscripted all males between the ages of sixteen and sixty, who did not already serve in some military unit, as part of a German Home Guard. ***Hitler Youth***. The Hitler Youth, founded in 1922, was based in Munich, Bavaria, and served as a recruiting ground for new Stormtroopers of the SA. The group was disbanded in 1923 but was re-established in 1926, a year after the Nazi Party had been reorganized. The second Hitler Youth began in 1926 with an emphasis on national youth recruitment into the Nazi Party. ***Harvest festival*** (*Erntefest*). In late October 1943, at Majdanek, prisoners were ordered to dig three huge trenches in the camp's southern sector. At morning roll call on 3 November, Jews were separated from the other prisoners, sent to the trenches, and shot, while dance music blared from the camp's loudspeakers to drown out the screams and machine-gun fire. The murders continued until nightfall. Intended to prevent prisoner revolts, Erntefest extended beyond Majdanek to other camps in the Lublin dustrict. ***Yitgodal veyitkadach shmé . . .*** See note for *from* "Kaddish" under Melanie Kaye/Kantrowitz, below (because Hebrew must be transliterated into English, alternate renderings in English are often spelled differently). ***Block II at Auschwitz***. See "Auschwitz" in *Glossary*.

William Heyen

"Riddle": ***Albert Speer*** (Berthold Konrad Hermann Albert Speer, 1905–81). An architect, author and high-ranking Nazi German government official, sometimes called "the first architect of the Third Reich." His two best-selling autobiographical works, detailing his often close personal relationship with Adolf Hitler, have given readers and historians an unequalled personal view inside the workings of the

Third Reich. Speer was Hitler's chief architect before becoming his Minister for Armaments during the war. He reformed Germany's war production to the extent that it continued to increase for over a year despite ever more intensive Allied bombing. After the war, he was tried at Nuremberg and was sentenced to twenty years' imprisonment for his role in the Holocaust. He was the only senior Nazi figure to admit guilt and express remorse.

Edward Hirsch
"Paul Celan: A Grave and Mysterious Sentence": Paul Celan (born Antschel, in Czernovitz, Bukovina, Romania, 1920) is best known for his "Todesfuge" ("Death Fugue"). His parents were murdered by the Nazis, and he was sent to forced labor. After the war, Celan went to Paris and became a French citizen, though he continued to write in German until his suicide by drowning in the Seine river in April 1970. During the last twenty years of his life, Celan published seven volumes of poetry in German, in addition to various translations. He is widely considered to be one of the finest lyric poets of his time and one of the most profound, innovative and original poets of the twentieth century.

Marilyn Kallet
"After a While, at Theresienstadt": ***Rexingen***. A town in Baden-Württemberg, a region of Germany.

"Mezuzah": ***Judenhausen*** (Ger.). Literally, Jewish buildings. They were usually overcrowded and poorly maintained.

"To My Poem of Hope": ***"Sara" and "Israel"***. By 1937, only Jewish names like "Sara[h]" and "Israel" could be given to Jewish children. ***Für Tot erklärt*** (Ger.). Declared dead.

"Survivor": ***Night of Broken Glass***. See "Kristallnacht" in *Glossary*. ***Muhringen***. ***Horb***. Towns on the eastern margin of the northern part of the Black Forest, just above the confluence of the river Grabenbach with the Neckar. Though the towns are nestled near each other, Horb is substantially larger. ***Shavei Zion*** (Heb.). Return to Zion. ***The East***. "Resettlement in the East" or "Deporting to the East" were Nazi German euphemisms for the forced removal of Jews to concentration camps and extermination camps during the Holocaust. ***Brundibár*** (Czech colloquialism for "bumblebee"). The name of a children's opera by Jewish Czech composer Hans Krása, with a libretto by Adolf Hoffmeister and performed by the children of Theresienstadt, in occupied Czechoslovakia.

Rodger Kamenetz
"My Holocaust": ***Jebusites***. According to the Hebrew Bible, the Jebusites were a Canaanite tribe who inhabited the region around Jerusalem prior to its capture by King David; the Books of Kings state that Jerusalem was known as *Jebus* prior to this event, which, according to some Biblical chronologies, would have happened around 1004 BCE.

Marc Kaminsky
"Medium": ***Kapoteh***. A long black frock coat worn by most married Chabad Hasidim. Many non-Hasidic rabbis wear a Kapoteh as well. ***Tish mit mentshn***. Sabbath table. ***Nign*** (Heb.). Also *Nigun* (pl. *nigunim*). A term meaning "humming tune." Usually, this refers to religious songs and tunes that are sung by groups. It is a form of voice instrumental music, often without lyrics or words, although

sounds like "bim-bim-bam" or "Ai-ai-ai!" are often used. Sometimes, Bible verses or quotes from other classical Jewish texts are sung repetitively in the form of a *nigun*. *Nigunim* are largely improvisations, though they can be based on thematic passages and are stylized in form. They are often sung as prayer in the form of a lament but may also be joyous and uplifting.

Peretz Kaminsky
"Identifications": ***"Lord , from the depths I call"***. A prayer asking God to hear us in our moments of despair. See Ps. 130:3.

Rosa Felsenburg Kaplan
"Kol Nidre": ***S'lach lanu, m'chal lanu, kaper lanu*** (Heb.). Forgive us, be with us, help us atone (for our sins). A prayer from the High Holiday prayer book. ***Kati Neni*** (Hun.). Aunt Kathrin.

Dori Katz
"Line-Up": ***Andrzei Munk*** (1920–61). A Polish film director, screenplay writer and camera operator and one of the most influential artists of the Polish Film School. Munk was born in Kraków. During the German occupation of Poland, he moved to Warsaw, where he was forced to hide because of his partially Jewish ancestry. Using a false name, he found employment as a construction worker. In 1944, Munk took part in the Warsaw Uprising. He died near Warsaw in a car accident while filming *Pasazerka* (*The Passenger*).

"The Return": ***Malines***. A city in Belgium that served the Nazis as a clearing center for deportation during the war. All Belgian Jews arrested were first sent to Malines, registered, and 'cleared'; then they were assigned to a transport to a concentration camp.

Eliot Katz
from "Liberation Recalled": ***Oradea Mare-Nagyvárad***. Originally, one of four independent town-states of Oradea, which is located in the northwestern part of Romania (near the Hungarian border) and is the tenth largest city of the country. Geographically, Oradea is situated at the crossroads of the trading route that linked central, eastern, and southeastern Europe to the Orient. The city has a rather complicated and controversial historical background due to its location and the diversity of its population. It has been known by several names, each used during a particular historical era and dependant on who ruled the region. In the Western world, that region is better known as Transylvania. ***Julius Streicher*** (1885–1946). A prominent Nazi and the publisher of *Der Stürmer* newspaper, which was to become a part of the Nazi propaganda machine. His publishing firm also released three anti-Semitic books for children. After the war, he was convicted of crimes against humanity and executed. ***Goebbels' newspaper, Attack***. Paul Joseph Goebbels (1897–1945). A German who joined the Nazi Party and was appointed district leader in Berlin by Adolf Hitler in 1926. A persuasive speaker, Goebbels edited the party's journal and began to create the Führer myth around Hitler; it was also Goebbels who instituted the party demonstrations that helped convert the masses to Nazism. Named chancellor in Hitler's will, he remained with Hitler to the end.

Alan Kaufman
"My Mother Doesn't Know Who Allen Ginsberg Is": ***Kathy Acker*** (1947–97). An experimental novelist, prose stylist, playwright, essayist, and feminist, whose work first achieved notoriety when she was part of the New York literary underground in the mid-seventies. ***Maya Angelou*** (born Marguerite Johnson, 1928). An American poet, memoirist,

and actress, and an important figure in the American Civil Rights Movement. Her best known book is probably the autobiographical work, *I Know Why the Caged Bird Sings* (1969). ***Charles Bukowski***. Henry Charles Bukowski (1920–94) was a Los Angeles poet and novelist, whose writing was heavily influenced by the geography and atmosphere of his home city. A prolific author, Bukowski wrote thousands of poems, hundreds of short-stories, and six novels, and eventually had more than fifty books in print. ***Anne Waldman***. During the sixties, along with Gregory Corso and Allen Ginsberg, Waldman became part of the East Coast poetry scene and gave frequent readings at the St. Mark's Church Poetry Project, which she ran from 1966–78. She has published more than forty books. ***On the Road***, ***Leaves of Grass***, ***The Awful Rowing Towards God***. Famous American literary classics by, in turn, Jack Kerouac (1922– 69), Walt Whitman (1819–92), and Anne Sexton (1928–74). ***The Kaddish***. The Jewish mourner's prayer but, in this context, also Ginsberg's famous long poem for his mother, Naomi. ***Mission and the Haight***. The Inner Mission, often called "The Mission" or "The Heart of the Mission" (*La Misión* or *El Corazón de la Misión* in Spanish) is an ethnically and economically diverse neighborhood in the Mission District of San Francisco, California, that is built on what used to be Spanish-Mexican ranchos. The Haight[-Ashbury] is another district of San Francisco and is named after the intersection of Haight and Ashbury streets, commonly known as The Haight. The district is famous for its role as a center of the 1960s hippie movement.

Melanie Kaye/Kantrowitz

from* "Kaddish":** ***Warsaw Ghetto Uprising. Between 1941 and 1943, underground resistance movements formed in about one hundred Jewish groups. The most famous attempt by Jews to resist the Germans in armed fighting occurred in the Warsaw Ghetto. In the summer of 1942, about three hundred thousand Jews were deported from Warsaw to Treblinka. When reports of mass murder in the extermination camp leaked back to the Warsaw Ghetto, a surviving group formed an organization called the Z.O.B. (abbreviation for Zydowska Organizacja Bojowa, Polish for Jewish Fighting Organization). The Z.O.B., led by twenty-three-year-old Mordecai Anielewicz, issued a proclamation calling for the Jewish people to resist going to the rail cars. On 19 April 1943, the Warsaw Ghetto uprising began after German troops and police entered the ghetto to deport its surviving inhabitants. Seven hundred and fifty fighters fought the heavily armed and well-trained Germans. The ghetto fighters were able to hold out for nearly a month, but on 16 May 1943, the revolt ended. Of the more than fifty-six thousand Jews captured, about seven thousand were shot, and the remainder were deported to killing centers or concentration camps. ***Yisgadal V'yiskadash sh'me rabbo, b'olmo deevro chiruseh v'yamlick malchuseh*** (Heb.). Transliteration of the opening words of the mourner's prayer: "Let the name of God be glorified and sanctified in the world, which He hath created according to His will. May He establish His kingdom [His rule]." ***B'chayechon uvyo-mechon, uv'chayey d'chol beys yisroel***. Continuation of the Kaddish: "During your life and during your days, and during the life of all the House of Israel." ***Covner-Gberna*** (in Polish, *Kowno Gubernia*). A province in Poland.

Irena Klepfisz

from* "Bashert":** ***Bashert (Yid.). Destiny. ***Shegetz*** (Yid.). Refers to a non-Jewish boy or young man. Although *shegetz*, like its feminine counterpart *shiksa*, comes from the Hebrew *sheketz* ("detestable," "loathed", "blemished") and literally translates as "rascal" or "scoundrel," its pejorative connotations now range from minimal to severe, depending on the context. ***Żyd***, ***Juif***, ***Jude***. "Jew" in Polish, French, and German. The word "Jude" was displayed on the yellow star Jews had to wear under the Nazi regime between 1936 and 1945.

"Solitary Acts": ***Neglinge***. A place in Sweden.

David Koenig

"After the Holocaust, No Poetry": The title is a reference to the famous statement by German sociologist and music critic, T. W. Adorno, in "Engagement," in *Noten zur Literatur III* (Frankfurt: Suhrkamp Verlag, 1965): "I do not want to soften the proposition that continuing to write lyric poetry after Auschwitz would be barbaric; negatively expressed in it is that impulse which inspires a committed poetic work" (125, translation by Marina Roscher).

Yala Korwin

"The Little Boy With His Hands Up": Author's note — "In Poland under the German occupation, Jews were ordered to wear white armbands with a blue Star of David (not a yellow star)."

"Noemi": Author's note — "According to a typical Polish prejudice, Jews could be recognized by dark, curly hair and brown eyes. My older sister, Noemi, was a brunette, while I was the only blonde with blue eyes in my immediate family. We both obtained false identity papers. Hers didn't help. She perished. How? Where? I do not know."

"Passover Night 1942": Pillars of clouds and pillars of fire refer to "the pillar of cloud by day, and the pillar of fire by night" in Exodus 13:22.

Aaron Kramer

"Westminster Synagogue": ***Westminster Synagogue***. Perhaps the prime center of Jewish worship in Great Britain. As soon as it was possible, following the war, this synagogue became headquarters for archiving and restoring many Central and Eastern European torahs that had belonged to annihilated congregations. Among the functions of this great center has been the transfer of restored torahs to new congregations, generally in North and South America.

"Zudioska": ***The Placa***. A main square in Dubrovnik. Many side streets lead down from the hills on all sides into that square.

Norbert Krapf

"*Tannenbaum*, 1940": ***Tannenbaum*** (Ger.). Fir tree. ***Wie treu sind deine Blätter*** (Ger.). How true are your leaves. ***Ihr Kinderlein kommet*** (Ger.). Oh, Come, Little Children. ***Stille Nacht, heilige Nacht*** (Ger.). Silent night, holy night. ***Glühwein*** (Ger.). Red wine, heated, with spices. ***Knabenchor*** (Ger.). Boys Choir. ***Stollen*** (Ger.). Fruit cake.

"The Name on the Wall": ***Altenheim*** (Ger.). Old-age home. ***Lohr am Main***, ***Hesslar***, ***Kreuzthal***, ***Tugendorf***. Towns, villages, and hamlets in Lower Franconia. ***Frankenwein***. Franconian wine. ***Riemenschneider***. Tilman Riemenschneider (c. 1460–1531). A German sculptor and woodcarver active in Würzburg from 1483 and one of the most prolific and versatile sculptors of the transition period between late Gothic and Renaissance art.

"A Freight Yard in Würzburg": ***Roland Flade***. A contemporary German writer, author of *The Lehmans: From Rimpar to the New World: A Family History* and other books. See Krapf's comments in the *Poets' Statements* section. ***Dürerstrasse*** (Ger.). Dürer Street. For more information about the Krapfs, see www.krapfpoetry.com.

Maxine Kumin
"The Amsterdam Poem": ***Concertgebouw***: The name of the hall. ***Eroica***. Beethoven's Symphony no. 3, op. 55 (1803), first performed 7 April 1805. ***Mijnheer and mevrouw*** (Dutch). Mr. and Mrs. ***Bittere Jaren*** (Ger.). Bitter years. ***Iron cross*** (Ger.: *Eisernes Kreuz*). A military decoration of the Kingdom of Prussia, and later of Germany, established by King Frederick William III of Prussia and first awarded on 10 March 1813. ***Walker Evans***. Like Ben Shahn and Edward Steichen, Evans (1903–75) was an important portrayer of the social forces at work in the United Stated during the thirties. A photographer, editor, and teacher, he was best known for his photographic documentation of poverty in rural America during the Depression. His work is collected in *American Photographs* (1938) and *Let Us Now Praise Famous Men* (1941). ***Vondelpark***: A park in Amsterdam, the Netherlands, named after the seventeenth-century writer, Joost van den Vondel. ***Westerkirk***: The name of the church.

Aaron Kurtz
"A Million Pairs of Shoes": The camps were death factories. With macabre efficiency, inmates were stripped of everything of the slightest use to the home front of the Third Reich. Everything was sorted and carefully warehoused. A roomful of long hair, cut from the heads of women prisoners, was saved for stuffing mattresses. Gold fillings in the mouths of the dead were extracted. Eyeglasses were saved. Most pathetic, perhaps, were the shoes of the victims, piled up and ready to be shipped for reuse by citizens of the Reich. This poem was published in 1945, in Yiddish, soon after the camps had been liberated and the atrocities revealed.

Carol Glasser Langille
"Babi Yar": ***Anatoly Kuznetsov***. Anatoly Vasilievich Kuznetsov (1929–79). A Ukrainian Soviet writer who described his experiences in German-occupied Kiev during World War II in his internationally acclaimed novel *Babi Yar*. The book was originally published in a censored form in 1966 in Ukrainian. An uncensored and expanded version was translated by David Floyd and published by Farrar, Straus & Giroux in 1970.

Alyssa A. Lappen
"How It Happened": ***Dobrinka***. The endearing nickname for Dobra, a small Jewish shtetl in Ukraine, near Nikolayev, destroyed during the Holocaust in 1941. Most often, the suffix "-inka" (meaning "the little one") is affectionately attached to names of small children, but it can also be applied to much-loved little places.

Denise Levertov
from* "During the Eichmann Trial":** ***Lemburg. Probably Lemberg, the German name for Lwów ("Lviv" is the Ukrainian name), a major city in western Ukraine. Lwów was the second largest Polish city, and both the city and its population suffered greatly from the two world wars, the Holocaust, and the invading armies of the period. ***Wienerwald*** (Ger.). Vienna Woods.

Alan Lupack
"Auschwitz Reportaż": ***Reportaż*** (Pol.). A report. ***"Abandon all hope. . . ."*** Words from the inscription on the gate mentioned at the opening of Canto III, the "Vestibule of Hell," in Dante's *Inferno*.

Yaacov Luria
"There Is One Synagogue Extant in Kiev": ***Ninth of Ab***. The ninth day of the Jewish month Ab (July-August on the Gregorian calendar). It is commemorated as a national day of misfortune for Israel that recalls a series of disasters, dating back to Exodus and including the destruction in 586 B.C.E. of Solomon's Temple in Jerusalem by the Babylonians and the razing of the Second Temple by Roman forces in 70 C.E. It is a day of mourning and fasting.

Arlene Maass
"Opa the Watchmaker": The ten Boom family of Holland ran a watchmaker's business and maintained living quarters in an old three-story building in the heart of Haarlem. During the Nazi occupation, they concealed a number of Jewish people in an obscure attic room. "Opa," the ten Boom patriarch, was a devout Bible-believing Christian; his convictions and his love for the Jewish people led to his eventual arrest, incarceration, and death at the hands of Dutch traitors and Nazis. ***Hiding place***. A reference to Ps. 32:7: "Thou [the Lord] art my hiding place." ***Moriah***. The name given to a mountain range in Genesis. Traditionally, the name of the specific mountain where Abraham was commanded by God to bind his son, Isaac, and offer up his life. Abraham stood ready to obey the command, but, at the last moment, God spared Isaac. In his place, a ram was sacrificed. ***Opa*** (Ger.). Grandpa. ***No justice in the streets***. A reference to Lam. 4:18: "Men stalked us at every step so we could not walk in our streets; our end was near, our days numbered, for our end had come." ***Root of Jesse***. A messianic reference from Isa. 11:1: "A root [shoot] will spring up from the stump of Jesse; from his roots a branch will bear fruit."

Channah Magori
***from* "Holocaust Archives I":**

'By My Father's Hand . . .': ***Die Aschen heben sich*** (Ger.). The ashes are rising. ***Kleine Kinder*** (Ger.). Little children.

'In My Mother's Voice': ***Shtocht me*** (Yid.). Pierced me. ***Tateh*** (Yid.). Father. ***Rosh Chodesh Nisan*** (Heb.). First day of the month of Nisan. Nisan usually occurs in March or April on the Gregorian calendar. ***Yah, ich gedenkt azoi*** (Yid.). Yes, that's what I remember. ***Mit*** (Yid.). With. ***Mameh*** (Yid.) Mother. ***Tzeteleh*** (Yid.). A little note. ***Gutten ort*** (Yid.). Cemetery.

Sandra Cohen Margulius
"Aunt Betty": ***Juden raus!*** (Ger.). Jews out!

David McKain
"For the Children": ***Führerbunker*** (Ger.). Literally, "shelter for the leader" or "the Führer's shelter." A common name for a complex of subterranean rooms in Berlin, Germany, where Adolf Hitler committed suicide during World War II. The bunker was the thirteenth and last of Hitler's *Führerhauptquartiere* or Führer Headquarters (one of the most famous being the Wolfsschanze [Wolf's Lair] in East Prussia).

Richard Michelson
"The Jews That We Are": ***Nazis march through Chicago***. In 1977, a group of neo-Nazis, a branch of the National Socialist Party of America (NSPA), created a furor by announcing its intention to stage a march through Skokie, the most sub-

stantially Jewish of Chicago's suburbs and the home of many Holocaust survivors. Although court battles and public pressure forced the demonstration to Chicago's Marquette Park, the confrontation became a *cause célèbre* when the American Civil Liberties Union defended the First Amendment rights of the NSPA to march. ***Peretz***. Isaac Leib Peretz (1852–1915). A prolific writer of poems, short stories, drama, humorous sketches, and satire, who — along with Mendele Mocher Seforim and Sholem Aleichem — helped set the standard of artistic expression for Russian Yiddish literature in the late nineteenth and early twentieth centuries.

Bernard S. Mikofsky

"Mame-Loshen, Yiddish": ***Mame-loshen*** (Yid.). Mother tongue. Mikofsky comments: "Mame-loshen (pronounced MAH-meh LAW-shun) has nearly a millennium of history, Yiddish having started as the Middle High German that Jews invited into medieval Poland spoke. This period of time is about the same as that of the development of English out of Anglo-Saxon, following the Norman conquest of England in 1066. And just as English was enriched by Old French (itself from Latin), as well as savant Latin and Greek words, just so was Yiddish tremendously enriched by Hebrew and Aramaic words (the Loshen-Koydesh, the Holy Language), as well as words from Slavic and other European Languages." [1985]

Marilyn Mohr

"Tsena Tsena": ***Tsena Tsena*** (Heb.). Go forth. A popular Hebrew song.

David Moolten

"Photograph of Liberated Prisoner, Dachau, 1945": ***Verboten*** (Ger.). Forbidden.

Sarah Traister Moskovitz

"December": ***Janet Hadda***. Dr. Hadda is a practicing psychoanalyst and a professor of English at UCLA. Her books include *Yankev Glatshteyn* (1980); *Passionate Women, Passive Men: Suicide in Yiddish Literature* (1988); and *Isaac Bashevis Singer: A Life* (1997).

"The Dress": ***Biala Podlaska***. An important village during the fifteenth century when it belonged to the Radziwill princes. Its aircraft industry was destroyed, along with most of the city, in World War II.

"The Teaspoon": ***NBG***. An abbreviation for Nuremberg. ***Justiz*** (Ger.). Justice.

Stanley Moss

"Ghetto Theater, Vilnius, 1941": ***"To sit. . . . Those are the questions."*** A take-off on Hamlet's soliloquy. See *Hamlet*, 3.1.64–98. "A Visit to Kaunas": *Das Lied von der Erde* (Ger.). Song of the earth.

Elaine Mott

"On the Wings of the Wind": ***Hannah Senesh [Szenes]*** (1921–44). Senesh was a diarist, poet, playwright and a parachutist in the Jewish resistance under the British Armed Forces during World War II. Now part of the popular heritage of Israel, the diary and letters of Hannah Senesh provide a primary source of information concerning Jewish life in Budapest during the rise of Nazism in Europe and the work of early Zionists in Palestine. Her literary work also includes several poems, most notably, "Blessed is the Match," and two plays. Senesh won even greater renown after suffering torture and death for her role as a parachutist in a 1944 Hagana campaign to assist Jews in Nazi-occupied Hungary. Her life has been eulogized as a 'lesson in courage.'

Mark Nepo
"Hill Where the Lord Hides": ***Commandant Jäger . . . Dr. Elkes***. Dr. Elkhanan Elkes was a legendary physician elected by his peers in the Kovno Ghetto in Lithuania to head the *Judenrat*, the so-called Jewish Council that was charged with dealing with the Nazis. *Judenräte* were administrative bodies that the Germans required Jews to form in each ghetto in the General Government (the Nazi-occupied territory of Poland) and later in the occupied territories of the Soviet Union. These bodies were responsible for local government in the ghetto and stood between the Nazis and the ghetto population. They were forced by the Nazis to provide Jews for use as slave labor and to assist in the deportation of Jews to extermination camps. Those who refused to follow Nazi orders or were unable to cooperate fully were frequently rounded up and shot or deported to the extermination camps themselves. When the remaining Jews in the Kovno Ghetto were sent to various concentration camps, Dr. Elkes found himself in Auschwitz where he was under the authority of Commandant Jäger. Ordered to perform experiments on his own people, Dr. Elkes underwent a hunger strike that killed him. Part of this note is based on the author's conversations with Dr. Elkes's son, Joel Elkes, and on his son's book, *Dr. Elkhanan Elkes of the Kovno Ghetto: A Son's Holocaust Memoir* (MA: Paraclete Press, 1999).

Lois E. Olena
"Homeland": ***Eretz Yisroel*** (Heb.). The land of Israel.

Jacqueline Osherow
"Ponar": ***Rabbi Akivah***. One of the great rabbis, he lived after the destruction of the Temple in the time of the Hadrianic persecutions. He and many of his colleagues were martyred by the Romans. Although the study of Torah was forbidden, some of the greatest literature of Torah scholars was written during that time. ***Alef-bet***. The Hebrew alphabet, which many believe to be sacred.

Alicia Ostriker
"Poem Beginning with a Line by Fitzgerald/Hemingway": ***Oskar Schindler*** (1908–74). A Sudeten German industrialist credited with saving almost 1,200 Jews during the Holocaust by having them work in his enamelware and ammunitions factories located in Poland and what is now the Czech Republic. He was the subject of Thomas Keneally's novel, *Schindler's List*, and the 1993 Steven Spielberg film of the same name that was based on it. ***André Trocmé*** (1901–71). A pastor in the French town of Le Chambon-sur-Lignon, who urged his Protestant congregation to hide Jewish refugees from the Holocaust. Inspired by spiritual leader Charles Guillon, Trocmé and his wife Magda organized the rescue of between three and five thousand Jews who were fleeing the Nazis' efforts to implement their Final Solution. ***Raoul Wallenberg*** (1912–1947?). A Swedish diplomat and businessman who helped save as many as one hundred thousand Hungarian Jews from Nazi extermination. To accomplish this, he handed out Swedish passports to as many Jews as possible, until his arrest by arriving Soviet authorities in January, 1945.

Linda Pastan
"Landscape near Dachau": ***Adolf Hölzel*** (1853–1934). German artist.

"Rachel (ra'chal), a Ewe": ***Rachel***. The younger of the daughters of Laban, the wife of Jacob (B.C.E. 1753) and mother of Joseph and Benjamin. The incidents of her life may be found in Gen. 29–33, 35. ***Pequod***. The fictional 19th century Nantucket whaling ship that appears in the 1851 novel *Moby Dick*, by American author Herman Melville. Also a place mentioned in Jer. 50:21. The word means "to punish."

Edmund Pennant

"Thoughts Under the Giant Sequoia": ***Massacre at York***. On the night of 16 March 1190, the feast of Shabbat ha-Gadol, the small Jewish community of York was gathered together for protection inside Clifford's Tower, the keep of York's medieval castle. Rather than perish at the hands of the violent mob that awaited them outside, many of the Jews took their own lives; others died in the flames they had lit, and those who finally surrendered were massacred and murdered. This event has become the most notorious example of antisemitism in medieval England, yet it was by no means an isolated incident, but rather the culmination of a tide of violent feeling which swept the country in the early part of 1190. ***Francis Parkman*** (1823 – 93). An American historian, best known as author of *The Oregon Trail: Sketches of Prairie and Rocky-Mountain Life* and his monumental seven-volume *France and England in North America*. His two-volume *Conspiracy of Pontiac* is considered a classic. ***Emanuel Ringelblum***. See note to Florence W. Freed's poem, "God's Death." ***Pontiac's despair***. Pontiac or Obwandiyag (c. 1720–69) was an Ottawa leader who became famous for his role in what is remembered as "Pontiac's Rebellion" (1763–66), a Native American struggle against the British military occupation of the Great Lakes region, following the British victory in the French and Indian War. Historians disagree about Pontiac's importance in the war that bears his name. ***Sharm el-Sheik***. A city situated on the southern tip of the Sinai Peninsula, in Egypt, on the coastal strip between the Red Sea and Mount Sinai, on a promontory overlooking the Strait of Tiran at the mouth of the Gulf of Aqaba. Its strategic importance led to its transformation from a fishing village into a major port and naval base for the Egyptian Navy. It was captured by Israel during the Sinai conflict of 1956 and restored to Egypt in 1957. A United Nations peacekeeping force was subsequently stationed there until the 1967 Six-Day War when it was recaptured by Israel and officially renamed Mifratz Shlomo (Heb.: "Gulf of Solomon"). Sharm el-Sheikh remained under Israeli control until the Sinai peninsula was returned to Egypt in 1982.

"Yom Hazikaron": ***Yom Hazikaron*** (Heb.). Israel's Memorial Day for those who lost their lives in the struggle that led to the establishment of the State of Israel and for all military personnel who were killed while in active duty in Israel's armed forces. ***Mount Herzl***. A high hill-top in Jerusalem, Israel, that is named for, and is the final resting place of, Theodor Herzl, considered to be the founder of modern political Zionism.

Marge Piercy

"Black Mountain": ***Sten guns***. A family of 9 mm submachine guns used extensively by the British Empire and Commonwealth forces throughout World War II and the Korean War. They were notable for their simple design and comparatively low cost of production. The name STEN is an acronym, derived from the names of the weapon's chief designers, Major Reginald Shepherd and Harold Turpin, and ENfield, the location of the Royal Small Arms Factory (RSAF) at Enfield Lock in London. ***Mogen David*** (Heb.). Star of David. Pronounced *Mag-en Da-vid* in Israeli Hebrew and *Mo-gein Do-vid* or *Mo-gen Do-vid* in Ashkenazi Hebrew and

Yiddish. It is named after King David of ancient Israel and is sometimes called the Seal of Solomon after his son, King Solomon. The six-pointed star is a generally recognized symbol of Judaism and Jewish identity and is also known colloquially as the "Jewish Star."

"The Housing Project at Drancy": ***C'est pas notre affaire*** (Fr.). It's not our business. ***Inkster***. A city in Wayne County, Michigan, USA. **Pitchepois**. Alt. spelling of "Pitchipois." See poem by George Bogin.

William Pillin
"Farewell to Europe": ***The Presence***. God (Jewish mystical tradition). ***Basta! Genug! Assez! Dostatochno!***. Enough! in Italian, German (and Yiddish), French, and Russian. ***Bris***. The circumcision of a Jewish male on the eighth day following his birth. See Gen. 17:10–14. ***Blood mysteries***. The ancient "blood libel" against the Jewish people that accuses Jews of preparing the Passover matzoth (unleavened bread) with the blood of Christian children — and similarly vicious and obscene libels used for centuries to incite violence against Jews.

"Miserere": ***Miserere*** (L.). The imperative of "misereri" — to have mercy or pity.

"The Ascensions": ***Clair-de-lune*** (Fr.). Moonlight.

Evelyn Posamentier
"Heinz Rosenberg on the Platform": Heinz Rosenberg, born in 1921 in Germany, survived eleven Nazi camps. Source: USHMM, Washington, DC. ***Meine güte*** (Ger.). My God!

"Toska": ***Bahnhof*** (Ger.). Railway terminus. Third Reich buildings in Berchtesgaden included the Bahnhof (station), which had a reception area for Hitler and his guests, and the Postamt (postoffice) next to the Bahnhof. See note to Simpson's poem, "A Story About Chicken Soup." ***Operation Reinhard*** (*Aktion Reinhard* or *Einsatz Reinhard*, Ger.). The code name given to the Nazi plan to murder Polish Jews in the General Government, which marked the beginning of the most deadly phase of the Holocaust, the use of extermination camps. During the operation, as many as two million people were murdered in Bełżec, Sobibór, Treblinka and Majdanek, almost all of them Jews. Source for Toska Feuchtbaum's story: Museum of Tolerance (Los Angeles).

Anna Rabinowitz
from Darkling: A Poem: ***Zum Abiken Andenken*** (Ger.). For endless remembrance. Author's note — "I guess, technically, the word 'abiken,' since it is an adjective, should not be capitalized, but the convention among these Polish Jews seems to have been to use the phrase as inscriptions on their [postcards and] photos and I guess they were a bit careless, or less than completely knowledgeable about German capitalization. I simply copied the way they wrote the words." She continues: "*Andenken* is a German word that translates as 'to think of a friend with kind regard in relation to an object they've given you.' ***Ostroleka***. One of the oldest cities in the Mazovian Lowland, northeastern Poland. ***"as they were . . . Efface. . . ."*** This quotation is from the notebooks of James McNeill Whistler. *Fotographia / Rafael, Lomza — Foto Bekker, Brok*. Photos from Lomza and Brok. ***Cartolina Postale . . . Posztówka***. Postcards from Italy, Germany, Belgium, Spain, and Poland.

David Ray
"Houses": ***Lion Feuchtwanger*** (1884–1958). A German-Jewish novelist who was imprisoned in a French internment camp in Les Milles and later escaped to Los Angeles with the help of his wife, Marta. See note to Forché's poem.

"Visitors from America": ***Golden apples of paradise***. In Greek Mythology, either a single tree or a grove of immortality-giving golden apples that grew in the Garden of the Hesperides. The apples were planted from the fruited branches that Gaia (the Earth Mother) gave to Hera (the goddess of marriage and birth) as a wedding gift when she accepted Zeus (the god of thunder and the sky). The Hesperides were given the task of tending to the grove, but occasionally plucked from it themselves.

Lisa Ress
"U.S. Army Holds Dance for Camp Survivors. Germany, 1945": ***Czerny exercises***. Finger exercises for piano, created by Austrian composer, Karl Czerny (1791–1857).

Elaine Reuben
"After Generation After": ***Churban*** (Yid.). Destruction. See note to Rothenberg's "IN THE DARK WORD, KHURBN," below. ***Galut*** (Heb.). Diaspora. ***Sheyres-Hapleyte*** (Yid.). Survivors.

Charles Reznikoff
from Inscriptions: 1944–1956: ***Lion of Judah***. In Genesis, the symbol of the Israelite tribe of Judah.

Liliane Richman
"After Claude Lanzmann's *Shoah*": The episode described is based on the 1985 documentary. Lanzmann interviewed survivors and witnesses of the Holocaust, as well as concentration camp guards and residents of towns near the camps. Richman states: "The poem is based on the recollection of a man who was a boy when the Nazis liquidated the people in his village." [1985]

Michael D. Riley
"Photograph of Bergen-Belsen, 1945": ***Death's-head guard***. The "Death's Head" was the symbol of the SS-Totenkopfverbande (one of the original three branches of the SS, along with the Algemeine SS and the Waffen SS), whose duty was to guard the concentration camps. Most of the original members of this organization were later transferred into and became the core of a Waffen SS division, the Death's Head Division. The symbol was most often seen as a tattoo, which sometimes indicated that its wearer had murdered one of the movement's enemies (e.g., a Jew or other minority).

Curtis Robbins
"In der Nacht"* ("In the Night"):** ***Ner tamid (Heb.). The eternal flame, or eternal light, that hangs in front of the ark in every synagogue. It is meant to represent the menorah of the Temple in Jerusalem.

Jennifer Rose

"At Dachau with a German Lover": ***Stau*** (Ger.). Updraft. ***Heil*** (Ger.). Hail! *"Sieg Heil!"* Literally, "Hail [to] Victory." During the Nazi era, it was a common chant at political rallies. When meeting someone, it was customary in Nazi Germany to give the Hitler salute and say the words "*Heil* Hitler." *"Sieg Heil"* was reserved for mass meetings, such as those held at Nuremberg where it was shouted in unison by thousands. At such rallies, there was often a display of banners carrying the slogan *"Sieg Heil,"* along with the swastika. ***Chart of stars***. Identification patches were given to all prisoners, according to their classification. For example, Jews were given yellow stars; political prisoners were assigned red triangles; homosexuals received pink triangles. Dual classification was also possible; for instance, Jewish political prisoners wore stars made from a red and a yellow triangle.

Elizabeth Rosner

"Almost Beautiful": ***Gänsemarkt*** (Ger.). Goose market. This triangular square has a misleading name, for there has never been a market there, let alone one that sells geese. In the Middle Ages, it served as a traffic junction. After being rebuilt in the 1980s, it became a new focal point for the city centre. ***Binnenstück*** (Ger.). Stuffed pastry.

Jerome Rothenberg

"Dibbukim"* ("Dibbiks"):** ***Dibbukim (Heb.). Usually spelled "dybbukim." The plural of "dybbuk." In European Jewish folklore, a dybbuk is a malicious possessing spirit, believed to be the dislocated soul of a dead person. ***Dibbiks*** (Yid.). See above. ***Ruakh*** (Heb.). Spirit.

"Dos Oysleydikn"* ("The Emptying"):** ***Shadai. A name of God used in Genesis when God addresses the patriarchs, Abraham, Isaac, and Joseph. Associated with progeny and nationhood. ***Bialo forest***. Probably the Bialowieza Primeval Forest, which is world famous for its unique lowland woods and is the only such complex in Europe. Poland and Belorussia both include parts of the Forest.

"IN THE DARK WORD, KHURBN": ***Khurbn*** (Yid.). Destruction, disaster. Khurbn is the Yiddish word for what is more commonly known as the Holocaust (from the Greek) or Ha-Shoah (Heb.). The term refers to the genocide of European Jews during World War II by Nazi Germany and its collaborators. Early elements of the Khurbn include the Kristallnacht pogrom, the T-4 Euthanasia Program, and the use of mobile killing squads.

"The Other Secret in the Trail of Money": ***Gematria*** (Heb.). Numerology using the Hebrew language and Hebrew alphabet, in which each letter also represents a number. ***Gold's orchestra***. Ernest Gold (1921–99) is best remembered as one of Hollywood's most successful film composers and one of the busier composers in television during the seventies and eighties. If things had been different in the world of the thirties, however, Gold might have been one of the last of the post-romantic composers on the European continent, making his way melodically in stark opposition to a musical world increasingly dominated by atonalism and jarring non-melodies. What made that impossible and sent Gold to the United States, was Hitler. So *Ernst* Gold came to Hollywood as *Ernest* Gold and became one of the last European romantic music figures to carve a name for himself in film music.

Mark Rudman

"Easy Leaving in Terezín": ***Shekel*** (Heb.). Israeli currency. ***Shtetl*** (Yid.). A small town with a large Jewish population in pre-Holocaust Eastern Europe. Both words are intentionally misspelled in the first stanza. ***Arendt*** (1906-75). See note to Hecht's "'More Light! More Light!'"

Biff Russ

"The Way to Be Haunted": ***Ugolino***. Ugolino della Gherardesca (c. 1220–89), count of Donoratico. An Italian noble and naval commander, head of the powerful family of della Gherardesca, the chief Ghibelline house of Pisa. He is best known from Dante's fictional depiction of him in the *Inferno*. Alleged to have betrayed his native city of Pisa to its enemies in Genoa, he was betrayed by his co-conspirator, the Archbishop Ruggieri, and imprisoned, along with his two sons and two grandsons.

Reg Saner

"Aspen Oktoberfest": ***Lily Tofler***. According to war crimes witnesses' testimony, Lily Tofler was nineteen when she died. Her usual answer to the question, "How's it going?" was "With me, it always goes well." *Boger*. The German lieutenant who raped Tofler, then killed her with his pistol. ***Oktoberfest*** (Ger.). October festival.

Rebecca Seiferle

"'A lonely man in his greatness'": Seiferle states that the title quote, along with the phrases "smelled of the absence of all scents," "no human presence should mar his daily stroll in the gardens," and "pure white wraith" — as well as some of the facts — are from *Hitler's Pope: The Secret History of Pius XII* by John Cornwell (New York: Viking Penguin, 1999). ***Pius XII***. Pope Pius XII, born Eugenio Maria Giuseppe Giovanni Pacelli (1876–1958), reigned as the two hundred sixtieth pope, the head of the Roman Catholic Church, and sovereign of Vatican City State from 2 March 1939 until his death. Before election to the papacy, Pacelli served as secretary of the Department of Extraordinary Ecclesiastical Affairs, papal nuncio and cardinal secretary of state, in which roles he worked to conclude treaties with European nations, most notably the *Reichskonkordat* with Germany. After World War II, he was a vocal supporter of lenient policies toward vanquished nations and a staunch opponent of communism. His leadership of the Catholic Church during World War II remains the subject of continued historical controversy. ***Concordat with Hitler***. The *Reichskonkordat* was ratified on 10 September 1933. In the Concordat, the German government achieved a complete proscription of all clerical interference in the political field (articles 16 and 32). It also ensured the bishops' loyalty to the state by an oath and required all priests to be Germans and subject to German superiors. Restrictions were also placed on the Catholic organizations. Shortly before signing the Reichskonkordat, Germany signed similar agreements with the major Protestant churches in Germany. Many historians consider the Reichskonkordat an important step toward the international acceptance of Adolf Hitler's Nazi regime. ***Gates of Ileum***. The ileum is the final section of the small intestine. Its function is to absorb the products of digestion.

Reva Sharon

"Unanswerable Questions": ***Haim Guri*** (b. 1923). An Israeli poet, novelist, journalist, and documentary filmmaker born in Tel Aviv and currently living in Jerusalem. Following time in Europe where he helped Jews emigrate to Palestine after World War II, he fought in the 1948 Israeli War of Independence. The impact of these events on Guri is evident in his writing. He was awarded the Bialik Prize for Literature in 1975 and the Israel Prize for Poetry in 1988. The film *The 81st Blow*, which he wrote, co-produced, and co-directed, was nominated for the 1974 Academy Award for Documentary Feature. ***Jhirka***. Jhirka was five years old and shared a bunk with Norbert Troller, an artist. Troller, who survived, and whose sketch of Jhirka has been preserved, described Jhirka as a "clever companion" with a thousand questions nobody could answer. Jhirka died at Theresienstadt. ***Pavel Friedmann***. Born 7 January 1921 in Prague. He was deported to Theresienstadt (Terezín) on 26 april 1942 and died at Auschwitz 29 September 1944. ***River Ohře***. After the Nazis burned the bodies of Jews in the crematorium, they put the ashes in boxes and numbered them to identify them. When the Nazis knew that their atrocities at Theresienstadt would be discovered, they emptied as many of the boxes as they could into the surrounding fields and into the River Ohře, which flows near to the site of the camp.

Enid Shomer
"Women Bathing at Bergen-Belsen": This sonnet is based on *A Memory of the Camps*, a documentary film made by British troops and edited by Alfred Hitchcock. The film was not made public until April 1985, on the fortieth anniversary of the Allied liberation of the camps.

Joan I. Siegel
"Haggadah": ***Primo Levi*** (1919–87). Jewish Italian chemist, Holocaust survivor and author of memoirs, short stories, poems, and novels. He is best known for his work on the Holocaust, and in particular for *If This Is a Man* (published in the United States as *Survival in Auschwitz*), his account of the year he spent as a prisoner in Auschwitz.

Louis Simpson
"The Bird": ***Ich wünscht' ich wäre ein Vöglein*** (Ger.). I wish I were a little bird. ***Wiener Blut*** (Ger.). Viennese blood or Viennese spirit. A waltz by Johann Strauss II, first performed by the composer on 22 April 1873. The new dedication waltz was composed to celebrate the wedding of Emperor Franz Josef's daughter, Archduchess Gisela Louise Maria, and Prince Leopold of Bavaria. ***Herr Ober-Leutnant*** (Ger.). Lieutenant Colonel, Sir.

"A Story About Chicken Soup": ***Berchtesgaden***. The area of Obersalzberg was appropriated by the Nazis in the 1920s for their senior leaders to enjoy. Hitler's mountain residence, the Berghof, was located here. Berchtesgaden and its environs were fitted to serve as an outpost of the German Reichskanzlei office (Imperial Chancellery), which sealed the area's fate as a strategic objective for Allied forces in World War II.

Myra Sklarew
from* "Lithuania":** ***Keidan. After World War I, the provincial capital of Lithuania. Jews had a long history in Lithuania that reached back at least to the 12th century, when Jews immigrated to the country to escape the persecutions of crusaders in other parts of Europe.

Kirtland Snyder
"City Children at a Summer Camp. Slonim, 1936": ***Slonim***. A city in White Russia, near the Polish border, where the summer camp was located. The camp, which was operated by the Jewish Health Society, ministered to the needs of poor, handicapped, and retarded children. ***Dresden dolls***. Dresden china (porcelain) has been world famous since 1710.

Jason Sommer
from* "Mengele Shitting":** ***Kustanovice. A small village about an hour's walk from the city of Munkács in Czechoslovakia. ***Latorica***, ***Laborec***, ***Ondava***, ***Topl'a***, ***Torysa***. Rivers on the southern slope of the Eastern Carpathians that flow into the Tisza, one of the major rivers of Central Europe. ***Polizei*** (Ger.). Police. ***Jundiai***. A city and municipality in the state of São Paulo, Brazil.

"Meyer Tsits and the Children": ***Munkács***. Diocese in Czechoslovakia but originally in Hungary, mentioned for the first time in 1458 in a document issued by King Mathias. ***Shtreimel*** (Yid.). A fur hat worn by married members of Hasidic sects, on the Sabbath and during Jewish holidays. It is made of genuine fur, typically from sable. ***Boco Corsi*** (Czech.). Soldiers' Promenade. ***Rabinovitz's court***. Rabbi Baruch Yehoshua Yerachmiel Rabinowicz (1913–99), or "Reb Burechel," as he was known, was born into a distinguished Hasidic dynasty and became a renowned rebbe, but he renounced his position following the turmoil of World War II. ***Kertvarosh***. The name of a street. ***Mydlow***. A city in Poland.

Hans Jörg Stahlschmidt

"November Rain": ***Wannsee conference***. The Wannsee Conference was a meeting of senior officials of the Nazi German regime, held in the Berlin suburb of Wannsee on January 20, 1942. The purpose of the conference was to inform senior Nazis of plans for the "Final Solution to the Jewish Question" — the mass killing of *all* eleven million Jews who lived in Europe at that time.

"Visit to the Fatherland": ***Ja*** (Ger.). Yes. ***Eine Jüdin*** (Ger.) A Jewess. The word, which refers to a Jewish woman or girl, is now rarely used in English and is usually considered offensive (Cf. "Negress").

Jan Steckel

"The Maiden Aunts": ***Höcher Menschen*** (Ger.). Higher (better) people, gentlewomen. ***Widow Romm and Sons***. The family name Romm relates to a Jewish family of printers and publishers of Hebrew books in Grodno and, later, Vilnius. The Romm Hebrew printing-office, established in 1789, was the first in Lithuania, and its authorization by King Stanislaus Augustus was considered an important event.

Martin Steingesser

"The Three": Miroslav Kosek, Hanus Löwy, and Bachner have four poems in *I Never Saw Another Butterfly: Children's Drawings and Poems from Terezín Concentration Camp 1942–1944*. ***Koleba***. A blend of the children's surnames that also evokes the Czechoslovakian *koleda*, a children's fairy tale, and *chleba*, bread. According to Steingesser, the three wrote the poems together, signing them "Koleba," while imprisoned in Terezín.

Gerald Stern

"Adler": ***Adler***. Jacob Adler (1855–1926), the founder of the acclaimed U.S. theatrical family and one of the leading Jewish actor-managers and reformers of the early Yiddish theater. According to Stern, Adler "was the most famous of all Jewish [Yiddish] actors — Lower East Side — a hero among women — who wrote, and acted in, *The Jewish King Lear*." ***Regan, Goneril, Gloucester, Cordelia, Albany, Kent, Edgar***. Characters in Shakespeare's tragedy, *King Lear*.

"Soap": ***Amelia Earhart*** (1898–1937). A famous U.S. pioneer aviator who disappeared mysteriously over the Pacific in the forties, but also, Stern says, the name of a former restaurant in Iowa City.

Rabbi Michael Strassfeld

"Who Knows One?": ***Lo dayenu*** (Heb.). [It is] not enough.

Lynn Strongin
"Erasing the Blue Numbers": ***Volksdeutsch***. An historical term that arose in the early twentieth century to describe ethnic Germans living outside of the Reich, often to more sharply differentiate them from the "Reichsdeutsch" (Imperial Germans).

"Her Velocity Had Been Taken": ***Jamais vue*** (Fr.). Never seen. ***Petit mal*** (Fr.). A type of abnormal electrical discharge in the brain that most often occurs in children. Other types of seizures include grand mal seizure and temporal lobe seizure.

"Theresienstadt": ***Bas Mitzvah*** (Heb.). According to Jewish Law, every Jewish girl becomes a *bas mitzvah* at age twelve, a year earlier than a Jewish boy becomes a *bar mitzvah*. Bas means "daughter." Mitzvah (plural, mitzvot) is a word used in Judaism to refer to any of the 613 commandments that are given in the Torah or any other Jewish law. The term can also refer to the fulfilment of a *mitzvah*, as defined above. ***Rabbi Nachman*** (1772–1810). The great grandson of Rabbi Israel, the Baal Shem Tov — 'Master of the Good Name' — founder of the Chassidic movement and an outstanding Tzaddik, Torah sage, mystic, teacher, Chassidic master and storyteller. During his lifetime he attracted a devoted following of Chassidim who looked to him as their prime source of spiritual guidance in the quest for God. His gravesite in the Ukrainian town of Uman is visited by many Jews even today.

"What a Waste of World": ***Casper Hauser***. Kaspar Hauser or Casparus Hauser (1812–33). A mysterious foundling in nineteenth century Germany who was suspected of having ties to the royal house of Baden. ***Schwesterlein*** (Ger.). Little sister.

Yerra Sugarman
"Because": ***"Because the spirit of man / is a candle."*** See Proverbs 20:27. ***"the dead are asked to intercede."*** — Quoted from *The Jewish Book of Why*, by Alfred J. Kolatch (Jonathan David Publishers, Inc., 1993), p. 81. ***"Some of the children were listed only by number . . ."*** and ***"the infants were too young / to say their names . . ."*** are statements Serge Klarsfeld makes in the brochure for *French Children of the Holocaust: A Memorial Exhibition*, which took place at The New School University in New York. ***Champs-Élysées*** (Fr.). A broad avenue in Paris that is one of the most famous streets in the world. Its full name is "Avenue des Champs-Élysées," which refers to the Elysian Fields, the place of the blessed in Greek mythology. ***Shuckle***. A transliteration of the Yiddish word for swaying while at prayer.

Yuri Suhl
". . . And the Earth Rebelled": ***Shema*** (Heb.). Hear. The first word of a section of the Torah that is used as a centerpiece of all morning and evening prayers.

Zahava Z. Sweet
"Dark Whispers": ***Konwalia*** (Pol.). Lily of the valley.

"In Ravensbrück": ***Julian Tuwim*** (1894–1953). One of Poland's most renowned poets and also a translator and dramatist.

Marie Syrkin
"Niemand": ***Zbonzyn***. Variant of Zbąszyn, a small town in western Poland. From 1919 to 1939, it was a frontier station on the German border on the main Berlin-Warsaw line. Dawidowicz comments: "On October 28 [1938] the Gestapo, on orders from the Foreign Office, began rounding up Polish Jews in Germany to transport

them to the Polish border. Prevented from entering Poland, they were kept in appalling conditions in a no-man's-land on the Polish side at Zbąszyn, near Posen [Poznan]" (100).

Marilynn Talal
"For Our Dead": ***Heraus*** (Ger.). Out! An order to move out from a place.

Philip Terman
"With the Survivors": ***Rehmuh Synagogue***. A synagogue in Kazimierz, Poland (the old Jewish section of Kraków), which is probably the only synagogue in Kraków that still functions as a working synagogue: all the others appear to be museums or historical sites. Only elderly Orthodox Jews remain. ***Shabbat shalom*** (Heb.). Sabbath peace. A common greeting used on the Jewish sabbath.

Susan Tichy
"Gaby at the U.N. Observation Post": Yehuda Amichai (1924–2000). An Israeli poet. Amichai is considered by many to be the greatest modern Israeli poet and was one of the first to write in colloquial Hebrew. His poems often dealt with the issues of day-to-day life and are characterized by gentle irony and the pain of damaged love. His was a love for people, for the Torah and Eretz Yisrael, and, most of all, it was a love for the city of Jerusalem.

Derek Walcott
from Midsummer '81: ***Sachsenhausen***. A concentration camp in Germany that operated between 1936 and April 1945. It was named after the Sachsenhausen quarter, part of the town of Oranienburg, and is sometimes referred to as Sachsenhausen-Oranienburg. It was located at the edge of Berlin, which gave it a special position among the German concentration camps: the administrative centre of all concentration camps was located in Oranienburg, and Sachsenhausen became a training centre for SS officers (who would often be sent to oversee other camps afterwards). While some Jews were executed at Sachsenhausen and many died at Sachsenhausen, the Jewish inmates of the camp were relocated to Auschwitz in 1942. About one hundred thousand inmates died there from exhaustion, disease, malnutrition or pneumonia from the freezing cold, and many others were executed or died as the result of brutal medical experimentation.

George Wallace
"An Apple for Wolfgang Granjonca": ***Oroville***. The county seat of Butte County, California. ***Jameson Canyon***. A tourist attraction in the wine country of Napa Valley, California. ***Joplin Airplane Zeppelin Cream***. Janis Lyn Joplin (1943–70) was an American blues-influenced rock singer and occasional songwriter with a powerful and distinctive voice. She was inducted into the Rock and Roll Hall of Fame in 1995. Jefferson Airplane was an American rock band from San Francisco, a pioneer of the LSD-influenced psychedelic rock movement. Led Zeppelin was an English rock band formed in 1968 that became one of the most successful groups in popular music history. Cream was a 1960s British rock band that has been celebrated as one of the first great power trios and supergroups of rock; their sound was characterized by a mix of blues, pop and psychedelia. ***Jerry Garcia and the Dead***. Jerome John "Jerry" Garcia (1942–95) was the lead guitarist and vocalist of the psychedelic rock band, The Grateful Dead. ***Live Aid concerts***. "Live Aid" (not to be confused with "Live 8") was a multi-venue rock music concert held on 13 July 1985. The event

was organized by Bob Geldof and Midge Ure, in order to raise funds for famine relief in Ethiopia. It was one of the largest-scale satellite link-ups and television broadcasts of all time: an estimated 1.5 billion viewers, in one hundred countries, watched the live broadcast. ***Ken Kesey***. Kenneth Elton Kesey (1935–2001) was an American author, best known for his novel, *One Flew over the Cuckoo's Nest*, and as a counter-cultural figure who, some consider, was a link between the "beat generation" of the 1950s and the "hippies" of the 1960s.

Ruth Whitman
"The Death Ship": ***Lord Moyne***. The British official who refused to allow the ship to land in Istanbul. For a concise account of the fate of the *Struma*, see Sachar, 178–180.

C.K. Williams
"Spit": ***The Black Book***. Subtitled *The Nazi Crime Against the Jewish People*, *The Black Book* was one of the first publications to include captured wartime documents of the Holocaust period.

Barbara Wind
"Hating Shakespeare": Wind writes: "Sending ashes to the families of their victims was an egregiously devious method employed by the Nazis. It served to line Nazi coffers while subduing the population into believing that those deported were being treated with a modicum of care and respect. The ashes were, in fact, completely random."

Kenneth Wolman
"The Drapers: A History Lesson": ***Ignorant son***. The Passover Haggadah introduces "four sons," each of whom represents a distinct personality type: the wise son, the wicked son, the simple (or lazy) son, and the son-who-doesn't-know-enough-to-ask. The Haggadah gives brief descriptions of each of these types and suggests a way to explain the history and significance of the Passover narrative to each. The ignorant son is the fourth of these types.

Carolyne Wright
"After Forty Years": ***Tribunal of Embú***. On 7 February 1979, Josef Mengele went for a swim and was felled by a heart attack or stroke. He was buried in Embú, Brazil, where he had lived in hiding with his family, under the name "Wolfgang Gerhard." Wright states: "The tribunal of Embú was the meeting of officials after the remains of Mengele were discovered and tentatively identified, in early June 1985. The purpose was to identify his remains definitively. Mengele's family members, in Germany and elsewhere, had kept silent as to his whereabouts, though he had lived quite openly in South America [Buenos Aires, Asunción, Paraguay, then Embú] under the protection of various pro-fascist dictators." In the end, forensic testing established, with 99.9% accuracy, that the remains belonged to Mengele. ***Angel of Death***. Embedded in Mengele's name is the German word "Engel," angel. This irony was not lost on those who suffered by his whim and died at his command.

"KZ": ***KZ*** (Ger.). Abbreviation for *Konzentrations Lager* (concentration camp).

Poets' Statements

Sherman Alexie * *from* **"Inside Dachau"**
I've always felt a certain kinship with Jewish people due to our shared history of genocide, which felt even closer after being at Dachau. I didn't realize how close the houses were to the camp and how everyday and ordinary the camp was. That a death camp could be ordinary was both shocking and not surprising at all. The parallel between Nazi death camps and Indian reservations was all the more clear to me.

On another level, though, the German people's insistence on remembering what they did and the sense that they will always have to make amends doesn't exist here at all. In the U.S., there is a bureaucratic sense of atonement but not a spiritual one.

Karen Alkalay-Gut * ***"Hitler Builds a City for the Jews,"*** **"Mr. Panitz," "Night Travel," "Voices in My Skin," "Voyage Home"**
My parents' arrival in Holland was the turning point in their lives — after years of persecution and statelessness, before the Nazi occupation. As a communist ex-convict, my father had no papers, and was repeatedly attacked by the Nazis because of his Jewishness and by the authorities in Danzig because he had been a communist (at the age of 16). So my parents had been hiding in a series of rented rooms in Danzig for a few years, trying various ways to get out. Twice they went to international Esperanto conferences in Stockholm, asked for refuge, and were sent back. Once they even got to Palestine, but they were turned over to the authorities by informants and were sent back to Danzig on the eve of Hitler's invasion. Agricultural visas to England saved them at the last moment. And my mother was the only survivor of a large family.

There was no decision to write poems in response to the Holocaust. I once wrote that even the milk my mother nursed me with was salty with the tears she shed for her family as she learned of their losses, one by one. And almost every memory of my childhood is tainted with those terrible events. When we moved to the United States, and eventually bought a house, we were immediately joined by families of refugees who lived with us until they got settled. The German-speaking man who taught me to ride a bicycle when I was seven would hold on — with hands deformed by torture — as I careened down the street: only the index fingers and thumbs had nails. He never spoke of it, and my brother and I would tease each other with speculations. Once, at a wedding, we teased one of the haunted bachelors. "Who's getting married?" we whispered on either side of him. A week later, he hung himself in his room at the Y. The "Farband"* picnics on Sunday afternoons were all felt as triumphs of our survival, as were all the cultural activities of the refugees. Although rarely was the subject mentioned, the Holocaust was in our bones.

Long before I knew who Kurt Gerron was, I studied his portrait and wrote poems about it — it was always clear to me that he was someone who played roles with parodic depth. As I gradually discovered the stories of the person behind the portrait, I was even more convinced of his complexity as an individual. Nevertheless, the first film that came out about him, *Kurt Gerron's Karussell*, by Ilona Ziok (1999), emphasized his qualities as an entertainer. *Prisoner of Paradise* came out in 2002 and presents him as a somewhat childish man who made the wrong decision to direct the propaganda film for Hitler, in order to save his skin. This bothered me very much, because it seems clear that Hitler didn't give him a choice, and he couldn't refuse. [During his life,] Gerron had been known as a generous and kind man, and I felt he had been maligned in this otherwise exceptional documentary, and thought he deserved a voice. I can't be sure that the motives I attribute to him are right, but I know that even though he had taken great measures to make sure his parents and his wife got to accompany him to Theresienstadt, he went to the gas chambers childless and alone, and he deserved an evaluation that was more fair.

**Farband (Yid.). Brotherhood. It is also shorthand for the Yiddisher Natsyonaler Arbeter Farband (the Jewish National Workers' Alliance), a labor Zionist fraternal order founded in the beginning of the twentieth century. The Farband provided insurance and medical plans, and it also organized schools and Yiddish cultural activities and participated in political affairs.*

John Amen * "Verboten"

My grandparents left Europe in 1938. As soon as they reached America, they worked hard at assimilating, essentially shedding their Jewishness. "Verboten" represents an attempt to reconnect with my Jewish roots, to approach the Holocaust as an event that deeply impacted, and continues to impact, my own life and family.

Brett Axel * "Morning After a Fight, He Says"

The speaker of the poem is my grandfather, who is addressing my grandmother; to the best of my knowledge, the details are true. The diction is my grandfather all the way, although he, himself, never told me the gruesome details. When I did hear that part, it was in hushed whispers where he could not see.

David B. Axelrod * "The Suffering Cuts Both Ways"

I wrote the poem so the story within it — which is essentially true — the "pot roast cooking" — would be preserved. Bill Heyen has poems about going back to Germany and certainly asks the question in his book entitled *Swastika Poems*, "How could it have happened?"

There is a subtext for the poem, however. I wrote the poem after meeting Bill Heyen for the first time, when he came to read at our college campus. I had never met him before or heard him read his poetry. He had just published his *Swastika Poems,* and I was horrified that someone would give a book that name, so I went to the reading with a negative mind set.

I grew up fearing pogroms and ducking vehement anti-Semitism. My grandmother, who raised me, had fled the Russian shtetl and Cossack attacks. I felt like a first-generation American and absorbed her fears and regrets. When I was a child growing up in Beverly, Massachusetts, it was a miserable place for a Jew. I still have a major repulsion for anyone with a tattoo because the only people with tattoos when I was little were not only *not* Jews; they wanted Jews dead!

At the reading, I walked up to Bill, and this big, tall, very white, very blond, very blue-eyed fellow reached out to shake my hand. For a minute, I imagined he was wearing jack-boots. It was frightening. But Bill is a major gentleman, a true anti-fascist, anti-Nazi. I've learned that through years of good will and working with him. I couldn't have known that when I met him. I was just scared!

Even though his poems were well-intentioned, I went home and had a dream that I was being chased by the SS, who had come to my house to take me and my family away. We were hiding under a cliff in Rocky Point (known for its high cliffs hanging over Long Island Sound), fearing the sand would fall down on us and smother us. My little daughter was with us, and I was sure we would be found and dragged off.

Some dream! After that, I made up my mind that I would get over my "prejudice" and fear of German people, so that I wouldn't feel fear when I met otherwise good people like Bill Heyen. The poem was my way of understanding how the Holocaust happened and how the suffering cuts both ways.

However, I must note that while the father and son in my poem are part of the story Bill Heyen lays out regarding his own father (who worked building DC-3's), the actual aunt who told her story within the poem, pretty much as I retell it, was my German professor at Penn State in the fall of 1966, one Dr. Boggs. "It smelled like pot roast cooking" is a line I couldn't forget and probably could not even make up! Professor Boggs had an aunt who "stayed behind," who told him the story about the "pot roast." Bill asked his family how it could have happened. It's just that Dr. Boggs, when he asked the same question, got a more dramatic answer! The story stunned me. My hope is the poem stands on its own as a troubling answer to certain questions.

Yakov Azriel * "We, the *Tefillin* of Once-Was Europe"

I write poems on Jewish and Biblical themes extensively. Saying that, I do not often write poems about the Holocaust. It seems to me almost sacrilegious for someone who did not experience the Holocaust, indeed for someone who was born after the end of World War II, to attempt to write about it. Just as Moses was told in the Bible to take off his shoes when he approached the burning bush, for it was sacred ground, so, too, do I feel that when approaching the burning bush of the Holocaust, one must come with trepidation, with trembling, with the utmost humility. On the other hand, the Holocaust was such a central event in Jewish history and consciousness, and indeed in the history of human suffering, that it borders on the sacrilegious to simply walk away from it, to ignore it, to leave it in silence. Is it not disrespectful to those who were murdered not to speak of them, not to acknowledge their torment?

When I do write a poem about the Holocaust, I try to place it within the context of the Jewish tradition and a Biblical set of reference and framework, as in my poem, "We, the *Tefillin* of Once-Was Europe." Perhaps this tradition and this framework can help us — who know of the Holocaust only second-hand, through testimony of the survivor and the witness — to somehow grapple with the legacy of the Holocaust, the way Jacob wrestled with the angel.

Crystal Bacon * "Kristallnacht, 1991"

My mother grew up in Nazi Germany and came to the U.S. as a "war bride" in the late 40s. My childhood was peppered with stories about her German life but [she said] very little about the war and next to nothing about the Holocaust. Whatever I've written about, it is slim and based on the few details my mother shared during my early life. Often, what she said about that time was very much from the perspective of the child and young woman she'd been while living in Hitler's world: the paradoxical views of a child, once lifted up by Hitler onto the running board of his car during a parade, who was taught by every institution to honor the Führer, and of her father, who risked his life to listen to the Voice of America on the radio even after a neighbor was taken away by the SS for the same act. His family received his wedding ring and watch in an envelope one day, but the husband, the father, was never seen again. My grandmother, my mother, and my aunt had to station themselves around the house to keep watch while my grandfather performed this quiet sedition of listening to the radio. He resisted the war in his quiet ways, refusing to wear the wedding ring that he had fashioned in his masonry guild sign, the skull and crossbones, when the SS began to wear the same symbol in silver on their uniforms. My mother took the ring, and I wear it today with all its powerful history. My mother still does not talk about the Holocaust, but she has read these poems and borne witness to their telling.

Stanley H. Barkan * "The Mothertree"
I was visiting with Rivke Katz, the widow of the Yiddish poet, Menke Katz, at her shtibl-like country home in Spring Glen, a small town in the Catskills. She told me about her son, Dovid Katz, who, among other things, like starting the Yiddish program at Oxford University and authoring a half dozen books on Yiddish grammar and original stories and teaching Yiddish in Vilnius, has made it a life's work to gather Yiddish data firsthand from the remnant in Eastern Europe. On one occasion, he met Blumke Katz (alternately spelled Bluma Kac with an acute accent on the c), who told him her story about what happened to her during the German and then Russian occupation of her shtetl. Rivke told me the story. I immediately wrote the poem. After we had lunch together at the Nevele gold club, her favorite place for lunch, I read her the poem from my journal, based on what she had told me about Blumke Katz. Amazed, she asked, "When did you write this?" I told her, just after our initial visit at the little forest home where she and Menke shared so many good years together. That's the story.

Tony Barnstone * "Parable of the Jew Without a Name"
Like the hidden Jews of New Mexico, the crypto-Jews forced to convert to Catholicism, I am the product of the force of assimilation. My Germanic family name, Bornstein, means "burning stone," and refers to the fiery yellow stone, amber, suggesting that perhaps my ancestors were dealers in precious jewels. When my great-uncle Vincent convinced my family to change their name, he must have discovered that the Old English word for amber was "barnstone," clearly a cognate of "Bornstein." It was a good translation, but it translated us out of our ethnicity. With a name like Tony Barnstone, I am usually assumed to be English in origin. In fact, I was not raised religiously or culturally Jewish, and orthodox Jews would not consider me Jewish because while my father is Jewish, my mother is Greek and was raised Greek Orthodox. I am, as I say in my poem, a "lousy Jew."

And yet, I know that my great-grandparents came from Poland and that over ninety percent of the Polish Jews died in the Holocaust, and so it seems likely that whatever town I came from is populated by the ghosts of Bornsteins. For me, this has always been immensely moving, that my roots stretch back towards a severed past, that my personal genealogy is a genealogy of absence, of phantoms, and of unknowing. I know also that for the Nazis the question of my mother's origin was moot. I was Jewish enough to be killed. I am probably more Greek than I am Jewish, because my family visits Greece often, and I speak the language somewhat, but my Jewish identity has been strangely important precisely because it is hidden enough that people feel comfortable expressing their anti-Semitism to me.

When I think of the writing of Hemingway, I think of a writer who predicated his writing on the idea of being part of the cultural elite, "one of us" who have suffered the War and shown grace under pressure, but which excludes the Robert Cohns of the world. When Jake Barnes describes the "nigger drummer . . . all teeth and lips" or talks about his desire to punch a gay man, "to shatter that superior, simpering composure," the reader is meant to sympathize, because if you are gay, or black, or Jewish, you are less than fully human, worthy only of attack. His mean-spirited and clannish bigotry will always undermine his brilliance. I am a different writer. I find myself sympathizing with minority over majority, with the outcast over the insider, with the despised over the praised. I do feel that as a lousy Jew, as an ignorant Jew, a Jew that some Jews do not accept, a Jew who has white skin and an English name, I have nonetheless been shaped by Jewishness. In some way, my Jewish heritage has given me a critical distance from mainstream American culture, a step away from the assumption of privilege that my white skin gives me. The "Parable of the Jew Without a Name" is an attempt to imagine into being my relatives who are smoke, is an attempt to rename myself back into Jewishness, to cease being hidden, and to let my past burn back into being, like fire, like amber.

Judith Barrington * "Ineradicable," "History and Geography"
I was born on the south coast of England in 1944 in the middle of an air raid and grew up with many stories about World War II. However, it was not until I became part of a large Jewish family, some thirty-five years later, that I realized how little those stories included about the Holocaust, although many people I knew had lost family members as a result of bombings or being in military service. My Jewish partner's grandmother had died at Auschwitz and her father had escaped after twice being taken to Dachau.

Every group has its own stories about such a huge historical event. I realized that those of my growing-up years, like those of many others, were partial: they were particular to that British, middle-class milieu. I write now about the Holocaust because I am part of a new family. I have grown beyond the boundaries of my first culture and acquired a wider view of history.

Marvin Bell * "The Extermination of the Jews," "Oft-Seen Photo from the Liberation of Auschwitz"
"The Extermination of the Jews" was first collected in *A Probable Volume of Dreams* (Atheneum, 1969). It came from a conversation with the poet Donald Justice in which I spoke the first sentence of the poem. "You should start a poem with that," he said, so I did. As readers can see, I believed that the hatred that produced the Holocaust, and the heroism within the ranks of the victims, would prove to be ongoing. "Oft-Seen Photo from the Liberation of Auschwitz" was written in January, 2007, thirty-eight years after "The Extermination of the Jews." It marks Holocaust Day, for which the United Nations passed a resolution. One country voted against it.

Lora J. Berg * "Maschlacki"
The Holocaust is a new subject for me. I grew up without relatives. Shortly after my father's arrival in America, his family in Warsaw was destroyed. My mother's father, a Russian, was alone here; we have no records of his relatives (only yellowed photos). In my life, there is a hollowness where relatives should be. I respond in part by creating, in part by teaching minority students — encouraging them to explore their past . . . perhaps to fight my battles? To become adopted family? Even for those who 'choose to forget,' the past perpetuates itself in needs.

I write about the Holocaust when other fears press in on me — it has become the symbol of fear for me, casting shadows over areas of my life that, in reality, may not be touched by 'race.' In a sense, I want to be free of this . . . I feel that I am sustaining a chord of evil; yet it is a chord I am not trustful enough to silence. So I participate in the passing on of this story, and I am sorrowful about my role, about its possible consequences. The violence seems impossible to erase. We are atheists in my family. Both of my parents are scientists, 'optimists'; they turned away from tragedy. But I can't. [1985]

Michael Blumenthal * "Juliek's Violin"
I wrote "Juliek's Violin" many years ago, after first reading Elie Wiesel's heartbreaking memoir, because I was touched and moved — even shattered — by the juxtaposition of the divinely beautiful and the satanically daemonic that the scene provided, just as I was once again similarly moved, only a few years ago, by the sight of the to-me-somehow-visually-beautiful sterilization vats in the concentration camp at Terezín near Prague.

This juxtaposition — of good and evil, extreme beauty and extreme (often human) ugliness — has always moved, and perplexed, me. It represents to me the extremes of the human condition and predicament, and the fact that the two can sometimes coexist so closely is, for me, a subject of the gravest, and most serious, meditation and puzzlement.

Emily Borenstein * "Night Journey to Poland," "The Shoah," "Triumph of the Dead," "Verdi's Requiem Played and Sung by Jews in Terezín Concentration Camp / Summer, 1944"

During the 1930s, my grandmother, Rebecca, shipped to our relatives, by boat, huge bundles filled with articles of clothing and shoes, from raids on our closets, so that she could provide for the poorest of our relatives in Russia and Poland. She wrote to them and received heartfelt responses telling her of the increasingly difficult time they were having as life for them began to take on the dimensions of a nightmare and life itself hung precariously in the balance. In the late thirties and early forties, the letters from the relatives stopped coming. My great-aunts, great-uncles and cousins may well have been among the thousands killed at Babi Yar and Ponary, falling into mass graves, layer upon layer. Other relatives of mine in Russia and Poland were also shot on the spot or forced into cattle cars traveling by day and by night enroute to unspeakable torture and death.

"Night Journey to Poland" makes no direct reference to the Holocaust. The connection is implicit. "The mysterious fires . . . burning" suggest the cremation furnaces toward which the night journey in the poem is moving. The fires also conjure up the torched synagogues that went up in flames in Russia and Poland and in other countries in Europe. Even the reddish, bloody-looking moon "hangs fire" and casts evil shadows. The wounded songbird is a metaphor for the poet and for writers and musicians, in particular, who were murdered by the Nazis as well as those who miraculously escaped death and those who did not.

My poem, "Verdi's Requiem Played and Sung by Jews in Terezín Concentration Camp / Summer, 1944," draws its *raison d'etre* and its life from the Czech publication of Josef Bor's book, *The Terezín Requiem.* In writing this poem, I was concerned with finding the right balance in the organization of its stanzas and in the joining of its parts with my own transformational thoughts and feelings expressed *sotto voce*. I hoped to transmit and underscore for readers that, during the Holocaust, survival itself was a form of resistance and that Schächter, the Jewish conductor, and his orchestra and soloists, retained an important measure of their humanity and dignity by withstanding humiliation and persevering against all odds. My own thoughts and feelings were focused on moving the action forward and showing under the surface of the poem the forces of good and evil on a collision course. In writing my poem, it was as if I were leaping naked through the historic dimensions of the Holocaust from which the poem derives its life. The book carried me away. I was filled again, and more than ever, as a musician, a poet and a psychotherapist, with the moral imperative of *remembering* or, in my case, *testifying* as a poet.

Laure-Anne Bosselaar * "The Feather at Breendonk," "The Pallor of Survival," ***from*** **"Seven Fragments on Hearing a Hammer Pounding"**

I am often asked — tactfully and sometimes less diplomatically — why I continue to write about my childhood in post-war Belgium and why I'm so very much involved with denouncing, and thus fighting, anti-Semitism. My answer to that question is always the same: "*Not* writing about it seems out of the question: I believe it's my responsibility, particularly as the daughter of Nazi sympathizers, to keep the memory of what has happened alive."

To those who complain that we are constantly deluged with stories, memoirs, documentaries, poems, and photographs of the Holocaust, I can only reply that as long as there are writers, journalists, philosophers and scholars who actually *deny* the existence of the Holocaust, it is vital that witnesses keep coming forward. Although what I witnessed is only a minuscule aspect of the unspeakable terrors and crimes that shaped the twentieth century, the Holocaust is an integral and irrefutable part of my generation's identity, and I continue to be haunted by it — and, as a result, it will continue to appear in my work.

Allen Brafman * "Gardens of Smoke," "Rivkah"
I was born in Brooklyn, New York, in February 1942. If my grandparents had not left Eastern Europe earlier in the century, I probably would not have been born. Had I been born, most likely I would not have survived. Many of my family — great-uncles, great-aunts, their children, my great-grandmother — were murdered in 1942, some in the same towns my grandparents had left. The blood of those who perished flows in my veins.

After the war, a trickle of survivors appeared in our living room. The language they spoke was Yiddish punctuated with gasps, with sighs, with sobs. The grownups leaned close in to one another, whispering and crying, as though trying to muffle something unutterable, to stifle it into extinction. I grew older. I met other relatives. I listened to the narrative of their experiences and realized that any of those great-aunts could have been my mother; any of those great-uncles could have been my father. Any one of them might have been me.

Over the years, I have spoken with hundreds of survivors — teachers, friends, chance encounters — and it has become clear to me that we are a family: those who perished, those who survived, those who were not there. My bones ache from our suffering. I exult in our success at surviving.

In recent years, as I see fewer and fewer people with numbers tattooed on their forearms, I think about the Holocaust more frequently. I write about the destruction of the Jewish culture that flourished in Eastern and Central Europe. I write about the murder of untold millions, including those who will never be born because the men and women who would have been their parents were consumed in flames. I produce written objects that concern themselves with the events and the experiences of the Holocaust in an effort to understand that which refuses to be understood.

The vitality of those who survived, as well as those who were murdered, will endure much longer than the inhumanity that sought to destroy us. If we continue to think and talk about the Holocaust, we will continue to prevail. I write about the Holocaust because I write about myself — my past, my present, my future, my people.

Van K. Brock * "The Hindenburg," *from* ***This Way to the Gas***
Some survivors insist metaphor is an inappropriate approach to the facts of the Holocaust. Fact and metaphor are both needed. And better myths, not absence of myth, by which to shape our lives and civilization. After long immersion in the facts of the Holocaust, events far less horrible became occasions for metaphors that touched the greater horror. One, a news article about the Hindenburg, casually noting that eight hundred fifty thousand skins of cattle were used in making it, prompted this poem, which draws on a theme that emerged in the poems, the dominance of a rapacious human technology over all nature.

I wrote *This Way to the Gas* because Borowski, and all he lived through, did, and wrote, by the time he killed himself, before thirty, was powerful because he lived through the ravaging of Poland, being a prisoner in Auschwitz, and finally being oppressed again by the Cold War. And his suicide followed the pattern of survivors succumbing, ironically, to gas. Battered by Western and then Eastern dominations, he embodied Poland's old tragedy, leaving a lucid record.

Louis Daniel Brodsky * "Learning the ABC's of Wartime Germany," "Phoenixes," "*Schindlerjuden*," "Speaking for Survivors," "Yom Kippur for a Survivor"
In my Holocaust poems, I address what I believe to be my second-generation "survivor"'s responsibility to deal with man's seemingly ineradicable legacy of bigotry, cruelty, and destruction. My compulsion to confront this subject does not result from a desire to interpret the accounts of victims, refugees, their children, and historians of the Holocaust but rather from a need to express, imaginatively, the torment I feel as a besieged American born too late to really remember — but not late enough to forget — the Nazi atrocities of World War II.

In *Holocaust Testimonies: The Ruins of Memory*, Lawrence L. Langer isolates one notion common to virtually all Holocaust survivors. He quotes one victim: "To understand us, somebody has to go through with it. Because nobody, but nobody fully understands us. You can't. No [matter] how much sympathy you give me when I'm talking here, or you understand. . . ." Langer says, "A statement like 'to understand, you have to go through with it,' however authentic its inspiration, underestimates the sympathetic power of the imagination. Perhaps it is time to grant that power the role it deserves."

I write about the Holocaust from secondhand experience — books, radio, TV, newspapers, movies, and word of mouth. My work is *imagined*; thus, my evocation and recreation of events are, with few exceptions, *sympathetic*, in Langer's terminology, *vicarious*, in my own.

Occasionally at public readings of my Holocaust poems, I have been confronted by survivors and refugees, who have accused me of trespassing on their sacred territory, desecrating it, them, and their relatives by composing poems that dare to address the Holocaust. They believe I have no right to their shared experience. Others, including some of my own contemporaries, have even gone beyond this, pontificating that only the children of the victims have any right to speak for the dead. To accept either of these positions is to deny imagination its capacity to counterbalance spiritual annihilation and to refuse art its power to survive reality's fact-camps with its own liberating forces. More important, these arguments have inherent in them germs that can exterminate their best intentions, because, unwittingly, they promote their own brand of intolerance.

A child of neither victims nor survivors, I have never presumed to speak for the dead. All I have really desperately, obsessively, wanted to accomplish with my Holocaust poems is to speak *to* and, if my work does not seem contrived or inauthentic, *for* the living. This is my inalienable right, my freedom of speech, my responsibility as an artist. I consider my poems neither a Jewish response to the Holocaust nor a Jew's response (although I am Jewish) but rather one man's voice raised against hatred, racial prejudice, and violence, one plea for universal peace.

Michael Dennis Browne * "Mengele"
I wrote "Mengele" in anger after reading a 1985 newspaper report that an Israeli expert had identified the bones of Josef Mengele in Brazil; the suggestion in the report was that *that* chapter was now closed. Something in me protested against the naiveté of that assessment.

I write poems on themes of social justice — on the Shoah, Vietnam, Iraq, civil rights, and the like — because these are wounds that will not close; lines, images, rhythms keep proposing themselves to me, year after year, and I see it as my job to get them down and arrange them, as rhythmically and urgently as I can. These are stories that must always be told; each generation has the responsibility to keep them alive for the generations that follow, so that the young have the best possible chance of understanding and feeling the complexity of the world we live in.

Michael R. Burch * "Pfennig Postcard, Wrong Address"
I write about the Holocaust for two reasons: to try to come to terms with it myself, and to try to put it into some sort of intelligible perspective. Having been born in 1958, and not having lived through World War II, I struggle personally with the horror of the Holocaust. I know it happened. And yet I find it nigh impossible to imagine that so many Germans enslaved, tortured and murdered millions upon millions of Jews and other "undesirables." As a poet, I have to war with myself on two fronts. On one hand, I want to recoil from the horror, to protect myself from it. On the other hand, it is far too easy (and therefore dangerous) to "poeticize" or "wax sympathetic" about the victims. I think poets and readers must steel themselves not to recoil from the truth of the Holocaust, and yet they cannot allow meaningless pity or shallow "empathy" to overwhelm them either. We cannot put ourselves in the shoes of the victims, many of whom went to death barefooted. Perhaps the best we can do is celebrate the love, kindness and heroism so many of them displayed toward each other, while admitting to ourselves the inadequacy of our own words and thoughts on their behalf.

Cyrus Cassells * "Auschwitz, All Hallows," "Juliek's Violin," "Life Indestructible," "Poem for the Artists of the Holocaust," "The Postcard of Sophie Scholl"
In late October [2005], I visited the Slovak Republic, then traveled with a musician friend on a rickety old train to Kraków to visit the remarkable Polish poet, Adam Zagajewski. I remember the gasp of coming awake after a long nap to find our limping train stopped at the Auschwitz station, just as it was getting dark. I vowed in that jostled moment to make the pilgrimage to the notorious camp. The only time possible to go, in terms of my travel schedule, turned out to be November 1 — the traditional day of the dead: a daunting prospect. Did I have the strength to face the juggernaut of Auschwitz at the symbolic moment when the veil between worlds is said to be at its thinnest? Despite my initial dread, it turned out to be an exceptional day: groups of Israeli schoolchildren were visiting the camp, bearing eye-catching blue-and-white flags, so the Star of David was everywhere triumphant and aloft in Auschwitz-Birkenau. Pilgrims had poignantly brought flowers and candles and placed them in various parts of the camp — most strikingly before the iron maws of the still-extant ovens in Auschwitz I. My guide said quietly, matter-of-factly, as we walked near the ruins of the blast crematoria of Birkenau: "Here, everywhere you walk, you are walking on human ash." And so we must leave for the irreplaceable, the betrayed, a balm of flowers and revering light, a language of banners, poems, and prayers, lest we forget.

"Juliek's Violin" was inspired by a passage in Nobel Laureate Elie Wiesel's *Night,* and is dedicated, with deepest respect, to Elie Wiesel, who was born in Hungary in 1928, and deported with his family to Auschwitz and Buchenwald. A visit to Hungary and to the Nobel Peace Prize Museum in Oslo helped to further this poem.

I wrote "Life Indestructible" in response to the awe-inspiring power of Etty Hillesum's riveting diaries. More than anything I have read, her work reminds me that always during the Shoah the whole spectrum of life was going on — joy and spiritual illumination as well as the ferocities and agonies of the camps. Recent trips to Anne Frank's Secret Annex and Terezín, where my friend Eric Kahn was interned as a child, have strengthened my personal dedication to bear witness in poetry to the ignoble events of that time.

Judith Chalmer * "The Archivist," "Personal to Kaplan"
Though I know it's not a certainty, I assume human life will exist centuries and centuries from now and that Jewish life will be part of it, but I wonder about that distant future — how the Holocaust, for Jews, will be woven into the value systems that have sustained our cultures for so long. I don't assume my poems will be among those that last. But I do believe our collective effort at forming language moves us forward in creating a lasting meaning, and I'm glad to take part in the multiplicity of drafts.

David Citino * "Swastika"
There are times when the news — local, state, national — breaks us out of the here-and-now we're caught in and propels us into the halls of history, connecting the type to its archetype, the moment to the momentous, the days of our lives to ages and eons. The breaking news of the discovery of a natural swastika formed of trees planted by a detachment of Hitler Youth and visible only from the air was one such occasion of dislocation for me.

A post-World War II baby, I learned early on to estimate any new massive act of evil landing on my porch with the daily news by setting it against the Holocaust. The Nazi war against the Jews was, and remains, my moral measuring tape. Always, the Holocaust "wins" contests of comparative perversity.

The Holocaust was the world's worst idea: a state-devised and supported, multinational, technologically sophisticated program that roared, chugged, and hissed for decades, long trains chugging up and down numerous main lines, tracks and sidings. It was instituted and carried out to exterminate a people and their culture from the face of the earth, and to do so in secret. The prejudices that supported these crimes against the Jews were ancient, but it was the modern world and its technology, its ready acceptance of the latest "isms," no matter how morally bankrupt, its lack of human connectivity and communion, that enabled the strong to crush the weak with impunity for so long.

The trees provide an eloquent memorial that renews itself each season, rings tolling the anniversaries of the suffering of the lost and their survivors, the birds in their branches singing the truth. As the speaker of the poem urges, the swastika must be allowed to stay, to say to each generation, even beyond words, how nature's goodness — root, trunk, leaf, fruit, and nesting birds — can be defaced and rendered obscene by the worst that men and women can think and do. Let it stand. It will always be news.

Vince Clemente * "From the Ardeatine Caves"
In 1975, my wife and I and two daughters lived in Rome, Italy, for a year. I taught, Annie worked on translations — she is fluent in Italian — and our daughters were in local Italian elementary schools. We visited the Ardeatine Caves on four separate occasions. With each visit, I felt a part of me — my deepest part — was left there. We also observed the Italian National Day of Mourning, on 24 March. I spoke to many Romans and our Italian relatives that year about the atrocities, so close to Rome.

My journals contain these exchanges. It wasn't until February 1978, when I read of the death of "Nazi war criminal, Herbert Kappler, former police chief of Rome," in the *New York Times*, that I began working on the poem that took three years to complete. The poem is more transformation than transcription, as only the "hard" facts are there. Much was given me through conversations with my Roman friends — my sense of loss.

Helen Degen Cohen (Halina Degenfisz) * "And the Snow Kept Falling," "Habry," "I Remember Coming into Warsaw, a Child"

I was born in Grojec, a shtetl about forty kilometers south of Warsaw. Shortly after the Nazis invaded the shtetl, my parents and I fled to Lida, White Russia. When eventually the Nazis invaded White Russia as well, my family was put, along with other Jews, into the Lida Ghetto. My father was then working in Lida's little prison — as barber, plumber, and distributor of provisions (food). Because he'd become indispensable as a jack-of-all-trades, he was able to use his influence to get my mother and me out of the ghetto, to live with him in semi-hiding in a little room over the guardhouse in the prison. When, finally, ALL remaining Jews were rounded up to be exported to the Camps, and my family stood at the train station among the crowd waiting to board the train, my mother gave me a cup and told me to pretend I was going for water at the water-pump, and to keep on walking, until I found the house of the prison cook my parents had befriended. Which I did. I was then not quite eight years old. The prison cook, who had three children of her own, took me in and, within a few days, found Maria Szumska, a devout Catholic woman, who agreed to hide me. Szumska sold her belongings and, with the money, rented a cabin in the country in which she hid me for the last year of the war. Meanwhile, back at the train station, my parents had boarded the train; but, within hours, my father helped to organize an escape party, and he and my mother were among the eleven people (out of approximately five hundred) who jumped the train at night. Four were shot immediately, and the remaining seven joined the Underground/the Partisans. After the war, after many efforts, they found me in the cabin among the farm fields — in a long dress and with long braids, looking "like a nun."

I write about the War — among other topics, I want to stress — because it is my childhood (I am a Survivor), and therefore, as for most poets or writers, compelling. Even magnetic. To quote myself from an interview for *Spoon River Quarterly* (now *The Spoon River Poetry Review*), when asked if my birthplace influenced my work, I said, "The War was my birthplace."

Regarding "And the Snow Kept Falling," the Jewishness I denied [while in hiding] is in that poem, like a lost world I was a part of only for a tiny period of my life. Though it was a difficult world, it had a powerful character, a substance. I think this poem is about the loss of that substance, as horrible as it may have been. All of us look for it. And there it is, forever, colorful and strong, that world, as though under a glass bubble we are trying to get into, because we are nowhere.

David Curzon * "The Gardens"

"The Gardens" is a series of adult recollections of childhood memories of my father, who emigrated from Poland to Australia in 1939 and eventually committed suicide, presumably in part because of what had happened to the family and community he left behind. It is a midrash in the sense that it has an epigraph from Psalm 137, which is set in the Babylonian exile, is in the voice of one of the exiles, and ends with a reference to Babylon, which is meant to evoke a comparison between those exiles and the situation of my father in exile in Australia after the Jewish community he came from had been destroyed.

The phrase "Australian picnic" is used in the poem by an Australian child trying to tell his immigrant father that leaving lobster shells on the steps of a synagogue was not a deliberate act of desecration, as it would have been in Europe, but just the result of some boorish Australians who ate a picnic lunch there and didn't clean up when they left.

Ruth Daigon * "Dachau Revisited 1971"
In 1971, my husband had a sabbatical leave from the University of Connecticut and we packed our two sons up and took off for Europe. Since we had never been there before we had much to see and even more advice on *what* to see. In our stay in Germany, when we spent a few days in Munich, we knew that the concentration camp of Dachau was nearby, but no one would give us information on where it was and how to get there. Finally after driving around the area, I noticed a very small sign saying *Gedenkstade*, and even my inadequate knowledge of German led me to believe that this was indeed the way to Dachau. We followed the signs that led us to huge gates decorated with huge letters — ARBEIT MACHT FREI — and smaller letters spelling out *Dachau*. We had reached our goal, and since it was our son's thirteenth birthday, we thought his exploration of Dachau was a "real bar mitzvah." And so it was for all of us. The buildings were all there and the photographs of the people passing through that "initiation" made us feel more Jewish than all the stories of our parents, the books and articles we read, the speeches and witnessings we heard. I felt as though I had come home. And somehow the only way I could really express my feeling was to wear the skin and skeleton of a survivor who had come back and relived [the part of] her own life that had been spent in Dachau.

Enid Dame (1943–2003) * "Soup"
The following comments were written by Enid Dame's husband, Donald Lev —

Enid had seen musician and documentary film-maker Josh Waletzsky's 1986 documentary film, *Partisans of Vilna*, either on television or in some theater; I don't remember which. But she was very taken with the film — this I do remember. So she composed the poem "Soup," imagining a survivor, a woman, now resident in the Brighton Beach section of Brooklyn, where Enid and I lived at the time, watching this same documentary on television, herself a participant in the events. She had been making soup in the Vilna Ghetto and she is now warming (Chinese take-out) soup in Brighton Beach, for herself and her daughter, with whom she has never discussed this family history.

The poem is published in Enid's 1992 collection, *Anything You Don't See* (West End Press). It concludes the first section of the book which is wholly composed of dramatic monologues. Enid speaks in the voices of Eve, Lot, and Lot's wife from the Bible, Cinderella from the fairy tale (an immensely popular feminist poem of Enid's), Persephone from Greek mythology, an old woman — an ex-radical — a character so well represented in the Brighton Beach of the time, and finally this survivor — also significantly represented in the population of Brighton Beach in those days.

Besides exploring the specific moment of history the film refers to, the poem also revisits many of Enid Dame's perennial themes: family, sibling rivalry, the mother-daughter dialogue, the role of politics in life, and survival itself — particularly Jewish survival — "that oversensitive tribe / with their knack for survival" she says elsewhere ("Lilith Talks About Men" in *Lilith and her Demons*, Cross-Cultural Communications, 1986) — and, ultimately, Jewish survival in America.

Kate Daniels * "For Miklós Radnóti: 1909–1944"
I wrote this poem in the early 1980s after discovering the marvelous English-language translation of Radnóti's poems called *Clouded Sky* (translated by Steven Polgar, Stephen Berg, and S.J. Marks). The harrowing testimony of the poems was unbearably intensified by the details of Radnóti's life. How, I wondered, could anyone have sustained such an affirmative view of life? How could anyone in those circumstances go on loving, and desiring, and believing in the love of another? Later, I would discover a few other poets as large, as loving: Nazim Hikmet, for instance. But for a long time when I was young, Radnóti was the only poet I carried about with me whose darkness was matched by his vision of light. I loved him not only for his beautiful words (a few of which I could read in Hungarian) but for that heavy burden he carried so effortlessly, and for the way he took on some of my own burden in those days when I easily grew discouraged, repelled, or sickened by the world and by the ways of the world. His poems re-lit the light for me, and connected me with him, and with everyone else struggling in darkness.

Theodore Deppe * "School of Music"
Zhanna Dawson, the mother of one of my best friends in childhood, is a concert pianist who once escaped from a death march out of Kharkov during World War II. She is my direct source for "School of Music." She remembers being lined up, six in a row, and marched out of town during a snowstorm. In her row were her father, her mother, her grandparents, her sister, and herself. Her father managed to bribe a Ukrainian guard with a family heirloom, an old watch, and the guard allowed her to escape. Later, her sister also escaped, but the others were killed in the death camps.

Norita Dittberner-Jax * "Name Tag"
I grew up in a strong German-American home full of music and political talk, but no one mentioned the Holocaust. Learning about it as a young adult, I was stunned. The Holocaust became the yardstick by which I judge evil. When I first began writing poetry, I wrote about my childhood home and working class neighborhood. It wasn't until I had done that, that I was able to see the connection between the personal and the political, the small life hidden in the large. I applied for and received a grant from the Jerome Foundation to study in Eastern Europe. My husband and I undertook that journey together. It was an arduous trip emotionally, but exactly where I wanted to be. The poems in *Longing for Home,* the manuscript from which "Name Tag" is taken, came out of that journey, as well as from the reflection on growing up in a German-American home.

Visiting Auschwitz was overwhelming. What made it more particularly so for me was the huge room of the suitcases, one piled on top of the other, some with the names showing. My husband pointed her name out: *Fanny Klinger.* I remember saying her name out loud. I could imagine her. We looked up her name at Yad Vashem, in Jerusalem, but couldn't find it. She remains with me.

Sharon Dolin * "Three Postage Stamps"
As a Jewish girl growing up in Brooklyn in the sixties and early seventies, the only way I could understand the enormity of the Holocaust (not having had a close relative who had lived through it directly) was through reading Anne Frank's diary. Many years later, when I was living in Italy one summer, my German room-mate gave me a newly issued German postage stamp commemorating what would have been Anne Frank's fiftieth birthday. I was struck by the macabre drawing of Anne Frank on it, and so I held onto the stamp. About a year later, while I was a graduate student at Berkeley, a Dutch friend gave me the second stamp, with a photograph of Anne Frank's smiling face on it that I found so poignant. That's when

I decided I had to write a poem where I would communicate my reactions through the description of each stamp. But I felt it was not enough to describe the two stamps, that I had to bring something of myself and my own childhood identification with Anne Frank into the poem (I was a girl like Anne who liked to stay up late and write poems and by sheer happenstance and luck lived in a time and place where I never experienced any anti-Semitism). Before starting to write, I knew the poem would be called "Three Postage Stamps" and would consist of three blocky stanzas shaped like postage stamps; each one would describe a stamp, with the last one being my imaginary American stamp.

Wendy Drexler * "On Hearing a String Quartet Written by Prisoners of Theresienstadt"

On Holocaust Remembrance Day several years ago, I was listening to the radio in the kitchen while peeling and slicing cucumbers for a salad. A poignant string quartet, composed by prisoners in Theresienstadt, began to play, releasing a flood of emotions — among them, the horrors of the camps, the human impulse to create art under even the most dire circumstances, and a fresh, visceral stab of pain as I recalled my beloved's personal narrative of an encounter between his mother and an SS officer that in all likelihood saved her life. His mother was studying medicine in Italy in the late 1930s (as a German Jew, she was unable to attend school in Germany). She had gone to the German Embassy to obtain a visa to return home to visit her parents in Würzburg, Germany. The officer's warning in a coded message about the weather induced her not to return. She never saw her parents again.

Shoshana Dubman * "Istanbul 1967," "Memories"

I write because I need to put some order to the disturbed childhood I remember. I grew up in a community of Holocaust survivors. I didn't hear as many stories as one would in an average extended family. Instead, I saw numbers on arms and heard different European languages. There was no talk of war or the difficulties anyone endured. Only talk of a better life, a better car, a better house. It seemed that so much of life was not about the past but about being American. I heard the whispers of how thankful I should be for their taking me out of Germany. I had more questions than answers and no one to turn to for the answers. Making art in whatever way I decide is a vessel for so many questions that will never be answered. When I moved to New Mexico, I eventually became a teacher in a community where I learned how families connect with aunts, uncles, grandparents, great-grandparents. I learned there are stories not of a Holocaust but of grandparents who struggled to come to this country and who raised fifteen kids. I now teach their kids and hear their stories, and suddenly I realize I never had grandparents, not even for one day. So, I write or make art for all the stories I never heard from my grandparents who I never knew. Sometimes I feel that I write or make art for all my brothers and sisters and aunts and uncles and friends who never were able to see the end of the war.

Jehanne Dubrow * "Shulamith Rereads *The Shawl*," "Shulamith, in White," "Shulamith Writes *Fuck You*"

"Shulamith Rereads *The Shawl*," "Shulamith, in White" and "Shulamith Writes *Fuck You*" come from a series of poems written in the voice of Shulamith, a composite inspired both by the Shulamite woman of the *Song of Songs* and also by a character who appears in Paul Celan's "Todesfuge," perhaps the most important poem in the canon of Holocaust literature. In the *Song of Songs*, the Shulamite woman embodies sensuality and sexual ecstasy. Celan's Shulamith, on the other hand, is the personification of Jewish suffering and destruction, a figure reduced to ash.

I wrote the Shulamith cycle throughout the year leading up to my wedding. Our rabbi had suggested that my husband and I write something marriage-related for the ceremony, an idea that baffled me. At the time, the work of my dissertation centered on Holocaust texts; I couldn't escape the Shoah. So I spent the year trying to figure out how one speaks of joy even while facing atrocity. Since I couldn't avoid reading or writing about the Holocaust, the poems ended up as post-Auschwitz wedding poems, simultaneously erotic and necrotic. Most of the pieces play with received forms. It interested me that Polish poets had rejected formalism after the Second World War. They believed formalism represented an innocence and Romanticism made irrelevant by the Holocaust. I wondered if form might be reclaimed.

Shelley Ehrlich * "Vilna 1938"

My writing about the Holocaust is shaped by how the word *visas* hung over my childhood in New York — my father struggling to rescue family members from Europe. Confused by that word as a child, I nevertheless breathed in my father's anguish and foreboding. I sensed then that words connect to hidden meanings and realities.

Frederick Feirstein * "'Grandfather' in Winter"

In 1968, during the Nigerian Civil War, I had been directing publicity for the American Committee to keep Biafra Alive. I hadn't fully understood then why I wanted to help the children under siege or how it was connected to my mother, until I wrote this poem. Only after I wrote such poems as these did I press my mother for details about her background and begin to understand how much my mother's childhood experiences were part of me and my poetry.

My mother escaped two pogroms in Russia before she came here at eleven. Though, like many pogrom survivors, she never talked about the details of her experiences — hiding in a cemetery above the town during the first; fleeing to America during the second — it was part of the dynamics of our family life: my family's solidarity, for instance, and its overprotectiveness. In some ways, I think of myself as a survivor's son. That feeling, plus an early awareness of the Holocaust (which in some ways I see as a culmination of the pogroms), moves me to write about the Holocaust sometimes and the persecution of Jews often.

Irving Feldman * *from* **"Family History," "The Pripet Marshes"**

Over the years, in trying to make the murder of the Jews as real to myself as I could, I often pictured my family and friends in a Jewish town just before it is overrun by the murderers. Then, one day in 1964 (I remember crowded streets, and twilight), in the midst of my fantasy it struck me that I could write it down as a poem. But this poem wasn't — from its first words, couldn't be — a simple transcription of my wordless mental pictures. It would be as well about the picturing: I am distant from the scene I imagine; with empty, terrible power, I tear my family and friends out of their lives, I put them in mortal danger; unable to end or alter or face what will happen, I return again and again; each time, beyond my control, it is happening in me.

Ruth Feldman * "Survivor"

"Survivor" was inspired by a short story by Giorgio Bassani about a man who returns unexpectedly to Ferrara on the day in which a marble plaque is being put up on the synagogue wall with the names — including his — of the Jews who had perished in concentration camps. The story, *"Una Lapide in Via Mazzini"* ["A Memorial Tablet in Via Mazzini"] haunted me for two years, and I finally "exorcized" it by writing the poem.

Tamara Fishman * "I Did Not Know, but I Remember"
I wrote this poem when I was very young. It was my immediate reaction to learning the scope and depth of what happened during the Holocaust. I felt my own horror and sorrow rise, viscerally, acutely, and I knew that I was tied to these events and these lost souls; I was a living echo of their breath. Although the Holocaust took place decades before I was born, I am still a witness.

Mike Frenkel * "Quiet Desperation"
My mother watched her house burn as she and her family hid in a park across the street. She peered through the living room window and watched her piano burst into flames. That image was vivid in her mind many years later as she told me the story of that day, and that image was my starting point for this poem. I had been a typical child of the sixties, disdainful of the mundane, safe, middle-class comfort my parents had constructed for us. My opposition to the Vietnam War was one thing my parents and I could agree on, but I embraced the excitement of the counterculture, and my parents cared only for my safety. The writing of this poem began to help me understand why my parents would always discourage me from taking chances and why they seemed to so enjoy what I considered their modest successes and simple pleasures. Children often have trouble reconciling the idea that the boring, old people who are now their parents once had love affairs or drove motorcycles or got drunk at parties. Children of survivors see their seemingly "normal," boring, parents and struggle to imagine how they could have heroically survived the horrors they recount as part of their dinnertime conversations. What did they lose, and what did they gain from these experiences, and what did their children lose and gain from the "ripple" effect? And how were the births of their children a major part of their survival?

Alice Friman * "At the Holocaust Museum," "The Waiting Room"
What a strange thing, to be asked to write a statement about why I've written about the Holocaust. Why indeed. One might as well be asked why write at all. I suppose I could tell how, being a child in New York City during the war, I remember the war bonds, the rationing, and the refugee children — Ellen and Gitta — who became my best friends. I could talk about Walter from somewhere in Germany whom no one spoke to because he had funny clothes and a haunted look in his eyes. I could tell you about the second and third cousins who probably perished in the camps, if I knew their names. Or I could wax eloquent about how I felt years later walking through Auschwitz and Birkenau, and how I sobbed to see the piles of shoes. The shoes, the empty shoes. And how pedestrian I found evil to be, how decidedly ordinary. Maybe that was the worst part.

But why write about the Holocaust when probably everything that can be said about it has been said? Perhaps the answer to that question has less to do with the Holocaust than about the nature of poetry. Although my husband and I didn't plan it, we found ourselves at Washington's Holocaust Museum the last day of the last month of the last year of the last century, December 31, 1999. And what surprised me, intrigued me most, was other people's reactions. How they seemed to soften to each other, to apologize for the slightest jostle; how the further down they spiraled, the quieter they got, and how in their growing horror, they seemed to lean in toward each other as if wanting to touch. In the face of such evil, all distinction between friend and stranger seemed to fall away, leaving only the kernel of what's decent in us and essentially vulnerable. I wanted to write about that.

Patricia Garfinkel * "The Tailor"
The Ulezalka poem was about our neighbor during the 1950s in Flushing, Queens. He was just a slip of a man, less than five feet tall and weighing no more than eighty pounds. He was the only survivor of the brutal camps in his family. The description in the poem of the guards throwing him against the stone walls is factual, and he finally died of brain cancer in his forties. Years later, when I visited the Holocaust Museum, I could hear his voice and see his face in every room. I wrote "The Tailor" because his story is an amazing tale of survival. He lived through the horrors of two concentration camps as the only survivor in his family. At the time I knew him, he lived two doors down from us in Flushing, New York. He practiced the tailoring trade and actually did the alterations on my wedding dress in the summer of 1959.

Kinereth Gensler * "For Nelly Sachs"
I think of the poem as a form of personal exorcism, as well as a belated response to *O the Chimneys*. Brought up in the late 1930s, I was an American teenager during World War II, during my high school years, when we lived in Jerusalem. When the news of the concentration camps trickled out, and then the full magnitude of the Holocaust became known, I was a college student at the University of Chicago. I felt then, as I still feel, "There but for the grace of God go I." Surely all Jews of my generation share that feeling. Although I am not a member of One Generation After [children of Holocaust survivors], I *am* a member of the generation of the Jews of the Holocaust and have always felt part of them, one of the lucky ones. Nelly Sachs, too, managed to find a safe harbor during the war; her book spoke for me, and I was sorry not to have written to her before her death. [1985]

David Gershator * *from* **"The Akiva Poems," "Last Night's Doubleheader"**
Early on, no one realized the magnitude of the slaughter. It was unimaginable. There were no special words for it then. When I was a child, I heard the words *tevach* (slaughter) and *haregah* (massacre). My father lost his entire family in the war. His own life was spared only because he'd left Lithuania to study rabbinics (one excuse for leaving Europe for the Promised Land). He reached Jaffa in 1926, with a make-believe bride, at a time when the British were already making it difficult for Jews to enter Mandated Palestine.

During the war, I was knocked flat by an Axis bomb meant for the Haifa oil refineries. I remember the dusty bombshelter we ran to whenever the sirens sounded for a Mussolini air raid, and I remember the bad news breaking after the war — and breaking and breaking. My family left for New York in 1945 on one of the first civilian ships to cross the Atlantic. But in our Brooklyn tenement across from the fire house, the nightmare continued.

Thomas A. Goldman * "Rotterdam — 1946: The Pre-War Visa Files"
In 1945, I was discharged from the Army and entered the U.S. Foreign Service. My first assignment was as Vice Consul at the consulate in Rotterdam, where I was put to work in the visa section. Several months after my arrival, one visa applicant brought up the fact that he had registered for a visa before the war. The head of the visa section told me to go to the basement and look for his records in the files. The basement was a low-ceilinged room of large size, not divided into smaller rooms as were the other floors. It was completely lined with file cabinets containing folders tightly compressed, many thousands in all. The realization that these people, with few exceptions, had all died in concentration camps was a shock I shall never forget. [1985]

What I would like to leave in the reader's mind, without making a specific reference, is the contrast of the generous, even self-sacrificing, attitude of someone like [Swedish diplomat Raoul] Wallenberg, who sought to save as many people as possible, even if it meant disregarding regulations, or even Swedish laws, with the narrow-minded, bureaucratic approach of the American consular service, which sought to admit as few people as possible, presumably on orders emanating from Washington. In my concept of the poem, the focal point is the penultimate sentence: "We buried here one vital organ, hope."

Rachel Goldstein * "Prosciowiece, 1942," "There Is No Time," "Those Who Remain"

My writing is an attempt to capture the essence of my parent's stories and their impact on my life. Even though I did not live through the Holocaust, it has shaped my identity. My parents' wartime experiences weave their threads through my daily existence — even into the most ordinary times, like putting my daughter to bed or cooking a meal. My poetry is the resulting fabric. Once, when speaking to my mother about her youth, she claimed that she had had a "normal" childhood. "What about the War?" I asked, to which she replied, "Oh, except for that." Therefore, the title of my poetry manuscript is called "Except for That." Except for the war and its lasting effect on my perceptions, I too had a "normal" upbringing.

Louise Bogin wrote about the creative process: "In a time lacking in truth or certainty and filled with anguish . . . no one should be shamefaced in attempting to give back to the world through his or her work a portion of its lost heart." Responding through poetry is my attempt to do so. I believe that the making of art is an act of hopefulness. To remain human, one must be hopeful.

John Z. Guzlowski * "How Early Fall Came This Year," "Hunger in the Labor Camps," "Night in the Labor Camp," "What the War Taught My Mother"

My primary subject is the experience of my parents before, during, and after the Second World War. Both were taken into Nazi Germany as slave laborers. My father was captured in 1940 outside of Poznan, Poland. My mother was captured near her home west of Lwów, Poland, and transported in 1942. They worked in concentration camps and the associated factories and farms until the end of the war. Afterwards, they lived in refugee camps in Germany until 1951 when they came to the United States with their two children as Displaced Persons (DPs).

My poems give my parents and their experiences a voice. They had very little education. My father never went to school and could barely write his name. My mother had two years of formal education. I felt that I had to tell the stories they would have written if they could. For the last twenty-five years, I have been writing poems about their lives, and I sometimes think that I am not only writing about *their* lives, but also about the lives of all those forgotten — voiceless refugees, DPs, and survivors — that the last century produced. These are the sorts of poems that I write and that I have published in *Language of Mules.*

In terms of my treatment of their lives, I've tried to use language free of emotions. When my parents told me many of the stories that became my poems, they spoke in plain, straightforward language. They didn't try to emphasize the emotional aspect of their experience; rather, they told their stories in a matter-of-fact way. This happened, they'd say, and then this happened: *The soldier kicked her, and then he shot her, and we moved on to the next room.* I've also tried to make the poems story-like, strong in narrative drive, to convey the way they were first told to me. The title *Language of Mules* comes from something my father used to say about the Nazis, that they treated the slave laborers and concentration camp inmates as if they spoke the language of mules and not the language of people.

Leo Haber * "The Book of Lamentations," "Rachel at the Well," "Sanctification"
All poetry is profoundly personal. My father came to the Passover seder table in the spring of 1940 with joy on his face that I had not seen since Rosh Ha-Shanah. He happily waved the first letter that he had received from his beloved younger brother, a *shochet* and *dayan* in Radom, Poland. His brother, wife, and children, my unseen uncle, aunt, and cousins, had escaped the Nazi onslaught in the Soviet sector. "Now," my father exclaimed, "we can have a happy Peysach and a joyful *simcha* in two months." He was referring to my upcoming bar mitzvah. But that was the last time we heard from Uncle Layzer. After the war, my father spent years tracking down survivors from the area in the struggle to find out what happened to his family, all to no avail. After my father's passing, I continued the effort through Yad Vashem, the Red Cross, the Polish consulate, with similar fruitless results. When my wife, Sylvia, gave birth to our first child in 1952, she, according to tradition, chose the child's first name, but she asked me to choose a middle name. I told this to my father. He turned away, hiding his emotions, and said, "Name him Layzer."

These events are seared into my soul. Every Jew of that period, no matter where they were in the world, has a story. This is my story in the safety and glorious refuge of America.

Israel I. Halpern * "Being Seemingly Unscathed," "Love in a Death Camp"
My father had eleven brothers and sisters. Three (Dora, Hershel, and Leo) managed to escape and survive; I knew them and loved them. They told me of my Tante and her travails and martyrdom. Subsequently, my three sisters, Selma, Ruth and Shirley, all survivors, re-affirmed the details, as they are all older than me — Selma and Ruth were born in Vienna, Shirley in Amsterdam. I was in-utero when my mother and father and three sisters caught the last ship, the Pennland, out of Holland, in May of 1940. Hence, I was born in New York but conceived in Nazi-occupied Europe. Perhaps that makes me one of the youngest survivors of the Shoah. I don't know, to this day, what to make of this, so I rarely ever mention it. I want to add that the murders of six million Jews, and the concomitant slaughter of Gypsies, homosexuals, people of color, socialists, and the disabled, along with the stifling of dissident voices of people who opposed Fascist racism, remains an integral part of my mentation and daily sensibility. My impulse to write came from finding lost pencils and pens on the sidewalks and byways of my childhood and deciding that I would have to use these implements to etch whatever potential for texts they might contain, to say in writing whatever strikes me. The Holocaust strikes me.

Annette Bialik Harchik * "Earrings," "Requiem"
Auschwitz was an extermination camp in Poland where more than a million Jews were worked, beaten, starved, and gassed to death. And a whole industry was created around the disposal of the bodies. Although my mother physically survived the camps, mentally and emotionally, she never recovered from the trauma of her tortures and family losses. She was the only survivor of her family, which included two sisters, one brother, parents, grandparents, six aunts, seven uncles, and many cousins. For Franja Bialik, life lost all meaning after her arrival at Auschwitz, and she continued to be lost in her protective mental illness and isolation until age sixty-seven, when she died of diseases and conditions induced in the death camp.

Geoffrey Hartman * "Day of Remembrance," "In Memory of Paul Celan"
Paul Celan is impossible to take as a model for poetry that tries to cope with the Shoah. He subdued the more conventional lyrical élan that marked his early poems, fashioning a constricted, if powerful, style that no longer, or rarely, resembles the previous tradition of German lyricism. It is as if he were expressing the equivalent

in his poetry of the impulse of some survivors who did not wish to bring children into the kind of world the Holocaust had revealed. "The herod of waters" refers at once to Celan's suicide and the massacre of the innocents. How to emulate or at least honor Celan's poetry? Someone must travel his pages and be inspired by them — both by their attempt to keep writing in an eloquence tainted by an unspeakably cruel and inhuman event and by the poet's later ascetic and elliptical manner, which this epitaph suggests is akin to a self-maiming.

Leslie Woolf Hedley * "Chant for All the People on Earth"
"Chant" (now known as "The Holocaust Cantata") has had numerous lives. The Polish-American composer, Marta Ptaszynska, used it for full symphony orchestra conducted by Lord Yehudi Menuhin at the Schleswig-Holstein Festival and Sinfonia Varsovia in Warsaw. French composer, Depraz, used "Chant" for the French Radio TV Symphony Orchestra. It also was performed by the St. Paul Chamber Orchestra at the Macalester College Music Festival. The poem was read over BBC (London) and CBC (Canada). Yehudi Menuhin told me he hoped to conduct this work at the UN. Arab states stopped it.

Chaia Heller * "A Jew's Love for Language," "The Yiddish I Know"
I do not think there can ever be enough writing about the Holocaust. Each poem is a tiny stone placed on the missing grave of a child, mother, father, or cousin who lost their life simply by being born into the wrong time, place, and ethnicity. Poems serve not only to sustain the memory of lost peoples and cultures; they also serve as necessary reminders that racism and ethnocentrism are still very much alive and must always be actively and consciously transcended.

Michael Heller * "Bandelette de Torah," *from* **"Bialystok Stanzas"**
"Bandelette de Torah" is the result of an intersection, both physical and psychic, with the subject of the Holocaust. The poem's genesis began in Paris amidst the marvelous treasure trove of Eastern European artifacts housed in the Musée de Judaism on Rue du Temple in the Marais. The museum stands at the end of a line one can draw across the streets of the Marais to the primary school where, during the Occupation, as the plaque in front instructs, 138 Jewish school children were removed by the Nazis and the French gendarmes, put on transports and sent to Auschwitz. It is no longer possible to walk by a public school in Paris without seeing a similar plaque; since the early 90s, an organization, dedicated to memorializing these kidnappings, has placed such plaques on almost every school building in the city, each one noting that these acts were done "with the aid of the Paris Gendarmerie." This same line, inscribed for me across the conscience of Paris, on its way from museum to school also strikes tangentially the Jewish-European restaurant, Goldenberg's, where, on a pleasant sunny August afternoon in 1982, Abu Nidal's terrorists machine-gunned the outdoor tables, leaving six diners dead. The murder of children (and of all innocents), for which no explanation or justification on earth will suffice, for which no mourning can ever be enough, set me to writing this poem with its odd triangulations of Western thought. Some of its terminology comes from Gillian Rose's book, *Mourning Becomes the Law*, which addresses European history, including the Shoah, through the conflictive systems of Athens, the city of intense rationality; Jerusalem, the city of visionary religious fervor; a third, as yet unnamed, imaginary city of love; and the fourth "city," Auschwitz, a hell where arbitrary decisions of who shall live or be murdered prevail over any other systemization.

A similar intersection occurred in the writing of "Burnt Synagogue," a section of a poem I wrote in the early 1970s, "Bialystok Stanzas." There was a time in my life when I wanted to write an historical novel, and my father, a Bialystoker by birth, referred me to a book by his friend, David Sohn, *Bialystok: Photo Album of a Renowned City and Its Jews the World Over.* In fact, the book, with its movingly captured history, impelled me to write the poem. My intentions were to honor a way of life fiercely attacked in the pogroms at the beginning of the century and then totally destroyed and erased by the Nazis. In the book's "Yizkor Calendar" of annihilations, the first horrific act described is the burning alive of over two thousand Jews who had been locked in the main synagogue of the city, a vast wooden structure of delicate beauty and craftsmanship. The calendar and the before and after photographs of the synagogue led me into the poem. It is, like "Bandelette de Torah," a part of my hunger to articulate a vision beyond the resonances of the Holocaust, indelible as they are.

Stephen Herz * "Fried Noodles Topped with Raisins Cinnamon and Vanilla Cream," "In Your Lager Dream," "Jedwabne," "Marked," "Shot"
Writing poems on the Holocaust sometimes leaves me doubting my words. Are they sufficient? Can they speak history? Are they capable of awakening historical amnesia? Can they give us a clue, an answer, to the everpresent question: "Why?" Maybe the only answer can be found in the stark words spoken to Primo Levi by a guard at Auschwitz: "*Hier ist kein warum.* Here there is no *why.*"

Walter Hess * "Oma"
I grew up in a small farming village in the German Rhineland. Most of that growing up took place in my grandmother's house. "Krystallnacht," I saw my father taken off to Dachau. Soon after his return, my family left Oma's house for Ecuador; it was the summer of 1939; I was eight. That leaving, of a place and of people that I loved, has been present with me ever since. Of course, the consciousness of that presence did not appear till many years later. As a teenager growing up in New York's Washington Heights, in which lived a large colony of refugees with histories similar to mine, I heard the almost constant repetition of "Kaddish" and "El Mole Rachamin," prayers for those who had died in the camps. The Holocaust became very personal and painful. Probably, because of that pain, I needed, for a very long time, to distance myself from it. For many years, I could not, for instance, read anything about the Holocaust. Only when I began to write poetry, in the late seventies, did that begin to change. One of the early poems became "Oma."

William Heyen * "The Candle," "The Legend of the Shoah," "Riddle," "The Secret," "Simple Truths"
The danger is that Holocaust poetry may console, may give pleasure, may be beautiful despite its best intentions to portray/embody/condemn/remember. Even as it recedes from us, the Holocaust must quail the spirit, but poetry remains seductive, its whole tradition of formful song seeking to enlist us in the human dream of love/grace/redemption while, in Lawrence L. Langer's words, "the Holocaust still mocks the idea of civilization and thereafter our sense of ourselves as spiritual creatures" (*Admitting the Holocaust*, 1995). Looking at them now even long after I wrote them, I sense that my own Holocaust poems have in some ways betrayed me and my reader, that they often aspire to aria and enlightenment while, in Elie Wiesel's words, "Auschwitz signifies death — total death — of man and of mankind, of reason and of the heart, of language and of the senses. Auschwitz is the death of time, the end of creation; its mystery is doomed to stay whole, inviolate" (*A Jew Today*, 1978). So it must be, despite poetry, which refuses to acknowledge this truth, such refusal being at once our abiding hope, and fall.

Rick Hilles * "Amchu," "Yom HaShoah in Florida"
Both "Amchu" and "Yom HaShoah in Florida" (and other poems from the poetry collection, *Brother Salvage*) were inspired by stories told to me by Dr. Tadeusz (Tadzik/"Ted") Stabholz, my former pediatrician and now friend. Several personal revelations occurred to me in and around these poems: Firstly, in my mid-thirties, I learned that my mother's father's mother, Mary, was Jewish, making my grandfather Jewish by rabbinical law. I also learned (first through Ted and then from other sources) that the Nazis considered anyone who had a Jewish grandparent to be Jewish. The Holocaust (Ted's stories and those of countless others less fortunate) could have been my story, had circumstances been different. It is with this terrifying yet clarifying recognition that I've tended to Ted's stories, trying to make a home for them and, by extension, him, raising them as if they were my own. These poems, and my deepest gratitude for a most life-affirming friendship and many luminous conversations, which I hope are still to come, are for him.

I've spent many hours in the U.S. and in Poland researching Warsaw's Jewish and Polish Uprisings. In Poland, such research was not always encouraged and was often openly thwarted, particularly at the Archives at Auschwitz and at Warsaw's Institute for National Memory (one is far better off going instead to Warsaw's Jewish Historical Institute, where the archivists pursue answers to all questions with a kind of avenging spirit that can revive event the weariest of researchers). The archivists at Auschwitz, located in an old cell block at Auschwitz I, were helpful — up to a point — but it took me ten separate visits and a formal letter of introduction to be granted any real access to information. On the tenth visit, an archivist named Eva confessed that they feared I was a journalist and decided only to be of minimal help.

For those interested in reading more about Dr. Stabholz, I recommend his only book, *Siedem Pikiel* (*Seven Hells*), which was first written and published in a DP camp near Stuttgart in 1946. From this book, at least two people I know of have learned the fates of loved ones lost without a trace during that time, since he cites many, many names. *Siedem Pikiel* has since been translated into Hebrew, German, and English. In English, regrettably, the volume is now out of print.

I have tried to be as historically accurate as possible in these poems, while remaining faithful to the imaginative possibilities in language while writing them. There is one historical inaccuracy that I know of and have been unable to correct, and I will try to do so here. The prisoner race mentioned in "Yom HaShoah in Florida" — the one that Henio Grin won and, in so winning, unwittingly secured his death, actually took place at Treblinka (not Maidanek). Henio's sister, Fredzia Grin (who at the time was Ted's fiancé), was also lost at Treblinka, as was their friend, Natek Remba. Pinek, like Ted, managed to escape Treblinka and Maidanek, but he was murdered at Auschwitz-Birkenau. It seems important now to tell you this.

Edward Hirsch * "Paul Celan: A Grave and Mysterious Sentence"
I adore Paul Celan's "Fugue of Death" ["Todesfuge"], which may be the greatest Holocaust poem written. It stunned me the first time that I read it, and I've carried its music around in my head for years now. I wish I'd written "Black milk of daybreak, we drink you at nightfall." And the poem's structure is astonishing. Celan himself later renounced the poem for its "simplicity" and "clarity," its easiness. I suppose this is what first got me going on my poem. Celan seemed to me a great voice who was forever haunted and crippled by the experience of losing both of his parents in the death camps and being interned in a camp himself. After the war, he moved to Paris and began to write his first major poems. That's when my own poem takes place, in 1948, Paris. Celan was obsessed by language, by the difficulty (even

the impossibility) of writing poems after the Holocaust, by the fact that he wrote in German, a language he both loved and despised, a language infiltrated by history. That's partially why he began to write a poetry which questioned language itself — and which by necessity had to use that language. And that's also one of the reasons that he became such a modern and hermetic poet.

I wanted to write a poem about Celan and his experience. I wanted to help account for his distrust of language itself — and his later hermetic poems — and yet I still love some of his early, more accessible poems — poems which are influenced by surrealism and expressionism. I also wanted to pay homage to "Death Fugue." I didn't at first want my own poem to be written in Celan's voice, from his point of view. I tried lots of other possibilities, but the poem just didn't work out. It always seemed too cool. Finally, I just gave up and decided to write it from inside the speaking subject — to give it intensity. I had to set it at a time when Celan was still writing clear poems. I wanted the poem to be true to its moment (Paris '48), and also to account for what was going to happen to Celan and to his poetry. I certainly didn't want to use or exploit Celan in any way. I just wanted to write a poem that would speak about the experience from inside — from inside and outside of language, from inside and outside of history, from inside and outside of human life.

Jean Hollander * "The Chosen"

In regard to "The Chosen," the background story is that I was born in Vienna and was a little child when the Anschluss occurred, at which time my parents were imprisoned. My mother was released, but my father was sent to a concentration camp. She spent the next year going from one official to another in Vienna and Berlin to get him released. She was a very heroic woman who would not leave until she succeeded. But that is another story, which I never wrote about.

Thea Iberall * "Keeping the Ground"

In Prague, there are two Jewish cemeteries. The Old Jewish Cemetery of Prague was established during the 15th century and is the oldest existing Jewish cemetery in Europe, left by the Nazis because it was to become part of Hitler's Jewish museum. Expanding as much as it could through the purchase of additional land sites, it eventually filled up the small space between two synagogues in the Jewish ghetto. There are about a hundred thousand people buried in the cemetery, although many fewer gravestones because graves were layered — in some places, twelve deep. The most recent gravestone dates from 1787.

In contrast, the New Jewish Cemetery of Prague was opened in 1891 and is still in use today. It is on a hill in a more modern section of Prague. Near the entrance is a memorial to victims who died in the concentration camp or as fighters in the resistance movement. Prominent rabbis and scholars are buried there, including Chief Rabbi of Prague, Ezekiel Landau. The great Czech writer, Franz Kafka, is also buried there. A tall hexagonal stone marks the site. Tourists to the cemetery go to the famous names, but I tried to be open to other aspects of it. I was struck by how time was vertical in the old cemetery and horizontal in the new one. The individuals named in the poem are ordinary people, many of whom were women (as is obvious from their names: a married Czech woman adds 'ova' to her husband's surname). It was in looking for the unfamous that I stumbled across the area of the cemetery mentioned in the poem.

Concerning why I write about the Holocaust: Something early I remember is my mother telling me we could not buy any product made in Germany. Even as a child, I prided myself as being open and accepting, so I tried to learn everything I could that might help me understand why she felt so strongly about this. The deaths of my great-grandparents in the Holocaust were far removed from me. I studied German, I read books on WW II and post-war Europe, and in 11th grade, I went to Germany with my German Club. I saw impressive churches, enormous cathedrals. In subsequent years, I went back to Europe. One year, I went to Dubrovnik and searched up and down the winding streets of the Old Town until I found the one remaining synagogue. In the Athens Jewish Museum, they display the synagogue from Patras. In Prague and in Kraków, the synagogues are museums. After forty years of trying to grasp what happened, I am left with anger, seeing this evidence of how close a group of people came to destroying my race. It is in this anger that I write my Holocaust poems.

Judith Irwin * "1985 — In a Small American Town"
"1985 — In a Small American Town" is a poem written after thirty years of marriage to a man who, as an American MP, witnessed the open graves and has been so deeply wounded by what he felt that it has been like a bottomless grave in his life. I do not mean to say he would express his feelings this way. I mean, rather, that as his wife, I have come to understand that the photos he carries in his wallet and his sometimes sleeplessness relate to experiences I have not been able to share.

When I first met him, my husband would have nothing to do with American women. He said that we were too shallow, thinking of nylons and dances, of cottages and flawless children. Fortunately, having myself been raised on a farm and living through the Depression, I could at least empathize with the painful experiences he related to me from those days of the Holocaust and of European cities all but decimated. Yet, I realize, there is much I cannot share with him — or, perhaps, he cannot share with me. There is a residual pain like slow death. I am writing this poem from the point of view of a wife who realizes that pain and feels helpless. [1985]

Dan Jaffe * "In a Holocaust Memorial Garden"
Can any sensitive person learn about the Holocaust without shuddering, without asking questions about God and man, about evil and conscience? I believe such questioning inevitably affects whatever poems we write. I suspect that fine work that follows from the awareness of the terrors of history, especially from the Holocaust, may not refer explicitly to the source of the work's feelings and insights. Often I have written poems out of my sorrow and revulsion, out of my sense of loss and love for those who have suffered and are vulnerable. At times, only afterwards did I realize that the Holocaust was continuously present. One's awareness of the Holocaust can transform all experience. That includes how one responds to poems written prior to World War II. It includes our reactions to writing about other situations and other people. Poems have a way of absorbing the wisdom of the world. Take Robert Frost's "Fire and Ice." Think about it deeply and it becomes a Holocaust poem.

Katherine Janowitz * "The Third Generation"
In the years since writing the poem, all my beloved survivors have passed away. I find it hard to be optimistic about the future but I try, now that there's a fourth generation, two small grandsons.

Sheila Golburgh Johnson * "Shoes"
I hesitate to write poetry or prose about the Holocaust because so much has been written on the subject that words seem to become clichés as soon as they appear on the page. When I visited the United States Holocaust Memorial Museum in

Washington D.C., I found myself numbed by the photographs, the stories, even by the personal identification card I took home that tells the short life of an eighteen year old boy, Moshe Finkler, who lived in The Hague during the Holocaust. The card faces me now as I write this, with Moshe's vulnerable dark eyes staring out from the picture. I raise walls around my heart to spare myself further pain when confronted by this overwhelming event.

The stack of shoes, placed near the end of the walk through the museum, was different. With the humble tenacity of inanimate objects, they had survived. As I stared at the shoes, at their different shapes and sizes and purposes, I had a vision of the people who had worn them; ordinary people going about their varied activities and then cut off, annihilated, exterminated, all aspirations and hopes snuffed. The shoes cracked that wall around my heart and their image kept recurring for a couple of years. The poem allows me some peace.

Laurence Josephs * "Passover at Auschwitz"
I came to write "Passover at Auschwitz" when I read that the people detained in such places did not really have anything like calendars to keep them abreast of days, months, years, and holidays of the religious year. Since for us calendars are so important in the joy of planning holidays like Pesach, to which we look forward with such anticipation, I began to think how terrible it must have been for them not even to know — in addition to all the other horrors of their life — what month or year they were suffering through, and that even *that* had been wrenched away from them. Somewhere, too, I felt the extreme irony and bitterness of the fact that this place had become their Egypt and that they were all suddenly and cruelly the "firstborn" who were terribly in danger.

Marilyn Kallet * "After a While, at Theresienstadt," "Mezuzah," "To My Poem of Hope," "Survivor"
After my mother died in 1997, I found a picture of two Schwarz brothers, with a caption: "The Nazis got the rest." My mother had never spoken about this. I canvassed my relatives and found one cousin who knew the town where the Schwarzes had lived. I went to the Holocaust Museum with only this bit of information, thinking that they would never be able to help me. A German Jewish volunteer, Peter Lande, took me by the hand and showed me on a map the little town on the Neckar River. And he directed me to a microfilm of thousands of file cards. The Nazis had required that German Jews register in 1939. He told me it might take a very long time to find my family, as the files were not alphabetized, but within a few minutes, I found them all living together in a few houses. I recognized most of the first names, as these names are still in use in my family. This follows the Jewish tradition of naming our children after the deceased.

In March 2004, I went to Horb/Rexingen with my daughter, Heather, my sister, and her daughter. We were aided by an elderly German in Horb, Herr Sayer. He knew my family. He introduced us to others who gave us documents and family trees. I learned about Hedwig Schwarz, who survived deportation, even though she was crippled. Heroic and amazing stories, with Righteous individuals who hid Hedwig and who later cared for her. She was buried in the old Jewish cemetery in Rexingen in 1952. I'm happy to say that I have also found living relatives, one who survived Riga and one who escaped from Germany. I wrote up my research as poems for my book, *Circe, After Hours*, which was published by BkMk Press in 2005. In July, 2006, the next phase of my research took me to Riga, where I said Kaddish for those who were killed there. The survivors gave me lists of names. They won't go back there. Why should they?

Rodger Kamenetz * "My Holocaust"
I wrote "My Holocaust" as a response to two events: the opening of the Holocaust Museum in Washington D.C. and the screening of the film *Schindler's List*. Though I've written a great deal of Jewish material, I never felt comfortable writing about an experience that others were more immediately witness to, such as Primo Levi and Paul Celan. However, I found I could write about how the Holocaust was 'mediated' and my response to that mediation and what it means for the "future" of the Holocaust. In that sense, my poem is both a response and an enactment.

Peretz Kaminsky * "Bramble," "Identifications"
Raised as a Yiddishist/atheist in a house where poets and poetry were tabletalk and table presences, that I became a poet is hardly a surprise (I am the son of a poet and the father of a poet). After the early forties, anyone writing in Yiddish, who had any knowledge of Jewish history — and who was dedicated to Jewish survival — had no choice but to look at the Holocaust and deal with it in some way. My movement away from earlier concerns was gradual.

The instruction contained in the Pesakh ritual — to teach our children about the slavery in Egypt, *as if we ourselves had been there* — can be taken to mean that we are also seeing ourselves as present at every event in our past. Jewish history becomes personal Jewish memory. The Holocaust, in addition to being the largest moral question in our history, and in the history of the world, is one of the many events in which I participate in my life as a Jew. It is for this exact reason that most of my writing is in the first person. I also intend for the readers of these poems of mine to see *themselves* when they read the "I" of the poems — that the self I intend for myself is also to become the self of the reader within the moment of reading.

Rosa Felsenburg Kaplan * "Kol Nidre"
The first part of the poem refers to the following events: One way of leaving Austria in 1938 was to get a visa to Luxembourg and cross the border from there to France where Jews were permitted to remain — provided they did not work, live in Paris, or retain their nationality. Since it was difficult to go through this maneuver with five children, our parents sent us to relatives in Hungary and Czechoslovakia on the passport of people whose children's ages and genders corresponded to ours. Once our parents were settled in Chelles, they located other people who brought us to France. To do so required much ingenuity and luck on the part of our parents and inordinate courage and commitment on the part of the people who did the supporting. For instance, Mrs. Shmuel (Mulo) Cohen, a French woman in her early thirties, transported five children from different families, none of whom spoke French, across Czechoslovak, Hungarian, German, and French borders. Mrs. Cohen is still alive, though she lost her husband, who fought in the French Underground. I do not know what happened to the people who transported me and my cousin Rosa.

Although I considered myself rather sheltered among Holocaust survivors, I found myself having to come to grips with my losses and the unfinished business. It is these areas, rather than so-called "survivor's guilt," which I wished to address in my poem — which started on the way home from a Kol Nidre service. I puzzled why it was that Jews, who have good mechanisms for dealing with guilt, still felt so guilty and concluded that as incest survivors or abused children [often] blame themselves for their victimization, so do we. Our victimization, generation after generation, has been the losses — the unfinished business — which make it necessary to recite *Kol Nidre* three times.

I am currently a clinical specialist in mental health and substance abuse. Some of my recent experiences at work make me aware of the fact that with all the disruptions in my early life, I have been relatively sheltered: I have never been in a situation where the people who were to raise me, teach me, nurture me, were people who abused or exploited me. My Holocaust experiences also taught me that if anybody is not treated decently, nobody is safe. [1985]

Dori Katz * "Line-Up," "My Face Before," "The Return"
"Line-Up" was inspired by the last, unfinished, film by Andrzej Munk, *The Passenger* [*Pasazerka*, 1963]. It concerns a former German concentration camp guard who is honeymooning with her new husband years later on a cruise ship and recognizes a former inmate among the passengers. The film is her "false" recollections of her experience as a guard in the camp, i.e., the story she feels forced to tell her husband.

"The Return": The tattooed number was my father's actual number. In an earlier draft, I had invented a number, but when I found out what his actual number had been, I decided to use it and changed the line. I learned as a child that my father had had a leg amputated in Auschwitz; I always pictured him with one leg after that.

Eliot Katz * *from* **"Liberation Recalled"**
"Liberation Recalled," composed from 1994–97, is a long poem written in alternating sections that shift between my mother's testimony about her experiences in World War II concentration camps — where her parents and five brothers and sisters were killed — and my own stylistically varied verses on a range of historical and contemporary themes. Employing elements of modernist experimentation, the poem, through its juxtapositions, attempts to explore questions of historical and intergenerational legacy, psychic reconstruction, political-literary theory, and the challenge of building a more humane future. My mother's account, originally recorded on tape in one long interview, is transcribed in somewhat flexible ten-syllable lines — alluding, in my own mind at least, to the narrative style of "Paradise Lost" — in an attempt to add a formal layer of timelessness to her story. The poem was written at a time when I'd been studying the modernist long-poem tradition, including Muriel Rukeyser's "Book of the Dead," William Carlos Williams's "Spring and All," Langston Hughes's "Montage of a Dream Deferred," H.D.'s "The Walls Do Not Fall," Ezra Pound's *Cantos*, Pablo Neruda's *Canto General*, and, of course, Charles Reznikoff's *Holocaust* — as well as re-reading longtime influences, Walt Whitman's "Song of Myself" and Allen Ginsberg's "Howl" and "Kaddish." The juxtaposition of forms and themes (and their exploration of historical and intergenerational legacy) was part of my original concept for the poem, as well as one of the things that I hoped would make the poem a bit new and different as Holocaust-related poetry.

Alan Kaufman * "My Mother Doesn't Know Who Allen Ginsberg Is," "Who Are We?"
In my estimation, the methodical destruction of European Jewry by Germany — a modern industrialized Western nation — constitutes the single most significant event in human history, one whose impact will continue to be felt for centuries to come. As the son of a survivor, I have seen firsthand its effects not only upon my mother, Marie, but upon the entire world: its politics and culture, its visions and values. And I have seen its effects on me. It has influenced not only every choice I have made in my personal and professional life but also my very perception of the most ordinary things. I cannot shower without thinking about it. I cannot turn

on a lamp without referencing its horrors. I cannot wait on a queue in a restaurant or supermarket without a subtle sense of panic that the melting line brings me ever closer to it. It hides in my very skin, an invisible tattoo deep beneath the real tattoos that I wear. It is in the food I eat, a memory of homicidal deprivation. The very clothing that I wear — a trace of killing cold.

It will always, forever, be in fire.
The gas jet on a stove.
The oven.

Tsipi Keller * "The Shower"
My parents were Holocaust survivors (Czechoslovakia) and, unlike many other survivors, spoke about their experiences. My father, especially, encouraged me to read about the Holocaust and, over the years, I've read the books and watched the documentaries. "The Shower" was written after I watched actual footage of female inmates taking a shower after the liberation of Bergen-Belsen.

Steve Klepetar * "Burial," "The Spells of Earth"
My father was driven from his home and profession by the Nazis in 1939; my mother was incarcerated at Terezín, Auschwitz, and the labor camp at Oederon; three of my grandparents perished at Auschwitz. I grew up marked by the Holocaust and the refugee experience. While the Holocaust was not a forbidden topic in my parents' home, it was rarely discussed, and not in any detail. My interests in literature and writing did not connect with this crucial part of my family background until I was in my early forties, and a friend remarked that my poems were infused with violence and loss. "You are writing about the Holocaust, you know," she said, "without mentioning the word. You need to start naming it." I reread the work she referred to and discovered she was right. From that point on, I began trying to write directly about the Holocaust.

I began with poems connected to the stories my parents had told me, and I asked my mother for more detail. She began writing letters, and from those I pieced their story together, and tried to write poems in response. I think my work began as documentary and has become more lyrical over the past few years. The poems try to honor my parents and grandparents, to witness and acknowledge their suffering and courage, and to express my sorrow and loss, and also my deep personal connection with the fate of all the victims.

Irena Klepfisz * *from* "*Bashert*"; "Solitary Acts"
Since the age of twenty-one, I have been writing poetry in which the Holocaust is a recurrent theme. Because I'm a child survivor, my early writing was experiential and very private. Later, I began consciously exploring larger implications. Fearing I might become trapped in the past, I sought connections between the Holocaust of the Jews and the experiences of other groups who lack political power and privilege — women, working-class, Third World, gay. Increasingly, I found that an understanding of the Holocaust broadened my understanding of present political situations and conflicts and of genocides since 1945. These concerns as well as a very strong feminist perspective are, I believe, reflected in my poems "*Bashert*" and "Solitary Acts." So that is one direction of my writing in relation to the Holocaust.

Ruth Kluger * "Halloween and a Ghost"
"Halloween and a Ghost" is a poem about a survivor of the Holocaust whose teenage brother was murdered by the Nazis. She identifies her own children and those who come trick-or-treating with the lost child. In a way, it's an attempt at exorcism, but an exorcism that doesn't in the end succeed. And yet there is some irrational comfort in the poetic act itself, and this is what I was searching for. I wrote this poem more than forty years ago.

Yala Korwin * "The Little Boy with His Hands Up," "Noemi," "Passover Night 1942," "You, Who Did Not Survive"
I am one of the few who were lucky to escape the hell of the camps. I survived not because I was smarter or stronger than others but because of my "Aryan" appearance. It was easier for some righteous gentiles to save me, rather than my dark-eyed sister. Remembering hurts, but I cling to it. It is my way of keeping alive those I was unable to help: parents, sister, friends, neighbors, strangers. My sacred duty is to preserve and transmit these memories as lessons about human nature. The most palatable way is through art.

I wrote "Passover Night, 1942" years ago, as an assignment for a poetry workshop I attended at that time. It was spring, Passover was around the corner, and the group was told to write about this holiday. Being a Holocaust survivor, my thoughts went back to a time when there was hunger and fear.

In regard to "The Little Boy with His Hands Up": When I saw, for the first time, probably in 1956, the photo showing a group of women and children, and an SS man holding a gun directed at the frightened little boy who, hands up, is standing in the foreground, I was deeply touched. I remember my feeling of extreme tenderness toward him. A Holocaust survivor, I was then a young mother of two youngsters, struggling with the dilemma of how to answer their questions without lying, but trying hard not to upset their childhood innocence. In the little boy's face, I saw what I wanted to protect my children from: the premature loss of innocence. It took many years before I was ready to write this poem. The boy was still alive when the photo was taken. Speaking to him directly was my way of rescuing him.

Norbert Krapf * "*Tannenbaum*, 1940," "The Name on the Wall," "A Freight Yard in Würzburg," "Meditation in the Israelite Cemetery, Würzburg"
It was very moving that, five years after *Blue-Eyed Grass* appeared [in 1997], the family of Klara Krapf, the Jewish Krapfs from my ancestral region, found me and the Klara Krapf poems through my website. We have exchanged many messages and all the information I gathered, with the help of Catholic German researchers who study the history of the Jews of Lower Franconia. Deborah Lipman Cochelin, a Klara descendant from Charleston, South Carolina, who lives in Seattle, visited with me and my wife in New York in 2003, and we visited her in Seattle in 2005 and 2006. So the poem "Letter to the Brothers and Sisters of Klara Krapf from Wonfurt," which asks that any readers who are relatives of Klara please contact me, did indeed receive the reply I was hoping for. As a result, the Jewish Krapfs and I have been able to ask and answer many questions together.

I talk about the importance of Klara Krapf, the poems I wrote about her, and the significance of the Holocaust as a subject for my poems, in the essay "The Complications in Making an American Book of Poems about Germany," which Winfried Fluck and Werner Sollors included in their anthology *German? American? Literature?* [2002] and which I have reproduced on the "Prose" page of my website [www.krapfpoetry.com]. I hope it is clear to the reader of *Blue-Eyed Grass* that in these poems I try to speak to Klara Krapf, communicate with her, and approach her as closely as is humanly possible. There is no way I could begin to speak *for* her or her family.

"The Name on the Wall," which describes my discovery of Klara and her fate, "A Freight Yard in Würzburg," and "Meditation in the Israelite Cemetery, Würzburg" are the only three of the dozen Klara poems set in Würzburg. When she was deported, Klara lived in a Jewish nursing home in that city, the capital of the region (Lower Franconia / Unterfranken). I went to that nursing home in 1992 with German historian and journalist, Roland Flade, who also took me to the train station and introduced me to the rabbi. This 1992 trip was the same one that my family and I took to Klara's hometown of Wonfurt and to Theresienstadt/Terezín in what is now the Czech Republic. Later, after *Blue-Eyed Grass* appeared in 1997, I was invited to give a reading of my poems in English at the Würzburg City Archives, with the understanding that I would introduce the poems in German and a couple residing in the city would read them first in German. The day before, there was a press conference in the Jewish Archives. David Schuster, president of the Jewish congregation of Würzburg and Lower Franconia, spoke movingly and produced the deportation list which included the name of Klara. He died not long after that.

"*Tannenbaum*, 1940" was inspired by photos in an exhibit, "The Fate of the Erlangen Jews in the Nazi Period," in the Erlangen City Museum when we were living there in 1988–89.

Carolyn Kreiter-Foronda * "Leaving a Country Behind"

There's a certain amount of truth to the assumption that many German descendants carry with them a collective guilt for the crimes their forefathers committed during World War II. There is also truth to the fact that countless Germans living today are so attached to this guilt that they willingly support whatever efforts they can to prevent similar abominations from occurring. In fact, some of these individuals through documentaries or docudramas have admirably educated Americans about the brutal realities of Hitler's concentration camps. Others on a small, though equally important, scale have educated American youngsters about the atrocities of World War II. As a teacher, I belong to this latter group. Interestingly enough, I have gone so far as to take my students to Dachau so they could catch a glimmer of truth about a war that stripped humans of their dignity. I have also spent hours in the classroom familiarizing students with the poems of such caring poets as William Heyen, a German-American who shares his own history of the Holocaust in the moving *The Swastika Poems* [later incorporated into Heyen's *Erika: Poems of the Holocaust*]. And I have written about a personal attempt to leave this collective guilt behind in "Leaving a Country Behind."

I had just returned from Dachau when the initial strains of "Leaving a Country Behind" began playing in my head. Having visited the concentration camp with a close Jewish friend had emphasized the reality of my German heritage and my inability to ignore these roots while confronting the horrors of Dachau. Once back in America, I came face to face in a recurring dream with an overwhelming sense of collective guilt. This dream initiated the first two segments of the poem. What I hoped to recreate with words was the fragmented nature of this haunting nightmare: the illusive image of my father on a flight home from Munich staring into darkness, his aunt coming into view out of memory, "cupping" fresh flowers, perhaps the last bouquet she'd hold before she lost touch with reality. The second segment provides a glimpse into her past and how her own sense of collective guilt led her eventually to lock herself in an attic "to sketch" the mad giant, Hitler. Flowing out of this image is a vision of my great aunt's funeral, a choirboy, innocent and seemingly unaware of history, singing "as if the past were but a moment he could bury with the dead."

As a young girl, I remember my father telling me I should be proud of my German heritage. I *was* until the day a friend accused me of being kin to Hitler. I can still see her tiny lips pursed as she spoke: *Anyone with a German name like Kreiter must be kin to him!*

Maxine Kumin * "The Amsterdam Poem"
"The Amsterdam Poem" is essentially a travelogue that focuses on how the citizenry survived or died in World War II. Anne Frank's story is of course an important part of that. On a personal level, the Holocaust is meaningful to me because I was in my early teens when news of the concentration camps began filtering into the safe suburb of Philadelphia where I lived. As I watched my father weep over letters from Poland, presumably from unknown cousins begging him for sponsorship, I grew up, seemingly, overnight.

Christine Lahey * "Dan's Shoe Repair: 1959"
Dan was our local shoe repairman in a suburb of Detroit where I was raised. As a child, I was fascinated by him, all the more because it was known that he "had been in the camps during the war." The *Life* photos mentioned in the poem I actually saw at home at an earlier age — I still have a mental photo of the one showing hundreds of bodies lying in a pit, twisted, torn beyond recognition. The ghastly horror I felt then (at seven? eight?) is forever impressed in my memory. So, seeing the photo, meeting Dan often (his shop was only about a block and a half from my house) as a local phenomenon, a "witness" to the horrors contained in that *Life* photo, plus my sensibility as a child whose father had passed away when I was just short of two years old, all this years later — in 1979, to be exact — came together in the poem. I should add that early in '79, the image of Dan would come to my mind again and again — the figure from my childhood started to haunt me, and the poem "wrote itself."

Alyssa A. Lappen * "How It Happened," "This, My Incarnation"
Masha Henley came to the U.S. as a refugee from Europe in 1947. She met my mother in a Hadassah meeting in New Haven, Conneticut in 1948, and they remained lifelong friends.

Masha lost her son and husband, in-laws, parents and siblings in the Holocaust. She remarried twice in the states. Her second husband died suddenly of a heart attack. Her third, she divorced after he had used, and betrayed, her. She had no more children; she feared recalling the instant her son's head was crushed against a tree, before her eyes.

The date of my December birthday was also hers. All my life, she called me "her kid." Though I had, and have, a mother, Masha frequently said she had "adopted" me. She also instilled in me the syndrome typical of children of Holocaust survivors.

In New Haven, I regularly visited Masha. In the mid-sixties, she moved to California; I made several trips especially to see her. Other than an interviewer who taped her oral history, I was the only person to whom she showed the transcript, which has since remained in a Holocaust archive, under seal.

I made my last special visit, at some personal sacrifice, in 2000. Masha was quite ill and seemed never again likely to come east, which in fact she never did.

According to Masha's camp sister, also from Vilna, my 2000 visit was a huge mitzvah. Masha had lost many of her Holocaust survivor friends, and her bitterness had alienated her from many younger friends. I spoke to her regularly by phone, each time for an hour or more.

In fact, I am an orphan soul only figuratively. Yet my family never understood Masha's and my close connection. She was a second mother to me, and left some imprints as important as those of my own mother. Our last visit was sad, but wonderful. I had grown up. Masha, now seeing me as an adult, was comfortable sharing with me still more, heretofore altogether secret, details — and the one remaining photograph of her murdered infant son.

Masha died in January 2003 in Los Angeles, California.

Alan Lupack * "Auschwitz Reportaż"
"Auschwitz Reportaż" was written after a trip to Auschwitz. The aura of the place seems tangible and creates both a physical and an emotional effect. It is as if the past — the voices of the victims, the cruelty of the guards — lingers. For someone like my wife, who lost relatives in the Holocaust, that emotion is overwhelming.

Yaacov Luria * "There Is One Synagogue Extant in Kiev"
I never write about the Holocaust itself. I feel that this is the province of survivors, their closest kin, and Holocaust scholars. They have the terrible obligation to bear witness and to record. Nevertheless, I live with the awareness that I escaped the Nazi murderers only because my grandparents brought their families to the United States at a time when immigration was relatively easy. I become emotional when the lifting of a sleeve reveals a number tattooed on a forearm.

One morning shortly after the Yom Kippur War [Fall 1973], I sit with a handful of old Jews in the courtyard of the only synagogue left in Kiev. When I ask how to get to Babi Yar, a woman shows me the palm of her hand. "*Dort iz gornit zu sehen* — there's nothing to see there. It's flat as this hand. Disappeared." How can I avoid expressing this sadness? [1985]

Arlene Maass * "Opa the Watchmaker"
Eichmann was on trial in Jerusalem when I was in third grade at a Catholic school. The only image I had of Jerusalem was from a little "holy land" prayer card from my grandma. The picture of the Mount of Olives contained a mustard seed illustrative of Jesus's explanation that faith even the size of the tiny mustard seed was capable of growing into a large tree where birds could nest. Because of my youth, I was inarticulate, so it was more by intuition that I sensed the incongruity. Of all people, it was Jesus's kin who were so barbarously tortured. I asked a priest why/how God would allow this and, of course, he could not answer my question.

In my early teens, I lost my mustard seed of faith, lost faith both in my creator and in other created beings, but not in the creative process. My art was all I had: I was more comfortable with poetry than with theology and people. Yet the problem of evil — an intrinsically theological and people question — continued to haunt me and inform much of my writing. It's a long story how I came to finally put my trust in the suffering servant, Jesus, depicted so starkly in numerous Chagall paintings (I too was longing and searching for redemption). But nearly thirty years after that move of faith, human suffering remains a central theme in much of my poetry.

What I say may be offensive. But I'm not convinced that the possibility of "total depravity" in humans has been adequately explored and considered. There's a collaborative side to us that too easily succumbs to evil, loses faith, seeks its own self, and looks the other way. With fast and furious technology, the redefining of life and death that stretches the bounds in an already nightmarish world, it is not incomprehensible to imagine where our technical prowess and progress could take us. Writing about the Holocaust is both a memorial to the dead and a reminder that the task of moral responsibility and spiritual accountability is ours and ours alone as long as we have our being. [1985]

Channah Magori * *from* **"Holocaust Archives I" & "Holocaust Archives II"**
My manuscript-in-progress, *Holocaust Archives*, is a collection of second-generation Holocaust Poetry. Asked why I choose to write about the Holocaust, my answer can only be that in so far as the Holocaust chose my grandparents for extermination and my parents for torture and suffering, so, too, it chooses me to give testimony to the toxicity and post-traumatic terror inflicted on the following generations. We are all tattooed. It is that invisible but indelible ink that lies under my skin and over my heart that I draw out, to write these Holocaust archives.

Sandra Cohen Margulius * **"Aunt Betty"**
When I married in mid-August of 1971, I became part of a family of Survivors. As a Jew, I'd always felt a connection and curiosity about the Holocaust, but had no idea of the difference being part of a family who had actually lived through the experience would mean to me. Stories of death and work camps, torture, hunger, sacrifice, murder, and rape, now became personal, as I slowly learned some of the history of this family. Yet, they rarely wanted to discuss it. It was their special secret.

The poem "Aunt Betty," was written as a personal tribute to my husband's Aunt Betty who survived Auschwitz and later moved to Milwaukee to join her younger brother (my father-in-law) and sister, the only other survivors of what had been a large family. As a poet and Jew, I feel an obligation not to ever let the stories of these incredibly strong and proud people be forgotten. Their survival, and the survival of their histories, serves as a daily reminder that life is truly a precious gift.

David McKain * **"For the Children"**
As a small boy during World War II, I went to the movies on Saturday afternoons to watch Hopalong Cassidy, Woody Woodpecker, the "Adventures of Brick Bradford" (a serial), and the weekly horrors of the cattle cars, the barbed wire, the zebra-shirted men with sunken eyes, the gas chambers, and the human skeletons staked for burning outside the ovens. When this particular section of the newsreel came on, the announcer lowered his voice dramatically and the violins played in a discordant minor key. I must admit that the first few times I saw these newsreels, I thought they were part of the afternoon show. My mother told me otherwise, appalled that I did not make distinctions between the Pathfinder News and the "Adventures of Brick Bradford." When I finally realized what was going on, I believe the shock of the concentration camps hit me harder than it would have if I had understood from the beginning.

Sixty years later, I have not forgotten my own culpability and ignorance as I sat eating popcorn and watching the Pathfinder newsreels during Saturday matinees. Randomly now, when I least expect it, I see a pile of starved and naked children — on the street or in a restaurant — but the scene is no longer on film; it is part of my own past, my own memory, and I feel at once horror and responsibility. That is why I write about the Holocaust: to remind children now and tomorrow that we must never forget and that we must participate in the process of justice and punishment. That is why, in particular, I wrote "For the Children." [1985]

Robert Mezey * "Terezín"
The Shoah is a nearly impossible subject for a poem and, though I have read a good many attempts, the only one that seems to me wholly successful is Paul Celan's haunting round ["Todesfuge"]. The only possible way into such a poem, for me, was to focus on one person, in this case a young girl whose water-color I found in a book about the art of the children held in Theresienstadt. I suppose my poem is a kind of synechdoche, in which Nely Silvinová must bear the burden not only of her own suffering but of representing six million Jews.

Richard Michelson * "The Jews That We Are," *from* **"Recital"**
In 1949, my mother was given a family chart that diagrammed five generations of her relatives and detailed, with asterisks, those among generations three, four, and five, who had their lives unbearably stolen. I was born in 1953, and throughout the 60s, I spent an innumerable amount of time studying that chart: *We have 1119 members in our family. Those killed by the Nazis are marked with a *. Those who died otherwise in the war are marked **. The Nazis murdered 177, not counting children whose names we do not have.*

Why do I write poetry about the Holocaust? Yes, to me too it sounds sacrilegious. I cannot help but feel a certain pleasure as I manipulate language and form. I am often ashamed of my own vanities. Poetry, as Michael Wyschogrod has said, "*takes the sting out of suffering. . . . Any attempt to transform the Holocaust into art demeans the Holocaust and therefore results in poor art.*" I agree with those who take that point of view. And yet isn't silence the greater of two evils? If the imagination, which has many times confronted individual death, and in the best of cases transformed it into a beacon for those of us still alive; if the imagination must turn its eyes when confronted with meaninglessness and mass suffering; do we not, then, give Hitler his final victory? The physical act of putting words to paper is based on my belief in the importance of human perception. The systematic destruction of the Jews was based on the assumption of men and women's uselessness. If our poets, whose job it has traditionally been to unmask truths, will despair of their vision, how can we hope to avoid the advancing danger of a nuclear holocaust in today's world?

I'm surprised to notice that the two poems of mine included in this anthology were written twenty years apart, and yet the "themes" are not dissimilar: How can love flourish in a world such as ours? and What sustenance can be found in the making of art? The seeds for "Recital" were planted while watching my daughter perform at a Jewish nursing home, one of the "good deeds" undertaken prior to her bat mitzvah. The contrast of her belief in life's sweet possibilities with the terrors endured by some of those in attendance, all set against the backdrop of the first Gulf War, made me question how I could continue to pursue my own self-interested daily artistic agenda. And, paradoxically, the best way I know to explore such questions of poetry's ineffectuality in the face of genocide is within the poem.

In the end, the question, for me, is better phrased as: How can I *not* write about the Holocaust? How else can I hope to understand this world? All poets, if faithful to our time, must wrestle with what we now know of human capability. I submit that all poems written in the past fifty years are, implicitly or explicitly, by necessity, poems about the Holocaust.

Bernard S. Mikofsky * "Mame-Loshen, Yiddish," "1945"
We grieve for the millions lost in our holocaust and in, say, the Cambodian and Armenian holocausts. But whenever I look at the few precious photos we have of

my saintly, scholarly uncle, Zalman Moshe Mikowski, his dear wife, and my cousin Bernard and his two sisters (they were married and had children), the Holocaust becomes searingly personal. Bernard was in the Polish army and was killed during the opening weeks in which Nazi Germany cut its bloody swath through Poland. The others were murdered in the concentration camps.

Aaron Miller * "Not Dachau"
I was serving in Germany in 1961 with the U.S. Information Service. In the Interest of doing my work with a measure of equanimity, I had avoided visiting places like Dachau. But in the summer of 1961, on a fine Sunday afternoon, with nothing else to do, and with orders to head for East Africa on my desk, I decided to drive out from Munich. The camp and park were swarming with sightseers of all nationalities — French, German, Swedes, Americans, Hungarians, et. al. And what struck me very forcibly was that all of them seemed to be on the outside looking in, personally detached from what they were seeing, whereas I was experiencing my own humanity. I mean, at the ovens, I saw myself at both ends of the shuttle. The Nazis had merely been the personification, the incarnation, of the darkness in all of us. At that point, my ethnic identity disappeared; indeed, all of my personae were gone, stripped away to reveal the naked victim, naked killer.

Marilyn Mohr * "Tsena Tsena," "Yiddish"
I often write about the Holocaust because of my grief, my sense of loss, and my horror at the immense cruelty inflicted on my people. I write to remind the world that it failed. I write to release the pain. Along with my twin sister, I was born in 1944 to an immigrant family from Poland. Most of the family in Poland was lost in the Holocaust; the one uncle who emigrated to Paris suffered the same fate. I write because I am proud to be a Jew, inextricably bound to my history and my people.

David Moolten * "Photograph of Liberated Prisoner, Dachau, 1945," "Yellow Star"
I write poems about the Holocaust because of my heritage, because it is a sacred topic, and because not to address it is, at least for me, a form of forgetting, if not denial. I write poems about the Holocaust because there is denial and because I believe the best way to refute it is to write the truth, which lives deeper in the soul than facts or dates, because the Holocaust must be felt for understanding to even begin. I write poems about the Holocaust because there are stories that haven't been told or that must be told again to new listeners. I write them because Theodor Adorno was wrong; poetry is not barbaric after Auschwitz because, to paraphrase a line from one poem, there is no *after*.

Sarah Traister Moskovitz * "December," "The Dress," "The Teaspoon," "At the United States Holocaust Memorial Museum"
I am the daughter of Polish Jewish Yiddish-speaking immigrants who arrived in America in the 1920s. I am the niece of aunts and uncles and the cousin of those left behind who were killed in Warsaw, Biala Podlaska, Treblinka and Babi Yar during the Holocaust. By the time I was ten, I knew that uncles and cousins were in mortal danger. By the time I was sixteen, I knew that almost everyone had disappeared. My psychotherapeutic work with survivors and my poetry are the ways I have found to mourn and honor our dead as well as cherish and join with the survivors. When I write in Yiddish, I resurrect the dead. Poems come to me in both English and Yiddish. I do not consciously choose which river of language will carry them.

My father, Yitzkhok Traister, dedicated his life to Yiddish. For over forty-five years, he was a principal and teacher in the Workmen Circle schools in Springfield, Massachusetts, and Los Angeles. I followed in his footsteps by also becoming a teacher and scholar of human development. My mother's influence on my work as a psychotherapist was also profound. She was orphaned young and encouraged me to have a career when it was not popular for women to do so. Wise but without formal education, she said *"Fun yedn eynem menchn ken men epes lernen"* ("There is something to be learned from every single person"). My profound interest in children, orphans and Holocaust survivors came together in 1977 when, as a visiting professor from Cal State University Northridge, I spent ten days at Anna Freud's Hampstead Clinic and met Alice Goldberger, the matron of the Lingfield Children's Home for young ones who had survived the Holocaust and who had come to England after Liberation. Meeting Freud and Goldberger was a life-changing experience that resulted in my writing *Love Despite Hate: Child Survivors of the Holocaust and Their Adult Lives* (Schocken, 1982). This book, and subsequent video-taping, brought thirty-five Los Angeles child survivors out of isolation and into the first of many organizations of child survivors. These organizations now have memberships in the thousands all over the world.

I did not write poetry in my mother tongue until 1995 when a poem came to me in Yiddish the morning after I attended a Yiddish poetry seminar with Professor Avrom Nowersztern from Hebrew University. This seminar in Malibu was part of a program called "Dancing at Two Weddings" (*"Tantzndik Oif Tsvey Khasenes"*), conceived and organized by Aaron Lansky, founder of the National Yiddish Book Center. My creative return to Yiddish was inspired there. It is no accident that the first poem I wrote in Yiddish was one of mourning, "Detsember" ("December") or that the one that followed, an homage to Aaron Lansky, was called *"Yerushe"* ("Legacy").

I write in Yiddish because I love the language, its rich possibilities for intimacy, remembrance, and humor. I warm to its strong and tender sound. To tap that deep core in me where my Yiddish voice lives is the best way I know to honor its vitality, to protest the genocide of millions of its speakers, and to rail against its having been treated as a stepchild in Israel. When I write in Yiddish, I restore the bond between myself and my murdered family in Poland and all my people whose daily language it was. When I write in Yiddish, I contribute to the living river.

In 2003, with a grant from Cal State University Northridge and an invitation to serve as a visiting scholar from the United States Holocaust Memorial Museum, I undertook the work of translating the Yiddish poetry that was buried in the Ringelblum Archives in Warsaw during the Holocaust and unearthed after the war in two milk cans and ten tins. With the devoted and indispensable help of my computer-maven husband, Itzik, who was able to make some unreadable microfiche frames readable, I have translated this treasury of poetry from Yiddish to English. Among the poets are such great poets as Yitshok Katsenelson and Simkha Shayevitch, as well as wonderful poets who are less known to us, like Kalman Lis, Miriam Unlinower, Shmuel Marvil, Yosef Kirman, and Shmuel Rabon. There are also many poems whose writers are unknown. All of the above writers — and a staggering number more — were killed in that tragic era, and many wrote until they were taken. I feel privileged to have done this work, to have brought these tragically silenced, vital Yiddish voices to the attention of a wider group of readers.

Stanley Moss * "Ghetto Theater, Vilnius, 1941," "A Visit to Kaunas"
I went to a festival of poetry in Lithuania sponsored by the State Department (in the balmy Clinton days) and visited the Devil's Museum, which consists of a few hundred years of depictions of the devil, who always looked like either me or a close relative. My grandfather was trained in Lithuania as a shoemaker. "The

Shoemaker's Synagogue" is nothing but dust. Where it stood looks like the lots in Queens [New York] where I played baseball, in those days when I still thought I had a chance at making the Yankees. After seeing the death camps, I telephoned a friend, an Israeli poet, and wrote the Kaunus and Vilnius poems.

Elaine Mott * "The Balcony," "The Last Visa for Palestine," "On the Wings of the Wind"

From 1950 to 1957, I spent summers at a bungalow colony in the Catskills, where half the adults were Holocaust survivors with blue numbers tattooed on their arms. I played with the survivors' children and kept discovering more and more about the unthinkable things that had happened before I was born. Years later, I read my cousin Shimon Frost's memoir about his escape, as a teenager, from the Warsaw Ghetto. "The Last Visa for Palestine" was written in memory of Shimon's sister, who was killed. In this poem, I have imagined my cousin as she would have been if she had lived. The "I" of the poem is not me. I considered writing in the third person, but I thought it was awkward and lacked directness. All the rest of my Warsaw relatives perished, including Shimon's parents and sister, who an eyewitness had seen being rounded up for transport to Treblinka. I wrote my poems in memory of these family members who I never knew and for the millions like them.

Mark Nepo * "Hill Where the Lord Hides," "I Wake from a Dream of Killing Hitler"

The paradox of what life does to us and what we do to ourselves and each other is never far from me. As a Jew, this is only more pointed. I return to the Holocaust and its moral conundrums and unspeakable acts as a crucible in which most of human behavior is grossly unraveled. The twin responses are close to all of us. On the one hand, fighting to the death like those in the Warsaw Ghetto. On the other, the compliant — almost stoic — walking into the ditch at Babi Yar. Like everyone who ever lived, I am precariously capable of either and not sure what leads me to one or the other.

Amos Neufeld * "In the Heaven of Night," "A Shade of Night," "When Israel Went Forth"

As a writer who was born in Israel to survivors of the Shoah, I have felt compelled to do my part as a member of the generation born after, who somehow feel as if we were there with our families and community and must bear witness. To not write about an event that has shaped my life, for better and worse, would amount to living in exile not only from my community but from myself, from the deepest concerns and currents of my life, to cutting myself off from the search for meaning and purpose in my life.

Miriam Offenberg * "Reforger"

As the public relations officer for the naval unit that would be going to Germany as part of an annual exercise, I was expected to go along and report (favorably) on the activities. The poem was an expression of my feelings at the idea of having to spend a week in that country and having to meet and greet its dignitaries. Fortunately, I never went.

Lois E. Olena * "The Archivist," "Homeland"

My interest in Jewish Studies began at the end of my undergraduate work many years ago, when I took a course in Jewish-Christian relations. I knew I wanted to go on to graduate work, but it was only after that class that I really felt directed toward Jewish Studies. So many things about my own spiritual heritage became more clear when understanding Christianity in the historical context of first-century

Judaism. Also, having become aware of the terrible legacy of Christian anti-Semitism, I felt responsible to help Christians become increasingly mindful not only of their 'Jewish roots,' but also of Jewish-Christian history, so they could take active steps in our day to prevent a repeat of anti-Jewish sentiment and behavior.

Though I began transcribing tapes of interviews with Holocaust survivors in early 1990 for the Gratz College Holocaust Oral History Archive in Philadelphia, it was not until six years later that I wrote my first poem, "The Archivist," in response to being a part of this important historical effort. "Homeland," based on the survivor interview of Eva Bentley, was published by *Midstream* magazine. Other [poems in this group] were published by *European Judaism* and other poetry journals. As a Christian, I feel it is important for the Christian world to understand Jewish history and do all we can to assure nothing like what happened under Hitler will ever happen again. Poetry has a way of moving people to feel — in some small, but very personal, way — what the victims of the Holocaust suffered.

Jacqueline Osherow * "Ponar,"
"Villanelle from a Sentence in a Poet's Brief Biography"
I never wrote about the Holocaust until I married into a family of survivors. I heard a lot of astonishing stories and became embroiled in this subject matter through no will of my own. The first time I dealt with the Holocaust in poetry was when I wrote an elegy for the woman who would have been my sister-in-law. I thought she was born in a D.P. camp (indeed that's what it says in the dedication to my poem; in fact my (now-ex) father-in-law dealt in black market alcohol and cigarettes and had an apartment in Lansburg; he was, however, serving time in an American prison when she was born). Her having been born in 1947, the daughter of two people who'd met at Dachau, somehow meant that I couldn't write about her death without acknowledging the circumstances of her birth.

About five years after that, my dying step mother-in-law, having seen the movie *Shoah* and having returned with my father-in-law to Auschwitz (he was first at Auschwitz, then at Dachau) started talking to me about her experiences during the war. It was absolutely clear to me that she wanted me to write about this. I was, by then, in her mind, a writer. I had published a book of poems. She would even spell names out for me. I remember very distinctly feeling that I was obliged to get what she was telling me into a poem; I felt that she, a dying woman, was making this demand of me. The stories were amazing; but it was also clear that she wasn't always telling the entire truth.

I remember wondering how I was going to write her poem. First of all, I felt very strongly — and I still feel — that a poem's power should never come solely from its subject matter. You write a poem because the meanings you are trying to convey can't be conveyed any other way. So making a poem of this story, which would have been thoroughly compelling as journalism or prose, was a tremendous problem for me. What I attempted to do was to place myself and my dilemma in the poem.

Whatever my poems are, let me say, emphatically, that they are in no way poems of witness. I have never witnessed anything. Whenever anyone talks about the poetry of witness or giving voice to the voiceless I always become extremely nervous, particularly if the issue is the Holocaust. Primo Levi, who spent years in Auschwitz, tells us that if you survived, you aren't a witness. How much less of one is a middle-class Jewish girl from Philadelphia, born eleven years after the war ended? When I write a poem about the Holocaust I try to make utterly clear that I have no idea what I'm talking about. Otherwise, for me, at least, the enterprise would be obscene. But it would have been impossible for me to have been told what I've been told and not at least attempt to put some of it into my poems.

Alicia Ostriker * "The Eighth and Thirteenth," "Poem Beginning with a Line by Fitzgerald/Hemingway"

As a Jew, I am commanded to "choose life." It is in this spirit that I have written "Poem Beginning with a Line by Fitzgerald/Hemingway" and "The Eighth and Thirteenth." To fail to write, to choose life, after the Holocaust, or for that matter after any of the many horrors we have had to contemplate in our time, is to surrender to them. How can we keep going, how can we keep our spirits and our hope for humanity alive, how can we not be crushed by feelings of hopelessness?

These poems were written in homage to souls greater than my own — the souls of those who saved the lives of Jews during the years of the Shoah, at risk to their own lives, and the soul of Dmitri Shostakovich, who was able to compose a symphony of wrenching power and grief for his fellow Russians, dead in the siege of Leningrad, and also able to compose a symphony in memory of the Jews massacred at Babi Yar — the Jews still hated by most of his countrymen. It is for this reason that God gives us imagination: that we should use it to cross over, to cross over to the place of the other, to become more completely and effectively passionate and compassionate in the face of suffering.

Christina Pacosz * "Auschwitz: Oświęcim

This poem is a response to my journeying to Poland in 1986 to visit relatives and study Polish-Jewish relations at Jagiellonian University. It is an excerpt from my collection of poems about my experiences, *This Is Not a Place to Sing* (West End, 1987). I had learned about the Holocaust as a very young child from my father, Walter Pacosz, who grieved for the way of life [he had known] and for his community of friends in Modliborzyce, who were destroyed and murdered by the Nazis.

Mark Pawlak * "Like Butterflies"

A Jewish colleague of mine, a child of Holocaust survivors, once said to me that she could never become my friend because of my Polish heritage. I was dumbfounded that she could find me untrustworthy or in some way hold me responsible for, or complicit in, the atrocities perpetrated against her family and relatives when my own ancestors had emigrated from Poland forty years before those events took place and had had essentially no contact afterwards with our relatives back in the "Old Country." Until then, I had thought that I already knew everything I would ever care to know about the Nazis and the genocide against the Jews of Europe, but I found her response to me so profoundly troubling and incomprehensible that I was compelled to look deeper. I embarked upon reading everything I could lay my hands on about the Holocaust. This included a flood of scholarly books and survivors' memoirs that were appearing at the time, as well as novels and poetry. I recall how powerful and disturbing I found Claude Lanzmann's documentary film, *Shoah*, with its depiction of deep-seated anti-Semitism among Poland's country people.

Charles Reznikoff's city poems had long been influential in my own work, but when I discovered his collections, *Testimony* and *Holocaust*, I realized that I could emulate his found/documentary approach to bring my newly-gained understanding of the Holocaust to bear in the poems I was writing. I admired his emotional restraint in allowing "just the facts," although carefully selected, to speak powerfully without comment or embellishment. "Poetry presents the *thing* in order to convey the *feeling*." He liked to quote from an 11th-century Chinese poet. "It should be *precise* about the thing and *reticent* about the feeling."

I wrote "Like Butterflies" in one sitting after reading a newspaper account of the discovery and identification of Mengele's remains in Argentina in 1985. It was a "gift," as my mentor, Denise Levertov, used to say about poems that came out fully formed, requiring little if any reworking.

Louis Phillips * "Perhaps You Wish to Learn Another Language," "Words over the Entranceway to Hell"
The two defining moments of the twentieth century are easy to pinpoint: the Holocaust and the development of atomic energy for war and peace. Unfortunately, far too many modern and contemporary poets write poems that neglect politics, historical events, and the immense suffering caused by persons with weapons. Such neglect comes back to haunt us all. The language of the previous century was violence, and no doubt it shall also be the language of the twenty-first century. Perhaps we would all wish to learn another language — the language of healing, forgiveness, and empathy for other human beings, in short, the language of true poetry — but such a wish will not be easily granted.

Heidemarie Pilc * "Somewhere in Poland . . . Survivor's Lament"
"Survivor's Lament" was inspired by my friendship with a Czech artist who lost most of her relatives and friends during the Holocaust. She herself survived imprisonment in a concentration camp and tried to start a new life in the U.S. All her life she was haunted by the loss of her loved ones and unable to make the adjustment to a new culture. With my poem, I wanted to erect a lyrical monument in commemoration of her suffering.

John C. Pine * "The Survivor"
I first became aware of the Holocaust as a teenager in the early years of World War II. I remember seeing small news items about the extermination of the Jews in Europe buried in the back pages of the *New York Times*. I remember wondering why these reports of horrible atrocities committed on innocent people received such little space and occasioned so little reaction. It all seemed unnatural and unreal to me. When the death camps were liberated after the war, I was serving in the Merchant Marine. Consequently, I was scarcely aware of the events of those days and of the outpouring of rage and revulsion that swept over the world at the sudden revelation of the extent of the tragedy.

Ever since those days, we have all become "witnesses" to the Holocaust, either through the writings of famous authors or through the accounts of survivors. Kitty Hart's "Return to Auschwitz" (1979) was one of the most moving of these eyewitness accounts because, through the medium of television, we were able to vicariously relive her own return to the death camp after a period of thirty-five years. Those tiny news items buried in the back pages of the *Times* suddenly took on a new meaning and a new menace as I followed her through the entrance of the death camp and through all those secret, never-to-be-forgotten, places of fear, loathing and, yes, courage far beyond that which anyone should be called upon to exhibit in this life.

Karl A. Plank * "Ash Wednesday"
"Ash Wednesday" takes its point of departure from a scene narrated by Filip Mueller in his memoir *Eyewitness Auschwitz*. Mueller, a member of the Sonderkommando at Auschwitz, recalled how Hauptscharführer Moll — the glass-eyed "Cyclops" of the poem — ordered the digging of pits near Birkenau's Crematorium V, a site close to a field in which spring flowers were blooming. The poem deals with the

juxtaposition of this meadow with the deathly reality of blinding ash that obscures signs of life. It then appropriates the imagery of ash to suggest a reinterpretation and intensification of the Christian Ash Wednesday liturgy.

Anna Rabinowitz * *from* ***Darkling: A Poem*** **&** *from* **"Dislocations"**

Darkling is an homage to the old photographs I found in a shoebox after my parents died. All the italicized lines in this section, with the exception of the italicized passage confined between quotation marks, were inscribed on the backs of photographs of primarily unidentified relatives and friends of my parents who were murdered in the Holocaust. They represent a cacophony of many voices prematurely and cruelly silenced — voices I am trying to retrieve. The passage that begins "as they were . . . in great strong masses" and ends "night cannot / Efface" is from the notebooks of James McNeil Whistler. As for the SS Hamburg, it is one of the German ships that traversed the Atlantic, carrying many Jewish refugees — in fact, it is the boat that carried my mother to these shores. My parents emigrated from Poland to America, leaving their families behind. When World War II ended, my mother discovered that every member of her family had perished in the Holocaust. My father's family's fate was hardly better: only his brother and the son of his half-sister had survived.

After my parents died, I found myself with an inheritance of truncated histories, sketchy memories, anecdotes they occasionally shared with me, and the contents of a shoebox: old photographs of people I had never known, most of whom had not even been identified for me, and postcards and letters in Yiddish and Polish that I subsequently had someone translate into English. I was haunted by this legacy, fragmented but charged with the stuff of memory and loss, testimony to the senselessness and profound evil of the Final Solution.

I could not create a clear narrative for all the people who spoke to me through the letters and photographs, but I was determined to find a way to make the absent present, to create something that would allow their passions, their terrors, their longings to emerge. In 1989, I traveled to Russia, Poland, and Czechoslovakia, hoping to fill in at least some of the lacunae. Unfortunately, all I could find was documentation that my parents had married in Poland; no other records pertaining to their families remained, if, in fact, they had ever existed. The excerpts from "Purple Blood of Lilac," originally published in my book, *At the Site of Inside Out*, are from the diary I kept during that trip.

My annihilated Jewish forebears — all those disembodied voices and faces — continued to loom large in my consciousness. Finally, in 2001, I completed writing *Darkling: A Poem*. With Thomas Hardy's "The Darkling Thrush" as my acrostic armature, I had fulfilled my mission; my legacy of shards at long last had held together. Those who had not survived to tell their stories or write their memoirs were miraculously present between the covers of my book. And, in 2003, American Opera Projects, a company nationally known for innovative and challenging new work, began the process of transforming *Darkling* into an experimental multimedia theatre piece. Since then, *Darkling* has played to enthusiastic audiences at the Guggenheim Museum and at the off-Broadway 13th Street Theatre, both in New York City. Those who did not survive now have yet another life on the stage.

David Ray * **"Houses," "A Photograph from 1935,"**
"A Song for Herr Hitler," "Visitors from America"

I've always identified with victims, as I do in the book about the Iraq Wars [*The Death of Sardanapalus and Other Poems of the Iraq Wars*, Howling Dog Press, 2004] and in *Sam's Book*, where the victim was my son, Samuel, and in my memoir, *The Endless Search*, where my childhood abuse is discussed. When you've had a lot of abuse in your life, you can lose your self-absorption only by being caught up in, and concerned with, suffering far more cosmic and terrible than your own. Transcendence and a more objective perspective can be found only in compassion and getting out of the self.

John Dewey wrote in his *Psychology* (1887) that forgetfulness of self alone can help one get in touch, or become a part of what he calls the universal. He examines how hard it is to deal with hard facts, and how "knowledge implies reference to the self . . . an activity which the self experiences. . . ." In a way, he seems to be saying that we are all part of one another, and there's no way to separate out, as we now do when the bloody carnage elsewhere in the world is treated as if it takes place on a distant planet. And if it is the case that we are all part of one another, it is our duty to deal with any human tragedy. "To obtain knowledge," Dewey writes, "the individual must get rid of the features which are peculiar to him and conform to the conditions of universal intelligence. The realization of this process, however, must occur in an individual." There's no understanding by the group mind. Only getting out of the self can liberate, so your efforts to find universal truths by self-reflection are entirely in vain. Ultimately, your own problems cease to exist when they comparatively shrink to nothing. Seeking relief from your own suffering, you identify with victims, just as you do when you witness tragedy on stage, the Aristotelian notion of art as catharsis.

I hope this does not smack of "using" the history of other victims, but I find that inescapable. How did Eliot, quoting the *Upanishads*, describe the search for control? *"'Datta, dayadhvam, damyata'* — Give, sympathize, control." It begins with giving your attention, your compassion, your love, the I-Thou, not the evil that begins with the I-It. Almost at any cost, the artist must escape the self even to begin. And it is very serious business, for we are 'shoring up fragments against our ruin.' We never have more than what that effort provides.

Barbara Reisner * "Sweet Savour"
I've thought a lot about the question of why I write poems about the Holocaust. I cannot pinpoint exactly when the news of the Holocaust entered my bloodstream. When Eichmann came to trial, I was sixteen. This trial opened the floodgates of an obsession with the Holocaust and the fate of the Jewish people. Before that, I think there were many hidden stories in my family and my neighborhood that I will never know, but whose sub rosa quality — the voices calling out underneath the silence — made me want to know the unknowable. Dream, reality, and memory, ancient and current, entwined in consolation.

"Sweet Savour" tells the story of a family gathering during the evening of a young cousin's bat mitzvah. We were looking through old photographs of our European relatives whom we never knew, and whom we knew nothing about. There was writing on the back of some of these pictures, and these words haunted us. The modern shul and the ancient scripture was another set of forces that called to be reconciled.

Lisa Ress * "U.S. Army Holds Dance for Camp Survivors. Germany, 1945"
"'U.S. Army . . .' — and many of the other poems in this series in *Flight Patterns* (Virginia, 1985) — came into being out of the intersection of my own experiences as the child of Holocaust refugees and those recounted in Helen Epstein's book, *Children of the Holocaust* (Putnam, 1979). The poem is based on a combination of an account in Epstein's book and another concerning the experiences of a Viennese woman, a journalist, who as a child remained hidden by neighbors with her mother in the basement of their apartment building in Vienna during

the entire Nazi period. It was in fact she who continued her piano lessons on a board painted to simulate a piano keyboard, and I heard this story from her in 1958 while in Vienna."

Charles Reznikoff * *from* **"Massacres," "Mass Graves," &**
Inscriptions: 1944–1956
From correspondence with Nathan Pollack —

"Charles was my cousin. I have always admired his approach to history. . . . He developed a method of rendering human experience in its atomic form. As an American-born Jew, Charles agonized over the events in Europe [which occurred] while he was safe and comfortable in New York. It took him many years to accumulate and work over the experiences of Jewish victims of the Nazis. It was Charles's way of dealing with a very important aspect of his own life and history."

Michael D. Riley * **"Photograph of Bergen-Belsen, 1945"**
Like so many others in the postwar generation (I was born in 1945), my awareness of the Holocaust as I grew up was a lot like the country's emerging sense of what really happened, at least for the average citizen. I can still recall my first glimpse as a teen of the films from the camps. No other media of the time presented these facts, and even the films themselves were marketed, disgracefully, with considerable sensationalism. The effect was still traumatic for a boy in his teens who never knew how sheltered he had been.

The result for me was the deepest sort of unease, the sense that a terrible door into the nature of the world had opened and demanded an entry of some kind from me personally. Made palpable, evil, like good, must be encountered authentically. For me, the result was much reading, meditation, and writing. I have returned to the theme often in my poems to at least further some kind of imaginative grasp of what is often called, understandably, "unimaginable." But the job of art is to make the unimaginable imaginable again, for reality has already done so, and only imagination can rescue it, and us.

The poem included here is unique among my others on this theme, for it attempts to tell of a moment that "looks through death." To some degree, it is doomed to fail because of that prior reality mentioned above. Yet the photograph from which the poem arose (it appeared in *Time* magazine) became a powerful moment of strange hope for me, a "still point," both literal and figurative, that promised in its disturbing but beautiful combination of opposites that, indeed, even "horror is not final." Whether the poem communicates any of this intuition is not for me to judge. The experience, however, drew me to a new place in my spiritual encounter with this great subject, the final bastion of hope: beauty and the leap of faith, both embraced without looking away from all that seeks to defile them.

Nicholas Rinaldi * **"Auschwitz"**
"Auschwitz" was included in a sequence of poems that I wrote, a number of years ago, about the war against Hitler. I was a schoolboy during World War II, and the news-of-the-week movie-reels that were shown at the movie houses made a powerful impression on me, especially the images of the death camps that appeared at the end of the war. Some of my cousins, much older than I, served in the military, and one, with whom I often corresponded, was caught up in the Battle of the Bulge. All of that eventually fueled my researches into the war and boiled up into the long sequence of poems that was published as *The Luftwaffe in Chaos*.

Curtis Robbins * *"In der Nacht"* ("In the Night")
In 1988, just before Pesach, Rose Roseman and her hearing mentor came to Washington, DC, hoping to establish a small exhibit at the new National Holocaust Museum about the plight of deaf Jews, who had been led to their demise by a CODA [**C**hild(ren) **of D**eaf **A**dults)] Nazi soldier — to no avail. They were living in the same community in Berlin where the Jewish Deaf School had long been established (it's still there!). Rose had been married two weeks prior to the murder of her husband. She never saw him again and has not remarried. Most of her friends and relatives perished as well.

While still in Washington, Rose and her mentor gave a lecture and photo exhibition at Gallaudet while I was a professor in the graduate school. The story was movingly told — and it stuck in my mind. At the first seder, the stories from the Hagaddah that told of the Jews and Pharaoh reverberated for me with the atrocities Rose had lived through. While my family dined, I wrote down notes for the poem.

The photo exhibition now hangs at the Gallaudet University Visitors Center.

William Pitt Root * "Pastoral for the Twenty-first Century"
My writing of this poem came from a series of dovetailing circumstances, beginning with my learning that some of the elders in my mother's family, having come from a region that was sometimes Germany, sometimes Denmark, were persecuted by their neighbors in this country during World War II. Because I knew them only as gentle hard-working people, I asked why, and the answers, which were not answers, baffled me as a child. Later, I learned how Germans had been regarded then, and why, and felt a deep uneasiness about that part of my own blood.

Later still, much later, when Jacob Bronowski was narrating [the Public Television Series] *Ascent of Man* [1973] and was touring some of the concentration camps, recalling their horrors, he walked, fully clad, without interrupting his narrative, into a pond in which the ashes of some of those who had been cremated had been dumped for years decades earlier. So astonishing was that act, so inexplicably right and so thrillingly healing, that I found myself among the millions weeping at that moment as we witnessed the strange baptismal blessing of that extraordinary man. I wanted to write about it but couldn't find a point of entry, and the act itself far exceeded any gesture of language I might conjure.

Later still, in Sitka, Alaska, I was talking with an artist, Diane Katsiaficas, who works with constructions of natural "found" materials. She described finding in Germany, near the Belsen camp, hung on the barbed wire of farmers' fences after the seasonal floods, great patches of natural paper drying and curing in the sun. Instantly, I found myself associating those floodwaters with the waters in the pond Mr. Bronowski had walked into, waters in which the ashes of thousands upon thousands had settled, and felt beginning in me the elaborate series of further associations which ultimately took me back to paper again, this time to start the poem which, once begun, nearly wrote itself with my hands.

Marina Roscher * "The Lanternman"
I was born and raised in Germany. As a child, I wrote poems in German but, after the revelations of 1945, I knew I would have to grow into another language first before I could hope to write again. Although I have published prose and poetry in English for more than ten years now [1985], I was unable to write about the Holocaust until conversations with the editor of this volume helped liberate feelings and deeply submerged images.

Jennifer Rose * "At Dachau with a German Lover"
Making art about the Holocaust is a difficult endeavor for anyone, especially those of us who did not experience it directly. I have tried to keep in mind William Butler Yeats's wise observation: "From our quarrels with others we make rhetoric. From our quarrels with ourselves we make poetry."

Menachem Z. Rosensaft * "Birkenau Barracks," "The Second Generation," "Sosnowiec Visited," "Yad Vashem Museum Opening, March 15, 2005"
There is a darkness, a painful vacuum, within which the Shoah exists as an aberration of history. It has been called the "Holocaust Kingdom" or the "Planet Auschwitz." In fact, it is far more distant, far more incomprehensible.

Genocide has happened before and since. Oppression, persecution and mass-murder have occurred before and since. Anti-Semitism and other forms of racial, ethnic and religious bigotry have manifested themselves before and since. But the cold, deliberate, systematic and impersonally cruel process of attempting to totally dehumanize a people before annihilating it, the perpetrators' utter indifference to the suffering of their victims, and these victims' ability to defy, resist and confound their oppressors and murderers, are unprecedented and unequalled in the annals of humankind.

How does one express anguish, fear, suffering and death? How can one adequately describe the virtually unimaginable in words that are not so trite or so desensitized as to be meaningless? Poems, like atonal melodies or abstract colors on canvas, have the power to evoke emotions.

I reach into myself to try to imagine, to try to visualize the nocturnal universe of the Shoah. I cannot know, will never know, my mother's anguish at being separated from her five-and-a-half year old son, or her horror upon realizing that her child, her husband and her parents had been murdered. I cannot know, will never know, my brother's fear as the doors of a Birkenau gas chamber were slammed shut, or my grandparents' agony as they began to inhale Zyklon B gas.

I write poems because I was not there. I write poems to voice an anger within me that transcends mourning. I write poems so as not to lose unanswered prayers and nightmares, theirs, mine. I write poems to express the reflection of shadows.

Elizabeth Rosner * "Almost Beautiful," "Anything," "Chocolate," "Homework," "My Father's Souvenirs"
I am writing not only what I know, but what I *want* to know. As my biography suggests, much of my work is centered around questions of identity and inheritance — in my case, the Holocaust stories of my parents, their suffering and loss, as well as their survival and hope. I am constantly searching for ways to make sense of the impact of the past on the present; I write to explore the secret of what we are given at birth and what we carry beneath our skin. As a daughter of Holocaust survivors, I feel especially close to that particular history, but at the same time I believe the legacies of those events are shared collectively by all of us, even those with no obvious personal relationship to the war or its aftermath.

I work in many forms: essay, poetry, short- and long fiction. Yet more and more, I find there are no precise distinctions among those forms, because I am aiming primarily at the emotional truth of ideas, experience, memory; the structure and shape often come later, after I have allowed the questions and voices to pour through me. I write to examine inherited grief and trauma, as well as optimism and beauty; I write to locate myself in the path of history, even as I recognize myself among its gaps and mysteries. Sometimes finding language for these things feels nearly impossible, and yet I am dedicated to the attempt. The more I write, the more I want to know.

Jerome Rothenberg * *"Dibbukim"* ("Dibbiks"), *"Dos Oysleydikn"* ("The Emptying"), "IN THE DARK WORD, KHURBN," "The Other Secret in the Trail of Money," *from* **"Peroration for a Lost Town"**
Author's introduction to Khurbn & Other Poems*:*

"In 1987, I was a decade, more, past *Poland/1931*. I went to Poland for the first time & to the small town, Ostrow-Mazowiecka, sixty miles northeast of Warsaw, from which my parents had come in 1920. The town was there and the street, Miodowa (meaning 'honey'), where my father's parents had a bakery. I hadn't realized that the town was only fifteen miles from Treblinka, but when we went there (as we had to), there was only an empty field & the thousands of large stones that make up the memorial. We were the only ones there except for a group of three people — another family perhaps — who seemed to be picnicking at the side. This was in sharp contrast to the crowds of tourists at Auschwitz (Oświęcim / Oshvietsim) & to the fullness of the other Poland I had once imagined. The absence of the living seemed to create a vacuum in which the dead — the dibbiks who had died before their time — were free to speak.

"It wasn't the first time that I thought of poetry as the language of the dead, but never so powerfully as then. Those in my own family had died without a trace — with one exception: an uncle who had gone to the woods with a group of Jewish partisans and who, when he heard that his wife and children were murdered at Treblinka, drank himself blind in a deserted cellar & blew his brains out. That, anyway, was how the story had come back to us, a long time before I had ever heard a word like 'Holocaust.' It was a word with which I never felt comfortable: too Christian & too beautiful, too much smacking of a 'sacrifice' I didn't & still don't understand. The word with which we spoke of it was the Yiddish-Hebrew word, *khurbn* (*khurban*), & it was this word that was with me all the time we stayed in Poland.

"When I was writing *Poland/1931*, at a great distance from the place, I decided deliberately that that was not to be a poem about the 'Holocaust.' There was a reason for that, I think, as there is now for allowing my uncle's khurbn to speak through me. The poems that I first began to hear at Treblinka are the clearest message I have ever gotten about why I write poetry. They are an answer also to the proposition — raised by Adorno & others — that poetry cannot or should not be written after Auschwitz. Our search since then has been for the origins of poetry, not only as a willful desire to wipe the slate clean but as a recognition of those other voices & the scraps of poems they left behind in the mud."

Larry Rubin * "The Nazi in the Dock, at Sixty"
There was something (is something) grotesque about these old men, being exposed now [1985] after four decades and nearing death themselves — hideous crimes are associated generally with younger, more energetic monsters. I wanted to express not only the horror, but the pity of it — to be so old and to have so much to account for. The Fedorenko case in Fort Lauderdale (Miami Beach is my hometown) is, I think, what triggered the poem; but all the ingredients for writing it were already coming to a boil. . . . [Federenko admitted to having been a guard at Treblinka, a major extermination center in Poland, northeast of Warsaw and, in March 1981, was stripped of his U.S. citizenship for failing to disclose his wartime activities during his immigration to the U.S. in 1949.]

Mark Rudman * "Easy Living in Terezín"
My poem, "Easy Living in Terezín," has a very specific origin. In the fall of 2004, I went to the beautiful and harrowing "Terezín" exhibit organized around the presence of the artist and teacher Friedl Dicker-Brandeis at the Jewish Museum in New York. Not long after, I started to read Amos Oz's memoir, *A Tale of Love and Darkness*, with a growing sense of disbelief at its excellence. Two-thirds of the way through this magnificent memoir, for reasons peculiar to my own nature, I couldn't go on. The vividness of Oz's recreation of a world composed of people whose main occupation was to get at the meaning of things stirred up longings for something I had never experienced in just that way. The vanishing of Oz's Jerusalem mingled in my mind with the destruction of the children who would have been the candidates to keep this strain of artistic and spiritual pursuit going. My only recourse was to write a poem. To do this, I adopted a somewhat uncharacteristic form of irony to prevent myself from being owned by contemplation of their fate and a sense of loneliness. Who would not be appalled by the sickening duplicity the Nazis showed in using this ghetto as a facade to trick visitors, like the Red Cross, into thinking that there was something humane going on, that the "artistic" occupants would not simply be exterminated when that opportunity presented itself.

Biff Russ * "The Way to Be Haunted"
I generally prefer to let my work reveal its *raison d'etre*. However, in the case of "The Way to Be Haunted," [I'm willing to say that] I believe that the gift of poetry does not come without obligation. With whatever gift a poet is granted, he or she honors the human experience. The full magnitude of suffering engendered by the Holocaust is unimaginable. Ultimately, it is inexpressible. If, however, in some small way, poetry can alleviate any fraction of that suffering by giving grief a home, I aspire to that end.

Luada Sandler * "A Scene from *Shoah*"
Two factors have deepened my interest in the Holocaust: 1. My late husband was born in Latvian Russia and was twelve or thirteen years old at the outbreak of the Russian Revolution. Early in the revolution, his father was cut off from his family while on a business trip to Riga, and his mother was imprisoned, an alleged political prisoner, leaving four small children to fend for themselves (my husband was the eldest of the four). Their mother was sentenced to death, but that was commuted to ten years. Finally, she was released after about a year. The family immigrated to the U.S. when my husband was sixteen. From him and his family, I gained insight into the wanton destructive use of power in time of war and revolution.

2. During World War II, I served as a staff aide with the American Red Cross in military hospitals in the European Theatre of Operations. Immediately after the end of the war in Europe, I saw emaciated former prisoners of war coming through our hospital in Liège, Belgium, on their way home, for further treatment in U.S. hospitals. I remember meeting a man very briefly, a political prisoner who had been at Dachau and was on his way home to New York. Although he did not talk about his years at the camp, one felt the deep tragedy of his experience. In Marseille, I met a family of survivors who were related to one of our staff members, and I spent a day with them. I remember one of them said, "You can't imagine how horrible the camps were, especially for a young woman like me."

The enormity, the depravity, and the monstrosity of the Holocaust seem to me, metaphorically at least, as if an earthquake of cosmic dimensions had struck the universe. I believe the damage it caused is still being felt around the world. Whether that damage can be repaired may be debatable, but I feel it is incumbent on all of us to do our utmost to contribute to the restoration of the world's "balance." When

I think how much the world has been impoverished by the Holocaust, not only by [the loss of] those who perished but also by how much the rest of us have been diminished, the task of repair seems extremely formidable. . . . I feel that the telling of the history of even one survivor can help repair at least a small section of the psychic terrain traumatized by the giant upheaval of the Holocaust.

Reg Saner * "Aspen Oktoberfest"

In 1978, a visit to the prison camp at Dachau, twenty-minutes outside Munich, gave me a basis for appreciating one very pretty nineteen-year-old victim of the Nazis named Lili Tofler, who actually died at Auschwitz, but died there as the poem describes. Her answer when fellow prisoners asked, "How's it going, Lili?" was famous among them. "With me," she'd say, "things always go well." Ever since then, the words "Lili Tofler" have named, for me, an unimaginable kind of courage. My poem enacts an extreme instance — though entirely factual — of an experience we all have: feeling unusually happy while being aware of those who are not.

Dachau is a town about twelve miles north of Munich, with the former prison camp on the edge of town. Europe abounds with signage alerting motorists to points of interest, but no such signs pointed our way to the camp when my family and I cruised around looking for it. At Dachau's center, I queried several people who claimed not to know of any such place. One, a twenty-five-year-old male wearing a university sweatshirt, convinced me by his tone he genuinely did not know what I was talking about. Finally, a hard-eyed, apple-cheeked woman at a newsstand curtly directed me to it, as if she answered the same question many times a day.

Rebecca Seiferle * *"'A lonely man in his greatness'"*

This poem, "*A lonely man in his greatness*," was much informed by my reading *Hitler's Pope: The Secret History of Pius XII*, by John Cornwell. The poem's italicized phrases are taken from that volume, and, in some sense, I felt that the poem was buried alive within the book. The poem occurs in that contrast between an immaculate public image, and sense of self, and the secret life of the body, for it is the burial of Pius XII, his coffin carried through the streets, and the sounds of bodily decay decomposing within that coffin, that is the poem's pivotal image, contrasting [as it does] his immaculate sense of himself with the physical reality that he could not, finally, evade. *Hitler's Pope* shocked me, not because I was unaware of the historical realities of the Concordat between Hitler and the Vatican or other events of that time, but because of the level of intricate and subtle complexity involved in keeping the secret — the secret not only of the Pope, which was both personal and political, and woven into the fiber of his personality, but also the secret of the consequences of power, the secret of the physical reality of so many other lives, usually Jewish, destroyed by subtle alliances of public image and power.

The Holocaust is, I feel still, a horror of unspeakable significance in human history. The Holocaust's unspeakable significance is derived, I think, from the intersection of so many forces — scientific technology and research, the typology of human beings and the means of killing them and disposing of the remains, private assumptions and cultural myths, reason and logic — all aspects of human agency were involved in deliberately and consciously deciding to exterminate an entire people, so in that event, it is possible to see and discern all the elements that were attendant upon such a horror. In the case of Hitler's Pope, as elsewhere in the Holocaust, the power of the secret is most evident — secret alliances, secret assumptions, those people whose very existence was defined as secret — for Pope Pius XII said nothing of the Jews publicly; their lives and their deaths and terrible suffering became an unspoken secret — what is not spoken of does not exist.

I wrote this poem at the time that I was still a practicing Catholic, though I was not one who grew up in the Church but, instead, converted as an adult, and at a time when I was becoming more and more troubled by the Church's secrets, which as they were revealed seemed integral to its power. The public image, the immaculate self, is perhaps always dependent upon the maintaining of a secret existence, a secret existence to which not only aspects of the self but others, perhaps an entire people, can be relegated and so obviated, never spoken of, never acknowledged. In some sense, I feel that the Holocaust is still with us, intricately interwoven into our imaginations and assumptions, whether we are aware of it or not, though the lack of awareness means that our agency can be driven by those assumptions, as it is every time a person cultivates a public image, a reasonable policy, while also having a secret life that results in, and contributes to, cruel usages of others and, given enough power and agency, to endorsing and allowing the proposed extermination of a people. So I wrote it out of this sense of being profoundly troubled, of having the necessity of replying to an unspeakable reality.

David Shapiro * "For Victims"

The poem, "For Victims," was also planned as a poem to be carved into an architectural monument by the late John Hejduk. In memory of the Jewish victims of the Holocaust and, by implication, all victims of political and racist persecution, this poem was inspired by the old Jewish history volumes of Graetz, which I received from my politically-minded grandmother, who was influential in the early Pioneer Women [a Zionist organization]. I was reading about early atrocities when I had a vision, around age seventeen or eighteen, of all the horrors and Satanic dogmatists dissolving in a mist. This Dantesque vision emerged [and melded] with a line written by my four-year-old sister. I was taken aback by the force of this "vision" and didn't publish the poem for many years. I tucked it away in another poem, "How to Make Your Own Rainbow," which appeared in a book that in 1972 was nominated for the National Book Award. [At that time,] these lines came back to haunt me and, after hearing very late of the slaughter of my aunts in Poland, I began to think increasingly of the rage and virtue of this poem, which hitherto had seemed undeserved.

There is no doubt that the extreme sense of my mother, of her duties toward justice, influenced me. My mother told me throughout my youth of her activities in South Africa, where Berele Chagy was chief chazzan for a decade. My mother, dying young in 1974 at the age of fifty-five, was an indelible force in my life and a great anti-fascist. I dedicate this little poem to the memory of my mother's voice.

Gregg Shapiro * "Tattoo"

"Tattoo" is a poem that has taken on a life of its own. It has been anthologized numerous times, and it has also appeared in a few textbooks. I am proud of the way the poem has touched readers. I am especially grateful for the dialogues I have established with students of all ages who have been taught the poem in classrooms. It has been a privilege to be able to share the complex, but loving, relationship between the father and son in "Tattoo."

Harvey Shapiro * "Ditty," "Natural History"

Readers of "Ditty" might want to look at "I Sing of a Mayden," an anonymous poem of the fifteenth century.

Reva Sharon * "In the Absence of Yellow," "Holocaust Remembrance Day," "Shoshana," "Unanswerable Questions"

When I visited Terezín, the words of Pavel Friedmann's poem, "I Never Saw Another Butterfly," were a consistent refrain in my head as I walked through the cells, the prison, the crematoria.

It is sixty years since the liberation of the camps, but it is not sixty years since the Holocaust ended. I was born when the black buds of the "Final Solution" were uncoiling their sulfurous petals, and I live now because my grandparents left Europe behind to make their lives in America. But I know about the camps and the ghettos, and I know that not one member of the four families from which I am descended lives in Austria or Poland or Lithuania now. Almost all perished — the survivors live in America or Israel today. And I have grown up knowing about the horrors which humans are capable of — and I cannot know the extent of it. No, I was not there, but I cannot forget what I have read, seen, heard. The pictures, the reports, the diaries, the Prague Museum, Theresienstadt. I have seen the human ashes that remain in the ovens. I have touched the barbed wire that has been preserved. I have touched the bunks, walked through the cells. I remember no day when I have not remembered some fragment of the Holocaust.

I can only write about one boy of five who never lived to ask or hear the answers to his questions. I can only write to one young dead poet to tell him I remember. I can only write about one nameless woman whose faith in life was so great that even when she was dying she found hope in the fact of a chestnut tree blossoming in the heart of a camp. I can only write to my brother and tell him what I have seen and what I remember and what we share as a legacy. I walk with the legions who haunt me. The world has been denied the fruit of their lives and the seeds that should have one day flowered. I cannot breathe life back into ashes, but I carry them in my heart and, when I can, write something, a few lines in poems about a few: it is my only way to say Kaddish for all of them, for each of them.

Enid Shomer * "Women Bathing at Bergen-Belsen"

I chose the sonnet form for my subject because it is a very demanding form and I wanted to pay homage to the survivors as well as the dead on the day of liberation at Bergen-Belsen. The poem is factual [and is] based on the documentary film, "A Memory of the Camps," which was aired on TV [Spring 1985].

Joan I. Siegel * "Haggadah"

"Haggadah" reflects my deep admiration for Primo Levi, both as a writer and a human being. Some years ago, after reading *Survival in Auschwitz*, *The Reawakening, Moments of Reprieve,* and *The Drowned and the Saved* — Levi's harrowing personal account of the Holocaust and his ruminations on evil, suffering, human nature and the meaning of survival — I was compelled to write this poem. I did so with the greatest sense of humility and respect for both the survivors and the dead. The title and design of the work derive from the Passover *Haggadah*. The cadences and refrains are reminiscent of the "Dayenu" portion of the text, which reflects the good deeds of a merciful God during the Hebrews' exodus from Egypt. In contrast, my poem attempts to underscore the hopeless plight of Holocaust victims, for whom there was neither a merciful God nor an exit from suffering.

Maurya Simon * "Letter to Vienna from Paris, 1942"
This poem and several related poems arose from stories my mother-in-law, Margit Idelovici Falk, has told me. Both she and my father-in-law were born and raised in Vienna. Most members of their respective families died either in concentration camps, during the fire bombing of Dresden, or in Israel in 1948 during the war there. Margit was sent by her family to Indonesia in 1940, to stay with Dutch relatives. When the Japanese occupied the country, she was imprisoned in Bandung for four years. I felt not only justified, but compelled, to serve as witness for her, and for all those in my extended family — both living and dead — who cried out to be heard. Though one generation removed from the speakers in my poems, I am not at all removed from the anguish of their stories.

Louis Simpson * "The Bird," "A Story About Chicken Soup"
"The Bird" is a character study of a Nazi concentration camp guard that was written before they started turning up in South America. One critic remarked that the poem was based on my reading of Brecht. This is not true. I had been reading Heine, but the poem rose out of my imagining such a character and situation. The line about the little bird is taken from a German Romantic poem — by [Eduard Friedrich] Mörike, I seem to recall.

In "A Story about Chicken Soup," the mention of my grandmother and the old country are autobiographical. All those people in the old country, southern Russia, were indeed killed by the Germans. The second part is also autobiographical. In 1945, the 101st Airborne Division of the U.S. Army, in which I served, occupied Berchtesgaden. The poem was finished in a curious way. I had written most of it but was having trouble with the third part. A friend, Robert Bly, came to visit. As I explained to him what I wanted to say, he wrote down lines from my conversation. Then he showed them to me, and I had finished the poem.

Myra Sklarew * *from* **"Lithuania"**
[Regarding her travels in Eastern Europe in 2006 and previously] In Romania, I tried to help a friend find information about her father's town of origin and hoped to learn something about my father's people, but it was barely a beginning. In Lithuania — I've made ten trips there over thirteen years — I try to visit with the remaining survivors (only a hundred twenty left now), to see what is needed, and to offer help when I am there and after I return home. It has been a privilege to come to know this community over these years, rather miraculous to have had this chance.

Joan Jobe Smith * "Hollow Cost"
I was around four, just after the war, when the American public became informed of the atrocities inflicted upon the Jews and Poles. Hearing about those awful things 'ruined my life,' disrupted my innocence, just as a death in the family or sexual assault makes nothing ever the same again for a small child; and hearing about those horrible things from the quiet moment of my parents' safe, serene bed created an irony and truth that still shakes me — that there is no haven from harsh realities, not even in your mother's arms (my mother also told me how children were exterminated — snatched from their mothers' arms!). I wept for a long time after my mother told me; and so painful was the "mort dans l'ame" ("death in the soul") that I actually disliked my mother for some time for being the bearer of such bad tidings.

Kirtland Snyder * "'City Children at a Summer Camp. Slonim, 1936,'" "'Selma . . . A Pot of Soup . . . A Bottle of Milk. Łódź, 1938'"
The Holocaust has haunted my imagination for many years. It has seemed to me to be a central symbol of the human condition, a barbarity that smashes all neat conventions about "civilization." More particularly, it seemed to say something central about the bankruptcy of Christianity.

I felt a deep grief for the Jewish victims of Christian Europe under Hitler and wanted *to do something* for them, to perform some act of remembrance, to confer some dignity upon their horrible deaths. Just about all my attempts to do so in writing, until *A Vanished World*, failed for one reason or another. The difference, I think, has to do with the fact that the poems of the sequence focus on the living Jews before the Holocaust. This is the beauty of Roman Vishniac's photographs. There is enormous dignity in the lives as Vishniac reveals them, no matter how impoverished. These Jews live, even though most of them vanished.

I felt I could discover something essential about myself by writing about the Holocaust. As I wrote, I did indeed discover this essential thing: that I, too, was somehow its victim. It has to do with John Donne's idea that each man's death diminishes me, because I am involved in mankind. Which is, it seems to me, essentially a Jewish idea.

J. R. Solonche * "Another Book on the Holocaust"
Since I've written only three or four poems on this subject, I don't see myself as a Holocaust writer. I write about the Holocaust when it comes clearly into focus for me in some concrete form. Reading reviews of books about the Holocaust, for instance. Or hearing what other visitors said at the United States Holocaust Memorial Museum when my wife and I were there. Isn't this how people write poems about anything?

Jason Sommer * *from* **"Mengele Shitting," "Meyer Tsits and the Children," "The Property of the World," "What They Saw"**
I write about the Holocaust, or with it as the setting of some of what I have written, because my father is a survivor, as was his late brother, Harry, and Harry's wife, my Aunt Lilly. I write, then, to understand the people and the history that had a part in making me. Sometimes I have written on their behalf, telling what they would have me tell; I have also spoken of matters they would have as soon left unsaid. I came to feel as a result of the stories that were told around me, and the aftermath of the events as they played out in the lives of the people among whom I lived, that I write about the Holocaust because the extremities of the experiences reveal everything about what it is to be human.

What finally prompted me to attempt some of the poems here was a rough coincidence of events: the discovery of Mengele's bones in Brazil, the uncovering of accounts of the monstrous Auschwitz doctor's final years, and my aunt's sudden bursts of disclosure about her own direct experience of him, after so many years of silence. I began to sense that the stories that belonged to others also were mine, since they had to do with forming me. I thought I had something at last to give survivors in return for the pain of their testimony, a story they would not themselves have, since it was a twining of stories — theirs, mine, and the story of the story. Drawing on the resources of poetry, I might have a chance to make something durable enough in language to contain and give shape to experience at the junction of history and personality, a poetry that could preserve what was placed in my keeping: the voices of the tellers and what they told, even my voice among theirs, telling what was mine and not mine.

Gizela Spunberg * "Memories of December"
My city, Lwów, was occupied by the Russians and I wanted to cross the border to Rumania. I never saw my mother again.

Hans Jörg Stahlschmidt * "November Rain," "Visit to the Fatherland"
Although I knew a few German Jews in Berlin, I was confronted in a more profound way with the German past and the Holocaust when I came to the Bay area. Whereas in Germany the discourse was academic and political, in my new home the dialogue was direct and personal as well as emotionally charged and moving. Besides the deeply divisive issues, I also experienced the similarities and kinship between Jews and Germans.

Writing poetry is a way not only to process the complexity of my experiences, but also a way to initiate a dialogue. Writing about this difficult subject forced me to find ways to connect the universal issues with the personal and subjective and to search for ways to overcome the past while acknowledging history and its pervasive impact.

Jan Steckel * "The Maiden Aunts"
"The Maiden Aunts" is about my maternal grandmother, Selma Romm Raskin. It's based on stories Selma and her sister Estelle told me. I suspect the oral history got embellished along the way. When I was a child, my mother showed me the entry in the Library of Congress catalogue for my great-great-grandfather's treatise on Maimonides, and I know he was a rabbi in Riga. My Aunt Estelle's claim that his forebears were rabbis for nine generations before him could also be true. I've seen no direct documentation, however, that a Romm (also spelled "Ram") was Chief Rabbi of Riga. My family still has Yiddish and Hebrew books published by the Widow Romm and Sons (or Widow Romm and Brothers). The Romm family's close relatives, the Rosba family, owned lumber mills in Riga. My grandmother Selma's parents were first cousins: one was a Rosba, and the other a Romm.

My grandmother and aunt weren't the only Romms left alive in America. They were, however, the surviving members of the branch of the family that they knew, the descendants of Judith Romm, my grandmother's grandmother. Judith's husband, the rabbi (who wrote the treatise on Maimonides), died on a trip to Jerusalem when he fell asleep studying and knocked over a candle, causing the boardinghouse to burn down around him. His death eventually forced his widow to emigrate to the Lower East Side, saving their descendants from an even greater conflagration.

Bradley R. Strahan * "Yom Kippur"
"Yom Kippur" was inspired by a walk in the park, which made me think of nature's ability to regrow, despite assaults by man.

Rabbi Michael Strassfeld * "Who Knows One?"
I wrote "Who Knows One?" to be read at Passover seders. I tried to bring together elements of the liturgy recited during the ritual meal and celebration of Passover with thoughts on the crisis in Darfur. Using elements of the traditional Passover songs, I attempted to weave familiar phrases into our contemporary life. This piece reflects the remarkable paradigm of the seder itself that suggests that we have all experienced the slavery and redemption of Egypt, not just our ancestors. In our time, we are called to continue to work for the redemption of all people.

Lynn Strongin * "Erasing the Blue Numbers," "Her Velocity Had Been Taken," "Theresienstadt," "What a Waste of World"

Bergie was a woman I met in Berkeley during the sixties, less than two decades after World War II. Bergie was sinewy, appearing to be in her sixties, although she may have only been in her late forties. She had been in one of the concentration camps in Europe. It was warm weather, and we all had rolled up sleeves as we chatted on a Berkeley sidewalk. I remember how slight Bergie was, hunkering by the curb, smiling, smoking. All of a sudden, under purple blossoms, I saw the blue numbers on her arm. This was the most physical manifestation I'd ever seen of the concentration camps, and the contrast between those marks of brutality on Bergie's arm and the tensile beauty of spring cut me, incisive as glass, making Bergie and me soul-sisters for life. I wasn't surprised to learn, five years later, that Bergie had died. I grafted some of my own childhood hospital experience upon my imaginative recreation of her life in "The Blue Numbers."

Yerra Sugarman * "Because"

In an essay he wrote after the end of World War II, Theodor Adorno argued for the need of a new awareness in regard to art, one that recognized the paradoxical relationship between "culture and barbarism." He claimed in what are now often quoted words: "Even the most extreme consciousness of doom threatens to degenerate into idle chatter. . . . To write poetry after Auschwitz is barbaric." Although he revised his view, [his statement] never seemed to me a proscription against creating art after the Shoah. I understand it, instead, as a plea to counter moral and artistic complacency and as a gauge by which to measure and challenge western notions of progress that propel us to implicate ourselves in the world's depravity, even as we embrace its luminosity. His words also urge us to acknowledge the implicit impossibility of representing genocide — all genocide — even by "nonrepresentational" means, and to be humbled by our inadequacy.

It is with this sense of contradiction, language's insufficiency, and the survivors' own lessons of silence, that I try to approach my poetry. Risking the trivialization about which Adorno wrote, I aimed in my first book, *Forms of Gone*, to redress what, clearly, eludes reparation: the anomalous lives of survivors, those of my parents, our family and community. But I also wanted to write in earnest about the force of my upbringing and my often ambivalent and conflicted relationship to it, while illuminating the counterpoint that was the daily life of the survivors I knew and their children. This was a quotidian suffused by loss, which rendered speech itself a predicament, thus never truly "daily," because it was woven with a tragic history and, for the children, with an appropriation of losses they themselves had not experienced directly. In poems like "Because," an early piece and a point-of-departure, I hoped to find poetic means by which I could confront the problem of how to bear vicarious witness, how to write about a devastation that affected me each day, yet one I experienced "at a remove" from the actual events that had been its agent and marked the lives of those about whom I wrote.

Zahava Z. Sweet * "Dark Whispers," "The Line," "In Ravensbrück"

My Holocaust poems are about my mother and other members of my family and about the suffering during World War II. They are a retrospection of my experiences and, essentially, the reticent voice of my war-torn childhood returning unabashedly to free a silent suffering.

Marilynn Talal * "Another Holocaust Poem," "For Our Dead," "My Mother as Superhero,"
I came into consciousness during World War II when I saw grown men — my beloved father and uncles — crying for reasons I didn't understand; an uncle saying, "The world hates the Jews"; my mother anguished because she didn't have more to give Holocaust survivors who moved into our neighborhood. "My Mother as Superhero" is a prayer, a wish that I could have helped my mother enjoy her own goodness.

On the subway, in summer, I saw the numbers tattooed on the arms of attractive men and women, signifying a dark, unknown, unspeakable, terrifying horror they had experienced because they were Jews. Their suffering spoke to me so powerfully, I trembled when I saw them. Had my grandparents not fled, I would be dead or would have suffered as they did.

"For Our Dead" came out of my grief for our loss in their pointless deaths. "Another Holocaust Poem" arose out of the agony of feeling inadequate, of endlessly remembering that I'm a helpless bystander: the horror has already become history.

Sean M. Teaford * "A Pure Breath," "Warsaw Epidemic"
I originally set out to read Korczak's *Ghetto Diary* for the sake of learning about the history and experiences of the Holocaust. As I read further into this book, I came to an astonishing realization that *Ghetto Diary* is not [only] an historic text . . . it is a script of life's dark side. This is a page in our story that some may gloss over, feeling that they have missed nothing, but those of us who have read this page will never forget; we will always remember the blood with which those words were scribed, and we will know that the people who were murdered are not a footnote. They are the ones who will forever be our teachers. These poems will never be more than an echo of their whispers. This is not just the story of Janusz Korczak and his children but [my story] as well as yours; these poems, along with the eleven other poems in the series, are a "Kaddish Diary."

Philip Terman * "The Jewish Quarter in Budapest," "What We Pass On," "With the Survivors," "The Wounds"
I always avoided writing about the Holocaust. I detested the way in which so many — Jews and non-Jews alike — identified Judaism solely with that catastrophic event, and it was put upon me that, because of it, I had a responsibility to remain Jewish. In fact, though, what attracted me to Judaism at an early age were the poetic and sacred qualities of its rituals, symbols, language. In my poetry, I explored the plethora of images and tropes that living the life of the American Jew inspires.

I avoided the Holocaust for a long time until it, as it must, sooner or later with every Jew, confronted me. It did so in a conversation I had with my mother, who finally told me the story of her grandmother's family's tribulations in Eastern Europe. That door, finally, had opened. I felt my connection, and in what ways it affected my own life. These poems were written in response to a trip I made to Eastern Europe to witness former Jewish quarters and concentration camps. What drew me in was not only the past but also the present: these streets, these synagogues, these worshipers — wounded, but still here, in what the poet, survivor and Jew, Paul Celan, would call "heartspace."

Elaine Terranova * "1939"

This poem is based on the Middle Europe of my imagination and [Roman] Vishniac's camera, a place where my relatives who perished were living. I imagine, too, a child and her mother, in a world that is slipping away from them. The mother is confident that life will remain dependable and pleasant; the child is uncertain and uneasy, for the deeds of fairy tales are more real to her than the superficial calm. As it turns out, she is of course right. All of my mother's family, except for one brother and one sister, were lost.

Alfred Van Loen * "Auschwitz #1," "Auschwitz #6"

My Auschwitz poems were originally written in Dutch in 1946 and translated into English in 1948, after I came to this country. My parents, my sister, and I lived in Amsterdam and escaped the Holocaust. I was active in the underground from 1939 to the end of the war. It wasn't until then that we knew the fate of our relatives in Germany and other parts of Europe.

My grandfather, Simon Lowenthal, on the way to his office in Munich, made it his habit to sit on a bench in a nearby park and feed the birds and the squirrels. Early one morning, in the fall of 1941, he was attacked by a couple of Nazis and beaten to death. He was seventy-six years old. My grandmother and my father's brother, Hermann, who was a poet, were shortly thereafter sent to concentration camps. [At first,] Grandmother was held in Theresienstadt, where Father was able to send her packages; later, she was moved. From survivors returning to Amsterdam, we heard that Grandmother was seen in Bergen-Belsen, where she died. My Uncle Hermann was in Auschwitz, where he was part of the work crew for fourteen months until he, too, was murdered.

These facts and stories told by survivors prompted the writing of these Auschwitz poems. In my dream, I felt like I had been with my relatives and shared their suffering. As long as I live, I will never be able to forget or forgive the Nazi horror. [1985]

George Wallace * "An Apple for Wolfgang Granjonca"

I wrote this poem while stranded in the San Francisco Bay area in the week following September 11th. At the time, I was acutely aware of how an individual's circumstances can become dislocated through the machinations of governments and societies. Indeed, I felt stranded, imperiled and adrift, somewhat like a refugee. This was a subject I explored over and over again during that period, from varying angles — on this particular day's writing, it was through the medium of Billy Graham's personal odyssey after the Holocaust, his ability to overcome that trauma, and the life of accomplishment and personal decency he was able to achieve, despite the experiences he faced in his early life.

Florence Weinberger * "Marrowbones," "Speak to the Children," "Survivor"

My interest in the Holocaust began in the 1940s, while listening to my immigrant parents' well-founded fears that the families they had left behind in Hungary were in danger, then listening to them read aloud the letters arriving after the war from the few survivors.

In 1955, I married Ted (Tibor) Weinberger, a native of Miskolc, Hungary, and a survivor. All the reading and research I have done since then on the Holocaust has been part of an attempt to understand that which cannot be understood. The dedications on all the poems would have to read "For Ted."

"Survivor," of course, is for my husband. It was written in 1984, prior to our trip to Hungary with our two daughters. My husband had looked forward to this event with great anxiety. Coincidentally, the day we visited Miskolc marked the fortieth anniversary of the day the Jews of the city were removed from the ghetto and put on trains.

Barbara Wind * "Hating Shakespeare," "Math Test"
"Hating Shakespeare," which is autobiographical, was inspired by an article in the *New York Times*. Written about a decade ago, it spoke of the tremendous increase in anti-Semitism in Japan, a country in which very few people had ever met a Jew. The article attributed this irrational phenomenon to the growing popularity of Shakespeare, particularly productions of *The Merchant of Venice.* It was a revelatory moment and brought back a conversation I had with my father when I was twelve. At that time, and with all the arrogance of the adolescent daughter of an immigrant, I thought I knew more than my father about Shakespeare and so much else.

Don't all writers hate math? "Math Test" is a poem in which I "tell the truth slant but tell it slant." In fact, my parents did lose their immediate and extended families. Did I say *lose*? The Nazis and their cohorts terrified, humiliated, robbed, enslaved, starved, brutally beat, and killed everyone in their respective families, with the sole exception of my maternal grandmother. She was my favorite storyteller and always urged me to "Write it down!" I'm writing, Grandma. I'm writing.

Betty Wisoff * "Sanity"
"Sanity" is the story of a thirteen-year-old and his experience in a concentration camp. He witnesses a baby being bayonetted, and this marks him for life. The boy, now middle-aged [1985], is my grocery store manager. In telling me what he had seen, he prefaced the tale with an account of his dog's illness and the care he gave it. I thought he was rambling, but he was only trying to equate his love of an animal with the German's cruelty to a defenseless baby.

Kenneth Wolman * "The Drapers: A History Lesson"
This poem is of course autobiographical, but it is autobiography without me as the center. The two men — father and grown son — were real; my mother had hired them to cut and hang drapes in the apartment. In 1992 or '93 when I wrote it, what stuck was what sticks now: their silence. It was as thought they either didn't know how to speak or had lost the need for it. Maybe, I sometimes think, speech would have reminded them of the life before the War, before the experiences that changed them into forced-smiling mutes. I don't know their original nationality or where they were imprisoned. I don't know whether they were in an extermination camp, were "simply" interned, or were slave laborers. In the end, it makes no difference. For all they did not say, they were the first two people ever to show me the Shoah, and they did so by having their sleeves rolled up on a warm day in the Bronx. Those tattoos got my attention, their attention that I was paying attention, and a world of both curiosity and fear that has never left me.

If we are not ourselves the children of survivors, how old are we when we first learn about the Shoah? We are not born knowing about it; the knowledge creeps in gradually, perhaps even insidiously. I recall that when I asked my mother about the numbers, she was evasive. Only years later did I learn the frightful truth behind those obscene purple tattoos and intuit that those two men were the recipients of a miracle, but a backhanded one. Father and son both had lived, but they did so to enter a world of silence and memory. Wherever they are now — for I must presume by now they both are dead — may their souls have found rest and peace.

Carolyne Wright * "After Forty Years," "KZ"

I wrote "KZ" after a visit to the Dachau *Konzentrationslager Gedenkstette*, the Dachau Concentration Camp Memorial Site, in January 1986. It was an icy mid-winter day, with a light snow drifting over the open square, the guard tower, the one remaining barracks-style dormitory, the ovens, the original camp entrance with its grillework gate — the structures left standing from the original complex — as well as the memorial museum filled with photos of inmates and guards, documents, and articles of clothing and personal items. Looking at the 1940s black and white photos and then at the wintry scene out the window — the dilapidated buildings as gray and grim as when they were in use in their deadly functions, the branches of the few bare trees standing out stark and black against the snow — I was struck by how similar the site looked in the photos and out the window, how little had changed in the passage of forty years. Even though the scene was empty of inmates and guards, and very few other visitors had ventured out on this cold snowy afternoon, I could imagine myself in the camp as it was then, and felt myself able to enter empathetically into the experience of those who had suffered and died there. This poem is for Terrence Des Pres (1939–87).

"After Forty Years": In June 1985, the body of Nazi death camp doctor Josef Mengele was discovered in a grave in Embú, Brazil, where he had lived for decades in hiding (with the knowledge of his family and many local people who were aware of his identity) until his death by drowning. Embedded in his name is the German word *Engel*, angel. This irony was not lost on those who suffered and died at his hands. I heard the news reports of this discovery on National Public Radio and was riveted by the story. Later, I watched the television coverage — the pitiful bundle of bones and skin, stained brown by the soil they had been buried in — seemed an anticlimactic end for such a ruthless, sensationally evil, man, even one who had lived in disgrace under a phony name.

I never asked myself why I was drawn to the phenomenon of the Holocaust — I have gravitated to the deeply human stories of all people who suffer persecution: the African American stories of the Middle Passage, slavery, and Jim Crow-era violence in the South; the Native American genocide and Trail of Tears; and (from my own experience in Chile during the presidency of the doomed Salvador Allende) the suffering of Allende's supporters and sympathizers, thousands of whom were killed, *disappeared*, and exiled after the first 9/11, the September 11, 1973 military coup in Chile. For me, the Holocaust was among the most horrific exercises of human inhumanity — and one of the more recent and most thoroughly documented incidences thereof. My own experiences witnessing human cruelty in the case of Chile and elsewhere deepened my feeling for the Holocaust among other holocausts.

It wasn't until many years later that my brother and I found out that we are part Jewish through our mother. Through much genealogical sleuthing, my brother learned about our great-grandfather — our mother's father's father, Louis Lee — a gambler and *bon vivant* who claimed to have been born in London . . . and also in Florida! My brother's research uncovered the fact that Louis Lee was really a Jew of Eastern European parentage — which country of origin we have not been able to discover — possibly surnamed Levy or Levin and, on one document, Roselle. My brother discovered that Louis Lee had in fact been born in the early 1860s in New York City's Lower East Side, a district crowded in those years with immigrant Jews from Eastern Europe and Russia.

Likewise, Louis Lee's son — our mother's father, Harry Lee — also claimed to have been born in Florida. Even our Aunts Mabel and Harriet, our mother's younger sisters, believed in the story of their father's Florida birthplace; but in fact he, too, was born on the Lower East Side. Our mother always denied any Jewish ancestry whenever my brother tried to pry information from her. Unlike our mother, though, Aunt Mabel admitted to my brother shortly before she died that the three sisters knew their father was Jewish or half-Jewish. My brother later obtained a microfilm copy of Harry Lee's 1888 birth certificate from the New York City public records: on it were written the words "*Pater Israelita*," in the Latin phrasing of the era. My brother would joke in later years that my middle name, Lee — after our mother's maiden name — should really be Levy!

The secrecy surrounding my mother's Jewish ancestry has gone back at least as far as her father's father, Louis Lee, who may have been the one to Anglicize what most likely was a German or Eastern European surname. This secrecy is one reason that there has been no connection to any Jewish family remaining in Europe. My brother and I have no knowledge of Louis Lee's ancestors — his parents, who may have been the ones to emigrate from Europe, or their brothers and sisters, aunts and uncles, or cousins. Therefore, we have no idea if extended family members were still in Europe during the Third Reich, and thus we have no direct family connection with the Holocaust. But the stories of those who suffered and died during those years have haunted me, and prompted the writing of the poems included here.

Biographical Notes

Marjorie Agosín is the daughter and granddaughter of Jewish emigrants from Odessa and Vienna. She was raised in Santiago de Chile and arrived in the United States at sixteen, after her family escaped the tyrannical rule of Augusto Pinochet. Agosín is the author of almost forty books, including *At the Threshold of Memory: Selected & New Poems* (White Pine Press, 2003), and she has been honored by the government of Chile with the Gabriella Mistral Medal of Honor for lifetime achievement. Currently, she is the Luella Lameer Slain Professor of Latinamerican Studies at Wellesley.

Sherman Alexie has published seventeen books. His first collection of short stories, *The Lone Ranger and Tonto Fistfight in Heaven*, received both a PEN/Hemingway Award for best first book of fiction and a Lila Wallace-*Reader's Digest* Writers Award. He was named one of Granta's "Best of Young American Novelists" and won the Before Columbus Foundation's American Book Award and the Murray Morgan Prize for his first novel, *Reservation Blues*. Alexie's work was selected for inclusion in *The Best American Short Stories 2004* and Pushcart Prize XXIX of the Small Presses. He is a Spokane/Coeur d'Alene Indian.

Karen Alkalay-Gut was born on the last night of the buzz bombs in London to parents who had escaped from Danzig during the war, and she grew up in the US. She received her PhD from the University of Rochester (her thesis focused on Theodore Roethke). In 1972, she moved to Israel where she teaches English at Tel Aviv University. Alkalay-Gut has published over twenty books of poetry and is currently working on her third CD. Her most recent book, *So Far So Good*, was published by Sivan in 2004. Her critical study, *Open Secret: Poetry and Popular Culture* was released by the University of Washington Press in 2007.

Michael Alpiner is an English Teacher in New York City. His poems have appeared in such journals as *Jewish Currents*, *Soul Fountain*, and *New Works Review*. In August 2004, he received a grant to work at the Vermont Studio Center. During this residency, he completed *Pebbles from the Village*, a poetry memoir of his family's European immigrant experience, and began work on a second poetry manuscript that documents his successful battle with Hodgkin's Disease. Alpiner has been featured on Hofstra radio's "Calliope's Corner" and was also featured at the annual Jewish Arts Festival at Monmouth University in New Jersey.

John Amen is the author of two collections of poetry, *Christening the Dancer* (Uccelli Press. 2003) and *More of Me Disappears* (Cross-Cultural Communications, 2005), as well as one folk/folk rock CD, *All I'll Never Need* (Cool Midget. 2004). He is featured in the 2007 *Poet's Market*. Amen founded and continues to edit the award-winning online literary bimonthly, *The Pedestal Magazine*.

Frieda Arkin is a retired physical anthropologist who is also the author of many short stories and two novels, the latest of which, *Hedwig and Berti*, has the Holocaust as its subject and moving force. Members of Arkin's family, on both her mother's and her father's sides, were victims of the Nazis.

Brett Axel is a poet, social activist, father, and devout Unitarian Universalist living and writing in Utica, New York. His three collections of poetry are *First on the Fire* (GOTT, 1999), *Disaster Relief* (Minimal, 2002), and *Rules* (Minimal, 2004). He edited the critically acclaimed poetry anthology, *Will Work For Peace* (Zeropanik Press, 1999).

David B. Axelrod was raised in the home of his Russian Jewish grandmother, and his earliest consciousness formed around her fears concerning pogroms and the Holocaust. He has received three Fulbright fellowships, the third of these to serve as the first official Fulbright poet-in-residence in China. Axelrod has published fifteen books, the most recent of which is *Another Way: Poems Derived from the Tao Te Ching*, and his work has appeared in hundreds of magazines and anthologies. He directs Writers Unlimited Agency, Inc., a not-for-profit organization providing information on the writing arts (www.writersunlimited.org).

Yakov Azriel has published poems in the US, the UK and Israel. His first full-length collection of poetry, *Threads from a Coat of Many Colors*, was released by Time Being Books in 2005. Six of his poems have won prizes in international poetry competitions, including First Prize in the 2004 Miriam Lindberg Israel Poetry for Peace Competition. In addition, he was recently awarded a poetry writing fellowship from the Memorial Foundation for Jewish Culture. Azriel has been living in Israel since he was twenty-one.

Crystal Bacon is a 1998 New Jersey State Council of the Arts grant recipient. Her first book, *Elegy with a Glass of Whiskey*, received the 2003 BOA Editions "New Poetry America" prize, and her work has appeared in a variety of publications in the US and Canada. Bacon has also published essays on Elizabeth Bishop in *Divisions of the Heart: Elizabeth Bishop and the Art of Money and Place* and *In Worcester Massachusetts: Essays on Elizabeth Bishop from the 1997 Elizabeth Bishop Conference at WPI.* Until recently, she served as Assistant Dean of Academic Services at Warren County Community College in Pennsylvania.

Julius Balbin was interned by the Nazis in the Jewish ghetto of that city and then in four concentration camps, including Mauthausen. He was liberated in 1945 by American troops but lost nearly all of his family in the Shoah. Balbin has taught French, German, Spanish, and Russian at colleges in the U.S. and has served as president of the New York Esperanto Society. He has published two books of Holocaust poetry in Esperanto, *Strangled Cries* (1981) and *The Bitch of Buchenwald* (1986), both from Cross-Cultural Communications. In 1989, Edistudio (Pisa, Italy) brought out his collected poetry, *Imperio de l'Koroj* (*Empire of the Heart*).

Stanley H. Barkan is the publisher of Cross-Cultural Communications and editor of the *Cross-Cultural Review of World Literature and Art*. In 1996, the Small Press Center presented him with the Poor Richard's Award for "a quarter century of high quality publishing." His own poetry has been translated into twenty-one different languages, and he is the author of twelve poetry collections, several of which are bilingual. These include *Under the Apple Tree* (Polish), *Bubbemeises & Babbaluci* (Italian), *Naming the Birds* (Bulgarian), and *Crossings* (Russian). His latest book, *Mishpocheh*, is a poetic memoir about his and his wife's extended "family."

Tony Barnstone is Professor of English at Whittier College in California. His books of poems include *The Golem of Los Angeles* (Red Hen Press), winner of the 2007 Benjamin Saltman Award; *Sad Jazz: Sonnets* (Sheep Meadow Press, 2005) and *Impure* (University Press of Florida, 1998). Among his other books are *Chinese Erotic Poetry* (Everyman, 2007)*; Out of the Howling Storm: The New Chinese Poetry; Laughing Lost in the Mountains: Poems of Wang Wei*; and *The Art of Writing: Teachings of the Chinese Masters*. He is the recipient of many national poetry prizes and of fellowships from the National Endowment for the Arts and the California Arts Council.

Willis Barnstone is Distinguished Professor of Comparative Literature at Indiana University. He taught in Greece at the end of the civil war (1949–51) and in Buenos Aires during the "Dirty War" (1975–76) and was a Fulbright Professor of American Literature at Beijing Foreign Studies University (1984–85). He has published many books of poetry, scholarship, translation and memoir, including *The Other Bible* (1984); *Five A.M. in Beijing* (1987); *With Borges on an Ordinary Evening in Buenos Aires* (1993); *The Secret Reader* (1996); and *Sweetbitter Love: Poems of Sappho* (2006).

Judith Barrington is the author of three collections of poetry, most recently, *Horses and the Human Soul* (Story Line Press, 2004). Her awards include the Dulwich International Festival Poetry Prize (UK), the *Clackamas Review* Poetry Prize, the A.C.L.U. of Oregon's Freedom of Expression Award, and the Stuart Holbrook Award for services to the literary community, and she has been shortlisted for the Bridport Prize and the *Times*/Arvon Poetry Competition. Barrington has taught at numerous conferences and workshops across the U.S. and for the Poetry School and the Arvon Foundation of Britain. She lives in Portland, Oregon.

Marvin Bell has been called "a maverick" and "an insider who thinks like an outsider." Nonetheless, he served two terms as Iowa's first poet laureate. He taught forty years for the Iowa Writers Workshop and now serves on the faculty of a low-residency MFA program based at Pacific University in Oregon. He is the creator of the "Dead Man" poems, for which he is both famous and infamous. *Mars Being Red*, his nineteenth book, was published by Copper Canyon in 2007. He and his wife, Dorothy, live in Iowa City, Iowa, and Port Townsend, Washington.

Lora J. Berg worked for the U.S. Embassy in Tunis, Tunisia. Her first book, *The Mermaid Wakes: Paintings of a Caribbean Isle* (with Canute Caliste), was released by Macmillan Caribbean in 1989. Her father was one of the few survivors on the Glicksberg side of her family.

Michael Blumenthal is the author, most recently, of the memoir *All My Mothers and Fathers* (2002), and of *Dusty Angel* (1999), his sixth book of poems. His novel, *Weinstock Among the Dying* (1994), won *Hadassah Magazine*'s Harold U. Ribelow Prize for the best work of Jewish fiction, and his collection of essays from Central Europe, *When History Enters the House*, was published in 1998. Formerly Director of Creative Writing at Harvard, he has taught at universities in Hungary, Israel, Germany and France. From 2006–07, Blumenthal held the Darden Endowed Chair in Creative Writing at Old Dominion University.

George Bogin (1920–88) was the author of *In a Surf of Strangers* (University Press of Florida, 1981) and a booklength translation, *Selected Poems and Reflections on the Art of Poetry*, by the Franco-Uruguyan writer, Jules Supervielle (SUN Press, 1985). His poems also appeared in many literary magazines and anthologies, including *American Poetry Review*, *Paris Review*, the *Nation*, *Ploughshares*, and *Chicago Review*.

Emily Borenstein has worked as Music/Drama/Dance reviewer for the Middletown *Times Herald-Record* and Supervisor of Volunteer Services at Middletown Psychiatric Center, and she has served as poetry advisor to the Orange County Arts Council. Her books include *Cancer Queen, Night of the Broken Glass*, and three chapbooks, and her poetry has appeared in a number of anthologies, including *Voices Within the Ark: The Modern Jewish Poets*. A revised and enlarged edition of her book of Holocaust poems, *Night of the Broken Glass*, was published in 2007 by Timberline Press.

Laure-Anne Bosselaar is the author of *The Hour Between Dog and Wolf* and *Small Gods of Grief*, which received the Isabella Gardner Prize for Poetry in 2001. She is the editor of four anthologies, including *Outsiders: Poems About Rebels, Exiles and Renegades* and *Never Before: Poems about First Experiences*. She teaches a graduate Poetry workshop at Sarah Lawrence College and translates American poetry into French and Flemish poetry into English. With her husband, Kurt Brown, she completed a translation of a book of poems by Flemish poet, critic and essayist, Herman de Coninck, which the Field Translation Series published in 2006.

Allen Brafman lives and works in Brooklyn, New York. In the early sixties, he taught in Chasidic elementary schools in the Williamsburg and Crown Heights neighborhoods of Brooklyn, where many of the students were children of Holocaust survivors. His poems have appeared in a variety of print and online journals, including *Skidrow Penthouse*, *Downtown Brooklyn*, Poetz.com and *Mudfish*. In 2000, Elephantine Press (Maastricht) brought out a small edition of *Sonnets from the Yiddish*, work he had done in the early seventies.

Van K. Brock is the author of nine collections of poetry, including, most recently, *Lightered: New and Selected Poems* and *Unspeakable Strangers* (poems on the Holocaust). His poems have been anthologized in *The New Yorker Book of Poems; Strong Measures: American Poets in Traditional Forms*; *Blood to Remember: American Poets on the Holocaust*; *The Made Thing: Contemporary Southern Poetry*; and numerous others. At Florida State University, Brock helped launch the writing program, which he codirected, and also founded Anhinga Press and *Southeast Review*. During the 1990s, he founded and edited *International Quarterly*.

Louis Daniel Brodsky has written fifty-five books of poetry, including the five-volume *Shadow War: A Poetic Chronicle of September 11 and Beyond*. His *You Can't Go Back, Exactly* won the Center for Great Lakes Culture's 2004 award for best book of poetry, from Michigan State University. He has also penned thirteen volumes of fiction and coauthored nine books on William Faulkner. His poems and essays have appeared in *Harper's*, *The Faulkner Review*, *Southern Review*, *National Forum*, *American Scholar*, *Studies in Bibliography*, *Cimarron Review*, and *Literary Review*, as well as in *Ariel*, *Acumen*, *Orbis*, *New Welsh Review*, *Dalhousie Review*, and numerous other journals.

Michael Dennis Browne is Distinguished Teaching Professor of English at the University of Minnesota in Minneapolis, where he has been since 1971. His books of poetry include *Things I Can't Tell You* (2004), *Selected Poems 1965–1995*, and *Smoke from the Fires* (1985), all from Carnegie Mellon. Browne has also written extensively for music, mainly for the music of Stephen Paulus. His most recent collaboration with Paulus is *To Be Certain of the Dawn*, a post-Holocaust oratorio that premiered in 2006 and that will be recorded by the Minnesota Orchestra in 2008.

Michael R. Burch is the editor of *The HyperTexts* (www.thehypertexts.com), where he has published the work of three Pulitzer Prize nominees and recent winners of the T.S. Elliot, Richard Wilbur and Howard Nemerov awards. His own poems have appeared over four hundred times in such literary journals as *Chariton Review*, *Poetry Magazine*, and *Verse*, and in such anthologies as *Writer's Digest — The Year's Best Writing 2003* and *The Best of the Eclectic Muse 1989–2003*.

Olga Cabral (1909–97) was born to Portuguese parents in 1909 in the West Indies. As a child, she was taken to Winnipeg, Canada, and shortly thereafter to New York City, where she lived for the rest of her life. Cabral was married to the Yiddish poet, Aaron Kurtz. Her books of poetry include *Cities and Deserts* (1959), *The Evaporated Man* (1968), *The Darkness in My Pockets* (1976), *In the Empire of Ice* (1980), and *The Green Dream* (1990). *Voice/Over: Selected Poems* was published in 1993.

Joan Campion is the author of *In the Lion's Mouth: Gisi Fleischmann and the Jewish Fight for Survival* (University Press of America, luniverse.com). A freelance writer, proofreader, and editor, Campion is also the author of *Smokestacks and Black Diamonds: A History of Carbon County, Pennsylvania*. She has also been working on a memoir entitled *Jerusalem Journal: Adventures in a Desert Landscape*.

Cyrus Cassells is the author of four books of poetry: *Soul Make a Path Through Shouting* (1994), *Beautiful Signor* (1997), *The Mud Actor* (2000), and *More Than Peace and Cypresses* (2004). Among his honors are a Lannan Literary Award, a Lambda Literary Award, the William Carlos Williams Award, and two NEA grants. Cassells is an associate professor of English at Texas State University-San Marcos and lives in Paris and Austin. His fifth collection of poetry, *The Crossed-Out Swastika*, will be released by Copper Canyon Press in fall 2008.

Judith Chalmer is the author of a book of poems, *Out of History's Junk Jar* (Time Being Books, 1995). She is the creator of a dance/narrative with oral histories, *Clearing Customs/ Cruzando Fronteras/ Preselenje,* on the lives of immigrants in central Vermont (1999) and author and performer of a one-woman comedy, *Don't Go In There!,* on race consciousness and Jewish identity in central Vermont (2002). Chalmer's poems, essays and oral histories have appeared in numerous anthologies and journals. She is Executive Director of VSA Arts of Vermont, a nonprofit devoted to arts and disability inclusion.

John Ciardi (1916–86) was born in Boston Massachusetts, the child of Italian immigrants. He was the author of more than forty volumes of poetry, among them *The Collected Poems of John Ciardi* (1997), *The Birds of Pompeii* (1985), *The Little That Is All* (1974), *Person to Person* (1964), and *Other Skies* (1947). He is perhaps best known for *How Does a Poem Mean*? (1959), which became a standard text for college and high school poetry courses. Ciardi also wrote an acclaimed translation of Dante's *Divina Comedia* and served as poetry editor of *Saturday Review* for many years.

David Citino (d. 2005) was the author of twelve books of poetry, most recently *The News and Other Poems* (Notre Dame, 2002), and *A History of Hands* (2006) and *The Invention of Secrecy* (2001), both from Ohio State, and he also published *Paperwork* (Kent State), a book of essays. Citino was a contributing editor for *The Eye of the Poet: Six Views of the Art and Craft of Poetry* (Oxford) and taught at Ohio State, where he was poet laureate of the university.

Vince Clemente is a poet and biographer, whose books include *John Ciardi: Measure of the Man*; *Paumanok Rising*, an anthology of Long Island Poetry; and seven volumes of verse. His most recent collection, *Sweeter Than Vivaldi* (Cross-Cultural Communications, 2002), features the paintings of Ernesto Costa. Clemente's work has appeared widely in periodicals and also in a number of anthologies, including *Blood to Remember: American Poets on the Holocaust* and *Darwin*, a Norton Critical Edition. For many years, he was a trustee of the Walt Whitman Birthplace and was also a founding editor of *West Hills Review.*

Helen Degen Cohen (Halina Degenfisz) has received an NEA Fellowship in Poetry, First Prize in *Stand Magazine*'s fiction competition, and several Illinois Arts Council literary awards. For years, artist-in-education and instructor for Roosevelt University, she cofounded and coedits *Rhino* and coordinates its adjunct, the *Poetry Forum*. Her work has been the subject of two studies, "This Dark Poland — Ethnicity in the work of Helen Degen Cohen," in *Something of My Very Own to Say: American Women Writers of Polish Descent* (Columbia University Press), and "Rootlessness and Alienation in the Poetry of Helen Degen Cohen," in *Shofar*.

David Curzon was born in Melbourne, Australia, and has lived since 1970 in New York, where he worked at the United Nations until 2001, at which time he retired from the post he had held for fifteen years, Chief of the Central Evaluation Unit. Curzon has published collections of poetry with Cross-Cultural Communications, Penguin Australia and the Jewish Publication Society of America and has also published two anthologies of twentieth century poetry that respond to biblical texts. His poems and translations have appeared in many journals and several anthologies, including *World Poetry* (Norton).

Ruth Daigon was the founder of Poets On: and edited that journal for twenty years. Her poems have been widely published in online and print magazines and in anthologies and collections. Her awards include the Ann Stanford Poetry Prize (1997) and the Greensboro Poetry Award (2000). Daigon's most recent books include *Handfuls of Time* (2002) and *Payday at the Triangle*, based on the 1911 Triangle Shirtwaist Factory Fire in New York City (2001), both from Small Poetry Press, and *The Moon Inside* (Newton's Baby, 1999). Her poetry was distributed by the U.S. State Department in its literacy exchange with Thailand.

Susan Dambroff is a mother and a teacher of autistic children. Her poem "There Were Those" is from her book *Memory in Bone*, an introspective journey about herself as a Jew and a political person. Her work has also been published in the anthology *Ghosts of the Holocaust* (Wayne State University Press) and in a number of literary journals.

Enid Dame (1943–2003) coedited *Which Lilith? Feminist Writers Re-Create the World's First Woman* (1990). She was also a coeditor of *Bridges*, the Jewish feminist magazine, and *Home Planet News*, the literary tabloid she founded with her husband, Donald Lev, in 1979. Her work often reflected her Jewish background and culture. "Miriam's Seders," from *Stone Shekhina* (Three Mile Harbor, 2002), her last book of midrashic poems, was included in *Best Jewish Writing 2003*. Alicia Ostriker has called Enid Dame "one of the great midrashists of our time."

Kate Daniels is Associate Dean of the College of Arts and Science at Vanderbilt University. Her first book of poetry, *The White Wave* (1984), won the Agnes Lynch Starrett Poetry Prize, and the *Four Testimonies*, her third, was one of Dave Smith's selections for his Southern Messenger Series (1998). Daniels has also edited *"Say Your Life Broke Down": A Literary Companion for Psychoanalysis and Psychotherapy*; was coeditor of *Solitude and Silence*, a volume of critical essays on Robert Bly (1982); and edited Muriel Rukeyser's selected poems, *Out of Silence* (1982). She has also served as a judge for the National Book Award in poetry.

Sister Mary Philip de Camara taught English at the Georgetown Visitation Preparatory School in Washington, DC, from 1963–83. With Stephen Hayes, she coauthored the Monarch Notes study guide on Conan Doyle's Sherlock Holmes and another on the four novels that feature Holmes. Sister Mary Philip published poems and articles in the *Baker Street Journal*, and her poetry also appeared in *Christian Poetry Journal*, *Black Warrior Review*, *Wings*, and several anthologies.

Theodore Deppe is the author of four collections of poems, including *The Wanderer King* (Alice James Books, 1996) and *Cape Clear: New and Selected Poems* (Salmon Books, Ireland, 2002). He has received a Pushcart Prize and two NEA grants and is currently the Irish field director of the Stonecoast MFA program.

Norita Dittberner-Jax is an educator and poet, who lives in St. Paul, Minnesota, and works as a writing consultant for the St. Paul public schools. Her poems have been widely published in small press magazines, and her book of poems, *What They Always Were,* won the Minnesota Voices Competition and was nominated for a Minnesota Book Award. Dittberner-Jax is the recipient of a number of awards for her poetry and is one of the featured poets in *Thirty-Three Minnesota Poets.* She won a Travel and Study grant from the Jerome Foundation to study cities associated with the Third Reich and the concentration camps.

Sharon Dolin is the author of three books of poems, *Realm of the Possible* (2004), *Serious Pink* (2003), and *Heart Work* (1995), as well as three chapbooks. Her poems have appeared in numerous journals, including *Kenyon Review*, *New Republic*, *New American Writing*, *American Letters & Commentary*, and *Poetry*. She has been a Fulbright scholar in Italy and a recipient of a national award from the Poetry Society of America. Dolin is also the coordinator and cojudge of the Center for Books Arts' annual poetry chapbook competition, and she teaches at the Unterberg Poetry Center of the 92nd Street Y and Poets House in New York City.

Wendy Drexler is an editor of language arts materials and lives in Belmont, Massachusetts. Her poems have appeared in *Comstock Review*, *Barrow Street*, *Mid-America Poetry Review*, *Passager*, *Rhino*, *Ibbetson Street*, and other journals, and in two anthologies, *Mercy of Tides: Poems for a Beach House* (2003), and *Rough Places Plain: Poems for the Mountains* (2005), both from Salt Marsh Pottery Press. Drexler's chapbook, *Gas Stations, Drive-Ins, the Bright Motels* (2007) was published by Pudding House Press.

Shoshana Dubman was born in April 1946 or 1945 in Germany, probably in a displaced persons camp, and grew up in St. Louis, Missouri. After high school, she spent a short time in college, then wandered through Europe, and finally ended up in Israel, where she spent some time on a Kibbutz. She attended Bezalel University in Jerusalem and graduated in 1972. Eventually, she returned to the United States and settled in Albuquerque, New Mexico, where she received an undergraduate and graduate degree in art education. Dubman currently works as a special educator in the public school system.

Jehanne Dubrow was born in Italy and grew up in Yugoslavia, Zaire, Poland, Belgium, Austria, and the United States. She is currently completing a PhD in creative writing at the University of Nebraska-Lincoln. Dubrow's work has appeared in *Poetry*, *Hudson Review*, *Tikkun*, *New England Review*, and *Poetry Northwest*. Her chapbook, *The Promised Bride*, was published by Finishing Line Press in 2007. Also in 2007, the U.S. Holocaust Memorial Museum in Washington, DC, granted her a four-month fellowship to research materials for a book of narrative poems on the Shoah that will examine the nature of second and third generation trauma.

Shelly Ehrlich (1931–88) was a psychiatric social worker, teacher, editor, and poet. Her poetry was widely published in small press journals, and three of her books of poetry — *How the Rooted Travel*; *Dreaming the Ark*; and *Beneath All Voice* — were published by Juniper Press, the last of these three years after her death.

Kenneth Fearing (1902–61) was born in Oak Park, Illinois, and studied at the University of Wisconsin before settling in New York City. He published several collections of poetry, including *Angel Arms* (1929), *Dead Reckoning* (1938), *Afternoon of a Pawnbroker and Other Poems* (1943), and *Stranger at Coney Island and Other Poems* (1948), as well as several novels, among them *The Big Clock* (1946), which was released as a film in 1948.

Frederick Feirstein is a psychoanalyst, poet, and playwright. His books include *Manhattan Carnival*, a Pulitzer Prize finalist, and *Ending the Twentieth Century*, which won the *Quarterly Review of Literature*'s International Prize. His most recent collection is *New and Selected Poems* (1998). Among his many awards are a Guggenheim Fellowship and the Poetry Society of America's John Masefield Award. Feirstein's play, *The Family Circle*, was produced at the Provincetown Playhouse in New York City and published in the Modern Classics series in London. He has also written several acclaimed musical dramas.

Irving Feldman is Distinguished Professor of English at the State University of New York at Buffalo. Feldman's collections of poetry include *Beautiful False Things* (2000); *All of Us Here* (1986), a finalist for the National Book Critics Circle Award; and *Works and Days* (1961), winner of the Kovner Poetry Prize of the Jewish Book Council. Feldman has received a National Institute of Arts and Letters award and a grant from the National Endowment for the Arts, as well as fellowships from the Guggenheim, Ingram Merrill, and MacArthur foundations. His *Collected Poems 1954–2004* was published by Schocken Books.

Ruth Feldman is the author of five books of poetry and fifteen books of Italian translations, all poetry, with the exception of Primo Levi's concentration camp stories, *Moments of Reprieve* (1986). In 1999, Feldman and John P. Welle received the Raiziss/de Palchi Book Prize for their translation of Andrea Zanzotto's work, *Peasant's Wake for Fellini's Casanova and other Poems*. She has won the John Florio Prize in England, the Circe-Sabaudia Prize in Italy, and the Italo Calvino Prize in the United States, as well as a Literacy Translator's Fellowship from the National Endowment for the Arts. She lives in Massachusetts.

Charles Adés Fishman. Please see the note that follows this section.

Tamara Fishman is a singer-songwriter and news editor based in New York City. A passionate performer and eager traveler, she has also been known to write novels in her spare time. Her first CD, *The Hunger and the Silence*, was released in 2006.

Ephim Fogel (1920–92) was born in Odessa, Russia, and came to the United States in 1923. He served in the U.S. Army in World War II and taught at Cornell University from 1949 until 1990. Fogel's poems appeared in *Atlantic Monthly, The Oxford Book of War Poetry*, and *Poetry*, among other journals and anthologies, and a number of his translations of Mandelstam's work were published in *Granite, New Letters*, and elsewhere. Fogel's scholarship centered on Renaissance literature, on attribution of authorship, and on the use of computers in literary studies. "Shipment to Maidanek" (1945) was among the earliest literary responses to the Holocaust.

Carolyn Forché is the author of four books of poetry: *Gathering the Tribes*, which received the Yale Younger Poets Award; *The Country Between Us*, chosen as the Lamont Selection of the Academy of American Poets; *The Angel of History*, winner of the *Los Angeles Times* Book Award; and *Blue Hour* (2003), a finalist for the National Book Critics Circle Award. She compiled and edited *Against Forgetting: Twentieth Century Poetry of Witness* (W.W. Norton, 1993) and received the Edita and Ira Morris Hiroshima Foundation Award for Peace and Culture in Stockholm for her work on behalf of human rights and the preservation of memory and culture.

Florence W. Freed made her career as a clinical psychologist and professor of psychology at Middlesex Community College in Massachusetts. She has published research on attitudes toward abortion, battered lives, and the effects of corporal punishment. Since her retirement, her poetry and short stories have appeared in such journals as *Agada*, *The Bridge*, *Jewish Spectator*, *Jefferson Review*, *Midstream* and *Response*. Her husband, Charles Freed, is a laser research scientist at MIT's Lincoln Laboratory and is a Holocaust survivor.

Mike Frenkel was born in Paris, France, in 1950. His parents survived the Holocaust in Romania, but his grandparents and an uncle did not. He teaches English in Brooklyn Technical High School. Frenkel's poetry related to the Holocaust has also appeared in *Beyond Lament: Poets of the World Bearing Witness to the Holocaust* (Northwestern University Press, 1998) and *English Journal.*

Sari Friedman is a poet and short-story writer. Her family escaped from Nazi Germany.

Alice Friman is the author of eight collections of poetry, most recently *The Book of the Rotten Daughter* (BkMk Press, 2006). She has received the Ezra Pound Poetry Award from Truman State University and the Sheila Margaret Motton Prize from the New England Poetry Club. Her poems have appeared in *Poetry*, *Georgia Review*, *Boulevard*, *Southern Review*, *Gettysburg Review*, and *Shenandoah*, which awarded her the 2002 James Boatwright III Prize for Poetry. Friman has received fellowships from the Indiana Arts Commission and the Arts Council of Indianapolis and has won three prizes from the Poetry Society of America.

Patricia Garfinkel has published three books of poetry, including *From the Red Eye of Jupiter* (1990), a winner in the manuscript competition sponsored by Washington Writers Publishing House, and *Making the Skeleton Dance* (George Braziller Publishers, 2000). She has read at such diverse venues as the Folger Shakespeare Library, Prairie Lights, and the Virginia Festival of the Book, and gave the first poetry reading at the National Air and Space Museum. Garfinkel has been a senior policy analyst and speechwriter at the National Science Foundation since 1995.

Kinereth Gensler (d. 2005) grew up in Chicago and Jerusalem. She received her B.A. from the University of Chicago and her M.A. from Columbia University. She lived in Cambridge, Massachusetts and taught in the Radcliffe Seminars for twenty years. In addition to her three volumes of poetry with Alice James Books, Gensler was coauthor with Nina Nyhart of *The Poetry Connection*, a text for teaching poetry writing to children.

David Gershator came to the US after WW II. He has taught English and Romance Languages at Rutgers, Brooklyn College, and the University of the Virgin Islands. His translations, poetry, and reviews have appeared in numerous anthologies and journals, and he has received both an NEH grant and a CAPS award. Gershator translated and edited *Federico García Lorca: Selected Letters* (New Directions) and has coauthored six picture books for children. His poetry collections include *Play Mas* (Downtown Poets) and *Elijah's Child* (Cross-Cultural Communications). As an artist and printmaker, his work is represented by Gallery St. Thomas, U.S.V.I.

Jacob Glatstein (Yankev Glatshteyn) (1896–1971) published sixteen books of poetry — including *Songs of Remembrance (1943), Radiant* Jews (1946), and *Down-to-Earth Talk* (1956) — in addition to seven collections of essays and criticism and four novels. He immigrated to the United States from Poland at seventeen and lived and wrote in New York City until his death. With A. Leyeles and N. B. Minkov, Glatstein was coeditor of the important Introspectivist anthology, *In Zikh* (1930). He was the recipient of numerous literary prizes for his work.

Barbara Goldberg is the author of four books of poetry and three translations. Her work has appeared in *Gettysburg Review*, *Paris Review*, *Poetry* and other literary journals, and she is the recipient of two fellowships from the National Endowment for the Arts and four grants from the Maryland State Arts Council. She is senior speechwriter for a large nonprofit association. Her most recent collection, *The Royal Baker's Daughter*, received the 2007 Felix Pollak Poetry Prize and will be published by University of Wisconsin Press in 2008.

Thomas A. Goldman served as an Air Force radar mechanic in World War II and was later in the U.S. Foreign Service. As vice consul in Rotterdam, he interviewed survivors seeking to emigrate to the United States.

Rachel Goldstein is the daughter of two Holocaust survivors and was born after World War II in a displaced persons camp in St. Ottilien, Germany. She lived in South American and Canada before settling in Boston. After receiving her college degrees from McGill University in Montreal, she taught in the private and special education sectors. Later, she studied at Simmons College (Boston) and worked for a non-profit organization, "Facing History and Ourselves." In 2002, she received Second Prize in the Robert Penn Warren Poetry Award competition.

Ber Green (1901–89) was born in Russia and came to the United States in 1923. His books of Yiddish poetry include *Flowers Under Snow* (1939) and *Ever-Green* (1965). Green was a founder of the Proletpen, a group of leftist poets of the twenties and thirties, and he also founded the Yiddish Cultural Alliance and coedited the anthology *Union Square*. His memoir, *Blood, Fire, and Pillars of Smoke*, appeared in English in 1985.

John Z. Guzlowski is retired from Eastern Illinois University, where he taught contemporary American literature and poetry writing. His poems often deal with his parents' experiences as slave laborers in Nazi Germany, and a number of these poems appear in his chapbook *Language of Mules*. *Jezyk Mulow i Inne Wiersze*, a Polish-English edition of these and other poems, was published by Biblioteka Slaska in Katowice, Poland. His most recent collection, *Lightning and Ashes*, was published by Steel Toe Books in 2007. Guzlowski's essays on contemporary American authors have appeared in *Journal of Evolutionary Psychology*, *Polish Review*, and elsewhere.

Leo Haber is editor of the bi-monthly Jewish Zionist journal *Midstream*. His first novel, *The Red Heifer*, was published in 2001 by Syracuse University Press. Haber's poetry, fiction, and articles on current affairs, music, and literature have appeared in a wide variety of publications, including *Commentary*, *Midstream*, the *Carnegie Hall Program*, *Saturday Review*, and the *New York Times*. His poems and fiction have also appeared in several anthologies, including *Beyond Lament: Poets of the World Bearing Witness to the Holocaust*, *Best Jewish Writing 2002*, and *Best Jewish Writing 2003*.

Nathan Halper (1907–83), author, translator, and art dealer, was an authority on the writings of James Joyce. He also translated and published Yiddish literature, reviewed books, and operated an art gallery in Provincetown, Massachusetts, where he lived for half of each year.

Israel I. Halpern was born in Red Bank, New Jersey. He taught Mishnah at Diaspora University in Jerusalem while working for the Israel Archeological Society at the Kotel Western Wall on Mount Moriah. His work has been published by various literary journals, including *Beyond Baroque*, *Schuykill Review*, and *Angel's Gate*, and he is president of the Fresh Meadows Poets, a group of poets with whom he teaches poetry writing at Rikers Island Correctional Center and Bedford Hills Maximum Security Penitentiary, as well as at colleges, high schools, and community centers.

Annette Bialik Harchik is a poet, educator, and translator. Her poetry focuses on personal loss in the Holocaust, issues in Jewish identity, and the quest for selfhood. She is a life member of the Women's Jewish Poetry Project-NCJW in New York City and a former poetry editor of *Response* magazine. Her poems have appeared in *Sarah's Daughters Sing: A Sampler of Poems by Jewish Women*, *Ghosts of the Holocaust*, and *Bittersweet Legacy: Creative Responses to the Holocaust*. Currently, she is a reading specialist at the Dwight School and also teaches Yiddish language and literature and Jewish history in the Workman's Circle *Folkshules*.

Geoffrey Hartman, Sterling Professor Emeritus of English and Comparative Literature at Yale, has published *Akiba's Children* (Iron Mountain Press, 1978) and a brochure, *The Bible in Italy and Other Poems* (Vagabond Press, Australia, 2004). His publications in the field of Holocaust Studies are *Bitburg in Moral and Political Perspective* (Indiana University Press, 1986), *Holocaust Remembrance: The Shapes of Memory* (Blackwell, 1994), and *The Longest Shadow* (Palgrove, 2002).

Anthony Hecht (1923–2004) was a Chancellor Emeritus of the Academy of American Poets. His books of poetry include *The Darkness and the Light* (2001), *The Transparent Man* (1990), *The Venetian Vespers* (1979), and *The Hard Hours* (1967), which won the Pulitzer Prize. He was also the author of *On the Laws of Poetic Art: The Andrew Mellon Lectures, 1992* (1995) and *Obbligati: Essays in Criticism* (1986); cotranslator of Aeschylus's *Seven Against Thebes*; and editor of *The Essential Herbert* (1987). Hecht received many awards and honors, among them the Bollingen Prize and fellowships from the Guggenheim and Rockefeller foundations.

Leslie Woolf Hedley is the author of *Watchman, What of the Night* (poems, 1988) and several short story collections, including *The Day Japan Bombed Pearl Harbor* and *XYZ and Other Stories*. Hedley's "Chant for All the People on Earth" was put to music by Marta Ptaszynska under the title "The Holocaust Cantata," and the cantata was recorded for PolyGram with Lord Yehudi Menuhin conducting. Another version of the cantata, composed by Depraz, was performed on Television France. His short stories appear in many anthologies, and his play, "The Gigantic Crematorium," was performed by the Muse Theater, Cleveland.

Julie N. Heifetz is a psychotherapist, poet and author of short stories and feature articles. She was cofounder and director of the Child Development Project of the St. Louis Psychoanalytic Institute (1978–82) and served as the writer-in-residence for the St. Louis Center for Holocaust Studies. Her books include *Jordie's Present* and *Oral History and the Holocaust* (Pergamon Press, 1985).

Chaia Heller has taught ecological philosophy and feminist theory at the Institute for Social Ecology in Vermont for over two decades and is the author of *Ecology of Everyday Life: Rethinking the Desire for Nature* (Black Rose Books). She has also been involved in the feminist, anarchist, and global justice movements as an activist. Heller received her PhD in anthropology from the University of Massachusetts, Amherst. Her dissertation explores the controversy in France surrounding genetically modified organisms. Currently, she is a visiting assistant professor of anthropology at Mount Holyoke College.

Michael Heller is a poet, essayist and critic. His collection of essays, *Uncertain Poetries* was published in 2005. His many books of poetry include *Conviction's Net of Branches*, *Wordflow*, and *Exigent Futures: New and Selected Poems*. He has also published *Living Root: A Memoir* and wrote the libretto for the recently performed opera, *Benjamin*, based on the life of Walter Benjamin. Heller is the recipient of numerous awards, including fellowships from the National Endowment for the Humanities, the Di Castagnola Prize of the Poetry Society of America, and the Fund for Poetry. His most recent book is *Earth and Cave* (Dos Madres Press, 2006).

Stephen Herz is a former advertising copywriter turned poet. He's a recipient of the New England Poetry Club's Daniel Varoujan Prize, and his poems have been widely published in such journals as *Boulevard*, *Connecticut Review*, *Hollins Critic*, *Michigan Quarterly Review*, and *New York Quarterly*. His book of Holocaust poems, *Whatever You Can Carry*, was published in 2003 by Barnwood Press.

Walter Hess, a retired documentary film editor, was born in Germany and emigrated to the United States in 1940 via Ecuador. Films he has worked on have won prizes from Yale, as well as a Peabody and three Emmy awards. His poems have appeared in *American Poetry Review* and *Barrow Street*, and his translations from the German have been published in *Metamorphoses*. Hess received his MBA from the CCNY writing program in 2003.

William Heyen was raised by immigrant German parents on Long Island. A former senior Fulbright lecturer in Germany and a Guggenheim fellow in poetry, he is retired from SUNY Brockport where he was the poet-in-residence for many years. His collection, *The Swastika Poems* (1977), later expanded to *Erika: Poems of the Holocaust* (1984), was among the first volumes of Holocaust poetry by an American. Heyen's *Noise in the Trees*, was an American Library Association "Notable Book of the Year"; his *Crazy Horse in Stillness* won the 1997 Small Press Book Award for Poetry; and *Shoah Train: Poems* was a finalist for the 2004 National Book Award.

Rick Hilles received the 2005 Agnes Lynch Starrett Prize for *Brother Salvage*, his first collection of poems, which was published in 2006 by the University of Pittsburgh Press. He has received fellowships from the Institute for Creative Writing at the University of Wisconsin in Madison and the Wallace Stegner Program at Stanford and was the Amy Lowell Poetry Traveling Scholar for 2002–03. Hilles's work has appeared in *Harper's*, *The Nation*, *New Republic* and *Poetry*. He teaches at Vanderbilt University and lives in Nashville, Tennessee.

Edward Hirsch has published six books of poems, including *Wild Gratitude* (1986), which won the National Book Critics Circle Award, *The Night Parade* (1989), and *Lay Back the Darkness* (2003). He has also written three prose books, of which *How to Read a Poem and Fall in Love with Poetry* (1999) was a national bestseller. Hirsch is the editor of *Transforming Vision: Writers on Art* (1994) and *Theodore Roethke's Selected Poems* (2005). Among other honors, he has received the Prix de Rome and Guggenheim and MacArthur fellowships and is now the fourth president of the John Simon Guggenheim Memorial Foundation.

Jean Hollander has taught literature and writing courses at Princeton University, Brooklyn College, Columbia University, and elsewhere. Her book of poems, *Moondog*, was a prizewinner in the QRL Poetry Books Series, and her first collection, *Crushed into Honey*, won the Eileen W. Barnes Award. Hollander has given talks, readings and interviews at numerous venues, among them the Poetry Society of America, the Dodge Poetry Festival, and the Newberry Library, and her work has appeared in over a hundred journals and anthologies. With Robert Hollander, she has published a verse translation of Dante's *La Divina Comedia* (Random House).

Barbara Helfgott Hyett has published four collections of poetry: *In Evidence: Poems of the Liberation of Nazi Concentration Camps*; *Natural Law*; *The Double Reckoning of Christopher Columbus*; and *The Tracks We Leave: Poems on Endangered Wildlife of North America*. Her most recent collection, *Rift*, was released in 2007. Hyett's poems and essays have appeared in dozens of magazines, including *New Republic*, *The Nation*, *Hudson Review*, *Ploughshares*, and *Women's Review of Books* and are included in twenty-five anthologies. She directs POEMWORKS: The Workshop for Publishing Poets, in Brookline, Massachusetts.

Thea Iberall is a poet, playwright, and scientist. Her poetry chapbook, *Be Ye Love*, was published by Inevitable Press (1997) and a collection of her contextual poems, *The Sanctuary of Artemis,* was released by Tebot Bach in 2007. Iberall represented Los Angeles at the 1998 National Poetry Slam Competition, and she is featured in the documentary *GV6 THE ODYSSEY: Poets, Passion & Poetry*. Her musical *At Seven* was performed by the Toledo Repertory Company, and her *Primed for Love* had a run at the Eclectic Company Theatre.

Judith Irwin taught English and humanities at Lower Columbia College in Washington. She completed a book on the Cowlitz Indians of southwest Washington, and her poetry appeared in the *Bellingham Review*, *Bitterroot*, *Negative Capability*, and other publications. Her husband served in World War II with an American military police unit in Germany.

Dan Jaffe is the author of *Round for One Voice* (University of Arkansas Press), which includes many poems of Jewish content. His last three books, *Playing the Word* (BkMk Press), *Festival* (Florida International University) and *All Cats Turn Gray When the Sun Goes Down* (219 Press), deal with Jazz and classical music. Jaffe has often written about Jazz and has performed with remarkable jazz musicians. His CD, *Playing the Word: Mike Melvoin presents Dan Jaffe* (City Light Entertainment, 2006), features seventy-two minutes of poetry and Melvoin's brilliant piano-jazz.

Katherine Janowitz was born in Trencín Teplice, Czechoslovakia, in 1946. Her parents were sent to a labor camp in 1942, but they escaped in 1944 and hid in the woods of Slovakia until the war ended. She has spent twelve years working with second and third graders as a volunteer reading arts tutor, has been active in theater as a script editor and producer, and has written three short comic plays on the tribulations of the acting life. Janowitz also has devoted much of her time to drawing in pastels and has published poetry and short stories in *Ms.*, *Partisan Review*, and elsewhere.

Sheila Golburgh Johnson earned a BA in English literature from Wellesley and an MAT from Ohio Wesleyan University, after which she taught in the United States, Australia, and Mexico. Her poetry has appeared in numerous magazines, anthologies and newspapers, and also on calendars and tombstones. In 1995, she won the Association of Jewish Libraries Sydney Taylor Award for Fiction for her book *After I Said No* and, in 1998, she won the Reuben Rose Award for Poetry from Voices Israel. Johnson also writes articles for literary reference books on the work of such poets as Yehuda Amichai, Linda Pastan, Toni Cade Bambara, Dan Paget, and Karl Shapiro.

Laurence Josephs published four collections of poetry: *Cold Water Morning*; *Six Elegies*; *The Skidmore Poems;* and *New and Selected Poems* (1988). His work appeared in various anthologies and in *Southern Review*, *Poetry*, *The New Yorker*, and elsewhere. He was a professor of English at Skidmore for many years.

Marilyn Kallet is the author of eleven books, including *Circe, After Hours* (BkMk Press) and *The Art of College Teaching: 28 Takes*, coedited with April Morgan (UT Press), both published in 2005. Her poems have appeared in hundreds of journals, among them *New Letters*, *Prairie Schooner*, and *Tar River Poetry*. She has received the Tennessee Arts Commission Literary Fellowship in Poetry and in 2005 was elected to the East Tennessee Literary Hall of Fame. Kallet directed the creative writing program at the University of Tennessee from 1986 through 2004, and now holds the Hodges Chair for Distinguished Teaching.

Rodger Kamenetz teaches English and Religion at Louisiana State University in Baton Rouge. His books of poetry include *The Missing Jew: New and Collected Poems* (Time Being Books, 1991) and *The Lowercase Jew* (Northwestern, 2003). His poems have appeared in *Voices Within the Ark: The Modern Jewish Poets*; *Telling and Remembering: A Century of American Jewish Poetry*; and *The Best Jewish Writing*. Kamenetz's prose books include *The Jew in the Lotus* (1994) and *Stalking Elijah* (1997), which received the National Jewish Book Award for Jewish Thought. His most recent book is *The History of Last Night's Dream* (Harper San Francisco, 2007).

Marc Kaminsky is a poet, essayist, and psychotherapist. His books of poetry include *The Road from Hiroshima* (Simon & Schuster), *Daily Bread* (Illinois), and *A Table with People* (Sun). His books on the culture of aging and Yiddishkeit include *The Uses of Reminiscence* (Haworth) and *What's Inside You, It Shines Out of You* (Horizon). He is the editor of Barbara Wyerhoff's *Remembered Lives* and (with Mark Weiss) a collection of her posthumous work, *Stories as Equipment for Living*, both from Michigan. Kaminsky has also worked with the Open Theatre, the Talking Band, and Ballad Theater as a writer-in-residence.

Peretz Kaminsky (1916–2005) was a poet, sculptor, graphic artist, teacher of poetry, and lifelong activist in the Yiddishkeit movement. He wrote in Yiddish until the 1950s, then for many years pursued his artistic vocation as a sculptor before discovering the language and form of his mature achievement: writing Yiddish poetry in English. In rapid succession, he published four books, including *Reflection in the Eye of God* (1969), *The Book of Rituals* (1971), and *The Book of Questions* (1972). The poetry workshops he founded in the Amalgamated Housing Co-op and in Three Arrows (a summer colony started by socialists) ran for more than three decades.

Rosa Felsenburg Kaplan was born in Vienna and was a Holocaust survivor and the child of survivors. She was a social worker and mental health educator. Kaplan's poems appeared in *Shirim*, *Jewish Frontier*, *Voices Israel*, and other periodicals, and in *Women Speak* (1987).

Dori Katz, a professor of French and Comparative Literature at Trinity College, was born in Belgium in 1939 and survived the war by hiding with a Catholic family and in a home for Belgian orphans. She and her mother survived the war and immigrated to America, but her father and other members of her family died in Auschwitz. Katz has translated poetry by Eluard, Max Jacob, Guillevic and others, and has also translated novels by Marguerite Yourcenar and Henri Raczymow. Her book, *Hiding in Other People's Houses*, was published in a Spanish bilingual edition in Mexico.

Eliot Katz is the author of three books of poetry, including *Unlocking the Exits* (Coffee House Press). He is a cofounder and former editor of *Long Shot* literary journal and a coeditor of *Poems for the Nation*, a collection of political poems compiled by Allen Ginsberg. Katz worked for many years as a housing advocate for Central Jersey homeless families. He lives in New York City.

Alan Kaufman has been widely anthologized, most recently in *Nothing Makes You Free: Writings From Descendants of Holocaust Survivors* (W.W. Norton). He has published a novel, *Matches* (Little, Brown, 2005); a memoir, *Jew Boy* (Fromm/Farrar, Strauss, Giroux, 2001); and a poetry collection, *Who Are We?* (Davka Limited Editions, 1998). Kaufman has also edited *The Outlaw Bible of American Poetry, The Outlaw Bible of American Literature*, and *The Outlaw Bible of American Essays* — all released by Thunder's Mouth Press — as well as *The New Generation: Fiction for Our Time from America's Writing Programs* (Anchor/Doubleday).

Melanie Kaye/Kantrowitz has taught and lectured throughout the U.S. and Canada and has served as the Jane Watson Irwin Distinguished Professor of Women's Studies at Hamilton College and the Belle Zeller Distinguished Professor of Public Policy at Brooklyn College-CUNY. Her books include *My Jewish Face & Other Stories*; *The Issue Is Power: Essays on Women, Jews, Violence and Resistance*; and *The Color of Jews: Racial Politics and Radical Diasporism*. Kaye/Kantrowitz is cofounder of "Beyond the Pale: The Progressive Jewish Radio hour" in New York City and continues to guest-produce segments.

Tsipi Keller is a novelist and translator. She is the recipient of a National Endowment for the Arts Translation Fellowship and of CAPS and NYFA awards in fiction. Her most recent book is the novel, *Jackpot* (Spuyten Duyvil, 2004).

Miriam Kessler has published her work in such journals as the *Alchemist* (Canada), *Kalliope*, *Peregrine*, *Poets On:*, *River Styx*, and *Tabula Rasa*, and in numerous anthologies and scholarly works, among them *Blood to Remember: American Poets on the Holocaust*, *Cries of the Spirit* (Beacon Press), *Feminist Revision and the Bible* (The Bucknell Lectures in Literary Theory), and *I Feel a Little Jumpy Around You: A Book of Her Poems & His Poems Collected in Pairs* (Simon Pulse). Her collection of poems is entitled *Someone to Pour the Wine* (Ragged Edge, 1999).

Steve Klepetar was born in 1949 in Shanghai, China, the son of Holocaust survivors. Three of his grandparents perished at Auschwitz in 1944, and his mother survived Terezín, Auschwitz and the German labor camp at Oederon, near Dresden. Klepetar teaches literature and writing at St. Cloud State University in Minnesota.

Irena Klepfisz was born in Poland in 1941 and came to the U.S. at the age of eight. A recipient of an NEA poetry fellowship and translation grants, Klepfisz is the author of *A Few Words in the Mother Tongue* (poetry) and *Dreams of an Insomniac* (essays) and coeditor of *The Tribe of Dina: A Jewish Women's Anthology*; *A Jewish Women's Call for Peace: A Handbook on the Israeli/Palestinian Conflict*; and *Di Froyen: Women and Yiddish*. Her research focuses on the writings and activism of Eastern European Jewish women.

Ruth Kluger was born in Vienna in 1931. At eleven, she was deported to Theresienstadt. Later, she survived Auschwitz-Birkenau, the work camp Christianstadt, and the chaos and privations of postwar Germany, before arriving as a refugee in the United States. Professor Emerita of German at the University of California, Irvine, she is the author of five volumes of literary criticism and the recipient of numerous awards.

David Koenig is the author of six books of poetry, including *The Ladder of Memory*; *The Spiral Staircase*; *Butterfly (The Soul in Search of Transformation)*; and *Butterfly Songs (The Soul Transformed)*; as well as the poetic autobiography, *An Invitation to Life* (Harp Song Press). His first volume of poems, *Green Whistle* (William Caxton Ltd.) won the Friends of Literature Book Award. Koenig is currently working on a history of Jewish poetry. His parents fled from Vienna in 1939.

Yala Korwin, a poet and visual artist, was born in Poland. She survived a labor camp in Germany and lived in France as a refugee for ten years before immigrating to the United States with her husband and young children. In college, she majored in French literature and earned a B.A. degree magna cum laude and then a Master's degree in library science. Her book, *To Tell the Story — Poems of the Holocaust*, was published in 1987 by the now-defunct Holocaust Library. Her poetry has been published in numerous magazines, and her poem "The Little Boy with His Hands Up" has been included in a documentary film produced in Finland.

Aaron Kramer (1921–97) first gained national prominence with *Seven Poets in Search of an Answer* (1944) and *The Poetry and Prose of Heinrich Heine* (1948). He was a leading resistance poet throughout the McCarthy era and, later, a professor of English at Dowling College, in Oakdale, New York. Kramer published *The Prophetic Tradition in American Poetry* (1968) and other critical studies, and his many translations include *A Century of Yiddish Poetry* (1989) and the internationally acclaimed *The Emperor of Atlantis*, an opera created in the Terezín concentration camp. His later collections of poetry include *Indigo* (1991) and *Regrouping* (1997).

Norbert Krapf grew up in Jasper, Indiana, a German community, and taught for thirty-four years at Long Island University, where he directed the C.W. Post Poetry Center. His books include *Blue-Eyed Grass: Poems of Germany*; *The County I Come From*, which was nominated for the Pulitzer Prize; and *Looking for God's Country*. He is the editor of *Finding the Grain*, a collection of pioneer German journals and letters from his native Dubois County, and the translator/editor of *Shadows on the Sundial: Selected Early Poems of Rainer Maria Rilke*. Krapf has been a Fulbright professor of American poetry at the Universities of Freiburg and Erlangen-Nuremberg, Germany.

Carolyn Kreiter-Foronda is a painter, sculptor and educator, who is also Virginia's current poet laureate. She has published four books — *Contrary Visions*; *Gathering Light*; *Death Comes Riding*; and *Greatest Hits* — and is coeditor of *In a Certain Place*, an anthology. Foronda's poems and other writings have appeared in such journals as *Antioch Review*, *Hispanic Culture Review*, and *Prairie Schooner*, and in a number of anthologies, including *Blood to Remember: American Poets on the Holocaust*. Her honors include three Pushcart Prize nominations and three Artist-in-Education grants from the Virginia Commission for the Arts.

Maxine Kumin lives on a farm in central New Hampshire. Her fifteenth book, *Jack and Other New Poems*, was published in 2005, following *Bringing Together: Uncollected Early Poems 1958–1988* and *The Long Marriage*; a memoir titled *Inside the Halo and Beyond: Anatomy of a Recovery*; *Quit Monks or Die!*, a murder mystery about sensory-deprivation experiments on primates; and *Always Beginning: Essays on a Life in Poetry*. Her awards include the Poets Prize, the Ruth E. Lilly Poetry Prize, the Pulitzer Prize, and the Harvard Arts Medal.

Aaron Kurtz (1891–1964) was born near Vitebsk, Russia, and immigrated to the United States in 1911. Kurtz published eight books of Yiddish poetry, including *Khaos* (Chaos) in 1920 and *Marc Chagall* in 1947. *Lider* (Poems) was published posthumously in 1966. Kurtz was associated with the Insichist group of modern Yiddish poets and later with the proletarian poets.

Christine Lahey is an adjunct associate professor at the College for Creative Studies in Detroit where she specializes in interdisciplinary studies and fairy tales. Her chapbook, *Sticks and Stones*, was published in 1980 by Urban Despair Press, and her work has appeared in *Michigan Quarterly Review*, *All's Normal Here: A Charles Bukowski Primer*, and *Abandon Automobile: Detroit City Poetry*. A recipient of the Hopwood Award for poetry from the University of Michigan and a 1992 Creative Artist Award from the Michigan Council for the Arts, Lahey coedited *Planet Detroit: An Anthology of Urban Poetry* with Kurt Nimmo in 1983.

Carole Glasser Langille has published three books of poetry and two children's books. Her second volume of poetry, *In Cannon Cave* (1997), was nominated for a Governor General's Award and the Atlantic Poetry Prize. Her third collection, *Late in a Slow Time*, was published in 2003. The composer Chan Ka Nin put six poems from this book to music in a piece for violin and piano entitled "Late in a Slow Time," which premiered in Newfoundland in 2006. Langille's most recent children's book is *Interview with a Stick Collector*. Currently, she lives in Black Point, Nova Scotia, with her husband and two teenage sons.

Alyssa A. Lappen is a former senior editor of *Institutional Investor*, *Working Woman*, and *Corporate Finance* magazines and a former associate editor for *Forbes*. Her chapbook, *The People Bear Witness*, won the annual award from *Ruah: A Journal of Spiritual Poetry* in 2000. Her poems have also appeared in *Midstream*, *Blueline*, *Sow's Ear Poetry Review*, *New Works Review*, *Common Ground Review*, and in many other forums. Lappen, now a freelance journalist, is also a Senior Fellow at the American Center for Democracy.

Denise Levertov (1923–97) was born in Ilford, Essex, England. She married the American writer Mitchell Goodman in 1947 and moved with him to the United States a year later. Levertov became a naturalized citizen in 1955 and was an important voice in the poetic avant-garde of the fifties, as well as a major figure in the peace movement of the sixties. Her published work includes four collections of prose and twenty-five volumes of poetry, among them *The Sorrow Dance* (1967), *Relearning the Alphabet* (1970), and *Freeing the Dust* (1975), which won the Lenore Marshall Poetry Prize. *This Great Unknowing: Last Poems* (New Directions) appeared in 1999.

Philip Levine is the author of sixteen books of poetry, most recently *Breath* (Alfred A. Knopf, 2004). His other poetry collections, nearly all of which have won major awards, include *The Simple Truth* (1994), *What Work Is* (1991), and *The Names of the Lost* (1975). Levine has also published a collection of essays, *The Bread of Time: Toward an Autobiography* (1994); edited *The Essential Keats* (1987); and coedited and translated books by Gloria Fuertes and Jaime Sabines. For two years, he served as chair of the Literature Panel of the National Endowment for the Arts and, in 2000, was elected a Chancellor of the Academy of American Poets.

Leatrice H. Lifshitz (1933–2003) edited *Voices: Jews in a Circle*, which investigated the meaning of Jewish memory. Her novel, *One Crack, Two Crack, Three Cracks, Four* was a finalist in the 1998 Willa Cather fiction contest, and her novel, *And There Would Be No Wolves*, was a finalist in the Hemingway First Novel contest. She edited *Her Soul Beneath the Bone: Women's Poetry on Breast Cancer* (1988) and *Only Morning in Her Shoes: Poetry About Women* (1990). Lifshitz won many awards for her haiku, tanka, rengay and haibun, including the Haiku Society of America's Gerald Brady Senryu Award (1999).

Alan Lupack, Director of the Rossell Hope Robbins Library of medieval studies and an adjunct Professor of English at the University of Rochester, is the author of *The Dream of Camelot*, a volume of Arthurian poetry. His poems and stories have appeared in numerous literary magazines. He has been coeditor of *The Round Table: A Journal of Poetry and Fiction*, and he has edited four collections of post-medieval Arthurian texts. His latest book is *The Oxford Guide to Arthurian Literature and Legend*. His wife lost members of her family during the Holocaust.

Yaacov Luria served in the Army Air Corps (1943–46). He taught at Fordham University and worked as the New York theater critic for the *Baltimore Jewish Times*. Luria was the author of one book of poetry, *Not a Piano Key*, and published short stories, poems, essays, reviews, and other work in a wide range of periodicals and anthologies, including *The New Yorker, Harper's*, *Saturday Review*, *Christian Science Monitor*, and the *Los Angeles Times*.

Arlene Maass published poems in *Jewish Currents*, Voices Israel, and *Concert at Chopin's House: A Polish-American Anthology*. With her husband, the Rev. Eliezer Maass, she lived in Skokie, Illinois, where she was a contributing editor at *Cornerstone Magazine*. She also created a newsletter for young writers called *Chicago Poetry Factory*.

Channah Magori is an American-born poet living in Jerusalem. She recently finished her Master's Degree in the Creative Writing Program at Bar Ilan University. Her work has appeared in *Poetica*, *Works in Progress*, and *B'nai Brith Magazine*. She is currently working on a manuscript of second-generation Holocaust poetry, a manuscript of love songs, and her first novel. Magori works for the International Coalition for Missing Israeli Soldiers.

Sandra Cohen Margulius has published poems in *RUNES*, *Cream City Review*, *Radiance*, *Women Writing*, *Hey Listen*, *Laughing Boy*, and other journals. She completed her MA in Creative Writing in 2001 at the University of Wisconsin-Milwaukee, where she studied with Susan Firer and William Harrold. Margulius is the mother of three grown children and lives in Bayside, Wisconsin, with her husband, Simon.

David McKain is the author of *Spellbound: Growing Up in God's Country*, winner of the Associated Writing Program's award for creative non-fiction and a nominee for the Pulitzer Prize and the National Book Award. His other books include *The Common Life* and *Spirit Bodies: Poems*. McKain has received fellowships from the National Endowment for the Arts, the Lila Wallace Foundation, and the Woodrow Wilson Foundation.

Robert Mezey has received the Lamont Prize for *The Lovemaker*, a Bassine Citation and PEN prize for *Evening Wind*, and the Poets Prize for *Collected Poems 1952–1999*. He has held fellowships from the Ingram Merrill and Guggenheim Foundations and from the National Endowment for the Arts. Mezey's poems, prose, and translations have appeared in numerous journals, including *Hudson Review*, *The New Yorker*, *Paris Review*, *Kenyon Review* and *Poetry*. His other books of verse include *White Blossoms*, *The Door Standing Open*, and *Selected Translations*, and he recently edited *Poems of the American West*.

Richard Michelson is curator of exhibitions at the National Yiddish Book Center and owner of R. Michelson Galleries in Northampton, Massachusetts. His poetry collections include *Battles and Lullabies* (Illinois, 2006), *Tap Dancing with the Relatives* (Florida, 1985), and the limited edition fine-press book *Masks,* with etchings by Leonard Baskin (Gehenna Press, 2000). His work is included in the *Norton Introduction to Poetry* and other anthologies. Michelson is also the author of numerous children's books, including *Too Young for Yiddish* (Charlesbridge) and *Across the Alley* (Putnam), a finalist for the National Jewish Book Award.

Bernard S. Mikofsky taught Russian and other Slavic languages as well as Romance languages at Kent State, Indiana University, and elsewhere. From 1943 to 1946, he served as a Signal Corps intelligence officer. He also published articles on Slavic philology and linguistics and wrote op-ed pieces for the Bethlehem, Pennsylvania, *Sunday Globe* and other newspapers.

Aaron Miller was executive director of Universities Field Staff International, an educational corporation engaged in research and publication in international affairs. He lived and worked abroad and was the author of three books of poetry.

Marilyn Mohr is the author of two volumes of poetry, *Satchel* (1992), and *Running the Track* (1981). She has been published in numerous magazines and anthologies and has performed her work on radio and television. In 1989, her poem "*Tzena*" was choreographed by the Avodah Dance Ensemble. Recent work has appeared in The Jewish Women's Literary Annual and Home Planet News. A native New Yorker, she was coeditor of *Woodstock Poetry Review* and the Catskill Poets Series. Mohr is currently the coordinator of a monthly reading series, the Poets Forum, at the JCC of Metropolitan New Jersey.

David Moolten received the Samuel French Morse Poetry Prize for his first collection, *Plums & Ashes* (1994). His second book, *Especially Then*, was published by David Robert Books in 2005. His poems have appeared widely in such journals as *American Scholar*, *Georgia Review*, *Kenyon Review*, *Poetry*, and *Southern Review*, and he has received awards from the Academy of American Poets and the Pennsylvania Council on the Arts. Dr. Moolten is a practicing pathologist with special expertise in transfusion medicine. He lives in Philadelphia, Pennsylvania, where he works for the American Red Cross.

Sarah Traister Moskovitz is the daughter of Polish Jewish immigrants who left relatives behind in the 1920s, all of whom disappeared. Her book *Love Despite Hate* (Schocken 1982) brought attention to child survivors of the Holocaust for the first time. In 2003, as a scholar-in-residence at the U.S. Holocaust Memorial Museum in Washington, DC, Moskovitz translated all the Yiddish poetry in the Ringelblum Archives, which had been buried in Warsaw in milk cans and tins. Though this poetry had been unearthed in 1946 and 1950, only a handful of the over one hundred fifty poems had previously been translated into English.

Stanley Moss was born in New York City and was educated at Trinity College and Yale University. He makes his living as a private art dealer, largely in Spanish and Italian old masters, and is the publisher and editor of Sheep Meadow Press. His most recent books are *A History of Color: New and Collected Poetry* (2003) and *New and Selected Poems 2006*, both published by Seven Stories Press. In 2004, he published *Songs of Imperfection* in the U.K.

Teresa Moszkowicz-Syrop was born in Poland. Except for her only brother, Symcho Moszkowicz, an acclaimed visual artist, her family perished in concentration camps. After the war, she was reunited with Symcho in the USSR and later immigrated, with her husband, to the United States.

Elaine Mott is retired from teaching and lives in the Catskills. Her poetry has appeared in *Cream City Review*, *Midwest Quarterly*, *Green Mountains Review*, *The Ledge*, and other magazines.

Laura Rocha Nakazawa, a native of Montevideo, Uruguay, is a Spanish translator and interpreter working in the Boston area. She has translated several works by Marjorie Agosín into English, among them *The Angel of Memory*.

Mark Nepo is a poet and philosopher who has taught in the fields of poetry and spirituality for over thirty years. His most recent nonfiction books are *The Exquisite Risk* (Harmony Books, 2005) and *Unlearning Back to God*, a collection of his published essays from 1985–2005 (Khaniqahi Nimatullahi Publications, 2006), and his latest book of poems is *Surviving Has Made Me Crazy* (Cavankerry Press, 2007). Nepo's other books of poetry include *Suite for the Living* and *Inhabiting Wonder*, both 2004. His work has been translated into French, Portuguese, Japanese and Danish.

Amos Neufeld was born in Israel to survivors of the Holocaust and now lives with his wife and two children in New York City where he works as an attorney for an appellate court. His poems and film reviews have appeared in literary journals, newspapers, and poetry and film anthologies, including the poetry anthology, *Ghosts of the Holocaust*, and the film anthology, *Celluloid Power*, in which his review of Claude Lanzmann's documentary film *Shoah* appears. He has most recently written a series of psalms that wrestle with the difficulty of prayer and praise, in the wake of the Shoah.

Miriam Offenberg was a teacher, community relations coordinator, audiovisual specialist, writer, and editor. She also served as president of the Chaucer Guild in New Jersey.

Lois E. Olena is an ordained minister with the Assemblies of God. She has a Masters of Art in Jewish Studies from Gratz College in Philadelphia and received her D.Min. from the Assemblies of God Theological Seminary in 2006. Her doctoral dissertation is entitled "Pentecostals and the New Anti-Semitism: Walking in the Fruit and Fullness of the Spirit for the Sake of the Jewish People." While working for the Gratz College Holocaust Oral History Archive, Olena transcribed over 500 Holocaust survivor interviews, one hundred of which are in the oral history collection of the U.S. Holocaust Memorial Museum in Washington, DC.

Jacqueline Osherow is the author of five books of poetry, most recently *Dead Men's Praise* (Grove, 1999) and *The Hoopoe's Crown* (BOA Editions, 2005). Osherow has been awarded the Witter Bynner Prize and fellowships from the Guggenheim and Ingram Merrill foundations and the National Endowment for the Arts. Her work has appeared in many anthologies and periodicals, including *Twentieth Century American Poetry*, *The Norton Anthology of Jewish-American Poetry*, *Best American Poetry* (1995 and 1998), *The New Yorker*, and *Paris Review*. She is Distinguished Professor of English at the University of Utah.

Alicia Ostriker has published eleven volumes of poetry, including, most recently, *No Heaven* (Pittsburgh, 2005); has been twice a finalist for the National Book Award; has won both the William Carlos Williams Award and the Paterson Poetry Prize; and has received fellowships from the Rockefeller and Guggenheim Foundations and the National Endowment for the Arts. She is also the author of *The Nakedness of the Fathers: Biblical Visions and Revisions*. Ostriker is Professor Emerita of English at Rutgers, teaches in the New England College low-residency poetry MFA program, and leads a monthly midrash writing workshop in New York City.

Christina Pacosz has been an artist-in-the-schools for the Metropolitan Arts Commission in Portland, Oregon, and the Washington State and South Carolina arts commissions, as well as visiting artist-in-residence at colleges in North Carolina. Her books of poetry include *Shimmy up to This Fine Mud* (1976), *Notes from the Red Zone* (1983), *Some Winded, Wild Beast* (1985), *One River* (2001) and *Greatest Hits, 1975–2001* (Pudding House, 2002). She teaches urban youth in Kansas City, Missouri.

Linda Pastan has published many books of poetry, including *The Five Stages of Grief* (1981), *Waiting for My Life* (1981), *Carnival Evening: New and Selected Poems 1968–1998*, and *The Last Uncle* (2002). She has served as poet laureate of Maryland and was the 2003 recipient of the Ruth Lilly Poetry Prize. Her twelfth and most recent collection is *Queen of a Rainy Country* (Norton, 2006).

Mark Pawlak is the author of five books of poetry, including *Official Versions* and *Special Handling: Newspaper Poems New and Selected*. His poetry and prose can be found in such journals as *New American Writing*, *Off the Coast*, *Pemmican*, and the *Saint Ann's Review*, and in *The Best American Poetry 2006*. He has edited four anthologies, the most recent of which is *Present/Tense: Poets in the World*, a collection of contemporary American political poetry. Pawlak is Director of Academic Support Programs at the University of Massachusetts Boston, where he also teaches mathematics. He has received two Massachusetts Artist Fellowship awards.

Edmund Pennant (d. 2002) published five books of poetry, including *Misapprehensions* (1984), *The Wildebeest of Carmine Street* (1990) and *Askance & Strangely, New and Collected Poems* (1995). His poems appeared widely in newspapers and literary magazines and in over thirty anthologies. Pennant was the recipient of the Davies Prize and the Kreymborg Memorial Prize, both from the Poetry Society of America. He was an adjunct Professor of English at Adelphi University and, in 1994, served as poet-in-residence at the West Point Military Academy. He was also an associate editor of *Poetrybay Magazine*.

Louis Phillips is a poet, playwright, and short story writer. Among his published works are three collections of short stories, including *A Dream of Countries Where No One Dare Live* and, most recently, *The Woman Who Wrote King Lear* (2007); *Hot Corner*, a collection of his baseball writings; *R.I.P.*, a sequence of poems about Rip Van Winkle; and the *Envoi Messages*, a full-length play. Phillips's other books of poetry include *The Krazy Kat Rag, Celebrations & Bewilderments*, and *Into the Well of Knowingness*. His most recent book is *The Death of The Siamese Twins & other plays* (World Audience Books, 2007).

Marge Piercy received an honorary doctorate degree from Hebrew University in Cincinnati in 2004. She is the author of seventeen novels, most recently *Sex Wars*, a tale of the turbulent post-Civil War period. Her seventeenth volume of poetry, *The Crooked Inheritance*, was published by Knopf in 2006, and *Pesach for the rest of Us* — which presents a way for non-Orthodox Jews to create a meaningful contemporary seder for friends and family — was released by Schocken in 2007. Piercy's book *The Art of Blessing the Day: Poems with a Jewish Theme* (1999) is a favorite bar- and bat-mitzvah present.

Heidemarie Pilc grew up in Ludwigshafen-on-the-Rhine. She studied language arts and world history and researched the history of the White Rose, which had been part of the German resistance movement. In the late 1970s, she married a jazz historian and emigrated to California, where she was actively involved in the West Coast jazz scene. Pilc is a freelance writer, whose work has received prizes from Bay Area literary groups and has been published in a number of anthologies and magazines.

William Pillin (1910–82) was the author of *To the End of Time: Poems New and Selected* (Papa Bach Editions, 1980). His earlier books include *Theory of Silence* (1949), *Pavane for a Fading Memory* (1963), and *Everything Falling* (1971). Pillin, also a potter, was born in the Ukraine and died in Los Angeles, where he lived for many years with his wife, Polia, a visual artist.

John C. Pine was a librarian and the author of five books of poetry*: Block Island*; *Cliff Walk*; *Ice-Age*; *Chinese Camp and Other California Poems*; and *Silhouettes at Eventide* — all from Moveable Feast Press. After retirement, he lived with his wife in the Sierra foothills of California.

Karl A. Plank is the J. W. Cannon Professor of Religion and Chair of the Religion Department at Davidson College in Davidson, North Carolina. He is the author of *Mother of the Wire Fence: Inside and Outside the Holocaust*, a study in Holocaust hermeneutics, and has published numerous articles in journals, including *Judaism*, *Anglican Theological Review*, *Cistercian Studies Quarterly*, *Literature and Theology*, and *Shenandoah*. He was the winner of the 1993 Thomas H. Carter Prize for non-fiction.

Ginger Porter was a high school student when she wrote "I Am Babi Yar." She was editor of her high school creative writing magazine, *Metanoia*, and received a number of awards for her work in the graphic arts.

Evelyn Posamentier has published poems in *American Poetry Review*, *Crysalis*, *Mississippi Review Online*, the Virtual Museum of Genocide Studies, and in other on- and off-line places, as well as in several anthologies, including *Bittersweet Legacy: Creative Responses to the Holocaust* and *Ghosts of the Holocaust*. Posamentier lives in San Francisco, California.

Anna Rabinowitz is executive editor of *American Letters & Commentary* and a vice-president of the Poetry Society of America. Her most recent volume of poetry is *The Wanton Sublime: A Florilegium of Whethers and Wonders* (Tupelo Press, 2006). Her booklength acrostic poem, *Darkling*, also published by Tupelo, has been transformed into a multi-media opera theater work by American Opera Projects and had its world premiere at the 13th St. Theatre in Manhattan. Rabinowitz's other books include *At the Site of Inside Out*, which won the Juniper Prize. Among her other awards are a fellowship in poetry from the National Endowment for the Arts.

David Ray has twice been the recipient of the William Carlos Williams Award and has received an NEA Fellowship for Fiction, the Nuclear Age Foundation Peace Award, and several nominations for Pulitzer and Pushcart prizes. His most recent books are *The Death of Sardanapalus and Other Poems of the Iraq Wars* (Howling Dog Press); *Music of Time: Selected and New Poems* (Backwaters Press); *One Thousand Years: Poems About the Holocaust* (Timberline Press); and *The Endless Search: A Memoir* (Soft Skull Press). He lives in Tucson with his wife Judy, who is also a poet.

Richard C. Raymond (d. 1980) was born and raised in Boston. He joined the United Nations Relief and Rehabilitation Agency in Germany during World War II and helped with the rescue efforts in the camps following Liberation. His book, *A Moment of Bells*, was published by Plowshare Press in 1970.

Barbara Reisner lives in Allentown, Pennsylvania. Her work has appeared in *Manhattan Poetry Review*, *Bellingham Review*, *River Styx*, *Laurel Review*, *Yarrow*, *Blue Buildings*, *Stone Country*, *Poets On:*, *Massachusetts Review*, *Shirim*, and other journals. She has a chapbook published by Creeping Bent Press.

Naomi Replansky was born in the Bronx, New York, in 1918. She has been writing poetry since she was ten, but writes slowly. Her first book, *Ring Song*, was published by Scribner in 1952 and was a finalist for the National Book Award in poetry. Her chapbook, *21 Poems, Old and New*, appeared in 1988, and her book, *The Dangerous World: New and Selected Poems 1934–1994,* was published by Another Chicago Press in 1994. Replansky's poems have appeared in many anthologies, and some have been translated into French and German. She now lives and writes in New York City.

Lisa Ress was born (as Anneliese Reiss) to Viennese parents in Tangier, Morocco, in 1939. Her first book, *Flight Patterns*, won the 1983 Associated Writing Programs Award in Poetry and was published by the University Press of Virginia in 1985. Ress taught creative writing at Cornell; the University of California, Irvine; Hollins College; and Knox College in Galesburg, Pennsylvania.

Elaine Reuben is on the board of directors of The Feminist Press. She lives in Washington, DC.

Charles Reznikoff (1894–1976) had initially planned to be a journalist, but he ended up graduating from NYU Law School in 1915 and practicing law for a time. Some of his early poems were reprinted by the Objectivist Press, which he, Louis Zukofsky, and George Oppen formed, basically to print their own books. Reznikoff's seminal collection of poetry, *Holocaust*, was published by Black Sparrow Press in 1975, and Black Sparrow also issued a two-volume definitive edition of his *Complete Poems* in 1975 and 1976.

Liliane Richman was born in Paris, the child of a survivor. She moved to the United States in 1959, where her poetry and prose appeared in *Response*, *The Smith*, *Sackbut Review*, and elsewhere. Richman's doctoral dissertation was entitled "Ideology and Themes in the Vietnam Films, 1975–1985." She taught language arts at the arts magnet high school in Dallas.

Michael D. Riley is Professor of English at Penn State Berks in Reading, Pennsylvania. His first book of poems, *Scrimshaw: Citizens of Bone*, was published by the Lightning Tree Press in Santa Fe, New Mexico. A second book, *Circling the Stones (Poems from Ireland)*, was published by Creighton University Press in 2006. Riley's poems have appeared in many periodicals, including *Poetry*, *Poetry Ireland Review*, *Cumberland Poetry Review*, *Fiddlehead*, *Arizona Quarterly*, and *Southern Humanities Review*.

Nicholas Rinaldi is the author of three novels — *Between Two Rivers* (HarperCollins), *The Jukebox Queen of Malta* (Simon & Schuster), and *Bridge Fall Down* (St. Martin's Press). He has also published three collections of poetry — *The Resurrection of the Snails* (Blair Press), *We Have Lost Our Fathers* (University Press of Florida) and *The Luftwaffe in Chaos* (Negative Capability Press). Rinaldi's poems and stories have appeared widely in literary journals in the U.S. and abroad. He is retired from Fairfield University, where he taught literature and creative writing.

Charlz Rizzuto is a graduate of Long Island University. In the sixties, he was a member of the New York Poets Cooperative. In the seventies, he edited a multimedia magazine, *Come and Eat*. Rizzuto has published poetry in various literary magazines and has translated two volumes of Holocaust poetry from the Esperanto of Julius Balbin, *Strangled Cries* (1981) and *The Bitch of Buchenwald* (1986), both published by Cross-Cultural Communications. He lives in New York City.

Curtis Robbins was born in New York City in 1943. He is a graduate of Gallaudet University, has a doctorate from the University of Maryland, and is a lecturer at George Washington University, where he teaches American sign language and deaf culture. He has published several poems in *The Tactile Mind*, a creative writing journal owned by a deaf-blind publisher-editor, and his poems also are found in two anthologies, *No Walls of Stone* (1992) and *The Deaf Way II Anthology* (2002).

William Pitt Root served as first poet laureate for Tucson (1997–2002) while commuting weekly to teach creative writing in Manhattan. His books include *White Boots: New & Selected Poems of the American West* (2006), *The Storm and Other Poems* (2005), *Trace Elements from a Recurring Kingdom* (1994), and *Faultdancing* (1986). Root's poems have been translated into nearly twenty languages and have been published in more than one hundred anthologies and three hundred magazines. He has won fellowships from the Guggenheim and Rockefeller Foundations, Stanford University, and the National Endowment for the Arts.

Marina Roscher was born in Regensburg, Germany, and has worked as a professional translator in the United States and abroad. She was a founding member of New York Quarterly and has been a contributing editor to other periodicals. Her poetry, translations, scholarly articles, and fiction have appeared in many publications, including *New Letters*, *Southern Studies*, and *Poetry Canada Review*. Her translation of Sarah Kirsch's 1984 collection of poems, *Katzenleben*, was released as *Cat Lives* in 1981 by Texas Tech University Press.

Jennifer Rose was born in Evanston, Illinois, in 1959. She is the author of *The Old Direction of Heaven* (Truman State University Press, 2000) and *Hometown for an Hour* (Ohio University Press, 2006). Her poems have appeared in *Poetry*, *The Nation*, *Ploughshares* and elsewhere, and she has received awards and fellowships from the National Endowment for the Arts, the Massachusetts Cultural Council, and the Poetry Society of America. Rose works as a city planner, specializing in downtown revitalization. A number of her family members from Germany and Croatia perished in the Holocaust.

Harriet Susskind Rosenblum (1931–2002) taught poetry, women's studies, modern American literature and Holocaust studies at Monroe Community College in Rochester, New York and, prior to that, at the University of Rochester. In 1995, she published *To See the Speech of Trees*, a collection of her poems. She received two fellowships from the National Endowment for the Arts and was twice a finalist for the Pablo Neruda Poetry Award. She contributed to the thirteen-part TV series *Voices & Visions*. which highlighted thirteen of America's most famous modern poets.

Max Rosenfeld translated many books of Yiddish poetry, among them, *The Minsk Ghetto: Soviet-Jewish Partisans Against the Nazis* (1989), by Hersh Smolar, a leader of the Jewish underground in the Minsk region. He taught classes in Yiddish culture at Gratz College and at Jewish community centers in Philadelphia.

Menachem Z. Rosensaft is the son of survivors of Auschwitz and Bergen-Belsen. He is chairman of the editorial board of the Holocaust Survivors Memoirs Project, a former member of the U.S. Holocaust Memorial Council, and founding chairman of the International Network of Children of Jewish Holocaust Survivors. Rosensaft is also president of Park Avenue Synagogue and a past national president of the Labor Zionist Alliance. In 1985, he led a demonstration at Bergen-Belsen to protest visits by President Reagan and West German Chancellor Kohl to the camp's mass grave and the German military cemetery in Bitburg.

Elizabeth Rosner lives in Berkeley, California. Her first novel, *The Speed of Light*, was published by Ballantine Books in 2001. Winner of several literary prizes, including *Hadassah*'s Ribalow Prize, the Great Lakes Colleges Association Award for fiction, and the Prix France Bleu Gironde, the book was a national best-seller and has been translated into nine foreign languages. Rosner's second novel, *Blue Nude*, was published by Ballantine Books in 2006, and a related essay was published in the *New York Times Magazine*. Her poetry collection, *Gravity* (Small Poetry Press, 2003), is one of the titles in the Select Poets Series and is currently in its thirteenth printing.

Jerome Rothenberg is an internationally known poet with over seventy books of poetry and several assemblages of traditional and contemporary poetry, including *Technicians of the Sacred*; *Exiled in the Word* (a.k.a. *A Big Jewish Book*); and *Poems for the Millennium*. Among his most recent books of poetry, all published in 2004, are *Writing Through: Translations & Variations*; *25 Caprichos, after Goya*, with Spanish translations by Heriberto Yépez; *A Book of Concealments*; and *The Burial of the Count of Orgaz & Other Poems by Pablo Picasso*, coedited with Pierre Joris. His thirteenth book of poems from New Directions, *Triptych*, appeared in 2007.

Larry Rubin has published in many magazines and anthologies, including *Visiting Emily: Poems Inspired by the Life and Work of Emily Dickinson* (University of Iowa Press, 2000) and *Imported Breads: Literature of Cultural Exchange* (Mammoth Books, 2003). His fourth collection of poetry, *Unanswered Calls*, was published by Kendall/Hunt in 1997. Rubin retired from teaching at Georgia tech in 1999.

Mark Rudman has received the National Book Critics Circle Award, the Max Hayward Award for his translation of Boris Pasternak's *My Sister — Life*, and fellowships from the Guggenheim and Ingram Merrill foundations, the National Endowment for the Arts, and the New York State Council on the Arts. His volumes of poetry include *Sundays on the Phone* (2005), *Provoked in Venice* (1999), and *By Contraries* (1987). His prose works include *Realm of Unknowing: Meditations on Art, Suicide, and Other Transformations* and *Diverse Voices: Essays on Poets and Poetry*. Rudman is the editor of *Pequod* and teaches poetry part time at NYU.

Biff Russ was the winner of the 1991 Marianne Moore Poetry Prize for *Black Method* (Helicon Nine Editions). She lives and writes in the Pacific Northwest, where she meditates and studies Buddhist philosophy.

Luada Sandler was a teacher and social worker and, during World War II, served as a staff aide with the American Red Cross in military hospitals in the European Theater of Operations. More recently, she was engaged in recording the oral histories of Soviet Jewish emigrés to the United States.

Reg Saner received the first Walt Whitman Award conferred by the Academy of American Poets and is also the recipient of an NEA creative writing fellowship and the Colorado Governor's Award for Excellence in the Arts. His essays and poems have appeared in such journals as *Yale Review*, *Poetry*, *Paris Review*, *Ploughshares*, *Field*, and *New York Quarterly*, and in more than fifty anthologies. His recent collection of nonfiction, *The Dawn Collector*, published by the Center for American Places, explores flora and fauna near his house in Boulder, Colorado, in relation to our terrestrial and celestial situation.

May Sarton (1912–95) published over fifty books, including novels, poetry, memoirs, and journals. Her books of poetry include *In Time Like Air* (1958), *A Private Mythology* (1966), *Coming into Eighty* (1994), and *Collected Poems 1930–1993* (1993). Among her novels are *Faithful Are the Wounds* (1955) and *Mrs. Stevens Hears the Mermaids Singing* (1966). Sarton is probably best known for her journals, particularly *Journal of a Solitude* (1973), which is still in print. The memoirs, which she distinguished from her journals, include *Planet Dreaming Deep* (1968) and *World of Light* (1996), her celebration of lifelong friendships.

Richard Schaaf is a translator of contemporary Latin American poets, among them Roque Dalton and Cristina Peri Rossi, and he is the former editor of Azul Editions, which publishes works of contemporary poets in translation. His translation credits include *The Black Heralds* (1990) by Cesar Vallejo, *Toward the Splendid City* (1994) by Marjorie Agosín, and *Epic Song* (1998) by Pablo Neruda.

Rebecca Seiferle has been Jacob Ziskind poet-in-residence at Brandeis. Her third poetry collection, *Bitters* (Copper Canyon, 2001), won the 2002 Western States Book Award and a Pushcart Prize; *The Ripped-Out Seam* (Sheep Meadow, 1993) won the Bogin Memorial Award from the Poetry Society of America, the Writers Exchange Award from *Poets & Writers*, and the Writers Union Poetry Prize. Seiferle is a translator from the Spanish and founding editor of *The Drunken Boat*, a quarterly online magazine of international poetry and translation. She received a 2004 Lannan Literary Fellowship.

David Shapiro has published many volumes of poetry, art and literary criticism. He wrote the first monographs on Ashbery, Mondrian's flower studies, and Johns's drawings. He has also published essays on Jewish themes in David Rosenberg's anthologies. Shapiro published his first book with Holt at eighteen and was nominated for the National book Award in 1971. His poems have been translated into many languages, and he has translated, edited and written plays and movies. He taught for a decade at Columbia, has taught art and aesthetics at Princeton and Bard College, and currently teaches at Cooper Union and William Paterson University.

Gregg Shapiro is a pop-culture journalist, poet and fiction writer who lives in Chicago with his life-partner and their dogs.

Harvey Shapiro is the editor of the anthology *Poets of World War II* and the author of eleven books of poetry. In 2006, Wesleyan published his *The Sights Along the Harbor: New and Collected Poems.*

Reva Sharon. Please see the note that follows this section.

Enid Shomer is the author of four poetry collections, most recently *Stars at Noon: Poems from the Life of Jacqueline Cochran*, and two short story collections: *Imaginary Men*, which received the Iowa Prize as well as the LSU/Southern Review Prize, and *Tourist Season* (Random House, 2007). Her poems and stories have appeared in *The New Yorker*, *Atlantic, Best American Poetry,* and elsewhere. Her recent awards include the 2004 *Virginia Quarterly Review*'s Emily Clark Balch Prize in Fiction and *Prairie Schooner*'s 2006 Glenna Luschei Award. In 2002, Shomer became the poetry series editor at the University of Arkansas Press.

Joan I. Siegel has published poems in numerous periodicals, including *Atlantic Monthly*, *American Scholar*, *Gettysburg Review*, *Prairie Schooner*, and *Commonweal.* Her work is anthologized in *Poetry Comes Up Where It Can* (University of Utah Press) and *Beyond Lament: Poets of the World Bearing Witness to the Holocaust* (Northwestern), among others. She coauthored *Peach Girl: Poems for a Chinese Daughter* (Grayson Books, 2001) and has received the 1999 *New Letters* Poetry Prize and the 1998 Anna Davidson Rosenberg Award.

Maurya Simon is the author of seven volumes of poetry, including *Ghost Orchid*, which was nominated in 2004 for a National Book Award in poetry. Her two most recent books (2005–07) are *Cartographies* (Red Hen Press) and *Weavers* (Blackbird Press). Simon is the recipient of an NEA Fellowship in Poetry and an Indo-American Fulbright Fellowship. She teaches creative writing at the University of California, Riverside, and lives in the Angeles National Forest in Southern California.

Louis Simpson was born in Jamaica, West Indies, in 1923. He served in the Second World War with the 101st Airborne Division. The publication of *Three on the Tower* (1975), a study of Ezra Pound, T.S. Eliot, and William Carlos Williams, brought him wide acclaim as a literary critic. Simpson has also published over seventeen books of poetry, including *The Owner of the House: New Collected Poems, 1940–2001* (2003) and *At the End of the Open Road, Poems* (1963), for which he won the Pulitzer Prize. His Modern *Poets of France: A Bilingual Anthology* (1997) won the Academy of American Poets' 1998 Harold Morton Landon Translation Award.

Myra Sklarew, former president of the artist community, Yaddo, and professor of literature at American University, is the author of six collections of poetry, most recently *Lithuania: New & Selected Poems* and *The Witness Trees*; a collection of short fictions, *Like a Field Riddled by Ants*; and a book of essays, *Over the Rooftops of Time*. A nonfiction work, *Holocaust and the Construction of Memory*, is forthcoming from SUNY Press. Sklarew serves on the advisory board of the Center for Israeli Studies and has worked in the Department of Neurophysiology at Yale University School of Medicine.

Joan Jobe Smith is the founding editor of *Pearl Magazine* and the *Bukowski Review*. She is a Pushcart Prize recipient and has published poetry and prose extensively in the US and UK, most recently in *Beat Scene*, *Ambit* and *The North*. Her collection, *Pow Wow Café* was published by Smith-Doorstop (UK) in 1998. Smith lives in Long Beach, California, with her husband, poet Fred Voss, with whom she has performed on five reading tours in England and Scotland.

Kirtland Snyder has published two chapbooks of poetry — *Winter Light* and *Soldiers of Fortune* (a collaboration with the American painter, Leon Golub) — both from Innerer Klang Press, and his booklength manuscript, *House of Earth*, was a finalist in the 2001 *Paris Review* Poetry Prize Competition. Snyder has written two novels, *The Wolf Moon,* and *The Man Who Had Two Hearts*, which received a 2002 Mayhaven Award for Fiction. His first CD, "Walking with Thoreau," was released in fall 2003. He has also written a travel memoir, *Ah, Mykonos*; a memoir of his conversion to Judaism, *Diary of a Conversion*; and stories and essays.

J. R. Solonche is coauthor (with his wife, Joan I. Siegel) of *Peach Girl: Poems for a Chinese Daughter* (Grayson Books, 2001). His poems have appeared in *Visiting Frost: Poems Inspired by the Life and Work of Robert Frost* (Iowa), the *Tenth Anniversary Anthology of Atlanta Review*, *Hampden-Sydney Poetry Review*, *Fugue*, and elsewhere.

Jason Sommer teaches literature and writing at Fontbonne University in St. Louis, where he also directs the honors program. He has published three poetry collections: *Lifting the Stone, Other People's Troubles*, and *The Man Who Sleeps in My Office*. *Other People's Troubles* won the Society of Midland Authors Award for Poetry and was a finalist for PEN USA West's literary prize. In 2000, he was one of a small group of poets who participated in the "Speech and Silence: Poetry and the Holocaust" program at the United States Holocaust Memorial Museum in Washington, DC. In 2001, he was awarded a Whiting Foundation Writer's Fellowship for his work.

Gizela Spunberg was born in Lwów, Poland, and received her master's degree in law and political science at the University of Jan Casimirus, prior to practicing law (before World War II) as a *referendar* of VIII degree in government service. She survived as a political prisoner in Karaganda and Siberia and arrived in the United States in April 1946. Her entire family perished in the Holocaust.

Hans Jörg Stahlschmidt is a German writer, psychologist and building contractor, who in 1982, moved to Berkeley, California, where he lives with his Jewish-American wife and their children. He has been involved in exploring the complexity of the German-Jewish relationship for many years. Stahlschmidt's poetry has appeared in numerous journals and anthologies, including *Madison Review*, *Atlanta Review*, *Manoa*, *Texas Poetry Review*, and the *Anthology of Magazine Verse and Yearbook of American Poetry*. He has received several prizes in national and international poetry competitions.

Jan Steckel is a Harvard- and Yale-trained former pediatrician, whose work has been nominated for a Pushcart Prize. She served as a Peace Corps volunteer in the Dominican Republic and cared for Spanish-speaking families in California at a county hospital and at a large HMO. Five years ago, she left the practice of medicine to write full-time. Eighty of her short stories, poems and nonfiction pieces have appeared in a range of print and online publications, including *Scholastic Magazine*, *Yale Medicine*, *Pedestal Magazine* and *Lodestar Quarterly*. Her poetry chapbook, *The Underwater Hospital*, was published by Zeitgeist Press in 2006.

Martin Steingesser has published poems in a broad range of journals, including *The Progressive*, *Janus Head*, *Chautauqua Literary Journal*, *Paterson Literary Review*, *American Poetry Review*, and *Tiferet: A Journal of Spiritual Literature*. In addition to *Blood to Remember: American Poets on the Holocaust*, his poems appear in the anthologies *Poetry Comes Up Where It Can: Poems from the Amicus Journal* (2000); *Motion: American Sports Poems* (2001), and *The Maine Poets* (2003). His books include *Brothers of Morning* (Deerbrook Editions: Cumberland, Maine).

Gerald Stern was born in Pittsburgh, Pennsylvania, in 1925. His books of poetry include *This Time: New and Selected Poems* (1998), which won the National Book Award; *Bread Without Sugar* (1992), winner of the Paterson Poetry Prize; *The Red Coal* (1981), which received the Melville Caine Award from the Poetry Society of America; and *Lucky Life*, the 1977 Lamont Poetry Selection. He is also the author of *What I Can't Bear Losing*, a collection of personal essays. Stern's honors include the Ruth Lilly Prize, a Guggenheim Foundation Fellowship, and four NEA grants. In 2005, he received the Wallace Stevens Award for mastery in the art of poetry.

Bradley R. Strahan is the publisher and editor of Visions-International. He has published several books of poetry and over five hundred poems in such places as *America*, *Cross Currents*, *The Christian Science Monitor*, *Confrontation*, *Midstream*, *Poetry Australia*, and *Sources* (Belgium). For over twenty years, Strahan sponsored a series of international poetry readings, and he also led the Washington Poets Workshop for nearly thirty years.

Rabbi Michael Strassfeld is the rabbi at the Society for the Advancement of Judaism, a synagogue in Manhattan. His most recent book, *A Book of Life: Embracing Judaism as a Spiritual Practice*, was released in paperback in 2006 by Jewish Lights.

Lynn Strongin is a four-time nominee for the Pushcart Prize in Poetry. Her anthology, *The Sorrow Psalms: A Book of Twentieth Century Elegy*, was "Book of the Month" in England's "Poetry Kit" in October 2006 and is on the 2007 list of best-selling books in the U.K. The Summer 2007 double issue of "Ygradsil" was devoted to a symposium on Strongin's work, and two collections of her poetry, *Rembrandt's Smock* (Plain View Press) and *The Girl with Copper-Colored Hair* (Conflux Press), were published in spring 2007. With Glenna Luschei, she is co-editing a companion volume to *The Sorrow Psalms* entitled *Crazed by the Sun: Poetry of Ecstasy.*

Yerra Sugarman grew up in a community of Shoah survivors in Toronto, where she was born in 1955 and where her parents settled after World War II. She received the 2005 PEN/Joyce Osterweil Award for Poetry for her first book, *Forms of Gone* (Sheep Meadow, 2002), and has also received a "Discovery"/*The Nation* Prize, a Chicago Literary Award from *Another Chicago Magazine*, an Academy of American Poets Prize and the Poetry Society of America's George Bogin Award. Sugarman's poems have appeared in numerous publications and have been translated into French. She teaches creative writing and English at City College of New York.

Yuri Suhl (1909–86) was born in Galicia, a region of Poland that was then a part of the Austro-Hungarian Empire. He left Poland at the age of fifteen and settled in New York City. Suhl was the editor and translator of, and contributor to, *They Fought Back: The Story of Jewish Resistance in Nazi Europe*, and he also published four volumes of Yiddish poetry and other work.

Zahava Z. Sweet was born in Poland and survived the Holocaust. After the war, she lived in Israel and later emigrated to America. Her book of poems, *The Return of Sound* (Bombshelter Press, 2005), is a reflection on her life. Her poetry was selected by the Bumbershoot Library Festival for performance and publication. She lives in Monrovia, California.

Marie Syrkin (1899–1989) was born in Bern, Switzerland, and moved to the U.S. in 1907. From 1950 to 1966, Syrkin taught English and humanities at Brandeis University. In 1934, she helped found *Jewish Frontier*, a Labor Zionist monthly, and she served as its editor from 1948 to 1971. Following World War II, she traveled as a representative of B'nai Brith to displaced persons camps in Germany, and her interviews with survivors of the Jewish underground culminated in her work, *Blessed is the Match* (1947), a book about Jewish resistance movements during the war. Her later publications include a biography of Golda Meir and a volume of poetry.

Marilynn Talal received the Ph.D. in Creative Writing from the University of Houston where she was a Stella Erhart Fellow. Her poetry has won numerous awards, including a National Endowment for the Arts Fellowship, and has appeared widely in journals, including *Paris Review*, *Poetry*, *New Republic*, and *Louisville Review*. She lives in New York City with her husband.

Sean M. Teaford grew up in Bryn Mawr, Pennsylvania. He received a B.A. in English from Endicott College in 2005. While at Endicott, he was an editor for the *Endicott Review* and was the college's nominee for the Ruth Lilly Poetry Fellowship in 2003, 2004, and 2005. Teaford's poems have appeared in *The Mad Poets Journal*, *Poetry Motel*, *Zillah*, *Spare Change*, *Midstream*, *Poetry Church*, and other journals. He was the winner of the 2004 Veterans for Peace poetry contest.

Philip Terman teaches English and creative writing at Clarion University and codirects the Chautauqua Writers Festival. His books are *What Survives* (1993), *The House of Sages* (1998), and *Greatest Hits* (Pudding House Press) and *Book of the Unbroken Days* (Mammoth Books), both 2005. Recent poems and essays have appeared in a variety of literary journals, including *Poetry*, *Georgia Review*, *Gettysburg Review*, *Prairie Schooner*, and *Tikkun*. Terman's most recent book, *Rabbis of the Air*, was published by Autumn House Press in 2007.

Elaine Terranova is the author of *Not To: New and Selected Poems* (Sheep Meadow Press, 2006) and three individual collections, *The Dog's Heart* (Orchises Press, 2002), *Damages* (Copper Canyon Press, 1996), and *The Cult of the Right Hand*, which won the 1990 Walt Whitman Award from the Academy of American Poets.

Her translation of *Iphigenia at Aulis* is included in the Euripides III volume of the Penn Greek Drama Series (1998). Terranova is Associate Editor of the on-line book review, *Frigate*. She received an NEA Fellowship in Literature in 1997.

Susan Terris is coeditor of an annual anthology, *RUNES: A Review of Poetry*. Her book *Fire is Favorable to the Dreamer* (Arctos Press, 2003) was named "Best Poetry Book of 2003" by the Bay Area Independent Publishers Association. Her other books are *Natural Defenses* and *Poetic License*, both 2004; *Curved Space* (1998); and *Eye of the Holocaust* and *Angels of Bataan*, both 1999. Her fiction titles include *Nell's Quilt* (Farrar, Straus & Giroux, 1996). Terris's work has appeared in many journals, including *Field, Iowa Review, Ploughshares, Shenandoah*, and *Southern California Anthology*.

Hilary Tham was the author of eight books of poetry, including *Bad Names for Women*; *Men and Other Strange Myths*; *Reality Check*; *The Tao of Mrs. Wei*; and a memoir, *Lane With No Name: Memoirs & Poems of a Malaysian-Chinese Girlhood* (Three Continents Press, 1997). Tham was editor-in-chief for *Word Works* and poetry editor for *Potomac Review*. Her poems and stories have appeared in numerous literary magazines, and two of her books are used as Asian Studies texts by the University of Pittsburgh. She was featured on NPR and Maryland Public Television.

Susan Tichy is the author of *Bone Pagoda* (Ahsahta Press, 2007), *A Smell of Burning Starts the Day* (Wesleyan University Press, 1988) and *The Hands in Exile* (Random House, 1983). Her poems, collaborations, and mixed-genre works have appeared in the U.S. and Britain and have been recognized by awards from the National Poetry Series, the Eugene Kayden Foundation, and the National Endowment for the Arts. She teaches at George Mason University and also serves as Poetry Editor of *Practice: New Writing + Art*. When not teaching, she lives in a ghost town in the southern Colorado Rockies.

Alfred Van Loen (1924–93) was an artist and sculptor, who taught at C.W. Post College on Long Island for twenty-eight years. He was born in Germany and moved to Amsterdam in 1938, where he graduated from the Royal Academy of Art in 1946. He immigrated to New York City in 1947. During his life, Van Loen's work was exhibited in numerous galleries and museums, including the Louvre, the Museum of Modern Art, and the Whitney Museum. Among his most renowned sculptures is his chess set, "Liberty vs. Slavery," which was exhibited by both the National Museum in Jerusalem and the Metropolitan Museum of Art in Manhattan.

Derek Walcott was born in St. Lucia in 1930. He is the author of numerous books of poetry, among them *The Prodigal* (2004), *Tiepolo's Hound* (2000), *The Bounty* (1997), *Omeros* (1990), *Collected Poems 1948–84* (1986), *Midsummer* (1984), *The Star-Apple Kingdom* (1979), *Another Life* (1973), and *Selected Poems* (1964). He has also published four collections of plays and is the founder of the Trinidad Theater Workshop. Walcott's many honors include the 1992 Nobel Prize for Literature and a five-year fellowship from the MacArthur Foundation in 1981. He lives in Trinidad and, during the academic year, Boston, where he teaches at Boston University.

George Wallace is the author of twelve chapbooks of poetry, published in the U.S., U.K. and Italy. He is editor of www.poetrybay.com; has read his poetry at Carnegie Hall and the Algonquin Club and across the U.S. and Europe; and has conducted poetry workshops worldwide at universities and writers' retreats. He has appeared at such events as Bradstock, Lowell Celebrates Kerouac, Insomniacathon/Louisville, and the Woody Guthrie Festival in Okemah, Oklahoma, and has collaborated with musicians David Amram, Paul Winston, DJ Spooky, and Levon Helm. In 2003, Wallace was named the first Poet Laureate of Suffolk County, New York.

Michael Waters teaches at Salisbury University and recently joined the faculty of the New England College MFA Program. His recent books include *Parthenopi: New and Selected Poems* (2001) and *Darling Vulgarity* (2006), both from BOA Editions, as well as the new edition of *Contemporary American Poetry* (Houghton Mifflin, 2006). He chaired the poetry panel for the 2004 National Book Award and was Distinguished Poet-in-Residence at Wichita State University in spring 2006.

Florence Weinberger has published three books of poetry, *The Invisible Telling Its Shape* (1997), *Breathing Like a Jew* (1997) and *Carnal Fragrance* (2004). Her poetry has been published in numerous literary magazines, including *Another Chicago Magazine*, *Antietam Review*, *Comstock Review*, and *Rattle*, and in such anthologies as *Family Reunion: Poems about Parenting Grown Children*; *So Luminous the Wildflowers*; *Images from the Holocaust*; and *Lifecycles: Jewish Women on Biblical Themes in Contemporary Life*.

Theodore Weiss (d. 2003) was the William and Anne S. Paton Foundation Professor of Ancient and Modern Literature at Princeton University. With his wife, Renée, he edited the quarterly *Review of Literature* for nearly sixty years. He published more than a dozen books of poetry, most notably his collected poems, *From Princeton One Autumn Afternoon* (Macmillan, 1987). Among his numerous honors and awards were the Poetry Society of America's Shelley Memorial Award and the Oscar Williams and Gene Durwood Award for Poetry. Weiss was the subject of an award-winning documentary, "Living Poetry: A Year in the Life of a Poem."

Ruth Whitman (1921–99) published eight books of poetry, including *The Testing of Hanna Senesh* (1986), *Laughing Gas: Poems New and Selected* (1990), and *Tamsen Donner: Woman's Journey*, which is probably her best known and most highly regarded collection (the book is available in a 2002 reprint edition from Alice James Books). Whitman also translated poetry from Yiddish and received the Kovner Award from the Jewish Book Council of America. During her long career as an educator, she taught at Radcliffe and MIT.

C.K. Williams has published ten books of poetry, including his *Collected Poems* (Farrar, Straus & Giroux, 2006). Among his other books are *The Singing*, which won the National Book Award for 2003; *Repair*, which was awarded the 2000 Pulitzer Prize; and *Flesh and Blood*, which received the National Book Critics Circle Award. Williams has published translations of Sophocles's *Women of Trachis* and Euripides's *Bacchae*, as well as translations of poems by Francis Ponge and others. His book of essays, *Poetry and Consciousness*, was released in 1998, and his memoir, *Misgivings*, came out in 2000. He is a member of the American Academy of Arts and Letters.

Barbara Wind is the daughter of Holocaust survivors. She has written for the *New York Times* and other publications. *Jacob's Angels,* her chapbook of poems about the Holocaust, is in its second printing, and *Walking on Ash* was translated into German and published as *Auf Asche Gehen* by EOS Verlag in 2004. Wind is the director of the Holocaust Council of Metro/West (United Jewish Communities of New Jersey). A fellow of Leadership New Jersey 2006, she is a founder and serves on the boards of CHE (Council of Holocaust Educators) and GSI (Generations of the Shoah International).

Betty Wisoff served as founder and chairperson of the Long Island Writers' Network during the 1980s. Her grandfather and other members of her family were killed by the Nazis.

Kenneth Wolman was born in New York in 1944. He attended New York City public schools and Hunter College and earned the Ph.D. in English Literature from Binghamton University in 1976. In 1995, he was awarded a New Jersey State Council on the Arts Fellowship in Poetry and, in 1996, he was a scholarship attendee at the White River Writers Workshop at Lyon College, Batesville, Arkansas, where he worked with Stephen Dunn and had his ideas of what poetry could be permanently altered by C. D. Wright. Wolman has made his living primarily as a corporate writer and editor.

Carolyne Wright spent four years on Indo-U.S. Subcommission and Fulbright Senior Research Fellowships in India and Bangladesh and has published three collections of poetry in translation from Spanish and Bengali. Her *Seasons of Mangoes and Brainfire* received the American Book Award from the Before Columbus Foundation, and her new collection, *A Change of Maps* (Lost Horse Press, 2006), was a finalist for the Alice Fay di Castagnola Award from the Poetry Society of America. Wright's memoir of her experiences in Chile during the presidency of Salvador Allende, *The Road to Isla Negra*, received the Crossing Boundaries Award.

Barnett Zumoff is an internationally renowned teacher and researcher in the field of Endocrinology, who holds the title of Professor of Medicine at Albert Einstein College of Medicine in New York. Dr. Zumoff has also had a long and distinguished career in the field of Yiddish cultural activity and is a prolific translator of Yiddish literature. Among his twelve published volumes of translations are *I Keep Recalling* (Yankev Glatshteyn's collected Holocaust poems), *In the Valley of Death* (Chaim Lieberman's prescient 1938 essay about Nazi Germany and the coming Holocaust), and *God Hid His Face* (selected poems by Rajzel Zychlinsky).

Rajzel Zychlinsky (1910–2001) was born in Gombin, Poland, and died in Concord, California. She was an internationally acclaimed poet and one of the last whose mother tongue was Yiddish. Zychlinsky had been writing since the 1920s and, between 1939 and 1993, published seven books of poetry in Yiddish. A collection of poems, *God Hid His Face*, was translated into English and published in 1997. Zychlinsky was well known for her Holocaust poetry. Her work has been extensively translated and anthologized and appears in Aaron Kramer's anthology: *A Century of Yiddish Poetry*. In 1975, she received the Manger Prize in Israel.

About the Editor

Charles Adés Fishman created the Visiting Writers Program at Farmingdale State College in 1979 and served as director until 1997. He also developed the Distinguished Speakers Program for Farmingdale State and led that program from 2001 through 2007. In addition, he was cofounder of the Long Island Poetry Collective (1973), a founding editor of *Xanadu* magazine and Pleasure Dome Press (1975), and originator of the Paumanok Poetry Award Competition, which he coordinated for seven years (1990-97). He has also been series editor of the Water Mark Poets of North America Book Award (1980-83), associate editor of *The Drunken Boat*, and poetry editor of *Gaia*, *Cistercian Studies Quarterly*, and the *Journal of Genocide Studies*, and he is currently poetry editor of *New Works Review* (www.new-works.org) and a consultant in poetry to the U.S. Holocaust Memorial Museum in Washington, D.C.

Among Fishman's most recent awards and honors are the Walt Whitman Birthplace Association's Long Island Poet of the Year Award (2006) and the 2007 Paterson Award for Literary Excellence. His books include *Mortal Companions* (Pleasure Dome Press, 1977), *Blood to Remember: American Poets on the Holocaust* (Texas Tech University Press, 1991), and *The Death Mazurka* (Texas Tech, 1989), an American Library Association Outstanding Book of the Year that was nominated for the 1990 Pulitzer Prize in Poetry. His most recent poetry collections are *Country of Memory* (Uccelli Press) and *5,000 Bells* (Cross-Cultural Communications), both 2004, and *Chopin's Piano* (Time Being Books, 2006).

About the Artist

Reva Sharon is an artist, photographer, poet, and writer who has been living and working in Jerusalem for the past nineteen years. She was born in Brooklyn, New York, and has lived on Long Island and in Florida.

Sharon's honors include First Prize for Digital Photography in the second annual Nagler Photography Competition; a residency at Mishkenot Sha'ananim — Jerusalem; and grants from the Israeli Government, the Tel Aviv Foundation for Literature and Art, and the Women's League for Israel. Her work is in the permanent collection of the Judah Magnes Museum in Berkeley, California, and has been exhibited at the Royal Photographic Society in Bath, England, and at Hebrew University, the USIA American Cultural Center, and Hebrew Union College, all in Jerusalem. Her poems and essays have been published in many anthologies and journals, and she has published one book of poetry, *Pool of the Morning Wind* (Shemesh, 1989).

The cover image is a montage created from photographs at the Valley of Lost Communities at Yad Vashem.

Permissions

Marjorie Agosín: "Bicycles," "Cousins," and "[Would it have been possible to take in the Jews,]" from *At the Threshold of Memory*, © 2003 by Marjorie Agosín. Reprinted by permission of the author and White Pine Press.

Sherman Alexie: Excerpts from "Inside Dachau," from *The Summer of Black Widows*, © 1996 by Sherman Alexie. Reprinted by permission of Hanging Loose Press.

Karen Alkalay-Gut: "*Hitler Builds a City for the Jews*," © 2007 by Karen Alkalay-Gut. Used by permission of the author. "Mr. Panitz," "Night Travel," "Voices in My Skin," and "Voyage Home," from *In My Skin* (Sivan), © 2000. Reprinted by permission of the author.

Michael Alpiner: "David-Horodok," "Pebbles from Auschwitz," and "Postcard from Poland" first appeared in *New Works Review* (www.new-works.org), © 2005 Michael Alpiner. Reprinted by permission of the author.

John Amen: "Verboten," from *More of Me Disappears*, © 2005. Reprinted by permission of the author and Cross-Cultural Communications.

Frieda Arkin: "Pinochle Day" © 1998 by Frieda Arkin. First published in *Beyond Lament: Poets of the World Bearing Witness to the Holocaust* (Northwestern University Press). Reprinted by permission of the author.

Brett Axel: "Morning After a Fight, He Says" © 2005 by Brett Axel. First appeared in the *Journal of Genocide Research*. Reprinted by permission of the author.

David B. Axelrod: "The Suffering Cuts Both Ways," from *Home Remedies*, © 1982 by David B. Axelrod. Reprinted by permission of the author and Cross-Cultural Communications.

Yakov Azriel: "We, the *Tefillin* of Once-Was Europe," from *Threads from a Coat of Many Colors: Poems on Genesis*, © 2005 by Yakov Azriel. Reprinted by permission of Time Being Books and the author.

Crystal Bacon: "Kristallnacht, 1991" © 1998 by Crystal Bacon. First appeared in *Beyond Lament: Poets of the World Bearing Witness to the Holocaust* (Northwestern University Press). Reprinted by permission of the author.

Julius Balbin: "Lament for the Gypsies" from *Strangled Cries* (Cross-Cultural Communications), © 1981, 1986 by Charlz Rizzuto. Reprinted by permission of the translator and Cross-Cultural Communications.

Stanley H. Barkan: "The Mothertree," from *Bubbemeises & Babbaluci* (Coop. Editrice Antigruppo Siciliano, Trapani, Sicily), © 2001 by Stanley H. Barkan. Reprinted by permission of the author.

Tony Barnstone: "Parable of the Jew Without a Name" © 2004 by Tony Barnstone. First appeared in *Margie*. Reprinted by permission of the author.

Willis Barnstone: "Miklós Radnóti" and "The Rose of Blue Flesh" © 1985 by Willis Barnstone. Reprinted by permission of the author.

Judith Barrington: "Ineradicable," from *Horses and the Human Soul*, © 2004 by Judith Barrington. Reprinted by permission of the author and Story Line Press. "History and Geography," from *History and Geography*, © 1989 by Judith Barrington. Reprinted by permission of the author and Eighth Mountain Press.

Marvin Bell: "The Extermination of the Jews," from *Nightworks: Poems 1962-2000* (Copper Canyon Press), © 2000 by Marvin Bell. Reprinted by permission of the author. "Oft-Seen Photo from the Liberation of Auschwitz" © 2007 by Marvin Bell. Used by permission of the author.

Lora J. Berg: "Maschlacki" © 1985 by Lora J. Berg. Used by permission of the author.

Michael Blumenthal: "Juliek's Violin," from *Days We Would Rather Know* (Viking-Penguin, 1984), © 1984 by Michael Blumenthal. Reprinted by permission of the author.

George Bogin: "Pitchipoi" © 1985 by George Bogin. First appeared in *Jewish Currents*. © 1989 by the Estate of George Bogin. Used by permission of the Estate of George Bogin.

Emily Borenstein: "Night Journey to Poland," "Triumph of the Dead," and "Verdi's Requiem Played and Sung by Jews in Terezín Concentration Camp / Summer, 1944" © 2006 by Emily Borenstein. Used by permission of the author. "The Shoah," from *Night of the Broken Glass*, © 1981 by Emily Borenstein. Reprinted by permission of the author and Timberline Press.

Laure-Anne Bosselaar: "The Feather at Breendonk" and "The Pallor of Survival," from *The Hour between Dog and Wolf*, © 1997 by Laure-Anne Bosselaar. Excerpts from "Seven Fragments on Hearing a Hammer Pounding," from *Small Gods of Grief*, © 2001 by Laure-Anne Bosselaar. Reprinted by permission of the author and BOA Editions.

Allen Brafman: "Gardens of Smoke" and "Rivkah," © 2005 by Allen Brafman. "Gardens of Smoke" first appeared in *New Works Review* (www.new-works.org). "Rivkah" first appeared in *Rogue Scholars*. Both poems reprinted by permission of the author.

Van K. Brock: "The Hindenburg" and excerpt from *This Way to the Gas*, from *Unspeakable Strangers* (Anhinga Press), © 1995 by Van K. Brock. Reprinted by permission of the author.

Louis Daniel Brodsky: "Learning the ABC's in Wartime Germany" and "Speaking for Survivors" are reprinted by permission of Louis Daniel Brodsky. "Phoenixes," from *Gestapo Crows: Holocaust Poems*, © 1992 by Louis Daniel Brodsky. Reprinted by permission of Time Being Books. "*Schindlerjuden*" and "Yom Kippur for a Survivor," from *The Eleventh Lost Tribe: Poems of the Holocaust*, © 1998 by Louis Daniel Brodsky. Reprinted by permission of Time Being Books.

Michael Dennis Browne: "Mengele," from *You Won't Remember This* (Carnegie-Mellon University Press), © 1992. Reprinted by permission of the author.

Michael R. Burch: "Pfennig Postcard, Wrong Address" © 2005 by Michael R. Burch. Used by permission of the author.

Olga Cabral: "At the Jewish Museum," from *In the Empire of Ice* (West End Press), © 1980 by Olga Cabral Kurtz. Used by permission of the author.

Joan Campion: "To Gisi Fleischmann: Rescuer of Her People" © 1985 by Joan Berengaria Campion. Reprinted by permission of the author.

Cyrus Cassells: "Auschwitz, All Hallows," "Juliek's Violin," and "The Postcard of Sophie Scholl" © 2007 by Cyrus Cassells. First appeared in *New Works Review* (www.new-works.org). Reprinted by permission of Cyrus Cassells. "Life Indestructible" and "Poem for the Artists of the Holocaust," from *Soul Make a Path Through Shouting*, © 1994 by Cyrus Cassells. Reprinted by permission of the author and Copper Canyon Press.

Judith Chalmer: "The Archivist" and "Personal to Kaplan," from *Out of History's Junk Jar*, © 1995. Reprinted by permission of the author and Time Being Books.

John Ciardi: "The Gift," from *Thirty-Nine Poems* (Rutgers University Press), © 1959 by John Ciardi. Reprinted by permission of the author.

David Citino: "Swastika," from *The Discipline: New and Selected Poems, 1980–1992* (Ohio State University Press), © 1992 by David Citino. Reprinted by permission of the author.

Vince Clemente: "From the Ardeatine Caves" © 1978, 1985 by Vince Clemente. Reprinted by permission of the author.

Helen Degen Cohen (Halina Degenfisz): "And the Snow Kept Falling" © 1989 by Helen Degen Cohen. First appeared in *Spoon River Quarterly*. "Habry" © 1997 by Helen Degen Cohen. First appeared in *Akcent* (Lublin, Poland). "I Remember Coming into Warsaw, a Child" © 1985 by Helen Degen Cohen. Reprinted by permission of the author.

David Curzon: "The Gardens," from *Midrashim*, © 1991 by David Curzon. Reprinted by permission of the author and Cross-Cultural Communications.

Ruth Daigon: "Dachau Revisited, 1971" © 2005 by Ruth Daigon. Used by permission of the author.

Susan Dambroff: "There Were Those," from *Memory in Bone* (Black Oyster Press), © 1984 by Susan Dambroff. Reprinted by permission of the author.

Enid Dame: "Soup," from *Anything You Don't See*, © 1992 by Enid Dame. Reprinted by permission of Donald Lev and West End Press.

Kate Daniels: "For Miklós Radnóti: 1909–1944," from *The White Wave*, © 1984 by Kate Daniels. Reprinted by permission of the author and the University of Pittsburgh Press.

Sister Mary Philip de Camara: "Yellow Starred" © 1985 by Sister Mary Philip de Camara. Used by permission of the author.

Theodore Deppe: "School of Music" © 1985 by Theodore Deppe. First appeared in *Poem in a Pamphlet* (Andrew Mountain Press). Used by permission of the author.

Norita Dittberner-Jax: "Name Tag" © 2006 by Norita Dittberner-Jax. Used by permission of the author.

Sharon Dolin: "Three Postage Stamps," from *Heart Work: Poems*, © 1998 by Sharon Dolin. Reprinted by permission of the author and Sheep Meadow Press.

Wendy Drexler: "On Hearing a String Quartet Written by Prisoners of Theresienstadt" © 2005 by Wendy Drexler. First appeared in *Nimrod*. Used by permission of the author.

Shoshana Dubman: "Istanbul 1967" and "Memories" © 2005 by Shoshana Dubman. Used by permission of the author.

Jehanne Dubrow: "Shulamith Rereads *The Shawl*," "Shulamith, in White," and "Shulamith Writes *Fuck You*," from *The Promised Bride* (Finishing Line Press), © 2007 by Jehanne Dubrow. Reprinted by permission of the author.

Shelley Ehrlich: "Vilna 1938" © 1981 by Shelley Ehrlich. First appeared in *Jewish Currents*. Used by permission of the author.

Kenneth Fearing: "Ad," from *New and Collected Poems* (Indiana University Press), © 1956 by Kenneth Fearing. Reprinted by permission of the Estate of Kenneth Fearing.

Frederick Feirstein: "'Grandfather' in Winter," from *Survivors* (David Lewis), © 1975 by Frederick Feirstein. Reprinted by permission of the author.

Irving Feldman: Excerpt from "Family History" and "The Pripet Marshes," from *Collected Poems: 1954–2004*, © 2004 by Irving Feldman. Used by permission of the author and Schocken Books, a division of Random House, Inc.

Ruth Feldman: "Survivor," © 1972 by Ruth Feldman. First appeared in *European Judaism*. Used by permission of the author.

Charles Adés Fishman: "Eastern Europe After the War," "A Jawbone from the Reich," and "The Silence," from *Chopin's Piano*, © 2006 by Charles Adés Fishman. Reprinted by permission of the author and Time Being Books.

Tamara Fishman: "I Did Not Know, but I Remember," © 1985, 1989 by Tamara Fishman. Used by permission of the author.

Ephim Fogel: "Icon" (originally "Portrait of a General") and "Shipment to Maidanek" © 1945, 1957, 1984 by Ephim Fogel. First appeared in *Cross Section 1945* (L. B. Fischer Co.). "Yizkor" © 2006 by Daniel Mark Fogel. Poems reprinted by permission of Daniel Mark Fogel.

Carolyn Forché: Excerpts from "The Angel of History" and "The Notebook of Uprising," from *The Angel of History*, © 1989 by Carolyn Forché. Reprinted by permission of the author and Harper/Collins.

Florence W. Freed: "God's Death" © 1985 by Florence W. Freed. Used by permission of the author.

Mike Frenkel: "Quiet Desperation" © 1985 by Michael W. Frenkel. Used by permission of the author.

Sari Friedman: "Skin" © 1985 by Sari Friedman. Used by permission of the author.

Alice Friman: "At the Holocaust Museum" © 2005 by Alice Friman. First appeared in *North American Review*. "The Waiting Room" © 2005 by Alice Friman. First appeared in *The Southern Review*. Poems reprinted by permission of the author.

Patricia Garfinkel: "The Tailor" © 1979 by Patricia Garfinkel. First appeared in *Seattle Review*. Used by permission of the author.

Kinereth Gensler: "For Nelly Sachs," from *Threesome Poems* (Alice James Books), © 1976 by Kinereth Gensler. Used by permission of Daniel Gensler.

David Gershator: Excerpt from "The Akiva Poems" © 2002 by David Gershator. First appeared on *Poetry Superhighway*. "Last Night's Doubleheader" © 2006 by David Gershator. Poems used by permission of the author.

Jacob Glatstein (Yankev Glatshteyn): "Dead Men Don't Praise God," "I'll Find My Self-Belief" and "Nightsong," from *The Selected Poems of Jacob Glatstein* (October House), © 1972 by Ruth Whitman, translator. Reprinted by permission of Ruth Whitman. "Millions of Dead," from *I Keep Recalling: The Holocaust Poems of Jacob Glatstein* (Ktav), © 1993 by Barnett Zumoff, translator. Reprinted by permission of the translator and the Glatstein Estate. "Without Jews" reprinted by permission of Helen Marjorie Windust Halper.

Barbara Goldberg: "Our Father," from *Cautionary Tales* (Dryad Press), © 1990 by Barbara Goldberg. Reprinted by permission of the author.

Thomas A. Goldman: "Rotterdam — 1946: The Pre-War Visa Files" © 1985 by Thomas A. Goldman. Used by permission of the author.

Rachel Goldstein: "Prosciowiece, 1942" and "There Is No Time" © 2002 by Rachel Goldstein. First appeared in *Antigonish Review*. "Those Who Remain" © 2005 by Rachel Goldstein. Poems used by permission of the author.

Ber Green: "The Martyrs Are Calling" © 1985 by Aaron Kramer. Used by permission of the translator.

John Z. Guzlowski: "How Early Fall Came This Year" and "What the War Taught My Mother," from *Language of Mules* (DP Press), © 1999 by John Z. Guzlowski. "Hunger in the Labor Camps" and "Night in the Labor Camp," from *Lightning and Ashes* (Steel Toe Books), © 2007. Poems reprinted by permission of the author.

Leo Haber: "The Book of Lamentations" © 1998 by Leo Haber. First appeared in *Beyond Lament: Poets of the World Bearing Witness to the Holocaust* (Northwestern University Press). Reprinted by permission of the author. "Rachel at the Well" and "Sanctification" © 2005 by Leo Haber. Used by permission of the author.

Israel I. Halpern: "Being Seemingly Unscathed," from *The Toolbox Poems* (Anarchy Press), © 1982 by Israel I. Halpern. "Love in a Death Camp" © 2006. First published in *Freshet 2006* (Fresh Meadows Poets Press). Poems reprinted by permission of the author.

Annette Bialik Harchik: "Earrings" © 1985 by Annette Bialik Harchik. "Requiem" © 2006. Poems used by permission of the author.

Geoffrey Hartman: "Day of Remembrance" and "In Memory of Paul Celan" © 2006. Used by permission of the author.

Anthony Hecht: "'It Out-Herods Herod. Pray You, Avoid It.'" and "'More Light! More Light!'" from *Collected Earlier Poems*, © 1990 by Anthony E. Hecht. Used by permission of Alfred A. Knopf, a division of Random House, Inc.

Leslie Woolf Hedley: "Chant for All the People on Earth," from *On My Way to the Cemetery* (Ampersand Press), © 1964, 1981 by Leslie Woolf Hedley. Reprinted by permission of the author.

Julie N. Heifetz: "The Blue Parakeet," "Harry Lenga," and "The Wheel," from *Oral History and the Holocaust* (Pergamon Press), © 1985 by Julie N. Heifetz. Used by permission of the author.

Chaia Heller: "A Jew's Love for Language" © 1998 by Chaia Heller. First appeared in *Beyond Lament: Poets of the World Bearing Witness to the Holocaust* (Northwestern University Press). Reprinted by permission of the author. "The Yiddish I Know" © 2005 by Chaia Heller. Used by permission of the author.

Michael Heller: "Bandelette de Torah" © 2004 by Michael Heller. First appeared in *Shofar*. Excerpt from "Bialystok Stanzas," from *Exigent Futures: New and Selected Poems* (Salt Publishing), © 2003 by Michael Heller. Poems reprinted by permission of the author.

Stephen Herz: "Fried Noodles Topped with Raisins Cinnamon and Vanilla Cream," "In Your Lager Dream," "Jedwabne," and "Shot," from *Whatever You Can Carry: Poems of the Holocaust*, © 2003 by Stephen Herz. Reprinted by permission of the author. "Marked" © 2005 by Stephen Herz. Used by permission of the author.

Walter Hess: "Oma" © 2005 by Walter Hess. Used by permission of the author.

William Heyen: "The Candle," "Riddle," and "The Secret," from *Falling from Heaven: Holocaust Poems of a Jew and a Gentile*, and "Simple Truths," from *Erika: Poems of the Holocaust*, both © 1991 by William Heyen. Reprinted by permission of Time Being Books and the author. "The Legend of the Shoah," from *Shoah Train: Poems* (Etruscan Press), © 2003 by William Heyen. Reprinted by permission of the author.

Rick Hilles: "Amchu" and "Yom HaShoah in Florida," from *Brother Salvage* (University of Pittsburg Press), © 2006 by Rick Hilles. Reprinted by permission of the author.

Edward Hirsch: "Paul Celan: A Grave and Mysterious Sentence," from *Wild Gratitude* (Alfred A. Knopf), © 1983 and 1986 by Edward Hirsch. Reprinted by permission of the author.

Jean Hollander: "The Chosen," from *Crushed into Honey* (Saturday Press), © 1986 by Jean Hollander. Reprinted by permission of the author.

Barbara Helfgott Hyett: "And There Were Pits," "Too Weak to Stand, They Lay" and "You Know, the Funny Thing Is," from *In Evidence: Poems of the Liberation of the Nazi Concentration Camps* (University of Pittsburgh Press), © 1986 by Barbara Helfgott Hyett. Reprinted by permission of the author.

Thea Iberall: "Keeping the Ground" © 2006 by Thea Iberall. First appeared in *poeticdiversity*. Reprinted by permission of Thea Iberall.

Judith Irwin: "1985 — In a Small American Town" © 1985 by Judith Irwin. Used by permission of the author.

Dan Jaffe: "In a Holocaust Memorial Garden" © 2007 by Dan Jaffe. First appeared in *New Letters*. Reprinted by permission of the author.

Katherine Janowitz: "The Third Generation" © 1985 by Katherine Janowitz. Used by permission of the author.

Sheila Golburgh Johnson: "Shoes" © 2005 by Sheila Golburgh Johnson. Used by permission of the author.

Laurence Josephs: "Passover at Auschwitz," from *Cold Water Morning* (Skidmore College), © 1963 by Laurence Josephs. Reprinted by permission of the author.

Marilyn Kallet: "After a While, at Theresienstadt," "Mezuzah," "To My Poem of Hope," and "Survivor," from *Circe, After Hours* (BkMk Press), © 2005 by Marilyn Kallet. Reprinted by permission of the author and BkMk Press.

Rodger Kamenetz: "My Holocaust," from *The Lowercase Jew* (Northwestern University Press), © 2003 by Rodger Kamenetz. Reprinted by permission of the author.

Marc Kaminsky: "Medium," from *Daily Bread* (University of Illinois Press), © 1982 by Marc Kaminsky. Used by permission of the author.

Peretz Kaminsky: "Bramble" and "Identifications" © 1985 by Peretz Kaminsky. Reprinted by permission of the author.

Rosa Felsenburg Kaplan: "Kol Nidre" © 1982 by Rosa Felsenburg Kaplan. First appeared in *Shirim*. Used by permission of the author.

Dori Katz: "Line-Up" and "The Return." from *Hiding in Other People's Houses* (La Luciernaga Editores), © 1999 by Dori Katz. "My Face Before" © 2005 by Dori Katz. Poems reprinted by permission of the author.

Eliot Katz: Excerpts from "Liberation Recalled," from *Unlocking the Exits*, © 1999 by Eliot Katz. Reprinted by permission of the author and Coffee House Press.

Alan Kaufman: "My Mother Doesn't Know Who Allen Ginsberg Is" and "Who Are We?" from *Who Are We?* (Davka Limited Editions), © 1997 by Alan Kaufman. Reprinted by permission of the author.

Melanie Kaye/Kantrowitz: Excerpt from "Kaddish" © 1984 by Melanie Kaye/Kantrowitz. First appeared in *Sinister Wisdom*. Used by permission of the author.

Tsipi Keller: "The Shower" © 1987 by Tsipi Keller. First appeared in *Present Tense*. Reprinted by permission of the author.

Miriam Kessler: "Yahrzeit" © 1985 by Miriam Kessler. Used by permission of the author.

Steve Klepetar: "Burial" and "The Spells of Earth" © 2005 by Steve Klepetar. First appeared in *New Works Review* (www.new-works.org). Reprinted by permission of the author.

Irina Klepfisz: Excerpts from "*Bashert*" and "Solitary Acts," from *A Few Words in the Mother Tongue: Poems Selected and New / 1971–1990*, © 1990 by Irena Klepfisz. Reprinted by permission of the author and Eighth Mountain Press.

Ruth Kluger: "Halloween and a Ghost," from *Still Alive: A Holocaust Girlhood Remembered*, © 2003 by Ruth Kluger. Reprinted by permission of the author and The Feminist Press at the City University of New York, www.feministpress.org. All rights reserved.

David Koenig: "After the Holocaust, No Poetry" and "Onkel Fritz Is Sitting" © 1985 by David Koenig. Used by permission of the author.

Yala Korwin: "The Little Boy with His Hands Up," "Noemi" and "Passover Night 1942," from *To Tell the Story: Poems of the Holocaust* (Holocaust Publications), © 1987 by Yala Korwin. "You, Who Did Not Survive" © 2005 by Yala Korwin. First appeared in *Midstream*. Poems reprinted by permission of the author.

Aaron Kramer: "Westminster Synagogue" and "Zudioska," from *Carousel Parkway and Other Poems* (A.S. Barnes & Co.), © 1980 by Aaron Kramer. Reprinted by permission of the author.

Norbert Krapf: "*Tannenbaum*, 1940," "The Name on a Wall," "A Freight Yard in Würzburg," and "Meditation in the Israelite Cemetery, Würzburg," from *Blue-Eyed Grass: Poems of Germany* © 1997 by Norbert Krapf. Reprinted by permission of the author and Time Being Books.

Carolyn Kreiter-Foronda: "Leaving a Country Behind" © 1985 by Carolyn Kreiter-Kurylo and 2006 by Carolyn Kreiter-Foronda. Used by permission of the author.

Maxine Kumin: "The Amsterdam Poem," from *The Nightmare Factory* (Harper & Row), © 1970 by Maxine Kumin. Reprinted by permission of the author.

Aaron Kurtz: "A Million Pairs of Shoes," © 1965 and 1985 by Olga Cabral Kurtz (translator). Used by permission of the translator.

Christine Lahey: "Dan's Shoe Repair: 1959," from *Sticks and Stones* (Urban Despair Press), © 1980. Reprinted by permission of the author.

Carole Glasser Langille: "Babi Yar" © 1985 and 2006 by Carole Glasser Langille. Used by permission of the author.

Alyssa A. Lappen: "How It Happened," from *The People Bear Witness* (Ruah), © 2000 by Alyssa A. Lappen. "This, My Incarnation" © 2001 by Alyssa A. Lappen. First appeared in *Midstream*. Poems reprinted by permission of the author.

Denise Levertov: Excerpt from "During the Eichmann Trial," from *Poems 1960–1967*, © 1983 by Denise Levertov. Reprinted by permission of the author and New Directions Publishing Corporation.

Philip Levine: "On a Drawing by Flavio," from *New Selected Poems*, by Philip Levine, © 1991 by Philip Levine. Reprinted by permission of the author and Alfred A. Knopf, a division of Random House, Inc. "Survivor" © 1974 by Philip Levine. First appeared in *American Poetry Review*. Reprinted by permission of the author.

Leatrice H. Lifshitz: "A Few More Things About the Holocaust" © 1985 by Leatrice H. Lifshitz. First appeared in *Escarpments*. Used by permission of the author and Lawrence M. Lifshitz.

Alan Lupack: "Auschwitz Reportaż" © 1985 by Alan Lupack. Used by permission of the author.

Yaacov Luria: "There Is One Synagogue Extant in Kiev," from *Not a Piano Key* (Shira Press), © 1979 by Yaacov Luria. Reprinted by permission of the author.

Arlene Maass: "Opa the Watchmaker" © 1985 by Arlene Maass. Used by permission of the author.

Channah Magori: Excerpts from "Holocaust Archives I" © 2005 by Channah Magori. First appeared in *Poetica*. Excerpt from "Holocaust Archives II" © 2005 by Channah Magori. Poems reprinted by permission of the author.

Sandra Cohen Margulius: "Aunt Betty" © 2005 by Sandra Cohen Margulius. Used by permission of the author.

David McKain: "For the Children," from *The Common Life* (Alice James Books), © 1982 by David McKain. Used by permission of the author.

Robert Mezey: "Terezín," from *The Door Standing Open* (Houghton Mifflin), © 1970 by Robert Mezey. Reprinted by permission of the author.

Richard Michelson: "The Jews That We Are," from *Tap-Dancing for the Relatives* (University Presses of Florida), © 1985 by Richard Michelson. Reprinted by permission of the author. Excerpts from "Recital," from *Battles and Lullabies* (University of Illinois Press), © 2005 by Richard Michelson. Reprinted by permission of the author.

Bernard S. Mikofsky: "Mame-Loshen, Yiddish" © 1977 by Bernard S. Mikofsky. First appeared in *Detroit Jewish News*. "1945" © 1975 by Bernard S. Mikofsky. First appeared in *Friday Forum*. Poems reprinted by permission of the author.

Aaron Miller: "Not Dachau" © 1964 by Aaron Miller. First appeared in *World Union* (India). Reprinted by permission of the author.

Marilyn Mohr: "Tsena Tsena" and "Yiddish," from *Satchel* © 1992 by Marilyn Mohr. Reprinted by permission of the author and Cross-Cultural Communications.

David Moolten: "Photograph of Liberated Prisoner, Dachau, 1945" © 2001. "Yellow Star" © 2005. Both poems first appeared in *Southern Review*. Reprinted by permission of the author.

Sarah Traister Moskovitz: "December," "The Dress," "The Teaspoon," and "At the United States Holocaust Memorial Museum" © 2006 by Sarah Traister Moskovitz. Used by permission of the author.

Stanley Moss: "Ghetto Theater, Vilnius 1941" and "A Visit to Kaunas," from *A History of Color* (Seven Stories Press), © 2003 by Stanley Moss. Reprinted by permission of the author.

Teresa Moszkowicz-Syrop: "Lullaby" and "The Tomatoes" © 1985 by Teresa Moszkowicz-Syrop. Used by permission of the author.

Elaine Mott: "The Balcony" © 2005 by Elaine Mott. First appeared in *Poet Lore*. "The Last Visa for Palestine" and "On the Wings of the Wind" © 1985 by Elaine Mott. "On the Wings of the Wind" first appeared in *Day Tonight/Night Today*. Poems used by permission of the author.

Mark Nepo: "Hill Where the Lord Hides" © 2006 by Mark Nepo. "I Wake from a Dream of Killing Hitler" © 1985 by Mark Nepo. Poems used by permission of the author.

Amos Neufeld: "In the Heaven of Night" © 1985 by Amos Neufeld. First appeared in *Response*. "A Shade of Night" © 1985 by Amos Neufeld. First appeared in *Forum* (Israel). "When Israel Went Forth" © 2005 by Amos Neufeld. Poems used by permission of the author.

Miriam Offenberg: "Reforger" © 1985 by Miriam Offenberg. Used by permission of the author.

Lois E. Olena: "The Archivist" © 1998 by Lois E. Olena. First appeared in *European Judaism*. "Homeland" © 1997 by Lois E. Olena. First appeared in *Midstream*. Poems reprinted by permission of the author.

Jacqueline Osherow: "Ponar," from *Conversations with Survivors*, © 1994 by Jacqueline Osherow. Reprinted by permission of the author and University of Georgia Press. "Villanelle from a Sentence in a Poet's Brief Biography," from *Dead Men's Praise*, © 1999 by Jacqueline Osherow. Reprinted by permission of the author and Grove/Atlantic, Inc.

Alicia Ostriker: "The Eighth and Thirteenth," from *The Crack in Everything*, © 1996 by Alicia Suskin Ostriker. "Poem Beginning with a Line by Fitzgerald/Hemingway," from *The Little Space: Poems Selected and New, 1968–1998*, © 1998 by Alicia Ostriker. Both poems reprinted by permission of the author and the University of Pittsburgh Press.

Christina Pacosz: "Auschwitz: Oświęcim," from *This Is Not a Place to Sing*, © 1987 by Christina Pacosz. Reprinted by permission of the author and West End Press.

Linda Pastan: "Landscape near Dachau," from *Queen of a Rainy Country* © 2006 by Linda Pastan. Used by permission of the author. "Rachel (ra'chal), a Ewe" and "Response," from *PM/AM: New and Selected Poems*, © 1981 by Linda Pastan. Poems reprinted by permission of the author and W.W. Norton & Company, Inc.

Mark Pawlak: "Like Butterflies," from *Special Handling: Newspaper Poems New and Selected*, © 1993 by Mark Pawlak. Reprinted by permission of the author and Hanging Loose Press.

Edmund Pennant: "Thoughts Under the Giant Sequoia," from *Dream's Navel* (Lintel Press), © 1979 by Edmund Pennant. "Yom Hazikaron" © 1984 by Edmund Pennant. First appeared in *Moment*. Poems reprinted by permission of Doris Zaslow.

Louis Phillips: "Perhaps You Would Like to Learn Another Language" and "Words over the Entranceway to Hell," from *Savage Steps to the House of Meaning* (Prologue Press), © 1995 by Louis Phillips. Reprinted by permission of the author.

Marge Piercy: "Black Mountain," "Growing Up Haunted," and "The Housing Project at Drancy," from *The Art of Blessing the Day*, © 1999 by Middlemarsh, Inc. Reprinted by permission of Alfred A. Knopf, a division of Random House, Inc.

Heidemarie Pilc: "Somewhere in Poland . . . Survivor's Lament" © 2001 by Heidemarie Pilc. First appeared in *Bittersweet Legacy: Creative Responses to the Holocaust* (University Press of America). Reprinted by permission of the author.

William Pillin: "Farewell to Europe," "Miserere," "A Poem for Anton Schmidt," and "The Ascensions," from *To the End of Time* (Papa Bach Editions), © 1980 by William Pillin. Reprinted by permission of Boris Pillin.

John C. Pine: "The Survivor," from *Cliff Walk* (Moveable Feast Press), © 1985 by John C. Pine. Reprinted by permission of the author.

Karl A. Plank: "Ash Wednesday" © 1992 by Karl A. Plank. First appeared in *Anglican Theological Review*. Reprinted by permission of the author.

Ginger Porter: "I Am Babi Yar" © 1985 by Ginger Porter. Used by permission of the author.

Evelyn Posamentier: "Heinz Rosenberg on the Platform" © 2004 by Evelyn Posamentier. "Toska" © 2006 by Evelyn Posamentier. Both poems first appeared in *2 River View* and are reprinted by permission of the author.

Anna Rabinowitz: Excerpt from *Darkling: A Poem* (Tupelo Press), © 2001 by Anna Rabinowitz. Excerpts from "Dislocations," from *At the Site of Inside Out* (University of Massachusetts Press), © 1997 by Anna Rabinowitz. Poems reprinted by permission of the author.

David Ray: "Houses," "A Photograph from 1935," "A Song for Herr Hitler," and "Visitors from America," from *One Thousand Years: Poems About the Holocaust*, © 2006 by David Ray. Reprinted by permission of the author and Timberline Press.

Richard C. Raymond: "And Nothing Moved," from *A Moment of Bells* (The Plowshare Press), © 1970 by Richard C. Raymond. Reprinted by permission of Laura Raymond.

Barbara Reisner: "Sweet Savour" © 2005 by Barbara Reisner. Used by permission of the author.

Naomi Replansky: "Korczak and the Orphans" © 2005 by Naomi Replansky. Used by permission of the author. "The Six Million," from *The Dangerous World: New and Selected Poems* (Another Chicago Press), © 1994 by Naomi Replansky. Reprinted by permission of the author.

Lisa Ress: "U.S. Army Holds Dance for Camp Survivors. Germany, 1945," from *Flight Patterns*, © 1985 by Lisa Ress. Reprinted by permission of the author and the University Press of Virginia.

Elaine Reuben: "After Generations After" © 2006 by Elaine Reuben. Used by permission of the author.

Charles Reznikoff: Excerpts from "Massacres" and "Mass Graves," from *Holocaust* (Black Sparrow Press) © 1975 by Charles Reznikoff. Excerpt from *Inscriptions: 1944–1956* © 1959 by Charles Reznikoff. Poems and excerpts reprinted by permission of Marie Syrkin.

Liliane Richman: "After Claude Lanzmann's *Shoah*" © 1985 by Liliane Richman. Used by permission of the author.

Michael D. Riley: "Photograph of Bergen-Belsen, 1945" © 1999 by Michael D. Riley. First appeared in *Karamu*. Reprinted by permission of the author.

Nicholas Rinaldi: "Auschwitz," from *The Luftwaffe in Chaos* (Negative Capability Press), © 1985 by Nicholas Rinaldi. Reprinted by permission of the author.

Curtis Robbins: *"In der Nacht"* ("In the Night") © 1998 by Curtis Robbins. First appeared in *Beyond Lament: Poets of the World Bearing Witness to the Holocaust* (Northwestern University Press). Reprinted by permission of the author.

William Pitt Root: "Pastoral for the Twenty-first Century" © 1983 by William Pitt Root. First appeared in *Southern Poetry Review* (as "Late Twentieth Century Pastoral"). Reprinted by permission of the author.

Marina Roscher. "The Lanternman" © 1985 by Marina Roscher. Used by permission of the author.

Jennifer Rose: "At Dachau with a German Lover," from *The Old Direction of Heaven* (Truman State University Press), © 2000 by Jennifer Rose. Reprinted by permission of the author.

Harriet Susskind Rosenblum: "After That Time" © 1985 by Harriet Susskind. "Ritual at Auschwitz" © 2006 by Mark D. Rosenblum. Poems used by permission of Mark D. Rosenblum.

Menachem Rosensaft: "Birkenau Barracks," "Sosnowiec Visited," and "Yad Vashem Museum Opening, March 15, 2005" © 2006 by Menachem Z. Rosensaft. "Sosnowiec Visited" first appeared in *Rayonot: A Journal of Ideas*. "The Second Generation" © 1980 by Menachem Z. Rosensaft. First appeared in *Midstream*. Poems used by permission of the author.

Elizabeth Rosner: "Almost Beautiful," "Anything," "Chocolate," "Homework," and "My Father's Souvenirs," from *Gravity* (Small Poetry Press), © 1998 by Elizabeth Rosner. Reprinted by permission of the author.

Jerome Rothenberg: *"Dibbukim"* ("Dibbiks"), *"Dos Oysleydikn"* ("The Emptying"), "IN THE DARK WORD, KHURBN," "The Other Secret in the Trail of Money," excerpt from "Peroration for a Lost Town," and introductory comments by Jerome Rothenberg, from *Khurbn & Other Poems*, © 1989 by Jerome Rothenberg. Reprinted by permission of the author and New Directions Publishing Corp.

Larry Rubin: "The Nazi in the Dock, at Sixty" © 1981 by Larry Rubin. First appeared in *Midstream*. Reprinted by permission of the author.

Mark Rudman: "Easy Living in Terezín" © 2007 by Mark Rudman. Used by permission of the author.

Biff Russ: "The Way to Be Haunted," from *Black Method*, © 1991 by Biff Russ. Reprinted by permission of the author and Helicon Nine Editions.

Luada Sandler: "A Scene from *Shoah*" © 1985 by Luada Sandler. Used by permission of the author.

Reg Saner: "Aspen Oktoberfest," from *Essay on Air* (Ohio Review Books), © 1984 by Reg Saner. Reprinted by permission of the author.

May Sarton: Excerpt from "The Invocation to Kali," from *Collected Poems: 1939–1973* (W.W. Norton), © 1974 by May Sarton. Reprinted by permission of the author.

Rebecca Seiferle: "'*A lonely man in his greatness,*'" from *Bitters*, © 2001 by Rebecca Seiferle. Reprinted by permission of the author and Copper Canyon Press.

David Shapiro: "For Victims" © 1989 by David Shapiro. Used by permission of the author.

Gregg Shapiro: "Tattoo" © 1983 by Gregg Shapiro. First appeared in *Reconstructionist*. Reprinted by permission of the author.

Harvey Shapiro: "Ditty," from *This World*, © 1971 by Harvey Shapiro. Reprinted by permission of the author and Wesleyan University Press. "Natural History," from *A Day's Portion*, © 1994 by Harvey Shapiro. Reprinted by permission of the author and Hanging Loose Press.

Reva Sharon: "In the Absence of Yellow" and "Unanswerable Questions" © 1985 by Reva Sharon. "Holocaust Remembrance Day" © 2006 by Reva Sharon. Poems used by permission of the author. "Shoshana" © 1998 by Reva Sharon. First appeared in *Beyond Lament: Poets of the World Bearing Witness to the Holocaust* (Northwestern University Press). Reprinted by permission of the author.

Enid Shomer: "Women Bathing at Bergen-Belsen" © 1985 by Enid Shomer. First appeared in *Negative Capability*. Reprinted by permission of the author.

Joan I. Siegel: "Haggadah" © 2000 by Joan I. Siegel. First appeared in *Journal of Genocide Research*. Reprinted by permission of the author.

Maurya Simon: "Letter to Vienna from Paris, 1942" © 1985 by Maurya Simon. Used by permission of the author.

Louis Simpson: "The Bird" and "A Story About Chicken Soup," from *The Owner of the House: New Collected Poems 1940–2001* (BOA Editions, Ltd.), © 2003 by Louis Simpson. Reprinted by permission of the author.

Myra Sklarew: Excerpts from "Lithuania," from *Lithuania: New & Selected Poems* (Azul Editions), © 1995, 1997 by Myra Sklarew. Reprinted by permission of the author.

Joan Jobe Smith: "Hollow Cost" © 1985 by Joan Jobe and 2006 by Joan Jobe Smith. Used by permission of the author.

Kirtland Snyder: "City Children at a Summer Camp. Slonim, 1936" and "Selma . . . A Pot of Soup . . . A Bottle of Milk. Łódź" © 1985 by Kirtland Snyder. Used by permission of the author.

J. R. Solonche: "Another Book on the Holocaust" © 1985 by J. R. Solonche. Used by permission of the author.

Jason Sommer: Excerpts from "Mengele Shitting," "Meyer Tsits and the Children," and "The Property of the World," from *Other People's Troubles*, © 1997 by Jason Sommer. "What They Saw," from *The Man Who Sleeps in My Office*, © 2004 by Jason Sommer. Reprinted by permission of the author and University of Chicago Press.

Gizela Spunberg: "Memories of December" © 1979 by Gizela Spunberg. First appeared in *Martyrdom and Resistance*. Reprinted by permission of the author.

Hans Jörg Stahlschmidt: "November Rain" and "Visit to the Fatherland" © 2001 by Hans Jörg Stahlschmidt. First appeared in *Bittersweet Legacy: Creative Responses to the Holocaust* (University Press of America). Reprinted by permission of the author.

Jan Steckel: "The Maiden Aunts" © 2005 by Jan Steckel. First appeared in *Pedestal Magazine*. Reprinted by permission of the author.

Martin Steingesser: "The Three" © 1978, 1980 by Martin Steingesser. First appeared in *American Poetry Review*. Reprinted by permission of the author.

Gerald Stern: "Adler" and "Soap," from *Paradise Poems* (Random House), © 1984 by Gerald Stern. Reprinted by permission of Gerald Stern.

Bradley R. Strahan: "Yom Kippur" © 1985 by Bradley R. Strahan. First appeared in *Jewish Spectator*. Reprinted by permission of the author.

Rabbi Michael Strassfeld: "Who Knows One?" © 2006 by Rabbi Michael Strassfeld. Used by permission of the author.

Lynn Strongin: "Erasing the Blue Numbers," "Her Velocity Had Been Taken," "Theresienstadt" and "What a Waste of World" © 2006 by Lynn Strongin. "Her Velocity Had Been Taken" and "Theresienstadt" first appeared in *New Works Review* (www.new-works.org). Poems used by permission of the author.

Yerra Sugarman: "Because," from *Forms of Gone*, © 2002 by Yerra Sugarman. Reprinted by permission of the author and Sheep Meadow Press.

Yuri Suhl: ". . . And the Earth Rebelled," from *Jewish Life Anthology: 1946–1956* © 1956 by Max Rosenfeld. Translated from the Yiddish by Max Rosenfeld. Reprinted by permission of the author.

Zahava Z. Sweet: "Dark Whispers," "The Line" and "In Ravensbrück" © 2006 by Zahava Z. Sweet. Used by permission of the author.

Marie Syrkin: "Niemand" and "The Reckoning," from *Gleanings* (Black Sparrow Press), © 1979 by Marie Syrkin. Reprinted by permission of David Bodansky.

Marilynn Talal: "Another Holocaust Poem" © 2003 by Marilynn Talal. First appeared in *Concrete Wolf*. "For Our Dead" © 1985 by Marilynn Talal. "My Mother as Superhero" © 2005 by Marilynn Talal. Poems used by permission of the author.

Sean M. Teaford: "A Pure Breath" and "Warsaw Epidemic," from *Kaddish Diary* (Pudding House Publications), © 2005 by Sean M. Teaford. Reprinted by permission of the author.

Philip Terman: "The Jewish Quarter in Budapest" and "With the Survivors," from *Book of the Unbroken Days*, © 2005 by Philip Terman. "What We Pass On" and "The Wounds," from *The House of Sages*, © 1998, 2005. Both collections published by Mammoth Books. Poems reprinted by permission of the author.

Elaine Terranova: "1939" © 1985 by Elaine Terranova. Used by permission of the author.

Susan Terris: "Train to Oświęcim" © 2005 by Susan Terris. First appeared in *New Works Review* (www.new-works.org). Reprinted by permission of the author.

Hilary Tham: "Daughter of Survivors," from *Bad Names for Women* (Word Works), © 1989. Reprinted by permission of Ilana Goldberg and Joseph Goldberg.

Susan Tichy: "Gaby at the U.N. Observation Post," from *The Hands in Exile* (Random House), © 1983 by Susan E. Tichy. Reprinted by permission of the author.

Alfred Van Loen: "Auschwitz #1" and "Auschwitz #6" © 1985 by Alfred Van Loen. Used by permission of Helen Van Loen.

Derek Walcott: Excerpt from *Midsummer '81*, © 1981, 1982, 1991 by Derek Walcott. First appeared in James Atlas, "Derek Walcott: Poet of Two Worlds," 23 May 1982, *New York Times Magazine*, VI, 38. Reprinted by permission of the author.

George Wallace: "An Apple for Wolfgang Granjonca" © 2006 by George Wallace. Used by permission of the author.

Michael Waters: "Dachau Moon," from *Fish Light* (Ithaca House), © 1975 by Michael Waters. Reprinted by permission of the author.

Florence Weinberger: "Marrow Bones" © 2005 by Florence Weinberger. First appeared in *Pedestal Magazine*. "Speak to the Children" and "Survivor," from *Breathing Like a Jew* (Chicory Blue Press), © 1997 by Florence Weinberger. Poems reprinted by permission of the author.

Theodore Weiss: "The Late Train," from *Fireweeds* (Macmillan), © 1976, 1987 by Theodore Weiss. Reprinted by permission of the author.

Ruth Whitman: "The Death Ship," from *The Testing of Hanna Sanesh* (Wayne State University Press), © 1986 by Ruth Whitman. "Maria Olt," from *Permanent Address: New Poems 1973–1980* (Alice James Books), © 1980 by Ruth Whitman. Poems reprinted by permission of Ruth Whitman.

C.K. Williams: "Spit," from *With Ignorance* (Houghton Mifflin), © 1972, 1974, 1977 by C.K. Williams. Reprinted by permission of the author.

Barbara Wind: "Hating Shakespeare" and "Math Test" © 2007 by Barbara Wind. Used by permission of the author.

Betty Wisoff: "Sanity" © 1985 by Betty Wisoff. Used by permission of the author.

Kenneth Wolman: "The Drapers: A History Lesson" © 2002 by Kenneth Wolman. First appeared in *The Drunken Boat*. Reprinted by permission of the author.

Carolyne Wright: "After Forty Years" and "KZ," from *Seasons of Mangoes and Brainfire* (Eastern Washington University Press / Lynx House Books), © 2000, 2005 by Carolyne L. Wright. Reprinted by permission of the author.

Rajzel Zychlinsky: "I Remember" and "The Undarkened Window," trans. by Barnett Zumoff, and "God Hid His Face," trans. by Aaron Kramer, from *God Hid His Face* (Word & Quill Press), © 1997 by Rajzel Zychlinsky. Poems reprinted by permission of the translators and Marek Kanter.

Sources Cited

Adorno, T. W. "Engagement." *In Noten zur Literatur III* (Frankfurt am Main: Suhrkamp Verlag, 1965).

Arendt, Hannah. *Eichmann in Jerusalem: A Report on the Banality of Evil* (Peter Smith, rev. ed., 1994).

Berenbaum, Michael. "The Urgent Task That Remains Undone: The Final Responsibilities of Survivors," *Midstream*, March/April 2007, 12–17.

The Black Book: The Nazi Crime Against the Jewish People (New York: Jewish Black Book Committee, 1946).

Bor, Josef. *The Terezín Requiem.* Trans. by Edith Pargeter. (Alfred A. Knopf, 1963).

Browning, Christopher. *Ordinary Men* (New York: HarperCollins, 1992).

Cattley, S. R., and George Townsend, eds. *Acts and Monuments*. Repro. of 1849 edition, 8 vols. (New York: AMS Press, ndg).

Cornwell, John. *Hitler's Pope: The Secret History of Pius XII* (New York: Viking, 1999).

Davidowicz, Lucy S. *The War Against the Jews 1933–1945* (New York: Holt, Rinehart & Winston, 1975).

Dewey, John. *Psychology* (1987), in *The Collected Works of John Dewey, 1882–1953.* 37 vols. (Carbondale: Southern Illinois University Press, 1967–1987).

Elkes, Joel. *Dr. Elkhanan Elkes of the Kovno Ghetto: A Son's Holocaust Memoir* (MA: Paraclete Press, 1999).

Epstein, Helen. *Children of the Holocaust: Conversations with Sons and Daughters of Survivors* (New York: Penguin repr. ed., 1988).

Etty: The Letters and Diaries of Etty Hillesum, 1941–1943. (Wm B Eerdmans Publishing Co., 2002).

Felstiner, John. *Paul Celan: Poet, Survivor, Jew* (New Haven: Yale University Press, 1995).

Gilbert, Martin. *Atlas of the Holocaust* (New York: Viking Penguin, 1982).

Goldhagen, Daniel Jonah. *Hitler's Willing Executioners* (New York: Knopf, 1996).

Hilberg, Raoul. *The Destruction of the European Jews.* Rev. and definitive ed., 3 vols. (New York: Holmes & Meier, 1985).

Kogon, Eugen. *The Theory and Practice of Hell.* Trans. by Heinz Norton (New York: Farrar, Straus & Co., 1950).

Kolatch, Alfred J. *The Jewish Book of Why* (Jonathan David Publishers, Inc., 1993).

Korczak, Janusz. *Ghetto Diary* (New Haven: Yale University Press, repr. ed., 2003).

Kuznetsov, Anatoly. *Babi Yar* . David Floyd, trans. (New York: Farrar, Straus & Giroux, 1970).

Langer, Lawrence L. *Admitting the Holocaust* (New York: Oxford University Press, 1996).

Langer, Lawrence L. *Holocaust Testimonies: The Ruins of Memory*, Reissue ed. (New Haven: Yale University Press, 1993).

Muller, Filip. *Eyewitness Auschwitz: Three Years in the Gas Chambers* (Ivan R. Dee, 1999).

Pryce-Jones, David. *Paris in the Third Reich: A History of the German Occupation, 1940–1944* (New York: Holt Rinehart & Winston, 1983).

Radnóti, Miklós. *Clouded Sky*. Trans. by Stephen Berg, S. J. Marks, and Steven Polgar (Harper & Row, 1972).

Rauschning, Hermann. *Hitler Speaks: A Series of Political Conversations with Adolf Hitler on His Real Aims* (Thornton Butterworth Ltd., 1940). Available in paperback from Kessinger Publishing LLC (2006).

Rees, Laurence. *Auschwitz: A New History* (Amazon Remainders Account, 2005).

Rose, Gillian. *Mourning Becomes the Law: Philosophy and Representation* (Cambridge University Press, 1996).

Sachar, Abram L. *The Redemption of the Unwanted: From the Liberation of the Death Camps to the Founding of Israel* (New York: St. Martin's/Marek, 1983).

Sohn, David, editor. *Bialystok: Photo Album of a Renowned City and Its Jews the World Over* (Bialystoker Album, 1951).

Stabholz, Thaddeus. *Seven Hells* (U.S. Holocaust Memorial Museum, 1991).

The Stroop Report: The Jewish Quarter of Warsaw Is No More! Trans. and annotated by Sybil Milton (New York: Pantheon Books, 1979).

Vishniac, Roman. *A Vanished World* (New York: Farrar, Straus & Giroux, 1983).

Vishniac, ICP Library of Photographers (New York: Viking, 1974).

Volavkova, Hana. *I Never Saw Another Butterfly: Children's Drawings and Poems from Terezín Concentration Camp 1942–1944.* Trans. by Jeanne Nemcova (New York: McGraw-Hill, 1964).

Vrba, Rudy, with Alan Bestic. *Escape from Auschwitz: I Cannot Forgive* (New York: Grove Press reprint ed., 1968).

Wiesel, Eli. *A Jew Today* (New York: Random House, 1978).

Wiesel, Eli. *Night* (first published in Buenos Aires in 1955; numerous editions in print).

Wyschogrod, Michael. "Some Theological Reflections on the Holocaust," *Response* (Spring 1975).

Young, James E. "Holocaust Memorials: Memory and Myth." *Moment* 14 (June 1989), 20–29, 59.

Principal online sources:

Wikipedia (http://www.wikipedia.org/)

Jewish Virtual Library (http://www.jewishvirtuallibrary.org/)

Index to Contributors

Authors

Translators

Editor

Charles Adés Fishman

Artist

Reva Sharon

Index to Poems

Acknowledgments

The special nature of this anthology spoke directly to a group of extraordinary individuals, all of whom deserve my gratitude and praise: Yala Korwin, in particular, who checked all of the historical and contextual notes for poems retained from the Texas Tech edition and who also helped me prepare many of the notes for poems new to the anthology: she has been a sustaining force through my editing of both editions of *Blood to Remember*; Judith Keeling, Director of Texas Tech University Press, who was my editor at the press while I was working on the first edition and who made archival materials available to me when I decided to bring out a new edition with Time Being Books; Kathleen Horan, whose research skills proved so helpful during my early efforts to locate contributors to the 1991 edition, as well as more recent poems that would be appropriate for this revised edition; and Heidi Silverstone, who retyped an important section of the manuscript, after a major hard drive crash in July 2006 temporarily brought my work on the anthology to a halt. Praise, too, for my northernmost sister-in-poetry, Lynn Strongin, whose editing of *The Sorrow Psalms: A Book of Twentieth-Century Elegy* (University of Iowa Press, 2006) was a model of judgment and exuberance. I'm also indebted to Marguerite M. Striar, whose 1998 anthology, *Beyond Lament: Poets of the World Bearing Witness to the Holocaust* (Northwestern University Press), provided me with another excellent model.

I owe special thanks to the many contributors who recommended the work of other poets and to the editors, anthologists, and publishers who put me in touch with contributors or sent poems and books for consideration. Thanks, too, to the permissions managers and permissions agents who efficiently and warmly followed up on my sometimes urgent requests. Here, I would especially like to express my gratitude to Frederick T. Courtright of the Permissions Company, who moved small mountains with grace and skill, and Bette Graber, Director of Copyright and Permissions at Random House, who made the near-impossible happen.

To Reva Sharon, the brilliant artist whose work illuminates the cover of this anthology: virtuosity, vision, passion, and generosity — all these gifts are yours.

Deep bows to Louis Daniel Brodsky for encouraging me to take on the holy task of assembling and editing a revised edition of this anthology, and to Trilogy Mattson, Jerry Call, and Sheri Vandermolen, of Time Being Books, whose intelligence, patience, and expert advice will not be forgotten. To Jeff Hirsch, whose genius for book design continues to amaze — heartfelt applause.

Finally, this needs to be said: In my life, I have been blessed by the steadying and nurturing presence of my wife, Ellen. Without her love and support, I could not have completed this work.

OTHER POETRY AND SHORT FICTIONS AVAILABLE FROM TIME BEING BOOKS

Yakov Azriel
Threads from a Coat of Many Colors: Poems on Genesis

Edward Boccia
No Matter How Good the Light Is: Poems by a Painter

Louis Daniel Brodsky
The Capital Café: Poems of Redneck, U.S.A.
Catchin' the Drift o' the Draft *(short fictions)*
Combing Florida's Shores: Poems of Two Lifetimes
The Complete Poems of Louis Daniel Brodsky: Volumes One–Three
Disappearing in Mississippi Latitudes: Volume Two of *A Mississippi Trilogy*
The Eleventh Lost Tribe: Poems of the Holocaust
Falling from Heaven: Holocaust Poems of a Jew and a Gentile *(Brodsky and Heyen)*
Forever, for Now: Poems for a Later Love
Four and Twenty Blackbirds Soaring
Gestapo Crows: Holocaust Poems
A Gleam in the Eye: Poems for a First Baby
Leaky Tubs *(short fictions)*
Mississippi Vistas: Volume One of *A Mississippi Trilogy*
Mistress Mississippi: Volume Three of *A Mississippi Trilogy*
Nuts to You! *(short fictions)*
Paper-Whites for Lady Jane: Poems of a Midlife Love Affair
Peddler on the Road: Days in the Life of Willy Sypher
Pigskinizations *(short fictions)*
Rated Xmas *(short fictions)*
Shadow War: A Poetic Chronicle of September 11 and Beyond, Volumes One–Five
Showdown with a Cactus: Poems Chronicling the Prickly Struggle Between the Forces of Dubya-ness and Enlightenment, 2003–2006
This Here's a Merica *(short fictions)*
The Thorough Earth
Three Early Books of Poems by Louis Daniel Brodsky, 1967–1969: *The Easy Philosopher*, *"A Hard Coming of It" and Other Poems*, and *The Foul Rag-and-Bone Shop*
Toward the Torah, Soaring: Poems of the Renascence of Faith
A Transcendental Almanac: Poems of Nature
Yellow Bricks *(short fictions)*
You Can't Go Back, Exactly
Voice Within the Void: Poems of *Homo supinus*

866-840-4334

HTTP://WWW.TIMEBEING.COM

Harry James Cargas ***(editor)***

Telling the Tale: A Tribute to Elie Wiesel on the Occasion of His 65th Birthday — Essays, Reflections, and Poems

Judith Chalmer

Out of History's Junk Jar: Poems of a Mixed Inheritance

Gerald Early

How the War in the Streets Is Won: Poems on the Quest of Love and Faith

Gary Fincke

Blood Ties: Working-Class Poems

Charles Adés Fishman

Chopin's Piano

CB Follett

Hold and Release

Albert Goldbarth

A Lineage of Ragpickers, Songpluckers, Elegiasts & Jewelers: Selected Poems of Jewish Family Life, 1973–1995

Robert Hamblin

From the Ground Up: Poems of One Southerner's Passage to Adulthood

Keeping Score: Sports Poems for Every Season

William Heyen

Erika: Poems of the Holocaust

Falling from Heaven: Holocaust Poems of a Jew and a Gentile *(Brodsky and Heyen)*

The Host: Selected Poems, 1965–1990

Pterodactyl Rose: Poems of Ecology

Ribbons: The Gulf War — A Poem

Ted Hirschfield

German Requiem: Poems of the War and the Atonement of a Third Reich Child

Virginia V. James Hlavsa

Waking October Leaves: Reanimations by a Small-Town Girl

866-840-4334

HTTP://WWW.TIMEBEING.COM

Rodger Kamenetz
The Missing Jew: New and Selected Poems
Stuck: Poems Midlife

Norbert Krapf
Blue-Eyed Grass: Poems of Germany
Looking for God's Country
Somewhere in Southern Indiana: Poems of Midwestern Origins

Adrian C. Louis
Blood Thirsty Savages

Leo Luke Marcello
Nothing Grows in One Place Forever: Poems of a Sicilian American

Gardner McFall
The Pilot's Daughter

Joseph Meredith
Hunter's Moon: Poems from Boyhood to Manhood

Ben Milder
The Good Book Also Says . . . : Numerous Humorous Poems Inspired by the New Testament
The Good Book Says . . . : Light Verse to Illuminate the Old Testament
Love Is Funny, Love Is Sad
The Zoo You Never Gnu: A Mad Menagerie of Bizarre Beasts and Birds

Charles Muñoz
Fragments of a Myth: Modern Poems on Ancient Themes

Micheal O'Siadhail
The Gossamer Wall: Poems in Witness to the Holocaust

Joseph Stanton
A Field Guide to the Wildlife of Suburban O'ahu
Imaginary Museum: Poems on Art